Real estate and urban development

Real estate and urban development

HALBERT C. SMITH, D.B.A., S.R.P.A.
Professor of Real Estate and Urban Land Studies
University of Florida

CARL J. TSCHAPPAT, Ph.D., S.R.P.A.
Professor and Chairman
Department of Real Estate and Urban Affairs
Georgia State University

RONALD L. RACSTER, Ph.D.
Associate Professor of Real Estate and Urban Analysis
The Ohio State University

 1973

RICHARD D. IRWIN, INC.   Homewood, Illinois   60430
IRWIN-DORSEY INTERNATIONAL   London, England   WC2H 9NJ
IRWIN-DORSEY LIMITED   Georgetown, Ontario   L7G 4B3

First printing, May 1973

Second printing, December 1973

ISBN 0-256-01462-0
Library of Congress Catalog Card No. 72–95397

Printed in the United States of America

To Ruth, Barbara and Janie

PREFACE

REAL ESTATE currently is experiencing a revival of interest from the academic community. The Gordon and Howell[1] and Pierson[2] reports of the 1950s, which analyzed education for business in U.S. colleges and universities, condemned much of the prevailing business education, and they were particularly devastating to the field of real estate. Undoubtedly the total effect of these reports was for the good, in view of the education process that prevailed in many collegiate schools of business. Too often the teaching of business subjects involved a how-to-do-it approach rather than the application of theory and research to business problems. The criticisms were particularly cogent for much of real estate education.

Undergraduate collegiate real estate education at that time was shackled by a proliferation of courses in Principles and Practices of Real Estate, Real Estate Brokerage, Property Management, Real Estate Salesmanship, Construction Techniques, and others. Too little attention was given the underlying disciplines of economics, land economics, psychology, and sociology. Real estate was most certainly thought not to be concerned with the great social problems of an urban society.

The effect of the reports on business education was dramatic. How-to-do-it courses were pared from business curricula; lip service (if not dedication) was given theory, research, and greater reliance on the underlying academic disciplines; behavioral and quantitative approaches and tools were used to analyze hypotheses suggested by literature of the basic disci-

---

[1] Robert A. Gordon and James E. Howell, *Higher Education for Business*, New York: Columbia University Press, 1959.

[2] Frank C. Pierson, *The Education of American Businessmen*, New York: McGraw-Hill Book Co., 1959.

plines. Organization theory, systems analysis, business logistics, and capital theory replaced many traditional courses in management, marketing, and finance.

In real estate, however, the experience was that many courses were dropped with few new programs or courses developing to take their place. At the doctoral level, where a field's teachers and researchers are educated, real estate was dropped or demoted. In some cases the emphasis was changed to urban economics or applied urban economic analysis. Real estate was almost never included in the core of courses for the M.B.A. degree; real estate was assumed not to hold much significance for middle and top managers of American industry.

More recently, however, the trend seems to have reversed. Centers for research in real estate and urban studies have been established at some major universities. Graduate courses have crept back into the curricula. Some schools have established departments of real estate and urban affairs, while others have recognized graduate degree programs in specialized aspects of real estate. For several years the demand for college and university teachers of real estate has been greater than could be supplied.

Forms of these new programs, centers, and curricula are considerably changed from previous experience. The how-to-do-it approach has been abandoned or de-emphasized in favor of approaches emphasizing urban sociology, economics, city planning, and business decision making. Unfortunately, however, an investment approach has taken a back seat in many of these programs. Research and curricula in urban planning and renewal, housing, and other urban problems have lacked sufficient understanding of the private decision-making process. Grandiose plans for development and renewal of our cities have often been implemented only to be rejected by those for whose benefit they were made, or to lie dormant because investors and developers would or could not carry them out.

Within business schools most traditional courses dealing with real estate for the businessman—real estate brokerage, property management, mortgage lending, and salesmanship—are gone. However, a more general approach recognizing the principles and interrelationships among investment decision making, city growth, and social problems has not been universally adopted.

The future direction of academic concern about real estate seems clear; the emphasis upon urban problems and development is unmistakable. The role of business education in real estate will be determined within this framework. It must concern the application of decision theory within an urban environment, determined by the framework of legal, social, and economic systems, to the special combination of factors of production—real estate. The additional requirement of progress toward the solution of urban problems must also be assumed.

Central in this concept of real estate education in schools of business or administration is the reliance upon the processes of investment decision making and implementation of the decisions. The combination of these two processes may be regarded as administration.

This book attempts to focus upon real estate investment decision making and execution of those decisions within the urban environment. It further attempts to shed some light from the micro decision-making point of view upon the macro problems of cities, and from the macro problems point of view upon the investment decision-making process. In so doing, much of the material that is traditionally taught in Principles of Real Estate courses is included. In order to comply with the new approach, however, some traditional material is inevitably omitted, while other such material is reorganized or de-emphasized.

Authors of a book owe many debts to numerous people. Our obligations begin with our parents, families, teachers, and friends, who have molded our lives and encouraged us along the road of academic pursuit. Economists of the past have developed our field and provided the base upon which a professional approach to real estate decisions can be built. And contemporary scholars, such as Richard U. Ratcliff, Arthur M. Weimer, Paul F. Wendt, Alfred A. Ring, William N. Kinnard, Jr., Raleigh Barlowe, and Hugh Nourse, have contributed immeasurably to our thinking.

We wish to acknowledge specifically the contribution of Robert O. Harvey, whose teaching, inspiration, and helpful comments have been an important force in the completion of the book. Other reviewers, such as Arthur Warner, James Graaskamp—and particularly Leonard Vidger—made numerous helpful comments and constructive suggestions. Special thanks go to Barbara Luse, who typed much of the manuscript and administered many of the daily chores associated with putting a book together.

The book is divided into five sections: Framework for Analysis, Value and Investment Analysis, Investment Opportunity and Constraint, Development Functions, and Real Estate Administration in the Public Sector. Effort has been made to relate each section and chapter to the others. Thus, we have tried to assure that the book "hangs together" as a unit and have sought to create a volume that is more than a compendium of facts and ideas.

Hopefully the book will serve the needs of students beginning their study of real estate in colleges and universities, either at the advanced undergraduate or graduate level. It should also be useful in the growing number of courses and programs required both for the licensing of the "new breed" of professional real estate business people and for entrance to and maintenance of standing in professional organizations.

April, 1973

HALBERT C. SMITH
CARL J. TSCHAPPAT
RONALD L. RACSTER

CONTENTS

proach. Mathematics of discounting. Valuation inputs. The highest and best use decision. Case example of the income approach. Value estimation by direct sales comparison. Value estimation by cost analysis: *Relation of cost to value. Reproduction cost. Accrued depreciation—penalties. Cost approach example.*

PART III
Investment opportunity and constraint

ferring partial ownership rights. Minimizing equity investment: The land contract. Selling the property. Other functions.

PART V
Real estate administration in the public sector

APPENDIXES

—————————————— PART 1
Framework
for analysis

chapter 1

INTRODUCTION

ALL PEOPLE use real estate. Upon it and within it we eat, sleep, walk, ride, sit, and perform every other activity of human endeavor. Businesses use real estate to support and protect employees, machines, and capital goods. Private and public institutions and governments similarly use real estate to house and protect employees, to protect equipment and other valuable items, to provide areas of recreation and training, and to create monumental symbols of prestige and status. Even spacecraft depend upon guidance and sustenance from the earth, and the space traveler of tomorrow will regard a certain area of the earth's surface as his home base. The preamble to the Code of Ethics of the National Association of Real Estate Boards emphasizes the all-pervasive influence of real estate on human affairs in stating the truism, "Under all is the land."

Because of the extent to which real estate must be used by human beings, it has received much attention by economists, lawyers, agronomists, geologists, archeologists, architects, and home gardeners. Our concern is primarily one of economic utilization of land resources, recognizing that within this viewpoint we must consider the privileges and limitations provided by the law and the utility characteristics imparted by factors such as fertility, mineral composition, and building design. The importance of economic theory is recognized as the basis for our analysis in the brief historical review in chapter 4.

The use of economic principles in controlling the use of real estate is manifested in decisions regarding the size of a parcel of land to be utilized for a particular purpose, the size and type of structure to be constructed, the legal rights to be obtained in a transaction, and many other kinds of decisions, such as whether to buy, sell, or improve a given

3

parcel of real estate or let it deteriorate. The rationale upon which such decisions are based, the process by which the decisions are made, and the considerations that enter into the decision-making process for real estate are all parts of the subject matter of this book. We attempt to provide an integrated study of real estate from the viewpoint of a decision maker who considers real estate to be an investment.

Hoagland has aptly chided the American public for its lack of knowledge about real estate and the decision-making processes affecting it by pointing out, "All Americans 'know' real estate. . . . At least most of us think we do." [1] The implication of this observation is, of course, that while usage of the physical commodity brings a feeling of familiarity, this is not sufficient for acquiring an understanding of the economic, social, and legal processes affecting land usage. Yet this knowledge is the key to maximizing successfully the usefulness of real estate. It is the source of understanding about how people explicitly or implicitly strive to obtain maximum benefit from the resources available.

Economic importance of real estate

Perhaps the first step in gaining an understanding of real estate is to obtain a feel for its relative importance and magnitude in the national economy. To grasp the importance of land resources, we may note that privately owned urban real estate constitutes approximately $1,500 billion (about 50 percent) of the national wealth. [2] New construction annually contributes almost 10 percent to the gross national product. The construction industry is the largest single industry classified and employs approximately 3.5 million people directly and millions more in related activities. Credit for real estate, which enables people to buy and build homes, offices, schools, apartments, churches, stores, and factories, is the largest single component of debt in the country and has expanded from 46.8 percent of private long-term debt in 1920 to approximately 60 percent in 1970. In actual amounts, mortgage debt increased from $25.5 billion to more than $450 billion during this period. The purchase of a home is often a family's single largest investment, and about 63 percent of the occupied housing units in the United States are owned by the occupants. [3]

Nature of real estate

Real estate is not simply the earth's surface. Rather, it is a term commonly used to denote the physical "good" involved in the legal concept

---

[1] Henry E. Hoagland, *Real Estate Principles* (New York: McGraw-Hill Book Co., 1955), p. 1.

[2] U.S. Bureau of the Census, *Statistical Abstract of the United States: 1971* (92d ed.; Washington, D.C., 1971), p. 328.

[3] Ibid., p. 672.

of real property. Although the term *property* connotes the exclusive right to control an economic good—in this case a parcel of real estate—the terms real estate and real property can usually be used interchangeably.

In addition to the earth's surface the concept of real property includes the air space above the earth's surface and the earth beneath the surface, extending theoretically to the center of the earth. Since this planet is a spheroid, the resulting shape of a square or rectangular parcel of surface land is an inverted pyramid, with the apex at the earth's center. The pyramid is not closed at the base because no limit is known in space.

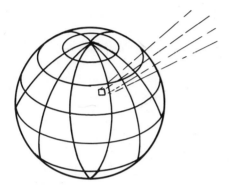

One may ask several interesting questions concerning this concept of real estate: Must a property owner allow airplanes, spacecraft, or rockets to fly through his real property? Does one theoretically own areas of other planets or stars when these space bodies are in the path of the outer fringes of the inverted pyramid? Although interesting, such questions have no practical significance. Public rights for the operation of aircraft have been decreed to exist a reasonable height above the earth's surface, and the concept of land would undoubtedly end at the outer limit of the earth's atmosphere. Also, the earth orbits and rotates in such a manner that no other heavenly body would remain in the inverted pyramid's path for more than an instant.

More practical questions arise concerning exactly what physical items within the inverted pyramid are considered to be real estate. The law makes a major distinction between real property and personal property. Usually real property consists of ownership rights in land, buildings permanently attached to the land, growing crops, trees, and other vegetation gaining its sustenance from the earth, minerals below the earth's surface, and the air space. Problems and disagreements often come about with respect to whether given items, such as carpet, drapes, television antennas, and so on, are part of the real estate when it is being sold. The tests that courts apply to such disagreements are discussed more fully in chapter 8, but suffice it to say now that if an item is considered a permanent part of a building it is legally considered to be real estate.

Finally, we may point out that there are many interests in real estate other than complete ownership. Life estates, reversions, remainders, and leaseholds are examples of real property interests that may have value and are governed by real property law. These interests are discussed more fully in chapter 8.

Real estate administration

Real estate resources are allocated among various economic units in the economy. Individuals, businesses, governments, and institutions acquire, hold, and dispose of real estate as the need arises and they are financially able to do so. The processes of making a decision as to the proper course of action and the carrying out of a decision once it has been made comprise the major processes of micro administration. An understanding of these processes is necessary for one to be assured that intelligent decisions are made and that they are properly carried out. Only when most individual investors understand this process will effective competition result in efficient utilization of land resources. Needless to say, when unintelligent decisions are made or proper decisions regarding real estate utilization are ineffectively executed, the macro result is a loss of benefit to society.

Micro administration. As suggested above, administration can be viewed in two perspectives—micro and macro. In the micro sense, administration involves the decision-making process and the execution process. As shown in Figure 1–1, these are further divided into the func-

FIGURE 1–1

Micro administration

DECISION MAKING	EXECUTION
1. Determine objectives	1. Plan the operation
2. Develop hypotheses	2. Organize the factors of production
3. Collect and analyze data	(land, labor, capital, and management)
4. Specify alternatives	3. Direct the operation
5. Formulate conclusions	4. Control the operation
6. Make a decision	

tions that must be performed in each process. The steps in formalizing a decision are essentially an application of the scientific method, while the execution process utilizes the management functions of planning, organizing, directing, and controlling. Although management theorists would undoubtedly prefer the entire decision-making process to be included as a part of the planning function, we feel that separating decision making from execution more accurately describes the concept of administration. The decision-making process employs micro economic analysis and is quite different from the action implied in the management functions of the executive process. Micro administration basically involves accomplishment of a given objective by working with people. Weimer, Hoyt and Bloom emphasize that it involves action.[4] Individuals, business firms, and government agencies make decisions and carry them out by seeing that the necessary tasks are accomplished by employees or professional agents.

Further, we should note that the activities concerning real estate of producing, marketing, financing, appraising, counseling, managing, and consulting are the functions to which the process of micro administration is applied. In accomplishing these functions, individual business firms and government agencies perform the administrative process. Decisions that arise in the performance of real estate functions are made by people in these economic units and are executed through people employed temporarily or permanently.

Although the administrative process implies rational behavior both in the decision-making phase and in the management phase, human emotions often result in irrational decisions and behavior. Psychological and sociological theories and research have provided much insight into how people react in certain situations; certainly synthesis of current knowledge and continuation of research in these two fields could be of great value to real estate businesses. For example, answers to such questions as which features attract home buyers and why, how various kinds of living arrangements in apartment buildings influence the behavior patterns of groups, and what factors businessmen consider to be most important in deciding where to locate offices and plants would provide better bases for decisions by sales people, planners, architects, and investors. We should hope for and expect much more of this type of investigation in the future. However, knowledge of individual and social actions does not negate the primary value of approaching the study of real estate within a functional, decision-making and executing framework. We assume that rational behavior in the solution of investment problems is always to be preferred to irrational, seat-of-the-pants decisions.

This point of view does not deny the value of using research results produced by the application of behavioral tools; indeed, we have incorporated such knowledge in various sections of the book, particularly in chapter 12 on marketing. Rather, a behaviorist framework constitutes another way of viewing the *same* problem or process, and it attempts to provide better data for the functional process. To state our position an-

---

[4] Arthur M. Weimer, Homer Hoyt, and George F. Bloom, *Real Estate* (6th ed.; New York: Ronald Press Co., 1972), p. 14.

other way, psychological and social factors may determine the nature of the inputs of the various steps in the administrative process, but these steps or functions are still present.

Steps two through five of the decision-making phase depicted in Figure 1–1 involve applied economic analysis. This analysis is often the least understood and the most infrequently used portion of the administrative process, particularly for decisions made by small-scale, individual investors. Nevertheless, it is essential, and its misuse or nonuse renders the remaining portion of the process meaningless. Thus, a major effort of this book is to present a logical framework for the economic analysis and to intergrate the determinants of economic objectives into the framework.

Macro administration. In the macro point of view we are concerned with the total effect of all the individual decisions. The *process* of *administering* is not the focus as in the micro viewpoint; rather, the organization for and the results of micro administration are the topics considered in macro administration. Under organization we study and analyze the units into which the economy is organized for accomplishing real estate functions or activities. Thus, the nature, organization structures, interrelationships, and effect on resource allocation of business firms, government agencies, and private investors, together with the laws, regulations, and policies affecting them are the topics of macro administration. In short, micro administration concerns the decision-making and managerial process, while macro administration concerns the manner in which economic functions are performed.

Functional activities for administration

Activities regarding real estate are performed by individuals, private businesses, and governmental agencies. In carrying out their activities or functions, these persons, businesses, or government agencies engage in the process of administration—they make decisions and execute them. Individuals purchase residential real estate for the purpose of consuming its services, and they invest in income-producing real estate for the purpose of earning a profit or return on their investment. They also must decide whether to sell, improve, expand, modify, or allow their properties to deteriorate. In making and carrying out such decisions, individuals may perform most or all of the activities to which real estate administration is applied. For example, an individual might appraise, finance, purchase, and improve a parcel of real estate. Usually, however, many of the functions are carried out by specialists or specialized firms, whose activities cause them to be considered part of the real estate business.

As with all businesses in a private enterprise economy, a real estate business will exist only so long as it performs a useful service for which members of society are willing to pay an amount sufficient to enable the business to earn a long-run profit. The various types of real estate businesses are discussed below under the activities they are organized to accomplish.

Governmental agencies perform the activities concerning real estate in carrying out the decisions and programs formulated by the legislative branches of government. Since the state legislatures and Congress are elected by the voting public, the nature and direction of these programs over the long run must be approved by society.

Producing.   The production of physical real estate resources involves the construction of buildings, the modification of existing buildings, the application to land of nonbuilding improvements (such as blacktopping for a parking lot or landscaping for a public park), and the development of raw land so that additional capital improvements may be applied. These activities are usually performed by firms that specialize in development and construction, remodeling, removal, landscaping, and paving. Construction firms usually specialize by type of structures erected; for example, some firms build only single-family residential houses, while others specialize in erecting the steel framework for skyscrapers.

Marketing.   Marketing activities are performed by real estate brokerage firms, speculative construction and development firms, individuals, government agencies, and businesses that wish to sell real estate without engaging a broker. Most of the real estate marketing activity is carried on by subdivision development and construction firms and by brokerage firms. Development and construction firms often build entire subdivisions and market each house on a speculative basis (that is, no buyer has agreed to purchase the house before construction). Brokerage firms enter into a contract, usually with the owner of real estate, agreeing to attempt to find a buyer for the property. If the broker is successful, he will earn a commission percentage on the property's sale price.

Financing.   The financing of real estate is performed primarily by private financial institutions. Commercial banks, mutual savings banks, savings and loan associations, and life insurance companies provide approximately 75 percent of the dollar value of all mortgage financing. Nevertheless, trust funds, pension funds, endowment funds, government agencies, and individuals are also sources of real estate financing. When obtaining financing, the borrower (mortgagor) usually signs a note evidencing the debt to the lender (mortgagee) and also executes a mortgage. The mortgage pledges the property for possible sale in case the mortgagor defaults on his debt to the mortgagee. The decision-making phase of financing concerns whether or not a loan will be made, while the management (or execution) phase involves the actual lending and supervision processes (refer to Figure 1–1).

Appraising.   Real estate appraisal has as its objective the estimation of value of specific parcels of real estate. The activity is performed primarily by professional appraisers and real estate brokers. Brokers are usually knowledgeable about markets and the factors which create value, but they frequently cut short most of the appraisal function in order to arrive quickly at a *listing price*. As will be seen in chapter 5, professional appraising involves rigorous analysis of various types of market data. Normally the broker has not been adequately trained in appraisal methodology nor does he usually maintain the files of market information required to perform the appraisal function. The appraiser is a specialized consultant and in recent years has gained much prominence in the shaping of real estate decisions. Three professional organizations—the Society of Real Estate Appraisers, the American Institute of Real Estate Appraisers, and the American Society of Appraisers—have been instrumental in upgrading the standards and educational requirements for those wishing to enter the appraisal field in the United States. In Canada, the Appraisal Institute of Canada, as well as the Society of Real Estate Appraisers, has performed this function.

Consulting and counseling. Various types of consultants are often required in matters concerning real estate. With the complexity of real property law, the lawyer is often required. Architects may be employed to design functional and aesthetically desirable buildings. Engineers may be required to design and oversee the construction of factories, bridges, roads, and other land improvements. Economists and business analysts may be needed to search out and analyze locations and to provide analysis, suggestions, and a continual review of micro administrative procedures.

Counseling is usually regarded as a more narrow term than consulting in the real estate field. The American Society of Real Estate Counselors (an affiliate of the National Association of Real Estate Boards) has popularized the term in regard to the type of service offered by its members, although the counseling function is not limited to those who are members of the organization. Counseling entails the rendering of investment advice to a client. An estimate of the value of a parcel of real estate may be one of the major considerations in the decision process of an investor but it is not the only important factor. The investor's financing requirements, his income tax situation, his portfolio of other investments, and his personal preferences should be considered by the counselor-consultant in advising a client about an investment decision.

Managing. The function of managing a property is often performed by a hired property management firm. For smaller investment properties the owner sometimes performs the management function. Whether a hired manager or the owner does it, however, management involves expense in terms of the manager's fees or the owner's time. Hired managers have become increasingly important since World War II because of the great mobility of the population which has led to increasing absentee ownership of real estate. It is not uncommon for the owner of a small parcel of investment real estate in the North to vacation in Florida during the winter months, leaving his property in the hands of a professional manager. The Institute of Real Estate Management (also an affiliate of the National Association of Real Estate Boards), which awards the C.P.M. (Certified Property Manager) designation to highly trained and qualified property managers, is the main professional organization in this field.

The investment process

It cannot be emphasized too strongly that the analysis and decisions concerning real estate are similar to the analysis and decisions concerning other factors of production and other investments which represent combinations of resources. Because real estate is often studied independently from other factors of production, the similarities between the various investments are obscured. Obviously, real estate, with its fixity of location and high unit value, can be differentiated from other resources (see chapter 5), and the law affecting real property is in many ways different from that affecting personal property. However, of primary importance is not the differences, but rather an understanding of the total investment process and how the *process is applied to real estate.*

The central theme of this book is that the theory of investment is relevant to the decision-making process involving real estate. The theory may be defined as the identification of factors causing people and firms to make decisions about income-producing assets and the description and measurement of the relationships among those factors. Investment theory boils down to the fundamental proposition that investors give up or pay a certain amount of valuable asset (often money) for the right to receive income or other valuable benefits in return. Algebraically, this proposition may be expressed in the following way:

$$P = (f)\,B$$

where P equals price or value, (f) is the functional relationship, and B equals the benefits to be derived, perhaps over a period of years. An understanding of investment theory allows one to analyze and predict how decisions will be made and thus how parcels of real estate will be developed. Analyzing patterns of decisions allows one to understand and predict city growth and development.

SUMMARY

If this brief overview of the real estate field seems to describe a large, multifaceted, complex sphere of activities, the impression is correct. In the segment of micro administration, decisions are made and actions are taken in a number of different types of business firms. Construction firms, real estate marketing firms, management firms, appraisal firms, consulting firms, land development firms, and financial institutions all play important roles in the field of real estate.

Many decisions involving real estate are also made by public or government agencies. Local governments pass zoning ordinances, building codes, housing codes and levy real estate taxes. State governments build highways and decide who can and cannot be in the real estate business. The federal government owns and leases much real estate and occasionally buys and sells property. More importantly, however, several government agencies, such as the Department of Housing and Urban Development, the Federal Home Loan Bank Board, the Federal Reserve System, the Federal National Mortgage Association, the Federal Housing Administration, the Government National Mortgage Association, the Federal Home Loan Mortgage Corporation, and the Farmers Home Administration, help channel funds into the mortgage market.

The results of all these decisions and influences produce patterns of types of institutions, funds flows, and land uses which can be studied in the area of macro administration. Basic mechanisms contributing to these patterns are commonalities in laws, economic behavior, psychological makeup, and social mores. The decision-making or investment process is the means by which these commonalities are translated into patterns of behavior. This process, the legal framework, functions performed, and the influences of public decision makers are the general topics for consideration in this book.

QUESTIONS FOR REVIEW

1. Why is the term *administration* important to an understanding of real estate?
2. How would you distinguish between administration and decision making?
3. What kinds of organizations serve mainly a macro administrative function?
4. What control do you have of activities that may occur in the air space above your land?
5. Can you identify real estate firms in your community engaged in each of the functional activities of producing, marketing, financing, appraising, counseling, managing, and consulting?
6. Why is investment theory important in understanding real estate?
7. Would you pay more or less than $2,000 for the right to receive $1,000 per year for the next two years? Would you pay more or less than $10,000 for the right to receive $1,000 per year for the next 10 years? Why?

REFERENCES

Calkins, Robert D.   "The Decision-Making Process in Administration." *Business Horizons*, vol. 2, no. 3 (Fall 1959), pp. 19–25.

Hoagland, Henry E.   *Real Estate Principles.* New York: McGraw-Hill Book Co., 1955, chap. 1.

Kinnard, William N., Jr.   "Reducing Uncertainty in Real Estate Decisions." Beyer-Nelson Distinguished Lecture at the Ohio State University, 1968. Published in *The Real Estate Appraiser,* vol. 34, no. 7 (November-December 1968), pp. 10–16.

Ratcliff, Richard U.   *Real Estate Analysis.* New York: McGraw-Hill Book Co., 1961, chap. 1.

Simon, Herbert A.   *The New Science of Management Decision.* New York: Harper and Row, 1960.

Weimer, Arthur M.   "Real Estate Decisions are Different." *Harvard Business Review,* vol. 44, no. 6 (November-December 1966), pp. 105–12.

Weimer, Arthur M.; Hoyt, Homer; and Bloom, George F.   *Real Estate.* 6th ed. New York: Ronald Press Co., 1972, chaps. 1 and 2.

chapter 2

MACRO EFFECTS FROM INVESTMENT DECISIONS

DECISIONS regarding the sale, purchase, rehabilitation, construction, and demolition of real estate are continually being made by people in real estate markets. Although most decisions are made by private individuals and business firms, governmental or public agencies also make these kinds of decisions. Most governmental units, from federal to local, buy and sell land, construct buildings and other improvements, modernize and rehabilitate buildings, and occasionally tear down buildings that have outlived their usefulness. Whether the decision is made by private investors or public agencies, action or administration to implement the decision must usually be taken in the private real estate market. The terms of sale, purchase, or improvement are not government controlled or dictated by any other super force. Even when using the right of eminent domain, governmental units must pay the *fair market value* to obtain a parcel of real estate.

PATTERNS OF DEVELOPMENT

Real estate markets are usually made up of a number of decision makers. Each decision maker, whether he be a private investor, government agency, or business firm, has various criteria upon which he bases his decision. For example, some home buyers demand five bedrooms, while others want three bedrooms; some buyers prefer a brick house, while others want frame or stone. Even when the same criteria are used, different weights are assigned to them by the various buyers in the market. For example, while the availability of water is important to all industrial firms in choosing a location, it is of relatively greater importance to a brewery than to most other types of firms.

Objectives

With the great diversity of people, motives, and criteria applied by these people, one might expect chaos to reign without public planning and dictated decisions. Such is not the case. Even with the diversity of criteria and weights applied to these criteria, investors, as well as business enterprises, have certain ultimate objectives in common. These have been termed the profit, service, and social objectives.[1]

Although there may be disagreement as to the relative importance of the three objectives, most people in the real estate market, as in other markets, attempt to fulfill these objectives in a variety of ways. We do not contend that one thinks explicitly about the objectives; rather, these objectives are in the nature of economic and social norms, the fulfillment of which determines in the eyes of his fellow man whether one has been successful or not.

Profit objective. Economic science is based upon the premise that people attempt to maximize their welfare by acquiring an optimal mix of valuable commodities and services. The extent to which one purchases any one commodity or service depends upon the benefit—financial or psychological—to be obtained from the item relative to the price that must be paid for it. Income is one of the primary benefits to be obtained from owning a productive commodity such as real estate. Income is desirable because with it one can purchase other commodities and services for ultimate consumption; the rental income to many landlords buys their groceries.

Another major type of benefit to be obtained from owning real estate is the psychological benefit (or amenities) one expects when he purchases residential real estate for self-occupancy. As in the case of the purchaser of income-producing property, the home purchaser is an investor in the sense that he attempts to buy the type of house at the lowest price which will give him the greatest psychological "profit" or satisfaction.

At times, business real estate is purchased for the prestige and status that may be attached to an impressive building. Business firms often construct buildings that are much more elaborate than would be necessary to carry on the firm's functions adequately and efficiently. The Seagram Building on Park Avenue in New York City, for example, is constructed of bronze, which is artistically more striking but also much more expensive than functionally comparable steel. In such cases it is doubtful

---

[1] See John F. Mee, "Management Philosophy for Professional Executives," *Business Horizons,* Bureau of Business Research, School of Business, Indiana University (December 1956), pp. 5–11.

whether the increased prestige will result in income that is sufficient to justify the increased cost of the building in a purely financial sense. Thus, profit must be measured in both financial and psychological terms.

"For one heady moment we considered challenging the Seagram Building for aesthetic honors rather than pursuing purely commercial ends, but then we decided what the hell . . ."

Service objective.   The service objective can be described from two points of view—both relative to the profit objective. First, service may be regarded as the ultimate objective. In this view each economic unit—a person or business—should strive to provide a service. If a needed service is provided at a reasonable price, the business or investor will indeed make a profit.

The second viewpoint regards profit as the ultimate objective. If a business firm or investor obtains a profit in the long run, he will indeed have provided a service.

Since arguing which of the two viewpoints is correct is a little like arguing which came first, the chicken or the egg, it may be well to regard profit and service as equally important. Certainly the two go hand in hand, and the accomplishment of both is necessary for the continued existence of an economic unit.

Social objective. If the profit and service objectives are regarded as having equal importance, they must share the glory with yet another motivating force. The social objective recognizes an investor's or a business' responsibility to society. This responsibility stems from the fact that no businessman or investor is truly "self-made." As Samuelson points out: [2]

If ever a person becomes arrogantly proud of *his* economic productivity and *his* level of real earnings, let him pause and reflect. If he were transported with all his skills and energies intact to a primitive desert island, how much would his money earnings buy? Indeed, without capital machinery, without rich resources, without other labor, and above all without the technological knowledge which each generation inherits from society's past, how much could he produce? It is only too clear that all of us reap the benefits of an economic world we never made.

How does the investor-businessman pursue the social objective? By engaging in an economically and socially useful activity which is both legal and ethical. The danger of engaging in illegal activities is evident. The danger of engaging in unethical activities is not so clear. Consider the case of a landlord who creates or maintains an unsafe, unhealthful, slum tenement. In most cases, refusal to improve undesirable conditions has been defended by landlords on the grounds that the additional rent cannot be sufficiently charged to justify the added expenditure of maintaining or improving property. In some cases this contention is valid. Particularly where government-imposed barriers exist—such as the long-standing rent control in New York City or confiscatory levels of the property tax—proper maintenance of existing units, as well as the construction of new units, is inhibited. Public policy should effect a more viable economic framework that will justify maintenance expenditures. However, in other cases slumlords have condoned unacceptable living conditions in their rental units when the income produced by the units would have justified greater maintenance expenditures. Such practices may be extremely profitable in the short run, and for any individual the short run may be a sufficiently long period of time to enable him to acquire desired wealth. Over a longer period of time, however, such activities will be limited or precluded by society.

In attempting to accomplish the three objectives, investors often arrive at similar conclusions about how best to go about the task. For example, in striving to maximize the benefits of home ownership within their capacities, many people have similar ideas of what type, size, and location of a house best fulfills their wants. Thus, we find districts and neighborhoods having homes with similar characteristics. Further, the residents of those homes would likely have similar income levels, educational attain-

---

[2] Paul A. Samuelson, *Economics* (6th ed.; New York: McGraw-Hill Book Co.. 1964), p. 435.

ment, and social status in the community. We discuss in this chapter the land use patterns that develop from these groupings and the relationships of the patterns to each other. These patterns and relationships constitute the macro effects that arise from many individual investment decisions. We also note in this chapter that certain types of limitations are placed upon the investment decision, and that these limitations affect the patterns of land usage that result from the micro decision-making process.

Land use patterns

If one categorizes the types of land use and makes a map showing the categories, he will find for all cities definite areas devoted predominately to a particular use. Figures 2–1 and 2–2 show two views (one, a close-up

FIGURE 2–1
Land use of map of Columbus, Ohio

view) of a land use map of Columbus, Ohio. The uses shown on the map are categorized into various degrees of residential density and other land uses, such as industrial, commercial and offices, and public and quasi-public facilities. One can notice that commercial usage predominates at the center of the city, while high density residential areas surround the core.

Relatively independent residential areas grow up as one moves outward from the older residential, commercial, and light manufacturing

FIGURE 2–2

Close-up view of land use map of Columbus, Ohio

areas. These may be communities within the major city or they may be suburban communities having separate governments. They are satellites to the major city, however, in that many of their residents work in the major city. In short, there is usually economic integration of the major city and outlying suburban communities, but segregation of economic classes, races, and social structure. The satellite communities, whether within the major city or politically separate, are served by stores selling primarily convenience goods, but with some stores having shopping goods. From an everyday living standpoint the satellite communities are independent; from the point of view of the breadwinner's source of income, location of major shopping purchases, and location of entertainment and cultural activities, the satellite communities are part of the major city.

Industrial areas are scattered somewhat sporadically around the city, although heavy manufacturing is usually located on the periphery of the densely occupied area or along railroad tracks or river fronts.

Theories of urban growth

In looking at land use patterns that have developed in the expansion of urban areas, one may begin to wonder what forces brought about the quiltwork of uses that at the same time seems to have both chaos and order. The identification and description of these forces would be an important step in the prediction of the future growth patterns of cities. Growth theory would also help to decide what is an optimal distribution or quantity of various land use types and at least provide some clues about how to cope with the social problems of poverty, crime, and juvenile delinquency which occur in overpopulated areas. If some of the expansionary forces that breed these conditions could be controlled and regulated, both privately and through action of city governments, perhaps these problems could be attacked more intelligently.

Concentric circle theory. Several theories of urban growth have been advanced. These are the concentric circle theory, the axial theory, the sector theory, and the multiple nuclei theory. The first of these, the concentric circle theory, was proposed by Ernest W. Burgess in 1925.[3] It states that cities grow in circular areas emanating from the central business district. Thus, at the center of the city the central business district contains the large office buildings, retail establishments, and governmental buildings.

The second circular area is called the zone of transition. Within this zone reside primarily immigrants and members of low socioeconomic classes. Although luxurious apartment buildings, night clubs, theaters, and restaurants also are located here, the living conditions constitute the slums of the city. Also within the zone are light manufacturing industries.

Zone 3 contains primarily the workers who work in zone 2. The housing tends to be typically large mansions converted into apartments, physically acceptable, but functionally out of date.

Zone 4 is composed of high-class apartment and single-family houses, along with entertainment and commercial establishments. Zone 5 is the commuters' zone, consisting of suburbs, or semirural areas. It would take from 30 to 60 minutes to ride the commuter train to the central business district from zone 5.

The axial theory. This theory is not traceable to one particular author. It has been recognized by several early authors in the field of urban analysis, and the implications of axial growth have been discussed by land value theorists. Basically, the theory says that an urban area tends to grow along its lines of transportation. This is due to the desire for the economic advantage of accessibility. Transportation time to the center of the urban area will tend to be equal from every point on the periphery. Therefore, the periphery will extend further out along the transportation lines and move in toward the center in areas not on major lines of transport to the central city.

---

[3] Ernest W. Burgess, "The Growth of the City," in Robert E. Park, Ernest W. Burgess, and Roderick D. McKenzie, *The City* (Chicago: The University of Chicago Press, 1925), pp. 47–62.

The sector theory. This theory, developed by Homer Hoyt in the 1930s, is concerned primarily with the growth of residential neighborhoods. In the sector theory residential neighborhoods are viewed as wedge-shaped sectors surrounding the central business district. Over time, the original high-rent and high-price areas near the center of the city deteriorate, inducing the wealthy and high-income population to move into new areas. Usually the new, high-class residential areas are developed along highways and other fast transportation facilities. Lower class areas remain in the deteriorated sections of the city and in other low-priced housing developments, often near places of employment. Intermediate class neighborhoods usually surround or adjoin the high-class neighborhoods.

The sector theory is based on the following general tendencies or premises: [4]

1. The various groups in the social order tend to be segregated into rather definite areas according to their incomes and social positions. While there are exceptions to this rule, it appears to have fairly general validity.
2. The highest-income groups live in the houses which command highest prices and rents, while the lower-income groups live in houses which are offered for the lower prices and rents. Generally the low-rent areas are located near the business and industrial center of the city and then tend to expand outward on one side or sector of the city, occupying the land which is not preempted by higher-rent residential areas or by business and industrial districts.
3. The principal growth of American cities has taken place by new building at the periphery rather than by the rebuilding of older areas. This means that some of our cities are beginning to resemble a hollow shell, with the major demands for land uses by-passing many of the "near-in" areas. In other cases these "near-in" areas become slums with little possibility of being rehabilitated through ordinary market processes.

The multiple nuclei theory. The multiple nuclei theory is essentially a modification of the sector theory and describes urban development in terms of various districts or areas which form around nuclei, or centralized activities. The theory, developed by Harris and Ullman,[5] advances four reasons why urban areas tend to develop in clusters around nuclei:

1. Certain activities require specialized facilities.
2. Certain like activities group together because they profit from cohesion.

---

[4] Arthur M. Weimer, Homer Hoyt, and George F. Bloom, *Real Estate* (6th ed.; New York: Ronald Press Co., 1972), p. 276.

[5] Chauncey D. Harris and Edward L. Ullman, "The Nature of Cities," *Building the Future City, Annals of the American Academy of Political and Social Sciences,* no. 242 (November 1945), pp. 7–17.

3. Certain unlike activities are detrimental to each other.
4. Certain activities are unable to afford the high rents of the most desirable sites.

Why a nucleus and cluster will develop in a particular location is determined by factors such as transportation, relative prices, communication possibilities, socioeconomic classes and ethnic groups residing nearby. Thus, heavy industry locates at the edge of cities on transportation facilities; principal business activities are located in the central business district, and financial, legal, and administrative offices congregate in close proximity just beyond the central business district.

FIGURE 2–3
Theories of urban growth

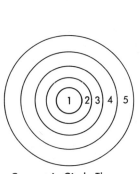

Concentric Circle Theory

Sector Theory

Multiple Nuclei Theory

Axial Theory

In forming conclusions about the adequacy of the so-called theories or hypotheses of urban growth, one may think of many exceptions to the ideas expressed in each. As Ratcliff points out:

Certain modern tendencies conspire to make the foregoing generalization less and less useful as a basis for forecasting coming urban patterns. The decline of public mass transportation is breaking down the structure of residential areas as it is described by Hoyt. The industrial worker neither depends on public transportation nor is his home necessarily near his place of employment. The executive drives to work, save in the largest metropolises, and lives where he will. This freedom of choice is leading to a greater diffusion, more mixture of neighborhoods, and less structuring of the metropolis.

Industrial development is no longer tied closely to rail lines, with the result that a greater scatter of industry characterizes recent development. Driven from central locations by the need for large acreage and by the congestion which hampers operations and employee movements, industrial plants are seeking suburban locations.

Retail conformations are changing to a lesser degree, but the change is significant. The central core of retail services remains dominant but is not growing in extent. New major suburban shopping centers are absorbing the added purchasing power of the growing metropolis. Suffering decline are the small neighborhood service centers, the older inlying retail sub-centers, and the string-street retail developments.[6]

To these trends we would point out that the increased emphasis that today is placed upon zoning, city planning, urban renewal, and public housing is additional cause why the theories of city growth developed 20 to 40 years ago cannot be expected to predict city growth in the future. To the extent that these arrangements modify the patterns people would otherwise develop in their real estate decisions, they lessen the value of theories which do not take them into account.

Although the theories may be inadequate for many predictive purposes, one may call to mind many instances in which the theories appear to have had some validity in describing the growth process. To the extent that each theory or combination of theories lends understanding to the urbanizing process, the decision maker should be able to analyze current developments more effectively. Whether more adequate theories will be developed remains to be seen; however, it seems doubtful.

Proportionality

Land uses. As one looks about him in any urban setting, he may notice that the city is composed of a variety of different land uses. Important

---

[6] Richard U. Ratcliff, *Real Estate Analysis* (New York: McGraw-Hill Book Co., 1961), p. 41.

uses typically are single-family residential, multi-family residential, commercial, and industrial. Subcategories of each are usually provided in zoning codes. In certain areas single-family residential housing predominates, while in other areas industrial or multi-family residential uses predominate.

When the city is viewed in its entirety, however, the amount of land devoted to each type of use bears some percentage relation to other uses. For example, residential uses may account for 60 percent; commercial, 15 percent; industrial, 10 percent; and other uses, 5 percent of the total land area. These relationships reflect the economic needs of the population and result in the macro effect of proportionality; economic forces tend to allocate approximately the right amount of land for each major use.

Proportionality and real estate markets. To most of us it seems only logical that there should be a variety and proportionality of types of land uses. Yet consider the system and the decision-making process which results in this diversity or proportionality of land use types. Proportionality of land uses results from many individual private decisions which have little or no external compulsion. The only force that in most cases dictates the decision for a particular use to be made of a parcel of land is the motive resulting from the market system of private choice. Each decision, therefore, was thought at the time it was made to be in the best economic interests of the investor-owner in competition with other investors and with the knowledge that other competing uses could also be applied to the land.

Although markets are discussed in considerably greater detail later in this book, it is well to note here two particular characteristics of the market system. First, a market, although not necessarily confined to one location, must consist of a number of buyers and sellers bidding against each other. How many buyers and sellers are necessary to constitute a market is not an answerable question; however, as the number of buyers and sellers in a market increases, the efficiency of the market increases. Conversely, as the number of buyers and sellers decreases, the efficiency of a market economy can be presumed to decline. It seems obvious, then, that individuals and groups of individuals should not be excluded from any market for noneconomic reasons. The exclusion of racial, ethnic, or religious groups from a market weakens the market and thus weakens the private enterprise system.

Second, to constitute a market freedom must be present. Freedom implies that there is no external compulsion in the decision-making process. The individual is free to choose that course of action which he believes will be in his own best interest. This requirement would exclude direct governmental intervention in the setting of market prices and would demand a minimum of social, racial, religious, ethnic, and class pressures, and the elimination of any other noneconomic external forces. Obviously these requirements are not met in the real-world real estate market. They do, however, represent market characteristics which would be desirable, even though unobtainable.

Structures. In addition to the proportionality of types of land uses that are observable in any land area, a proportionality exists with respect to the types and characteristics of structures within each use category. Within the residential category, for example, we find many styles of houses, different sizes, and different heights. In the commercial use category we find small single-story buildings, multifloor department stores, and office and industrial buildings. In the industrial category we would find small light-industrial manufacturing uses and a range therefrom all the way up to vast industrial complexes occupying thousands of acres of land. In the office building category are small single offices and a range all the way up to 100-story skyscrapers. In the office building use category, however, we do not find nearly as many 100-story skyscrapers as we would find 40- or 50-story skyscrapers. Nor do we find as many 50-story skyscrapers as we would find 10- to 20-story buildings, and we would not find nearly as many 10- to 20-story buildings as 1- to 5-story buildings.

The location of buildings having similar heights is another manifestation of proportionality. If one looks at the typical city which is large enough to have skyscrapers, he notes that the buildings at the outskirts are quite limited in height, usually being one, two, three, or four stories. As one moves toward the center of the city, he finds a few buildings of somewhat greater height, and as one enters the downtown area he finds a number of tall buildings. If he can obtain a cross-section side view of a city, he is likely to see something on the nature of a low-rising tent effect with the apex of the tent occurring near the center of the city in the highly commercialized downtown area. Of course, there are many modifications of this pattern, as seen from the sector theories and multiple nuclei theory.

Centers other than the downtown area may develop, and within these centers taller buildings may be constructed. However, the principles are the same in that the higher concentration of activity within the nucleus of the sector provides economic rationale for the construction of taller buildings. A good example of this latter effect is Houston, Texas, where many subnucleus areas with very tall buildings have developed in outlying areas from the downtown. The cross-section effect is something like a multicenter pole tent. The fact that in some cities, such as Los Angeles, Indianapolis, and Topeka, buildings are not so tall as in New York and Chicago does not negate the principle. Land has not sold at such premium prices to encourage more intensive use. The higher the land values at the center of the city, which result from the supply and demand conditions for land, the taller will be the buildings at the center of the city.

DIRECT LIMITATIONS

As noted above, the macro effects resulting from private decisions involve the premise that no or little external dictation of decisions is present. Nevertheless, the decision-making process for real estate resources operates within limitations upon real property ownership. A number of indirect economic influences that result from federal government monetary and fiscal policies are discussed in chapter 14. At this point we describe various limitations in the nature of direct regulations and controls within which private decisions are made. These direct limitations may be classified into the four categories of police power, the right of taxation, the right of eminent domain, and the doctrine of escheat.

Police power

The police power represents the right of governmental units to limit the rights that individual property owners have in their property. The justification of the police power is for the protection of the general welfare of all people in the regulation of public health, morals, and safety. McQuillan has noted that this power concerns "the inherent right of people through organized government to protect their health, life, limb, individual liberty of action, property, and to provide for public order, peace, safety, and welfare." [7] Examples of uses of the police power with respect to real estate are in the areas of zoning, building codes, fair housing laws, and the licensing of real estate brokers.

Zoning. Zoning involves the division of a city or other area into districts for various types of land uses. The zones or districts are usually delineated within a pattern established by a city plan. Within a zone such aspects as the height of buildings, the proportion of land covered by the building, and the uses to which the building may be put are regulated. In zoning residential areas, density may also be controlled by requiring a specified number of square feet of area or a given number of lineal feet of frontage per structure. Most zoning laws will not allow the invasion into one zone of a use from another zone. Thus, industrial uses are not allowed to enter a residential district.

Although zoning necessarily places limitations upon the rights of individual property owners, most experts as well as the general population seem to feel that zoning accomplishes worthwhile objectives such as raising land values, reducing traffic problems and nuisances, and improving the allocation of public utilities and recreational facilities. In order for zoning to be successful, however, the right amount of land must be set

---

[7] Eugene McQuillan, *The Law of Municipal Corporations* (3d ed.; Chicago: Callaghan and Co., 1949), vol. VI, p. 464.

aside for each type of use. If an oversupply of land is zoned for commercial use while insufficient land is zoned for industrial use, the prices of the latter will be bid up relatively out of proportion to the former. Thus, zoning authorities must be cognizant of the economic needs of the city both now and in the future. Furthermore, the zoning ordinance must not be a straitjacket of inflexibility. Exceptions are usually needed to allow the overall plan to be realistically workable; nevertheless, indiscriminate and unnecessary deviation should not be allowed. As with most restrictions, therefore, zoning must combine inflexibility with a tempering degree of flexibility so that legitimate exceptions to the rule may be made. (Appendix B describes some typical zoning requirements and procedures.)

Building codes. Building codes regulate the quality and strength of materials for the purposes of controlling safety, fire prevention, and sanitation. The thickness and height of walls, spacing of beams and girders and allowable stresses are usually governed, as well as the control over plumbing, vents, ventilation, height and size of rooms, and strength of materials that go into the building.

Building codes are established by local government agencies, usually the municipal governments. As with zoning ordinances, we should note that the regulations should stress a tempering of inflexibility with a degree of flexibility. In this case the flexibility refers to the ability of obtaining changes in building codes as new materials and construction processes replace older methods and materials. In too many cases in the past, building codes have not measured up to this requirement. A result has been in some cases a lack of progress. A good example is St. Louis, Missouri, which for many years enforced very restrictive, archaic building codes. In 1961 a change in the building code allowing utilization of newer materials resulted in a downtown building boom which continued for several years after the change.[8]

Although building codes by their nature must deal with some details, the amount of detail should be limited to an absolute minimum, while the emphasis is placed upon the objectives to be accomplished. The modern approach is to state standards in terms of *capacity to perform* rather than in terms of the *amounts* and *kinds* of materials going into the structure. Such criteria would encourage the introduction of improved building methods and materials.

A major problem with building codes has been that they differ among communities within the same metropolitan area. This situation forces construction firms to know several different code requirements, unnecessarily complicating their work. In many cities it also has resulted in special interest groups having a great deal of influence over the code.

---

[8] Robert L. Bartley, "Business Helps St. Louis Fight Decay," *The Wall Street Journal,* vol. 46, no. 159 (May 26, 1966), p. 14.

Dealers of presently approved products and craft unions understandably fight code changes which could weaken their profit positions. Such groups can form strong lobbies against major improvements, such as the acceptance of prefabricated units or more efficient new products. Recommendations for the improvement of building codes have included the placement of code formulation and enforcement at the state government level. The codes would be uniform for an entire state and would be less subject to pressures from local, special interest groups.[9]

Licensing of brokers. Licensing is required in practically every state before one may perform the functions of a real estate broker or salesman. Although this limitation is not directly concerned with an individual parcel of real estate, it does have considerable influence upon the total market activity for real estate resources. The license laws are designed to set a minimum standard of competence and honesty for real estate brokers. As is the case with respect to the licensing of physicians, attorneys, dentists, and other professional and business activities deemed to be in the public welfare, the licensing of real estate brokers has as its objective the protection of the public in an area where special, technical knowledge is required. It should be noted that the license laws presently do not contain standards that would elevate the real estate brokerage business to that of a profession. However, Realtor's associations in some states (such as Ohio, California, and Florida) have plans for proposing increasingly stringent licensing requirements over a period of 10 or more years. These plans generally call for the ultimate elimination of salesman licenses and the requirement of a college degree and specialized education in real estate for anyone seeking to become licensed. The Ohio plan is contained in Appendix C.

Open housing laws. Statutes and court decisions outlaw discrimination in real estate transactions on the basis of race, religion, or national origin. Although the federal fair housing law, some state fair housing laws, and the U.S. Supreme Court decision outlawing discrimination occurred in the late 1960s, a number of laws had been enacted in the early and mid-1960s by a few cities and states to forbid housing discrimination. These early efforts were sporadic and some suffered setbacks. For example, a state fair housing law enacted by the legislature in California was overturned by referendum. However, a 1966 decision of the California Supreme Court declared the referendum to be unconstitutional. Also in 1966, a federal fair housing law was introduced in Congress as part of civil rights legislation. And, in 1963 an order barring discrimination in transactions involving government underwritten loans was issued by President Kennedy.

---

[9] Carl J. Tschappat, "The Modernization of Building Codes," unpublished paper, September 1965.

On April 11, 1968, Title VIII of the Civil Rights Act of 1968 was signed into law by President Johnson. This law bans discrimination in the sale, rental, and leasing of housing *except* in the rental of apartments up to four units in size if the owner occupies one of the units, by religious organizations or private clubs, and by homeowners not using the services of an agent. These exemptions were negated by a decision of the U.S. Supreme Court in 1968 that the federal Civil Rights Act of 1866 outlawed all racial discrimination in housing. Additionally, some states also passed laws closing all avenues of discrimination in housing. For example, the Ohio fair housing law (House Bill 432) which took effect on November 12, 1969, outlaws discrimination in the sale, rental, or leasing of housing on the basis of race, color, religion, national origin, or ancestry. (See Appendix A for the provisions of these major antidiscrimination housing laws.)

Taxation

Although the right of taxation has been said to be the right to stifle or kill worthwhile projects, the lack of the right of taxation would be even more disastrous. Collective action through governments is a necessity for the operation of modern societies. Therefore, governments other than the federal government have the right to impose taxes upon the property within their jurisdictions. Much of the burden of providing needed services and facilities by local governments is incurred by the tax on real property. As with other liens, when tax payments are not made the property may be sold to satisfy the debt.

Real estate taxation procedures are archaic and sometimes produce inequities to some classes of property owners. Because of the reliance on the procedure of taxing building values, owners who modernize properties are penalized relative to those who let them deteriorate. The practice of estimating values by replacement cost less depreciation tends to cause new buildings to be taxed relatively more than older buildings. Often land is taxed under an agricultural use valuation after it has been developed commercially. Such practices obviously impede the proper allocation of real estate resources, and the system that permits them needs revising. Modern methods of valuation should be used, the level of competence of tax appraisers should be raised, and consideration should be given to removing the tax on improvements.

Although the federal government is prohibited from taxing property directly, the earnings produced by property are taxable in the form of federal income taxes. As we shall see, the federal income tax has an important bearing upon the micro decision-making process and will be considered in those investment calculations. Suffice it to note here that the income tax is in reality merely an *indirect* tax upon property of all types, real and personal.

Eminent domain

The right of eminent domain is the right of governments and other designated agencies to take private property for public use. When relinquishing private property for public use, the owner must be compensated for the value of the property taken. Although he has the right to be paid, the title holder does not have the option of refusing to give up his property. The right of eminent domain is one which can force an owner to sell for just compensation even if the owner does not wish to sell.

Often the governmental agencies cannot agree with the owner of the property as to what just compensation for the property is. When agreement cannot be reached, the governmental agency will conde... the property, and the court will determine the amount of just compensation. The right of eminent domain is vested in the federal government, the various state governments, municipal governments, and other public corporations such as public utilities whose function is regarded as essential to the public welfare.

Doctrine of escheat

The doctrine of escheat, although much less onerous than other limitations, nevertheless restricts the absolute control of property by private individuals. This doctrine is of common law origin and states, in effect, that when there are no longer any identifiable owners of a particular parcel of real estate, ownership or title to the real estate will vest in the state. This doctrine has greater influence upon private personal property such as bank accounts, savings and loan accounts, and so on, which many times go unclaimed by owners. With respect to real estate this type of occurrence is much less frequent, but nevertheless does occur.

SUMMARY

Decisions by many individual real estate investors result in identifiable patterns of market behavior. These patterns are reflected in types of land use, intensity of land use, growth characteristics of cities, and characteristics of structures within any given land use and intensity level. Growth patterns of cities have been observed and classified into several theories— the concentric circle theory, the sector theory, the axial theory, and the multiple nuclei theory. Each of these, either separately or in combination with others, can help in understanding where and why growth has occurred in a city and where future growth may be expected.

Several motivating and constraining forces serve to channel real estate investment decisions into observable patterns. Common objectives of profit, service, and social function stimulate investors to seek the same rewards. Common expectations about future growth and development tend to cause investors to evaluate similarly the various ways of achieving their objectives. And four main types of limitations on property rights—police power, taxation, eminent domain, and escheat—create a framework within which investment decisions are constrained. Although the approach of this book deals with the decision-making process by the individual real estate investor or firm, the resulting patterns and social consequences of this process must be continually observed, analyzed, and evaluated.

QUESTIONS FOR REVIEW

1. What is meant by the term *macro effects*?
2. What is the role of the three objectives of profit, service, and social in producing macro effects?
3. Why are the service and social objectives given equal weight with the profit objective?
4. Can you think of examples in a city or cities of the growth patterns suggested by each of the theories of urban growth?
5. How could a real estate developer use each of the theories of urban growth to identify desirable areas for residential development?
6. Visualize a side-section profile through the center of a large city. How does the height of buildings illustrate the principle of proportionality? How is the principle of proportionality related to the economic principle of increasing and decreasing returns?
7. What are the reasons for limiting private property rights of real estate owners? Do you believe additional limitations will be placed on ownership rights? If so, what types of additional limitations do you foresee?
8. The real estate tax is often cited as being an unfair and regressive tax. Can you think of reasons that it could be regarded in this way?

REFERENCES

Brown, Robert K. *Real Estate Economics,* Chap. 3. Boston: Houghton Mifflin Co., 1965, pp. 27–37.

Harvey, Robert O. and Clark, W. A. V. "The Nature and Economics of Urban Sprawl," *Land Economics,* vol. 41, no. 1, pp. 1–9.

Hoyt, Homer. "The Growth of Cities from 1800 to 1960 and Forecasts to Year 2000," *Land Economics,* vol. 39, no. 2 (May 1963).

Lynch, Kevin. "The Pattern of the Metropolis," in C. E. Elias, Jr., James Gillies, and Svend Riemer (eds.), *Metropolis: Values in Conflict.* Belmont, Calif.: Wadsworth Publishing Co., Inc., 1964.

Ricks, R. Bruce. "New Town Development and the Theory of Location," *Land Economics,* vol. 46, no. 1 (February 1970), pp. 5–11.

Weimer, Arthur M., Hoyt, Homer and Bloom, George F. *Real Estate,* Chap. 10, 6th ed. New York: Ronald Press Co., 1972, pp. 266–98.

chapter 3

AN OVERVIEW OF THE INVESTMENT APPROACH

DECISIONS must be made regarding almost every aspect of existence—what time to get up in the morning, what to eat for breakfast, where to go for a vacation, what person to marry, and what investments to purchase at what price and at what time. These are a few examples of choices that must be made by most people. Some decisions, after having been repeated often enough, become routine or habit and actually lose the characteristics of a decision. Some people become so accustomed to awakening at a particular time, for example, that they automatically wake up even though they might have decided to sleep another hour.

Other decisions are usually recognized as having a much greater potential influence on one's life and are given greater consideration and analysis. When one takes a job or purchases a home he usually considers the alternatives quite carefully and chooses the position or parcel of real estate that he believes to be in his long run best interest. The same can be noted for a business firm. Its officers will carefully consider the alternatives before hiring important personnel, purchasing a new machine, or building a new factory. A certain price must be paid to obtain such items, and the firm or individual wants to receive the maximum benefit from that price.

Premises

The investment approach to decision making in real estate is based upon the premise that many alternatives are available to the investor. The individual investor has a choice of purchasing stocks, bonds, real estate, a private business, or many other items. If he decides to purchase stock he has an endless variety of companies and industries from which to choose equity investments. If he decides to purchase bonds, an almost infinite variety of legal provisions and features are available from many firms in different industries. Similarly, real estate investments are as varied as all the individual properties and legal provisions compounded. The investor has almost an infinite variety of investment alternatives from which to choose.

A second premise is that market imperfections may cause the price of an investment property to be higher or lower than the property's value. If perfect competition reigned, the market price would by definition equal value, and the price the purchaser paid would be justified. Markets, however, are not perfectly competitive. For example, real estate prices may fluctuate during the year if the market is more active in some seasons than others. A seller may harbor an inflated opinion as to his property's worth. Or an owner may be under pressure to sell because he needs his capital quickly or because he is moving out of town. If an investor pays too high a price, his return on investment (R.O.I.) will be lower than necessary. But if the investor pays a price lower than the property's market value, his R.O.I. will be higher than market returns on properties of comparable risk. The smart investor should continually be watching for "good buys"—properties whose prices are less than their long-term values. Successful investment strategy usually requires the ability to exploit market imperfections.

A third premise—and a corollary of the first two—is that the investor (or his adviser) must collect, assimilate, analyze, and draw conclusions from a large quantity of market data. To make choices among the almost infinite variety of investments and to identify good buys or bad buys, information must be available concerning the types of available properties, income and expense characteristics of the properties, rates of return being obtained in the market by other investors, and rates of return obtainable from other types of competing investments. An investor who does not rely upon analyses of market data to guide his investment decisions is really not an investor; he is a gambler.

Investment criteria

The real estate decision maker needs to consider certain criteria in judging alternative investments. In effect he asks, "What is a good investment for my particular purpose? What purchase price should be paid?" The following criteria provide the standards by which to answer these questions.

Return on investment. Return on investment, or yield, is a percentage relationship between the price the investor must pay and the stream of income dollars he obtains from the investment. For example, if one paid $1,000 for a piece of land from which he expected to receive net $100 per year for as long as he holds the land, his return on investment would be 10 percent.

In the case of land, investors assume it does not wear out or lose value during the life of the investment, and therefore, the investor could recover his capital at any time simply by selling the land, which should bring about $1,000. The return on investment calculation becomes more complicated for investments such as buildings which wear out and lose value during the life of the investment. In addition to receiving a return *on* his invested capital, the investor must plan for the return *of* his capital from the income stream. For example, if an investor pays $10,000 for a building and the building loses value (depreciates) over the next 20 years, the investor must obtain in addition to his 10 percent on the outstanding balance of his investment 5 percent of $10,000 ($500) so that at the end of the 20th year he will have recovered the $10,000 invested capital. (Note: Compare this with the purchase of a corporate bond.)

Business risk.   Two types of risk enter into a determination of whether an expected return for a specific investment is sufficiently high—business risk and financial risk. Business risk concerns the probability that the income-producing ability of the investment (or business) will not be as great as expected. Although a return on the investment has been estimated, there is some probability that this expectation will not be realized. Any cause of such a loss that has its source in the investment itself would constitute a part of the business risk. For example, if an apartment building cannot be rented at the rates anticipated by an investor, the property may have to be sold to pay the investor's obligations. Manifestation of business risk will have resulted in loss of the investment.

Business risk stems from two sources—internal operating difficulties (or inefficiencies) and external factors. The R.O.I. calculation may assume that revenues and expenses will be kept at a particular level. Perhaps, however, poor management does not achieve a high tenant occupancy or does not take advantage of discounts in purchasing supplies. Because of such internal operating inefficiencies the return will be lower than expected.

Externally the demand for a particular product or the services provided by real estate may diminish. New apartment buildings may be erected, causing the relative attractiveness of older buildings to decline; or general economic conditions may force business tenants to get by with less office space, thus affecting the ability of management to lease space designed for this purpose.

The uncertainties associated with investment ventures of this kind can be compared to relatively riskless investments such as government bonds. With the latter type of investment there is virtually no business risk. The investor can be confident of receiving interest as scheduled and return of principal at the bonds' maturity. Obviously, the increased risk associated with real estate investments causes the investor to demand a greater return expectation before investing. The greater the business risk, the higher must be the expected return over and above the available rate on relatively riskless government bonds.

Financial risk. Most real estate investors use borrowed funds in the purchase of real estate. Although business risk is present even when no borrowed funds are used, financial risk is strictly dependent upon the amount of and legal provisions concerning borrowed funds. If the income produced by an investment falls below the payment which was specified in the debt agreement, the owner will have to either sell the property to satisfy the debt or make the payments from other resources. For most investments, of course, the property's income-producing ability is expected to cover all expenses including debt service.

In deciding upon an acceptable rate of return the investor should consider financial risk. He should not accept a return that barely compensates him for the burden of losing the property if debt payments cannot be made. On the other hand, if the investor has adequate personal resources to cover any such deficiency, the financial risk is lower.

Cost of capital. An investor's cost of capital determines whether the expected return on investment is sufficiently high. An investor should not purchase any investment which does not provide a return equal to the price he must pay for borrowed funds and the return he could obtain on competing investments. In calculating his cost of capital the investor should weight the cost from each source by the percentage of funds obtained from that source. For example, if a $100,000 investment property were financed by 60 percent debt funds and 40 percent equity (the investor's own funds), the cost rates of each would be weighted accordingly. Suppose the debt funds cost 8 percent interest on a mortgage and other equity investments with a comparable risk yield 12 percent. If the proportion of debt and equity funds employed by the investor is expected to remain constant, the cost of capital calculation would be as follows:

Mortgage debt (.60 × 8%) 4.8%
Equity (.40 × 12%) 3.6
Weighted average cost of capital 8.4%

The investment should not be purchased unless its expected return is at least 8.4 percent.

Stability of income. The stability of income can be of importance in an investment situation. Particularly with respect to the financial expenses, the income pattern can be crucial. If the income should fall below the debt service requirement for any period, the owner would either have to use other resources to make the payment, allow the property to be sold, or make special arrangements with the lender. Over a longer period the income might be adequate to provide the desired return; in the short run it could mean loss of the property.

This graph depicts a dangerous situation for an investor. During two months of the year the income is less than the debt service requirement. The difference of $250 per month will have to be paid out of the investor's personal funds, or he must be prepared to lose the property.

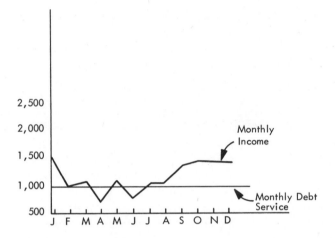

Liquidity. While the aforementioned criteria may be favorable, the investor might not find the investment desirable. He may realize that at any time he might have to sell the investment to meet a specific need. Real estate is sometimes vulnerable to a lack of liquidity, which is defined as the ability to sell the property quickly for at least as much as the amount invested. Therefore, in most such investments there should be a high probability that neither the equity funds nor the borrowed funds will be needed on short notice.

Investments providing high liquidity typically yield a lower return than less liquid investments. In other words, investors must be willing to pay for liquidity, and if they need a high degree of liquidity, they would probably resort to lower-yielding, high-grade corporate or government bonds.

The degree of liquidity for real estate is often a function of the type of property under consideration. Special-purpose properties of relatively high value are less liquid than general-use properties. Houses of medium-price range (say $20,000 to $40,000) are more liquid than very large or small houses. The wider the market for any investment, the greater is usually the chance for recovering the capital invested.

Applicability of the investment approach

In this book we include our entire study of real estate within the framework of the investment approach. We feel that this approach is superior to others because it facilitates the important aspect of decision making. Decision making was shown in chapter 1 to be the key element in the administration of real estate resources, and it is through the investment approach that decision making is understood.

We feel that it is of much less importance to memorize lists of characteristics about real estate, legal terminology and procedures, or the steps that are required to close a real estate transaction. Certainly these are important aspects of real estate, but they can be readily learned by one in a specialized situation or job. They will soon be forgotten when memorized by a person who does not have an immediate need for such information.

Nonincome-producing properties. The investment approach might be regarded as inappropriate for the analysis of properties that do not produce dollar income such as single-family residences, public parks, school buildings, or libraries. The benefits from properties of this type may not accrue in the form of monetary income and may be indirect or even immeasurable. Coons and Glaze have shown that in buying a home most people are concerned with consumption motives, such as the services the home will provide and the prestige and status to be obtained, rather than financial advantage.[1] A "good address" or an impressive architectural design for a home or the beauty of a park or attractiveness of a school are intangible benefits. Decisions are made whether to develop or purchase these types of properties. Upon what basis are these decisions made? What type of analysis goes into these decisions? We submit that the investment approach, which recognizes that the outlay must be justified by the expected returns—whether these returns be monetary or psychic—provides the best approach for understanding the ubiquitous decision-making requirement.

The expected future stream of psychic benefits (usually called amenities in real estate parlance) can be considered analogous to financial benefits in a dollar-income-producing investment. For dollar-income-producing investments a percentage relationship (or R.O.I.) is calculated between these benefits and the price that must be paid. For psychic-income-producing investments we cannot make such a calculation because the benefits themselves are not directly measurable in dollar terms. This does not negate the theory or analytical approach, however. Rather, it means that we must compare prices of alternative properties, as these prices are related to the benefits and to the other criteria discussed in this chapter.

The home purchaser should recognize that the business risk associated with a home purchase concerns the probability that the production of amenities by the home will not be as great as anticipated. Will the loca-

---

[1] Alvin E. Coons and Bert T. Glaze, *Housing Market Analysis and the Increase in House Ownership* (Columbus: Bureau of Business Research, The Ohio State University, 1964).

tion continue to provide the expected benefits? What is the probability the neighborhood will decline more rapidly than anticipated?

As with income properties, financial risk associated with amenity-producing properties concerns the probability that the mortgage payment cannot be met. To assess this probability the purchaser must weigh his expected future income against personal expenses, housing expenses, and the periodic mortgage payment. Two rough rules of thumb are that a purchaser having no abnormal personal expenses can pay up to two and one-half times his annual gross income for a home, and that he can afford to pay up to 25 percent of his monthly income in housing expense.

The home buyer should also consider the liquidity of his investment. Can he sell the home in a reasonable time if he should so desire? What is the probability he will need to sell within two, three, five, or ten years?

Lastly, stability of benefits should be considered. Will the home provide satisfactory benefits in winter as well as summer? Is it sufficiently well decorated that he will enjoy the benefits of home ownership as soon as he moves in, or will he have to wait some period of time until he can have the home redecorated?

The investment approach to home ownership thus involves a weighing of costs against returns. The principal returns are the psychic benefits or amenities produced by the property and the right not to pay rent. Costs include the interest that must be paid for borrowed money and the alternative monetary or psychic benefits that could be obtained from an alternative investment. These burdens comprise the home investor's cost of capital.

Social problems.   One last question about the applicability of the investment approach concerns its role in social analysis: How does the macro approach to real estate problems fit within this micro level framework? What justification would we have for including in this book a discussion of urban decay and redevelopment, mass transit, city planning, low-income housing, and so forth? A clue to our answer may have been noted in chapter 2. There we discussed the *patterns* that develop from many individual land use decisions. We described zoning ordinances and other regulations that attempt to control such patterns. We recognize that market imperfections and inadequate regulation and enforcement may contribute to the continuance of socially unhealthful consequences such as slums and racial ghettos. Understanding of the investment process may reveal ways the decision-making process can be altered to effect more desirable social results.

Additionally, however, knowledge of the investment approach can help identify those areas where social action must be taken to remedy patterns that cannot be changed efficiently through the private decision-making process.[2] One such area is urban renewal. The housing market is generally considered an inadequate device to renew and rehabilitate slum areas of our cities. The owner of one or several slum properties cannot fix up his property while the rest of the area remains deteriorated; rents cannot be increased to justify the expenditure. Furthermore, no one developer is large enough to accumulate all the properties in a slum area so as to be able to rehabilitate the entire area of blight. Clearly the market is inadequate and governmental assistance is needed. The investment in such a rehabilitation project must be justified from a social standpoint rather than from a private investor's potential return.

SUMMARY

The investment approach can be regarded as a philosophy of making decisions and solving problems. It entails identifying and measuring the benefits to be derived from a course of action and the costs that must be incurred to achieve that action. The costs are weighed against the benefits for alternative courses of action in order to decide which way to proceed.

Real estate analysis is particularly appropriate for the investment approach because benefits in the form of income or amenities are usually present and at least for income-producing properties are measurable. Similarly, the costs of purchase and maintenance can usually be identified and estimated. Relationships between costs and benefits for several properties or projects can then be calculated and evaluated.

Some of the relationships or investment criteria that can be noted are return on investment, the amount of cash generated after the payment of all expenses, the liquidity of the property, and the business risk and financial risk associated with the property. Another important criterion, the after-tax cash flow for income-producing properties, will be discussed later in the book. The cost of obtaining funds for investment is determined by a weighted average cost of equity and debt funds and is reflected in the rate of return on investment that is demanded by investors.

QUESTIONS FOR REVIEW

1. What is meant by liquidity? Look up in a finance book a definition of marketability. How do the two terms differ? Which is more important in real estate analysis? Why?
2. What are some of the considerations that should be taken into account when deciding what an appropriate R.O.I. should be?

---

[2] For one exposition of these problems, see Robert C. Weaver, *The Urban Complex* (New York: Doubleday and Co., Inc., 1964).

3. What would you say are the costs and the benefits of obtaining a college education? Can the question of whether to pursue a college education be regarded as an investment decision? Why or why not? Would everyone come to the same conclusion regarding the relationship between costs and benefits associated with four years spent at a college or university? Why or why not?

4. How would you measure business risk? In what way is business risk reflected in R.O.I.?

5. Why are investment criteria in addition to R.O.I. important? Can you think of a situation in which the expected R.O.I. might be acceptable but another criterion would cause a proposed investment to be unfavorable?

REFERENCES

Ratcliff, Richard U. *Real Estate Analysis.* New York: McGraw-Hill Book Co., Inc., 1961. Chap. 12, pp. 306–31.

Sauvain, Harry C. *Investment Management.* 3d ed. Englewood Cliffs, N.J.: Prentice-Hall, Inc., 1967. Chap. 1, pp. 3–20.

Seldin, Maury and Swesnik, Richard H. *Real Estate Investment Strategy.* New York: Wiley-Interscience, 1970. Chaps. 1–3, pp. 3–39.

Wendt, Paul F. and Cerf, Alan R. *Real Estate Investment and Taxation.* New York: McGraw-Hill Book Co., Inc., 1969. Chap. 1, pp. 1–12.

PART 2
Value and investment analysis

VALUE: THE CENTRAL IDEA

Decision making in real estate centers around the investment calculation. The potential purchaser of real estate wishes to pay a price which is sufficiently low to allow him to obtain a future return on his investment. The seller of real estate wishes to obtain a price high enough to allow him to have obtained a return on his investment in the past. Two processes, which constitute the investment calculation, are necessary to determine these returns. First is the estimation of net operating income (N.O.I.); second is a calculation of the effects of an equity investor's income tax and financing situation upon a prospective purchase. The latter process and procedure is reserved for chapter 6. In this chapter and chapter 5 we are concerned with understanding the concept of value and the procedures by which the value of real estate is measured.

The starting point is an understanding of value *theory*. Theories in general present an understanding of the world based upon the facts that are known. Theories describe what occurs and offer an explanation as to how and why phenomena occur. In other words, theory—at least good theory —is the best knowledge we have available. As such, theories should guide the practice of those who must make day-to-day decisions and should constitute predictive tools for increasing the probability of accuracy in decision making. Value theory deals with the nature and determinants of future returns in the marketplace—irrespective of an individual investor's personal situation—and how these returns are measured.

HISTORY AND DEVELOPMENT OF VALUE THEORY

Because of the great importance of decisions centering around value in explaining economic activity, the theory of value has occupied much thinking by the world's economists. Many of the analytical techniques used today by appraisers, counselors, and investors stem from the explanations and theories of economists who lived as long as 250 years ago. In some cases these theories have been replaced by newer, more accurate theories, while the technique based upon the outdated and discredited theories continues to be practiced. It is incumbent upon those practitioners who use analytical techniques not only to be well grounded in their underlying theories, but also to collaborate with theorists in striving to develop better theories and more meaningful practices.

Direct value theories

For the purpose of this rather brief discussion of value theory we may view the schools of thought as those concerned *directly* with value and those concerned *indirectly* with value. Theories that directly concern value attempt to explain its nature through one or more of the basic causes of value, such as supply or utility. Further, such theories are of a direct nature because they are concerned with an analysis of the value of an individual economic good, such as a machine or a parcel of real estate.

In contrast with the direct value theories are those dealing with economic factors or conditions that have implications for values in general. For example, Keynesian theory concerns analysis of an entire economy, but policies formulated under this theory may affect real estate values. Such a policy might require changes in tax regulations designed to stimulate or dampen economic activity. However, the tax change also may alter the values of real estate relative to other investments. For another example, changes in the rules and regulations of the legal or financial systems initiated by institutionalists could influence the desirability of real estate. Although such schools of economic thought are not concerned with the value of an individual good, the application of the theories to policy decisions may lead to profound effects upon investment decisions and values.[1]

Classical. The direct value theories can be classified according to the causal agent they espouse. The first is the supply factor, which was advanced by the classical economists—Adam Smith, Thomas Malthus, David Ricardo, John Stuart Mill, and Johann von Thünen. To the earlier of these economists—Smith, Malthus, and Ricardo—value was based upon the

---

[1] The distinction between direct and indirect value theories corresponds generally with that of micro and macro economics. However, our purpose in using the direct-indirect terminology is to focus upon those aspects of macro economics, as well as micro, that are concerned with value. Thus, some aspects of economics, e.g. welfare economics or business cycle studies, are far removed from our immediate concern with value theory but would fall under the heading of macro economics. We prefer to limit our scope of discussion to those aspects of macro economics holding some relevance, albeit indirect, to the developing concept of value.

factor of labor. Labor constituted the essential ingredient in production, and it was the cost of labor that measured the value of production. Since land was considered a factor of production, the labor cost theory was carried over to explain land income and value. However, these early economists encountered conceptual difficulties because the land was not created by human toil. Utility and productivity were not considered as value determinants except in the indirect sense that useful products resulted from labor productivity.

Adam Smith (1723–1790) also made the distinctions between value in use and value in exchange and between price and value. Value in exchange was producible only through a marketplace in which the economic good was being priced and bid for because of its scarcity and usefulness. Value in use referred to the necessity or desirability of a good (for example, air), which does not have value in exchange because there is no scarcity. Market value, as estimated by appraisers, is equivalent to Smith's value in exchange. Investment value or price recognizes that one buyer can afford to pay more or less than other potential buyers and is conceptually derived from Smith's value in use.

Price is in the nature of a fact. It is the sum of money a purchaser actually pays. Value is the price that *should* be paid in a viable market between informed, intelligent buyers and sellers. We might pay $.25 for a McDonald's hamburger. Its worth, however, may be open to question. A seller may ask $100,000 for a parcel of real estate, an appraiser may conclude its value is $95,000, and a buyer may actually pay $92,500. While value is never known with complete certainty, the price is quantifiable to the penny.

David Ricardo (1772–1823) went further than any of the early economists in dealing with land value. His work was an extension of Malthus' who had said that the return to land was price determined, i.e., was determined in other markets. Other economic factors were mobile and had a higher priority for achieving a return than did land. Thus, the return or price was determined in the markets for labor and capital. In his extension of the price-determined theory, Ricardo conceptually divided land into various grades of quality, from best to poorest. Landowners would use the best grade first, the next grade second, and so on until the last (or marginal) grade was brought into cultivation. Since the markets were demanding the products of this highest cost soil, the cost of the labor and capital equalled the value of the product. The higher grades of land were producing the same products but incurring lower costs. This greater productivity provided the owners of the higher grade land a surplus—or *rent*—which was unearned or unjustified by any greater contribution.

The German economist Johann Heinrich von Thünen (1783–1850) made a major contribution to value theory of land by adding the element of location to marginal productivity. He developed in great detail the explanation for the degree of labor and capital investment on a parcel of land. Unused or undeveloped land would not be brought into production unless the added revenue was expected to earn a return on the labor and capital investment equal to the current rate of interest. The revenue to be obtained was a function of the land's location relative to "the isolated city" or to its fertility relative to other parcels.[2]

The same type of analysis was applied by Thünen to land already in production. Increasing amounts of capital and labor would be applied to the land until the value of the last added worker and capital increment equals the value of the expected additional revenue. The distance of the undeveloped land from the city determined whether it would be more advantageous to develop the new land or to apply more labor and capital to land already in production. Today the last profitable application of labor and capital to developed land is called the intensive margin, while the point at which the development of additional land becomes profitable is termed the extensive margin. The cost of overcoming the friction of distance serves as the balancing force between the intensive and extensive margins.

Classical theory, which we have just discussed, is the origin of one of the three principal approaches used today in value estimation. This is the cost approach, and it is based upon the assumption that cost of production equals value. The weakness of this assumption is pointed out in the next chapter, but suffice it here to say that the cost theory ignores the utility or demand side of value.

Another major adaptation of the classical theory is the assumption in present-day appraisal practice that the income to land is residual. This assumption is based upon Ricardian theory and is manifested in the so-called residual techniques in which the income to either land or buildings holds lower priority to the other, depending upon the situation. We will deal with this assumption later in the section on modern value theory.

Marginal utility.   The marginal utility emphasis on value theory was developed by the Austrian economists Menger, von Wieser, and von Böhm-Bawerk around the turn of the century. These economists departed rather radically from the classicist's emphasis on cost of production (supply) to the emphasis on utility (demand). According to the marginal utility theory, the utility produced by the last unit of an economic good or service (*marginal* utility) determines its value. Cost of production does not enter into the value determination; the short-run decisions of marginal utility alone govern the theory.

To deny the long-run effect of production costs is, of course, as falla-

---

[2] Johann Heinrich von Thünen, *The Isolated State,* trans. Carla M. Wartenberg (New York: Pergamon Press, 1966).

cious as the classicists' noncomprehension of utility. Nevertheless, the marginal utility theory is a powerful concept in value theory. Utility is partially determined by expectations of relative supply, and who is to say how long the short-run market forces can endure? Perhaps the famous Keynesian adage about our all being dead in the long run is appropriate.

The marginal utility theory holds a close relationship to the income approach used in value estimation today. As developed more fully in the next chapter, the income approach attempts to measure the present worth —relative utility—of the future benefits expected to be obtained from an economic good. This approach, in fact, shows an even closer relationship to the Austrian school by virtue of the fact that von Bohm-Bawerk regarded interest as the payment for foregoing the present use of capital and the rate at which future goods must be discounted to determine their present values. "It (interest) therefore constitutes the most direct consequence conceivable of the difference in value between present and future goods." [3] As we shall see in the next chapter, capitalization rates used in real estate valuation and investment analysis are essentially interest rates added to capital recovery rates.

Neoclassical. With two basically different theories of value, economists began to think there must be truth in each and that they are not mutually exclusive. To Alfred Marshall, the brilliant English economist, (1842–1924) remained the task of synthesizing both types of theories into an integrated system. This he did in his famous book, *Principles of Economics,*[4] which became the world's leading economics textbook. In this book Marshall introduced the famous scissors analogy of supply and demand operating in the market. As each blade of a pair of scissors is necessary for the unit to function, so is supply and demand necessary for the economic unit—a market—to function. The interaction of both these forces is important in the determination of value.

The sales comparison approach to value estimation, developed more fully in the next chapter, is a direct application of the Marshallian analysis. It assumes an equilibrium of supply and demand forces in the market that culminate in a price. Note that if the market were a *perfect* market meeting the criteria of

a) Homogeneity of products
b) Many buyers and sellers
c) No buyer or seller large enough to influence the market
d) No external influence
e) Complete knowledge as to possible uses
f) Agreement as to expectations

---

[3] Eugen von Böhm-Bawerk, *Positive Theory of Capital,* trans. George D. Nuncke (South Holland, Ill.: Libertarian Press, 1959), p. 291.

[4] Alfred Marshall, *Principles of Economics* (8th ed.; London: Macmillan and Co., Ltd., 1920).

the price would, by definition, equal value. This is shown diagrammatically in Figure 4–1. Although real estate markets are far from perfect, real estate analysts look at many evidences of market activity in an effort to *estimate* value.

FIGURE 4–1

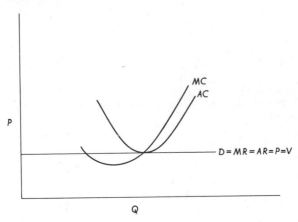

P = Price
Q = Quantity
D = Demand
MR = Marginal revenue
AR = Average revenue
V = Value
MC = Marginal cost
AC = Average cost

Modern value theory. The value theory relevant to today has elements of all the developments (and more) that are discussed heretofore. Additionally, however, modern theory seeks to explain the determinants of urban location values and to take a more realistic view of income production as found in affluent Western societies. The attempt to explain the value of agricultural land in a nontechnical society of 300 years ago is no longer the central task. (Yet try to detect after studying the next chapter how many appraisal applications stem from these theories.)

Perhaps the foremost advocate of reforming land value theories is Professor Richard U. Ratcliff. In his book on *Urban Land Economics* he views land, contrary to the classical view, as being a factor of production similar in nature and treatment to the other classical factors of labor and capital. In Ratcliff's own words:

We view land as a factor of production with an economic behavior little different from that of the other basic factors. We incline to the view that rent is a return to land for the contribution that it makes in creating want—satisfying goods and services; rent is compensation for the productivity of land in the same sense that wages are the payment for the productivity of labor. Land is valuable because it is scarce in supply in relation to the demand for its services. Rent is no more unearned than wages or interest, save in an abstract sense; in the same sense, wages might be considered in part a return on innate human intelligence. Rent is not exploitative, for it takes nothing from the worker, from the owner of capital goods, or from the consumer; rent is a measure of contribution not of extraction or reduction.[5]

Further, Ratcliff develops the thesis that land is economically mobile. "Though physically fixed there is a significant portion of the land supply of various grades that is appropriate for alternative uses. That portion is sufficient to impart to land the quality of mobility that is essential to participation in the competitive-equilibrium process of price determination." [6] Thus, he relies on the Marshallian equilibrium explanation of prices, giving no special significance to the marginal units or to their cost of production. In such analysis the distinction between price-determined and price-determining is irrelevant. Thus, land rent is not considered residual.

Indirect value theories

Although not directly explaining the value concept or how value decisions are made, much economic theory is indirectly concerned with value. These theories cannot be overlooked by the student of real estate, since they concern the bigger picture in which decision making occurs. Perhaps the most relevant of these indirect doctrines were formulated by the mercantilists, the physiocrats, the institutionalists, and the Keynesians.

The mercantilist economic doctrine was based upon international trade. A country's wealth and welfare were determined by the extent to which the country could develop a favorable trade relation with other nations. A favorable trade relation was one in which exports exceeded imports so that the gold and silver received in payment for the exports would increase the country's stocks of those valuable metals.

Modern international trade theory, of course, rejects this doctrine. Our old friend David Ricardo developed in 1817 the famous theory of comparative advantage, which showed that trading by one nation with another is mutually advantageous—even if the one country is inefficient relative to the other and has an unfavorable balance of trade. The point shown by this theory is, as students may recall from their economics principles courses, that a country is better off by specializing in the production of goods in which it is most efficient (relative to itself), rather than attempting

---

[5] Richard U. Ratcliff, *Urban Land Economics* (New York: McGraw-Hill Book Co., 1949), p. 365.

[6] Ibid., p. 367.

to produce all its own goods and not engaging in international trade because it would have an unfavorable balance.

As we shall see in chapter 11, the old mercantilist idea carries over into the economic analysis of cities in the form of economic base analysis. The need for development of better analytical techniques in this area is great. Mercantilism is also relevant today in emphasizing the role of a nation's relative international power in determining its general welfare. To the extent that world political opinion influences expectations as to a country's well-being and prestige, the value of its economic goods (including real estate) will feel the effect.

The physiocrats held sway in France under Louis XV and believed that agricultural production was the key to economic welfare. Their emphasis on productivity carries over today in its role in modern value theory. As you recall, the return to land in the modern view is for the contribution it makes in creating want-satisfying goods and services. The physiocratic doctrine also served to discredit the earlier mercantilist doctrine. Trade was thought to be of a secondary nature, and in fact not to contribute to a country's welfare.

The institutionalists are comprised of many economists covering no specific time period and advancing no integrated theory. Rather they are present in every socioeconomic system and serve the function of criticism and review. They observe society through economic lenses and describe social dangers and evils. They are the catalyst which often effects social change. Perhaps the best known such American economist is Thorstein Veblen, author of many remarkable books, the most widely read being *The Theory of the Leisure Class* [7] and *The Theory of Business Enterprise.* [8]

Veblen attacked the assumptions of standard economic science and scathingly criticized contemporary society. He argued that group behavior is in constant change, and the evolutionary nature of society cannot adequately be explained by the outmoded assumption that man is hedonistic in nature. Institutions in society are but one stage of cultural development; and in capitalistic society, the institutions of private property and technology lead to a "pecuniary culture." In such a society members of the so-called leisure class consume unproductively merely for the purpose of impressing others—the phenomenon of conspicuous consumption. On the production side, industries become businesses whose motive is not to produce needed goods but to obtain a profit or pecuniary gain through absentee ownership and hired managers. While regarding the future of capitalistic enterprise as leading to ever greater power and group conflict, Veblen was unwilling to predict the future of economic society. The

---

[7] Thorstein Veblen, *The Theory of the Leisure Class* (New York: Modern Library, 1934).

[8] Thorstein Veblen, *The Theory of Business Enterprise* (New York: C. Scribner's and Sons, 1915).

changing form of society could only be observed contemporarily or historically.

Another institutionalist who received a great deal of attention both in this country and abroad was Henry George (1839–1897). He contended that the private control of land led to the conditions of poverty that he viewed in the large cities. As in Ricardian rent theory, the land is not produced by human endeavor, and according to George, should belong in common to all people. His remedy was to discourage land ownership by imposing a heavy tax on land (but not improvements) and to tax no other factors of production. George's following was principally among the lay public—not the academic community. His own formal education had been meager, and although he wrote in knowledge of great economic thinkers, his writing style carried an emotional appeal rather than the systematic analysis of the professional economist. Nevertheless, the single tax idea developed by George in his widely read book, *Progress and Poverty,*[9] has many followers to this day.

The institutionalists' importance in value theory is transmitted through the way in which society functions and the resulting attitudes toward private property, the role of government in economic affairs, the types of controls placed on institutions, and the distribution of income. We need only point to the great social changes that have occurred in this country during the last 30 years to see the effect of some institutionalists. Still the criticism and espousal of even greater change continues:

The complaint that can be raised against the United States . . . is that it has lagged in applying the new knowledge we have about how to induce economic progress, and the new determination we have acquired to use this knowledge to our advantage . . . this unfortunate backwardness in American economic policy has serious effects not only for the welfare of large sections of its own people but also for both the direction and effectiveness of its foreign policy.[10]

John Maynard Keynes (1883–1946) shook the foundations of economic analysis with his startling new theories of economic analysis. He advanced the thesis that the equilibrium tendency of investment and saving are not necessarily the point at which full employment is achieved. The traditional equilibrium analysis was therefore held to be insufficient for the analysis of and formulation of policies for national economic welfare. His contention of the propensity to consume being a decreasingly steep curve and its subsequent empiric demonstration gave credence to his theory of underconsumption as constituting the primary source of depressions.

The policy implications of the Keynesian theories have important implications for real estate analysis. More than simply being familiar with

---

[9] Henry George, *Progress and Poverty* (New York: Robert Schalkenbach Foundation, 1948).

[10] Gunnar Myrdal, *Challenge to Affluence* (New York: Pantheon Books, 1965), p. 14.

the theory, real estate analysts must analyze current and expected national economic policies. Monetary, fiscal, and debt management policies are important tools in the Keynesian model for regulating the economy and, thus, in determining prices that occur for all economic goods, including real estate. The trend toward more and more planning for economic stability and growth forces the appraiser, analyst, and investor to consider these influences on real estate values.

THE CONCEPT AND NATURE OF VALUE

Having reviewed the economic thought that has been concerned either directly or indirectly with value, we now attempt to synthesize the various theories into the present-day understanding of the value concept. An understanding of the value concept is a necessary basis for the next chapter on the measurement of value. After all, one is usually better able to measure accurately that which he understands. And in order to understand an idea it is usually helpful to know its historical derivation. We have tried to provide this background for value in the preceding section.

In attempting to derive the concept of value from economic theory and logic, we may conclude unequivocally that value is a market concept. It is the resultant of interacting forces of supply and demand. It rests upon the presence of willing buyers and sellers freely bidding in competition with each other. Further, it is premised upon a system of free enterprise and private property.

But what about the various theories?—the classical emphasis upon the supply side through labor?—the unearned increment idea as contrasted from the marginal utility explanation?—the modern theory which holds that land is economically mobile? How do these seemingly contrasting approaches yield the supply-demand market concept?

The key is the synthesizing Marshallian theory—the neoclassical approach. In his theory Marshall integrated all the other relevant theories into the supply-demand model. He showed that the various theories advanced theretofore dealt only with the determination of either supply or demand and that the more explanatory and generally useful model is the one that incorporates all such possible determinants. It is this model of intersecting supply and demand curves to which we turn for our basic understanding of value.

We agree with the classical school that the supply of real estate, or any economic good, is an important determinant of value. We agree that labor is an important element in production cost and thus in supply. We would not agree, however, that this is the whole story—that once numbers have been assigned to these variables that the value of the good is known. Rather, there are important determinants identified by other theories that have a part in producing the final answer.

Another contention of the classical school (and of Henry George) with which we would not agree is that the income to land is a surplus—an unearned increment. Here we would prefer the modern view that land is necessary in the productive process and that the owners of land are thus entitled to the income derived from land—*provided the market system is working well.* This view correlates with the marginal utility theory and emphasizes the usefulness of land in the productive process. In addition, the productivity-marginal utility views incorporate conceptually the role of location. Location of land, because of its physical immobility, is a major determinant of its productivity. For example, even the most fertile farmland's productivity is diminished if it is located farther from grain and livestock markets than other fertile land. Location, of course, takes on an even more important role in determining the productivity of urban land.

A synthesis of the various value theories requires some further explanation. The resulting supply-demand model for the purpose of value *determination* carries the requirements of the perfectly competitive model of market behavior. If the requirements of this model were met, there would be no need for value estimates to be made. As shown above, the market price that actually occurs would, by definition, equal value. In analyzing any market, however, it soon becomes clear that the requirements are impossible to attain. For example, the wheat market is often cited as the market most closely approaching the idea of a perfect market; yet, even in this market the product is not homogenous (there are different grades of wheat). Additionally, the market is influenced by governmental activities and has within it buyers and sellers who do not have complete knowledge and are not in agreement as to the future. If the characteristics of the real estate market are compared with the requirements in this same way, the extreme imperfections become obvious—thus the need for professional value estimators of real estate.

Because real estate markets are considerably less than perfect, real estate appraisers have had to fall back on a definition of value which provides a workable, measurable concept, and which will be recognized by the courts. A definition of market value formulated by the Society of Real Estate Appraisers is as follows:

The price which a property will bring in a competitive market under all conditions requisite to a fair sale, which would result from negotiations between a buyer and a seller, each acting prudently, with knowledge, and without undue stimulus.[11]

Although the definition is somewhat similar to the definition of value under perfect competition, some of the perfect competition requirements

---

[11] Society of Real Estate Appraisers, *Real Estate Appraisal Principles and Terminology* (Chicago, 1971), p. 85.

are missing and some are less stringent. The real world thus dictates a compromise between the theoretically pure concept of a market and the necessity to make decisions and settle disputes.

In summary, then, a compromise market definition encompasses the classical, marginal utility, and productivity theories of land value. The costs of labor and capital certainly influence the supply of real estate. The short-run usefulness of the last unit of real estate produced determines demand. And the contention that land value is caused by its ability to contribute to productive processes, and that this ability may be shared to some degree by a number of parcels of real estate is one which helps explain both the demand and the supply sides of real estate markets.

Money and the value concept

An addendum to our explanation of the value concept is now necessary to clarify the role of money in economic (value) decisions. The role of money is often misunderstood because of its own characteristic ability to change in value. Although money serves both as a medium of exchange and a standard of value, the standard itself can change from year to year, day to day, or hour to hour. Some currencies, in fact, have experienced such rapid devaluation (for example, the German mark following World War I) that the change was noticeable almost minute by minute.

Since the values of economic goods are cited and compared in money terms, the value of an economic good may not have changed, even though the number of dollars measuring its value is different from one time to another. Thus, in order to compare dollar measurements of value over a time period during which the value of the dollar has changed, it is necessary to adjust the dollar measurements to conform to each other. This is done by the familiar method of inflating or deflating one of the dollar measurements to the level represented at the time of the other dollar measurement.

Value is a real concept. As expressed by Adam Smith, it is "the power of a good to command other goods or labor services in exchange."

An illustration of this definition of value and the clouding role of money is provided by two appraisals that were performed on the same downtown commercial building four years apart. The first appraisal estimated the building's value at approximately $200,000. The second valuation, with the differential depreciation added back in, estimated the value at $220,000. As measured by the consumer and wholesale price indexes, there had been about a 10 percent decline in the value of the dollar during that four-year period. It is clear that, disregarding depreciation, the value of the building was about the same four years after the first appraisal, even though the dollar measurement increased by $20,000. Stated differently, the real estate would command about the same goods in exchange as it did four years previously.

SUMMARY

Investment decisions are based upon an appraisal of a property's value. Although investment analysis requires consideration of other factors in addition to value (such as financing requirements and income taxes), the primary criterion is value. The process of estimating value can thus be regarded as a major portion of investment analysis.

The chapter traces the development of value theory. Economic theories directly concerned with the concept of value are divided among the classical, marginal utility, neoclassical, and modern schools of thought. Additionally, economic theories that do not deal directly with the value concept but which have important implications for value or its measurement are discussed.

The main conclusions from the theoretical aspects of value are that value is a market phenomenon which is the resultant of the interaction of supply and demand. In turn, supply and demand are the market effects of the relative scarcity and utility associated with an economic good. Under perfect competition value would equal the price paid for the good. There would be no necessity to measure value independently; it would be automatically measured by the price of each transaction. However, since markets are less than perfectly competitive (particularly the real estate market), value must be estimated independently by competent appraisers or analysts.

QUESTIONS FOR REVIEW

1. What concepts developed by classical economists are relevant today to our understanding of value?
2. What was the principal contribution to value theory of the marginal utility school of economic thought?
3. Can utility be measured? If yes, how? If no, why not?
4. What role does money play in the identification and measurement of value? How does money both help and hinder the measurement of value?
5. How did Alfred Marshall greatly increase our understanding of the nature of value?
6. Discuss the contention that "value is the basic criterion of all decision making."

PROBLEMS

1. A large home on the crest of a hill commanding a beautiful view of the river below was offered for sale at $250,000. The home had been built 15 years earlier by a wealthy business tycoon near the small town of his birth in southern Missouri. Although no one in the town could afford such an expensive property, all of the town's people agreed the home was probably worth at

least $250,000. A local businessman offered $100,000 but the offer was rejected. Finally, the property was sold for $150,000 to a Chicago family as a summer vacation home.

a) Did an effective market exist for the property?

b) In your opinion, what was the value of the property?

c) Does sale price necessarily equal value?

d) Would you have paid $150,000 for the property?

e) Would you have sold for $150,000?

2. Assume that you own a parcel of land for which you paid $10,000 three years ago. The annual real estate tax amounts to $175. You now need your money and want to sell. If inflation has been averaging 5 percent per year, would you accept $11,576 ($10,000 plus 5 percent compounded annually)? Why or why not? What additional costs might you want to cover in your asking price?

REFERENCES

Bell, John Fred.   *A History of Economic Thought*. New York: Ronald Press Co., 1953.

George, Henry.   *Progress and Poverty*. New York: Robert Schalkenbach Foundation, 1948.

Heilbroner, Robert L.   *The Worldly Philosophers*. 3d ed. New York: Simon and Schuster, 1967.

Ratcliff, Richard U.   *Urban Land Economics*. New York: McGraw-Hill Book Co., 1949, Chap. 12.

Rima, I. H.   *Development of Economic Analysis*. Homewood, Ill.: Richard D. Irwin, Inc., 1967.

Ring, Alfred A.   *The Valuation of Real Estate*. 2d ed. Englewood Cliffs, N. J.: Prentice-Hall, Inc., 1970, Chap. 2.

Spengler, Joseph J. and Allen, W. R.   *Essays in Economic Thought: Aristotle to Marshall*. Chicago: Rand McNally and Co., 1960.

What Veblen Thought: Selected Writings of Thorstein Veblen.   New York: Augustine M. Kelly, Bookseller, 1964.

chapter 5

THE MEASUREMENT
OF VALUE

As DEMONSTRATED in the last chapter, the problem of value measurement arises because of the existence of market imperfections. Price may or may not equal value in any less-than-perfect market; therefore, an independent measurement is required to arrive at a value figure. And after one obtains a value figure by an independent process, he is not certain the figure is the price that *would* have occurred in an active, viable market. Thus, the best that one can do is to *estimate* the value of an economic good.

Obviously, since real estate is an economic good, these general statements are applicable—even more so than for most economic goods—to the estimation of real property values. Real estate markets are fraught with hazardous variances from the concept of an ideal market, and therefore the estimate of value of a parcel of real estate requires a wider range of possible error than for other economic goods. The price obtained for a special-purpose, income-producing property valued at $300,000 might vary by as much as 25 percent in either direction from the appraised value. In contrast, the price of a bushel of wheat is probably so close to its value that there would be little discernible difference between value and price. These differences among markets in the efficiency and accuracy of the price-setting process largely result from the economic nature of the products themselves.

This chapter discusses the physical features of real estate that lead to its economic uniqueness. We attempt to relate the economic implications of each characteristic to its influence on value. Methods and procedures of value measurement which should incorporate the effects of economic characteristics into estimates of income, capitalization rates, costs, and market prices comprise the remaining portion of the chapter.

ECONOMIC CHARACTERISTICS

Because real estate markets are so imperfect, and because real estate is different from other economic goods, independent and specialized value measurement procedures are required to place a meaningful dollar worth on a parcel of real property. The differences between real estate and other economic goods concern its physical immobility, its length of economic life, and its economic size.

Physical immobility

The physical immobility of real estate, although an obvious characteristic, leads to several important economic considerations discussed in this section. These economic considerations in turn provide the reasoning and justification for the valuation procedures discussed in the latter part of this chapter.

Because of the physical immobility of real estate, the market for each parcel is largely determined by those who demand and supply properties in a localized area. Although the demand side of the market may contain buyers from outside the local area, in many instances prospective purchasers of real estate come from the local area. The supply side is, of course, local. To the extent, however, that a parcel in one locality may substitute for one in another locality, the supply side becomes broader in scope. The fact remains, however, that each parcel of real estate is imperfectly substitutable for other parcels.

The physical immobility of real estate has an important implication for the valuation of real estate. Since the parcel of real property cannot be moved from its location, its value is subject to the effects of economic, social, or political developments emanating from the national, regional, community, and neighborhood levels. With respect to moveable economic goods, such as a refrigerator or rug, purely local economic forces have much less effect on their values. Why? Simply because they can be moved to escape such influences.

Social, political, and economic developments at all levels require subjective assessment and often are tenuous in their relationship to value. Nevertheless, value estimates should be based upon some assumptions about future conditions in the society, although quantification of their effects is difficult. The appraiser or investment analyst considers these influences by beginning with the broadest influence and working down to more and more localized influences, i.e., from national to regional to city to district or neighborhood factors. Favorable trends tend to increase estimates of the gross income to be derived from a property or to increase one's confidence in a predicted level of income. Trends supporting demand have the effect of reducing vacancy expectations, reducing the risk factor in capitalization rates, or lowering one's expectation of future depreciation or obsolescence. Unfavorable trends would have opposite effects.

Examples of some of the large-scale social trends that might be considered in evaluating the worth of a property are those toward the formation of smaller families, delayed marriages, urban living, and longer-term apartment tenancy. These trends may be accentuated or mitigated within any one region or community, although social conditions in local communities are usually reflective of national trends.

Political trends are even more difficult to assess. The emphasis upon housing programs by Congress, the status of zoning laws, housing and building codes, open occupancy laws and programs, and school integration efforts are but some of the current political conditions that may affect property values.

Although it is fairly obvious that national economic conditions can influence a property's value (recall that during the Great Depression almost all real estate declined in value), the more localized types of influences may be more obscure. Examples: the decline in coal mining in southern Illinois from 1945 to 1960 caused the entire region to suffer economically and produced a commensurate loss in real estate values. Several cities, such as Evansville, Indiana, and Pittsburgh, experienced economic declines during the 1950s and early 1960s for a variety of reasons which were accompanied by sluggishness and value decreases in real estate markets.[1] Probably every reader can think of several examples of district and neighborhood developments that have adversely affected real estate values in an area.

Economic trends generally are more amenable to quantifiable analysis. Such considerations would include an analysis of income levels, availability of financing and interest rates, outlook for monetary policy, levels of savings, prices of housing relative to other economic goods, expected investment in housing and other kinds of real estate, and various demographic data, such as numbers of population and mobility trends.

Short-term analysis of the national economy is particularly helpful in determining an appropriate capitalization rate. As we shall see in the income approach to value, capitalization rates are simply interest rates added to capital recovery rates. Since capitalization rates are used to convert a parcel of real estate's earning expectancy to value, a property's value would tend to be inversely correlated with interest rates in the economy.

At the local level economic trends become more directly translated into market analyses for a particular type of property being considered.

---

[1] In the case of Evansville, the decline was caused by several large industries leaving the town following labor difficulties and mergers. The Pittsburgh decline was largely attributed to increasing automation in steel plants.

In assessing economic trends affecting housing, social and demographic factors are combined with income projections to estimate housing requirements and their predicted effects on rents, vacancy rates, and transaction prices. Similar types of analyses are important in the valuation and investment analyses of offices, commercial property (including shopping centers), and industrial property. Market analysis is discussed more fully in chapter 11, and an outline of market analyses conducted by the Federal Housing Administration is contained in Appendix E.

In addition to an analysis of social, economic, and politcal factors at the national, regional, and local levels, a thorough examination and analysis of the physical and legal characteristics of the property must be made. The physical immobility of real estate means that every parcel is different from every other parcel. If similar in every other respect, it differs in its location relative to other parcels; it is either closer or nearer the corner than the adjacent parcel. Similarly the legal rights and obligations may vary between two otherwise similar parcels. One seller may be contemplating the sale of his estate for life, another the sale of a leasehold, and still another a fee simple estate. The appraiser or investor must be aware of the exact physical items to be included in a purchase and of the legal rights and obligations accompanying the physical items.

Long length of economic life

The second major atypical characteristic of real estate is its relatively long economic life. Land, or more specifically location, lasts forever, and buildings usually are built to last from twenty-five to several hundred years. In contrast are other economic goods which last much shorter periods of time. For example, automobiles may last five to ten years, clothing two to five years, and groceries one day to a month. What is the implication of this characteristic for the economics of real estate? It is that the purchase of real property represents a long-term commitment. A purchaser's viewpoint should be long range, and he should be convinced of the ability of the property to provide the services desired over its entire economic life. The purchase of real estate thus requires a thorough analysis aimed at predicting the type, amount, and quantity of future benefits to be obtained from the property. It also requires a prediction of the *expected* expenses to be incurred by the property, for the resultant of the two—net operating income (N.O.I.)—is the generating engine of value. The two graphs in Figure 5–1 show diagrammatically one possible relationship between income, expenses, and economic life.

Net income prediction.   In attempting to predict future net income the most useful type of information is the historical experience of the property itself. In the case of a commercial, industrial, or apartment property, the first step is to analyze past years' income figures. How far back should

FIGURE 5–1

Determinants of economic life

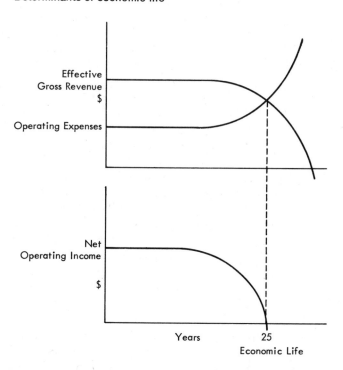

one go? There is no definite answer, but preferably the record for at least five years should be examined. In analyzing past revenues the following questions should be answered:

1. Is each source of revenue appropriate and reasonable?

Sometimes certain revenues should be discounted or eliminated. For example, some income statements show revenue from tenants for janitorial service. The offsetting expense will, of course, reduce or eliminate this item. But in some cases, even when the revenue is currently larger than the commensurate expense, it is unreasonable to *predict* this situation into the future.

Whether each amount of revenue is reasonable can be ascertained only in relation to other comparable sources. If an apartment rental is either too low or too high it should be adjusted to the proper or reasonable rent. This is called the market rent and is distinguished from contract rent which is the amount actually paid. Market rent is what *should* be paid and, therefore, is the amount that can be expected in the future.

2. What is the trend of revenues for the time being analyzed?

If the trend is either upward or downward, there may be some reason for the trend that the analyst has not discerned. Before proceeding he should decide whether he expects the trend to continue, or to change. This, of course, is the reason for analyzing a period of several years. Whether the past is an accurate predictor of the future can never be known for certain at the prediction stage of any analysis, but this makes it all the more important for the analyst to utilize the data he has available, his analytic powers, and his judgment derived from experience so as not to make investment decisions in a vacuum.

In analyzing past expenses, four questions should be considered:

1. Is each item of expense appropriate and reasonable?

The same comments that were made with respect to revenues are appropriate here. Additionally, however, we should mention that the problem of discerning and eliminating inappropriate expense figures from an owner's statement is usually greater than with respect to revenues. Most owners' income statements include expense items that are not appropriate to the property's value. Typical of such items are financing expense and income tax expense. These expenses are not allocable to the real estate. They do not necessarily have to be incurred by the real estate for it to produce income. Some owners would not need to bear such expenses, but all owners would have to expect janitorial or fuel expense. The former are thus personal or business expenses of the owner and should be eliminated from a statement of property expenses.

2. What is the trend for each expense?

As with the analysis for the trend of revenues, the trend of each expense should be noted and analyzed if necessary. If the trend of an expense is either upward or downward (and most expenses will be upward), there may be some reason for predicting higher or lower expenses in the future. On the other hand, the analyst may uncover an upward trend of some expenses that effective and efficient management could correct. If so, the analyst would then adjust the predicted expense downward under the assumption that effective and efficient management will be available for the property. The point to be emphasized with respect to analysis of the expense trend is that the trend should not be extrapolated blindly in the future. Often trends can be changed with proper management, and these possibilities will be detected by the analyst when he looks at the causes for basic factors underlying the trends.

3. Should any expenses not included in the owner's statement be included?

Often an owner's statement has been compiled for tax purposes or for other accounting reasons and not for the purpose of estimating the property's value. In these cases only the actual expenses incurred should be included. However, since the objective is to predict all the *future* expenses necessary for the property to have value—regardless of who owns the property—certain expenses should be added in. Two good examples of such expenses typically are vacancy and collection losses and management expense.

Vacancy losses and often collection losses involve little or no out-of-pocket expense. Yet, in predicting the future net income for a parcel of real estate, the analyst would be remiss in not recognizing the high probability that reductions from total possible gross income will result because of these reasons. Keep in mind that the objective is to predict future net income, and that particularly as buildings become older, an owner should expect to experience some periods between lessees when his property will not be drawing income and with some tenants who for various reasons will not pay their rent. Thus the analyst should include this expense as one expected for the future.

Particularly with respect to small, owner-managed investment properties the expense of managing the property is often not included in an owner's statement of income and expenses. The owner in these cases manages the property himself, and management does not represent an out-of-pocket expense for him; he thus does not enter it as a specific and identified expense. The function of property management, however, will have to be performed in the future for the property to obtain income for the owner. This reasoning provides the justification for including management as an expense that will be incurred by the property in the future— whether accomplished by the owner or by a hired manager. In cases where the owner has hired a manager and this expense is identified in his operating statement, and provided the expense is reasonable both with respect to amount and trend, this figure could be entered as the analyst's best estimate of the future expense. In those cases where the owner has not hired a manager and no management expense is indicated in his statement, the analyst should impute a future management expense to the property. The owner's time is worth money, since he could be earning during the time he spends managing the property. The amount imputed usually varies between 2 and 10 percent of effective gross income, which is the difference between total possible gross income and vacancy and collection losses.

4. Are large replacement item expenses amortized over the expected life of the replacements?

Some large components of a building such as its heating system, air-conditioning system, water heater, or roof can be expected to wear out faster than the building itself. A roof, for example, may have to be replaced every 15 years, while the building can be expected to last perhaps 50 to 100 years. Over its total life, then, the building will undoubtedly have several roofs. Many times the analyst will find that the owner has not amortized these large expenditures over their expected lives. Rather, as the large expense is incurred for replacing a roof or heating system, this expense will be included as a deduction from that year's income. This is not the proper procedure, however, for the value estimator. He recognizes that the roof wears out each hour each day and each year rather than all at once. It is fallacious to assign the entire expense of a new roof to one earning period only. Therefore, in predicting future expenses to the real estate he will attempt to include an amount allocable each period for major repairs and replacements of components of the building that last a shorter time than the building itself. These items are not included in any depreciation assignable to the building itself.

In predicting future revenues and expenses for a parcel of real property through the procedure of analyzing past operating statements of the owner, the analyst obtains a new statement of expected revenues and expenses which is called a reconstructed operating statement. An example of a reconstructed operating statement is shown in Figure 5–2.

FIGURE 5–2

Reconstructed operating statement
ABC Apartments

Gross possible income		$27,500
Less vacancy and collection losses		1,375
Effective Gross Income		$26,125
Operating expenses:		
Electricity	$ 750	
Fuel	1,025	
Water	100	
Repairs	300	
Decorating	300	
Trash collection	200	
Janitor's salary	1,500	
Supplies	200	
Miscellaneous	150	
		4,525
Net before Other Expenses		$21,600
Other expenses:		
Reserve for replacements	$ 400	
Fixed charges		
Real estate taxes	1,600	
Insurance	600	
		2,600
Net Operating Income		$19,000

Economic size

The third major atypical characteristic of most parcels of real estate is its relatively large economic size. To purchase a parcel of real estate one usually has to pay a price of anywhere from several thousand dollars on up. It is not unusual for a family to spend $30,000 to $50,000 for its home or for purchasers of investment properties to pay $500,00 or more. Contrast this with the price of groceries, clothes, or even automobiles. Thus, the single largest purchase of most families throughout their lives is for a home.

Long-term viewpoint. The relative size of most real estate transactions has two implications from an economics standpoint for real estate investors. The first of these is that the purchase of real estate must be viewed as an important, long-term commitment, and the second is that financing considerations are important determinants of the investment feasibility. Although one can trade in real estate—as one trades in stock, bonds, or other investments—the trader in real estate, even to a greater extent than with respect to other types of investments, should be convinced of the long-term soundness of his purchase. A real estate investment may be less liquid and less marketable than other types of investments. Even the trader in real estate may have to hold property one or perhaps even five years to expect to profit from his purchase. The investor, as contrasted with the trader or speculator, is concerned with the income-producing potential of the property. Thus, in purchasing property for trading, the trader's basic question is simply whether the price for which he can purchase the property is less than the price warranted by a long-term investment analysis.

Financing requirement. The second implication of the large economic size of real estate transactions impels the investor to consider the present state of financing conditions as well as to consider the impact of the specific financing arrangement on each transaction. A complex structure of financing institutions has evolved for the purpose of financing real estate transactions. Savings and loan associations, commercial banks, mutual savings banks, and life insurance companies are all important institutions in this area. The cost of borrowing funds and the terms demanded by these institutions are obviously important considerations to the real estate investor.

Because of the large amount of money that must usually be borrowed for a family to purchase its home, long-term amortized loan arrangements have been developed. It is not unusual for a family to agree to repay a large loan over a period of 25 years in monthly installments which include both interest and repayment of the principal amount of the loan. The real estate investor, whether he is a home purchaser or commercial property purchaser, should attempt to obtain the most favorable terms and interest rate possible from a reliable institution. But more important he must analyze the effect this will have upon his total income position. Will the income from the real estate or the amenities derived from home ownership be sufficient to more than offset the financing expense? What income will be left over after paying the financing expense, and how does this amount compare with the income to be obtained from other investments?

The individual terms and interest rates that an investor can obtain from various institutions vary from time to time in relation to the fiscal and monetary policies of the U.S. government. The investor should be aware of the basic determinants of interest rates and financing terms and should understand the relationship between fiscal and monetary policies and loan arrangements for real estate investment. One study of the cyclical effect of these policies showed a close relation between restrictive monetary and fiscal policies of the government and significantly decreased levels of real estate construction and investment.[2] In such times marginal buyers are excluded from the market because of the high cost and their inability to obtain financing. In the following chapter the procedure for taking into consideration the financing expense of a real estate transaction is developed.

VALUE ESTIMATION BY INCOME CAPITALIZATION

Relation of income capitalization to other approaches

There are three classical approaches, or frameworks of analysis, by which the value of a parcel of real estate is estimated. These are the income approach, the direct sales comparison approach, and the cost approach. Occasionally appraisal literature contains reports of newly developed approaches to real estate valuation; however, upon close examination it can be seen that even these so-called new approaches have their roots in one or more of the three classical approaches.

Although we discuss each of the three approaches separately from the others, each approach is highly related to the other two. Since all roads lead to the final objective—the concept of value—the three approaches can be regarded as being different ways of looking at the same problem. The analyst needs to understand clearly the relationships among the three approaches and to be able to discern which approaches are appropriate in a given situation.

Nature of the income approach [3]

The income approach focuses attention upon the value to investors of an expected future stream of net income to be derived from a parcel of real estate. The right to receive the income in future years is the right associated with property ownership. This legal right has value, and it is this value which the income approach measures. In carrying out the income approach several variables must be considered, all of which constitute inputs to the basic value formula that:

$$V = (f)\,I$$

---

[2] Halbert C. Smith and Carl J. Tschappat, "Monetary Policy and Real Estate Values," *The Appraisal Journal*, vol. 34, no. 1 (January 1966), pp. 18–26.

[3] A thorough treatment of the income capitalization approach to estimating market value is contained in William N. Kinnard, Jr., *Income Property Valuation* (Lexington, Mass.: D. C. Heath and Co., 1971).

where:

$$V = \text{Value}$$
$$I = \text{Income}$$
$$(f) = \text{Relationship between value and income}$$

In estimating value, we attempt to predict total income (I) and to estimate the appropriate, current (f) or capitalization rate. Income is composed of two elements—(1) net operating income (N.O.I.), and (2) reversion value. The capitalization rate is a composite of the discount rate and recapture rate. The latter rate is a function of the remaining economic life of the depreciating portion of the asset and the pattern of capital recapture. Before considering each of these inputs to the valuation process, we digress briefly to present the essential mathematical process of discounting. It underlies all capitalization procedures. Those students being exposed to discounting for the first time will have to give careful study to the following section. For those who are knowledgeable about present value concepts, the section may serve as a useful review.

Mathematics of discounting

The present value of any economic good is an amount less than the sum total of all of the future income payments to be derived from that economic good. There are basically two reasons for this. The first is that if the investor already had all of the payments to be derived in the future from the property, he could put these in a perfectly safe government or institutional investment and receive a return. The investor presumably would be incurring no risk of not obtaining his money at the end of the time. The second reason is that on top of the pure payment for the use of money, the investor must be compensated for added risk—the risk that he will not obtain his capital back. The percentage amounts for each of these two reasons, the pure interest rate and the risk rate, are the two components that make up the rate of return on investment (R.O.I.). The R.O.I. plus the straight line or sinking fund recapture rate make up the capitalization rate. The sinking fund recapture rate for estimating the value of an annuity is the amount necessary to be obtained each period, compounding at the discount rate, to accumulate to the original invested amount. Column 3 in Appendix G is a table of sinking fund factors. The R.O.I. is also often termed the discount rate.

$$\text{R.O.I.} + \text{R.O.C.} = \text{R}$$

where:

$$\text{R.O.I.} = \text{Return on total investment}$$
$$\text{R.O.C.} = \text{Rate of recapture of capital}$$
$$\text{R} \quad = \text{Capitalization rate}$$

To understand the discounting process it is convenient to discuss the compounding process and then to show how the discounting process is related to it. If one opens a savings account in a commercial bank and receives interest at the rate of 3 percent per annum, he would expect to have a value at the end of the year of his original investment plus 3 percent. Therefore, if he had invested one dollar, his investment at the end of the year would be $1.03. At the end of the second year he would have his investment of $1.03 plus 3 percent of the $1.03; thus, at the end of the second year the total worth of his investment is $1.0609. The 3 percent continues to compound in the future years similarly to the way in which it compounded the first two years for as long as the investor maintains his account drawing interest at 3 percent.

Illustrating with one dollar, we can explain the process of compounding by the formula $S = P(1 + r)^n$, where S is the compound sum, r is the interest rate and n is the number of years that the dollar earns the rate of interest. When the amount to be compounded is different from $1, the expression is multiplied by that principal amount (P). For example, in order to determine what the value of a $10 investment will be 10 years from today if it is invested at a rate of 4 percent, the formula would be $S = 10(1 + .04)^{10}$ and the answer would be $21.59. Columns 1 and 2 in Appendix G contain tables indicating the future values of $1 compounding and payments of $1 each period compounding over the designated number of periods.

The compounding process thus begins with a given investment and assumes that the investment draws interest at a specified rate, accumulating to a greater value at some future time. Compounding is contrasted from the discounting process in which one begins by knowing the future income stream and attempting to work backwards to find its present value (V). In other words, discounting is the reciprocal process of the compounding process, and thus it is given by the reciprocal of the compounding formula, or $V = P\left[\dfrac{1}{(1 + r)^n}\right]$. As in compounding, the expression is multiplied by P if different from $1. If, for example, one wanted to determine the value of $10 to be received 10 years from now which is to be discounted at a rate of 4 percent the formula would be $V = 10\left[\dfrac{1}{(1 + .04)^{10}}\right]$ and the answer would be $4.63.

If an equity investor in real estate expected to receive $1,000 for each of the next 25 years, the procedure for calculating the value of that level income stream would be to work out the formula for each of the 25 years and to sum the individual answers. This is, of course, an extremely lengthy process. However, there are two types of shortcuts which the analyst could take in order to avoid 25 lengthy calculations. The first of these concerns the fact that tables of present values of single payments of $1 due in the future have been calculated at various discount or interest rates. These are called Present Value of One tables, and Appendix G, Column 4 of this book contains such a table.

The second shortcut is a table which has already added the sums of various numbers of years' income of $1 discounted at various rates. It is called an annuity table and contains the present values of income streams of $1 at various rates of interest for various numbers of years. This table also is given in Appendix G, Column 5. Multiplying the first year's income by a factor from the level annuity table provides the value estimate.

Note that the level annuity factor obtained from the table is the reciprocal of the sum of the discount rate plus the sinking fund factor. In general, any factor from an annuity table is a reciprocal of a capitalization rate, and the following relationships hold.

$$I \times F = \text{Value}$$
$$\frac{I}{R} = \text{Value}$$
$$\frac{1}{R} = F$$

where:

I = Income
R = Capitalization rate
F = Factor

One may divide the rate directly into income to obtain the value estimate, or he may multiply by a factor obtained from the level annuity table (Appendix G, Column 5).

Valuation inputs

We now return to our discussion of the components of the income capitalization process. Decisions must be made regarding a property's expected net operating income, its remaining economic life, the expected pattern of the income stream, and the appropriate capitalization rate. When the decisions have been made the valuation process is reduced to arithmetic calculation.

Net operating income. The prediction of N.O.I. discussed earlier in the chapter is one of the most important considerations in the income capitalization approach to value. The net income calculation involves subtracting expected vacancy and collection losses, operating expenses, and replacement reserves from anticipated gross income. The analyst develops a reconstructed operating statement, with net operating income being the resulting figure.

Remaining economic life. The second variable to be considered is the length of economic life of the property. All material things wear out over some period of time, and buildings are no exception. Buildings wear out, meaning that expenses will increase over the life of the building, while revenues at some point will begin to decline and will decline more and more as time goes along. In time the expenses will become equal to and in fact may become greater than the revenues being produced by the property. The point at which expenses exactly equal revenues is the end of the economic life of the property; at this point the property no longer has value.

In the income approach the remaining economic life must be estimated because it is the period during which an owner can expect to obtain net income from his investment. Typically the economic life for buildings runs from 25 to 75 years, although exceptions can be found at both ends of the range. The actual measurement of this variable can only come from knowledge of construction techniques and judgment associated with long experience in dealing with buildings and estimating their economic lives.

Pattern of income. The third input in the income approach is the pattern of the income to be received over the remaining economic life of the building. The forecasted pattern is reflected in the process by which future income is converted to a present value. This conversion process is termed capitalization. An income stream's pattern will usually take one of the following two basic forms.

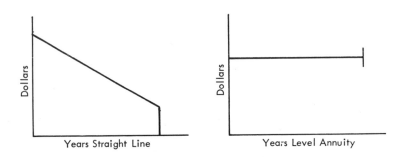

Years Straight Line   Years Level Annuity

The straight line pattern assumes that the net income will decrease by the same percentage every year to the end of the building's economic life, while the level annuity assumes the net income will remain constant.

The decision as to which pattern will be most realistic for a property being appraised must be based upon the analyst's assumption about the method of capital recapture. The straight line pattern assumes that an equal percentage of the capital investment in the building (thus, an equal yearly dollar amount) is recaptured every year.

If the remaining economic life of a building were estimated to be 25 years, a $100,000 investment cost would be recaptured by drawing equal annual amounts of $4,000 from the income stream each year for the 25-year period. The first year's income that would be produced would be the $4,000 plus the expected rate of return on the $100,000. If this rate were 8 percent the income would be $12,000 during the first year. For the second year the income would be $4,000 plus 8 percent of the remaining capital balance of $96,000, or $7,680, for a total income payment of $11,680. Each year the dollar return would be reduced because of the capital recapture assumption, as shown below. The value of the income stream would be estimated by dividing the capitalization rate of 8 percent plus 4 percent (12 percent) into the first year's income of $12,000. The resulting value is $100,000.

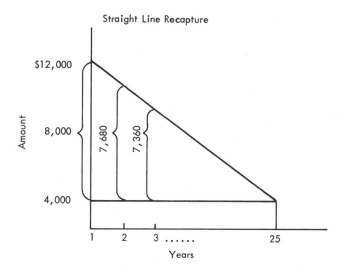

Straight Line Recapture

The crucial assumption contained in the use of the straight line method is that the amounts of recapture drawn from the income stream ($4,000 in the above example) are *not* reinvested and thus do not earn interest. These amounts presumably are deposited by the owner in his checking account or hidden in his mattress or at least used in some way in which no return is earned. Since this assumption is considered unrealistic by many real estate analysts, the straight line method of capitalization has lost favor in recent years.

The level annuity method of capitalization contains a more realistic assumption about the capital recapture portion of the income stream. In this method the capital recaptured each period is assumed to be reinvested in another property or investment yielding the same rate of return as the property being appraised. Thus, the amount of capital recapture before reinvestment is less than in the straight line method.

This sinking fund factor is added to the R.O.I. rate to obtain the total capitalization rate. If the same income used in the above example were capitalized by the level annuity method of capitalization, the capitalization rate would be .08 plus .01368, or .09368. Note that the capitalization rate is lower than in the straight line method and produces a higher value of about $128,000 (12,000 ÷ .09368). The higher value results because the income stream is level, rather than declining. It is level because additional income is produced through reinvestment.

When deciding whether to use straight line or level annuity capitalization, it is apparent that the net income pattern produced by the recapture assumption should be the basis for the decision. Do investors more typically place recapture dollars in nonincome-producing places for safe keeping? Or do they typically buy additional investments of a similar type? Most analysts of real estate, as well as securities and other analysts, today believe investors do reinvest and thus choose level annuity capitalization.

One additional point about the pattern of the net income stream: Although the actual amount of net income that will be received in any particular year may vary considerably from the amount forecasted for it by either the straight line or level annuity pattern, the deviations on either side are likely to cancel out—leaving the basic pattern. In other words, the estimate may turn out to be too low in some years but in other years the estimate will turn out to be too high. These theoretical income streams are thus estimates of the *pattern* and not of the actual amounts to be received in any particular year.

Estimation of capitalization rates. We now return to a determination of the capitalization rate to be used in discounting the future income stream. As we said previously, the two components of the discount rate are (1) the pure cost of the use of money, and (2) the additional business risk involved in a real estate investment. The addition of the discount rate and the recapture rate (straight line or level annuity) provides the capitalization rate. The reciprocal of the capitalization rate is a factor obtainable from a table. Discount rate determination, then, involves the question of what rate investors demand for a given level of risk in a particular real estate investment.

At any point in time the pure interest for long-term investments is determined by the yield on long-term government bonds. If this latter rate is say 4 percent, a real estate investor would demand an additional return to compensate for the added risk. Rather than trying to determine the rate to be added on to the pure rate of interest, however, the analyst or investor can usually more easily look at the overall rate of discount for similar real estate investments. If similar parcels were purchased for yields of 10 percent, the analyst would impute a 10 percent discount rate to the property in question. Similarly, if the going rate for the comparable parcels was 12 percent, this would be the return imputed to the parcel and to be used in the analysis. The idea is simple; only implementation is difficult. Other methods for determining capitalization rates are given in books on real estate appraising cited at the end of this chapter; in specialized valuation problems one of these methods may be appropriate and useful.

Site reversion. The only remaining variable to be determined in estimating the value of a property by the income approach is the value of the site. This is necessary, since the investor will be entitled to the continued use of the land after the building has worn out and no longer has value. For the analyst to estimate the value of the total property, therefore, he must estimate the value of the reversionary right to use the land after the building is gone.

Since no analyst has a crystal ball and can say what the value of the site will be say 25 or 50 years into the future, most real estate analysts, unless they have better information, assume that the value of the site at the end of the life of the building will be the same as the value of the site today. The problem, therefore, becomes one of estimating the value of the site today and discounting that value for the remaining economic life of the building. The valuation procedures for the site are (1) by direct sales comparison with comparable vacant parcels of land, and (2) by hypothetical highest and best use computation. The direct sales comparison approach is discussed later in this chapter.

The second procedure of estimating the value of a site is by capitalizing the difference between (1) the total income stream available to the real estate *if* it were improved with the most profitable, long-term use, and (2) the part of the income stream attributable to the building. The portion of the income stream remaining after building income is subtracted from total income is attributed to the site, and this income stream is capitalized to provide a present value for the land. In capitalizing an income stream to land, however, it must be recognized that this income stream theoretically can continue forever. That is, the legal right cannot be terminated so long as the owner lives up to the basic requirements of society. The income stream to a piece of land, therefore, is capitalized to perpetuity. This process involves dividing the site's first year income by the discount rate (R.O.I.) used in capitalizing the building's income.

The highest and best use decision

In both the income approach and the cost approach to value (to be discussed later in the chapter) it may be necessary to estimate the value of the site separately from the improvements. As developed in this chapter, both the income and cost approaches require a separate determination of site value. Other methods not requiring a separate site valuation are available for the income approach but are beyond the scope of a basic text. An excellent reference for these methods is Kinnard's *Income Property Valuation*. As discussed in the previous two paragraphs, one method of site valuation requires a decision as to the highest and best use of the site. Highest and best use is defined as that use of the land which will provide the greatest income to the site after deducting the capital and labor expenses of the improvements. The program of use to which the land is put must be long term in nature.

The highest and best use decision can be made whether the site is vacant or improved. If the site is vacant, all of the logical, feasible, alternative uses can be analyzed to decide which use would provide the greatest residual income to the site. This analysis involves estimating total N.O.I. under each proposed use and subtracting from it the portion of the income allocable to the improvement. The improvement's required income is calculated by multiplying the capitalization rate times the improvement's cost.

If the site is already improved, the existing improvement becomes one of the alternative uses to be considered as a candidate for highest and best use. Although considerable attention may be focused on an existing building, the analyst should not lose sight of the objective, which is to estimate the site's value *as though vacant*. The basic question in highest and best use analysis is: if the site were vacant (which it may or may not be) what use should be made of it? A parcel of land always has some value, and that value may exist independently from the present use. Potential uses often provide sites with higher values than would be justified by existing uses. For an existing improvement to qualify as highest and best use, reproduction of the structure in exact detail (including depreciation) would be justified if the site were vacant.

Whether a site is vacant or improved, the highest and best use decision may be simplified by constraining conditions. For example, in an area zoned for single-family residential structures, the analysis is limited to considering alternative homes. Commercial, industrial, or multi-family uses need not be considered; they are illegal. The problem may be further limited because structures over two or three years old cannot be considered highest and best use. If a building is older, the unavoidable physical deterioration and functional obsolescence would reduce the land's possible return sufficiently to remove the building from the range of highest and best use.

Although it is often easy to eliminate many potential uses, a decision about what *is* highest and best use may require a considerable amount of comparative analysis of several properties. For single-family residential properties, the highest and best use decision usually requires analysis of such factors as location, style, design, quality of construction, relation to lot, and size. All such factors must be considered in terms of the surrounding properties. Does the style, size, design, and so on blend in with neighboring uses? Too great a deviation in these factors would signify an over- or under-improvement.

For income properties the decision as to whether a particular improvement is highest and best use requires comparative analysis of income streams and economic lives. Where there is a wide variety of possible income-producing uses, the return provided to the land by each use must be calculated and compared with other possible returns. The following example should clarify how this determination is made.

Suppose that you have the opportunity to buy a vacant corner lot on a well-traveled, commercial "strip" street. The location is zoned for commercial usage but is adjacent to residential areas. Since you have available money to invest, you decide to analyze the financial aspects to determine the price you should be willing to pay. The present ower is asking $14,000 for the lot but you do not want to pay this price without an independent analysis.

In your preliminary analysis you note that the most apparent needs are for a supermarket or a dry cleaner. You call in a real estate consulting firm which conducts a demand-analysis survey which is favorable for both types of stores. Further, the consulting firm gives you the following cost and expected rental figures for two sizes of supermarkets and a dry cleaner store and processing unit:

Supermarket: $10/square foot
  10,000-square-foot supermarket $100,000
    Expected revenue 1% of gross sales of $1,000,000: $10,000
  8,000-square-foot supermarket $80,000
    Expected revenue 1% of gross sales of $900,000: $9,000
Dry cleaner: $10/square foot
  7,000 square feet: $70,000
    Expected revenue: flat $600/month or $7,200/year

All leases would provide net income to the owner. The investor would first decide the return he would demand on capital improvements and apply this rate to the three alternative projects. Suppose he would be satisfied with 10 percent (8% return and 2% straight line recapture for an assumed 50-year life). For alternative no. 1 the annual income required would be $10,000; no. 2, $8,000; and no. 3, $7,000. This would leave $-0-, $1,000, and $200 for the land. The conclusion is that alternative no. 2 is highest and best use. You would be willing to pay $12,500 for the land if the land income of $1,000 per year is capitalized to perpetuity at 8 percent.

Case example of the income approach

Estimating the value of the property described in this case illustrates many aspects of the income capitalization approach. The first step in a valuation problem is to estimate the future net operating income in the format of a reconstructed operating statement. Secondly, site value must be estimated, either by direct comparison of comparable site sales or by capitalizing the site income that remains after building income is deducted from total income under highest and best use. A level annuity factor representing a market-determined discount rate and the remaining economic life is then applied to the net operating income. The reversion value of the site is added to the capitalized N.O.I. to obtain the property's total present value.[4]

Assume that you are asked to estimate the value of the ABC Building, a two-story commercial structure, on a major artery near downtown. (See Figures 5-3 through 5-6). Other commercial buildings of fairly high

FIGURE 5–3

ABC Commercial Building owner's operating statement

Gross rents collected (1972)		$17,600
Expenses:		
Power	$1,800	
Real estate tax	1,600	
Garbage removal	100	
Supplies	400	
Mortgage payments	2,500	
Insurance	1,500	
Decorating	600	
Repairs	1,700	
Depreciation	2,000	
Janitor	1,500	13,700
Net Income before Taxes		$ 3,900

quality occupy the area, and this usage is expected to continue. Typical tenants in the area are service or specialty establishments, such as office machine firms, sporting goods stores, music stores, and carpet companies.

Although the building is 15 years old, it has been well maintained and has an expected remaining economic life of 40 years. Four suites of rooms occupy the first floor and are rented on long-term leases for $200 per month. The second floor also contains four suites, two of which are

---

[4] The income approach discussed in this basic text is one of several income capitalization methodologies used by appraisers to estimate property value. Other methodologies are: (1) the land residual method (used in the preceding highest and best use example); (2) the building residual method; and (3) variations on the property residual method, such as Ellwood's method, which explicitly incorporates financing. Discussion of alternative appraisal techniques and their merits is best reserved for a course in real estate appraisal. However, the authors agree with the contention that "the property residual technique is sufficiently elastic to meet any given appraisal problem. It is the preferred technique." See Sanders, A. Kahn, Frederick E. Case, and Alfred Schimmel, *Real Estate Appraisal and Investment* (New York: Ronald Press Co., 1963), p. 153.

SOLUTION:

FIGURE 5–4

ABC Commercial Building reconstructed operating statement

Potential gross income		$18,000
Vacancy and collection losses		600
Effective Gross Income		$17,400
Expenses:		
Power	$1,800	
Real estate tax	1,600	
Garbage removal	100	
Supplies	400	
Insurance	1,500	
Decorating and repairs	600	
Reserve for replacements	1,700	
Management	800	
Janitor	1,500	10,000
Net Operating Income		$ 7,400

FIGURE 5–5

Site value under highest and best use

Potential gross income	$22,800
Vacancy and collection losses	750
Effective Gross Income	$22,050
Less: Expenses	11,500
Net Operating Income (highest and best use)	$10,550
Value of site:	
Net operating income (highest and best use)	$10,550
Less: Building income: $80,000 ÷ 9.915	
(PV of annuity of 1, 10%, 50 years)	8,068
Site income	$ 2,482
Site Value ($2,482 ÷ .10)	$24,820

FIGURE 5–6

Valuation of ABC Commercial Building

Value of N.O.I. for 40 years:	
$7,400 × 9.779 (PV of annuity of 1, 10%, 40 years)	$72,365
Value of site reversion:	
$24,820 × .022 (PV of 1, 10%, 40 years)	546
Value of Property	$72,911, say $72,900

leased for $150 per month. The remaining two suites are rented on a monthly basis for $200 per month. One of these monthly rented suites tends to be vacant about 25 percent of the time.

The site measures 80 feet by 120 feet. Highest and best use of the site would be a new, more modern commercial structure costing $80,000. The building would have the same number of units, but all rents could be increased by $50 per month. Operating expenses would increase $1,500 per year. Investors in the market are able to obtain about a 10 percent rate of return on an investment in this type of real estate.

The present value of the property at a 10 percent rate of return is $72,900. A higher rate of return would produce a lower value, while a lower rate would produce a higher value. When market value is to be estimated, the rate of return should be justified from market experience.

The level annuity premise was used, which means that the capital recapture is assumed to be reinvested at 10 percent. The site's value at the end of the building's economic life is assumed to be equal to its current value. The site's reversion value was added to the present worth of the N.O.I. to obtain total property value.

VALUE ESTIMATION BY DIRECT SALES COMPARISON

The idea of the direct sales comparison approach is straightforward: by comparing prices for similar properties the analyst can judge the price (and thus the value) of the property under consideration. The properties for which these prices are compared must be similar; it would be fallacious to compare prices of dissimilar properties. But how similar to each other must the properties be? Although a quantitative answer is not possible, the general rule is that the properties must be sufficiently similar so that all the differences among the properties can be identified and dollar values assigned to these differences. For example, a comparison between two houses which have as their only difference the lack of a basement in one would be quite feasible. A value difference could easily be assigned to the basement, and the resulting market price imputed as one evidence of value.

In making comparisons it should be recognized that the determinants of supply and demand are operating to produce market prices, and that the analyst is looking at the end results of the market process. The actions of the market produce a price which can be viewed as a discounted value of the benefits that are expected from the property in the future. Thus, if buyers discount a property's expected benefits to a certain price they will tend to discount similar benefits available from other properties to similar prices.

This basic assumption of the direct sales comparison approach clearly shows its relation to the income approach. In the income approach the future net income to a property must, of course, be estimated, while this step is not necessary in the direct sales comparison approach. The benefits or income to a property are expected when the analyst employs the direct sales comparison approach, just as in the income approach. The fact that they are not estimated does not mean that a buyer will agree to forego these benefits.

By the same reasoning, the income approach must contain a measurement from the market to determine the value that should be placed upon the expected income. This measurement comes through the capitalization rate. In effect, there is a market of capitalization rates just as there is a market of prices. In the direct sales comparison approach, the analyst goes to the market to determine prices; in the income approach the analyst goes to the market to determine capitalization rates. He compares the capitalization rates for properties having similar risk and makes adjustments to the rate for any differences that are perceived.

In carrying out the direct sales comparison approach, probably the most useful technique is to construct a grid, showing on one axis each comparison property and on the other axis each item by which the properties are different. Such a grid is shown in Figure 5–7. Values are

FIGURE 5–7

Grid analysis, direct sales comparison

	A	*B*	*C*	*D*	*Subject*
Price	23,000	17,200	20,600	20,500	?
Date of sale	This year	3 yrs. ago +15% ($2,580)	2 yrs. ago +10% ($2,060)	1 yr. ago +5% ($1,025)	Now
Location	Equal	Equal	Better +$1,000	Equal	—
Architecture	Better −$400	Poorer +$400	Equal	Equal	—
Rooms	6½ −$500	6	7 −$800	6	6
Baths	1½	1 +$800	1½	1 +$800	1½
Condition of property	Better −$600	Poorer +$500	Equal	Equal	—
Terms of sale	25% down	30% down	All cash +$500	20% down	25% down
Conditions of sale	Same	"Hurried" sale +$1,000	Same	Same	—
Indicated value	21,500	22,480	23,360	22,325	

assigned to each difference and either added to or subtracted from the known price of the comparable to derive a price for the property under appraisal.

Adjustments that must be made reflect differences among physical characteristics (such as number of rooms and baths, lot size, physical condition, and architectural desirability), date of sale, terms of sale, and conditions of sale. Dollar or percentage adjustments are assigned to each differential in the comparables, based upon how much more or less the property would be expected to bring in the market with or without the feature. For example, lack of a second bath in a property being appraised results in a subtraction from price of a comparable property having a second bath. Similarly, better architecture or design of the subject property over a comparable property would require the addition of value to the comparable property's sale price.

Three items may require further explanation. These are Terms of Sale, Date of Sale, and Conditions of Sale. Terms of sale refers to the contractual provisions governing the amount, timing, type of repayment, and other obligations assumed by the buyer. The most stringent terms would be all cash at time of sale. In a real estate transaction the seller may take a mortgage from the buyer as part payment, sell on an installment contract, require no payment for a period of time, or lend the buyer funds at an attractive interest rate. For such relatively lenient terms the seller usually will obtain a higher price than if he sold for cash on the barrelhead. The analyst should compensate for such terms by adjusting all transactions to a figure the analyst believes would be appropriate for a normal or typical transaction. In the grid analysis of Figure 5–7 all the sellers except comparable C financed the sales. Buyer C paid all cash and obtained a somewhat lower price.

If the time of sale of a comparison property is over four to six months in the past, an adjustment often must be made to reflect the date of sale. The adjustment takes account of any change in the value of the dollar and the real estate market that may have occurred. With the value of the dollar having decreased an average of about 4 percent per year for the last five years and many real estate markets experiencing even greater price increases, an adjustment of at least 5 percent will often be required. This adjustment was made to the comparable properties in Figure 5–7.

Conditions of sale concerns the relationship between buyer and seller. Was each acting without undue pressure? Did each have knowledge of market conditions? Was the property on the market for a reasonable time? Was the transaction at arm's length i.e., is there a personal relationship between buyer and seller? In the example the sale of comparable B was hurried because the owner was moving out of the city immediately and needed his money. It was the appraiser's judgment that the property would have sold for $1,000 more had the property been left on the market for a reasonably longer period.

In conclusion, the direct sales comparison approach is appropriate for value estimation when there are active, viable markets for which sales prices are known and in which properties are truly comparable. Usually such markets exist for single-family residential properties and for some general purpose commercial and industrial properties. For more specialized types of properties, direct comparison of sales is impossible or implausible, and the appraiser must reply upon the income or cost approach.

VALUE ESTIMATION BY COST ANALYSIS

The cost approach to value estimation attempts to measure value by adding all the costs necessary to reproduce a building, subtracting therefrom any losses in value, and adding to this figure the site value. Because of its reliance on historical cost figures, the approach can be used when both market and income data are unavailable or unreliable. The main assumption upon which the cost approach is based, however, constitutes a theoretical weakness, and the task of measuring reductions in value on older buildings becomes its Achilles' heel in practicality.

Relation of cost to value

The principal assumption of the approach is that the cost of creating an economic good equals its value.[5] However, since value of improvements is determined by the forces of supply and demand in the market, the equality of cost and value only rarely exists. Investors pay only scant attention to the historical cost of the good, unlike the assumption of classical economic theory. Differences between value and reproduction cost can be identified and measured, but only with uncertainty.

There is, however, an important relation between cost and value. When a building or other improvement provides to the owner of the land the highest percentage return, the site is improved with its highest and best use. In this situation the cost of the improvement equals its value, and no further adjustments are required to estimate value. If too much capital is sunk into the building, the percentage return to land is lowered, and this condition is termed an overimprovement. If too little capital is invested in the improvement, which also would lower the land's return, an underimprovement results.

To repeat, then, value of the building equals cost when the improvement is highest and best use of the land. It is important that this relation-

---

[5] Recall from chapter 4 that the classical theory of land value is based upon the difference between the cost of labor and capital applied to the land and the total price obtainable. On the poorest (marginal) land, no income (rent) is obtainable, and no value accrues to the land. On better grades of land, surplus income (rent) is obtained by the landlord and constitutes payment for the original and indestructible powers of the soil.

ship be understood—specifically why value equals cost at highest and best use. The answer most simply is that when the improvement is highest and best use the cost incurred is justified. Intelligent, well-informed investors will gladly incur this cost so as to obtain the highest possible return.

Therefore, the cost approach is quite properly used whenever the analyst believes the improvement to be highest and best use of the land. When the building already on the land is not highest and best use, cost of the building would not be equal to its value. Accrued depreciation must be deducted from the building's reproduction cost new to estimate its value. And the value of the land must be determined either by direct sales comparison or by assuming a hypothetical highest and best use of the site and capitalizing the site's residual income (as demonstrated in the income capitalization section of this chapter). Reproduction cost new less accrued depreciation plus site value equals property value through the cost approach.

Reproduction cost

Estimation of reproduction costs can be accomplished in several different ways. These are by (1) quantity survey, (2) unit-in-place costs, and (3) comparison.

The quantity survey method of estimating costs refers to the costing of each item and service going into the building. All the nails, lumber, bricks, concrete, plaster, and services of laborers, plasterers, carpenters, electricians, and others would be added up. The total of all such items and services would be the final reproduction cost. The quantity survey method is a lengthy and onerous procedure that would be used by a contractor or architect to determine a bid price for a new building. For value estimation the additional accuracy is not usually great enough to warrant its use over more concise methods.

The unit-in-place cost method is a shortcut of the quantity survey method. It usually involves the use of a cost service—a manual that is updated periodically and shows cost figure for various components of a structure. Examples of cost services appropriate for a variety of types of buildings are the Marshall-Stevens *Valuation Quarterly* and the Boeckh *Building Valuation Manual;* Means' *Construction Costs* specializes in large buildings.

Basically, the method involves estimating cost of a unit of a major component or assembly of a structure and multiplying the cost of the unit by the number of units. For example, the cost of a square yard of roof would be multiplied by the number of square yards; the cost of a square foot of brick wall would be multiplied by the number of square feet; and the cost of a lineal foot of foundation would be multiplied by the number of lineal feet. The cost services provide such unit costs. They are kept current and are adjusted for regional cost differences.

The third method, the comparison method, requires the appraiser to keep personally up to date on construction costs and to keep current a set of "bench-mark" buildings about which the costs are known. A surprisingly small number—usually 10 to 15—of bench marks will provide the bases for estimating the costs of a fairly large number of types of buildings. The appraiser does this by applying the square foot or cubic foot cost of a bench-mark structure to the structure under appraisal and making adjustments for differences between them. For example, if a subject house had a downstairs bath while the bench mark did not, an adjustment would have to be made.

Cost estimating is a crucial part of the cost approach; however, this discussion can do no more than acquaint the reader with the fundamental ideas of cost estimating. The important point to remember is that costs are prices and prices occur in markets; therefore, it is imperative for the cost estimator to keep up to date on the current market prices of materials, labor, and services. The use of published cost services can help the process, but they should be used with caution. Costs vary from locality to locality, and costs that are not current or that have not been determined for a specific city are likely to be highly inaccurate.

Accrued depreciation—penalties

Deductions from the reproduction cost new of a building in order to estimate the value of an existing structure are of three types and are perhaps most appropriately termed penalties.[6] These are penalties for physical deterioration, functional obsolescence, and locational deterioration. The analyst measures each penalty in ways now to be discussed and deducts them from the reproduction cost.

Physical deterioration. The first penalty, physical deterioration, reflects the fact that all material things wear out. Every physical thing is on the road to the junk yard, and buildings are no exception. Therefore, in valuing a building over two or three years old, one must deduct accrued depreciation for both the building's structure and for its replaceable parts.

First, the analyst makes a schedule of replacement items such as water heaters, roofs, and bathroom fixtures that are worn out. He obtains cost figures for these items. Second, he makes a schedule of items and conditions that are partially worn out (depreciated). Such things as the furnace, water heater, roof, and paint job again would constitute candidates for this schedule. Again, they would be costed out (new), but the amount of

---

[6] Robert O. Harvey, "Observations on the Cost Approach," *The Appraisal Journal*, vol. 21, no. 4 (October 1953), pp. 514–18.

remaining useful life deducted from the penalty. This is usually done by prorating the cost over the total expected life of the item. For example, a three-year-old paint job that should last five years and costing $500 would have an indicated penalty of $300. Next, the analyst would recognize the physical deterioration in the building itself (sometimes termed the bone structure). This penalty would be measured by multiplying the ratio of the building's effective age to total economic life by its reproduction cost.

Functional obsolescence. Functional obsolescence is the loss of relative ability by a building to perform its function. The development of new materials and processes and the acceptance of different styles and designs causes older buildings to become less desirable. The second penalty in the cost approach recognizes those differences between modern buildings and the existing building.

Possible sources of functional obsolescence are lack of air conditioning and elevators, out-of-date kitchens, old designs, rooms too small, ceilings too high, and so on. In some instances such deficiencies can be corrected, and the value increase will be equal to or greater than the cost incurred. In other instances the cost incurred to remedy a functional obsolescence deficiency will be greater than the value produced by incurring the cost. The former is termed a *curable* penalty, while the latter is known as an *incurable* penalty. Obviously, these terms do not apply to the physical ability to make the change; any building can be completely changed. Rather, the terms curable and incurable refer to the financial justification for making a change.

The distinction between curable and incurable penalties is an important one for deciding how to measure functional penalties. The procedure is simple for curable penalties; the cost of correcting the deficiency is used, since this cost equals the value loss of the deficiency. For incurable penalties, however, the matter is a bit more complex. Since the cost of correcting the deficiency is greater than the value, some other method must be employed to estimate the value. Either the lost income can be capitalized, or direct sales comparisons can be made with properties that are similar but do not have the deficiency.

Measurement of the value loss by the income approach rests on the fact that many deficiencies will cause various types of expenses to be larger. For example, ceilings that are too high require larger fuel and maintenance expense; unattractive architecture and design results in vacancy losses; out-of-date kitchens result in lower sale prices, and inconvenient arrangements produce a need to hire additional, part-time help. These negative income (or loss) streams can be estimated and capitalized, and the resultant penalties are subtracted from the reproduction cost of the building.

The direct sales comparison approach can also be utilized to estimate incurable penalties. Ideally this would be accomplished by comparing transaction prices of properties that are similar in every respect except the deficiency. If, for example, houses similar to a house having an incurable kitchen deficiency sell for $2,000 more than other like houses having out-of-date kitchens, the penalty would be $2,000 (while the cost of putting in a new kitchen might be $3,000).

Locational deterioration. The third penalty of locational deterioration is defined as a loss in value of the building because the site is no longer as desirable for the purpose served by the building. It represents, in other words, a relationship between the land and the building that is less ideal than it once was. It does not, however, connote a value loss for the land. In fact the land has in many such cases increased in value due to its increased desirability for commercial or industrial uses. Keep in mind that the building suffers the penalties; the land is never penalized.

How then is the locational deterioration penalty measured? Answer: by deducting the present value of the income stream lost because of the lack of adoption to its site or by the increased value of similar buildings on sites more suitable. The theory is that the deteriorated relation between land and building will cause the building to be profitable a shorter time. (Physically, the building would be torn down sooner than would otherwise occur.) The percentage relationship of the present value of the income stream lost to the value of the income stream without the penalty can then be applied to the replacement cost less the first two penalties.[7] An example should clarify this complex description, as well as the entire cost approach.

Cost approach example

Assume that we wish to estimate the value of a 10-year-old school building. Although in good physical condition, the building is located in an area that has become ripe for industrial development. The school board has decided to determine whether the value of the building and land justifies abandonment of the school in favor of construction of a new building in a more desirable location.

By use of the *Stevens Valuation Quarterly* we have classified the building as "Class B", in "good" condition. Class B construction has reinforced concrete frame in which the columns and frames can be either formed or precast concrete. "Good" quality refers to the second from best, out of four quality classes. Such a building is designed for good appearance, comfort, and convenience. The cost cited of $19.96 per square foot totals $239,520 for the 12,000 square feet. From this we subtract the penalties for accrued depreciation as follows:

---

[7] The locational deterioration penalty also can be taken by capitalizing the loss of income attributable to this deficiency in the site. In the case of special purpose, amenity-producing properties, however, no loss of dollar income can be imputed.

1. Physical deterioration:
   Curable
       Repainting ....$ 2,000
       Roof leaks   1,000
   Incurable
       Structural decay 1% per year—10% 23,950 $26,950

2. Functional obsolescence:
   Curable
       Poorly fitting windows ....$ 3,000
       Needs acoustical tile in classrooms ....   5,000 $ 8,000
   Incurable
       Inefficient heating system requires an extra part-time janitor
       $1,000/yr. @ 6% for 15 years—life of heating system ....$ 9,712 $17,712

3. Locational deterioration:
   Life of new school at appropriate site 100 years:
       6% PV factor 16.62
   Life of new school at present site 40 years:
       6% PV factor 15.05

                                                1.57

$$\frac{1.57}{16.62} = 9.4\%$$

Reproduction cost $239,520
    Less: Total physical and functional obsolescence penalties   44,662

                                                $194,858

        $26,950
        17,712

        $44,662
9.4% ($194,858) locational obsolescence   18,317

Value of Building $176,541

The penalty for physical deterioration contains both curable and incurable elements. The painting and roof repair can be accomplished readily and relatively inexpensively. The structural decay cannot be remedied without complete reconstruction of the building. Such a task would not add as much value to the building as it would cost. With the total economic life of the building, if new, estimated at 100 years, approximately 10 percent deterioration is estimated to have occurred.

The functional penalty is also divided between curable and incurable components. The windows and acoustical problems can be remedied by spending $8,000, and such cost would be justified. The heating system requires supervision that a newer system would not require; nevertheless, its cost of installation would be greater than the value lost by the present system.

The locational penalty is estimated by the percentage of the present value of the economic life lost to the total economic life of the building at an ideal location. This percentage is applied to the building in its existing condition—that is, after deducting the first two penalties from reproduction cost.

To the building value of $176,541 would be added the site value. If the site value were, say, $50,000, total property value would be $226,541. The school board should not sell the property unless it could obtain at least that amount and construct a new school of comparable quality on a different site for a total cost (including land) not to exceed the price obtained for the old school. If the land value has appreciated sufficiently, this proposal could be feasible.

SUMMARY

This chapter describes the methods and techniques of value estimation. Emphasis is placed upon the valuation function because all decisions regarding real estate involve a consideration of value (price) or rate of return. Rates of return are a function of prices paid and received; and transaction prices in a market determine values. Although the following chapter emphasizes the rate of return and justified investment price to an individual investor, the central concept and beginning point for understanding investment analysis is that of market-determined prices—or value.

The valuation process requires a consideration of all factors believed to influence income expectancy and capitalization rates. These factors are complex and play an exceedingly important role in the valuation of real estate because of its physical nature. Immobility, long life, and large size make real estate particularly vulnerable to economic, social, and political-legal developments. Trends in each of these areas must be considered at the national, regional, community, and neighborhood levels. Since real estate investment decisions require a long-term, future-oriented point of view and great reliance is placed upon financing, a real estate investor's success or failure is in large measure dependent upon perceptive analysis and prediction of such value-determining trends.

The steps required in each of the three approaches to value are shown in the following diagram. Theoretically, if each approach were equally applicable to a valuation problem and if equally complete and reliable data were available, all three approaches would produce the same estimate of market value. Depending upon the nature of the property and the market in which it would be bought and sold, one approach is usually more appropriate than the other two. Before embarking on the appraisal procedures, the legal rights being valued must be identified.

The estimate of value is an important criterion in the investment decision-making process. Presumably, an investor would not want to pay more than the market value for a property—unless other investment criteria outweigh this consideration. Chapter 6 will discuss the way in

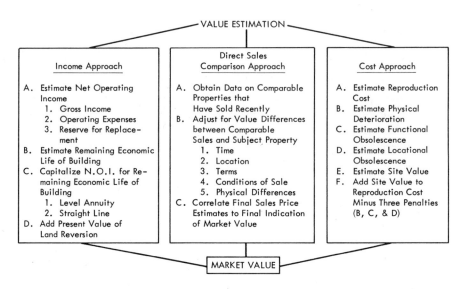

which additional factors, such as financing and income taxes, affect investment desirability. Advantages produced by these factors for a real estate investment can sometimes justify an investor's paying a price higher than the value of a property.

QUESTIONS FOR REVIEW

1. Why does the cost approach produce an estimate of market value? In other words, what market data are used in the cost approach?
2. Why does the income approach produce an estimate of market value? What market data are used in the income approach?
3. What is meant by terms of sale? Why would it be necessary to adjust the sale price of a comparable property which sold with unusually attractive terms of sale?
4. How does level annuity capitalization differ from straight line capitalization in its assumption about recapture of capital? Which is more realistic?
5. What is meant by functional obsolescence? Could a new building contain functional obsolescence? Why?
6. How is business risk reflected in a capitalization rate? Would a higher level of business risk result in a higher or lower value for a property, other factors remaining unchanged?
7. How does an analyst know whether expenses are reasonable or unreasonable?
8. What main difficulty would you foresee in attempting to estimate the value of a 30-year-old property via the cost approach?
9. In what situation does the cost of a building equal its value? Why?

PROBLEMS

1. Calculate the value of an income stream of $12,000 for the first year with a discount rate of 8 percent and capital recapture required over 25 years under straight line capitalization. What would be the value under level annuity? Can you explain the reason for the difference?

2. Estimate the value of the following property.

   " . . . the building is a frame five-apartment structure which was constructed in 1950, with additions in 1962 and 1967. The structure is in excellent physical condition, but the neighborhood is in rapid transition from residential to light-industrial usage. Four of the apartments rent for $100 a month each, with the owner paying all of the expenses. The owner, who functions as both janitor and manager, lives in one of the apartments. If vacant, his apartment would rent for $75 a month. The demand for apartments has been strong in the community and should continue at high levels."

   Other interesting data:

   Expenses:
Fuel, water, power, and telephone	$ 300
Building supplies	100
Mortgage payments	500
Decorating and painting	200
Repairs and maintenance	300
Reserve for wasting parts	200
Insurance	100

Land value (by market comparison)	$5,000
Estimated economic life of building	40 years
Rate of return derived from market	8%

   a) Convert the given information into a reconstructed operating statement.
   b) Identify the assumptions involved in your calculations.
   c) What is your final value estimate?

3. You have been asked to appraise a vacant site on the north side of town. The neighborhood is zoned C-2 (allowing small commercial uses), but is predominately residential in character. The residences are mostly around 40 years old; doubles and some small apartment buildings (up to eight units) are also in the neighborhood. The site is a double residential lot, 120 feet wide by 160 feet deep. After surveying the neighborhood and other comparable neighborhoods, you find the following sales that you believe can be used for comparisons purposes.

	1	*2*	*3*	*4*
Size	60 × 160	60 × 160	60 × 175	120 × 160
Terrain	Equal	Equal	Equal	10% better
Time of sale	1/72	11/72	9/72	1/73
Location	10% better	Equal	Equal	15% worse
Condition of sale	Arm's length	Forced purchase	Arm's length	Seller required to sell
Surroundings	5% better	Equal	5% worse	Equal
Price	$8,000	$7,500	$7,000	$14,000

The market has been rising about 5% per year; however, you believe no time adjustment is necessary for less than three months. Make any indicated adjustments and estimate the value of the site.

4. You are appraising the city hall of a town with a population of about 50,000. The building measures 100 ft. by 100 ft. and is one story in height (10 ft.) It was constructed in 1955, and the city is now considering selling the present city hall and erecting a new one in another location. You are unable to find any sales of buildings you feel would be sufficiently comparable to justify use of the direct sales comparison approach. Future economic life of the building is estimated at 25 years.

Highest and best use of the land, were it vacant, would be a 16-unit apartment building which would gross $24,480 per year and would net before depreciation about $9,800 per year. From comparable sales you feel that investors today must be able to foresee an 8% return on such an investment. You obtain cost estimates that indicate the 16-unit building could be constructed for $4,375 per unit.

The present building was built in 1955 at a cost of $89,500, and several contractors have told you the building could be replaced today for approximately $1.45 per cubic foot. Although the building has been well maintained, some wear and tear has occurred, and you believe physical deterioration of about 1½% per year should be counted. Also, because of the inefficient room arrangement, not all of the city employees have been housed in the city hall, and five rooms in other locations have been rented to house some employees. The rental on these rooms has run $350 per year, and (according to the employees) about $100 per year has been consumed in gasoline in going back and forth so that the outlying employees could use the candy and coke machines at city hall. The building needs decorating at a cost of $800.

You believe that the new city hall more centrally located will have an expected economic life of about 60 years, while the same building at the subject site would serve for only 30 years.

a) Estimate the value of the property.
b) How do you account for the difference between your value and original cost? Do you believe the property will increase in value in the future?
c) How do you account for the difference between the cost of a highest and best use structure and value of the existing property?
d) Would you recommend demolishing the existing structure in order to erect the 16-unit apartment building?
e) Should the cost of demolishment be deducted from the value of the land? Why or why not?

REFERENCES

American Institute of Real Estate Appraisers. *The Appraisal of Real Estate*. 5th ed. Chicago, 1967.

Brown, Robert K.   *Real Estate Economics*. Boston: Houghton Mifflin Co., 1965. Chap. 6, pp. 78–111.

Kahn, S. A.; Case, F. E.; and Schimmel, A.   *Real Estate Appraisal and Investment*. New York: Ronald Press Co., 1964.

Ring, Alfred A.   *The Valuation of Real Estate*. 2d ed. Englewood Cliffs, N. J.: Prentice-Hall, Inc., 1970.

Society of Real Estate Appraisers.   *An Introduction to Appraising Real Property*. Chicago; 1968.

chapter 6

THE INVESTMENT
CALCULATION

THE TWO PRECEDING CHAPTERS deal with the concept of value and its measurement. We emphasized that value is an opinion; transaction price is a fact. Professional appraisers are often called upon to estimate the value of parcels of real estate because the value figure is the basis for economic transactions. A buyer does not usually wish to pay more than the value nor the seller to take less than the value of the property. The law of eminent domain requires condemning authorities to pay the "fair market price" in taking private property for public use. Real estate taxes are based on a value estimate of the property.

Nevertheless, for many purposes the value estimate is not the whole story. It is only the first phase of the calculation for decisions having an investment motive, i.e., a conscious consideration of the expected returns in relation to the capital required. Since most decisions that determine the role of real estate resources in shaping the future of cities are made with the investment motive, it is our contention that the professional approach to the study of real estate and the making of intelligent decisions must employ as its base the investment calculation. Richard U. Ratcliff, also a strong proponent of the investment approach, has stated that "most of the critical real estate decisions which confront families, professional real estate operators, bankers, and businesses are, broadly speaking, investment decisions which call for predictions of productivity or value." [1]

---

[1] Richard U. Ratcliff, *Real Estate Analysis* (New York: McGraw-Hill Book Co., 1961), p. 4.

MARKET VALUE AND INVESTMENT VALUE

Market value, as estimated by the appraiser, reflects transaction prices and rates of return on investment resulting from competition among buyers and sellers in an imperfect market. A buyer in the market has a personal investment value (justified investment price) for each property he is considering for purchase. A buyer's investment value is the maximum that he would be willing to pay for a particular property. The buyer's assessment of risk and future productivity of the property is reflected in his investment value, in addition to his financing arrangements, tax situation, and other personal investment requirements. Each seller offering a property "for sale" also has a personal investment value for his property, which represents the minimum he would be willing to accept. If the seller cannot get at least $100,000, for instance, he will keep the property. The seller's investment value depends upon the same factors that determine a buyer's maximum offer.

In an effective (although imperfect) market, competition among buyers interested in similar properties establishes the "going" price for a property of that type. This price is sometimes referred to as the "consensus of the market" in regard to the value of that type of property. Each transaction price in this market will be equal to or below the investment value of the buyer involved and equal to or above the investment value of the seller of that property. A buyer may have an investment value that exceeds the going price and market value for the property purchased, perhaps reflecting his willingness to accept a lower return on investment, or other factors. In this instance, the buyer considers himself to have received a windfall profit—he has purchased a property for $110,000 for which he would have been willing to pay $120,000 if the seller had been able to bargain for the last dollar of the buyer's investment value. Competition among sellers of similar properties prevents differentiating among potential buyers and charging each buyer his maximum investment value. On the other side of the market, competition among buyers prevents differentiating among sellers, a circumstance which might result in the seller having to accept his investment value for his property.

Investment price calculation—Phase II

The investment calculation begins where the value calculation leaves off. We can regard the valuation calculation as Phase I and the investment calculation as Phase II. Actually both phases may be viewed as the investment process, with Phase II taking into account the personal and business considerations peculiar to the investor. Phase I will already have taken into account the general or average investment conditions in the market. To the extent that a particular investor's demands are different, the price he is willing to pay will differ from the market value.

The basic figure with which Phase II begins is net operating income as determined in the valuation phase. This figure, you will recall from chapter 5, is the resultant of the analyst's estimate of future gross income less future expenses attributable to the real estate. For income-producing real estate, this figure is a measure of its productivity. The sources and analysis of real estate productivity are examined in chapter 10. Our purpose in this chapter is to complete the framework of analysis so that the role of productivity in the investment approach may be clearly understood.

Although N.O.I. is the one best estimate of the future income to a parcel of real estate and would be the same under competent management (no matter who the owner), no such agreement may be reached with respect to the price each potential owner would pay. Personal considerations, such as the financing required for the potential investor to purchase the property, its expected effect on his income tax position, and other immeasurable influences, such as the disposition of the investor's spouse, may enter into the price he is willing to pay and the return he is willing to accept. It is the function of Phase II of the investment calculation to take into account the measurable personal and business influences (such as financing and income taxes) on the price an investor is willing to pay, or to determine his possible return given a price he must pay to acquire the property.

The injection of financing and income tax into the investment calculation produces several measures of income or flow in addition to N.O.I. These measures in turn can be related to appropriate investment amounts to measure profitability. These items are defined as follows:

1. *Cash Throw Off and Cash Flow*
   Net operating income (N.O.I.)
       Less: Annual mortgage payment (debt service)
   Cash throw off (before-tax cash flow)
       Less: Annual income tax liability
   Cash flow (after-tax cash flow)
2. *Taxable Income and Tax Liability*
   Net operating income (N.O.I.)
       Less: Depreciation for tax computation
       Less: Annual interest on mortgage debt
   Annual taxable income (or loss) from the investment times investor's tax rate
   Annual income tax liability
3. *Tax Shelter*
   Tax shelter is usually defined as a net loss for income tax pur-

poses. That is, if N.O.I. minus depreciation and interest is negative, the negative income is a loss for calculating income tax liability. The loss can be deducted from other income before computing the tax. Thus, if a tax loss of $1,000 occurs, and the investor's marginal tax bracket is 50 percent, he pays $500 less in tax on his other income than he would without the tax loss. This deduction from other, regular income is the tax shelter.

Of course, no investor wants a real loss. The tax loss occurs because the investor can deduct interest and higher levels of depreciation and possibly other expenses than he actually incurs. Thus, a tax loss may be claimed even though a positive net income is being produced by the property at more realistic depreciation charges and even though the property may actually be increasing in value.

In a broader sense, tax shelter occurs whenever an expense deducted for income tax is larger than the actual expense. Although, such an expense may not be great enough to produce a tax loss, the investor's tax liability is lower than it otherwise would have been.

Justified investment price

An investor seeking to determine the maximum price that he can pay for a property is ultimately concerned with his aftertax benefits. Essentially, the price he is justified in paying is the sum of these benefits capitalized at an appropriate equity yield rate plus the value of the debt component of the investment. As an example, let us start with the net income figure shown in the reconstructed operating statement in Figure 5–2 of $19,000 per year. From this figure we must subtract additional expense that an investor would incur if he purchased the property for investment. In most cases these expenses will consist of interest expense on the mortgage loan and income taxes incurred because of the greater income. The expenses will vary for each potential investor. One investor may require a large mortgage loan while another may pay all cash; one may experience a large jump in income taxes while another's taxes would be affected considerably less.

The investment calculation in Figures 6–1 and 6–2 shows the process of arriving at a justified price for a potential investor who would require a mortgage of $130,000 for 25 years and who has a taxable income before making this investment of $50,000 per year. Let us assume that this investor could obtain the loan at a 7 percent interest rate. The incremental income tax and the financing expense that the investor would incur are deducted from N.O.I. to estimate the investor's income after *all* investment related expenses. In order to calculate the incremental income tax, interest expense and depreciation are deducted from N.O.I. to obtain taxable income of the property. Both of these deductions are permissible

FIGURE 6–1

Calculation for determining investment price

N.O.I.		$19,000
Economic life of building ....40 years		
Land value (by comparison) ....$ 50,000		
Minimum return desired 8%		
Mortgage debt $130,000		
Annual mortgage payment at 7% for 25 years		11,154
Incremental income tax:		
Average for 1st 25 years		5,810
Average for remaining 15 years		8,254
Taxable income without investment		50,000
Present value of equity return—		
First 25 years:		
Net operating income		19,000
Less:		
Debt service ....$ 11,154		
Incremental income tax 5,810	16,964	
	$ 2,036	
Present value factor (8% for 25 years)	10.675	
Total		$ 21,734
Last 15 years:		
Net operating income	$19,000	
Less incremental income tax	8,254	
	$10,746	
Present value factor (8% for 15 years)	8.559	
	$91,975	
Discounted (8% for 25 years)	.1460	
Total		$ 13,428
Present value of land reversion		
$50,000 discounted at 8% for 40 years		$ 2,300
Total present value of equity return:		$ 37,462
Present value of mortgage debt		130,000
Justified Investment Price (for an 8% return)		$167,462

Note: Income tax rates are those applicable to a married taxpayer filing a joint return for 1972.

expenses for income tax computation, but are not of course deducted from gross income in arriving at N.O.I.

The problem of estimating the incremental income tax is complex and requires that we make some important but realistic assumptions. First, we assume an interest expense that is average over the life of the loan. Actually, the amount of interest will begin with 7 percent of $130,000 and decline to the maturity of the loan. Although using an average loan figure of $65,000 at 7 percent distorts the actual pattern of interest expense, the value estimate produced by averaging this expense is not significantly different from the result that would be produced by using each year's exact interest and discounting each year's income payment separately.

FIGURE 6–2

Calculation of incremental taxes

First 25 years:

N.O.I. $19,000

Less:

Average interest $\left(\dfrac{\$130,000}{2} \times 7\%\right)$ .... $ 4,550

Depreciation on building ($135,000 ÷ .025) 3,375   7,925

Taxable income to real estate $11,075

Annual income without investment: $50,000

Annual tax without investment: 17,060

Annual income with investment: 61,075

Annual tax with investment: 22,870

Incremental Tax .... $ 5,810

Remaining 15 years:

N.O.I. $19,000

Less depreciation on building 3,375

$15,625

Income without investment 50,000

Income with investment 65,625

Income tax with investment 25,314

Annual tax without investment 17,060

Incremental Tax .... $ 8,254

FIGURE 6–3

Chart of equity benefits

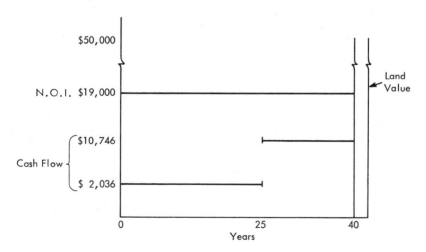

The second assumption involves the depreciation deduction. The investor's depreciation figure in actuality will depend upon the price he pays for the real estate; however, prior to purchasing the property he does not know what this figure will be. His analysis must, therefore, include an assumed price or value of the building which can be depreciated. In this example we use the cost of the building ($135,000) as the appropriate figure, and it is depreciated on a straight line basis over the building's expected economic life of 40 years.

After the interest and depreciation are subtracted from N.O.I., the investor's incremental tax can be computed. In this example the potential investor has $50,000 taxable income without the investment. The average additional income over the first 25 years resulting from the investment would be $11,075. At current tax rates the investor's total income of $61,075 would be taxed $22,870, while his tax on the $50,000 income without the investment would be $17,060. The average incremental tax for the first 25 years is thus $5,810. This figure along with the total mortgage payment is then subtracted from N.O.I. to arrive at the investor's equity return for the first 25 years. The equity return of $2,036 is then capitalized at the desired rate for the 25-year period.

The entire process must be repeated for the remaining 15 years of the building's economic life. Recall that the building has a remaining economic life of 40 years, while the mortgage is paid off at the end of the 25th year. Therefore, no interest deduction will be applicable for income tax determination during the last 15 years, and no mortgage payment need be deducted in arriving at the equity return. In our example the property's taxable income for years 26 through 40 is N.O.I. minus only depreciation (no interest expense), or $15,625. The investor's total income would, therefore, be $65,625 with the investment. The new tax of $25,314 is $8,254 greater than the investor's tax without the investment. Subtracting the incremental tax from N.O.I. gives $10,746 equity return during the last 15 years of the building's 40-year economic life. Again, the income stream is capitalized and then must be discounted back 25 years.

The mortgage payment, or debt service, is calculated by multiplying a "mortgage constant" from a table (see Appendix G, Column 6) for the appropriate number of years, at the assumed interest rate, and with the relevant amortization (monthly, quarterly, semiannual, or annual) times the face value of the loan. The resulting mortgage payment, as well as the constant, includes both interest on the loan plus a repayment of a portion of the loan.

The traditional assumption is made that the site will be worth the same at the end of the building's life as it is at present.[2] Since it has been

---

[2] Since site value may increase as well as decrease, appraisers historically have used the site's present value as a proxy measure of its expected future value. The practice has sometimes been further justified on the grounds that differences between such an estimate and the value that in fact pertains at the future time will be largely dissipated in the discounting process of estimating the present reversion value of the site. These reasons are insufficient justification for the traditional assumption when market evidence for a more valid procedure is available. An unrealistic assumption about future site value (or any other component of the analysis) can negate all of the procedural

estimated that the land is worth $50,000 today, this amount discounted at 8 percent for 40 years yields a reversion value of $2,300.

The face value of the mortgage loan is added to the investment value of the first 25 years, the investment value of the last 15 years, and the reversion value of the land in order to obtain the investor's justified investment price (J.I.P.). The mortgage loan is added in because it represents a portion of the total value of the investment. This portion has been excluded heretofore in the calculation process by the deduction of debt service from net income. Note that the debt service figure includes both principal and interest. We add back only principal (the face amount of the mortgage) because the part of the debt service which is interest presumably does not represent any of the investment worth. To repeat in a somewhat different way: in order to deduct mortgage interest from the investor's income we first deduct both interest and principal in the form of the mortgage payments and then add back the principal in the form of the face amount of the mortgage.

Interpretation of calculations

The calculation shows that this particular investor should be willing to pay $167,462 for the real estate. If he would purchase the property for this price and *if* the estimations of income, expenses, tax rates, and economic life of the building would prove to be accurate, the investor would obtain an aftertax return of 8 percent on his equity investment. Of course, if the estimates turn out to be inaccurate, his aftertax return will prove to be greater or less than 8 percent, depending upon the direction of the inaccuracies.

Although the estimates of certain crucial items such as the average future annual income, average future annual expenses, remaining economic life of the building, and income tax rates will never turn out to be absolutely accurate, the hope is that an investment price based upon such assumptions will turn out favorably to the investor more often than investment without such analysis. At least the investor knows what performance will be required in the future for his expected return to materialize. If, for example, he finds his operating expenses holding at about the expected level but his income being depleted because of vacancies, he will know where to place greater management effort. In this way, then, his investment calculation should continue to serve as a master budget after the transaction is made.

---

sophistication. We recommend that when adequate market data are available to allow meaningful predictions about a site's future value such estimates be used in calculating the site's reversion value. If site value trends cannot be discerned in the market, no other recourse is available than the traditional assumption that present value equals future value.

Varying the assumptions

Although the estimates of gross income and operating expenses are presumably based upon market experiences of comparable properties (as well as the subject property) the assumptions involved in calculating mortgage payments and income taxes may be variable. These *investment expenses* are usually dependent upon the investor's financial position and capacity, not just the project or property being considered for purchase. Furthermore, given a certain financial capacity, loan terms and depreciation expense may be variable within limits. For example, an investor may have the option of obtaining a 70 percent, 25-year, 7½ percent face rate loan or a 75 percent, 20-year, 8 percent face rate loan. He may be able to calculate depreciation for tax purposes over 25, 30, or 40 years or to use accelerated methods.

Role of computers

Differences among the variable assumptions will cause the value of the investor's equity position to change. Or, given a certain price or cost to obtain a property, the rate of return on the investor's equity will change with differing loan terms or tax requirements. When considering a proposed investment, the investor (or his adviser) should usually calculate several equity values or rates of return, using different assumptions about loan terms and taxes. It is normally desirable to project the calculations over several years, so that the expected rate of return can be seen separately each year.

Although investment values and rates of return can be determined by hand calculation, the computations are greatly facilitated by the use of electronic computers, especially when a variety of inputs are considered for each of several years. Among the inputs that might be varied, in addition to loan terms and income taxes, are gross income, expected vacancy rate, type of depreciation expense (straight line, declining balance, et al.), and individual expense items such as real estate taxes or maintenance expense. The estimated remaining economic life or expected holding period and the expected selling price of the property at the end of the holding period (reversion value) can also be varied. An investor or investment counselor can then see return rates (or investment values, given capitalization rates) within a range of most favorable to least favorable expected experiences.

A large firm may have its own computer and investment analysis programs. Medium and smaller size firms can more efficiently either (1) utilize their own programs on a time-sharing computer service, or (2) subscribe to a computerized investment analysis service. Perhaps the most widely used of the latter type of arrangement is provided by Realtron Corpora-

FIGURE 6–4

Realtron investment analysis

Input

MKT. VALUE	300,000	TAX BRKT.	22%
TTL. LOANS	220,000	IMPRVMNT.	70%
NET OP. INC.	25,000	DEPREC.	S/L
INT. RATE	8.50%	YRS. LIFE	30
ANNL. P. & I.	22,900	GRTH. RTE.	00%

Analysis

	Year 1	Year 5	Year 10	Year 15	Year 20
MKT. VALUE	300,000	300,000	300,000	300,000	300,000
TTL. LOANS	220,000	200,073	163,510	107,668	22,381
EQUITY	80,000	99,927	136,490	192,332	277,619
CAP. RATE	8.33	8.33	8.33	8.33	8.33
NET OP. INC.	25,000	25,000	25,000	25,000	25,000
INT. PAY.	18,532	16,770	13,539	8,603	1,064
DEPREC.	7,000	7,000	7,000	7,000	7,000
TAXABLE IN.	532–	1,230	4,461	9,397	16,936
GR. SPEND.	2,100	2,100	2,100	2,100	2,100
INCOME TAX	117–	270	981	2,067	3,725
NET SPEND.	2,217	1,830	1,119	33	1,625–
NET EQ. INC.	6,585	7,959	10,480	14,330	20,211
NET EQ. RTE.	8.23	7.96	7.67	7.45	7.28
ADJ. COST B	293,000	265,000	230,000	195,000	160,000

Cumulative Totals

TAXABLE IN.	532–	1,558	16,855	53,135	121,464
GR. SPEND.	2,100	10,500	21,000	31,500	42,000
NET SPEND.	2,217	10,158	17,295	19,816	15,287
NET EQ. INC.	6,585	36,214	83,146	146,445	234,742

tion. Realtron offers to subscribers who pay a monthly fee an investment analysis service in the format shown in Figure 6–4. (Output definitions for Realtron are shown in Figure 6–5.) The subscriber telephones the input data to a central computer and receives the output back within a few minutes. The example shown in Figure 6–4 shows the changing amounts and equity income rate given a property having a current market value of $30,000, total loans at time of purchase of $22,000, net operating income of $2,500, a mortgage interest rate of 8.50 percent, and annual principal and interest totaling $2,290. The investor is in the 22 percent tax bracket, improvements constitute 70 percent of the property's value, straight line depreciation is used for tax purposes, the property's remaining economic life is 30 years, and no change is expected in the property's value over the next 20 years (00% growth).

Some investment analysis computer programs such as those developed by the Educational Foundation for Computer Applications in Real Estate (EDUCARE), a number of universities, and some business firms are more

FIGURE 6–5

Realtron output definitions

Market value

This is the estimated value of the property and should be the List (sale) price of the property.

Total loans

The sum total of all encumbrances of record.

Equity

Determined by subtracting the total loans of record from the market value.
(Note: The above figures are as of the first of the year.)

Capitalization rate

Expresses the percentage of the return the property will produce when it is free and clear. Capitalization rate, from the appraiser's viewpoint, consists of the return on and the return of the investment.

Net operating income

That income which the property produces after proper deductions have been made for vacancy and credit losses and all operating expenses. Another method for arriving at net operating income is to multiply the market value and/or sale price by the capitalization rate. The result will be the net operating income.

Interest payments

All those interest costs for the loans that are of record.

Depreciation

The amount that the Internal Revenue Service will allow the taxpayer to deduct for the cost of the improvement over a given number of years as determined by the tax-payer. However, it should be noted that the government spells out specific guide lines with reference to the methods of depreciation and/or the economic life selected by the property owner.

Taxable income

That income that the property produces which will be subject to ordinary income tax. This often is expressed as a credit figure when the depreciation plus the interest exceeds that of the net operating income.

Gross spendable

The amount of income that remains after the property owner has deducted the principal and interest payments from the net operating income. This gross spendable is often referred to by many investors as "cash flow before income tax".

Income tax

As expressed in the analysis of an investment property, this is that tax liability which is created by the taxable income that the property produced. The amount of income tax to be payed will be determined by the income tax bracket or rate of the property owner.

Net spendable

What the property owner has to spend after he has deducted the income tax liability and/or credit from the gross spendable income. Sometimes called "cash flow after tax".

FIGURE 6–5 (Continued)

Net equity income

This is (1) the amount of principal reduction in the loans plus (2) the net spendable received and (3) the increase in value because of appreciation.

Net equity income rate

The net equity income divided by the equity in the property.

Adjusted cost basis

The book value of the property. (Initial cost basis less depreciation taken.)

Cumulative totals

The sum totals of the result of ownership. (1) Taxable income, (2) Gross spendable income, (3) Net spendable income, and (4) Net equity income are accumulated each year for that year and all previous years of ownership.

complex and provide greater sophistication in their output analyses. They require more input data and compute a greater variety of ratios and return rates while allowing more variables in the input data.

A case example projecting various rates of return under different sets of assumptions is presented in Appendix D, Queensworth Apartments. An investor's rates of return under three sets of assumptions are projected for the first year. The most logical and defensible of the three investment structures is then calculated for each of ten years—a normal holding period for such an investment. Although some of the concepts used in the case are not covered until chapter 7 (The Effects of Income Taxation on Real Estate Investment Decisions) and chapter 14 (Financing Real Estate), Appendix D should be studied in conjunction with this chapter as well as chapters 7 and 14.

Business risk and the investor's return

In the problem example of Figure 6–1 a discount rate of 8 percent was used with no explanation as to why. This rate is the discount rate for a specific investor. From the preceding chapter you will recall that the discount rate is composed of two parts—the pure rate for the use of riskless capital and the additional business risk associated with the parcel of real estate. Although the individual investor's return on investment may differ from the rate of return that is determined in the market, his return rate should have considered within it the elements of the discount rate. In other words, he must start with a consideration of the price of riskless capital and the business risk involved. Further, however, he should consider elements of risk that are individual and peculiar to his situation. The most common such element is financial risk.

Financial risk and the investor's return

Financial risk concerns the level and stability of income in relation to financing requirements. Mortgage payments are a contractual obligation upon the mortgagor, and any lack of income to meet these obligations would cause the investment project to fail. Obviously, then, the investor should be able to foresee an income stream that provides a considerable margin of safety above operating expenses, reserves, taxes, and financing charges. Since most real estate investors utilize credit and thus incur fixed charges when purchasing real estate, the capitalization rate would usually contain a "normal" level of financial risk. But when an individual investor's financial risk level becomes greater than some minimum level acceptable to the market, an additional percentage must be added in determining his necessary return rate. For example, if the analyst believes the market discount rate is 8 percent, but a particular investor would have to incur a greater-than-average financial obligation to purchase the property, his rate of return demanded should be increased proportionately to reflect the additional risk.

An investor's particularly strong financial situation and his ability to meet financial obligations out of personal funds can also be considered in determining his return rate. Since the discount rate includes a normal rate for financial risk, a lower-than-normal financial risk for a particular investor could serve to reduce his desired return below the market discount rate. He would then be in a position to bid a somewhat higher price for the property than could the "average" investor who would have to incur a normal level of financing.

INVESTMENT CRITERIA

In addition to calculating a justified investment price, an investor may find it desirable to determine the attractiveness of the investment by analyzing a number of ratios and by assuming a required seller's minimum price. These ratios can be grouped into three categories—multipliers, financial ratios, and profitability ratios. The ratios below are calculated using the data from the ABC Apartments for which a J.I.P. was calculated previously. The operating statement is shown on page 64. For the calculations assume the following facts:

Purchase price	$170,000
Mortgage	130,000
Equity	40,000
Gross income	27,500
Less: Vacancy and collection loss	1,375
Less: Operating expenses	4,525
Net operating income	$ 19,000
Mortgage payment	11,154
Cash Throw-off	$ 7,846

Multipliers

Two kinds of multipliers can be used. The net income multiplier is not often used since its reciprocal, the capitalization rate, is commonly employed in real estate analysis. The gross income multiplier is used more frequently; however, it must be used with great care. To compare gross income multipliers, the properties should be traded in the same market and should be equivalent in expense patterns, risk, location, physical attributes, time and terms of sale.

1. Gross income
$$\text{multiplier (G.I.M.)} = \frac{\text{Value or price}}{\text{Gross income}} = \frac{\$170,000}{\$\ 27,500} = 6.2$$

2. Net income multiplier $= \dfrac{\text{Value or price}}{\text{N.O.I.}} = \dfrac{\$170,000}{\$\ 19,000} = 8.9$

The multipliers can be used to obtain a quick estimate as to whether a property is priced reasonably in relation to its gross or net income. The gross income multiplier is usually regraded as less relevant for larger more complex properties, as their expense levels may vary greatly. However, one recent study showed that the use of the G.I.M. produces value estimates almost as accurate as more sophisticated techniques.[3] If expense patterns among a class of properties vary significantly, however, use of the G.I.M. as other than a rough guide to value is hazardous.

The multipliers for the ABC Apartments are within the realm of reasonable expectation for an apartment property. While multipliers vary greatly, the range for annual gross income multipliers is normally between 4 and 10. Net income multipliers for apartment properties usually range between 5 and 12. Appropriate multipliers for a specific property would be estimated from actual transactions of comparable properties in the same market area.

Financial ratios

These ratios deal with the income-producing capacity of the property to meet operating and financial obligations.

1. Operating ratio $= \dfrac{\text{Operating expenses}}{\text{Gross income}} = \dfrac{\$\ 4,525}{\$27,500} = 16.5\%$

2. Breakeven cash throw-off $=$
$$\frac{\text{Operating expenses} + \text{Mortgage Payment}}{\text{Gross income}} = \frac{\$15,679}{\$27,500} = 57.0\%$$

---

[3] Richard U. Ratcliff, "Don't Underrate the Gross Income Multiplier," *The Appraisal Journal*, vol. 39, no. 2 (April 1971), pp. 264–71.

3. Loan to value ratio $= \dfrac{\text{Loan}}{\text{Price or value}} = \dfrac{\$130,000}{\$170,000} = 76.5\%$

4. Debt service coverage $= \dfrac{\text{N.O.I.}}{\text{Mortgage payment}} = \dfrac{\$19,000}{\$11,154} = 1.7$

The operating ratio and breakeven cash throw-off ratios should be computed for all properties under investment analysis that will require the investor to incur operating expenses and financing charges. A relatively efficient property will exhibit a low operating ratio. Similarly, the breakeven cash throw-off ratio provides an indication of the magnitude of all cash charges relative to gross income. The margin of safety between cash inflows and cash outflows is the difference between 100 percent and the breakeven cash throw-off ratio. For the ABC Apartments both ratios are low, primarily because of the low operating expenses. Operating ratios typically range from 25 to 50 percent, while the breakeven cash throw-off ratio typically varies between 60 and 80 percent.

The loan to value ratio and the debt service coverage ratio are measures of the financial risk associated with the investment and should be computed for every investment using borrowed funds. The loan to value ratio on a newly financed property normally runs from 60 to 90 percent, while the debt service coverage ratio should normally be at least 1.3.[4] Legal requirements are usually imposed on the maximum loan to value ratios that institutional lenders can incur; the debt service coverage ratio provides an indication of safety from legal default in the event revenues would fall and the mortgage payment would be in jeopardy.

Profitability ratios

The ultimate determination of an investment's desirability is its capacity to produce income in relation to the capital required to obtain that income. Measures of relationship between income and capital for investment properties result in the following ratios:[5]

1. Payback period $= \dfrac{\text{Equity capital}}{\text{Cash throw-off}} = \dfrac{\$40,000}{\$\,7,846} = 5.1$ years

2. Equity dividend rate (before-tax return on equity) $= \dfrac{\text{Cash throw-off}}{\text{Equity}} = \dfrac{\$\,7,846}{\$40,000} = 19.6\%$

---

[4] When a borrower obtains a loan of 100 percent of value or price paid, he is said to have "mortgaged out." A loan in excess of 100 percent produces a "windfall."

[5] Other ratios might be computed, such as an average rate of return. See Maurice D. Kilbridge, Robert P. O'Block, and Paul V. Teplitz, *Urban Analysis* (Boston: Division of Research, Graduate School of Business Administration, Harvard University, 1970), pp. 120–23.

3. Overall capitalization rate $= \dfrac{\text{N.O.I.}}{\text{Total investment}} = \dfrac{\$\ 19{,}000}{\$170{,}000} = 11.2\%$

4. Aftertax equity dividend rate (aftertax return on equity) $= \dfrac{\text{Aftertax cash throw-off}}{\text{Equity}} = \dfrac{\$\ 5{,}896}{\$40{,}000} = 14.7\%$

Calculation of tax and aftertax cash throw-off

N.O.I.		$19,000
Less: Average mortgage interest	$ 9,100	
Less: Tax depreciation (5% double-declining balance, 40 years × $120,000 improvements)	6,000	15,100
Taxable income		$ 3,900
N.O.I.		$19,000
Less: Debt service	$11,154	
Less: Tax (50% marginal tax rate × $3,900)	1,950	13,104
Aftertax Cash Flow		$ 5,896

5. Gross yield on equity $= \dfrac{\text{Cash flow} + \text{mortgage principal repayment}}{\text{Equity}}$

$$= \dfrac{\$\ 7{,}950}{\$40{,}000} = 19.9\%$$

While most investors do not usually calculate all five of the above ratios in evaluating an investment, they are useful indexes of a project's profitability for a given year. We recommend that when the necessary data are available, at least four of the five ratios be calculated—and preferably for each of several years. The pay-back period is less important, since it is the reciprocal measure of the equity dividend rate. It also has the theoretical weakness, of course, of not discounting future years' earnings.

The equity dividend rate shows the investor what percentage of his equity investment will be returned to him in cash before income taxes for one year. Although the noncash expense of depreciation is not deducted, the amount of mortgage repayment is deducted in arriving at cash throw-off. Thus, if mortgage principal repayment approximates actual depreciation, the ratio is a good approximation of the true before-tax yield on equity. The aftertax equity dividend rate provides a comparable yield on an aftertax basis, while the gross yield adds back the mortgage principal repayment. The latter ratio would be a more accurate aftertax yield *if* the property were believed not to be depreciating in value.

The overall capitalization rate measures the profitability of the entire property. It is produced by both the equity and debt portions of the investment and thus falls between the mortgage interest rate and the equity yield. This ratio is often used by appraisers in estimating the market value of an entire property—not just the equity portion.

It should be recognized that each of these ratios has been calculated for one year only. The changing mortgage balance, depreciation, and income tax would cause some of the ratios to change each year. It is often advisable to calculate them for each of several years, as demonstrated in Appendix D.

6. *Internal rate of return.* The internal rate of return (I.R.R.) is a measure of profitability. It differs from the previous five ratios, however,

		Year		
	1	*2*	*3*	*4*
N.O.I.	$19,000	$19,000	$19,000	$19,000
Less: Interest	9,100	8,956	8,802	8,638
Less: Depreciation (200% declining				
balance, 40 years)	6,000	5,700	5,415	5,144
Taxable Income	3,900	4,344	4,783	5,218
N.O.I.	19,000	19,000	19,000	19,000
Less: Mortgage payment	11,154	11,154	11,154	11,154
Less: Taxes (50%)	1,950	2,172	2,392	2,609
Aftertax Cash Flow	5,896	5,674	5,454	5,237
Sale price			$170,000	
Less: Outstanding mortgage balance			120,880	
Equity			$ 49,120	
Less: Capital gain tax			8,129*	
Aftertax Cash Reversion			$ 40,991	

* Calculated as follows:

Total depreciation charged......................	$22,259	
Less straight line depreciation..................	12,000	
Excess Depreciation.........................	$10,259 × 50 % =	$5,129
Plus straight line depreciation at 25 %..........		3,000
Capital Gain Tax............................		$8,129

SOLUTION:

$$\$40,000 = \frac{5896}{(1+r)^1} + \frac{5674}{(1+r)^2} + \frac{5454}{(1+r)^3} + \frac{5237}{(1+r)^4} + \frac{40,991}{(1+r)^4}$$

15%	*14%*			*15%*	*14%*	
5,130	5,130	=	5,896 ×	.87	.87	(PV of 1, 1 year)
4,312	4,369	=	5,674 ×	.76	.77	(PV of 1, 2 years)
3,600	3,654	=	5,454 ×	.66	.67	(PV of 1, 3 years)
2,985	3,090	=	5,237 ×	.57	.59	(PV of 1, 4 years)
23,365	24,185	=	40,991 ×	.57	.59	(PV of 1, 4 years)
39,391	40,428	≈	almost 14½%			

r = aftertax internal rate of return
  = approximately 14.4%

in that it discounts a stream of earnings to be obtained over several future years. The internal rate of return, as is the J.I.P., is based upon the present value concept. To compute an internal rate of return, the following data must be known: equity investment price, aftertax cash flow, holding period or economic life, and selling price of the property at the end of the holding period or economic life. The following calculations produce an internal rate of return for the ABC Apartments over a holding period of four years. It is assumed that the property can be sold for the price paid, $170,000.

Notice that the rate produced is considerably higher than the 8 percent rate used to obtain J.I.P. It is higher because we assumed no depreciation in the I.R.R., whereas J.I.P. assumed depreciation over the 40-year economic life. Also, the I.R.R. calculation was made for only the project's four earliest years. The earnings of the later years, which would be discounted more heavily, were not included, as they were in the J.I.P. calculation.

The internal rate of return is the most defensible of all profitability ratios. Unfortunately, as reported below, it has not received widespread usage among real estate investors. We recommend the internal rate of return measure of profitability whenever adequate data are available and the necessary predictions about the holding period and selling price can be made realistically.

Motivation of investors

A recent survey of apartment investors by the U.S. Department of Housing and Urban Development shows that cash flow is the most important criterion considered by all types of investors.[6] Individuals ranked tax shelter as the second most important motive, while real estate groups and investment trusts ranked this consideration third in importance.

The study indicated that the aftertax return for a 50 percent tax bracket investor on a property five years old or less amounted to 17.5 percent. This figure consisted of 14 percent return on cash equity plus a tax saving of 3.5 percent on other income. For properties between 11 and 20 years old the average aftertax annual return given as a percentage of cash equity came to 7 percent. Cash distribution was 9 percent, but there was a 2 percent tax liability instead of tax loss.

Other important reasons for investing were financial leverage, capital appreciation, and low risk. Location, demand for housing, the housing supply, and mortgage financing opportunities influenced active investors,

---

[6] Arnold H. Diamond, "Tax Considerations Affecting Multi-Family Housing Investments," Annual Meeting of American Real Estate and Urban Economics Association, New Orleans, Louisiana, December 28, 1971.

while passive investors rated location and builder reputation high among nonfinancial criteria for investment.

With respect to earnings, over two thirds of the active investors spoke in terms of the average annual rate of return. Thirteen percent used total dollar return, and 11 percent used pay-back period. Only 4 percent used the discounted rate of return, which gives less weight to earnings in future years and more weight to early earnings. This result is surprising in view of the emphasis given to present value concepts in real estate and financial investment courses.

About one third of the apartment investors believed that apartments yield more tax shelter than other real estate investments, 25 percent thought apartments yield a higher return, and 20 percent believed apartments provide a better hedge against inflation than other real estate investments.

A previous study by Ricks showed that equity investors and other participants in the real estate investment process regard the rate of return on equity investment as the most important measure of profitability and the rate of return on cost as the second most important measure.[7] The after-financing, before-tax return on equity was listed as the most important decision guide. Second and third in importance were the before-financing, before-tax return and the after-financing, aftertax return.

Among the factors considered in making a decision to commit funds to a real estate investment, Ricks found that investors and other participants regard market value appreciation, safety of investment funds, and a high rate of return on equity as first, second, and third in importance. Loan terms were generally more important than characteristics of the property in decisions to commit funds.

SUMMARY

The valuation process, as described in chapter 5, may be regarded as Phase I of the investment calculation. Phase II, discussed in this chapter, extends Phase I to include personal or business expenses that would be incurred with an investment but which are omitted in the valuation process. Income taxes and financing charges are the two most important investment-related expenses which are not directly associated with real estate for valuation purposes.

Phase II may also involve a different discount rate from the rate which is appropriate in estimating market value. The market rate includes risk levels applicable to the average or typical buyer; any individual investor's risk situation or return requirements may justify a higher or lower

---

[7] R. Bruce Ricks, *Real Estate Investment Process, Investment Performance and Federal Tax Policy*, Report of the Real Estate Investment Project for the U.S. Treasury Department (Los Angeles: University of California, 1969).

discount rate. Financial risk, to the extent that it is greater or less than the normal market level, is also reflected in the investor's discount rate.

Assumptions about financing terms, depreciation expense, and income taxes can be varied; investment prices and rates of return can be calculated under several different combinations of assumptions. The calculations can be carried out for several years to show trends. Electronic computers greatly aid the calculation process and are a necessity if several investments are to be analyzed.

Other investment criteria, in addition to justified investment price, include multipliers, financial ratios, and profitability ratios. Given a selling price, a limited holding period, and aftertax cash flow, an internal rate of return can be computed for an equity investment.

Finally, we have noted some attitudes that investors claim to hold with respect to investment criteria. Cash flow and tax shelter are the two most important factors. Rate of return on equity is the most important profitability measure, while there would seem to be little attention paid to discounting processes that weigh future earnings less heavily than immediate earnings.

QUESTIONS FOR REVIEW

1. Why might an investor be willing to pay more for a property than its market value?
2. Why might an investor not be willing to pay as much as market value for a property?
3. Why might an investor not be willing to purchase a property at any price?
4. What is financial risk? How is it accounted for in investment analysis?
5. What is business risk? How is it accounted for in investment analysis?
6. What is J.I.P.? How does it differ in concept from market value?
7. Why is the face value of the mortgage loan added to the value of the equity benefits in arriving at total J.I.P.?
8. How do you explain the results of investor surveys that show that little reliance is placed upon discounted cash flows in evaluating investments?
9. Do you believe that the Queensworth Apartments case contained in Appendix D describes a realistic investment situation? Why or why not? What types of investment calculations are presented in the case?
10. What is tax shelter? Would you purchase a parcel of real estate to obtain tax shelter? Why or why not?
11. Distinguish between depreciation for tax purposes and capital recovery for valuation or investment analysis purposes.
12. What is profitability? Upon which profitability ratios would you place primary reliance in evaluating an investment?
13. What is an internal rate of return?

PROBLEMS

1. An investment is expected to produce $10,000 per year to perpetuity. If a 12 percent annual rate of return is required, how much is the investment worth?

2. If the life of the investment in problem no. 1 was expected to be 20 years, how much would the investment be worth?

3. A purchaser paid $80,000 for an investment property. How much annual income must the property produce to yield an 11 percent rate of return?

4. A home purchaser obtains a $40,000 mortgage loan at 7 percent for 20 years to finance the deal. How much would his total mortgage payments be, including both principal and interest (annual debt service), if payments are made annually? If payments are made monthly?

5. In problem no. 4, how much of the first year's payment would be interest? How much interest would be paid in the second and third years? Approximately how much total interest would be paid over the 20 years? What would be the amount of *average* annual interest paid?

6. Look in a Federal Tax Rate Schedule and determine the tax liability of a married taxpayer having a $20,000 taxable income, filing a joint return, and having one dependent. What amount of tax would the same individual pay in the succeeding year if his income were increased to $25,000? How much is the difference in tax on the two amounts (or incremental tax)?

7. A property produces $10,000 annual N.O.I. The owner charges $2,000 per year depreciation and pays $5,000 in interest on an outstanding loan. Total annual debt service on the loan is $7,500. The owner is in the 34 percent tax bracket.
   a) How much is the cash throw-off?
   b) How much income tax must the owner pay on the income generated by the property?
   c) How much is the owner's aftertax cash flow?
   d) If the owner has $20,000 of his own funds (equity) invested in the property, what is his equity dividend rate?

8. An individual has been willed a remainder estate in a parcel of land which allows him to obtain possession at the termination of a lease 10 years from now. If the land is forecast to be worth $25,000 at that time, how much could he sell his estate for today to an investor demanding a 10 percent rate of return?

9. A property is expected to generate N.O.I. of $10,000. Debt service will amount to $6,000 per year. If the investor contributes $25,000 in equity, how long is the pay-back period?

10. Calculate the internal rate of return for an investment property which is expected to yield $30,000 per year N.O.I. and which can be purchased for $225,000. The investor plans to sell the property after five years for $250,000. He will pay all cash, use straight line depreciation, and is in the 40 percent tax bracket.

11. Calculate a justified investment price for Projection 1 in the Queensworth Apartments case (Appendix D).

REFERENCES

Beaton, William R. *Real Estate Investment.* Englewood Cliffs, N. J.: Prentice-Hall, Inc., 1971.

Kinnard, William N. *Income Property Valuation.* Lexington, Mass.: D. C. Heath and Co., 1971.

Ring, Alfred A. *Real Estate Principles and Practices.* 7th ed. Englewood Cliffs, N. J.: Prentice-Hall, Inc., 1972. Chap. 14, pp. 231–44.

Seldin, Maury and Swesnik, Richard H. *Real Estate Investment Strategy.* New York: Wiley-Interscience, 1970.

Smith, Halbert C. "Investment Analysis in Appraising," *The Real Estate Appraiser,* vol. 32, no. 9 (September 1967), pp. 19–25.

Wendt, Paul F. and Cerf, Alan R. *Real Estate Investment Analysis and Taxation.* New York: McGraw-Hill Book Co., 1969.

PART III

Investment
opportunity
and constraint

chapter 7

THE EFFECTS OF INCOME
TAXATION ON REAL ESTATE
INVESTMENT DECISIONS*

THE IMPORTANCE of federal income taxation in real estate transactions cannot be overemphasized. The value of a property must increase substantially if aftertax appreciation is to be realized upon sale, and the cash to be collected in selling mortgaged property usually must be adequate to pay the gain taxes created by the sale.

In terms of annual operations, real estate provides opportunities for investors to deduct from taxable income the interest on debts, property taxes paid, and depreciation as well as ordinary operating expenses. These items are routinely deductible from corporate returns, and they can become deductible from individuals' returns through ownership of real estate.

The burden of holding land awaiting future appreciation is lessened somewhat by the fact that all payments except those applying to principal on debt are deductible from income taxable revenue. Thus, an investor in a syndicate who pays $1,000 toward interest, taxes, and management fees during the current year can deduct the full $1,000. If he is in the 40 percent marginal tax bracket, he will be entitled to reduce his reported tax liability by approximately $400. This lowers the net cost of his annual investment payment to $600.

The investor in depreciable real estate fares even better than the acreage investor. His deductions are greater because of depreciation taken on buildings and other improvements, and he does not have to pay cash for

---

* This chapter includes several complex subject areas that cannot be covered comprehensively within the scope of the text. Expansion and clarification of these areas can be obtained from *Federal Taxes Affecting Real Estate,* published by the National Institute of Farm and Land Brokers, or from other references cited at the end of the chapter.

the depreciation deduction. He normally is reducing a mortgage balance via nondeductible principal payments, but the depreciation taken frequently exceeds the nondeductible items and permits avoidance of income tax liability for several years.

A keen awareness of all income tax implications of real estate investments is essential to the investor who seeks to optimize his investment position. The materials in this chapter summarize the key points regarding many of the tax variables. However, the investor is cautioned to retain competent tax counsel whenever questions arise; income taxation is one of the most complex issues with which he must deal.

The Internal Revenue Code is updated periodically, and the Tax Reform Act of 1969 incorporated a number of major changes from earlier laws regarding real estate investments. A special surtax was levied against income that is sheltered from ordinary taxation; a limit was placed upon the amount of interest that an individual may deduct; and the use of rapid depreciation techniques was restricted. On the positive side, special short-term depreciation deductions were established for certain carefully designated property owners in an effort to encourage renovation of housing for low-income families. These and other provisions of the current code are now considered.

CAPITAL GAINS AND LOSSES

Capital gain sources.   A distinction is made between capital gains from different sources. Section 1201 capital gains are net long-term capital gains minus net short-term capital losses. Subsection (*d*) gains are those resulting from (1) sales prior to October 9, 1969; (2) liquidating dividends from a corporation whose plan for complete liquidation was adopted on or before October 10, 1969; and (3) any other long-term capital gain up to $50,000 ($25,000 for married person filing separate return) above the first two.

Capital gain computation.   An individual's tax is computed as the sum of three elements.

1. Tax on ordinary income (without considering Section 1201 capital gains or losses), plus
2. 25 percent of the lower of Subsection (*d*) gains or the amount of Section 1201 gains, plus
3. The amount by which Section 1201 gains exceed Subsection (*d*) gains.

Example

In 1971, Mr. Z earned a salary of $100,000 and a long-term capital gain of $80,000. He had $5,000 in short-term capital losses, and a Subsection (*d*) gain of $58,000. His tax was computed as follows:

Step 1
    Tax on ordinary income ($100,000) $45,180
Step 2
    A. Net Section 1201 gain $75,000
    B. Subsection (*d*) gain 58,000
       25% of $58,000 (lesser of A and B)   14,500
Step 3
    C. 35% of $17,000   5,950
        Total tax before surcharge $65,630

This example fails to show one alternative open to the taxpayer. If a smaller tax results he may compute his tax on the excess of net Section 1201 gain over Subsection (*d*) gain as follows: (tax on the total of ordinary income plus 50% of net Section 1201 gain) minus (tax on the total of ordinary income plus 50% of Subsection (*d*) gain). Such a computation yields a Step 3 tax of $5,440, providing a total tax of $65,120.

Corporation capital gains. A corporation will pay 25 percent on the lower of 1201 or Subsection (*d*) gains plus 28 percent on the excess until 1974. In 1975 and thereafter, *1201 gains* will be taxed at 30 percent for corporations. Real estate investment trusts are treated like corporations for this purpose.

Capital losses

Prior to 1970, a taxpayer was required to net his capital gains and losses to determine his tax position. If the net position was a loss, he could deduct up to $1,000 per year from his ordinary income. Under the 1969 act, the taxpayers are permitted to offset only $.50 of ordinary income for each $1.00 of long-term capital loss. Short-term capital losses are permitted to offset ordinary income on a dollar for dollar basis.

Capital loss limitations. Under the 1969 act, capital losses in excess of capital gains are limited to the smallest of three amounts:

1. Taxable income for the year.
2. $1,000 ($500 for married taxpayer separate return).
3. Sum of:
   a) Excess of net short-term capital loss over net long-term capital gain.
   b) One half of the excess of net long-term capital loss over net short-term capital gain.

The last element of the calculation 3(*b*) is where the 50 percent deductibility of long-term capital gains appears. A formula provides for an amount somewhat in excess of 50 percent for long-term capital gain for carryover purposes, but every application of long-term capital loss against ordinary income requires halving (except for pre-1970 losses). Note that this halving situation only involves amounts that total *less than the $1,000 limitation.*

Example

Mr. Noah, a single taxpayer, had a $15,000 ordinary income in 1970 and the following capital gains and losses.

	Long term	Short term
Gains	$400	$ 600
Losses	700	1,200
Short-term loss ($1,200) minus long-term gain ($400)		800
One half of long-term loss ($700) minus short-term gain ($600)		50
Amount deductible		$ 850

Under the pre-1969 law, Mr. Noah could have deducted $900.

Capital loss carryovers and carrybacks. The Tax Reform Act of 1969 establishes revised rules regarding capital loss carryovers and carrybacks. In carrying over a short-term capital loss, the full undeducted balance is applied on a dollar-for-dollar basis in the following sequence against (1) the following year's net short-term capital gain, (2) the following year's net long-term capital gain, and (3) ordinary income to the extent of the lower of $1,000 or taxable income.

In carrying over a long-term capital loss, the following three factors are totaled to determine the proper carryover amount.

1. Short-term capital gain for the loss year.
2. The amount deductible in loss year from ordinary income.
3. Deductible amount minus the net short-term loss in the loss year.

The resulting amount is then applied against the following year's net long-term capital gain. If a loss still results, the long-term capital loss limitations prevail in determining the offset against ordinary income.

Capital losses may be carried forward indefinitely by individual taxpayers. However, in each year the carryover amount is recomputed downward. The taxpayer should make every effort to offset the loss with capital gain as quickly as possible.

Example

Mr. Mitty incurred a $6,000 long-term capital loss in 1970, a year in which his ordinary income was $25,000. He had no short-term capital gains or losses. In 1970 he could offset $1,000 of ordinary income. He then subtracts from his $6,000 long-term capital loss the sum of (*a*) short-term capital loss ($0); (*b*) deductible amount ($1,000); and (*c*) deductible amount minus short-term loss ($1,000 − 0) to derive $4,000. The $4,000 is carried over to 1971.

In 1971, he had no capital transactions. He deducts $1,000 and applies the formula: $4,000 − ($0 + $1,000 + $1,000) for a $2,000 carryover in 1972.

In 1972, he incurred a short-term capital gain of $1,000. His $2,000 long-term loss is offset by $1,000. This leaves $1,000 for offsetting ordinary income, but the 50 percent rule limits him to $500. He deducts $500 to eliminate the loss.

Note that Mr. Mitty's $6,000 long-term capital loss was dissipated by writing off a total of $3,500. He would have been able to deduct $5,000 had he taken a $4,000 capital gain in 1971.

Corporations, but not individuals, are permitted a three-year carryback and a five-year carryover for net capital losses. This rule excludes losses due to foreign expropriation and those involving Subchapter S filings.

Opportunities for tax planning. The majority of real estate investors benefit from capital gain provisions through reporting one half of their gains rather than reporting the entire gain at the ceiling rate. The use of the tax-free exchange and installment sale provisions discussed later in this chapter helps investors spread their gains over several tax years, thereby keeping their marginal tax rates low enough to benefit from the one-half option.

The most significant planning in disposing of an asset is to avoid the need to carry forward a long-term capital loss under the 1969 Tax Reform Act. This loss dissipates over time, and the maximum benefit is derived by offsetting such losses with gains as quickly as possible after the loss is incurred. One way to save the loss for a short period is to sell the asset to a self-owned corporation at its depreciated cost basis, hold it six months, and let the corporation take the loss. This allows a five-year carryover, but a gain still must be matched against the loss. Obviously one cannot match every loss with a gain, but he should study his portfolio carefully when a long-term loss must be taken.

DEPRECIATION

Depreciation is a tax deduction that is taken on assets held for the production of income or for use in a trade or business. The Internal Revenue Service requires that the method of depreciation used by a taxpayer be reasonable, but any method is acceptable if it does not result in higher amounts of depreciation than those resulting from the maximum "rapid" method permitted for the appropriate category of property.

Several constraints in calculating depreciation are placed upon the taxpayer. First, the maximum amount that can be depreciated is improvement cost. Land cannot be depreciated, nor can value in excess of cost. Second, guideline lives that represent the shortest period of time over which depreciation may be taken are established by the Internal Revenue Service for various categories of property. Third, salvage value must be subtracted from improvement cost in calculating depreciation for those assets that typically are replaced before their values reach zero.

Determination of useful life

The useful economic life of a given parcel is basically a function of wear and tear, decay, climate, and maintenance. No two parcels are identical, and past experiences of the taxpayer and his industry provide a justification for an economic life that follows the established trend.

In absence of firm support for a short life, the Internal Revenue Service follows preestablished guidelines. These guidelines are long term, several examples being the following:

Type of building	*Years*
Offices	45
Hotels	40
Stores	50
Warehouses	60

Usually it is desirable to achieve a shorter life than the guideline life, but the taxpayer must defend any shorter estimate.

Depreciation provisions of Tax Reform Act of 1969

Three changes arose in the Tax Reform Act of 1969 regarding depreciation. First, permissible methods were revised to eliminate many properties from the more rapid forms of write-off. Second, the period of time for which depreciation in excess of straight line could be "recaptured" was lengthened substantially for most types of property. Finally, special provisions were established for residential property in which incentives were provided for constructing selected types of units.

Permitted methods

1. *Straight line.* The cost of property minus estimated salvage value is deducted in equal amounts each year over the estimated useful life of the property. Improvement expenditures can be depreciated in equal annual amounts over the remaining life of the property (or of the improvement if it has a shorter life).

Example

Cost of improvements	$150,000
Less salvage value	20,000
Basis for depreciation	$130,000
Estimated remaining life	20 years
Depreciation permitted each year ($130,000 ÷ 20)	$ 6,500

2. *Double-declining balance or 200 percent method.* This method accelerates depreciation more rapidly than any other permitted method. It is computed by applying during each accounting period a rate twice as great as the straight line rate to the property's value after that value has been reduced by depreciation taken to date.

Example

Cost of improvements $100,000
Salvage value (not considered in this method) ....None
Estimated economic life ....33 years
Straight line rate ....3% per year
Double-declining balance rate ....6% per year

Year	*Remaining basis*	*Depreciation taken*
0	$100,000	—
1	100,000	$6,000
2	94,000	5,640
3	88,360	5,302
4	83,058	4,983

(Steadily declining basis leads to steadily declining depreciation amount for each of 33 years.)

This was the most popular method of accelerated depreciation prior to 1969, and it now can be taken only on first owner *residential* property. It is disallowed for all forms of nonresidential property and for second or subsequent owner residential property.

3. *150 percent declining balance method.* Depreciation is calculated in this method in the same manner as in double-declining balance, with the exception that the maximum rate permitted is 150 percent of the straight line rate. This is the most accelerated depreciation method permitted for new nonresidential depreciable property. It can be taken only by the first owner of nonresidential property; all subsequent owners of such property are not permitted to take depreciation in excess of the straight line rate.

4. *125 percent declining balance method.* This method was created in 1969 to serve as the maximum accelerated method for second or subsequent owner *residential* property. The owner may take as depreciation 125 percent of the straight line rate per year applied to a declining balance.

The idea of separating residential property for depreciation purposes is new in 1969. This requires that residential property be defined, and the act defines it as follows:

A building or structure shall be considered to be residential property for any taxable year only if 80% or more of the gross annual income from such building or structure for such year was income rental from dwelling units. The term dwelling unit means a house or apartment used to provide living accommodations in a building or structure, but does not include a unit in a hotel, motel, inn or other establishment more than ½ of the units in which are used on a transient basis.

5. *Sum-of-the-years'-digits method.* This is a method of accelerated depreciation in which a changing fraction is applied to the original depreciable balance of the property, starting with a large fraction of improvement cost and moving towards a small fraction. The sum-of-digits method shall not be permitted for second owners of any type of property, including residential property. It can be used for new property as long as it does not exceed the maximums of 200 percent declining balance for new residential properties or 150 percent declining balance for new nonresidential property.

Example

Cost of property $120,000
Salvage value 20,000
Basis for depreciation $100,000
Estimated useful life ....10 years

Year	Changing fraction	Basis	Depreciation
1	10/55	$100,000	$ 18,180
2	9/55	100,000	16,370
3	8/55	100,000	14,560
4	7/55	100,000	12,730
5	6/55	100,000	10,910
6	5/55	100,000	9,090
7	4/55	100,000	7,270
8	3/55	100,000	5,460
9	2/55	100,000	3,630
10	1/55	100,000	1,800
			$100,000

6. *Component depreciation.* One means of accelerating the amount of depreciation that may be taken in the early years of a project's life is to divide depreciable components into separate accounts and depreciate each over the shortest life permitted by the Internal Revenue Service. Furnaces, fixtures, and equipment all have shorter lives than total buildings, and a separate depreciation account for each based on its shortest possible life usually leads to exceptionally rapid depreciation in the early years of project life. Other replaceable components such as roofs and pavement can also be broken out for separate depreciation.

7. *First-year special depreciation allowance.* Certain properties can qualify for a special depreciation allowance of 20 percent of cost to be taken in the first year of ownership. This does not apply to real estate, but furniture and fixtures usually qualify. Individuals can get up to $4,000

extra first-year deduction in this manner. To qualify, the property must be tangible personal property having a useful life of six years or more. It can be new or used property.

Depreciation recapture

The 1962 tax act established a procedure wherein taxpayers utilizing rapid depreciation techniques had to report *ordinary income* at the time the property is sold on all excesses of actual depreciation taken over straight line depreciation. This was true for the first 20 months, followed by a 1 percent per month reduction in the amount to be reported as *ordinary* income. After 10 years (120 months), all recapture would disappear. Note that in the absence of recapture, all of the amounts to be reported as ordinary income would qualify for capital gain treatment.

The 20-month rule applied to depreciation taken between 1963 and December 31, 1969. Excess depreciation taken after January 1, 1970, follows the rule described in the next paragraph.

The 1969 act divides residential and nonresidential properties in determining recapture. The excess of actual depreciation over straight line depreciation for *residential property* (only) must be reported as ordinary income on property acquired after January 1, 1970, during the first 100 months (8⅓ years), after which time 1 percent of the excess would be permitted as depreciation. All excess depreciation on nonresidential property is recaptured, regardless of when the property is sold.

Obviously a taxpayer who utilized an accelerated method for 10 or more years eventually "uses up" any excess depreciation balance as annual amounts grow increasingly smaller. This rule affects primarily the taxpayer who converts to the straight line method while a substantial amount of excess depreciation remains on his books.

Example

Mr. H. built a special purpose building that was placed in use on January 1, 1965. It cost $500,000, and it had a useful life of 25 years. He sold the building on December 31, 1977, after 12 years, for $460,000. During his holding period, he depreciated the building at a 6% rate based upon the 150% declining balance method.

Amount deducted	$348,360
Straight line amount	240,000
Excess depreciation	$108,360
Post-1969 excess (7 years)	$ 61,350
Pre-1970 excess (5 years) $47,010	
Recapture (100% minus 40% for 40 mos. held past 20 mos.) ... 60%	
Pre-1970 recapture	$ 28,206
Total Section 1250 recapture	$ 89,556
Amount of excess depreciation allowed	$ 18,804

The $89,556 is subject to taxation at ordinary income tax rates, and the $460,000 selling price minus the adjusted basis of $258,804 yields a long-term capital gain of $201,196.

Rapid write-off for rehabilitation costs

Capital expenditures made after July 24, 1969, and before 1975 for the rehabilitation of substandard housing rented to low- or moderate-income families may be depreciated on a five-year, straight line basis (without allowing for salvage value). To be eligible for this provision, the expenditure must be $15,000 or less per dwelling unit. The expenditure for any unit must exceed $3,000 during any two consecutive taxable years.

Other aspects of depreciation

Corporate reporting. The new act requires that corporations report earnings and profits for taxable years after June 30, 1972, in a manner that straight line depreciation is shown on the tax return. Qualified excess depreciation may still reduce a taxable income, but the practice of minimizing retained earnings shown for tax purposes, thereby maximizing the opportunity to issue "return of capital" (tax-free) dividends, is prevented. Under the old law, the corporation would follow the procedure as follows.

1. Report rapid depreciation—minimize profits and retained earnings.
2. Pay cash dividends in excess of earnings as tax-free return of capital.

The stockholder's basis was reduced by each tax-free distribution until zero basis was established, after which distributions were taxed as capital gains rather than ordinary income.

Real estate investment trusts. The straight line provision of corporations applies to real estate investment trusts (REITs) as well as corporations. However, the computation of whether or not the trust pays out 90 percent of taxable income (to qualify for conduit treatment) is not affected.

Tax planning opportunities. The investor who seeks to optimize his tax shelter position through ownership of depreciable property can do so today only in the form of residential property. All special depreciation benefits—reduction of recapture after 100 months; fast write-off of qualified rehabilitation properties; and use of the 200 percent declining balance method—apply only to residential property. Nonresidential property is somewhat less tax-oriented, but it does offer a fair measure of tax benefit in addition to operating benefit.

The investor can maximize his deductions through the many depreciation devices and through a sale-leaseback of the land underlying the depreciable buildings. This maximizes the amount of property that can be depreciated as well as gaining the fastest depreciation write-offs. His careful planning must be done in determining an optimal holding period and proper method of disposition of the building. The latest code provisions encourage long-range asset ownership, and the investor must balance his tax detriment against his capital gain benefit in considering the advisability of an early sale. Further, high percentage financing could lead to a situation in which the cash to be received from a sale is less than the gain tax liability to be incurred. The investor who can work out a depreciation-based investment program must be able to solve the capital gain/loss, 10 percent surcharge, and interest deduction limitations equations simultaneously. This usually calls for expert professional tax counsel.

PERSONAL HOLDING COMPANIES, SUBCHAPTER S CORPORATIONS, AND COLLAPSIBLE CORPORATIONS

The Internal Revenue Service is required to prevent individuals from utilizing sophisticated ownership forms to achieve tax benefits to which they would not be entitled in the ordinary course of business. An accumulated earnings tax can be levied against any entity that fails to distribute its earnings to owners and cannot show just cause for doing so. A rate of 27.5 percent is levied against the first $100,000 of unjustified accumulated earnings, and a rate of 38.5 percent is applied to accumulated earnings in excess of $400,000.

A special tax can be levied against corporations that are deemed personal holding companies, i.e., corporations into which individuals assign assets and generate a reservoir of money and other assets that are subject to corporate tax, but that escape personal income taxation. Once deemed a personal holding company, a corporation's undistributed income is taxed at a rate of 70 percent per annum.

Subchapter S corporations are those that are taxed as partnerships. Individual owners secure the tax benefits of an individual and the liability limitations of a corporation. The Subchapter S device is not permitted for passive investments such as those which yield tax-sheltered income plus tax shelter of other income. The collapsible corporation rule comes into effect when an individual or a group of individuals sell all of the stock of a corporation which holds depreciable property. If the depreciable property is 15 percent or more of the entity's assets, then gain on the stock sale results in ordinary income rather than capital gain.

LIMITED TAX PREFERENCE

The limited tax preference provision of the Tax Reform Act of 1969 is an attempt to prevent income-producing taxpayers from sheltering substantial amounts of money from taxation. A tax of 10 percent is levied against any financial benefits that are not subjected to ordinary or capital gain taxation. The major tax preference items that relate to real estate are (1) the untaxed half of capital gain; and (2) accelerated depreciation.

Capital gains

For individuals, tax preference equals 50 percent of long-term capital gain in excess of net short-term capital losses. For corporations, the formula for determining tax preference income is as follows:

$$\text{Net long-term capital gain minus net short-term capital loss} \times \frac{\text{(Corp. regular tax rate—Corp. capital gain tax rate)}}{\text{(Corp. regular tax rate)}}$$

Tax preference income is taxed at 10 percent for both individuals and corporations.

Accelerated depreciation

Any excess of accelerated depreciation over straight line depreciation is subject to the 10 percent extra tax during each year that the excess occurs.

Exemptions and deductions. A $30,000 exemption is allowed in computing the 10 percent tax. For married taxpayers filing separate returns, only $15,000 per return is exempted.

Income taxes imposed in the year, other than accumulated earnings tax and personal holding company tax, are deducted from tax preference items before the tax is applied. Tax credits permitted are also considered before the tax is applied.

Example

Mr. Spinoza earned $100,000 during 1970, and he reported $75,000 as one half of his long-term capital gain. His taxes were $97,180, and his tax preference items were $75,000 for one half of capital gain and $45,000 excess depreciation. His 10% tax is $282, as follows:

50% of capital gain		$ 75,000
Excess depreciation		45,000
		$120,000
Less:		
Exemption	$30,000	
Income tax	87,180	$117,180
Subject to 10% tax		2,820
10% tax		$ 282

Limited tax preference in loss years. If a taxpayer incurs a net operating loss to be carried over, the law permits the 10 percent tax to be deferred. If the loss carryforward is not used up within five years, the 10 percent tax will never be imposed.

Tax preference treatment of real estate investment trusts

In general, real estate investment trusts are accorded conduit or "flow-through" treatment. Tax preference items are apportioned between the trust and its shareholders according to the ratio between the dividends (other than capital gain dividends) paid each shareholder and the taxable income of the trust (ignoring the dividends-paid deduction). The ratio for finding the noncapital gains tax preference items of the shareholder is as follows.

$$\frac{\text{Tax preference items}}{\text{Tax preference items}} = \frac{\text{Dividends (noncapital gain)}}{\text{Taxable income of the}}$$
of shareholder = paid to shareholder
Tax preference items = Taxable income of the
of the trust = trust (ignoring dividends-paid deduction)

Tax planning opportunities. The 10 percent surcharge can be deferred when the investor incurs a net operating loss that can be carried forward, and the careful taking of short-term losses can at times reduce the amount of surcharge-eligible income to within the $30,000-plus-taxes-imposed limit. If the loss is carried forward continues for five years, the 10 percent surcharge is not levied.

LIMIT ON INVESTMENT INTEREST DEDUCTION

A special category of interest expense has been created for investments. Any interest paid on funds borrowed to hold investments is labeled investment interest expense.

The tax preference provision relating to investment interest relates only to individuals, tax option corporations, and personal holding companies. Ordinary corporations are not affected.

Beginning in 1972, a limitation is placed upon the amount of excess investment interest that an individual is permitted to deduct. This limitation is the sum of four amounts:

1. $25,000 ($12,500 for married person's separate return).
2. Net investment income before interest.
3. The excess of net long-term capital gain over net short-term capital losses. If this provides a deduction, the amount deducted must be added to ordinary income in calculating capital gains tax, capital gains deductions, and tax preference items.
4. One half of the excess of investment interest over (1) + (2) + (3).

Carryover of loss

Any excess investment interest that is not allowed may be carried over into the following tax year. The maximum amount that can be deducted in the following year is computed as follows:

$$\text{Carryover deduction} = \frac{\begin{array}{c}\text{(Net investment income} \\ \text{for carryover year} \\ \text{plus \$25,000)}\end{array} - \begin{array}{c}\text{(The greater of} \\ \text{investment interest} \\ \text{paid or \$25,000)}\end{array}}{2}$$

If excess interest beyond this limitation remains undeducted, the amount that can be carried over to a third year is reduced by the amount of the taxpayer's 50 percent capital gains deduction.

Example

	1972	1973
Investment interest	$150,000	$60,000
Long-term capital gain	15,000	15,000
Net investment income	15,000	40,000

1972

a) Investment interest	$150,000
b) Exemption	$25,000
c) Net investment income	15,000
d) Capital gain	15,000
e) Total	$55,000
f) One half of $95,000 (difference between (a) and (e))	$47,500

1973

g) Deduction allowed	120,500
h) Amount disallowed	$ 47,500
i) Net investment income ($40,000) + $25,000	$ 65,000
j) Greater of investment interest or $25,000	60,000
k) Investment interest deduction (½ of (i) less (j))	2,500
l) Nondeductible (h) less (k)	45,000
m) 50% of capital gain	7,500
n) Disallowed investment interest which can be carried to 1974 (l) less (m)	$ 37,500

Special rules and exceptions

Several special rules and exceptions are particularly important in computing investment interest limitations.

1. Property owned and leased on a net basis is treated as investment property if (*a*) business expenses are less than 15 percent of rental

income, or (*b*) the lessor is either guaranteed a return or guaranteed against loss.
2. Construction interest is not investment interest.
3. A trust cannot add $25,000 to net investment income nor use the $25,000 floor on investment interest in computing deductible interest.

Tax planning opportunities. The purpose of the interest deduction limitation is to encourage speculators to acquire income-producing property or to recognize long-term capital gains that otherwise would be deferrable through installment sales or tax-free exchanges. Either of these methods would permit deduction of a greater amount of interest, but either penalizes the successful acreage speculator who might not have experience in operating income-producing property.

The investor can plan his investment interest amounts for long periods into the future. His investment income and capital gains are predictable with less certainty than the interest payments, but they are predictable and he can devise a balance among the three to ensure the deductibility of his interest. When his planning fails, the carryover provision prevents a total loss of the deduction.

TAX-FREE EXCHANGES

The Tax Reform Act of 1969 did not change the prior law's tax-free exchange provisions. Real estate held for investment purposes meets the "like kind" and "investment property" tests, and it can be exchanged for any other real estate on a tax-free basis. Only "boot" is taxed.

Boot

Boot is any asset or liability transferred as part of the realty exchange. The most typical forms of boot are cash, mortgages existing prior to the exchange, purchase money mortgages created within the exchange, and debt instruments transferred in lieu of cash.

Neither party in a tax-free exchange is permitted to recognize a loss at the time of exchange. The party receiving boot in any form will likely have a gain that is subject to taxation, but the party who gives up boot may only add the surrendered boot to his tax basis. The following rules apply to boot.

1. Cash received is subject to taxation; cash paid is added to basis.
2. Mortgages exchanged as a part of the property exchange are netted against one another. The party who ends up with a smaller mortgage must report taxable boot on the difference in mortgages. The party who accepts the larger mortgage adds the difference in mortgages to his tax basis.

3. Notes made in lieu of cash are treated as mortgages. The party making the notes adds the amount of the notes to his basis.

For each party in a tax-free exchange, the adjusted basis after the exchange is calculated as follows.

To original basis of original property:
  Add: Cash paid
        Notes issued
        Mortgage obligation accepted
                (assumed or taken subject to)
  Deduct: Mortgage obligation passed to other party(s)
          Cash received
          Notes accepted

This yields the new basis. If the exchange caused the party to achieve a taxable gain, any gain recognized (taxed) is added back to his basis. This permits him to avoid double taxation at the time he sells the property.

Example

Mr. Dillon owns a hotel property that has a depreciated tax basis of $600,000 and a fair market value of $950,000. He has an outstanding $500,000 mortgage.

Mr. Cartwright would like to acquire Mr. Dillon's hotel by trading a vacant tract of land having a fair market value of $800,000 plus $200,000 cash. Mr. Cartwright will not assume Mr. Dillon's mortgage; it must be paid at the time of closing. Mr. Cartwright has a tax basis of $300,000 in his land and no mortgage.

If Mr. Dillon were to sell his property outright, he would report a $350,000 capital gain. Mr. Cartwright's gain would be $500,000 in the event of a sale.

This is not an even exchange. Mr. Dillon is giving up a $950,000 value for $1 million. Thus, Mr. Dillon's maximum gain is increased to $400,000 and Mr. Cartwright's drops to $450,000 after the exchange.

Mr. Dillon must report a gain of $200,000 in this exchange—the amount of cash boot he received. Mr. Cartwright incurs no gain and pays no tax. He adds $200,000 to his basis.

Apportionment of basis

In effecting the exchange, the relative values of land and depreciable improvements become very important. Both parties normally wish to achieve depreciable status on as much of their bases as possible, and increasing the building-to-land ratio is desirable in nearly any exchange of properties.

Example

	M	T
Fair market value of property	100	100
Building value	70	70
Land value	30	30
Tax basis at time of exchange	20	40

In this example, an exchange of equal value properties would affect future depreciation, thereby affecting future tax basis. M would take T's property, retaining his old basis of $20,000. He would split the $20,000 on a 70% building ($14,000), 30% land ($6,000) basis. T would allocate his $40,000 basis in the same way—$28,000 building and $12,000 land.

Assumption of a mortgage increases one's tax basis, as does paying cash. Also, payment of tax on gain recognized at the time of exchange is added back to basis. The total of these items is apportioned to buildings and land on the basis of relative appraisals.

Depreciation recapture

Depreciation recapture must be considered at the time a tax-free exchange occurs. Unpermitted excess depreciation must be reported as ordinary income in the tax year that the exchange is consummated.

Example

Mr. W. purchased improved land on January 1, 1970, for $100,000— $80,000 building and $20,000 land. During 1970, 1971, and 1972, he deducted $10,321 at a 150% rate of a 33⅓-year life. His adjusted basis on December 31, 1972, is $89,679 and he exchanges the property (without boot) for unimproved land valued at $93,800.

Straight line depreciation during the three years was $7,200 at 3% per year. Mr. W. is entitled to no excess depreciation (100% recapture), so he must report ordinary income of $3,121 ($10,321 − 7,200).

In this example, gain on property equals recaptured depreciation. Had the gain been less than the recaptured amount, only the amount of the gain would be recaptured. This rule recognizes the fact that actual incurred depreciation is certain at the time of disposal and sets the gain limit. In other words, recapture cannot of itself create a loss in which basis exceeds the value of property held after the exchange.

Tax planning opportunities. The tax-free exchange creates a substantial amount of flexibility for the real estate investor. Any type of real property can be exchanged for another, without regard to whether it is raw land or improved property. Thus, the investor who wants to acquire a particular parcel of property can find a substitute property that the desired property's owner would accept in trade, purchase it, arrange for financing that is identical in amount to that of the desired property, and exchange the two parcels on a tax-free basis.

The original owner transfers his old tax basis to the new property, and he incurs no tax detriment in the exchange. Normally he hopes to secure a greater value in the new property than that of the old one.

The investor is able to secure the desired property, which usually is ready for immediate development. He may wish to use the exchange technique to upgrade his tax basis by assuming a larger debt in the exchange, or he might wish to transfer from a parcel of raw land to an income-producing property. Through careful planning, nearly any property acquisition or disposal can be worked out as a tax-free exchange.

INSTALLMENT SALE

The installment method of reporting permits the seller to defer taxable gain on each dollar of selling price until that dollar is collected. If the total gross profit is 25 percent of the contract price, then 25 cents per dollar collected is taxable in the year of collection. Any property eligible for long-term capital gain can retain its eligibility and be taxed accordingly.

The installment treatment helps the buyer avoid bringing together dollars needed to purchase the property, and it permits the seller to pay tax only when he has received money. Income averaging is accomplished easily in this manner.

Most installment sales are set with a 29 percent downpayment. This figure is below the 30 percent maximum established by the Internal Revenue Service, probably because it offers the opportunity to make a slight error without upsetting the installment treatment.

Qualifying for installment treatment

The seller must comply with two conditions to qualify for installment treatment:

1. Not more than 30 percent of the gross selling price can be received in the year of sale.
2. The seller must elect the installment method in a timely return.

Terms must be defined carefully in dealing with installment sales. Two objectives are to be accomplished, one of which is to verify that 30 percent or less of the selling price is received by the seller in the year of the sale. The other objective is to establish a system wherein 100 percent of the taxable gain is reported as dollars of the selling price are received.

Gross selling price

The total gross sales price is used in determining whether or not 30 percent or less was realized in the year of sale. The seller may receive up to 30 percent of this amount in the year of sale, including downpayment and installment payments received (both principal and interest).

The total gross selling price includes the following:

1. Cash received by the seller.
2. Payments made on behalf of the seller such as liens, taxes, etc.
3. Mortgage on the property to the extent that it exceeds the seller's tax basis.
4. Any property accepted in lieu of cash.
5. Option payments that apply toward purchase price, regardless of when received.

Mortgage assumed

Note that assumed mortgage assumption is not considered part of the selling price unless the seller is "mortgaged out" (e.g., borrowed more than his tax basis in the property). The assumed mortgage involves money that will never be paid to the seller, and there is no reason to assume that the mortgage will be paid to the seller in the year of sale. The mortgage in excess of basis is actually income, and since the income was received prior to the date of sale (at the time of mortgage financing), then it must be reported as immediate income.

Marketable bonds are part of first year collections

In the past, an installment seller could accept buyer's notes, discount the notes, and not include the proceeds of the discounted sale as part of the first year collections. Under the 1969 act, a bond or other evidence of indebtedness which is payable upon demand or which is tradable in an established securities market shall be treated as cash rather than as evidence of indebtedness of the purchaser. This is also true of marketable obligations of a government or corporation. Thus, only relatively non-marketable securities such as those that are unsecured, nonnegotiable, subjected to extended repayment terms, or containing contingencies are exempted from treatment as income in the year of sale.

Imputed interest

The code contains special provisions for users of the installment sale method regarding interest-free payment plans. The installment sale permits capital gain treatment, and most sellers would prefer to receive all proceeds as principal rather than interest, with the Internal Revenue

Service being required to impute 6 percent interest unless at least 4 percent is charged by the seller. The imputed interest applicable to the year of sale is considered in calculating the 30 percent for installment sale qualification.

Tax planning opportunities

The benefits of an installment sale are obvious to a property seller. The buyer does not appear to achieve any personal benefits, yet he is usually able to accommodate the tax needs of the seller while securing low-cost financing on more than 70 percent of the contract price. In practice, most installment sales involves much less than a 30 percent downpayment, and the seller usually gets a lower-than-market interest rate on the unpaid balance.

The major problem that can arise in an installment sale transaction is that the buyer must arrange for property title releases to match his development schedule. If partial releases are established according to a fixed payment schedule, then the buyer might be unable to gain clear title when needed. Solving this problem usually leads to an installment sale that benefits both parties.

Example

Mr. Lsmft desired to sell a parcel of property on the installment basis. This property was purchased five years ago for $10,000.

Mr. Kreosote offered to buy the property on the following basis: $5,000 down on January 1, 1969, and $5,000 per year for three years payable each January 1 starting January 1, 1969. Mr. Lsmft accepted this offer with no mention being made of interest costs.

Mr. Lsmft must separate his gain into capital gain and interest income. He must report at least 4 percent per annum interest to avoid an Internal Revenue Service assumption that 6 percent has been charged.

Answer

	Year				
	1	*2*	*3*	*4*	*Total*
Recapture of investment	$2,500	$2,500	$2,500	$2,500	$10,000
Interest: 4 percent on balance each year	600	400	200	0	1,200
Long-term capital gain	1,900	2,100	2,300	2,500	8,000
Total	$5,000	$5,000	$5,000	$5,000	$20,000

TAXES AND OWNERSHIP FORM

Taxes represent only one of several motives considered in the selection of an ownership form, but a very important one. The corporation and the real estate investment trust have been practical vehicles for some income tax purposes, and with minor exception, their tax benefits carry through the Tax Reform Act of 1969. The following important changes occurred.

1. Corporate capital gains were taxed at a 28 percent rate in 1970, and the rate increased to 30 percent beginning in 1971. The ordinary rate on corporate income stays the same as before 1969 at a 22 percent rate on the first $25,000 and 48 percent on income above that amount.

2. Subsection 1201 (*d*) gains hold at 25 percent for corporations as well as individuals until 1975. After that year, all corporate capital gains will be subject to the 30 percent rate.

3. Real estate investment trusts now must issue capital gain dividends to holders of shares in two stages. First are those that are to be taxed at 28 and 30 percent, respectively, and second are the 25 percent subsection (*d*) gains.

4. Corporations are permtited to carry back capital losses for three years on all losses incurred during 1970 or after. The loss carryback is not limited in general, but it cannot create or increase a net operating loss.

5. After June 30, 1972, corporations and tax-free real estate investment trusts must report straight line depreciation in computing earnings and profits. However, this provision does not apply in determining whether or not the trust paid dividends of 90 percent or more of its taxable income to retain conduit treatment.

An important point to remember regarding corporations is that the collapsible corporation rules were not changed by the Tax Reform Act of 1969. One cannot achieve capital gain on the sale of stock in a corporation that holds depreciable assets within three years of completion of the assets unless the depreciable assets are less than 15 percent of the corporation's net worth.

Partnerships. Many real estate transactions are structured as partnerships in order to achieve direct tax deduction benefits for individual property owners. The partnership can be general or limited; the former involves partners sharing personal liability and management responsibility, while the latter involves a general partner or general partners who assume these liabilities and responsibilities to protect a group of limited partners. The limited partnership has been extremely popular among professional people who seek the earnings and tax deductions of real property without the attendant management responsibility and risks of liability.

The general partner can offer his limited partners an opportunity to deduct interest on mortgage indebtedness only if he is careful not to become *personally* liable for the entire indebtedness. Most mortgages on partnership-owned properties are written with an exculpatory clause which makes only the property collateral for the indebtedness. Since no single individual is liable, then liability is shared by all partners in proportion to their relative ownership. When the lender will not accept the exculpatory clause, a third party can purchase the property, obtain the mortgage, and sell the property to the partnership subject to the debt.

Tax planning opportunities

The terms *syndication* and *joint venture* describe relationships among investors that are not forms of ownership structure. The distinction between these terms lies in the extent of continuity of the relationship among the investors. The syndication can invest in numerous projects simultaneously, while the joint venture is normally thought of as a single project. In practice, however, the two terms are usually used interchangeably.

Joint ventures and syndications can be structured as corporations, trusts, partnerships, or tenants in common. Investors in these groups can also be corporations, trusts, partners, or tenants in common. Thus, a syndication structured as a partnership might have one share owned by a corporation, a second owned by an individual, a third owned by three men as tenants in common, a fourth owned by a general partnership, and a fifth owned by a trust.

The ability of the underlying property to satisfy different investor objectives determines the proper structure to use. A partnership or tenants-in-common structure allows depreciation deductions and operating losses to be taken by individuals on their tax returns. A corporation structure permits investors to achieve liability limited to their original investments. The proper structure for each situation must be custom designed to meet the needs of investors based upon the individual property's merits.

OTHER INCOME TAX ISSUES

Dealer status

Real estate investors must plan dispositions of real property in a way that avoids their being classified as real estate dealers. Dealers cannot achieve capital gain status; all gains they receive are treated as ordinary income.

To avoid dealer staus, investors must remain passive by not improving their property for sale purposes and by selling it in large parcels rather than subdividing it into many small sales. Limiting the number of sales to less than five per year and refraining from promoting the property heavily usually helps retain investor status.

Involuntary conversion

Investors whose land is taken by a public agency are permitted to reinvest the proceeds from the taking without incurring a capital gain or loss. They can treat the taking as a taxable disposition if they wish, but the involuntary conversion privilege offers the option of avoiding a tax payment. The rules regarding involuntary conversion are exceptionally articulate, and every provision must be followed carefully to avoid the incurrence of a taxable event status.

Housing for low-income families

Several steps were taken in the Tax Reform Act of 1969 to facilitate owner occupancy of homes by low-income families and to encourage the development of more moderately priced housing.

The first change in the act established an involuntary conversion type treatment for those who sell qualified properties to qualified buyers and then reinvest the proceeds of sale in qualified property.

A qualified property is one that provides rental or cooperative housing for lower income families and (1) is insured under the National Housing Act; (2) the owner (seller) operates as a limited dividend sponsor; and (3) rentals or payments charged to occupants are limited. A qualified buyer would be a tenant-occupant or a nonprofit, not-for-profit, or charitable entity.

In the sale, gains to be recognized are limited to the excess of sale proceeds over the cost of replacing the housing project. The basis of the replacement project is reduced by unrecognized gain (e.g., the seller's old basis carries over). Replacement property must be acquired, built, or reconstructed within the period beginning one year before the approved disposition and ending one year after the end of the first taxable year in which any of the gain is realized.

Recapture of depreciation applies in computing gain upon disposition of the qualified property. This gain is limited to the greater of (1) the recognized gain or (2) the amount of gain that would have been ordinary income under Section 1250 (in which most gains are capital gains while most losses are ordinary losses) minus the cost of Section 1250 property acquired in the replacement. A formula is provided in the Internal Revenue Code for computing depreciation recapture with component depreciation.

Charitable gifts of property

In the past, a taxpayer could deduct the fair market value of property donated to a qualified charitable organization. He would have no tax to pay on the difference between his cost basis and fair market value at the date of donation.

After December 31, 1969, the amount of charitable contribution deduction on individual parcels is limited. The Tax Reform Act of 1969 increased the percentage of one's adjusted gross income that he could give away from 30 percent to 50 percent. However, a special provision excludes capital gain property from the 50 percent limit. A 30 percent (of gross income) ceiling applies to capital gain property, with a five-year carryover of contributions in excess of the 30 percent limitation.

There are no exceptions to this rule. The taxpayer may elect to apply the 50 percent limitation when he makes a contribution to a public charity or to certain qualified foundations. However, if he makes this election he must give up that part of his charitable deduction that equals 50 percent of the capital gain that he would have realized had he sold the property on the date of sale. Thus, the 50 percent option is expensive and would be of value primarily when gross income is disproportionately high in a given tax year.

Example

Taxpayer has adjusted gross income of $120,000
Contribution to church–land
  Fair market value 140,000
  Basis 20,000
Using 30%, he could deduct 36,000
He would then carry over to future years 104,000
Using 50% of adjusted gross, he could deduct 60,000
He had $140,000 − 20,000 = $120,000 in gain; 50% of
  $120,000 = $60,00 not allowed; amount allowed in total 80,000
Amount carried forward ($80,000 − $60,000) 20,000

Ordinary income property

Ordinary income property, e.g., property not qualified for long-term capital gain treatment, is treated differently. With ordinary income property, *the maximum deduction equals the taxpayer's basis in the property.* Appreciation is not considered. He can make a gift equal to or less than 50 percent of his adjusted gross income.

Bargain sales to charity

Under the new act, one's benefits from selling property to charity are limited. He must prorate the fair market value of property given between gift and sale. The gift portion is subject to charity treatment, while the sale portion results in a taxable gain or loss.

Example

Taxpayer sells land to church
  Fair market value $40,000
  Cost basis 12,000
  Sale price to church 24,000

The "sold" portion of value is 60%
The "gift" portion of value is 40%
His basis is:
  Gift ....$ 4,800
  Sale 7,200
Taxable income subject to capital treatment ($24,000 − 7,200) 16,800
Donation subject to 30% of adjusted gross income limitation 16,000

This is less beneficial than the pre-1970 rule, but it is still more beneficial than selling property and making cash donations.

Gifts of property use

Under the pre-1970 rule, a taxpayer could permit a charitable organization to use property such as office space, reducing his gross rental income and establishing a charitable deduction equal to the rent foregone. Under the 1969 act, he cannot obtain the charitable deduction unless he gives the entire property (fee simple interest) or an undivided tenant-in-common interest to the charity.

SUMMARY

Income taxes must be considered in acquisition, operation and disposition of real estate assets. Capital gain and capital loss rules have become less favorable for real estate investors, with the maximum capital gain tax rate having increased to 35 percent while the loss and loss carry forward deductions have been limited to less than their pre-1969 levels. Charitable gift deductions have been reduced somewhat, and rules about bargain sales to charities are more stringent.

Operators of real estate assets are experiencing reductions in opportunities to use rapid depreciation techniques. Depreciation recapture provisions have become more complex and restructive, and only residential properties are granted the liberal deduction treatment enjoyed formerly on all types of properties.

A limit has been placed upon investment interest deductions which exceed investment income, and a new 10 percent tax has been added which applies to items such as rapid depreciation and untaxed portions of capital gains. Careful planning is needed to secure maximum benefits from these items.

Opportunities for income tax planning abound. The subject is complex, but the rewards from careful programming of gains, losses, depreciation deductions, and interest deductions can be great. Sophisticated transactions such as tax free exchanges and installment sales can save a large portion of the taxes on potential gains. The assistance of a tax expert is important in this aspect of real estate.

QUESTIONS FOR REVIEW

1. How is the annual capital loss limitation for an individual computed?
2. In what manner is a capital loss carryover lost over time?
3. Indicate the general constraints that are imposed in computing asset depreciation.
4. What are the methods of depreciation that are generally approved by the Internal Revenue Service?
5. Describe depreciation recapture.
6. How does one calculate the exemption from the limited tax preference provision?
7. What is the limit on the amount of investment interest that can be deducted?
8. What is "boot"? How is boot computed?
9. Why must the investor worry about apportionment of basis in a tax-free exchange?
10. What conditions must be met to qualify for an installment sale?
11. Why must interest be charged on the unpaid balance in an installment sale?
12. What are the advantages and disadvantages of the partnership ownership form?
13. Evaluate the Tax Reform Act provisions regarding housing for low-income families.
14. Do you feel that the latest tax laws regarding charitable contributions are reasonable or unreasonable? Why or why not?

REFERENCES

Berman, Daniel S. and Schwartz, Sheldon. *Tax Saving Opportunities in Real Estate Deals.* Englewood Cliffs, N.J.: Prentice-Hall, Inc., 1971.

Boyd, Orton W. *Atlas' Tax Aspects of Real Estate Transactions.* Washington, D.C.: Bureau of National Affairs, Inc., 1971.

Casey, William J. *Tax Shelter in Real Estate.* New York: Institute for Business Planning, Inc., 1971.

J. K. Lasser Tax Institute. *J. K. Lasser's Successful Tax Planning for Real Estate,* Bernard Greisman (ed.). Rev. ed. Garden City, N.Y.: Doubleday and Company, Inc., 1972.

McCoy, John O.; Olsen, Harvey A.; Reed, Charles H.; Sandison, Robert W.; and Wright, Robert F. *Federal Taxes Affecting Real Estate,* 2d ed. Chicago: National Institute of Farm and Land Brokers, 1970.

Tax, Legal, and Financial Reporting Services:

American Institute of CPA's, 666 5th Avenue, New York, N.Y. 10017.
Commerce Clearing House, Inc., 4025 West Peterson, Chicago, Ill. 60645.

Federal Tax Press, Inc., 19 Roosevelt Avenue, West Haven, Connecticut 06516.

Prentice-Hall, Inc., Englewood Cliffs, N.J. 07632.

Weiss, Robert M. *How to Maximize Tax Savings in Buying, Operating, and Selling Real Property.* Englewood Cliffs, N.J.: Prentice-Hall, Inc., 1971.

Wendt, Paul F. and Cerf, Alan R. *Real Estate Investment Analysis and Taxation.* New York: McGraw-Hill Book Company, 1969. This book does not contain the Tax Reform Act of 1969.

—————————————————— chapter 8

PROPERTY OWNERSHIP
RIGHTS

IN MOST INSTANCES, the real estate investor is in the fortunate position of being able to choose consciously the precise legal form of ownership he is to employ. He has the prerogative to make decisions as to whether he wishes to lease or own outright, and he can elect to own individually or jointly with others. He is able to specify the fixtures which he wishes to acquire with land, and he is in a position to adjudge the impact that various easements, private deed restrictions, and zoning ordinances will have on the use he wishes to make of the land. He also has the options of establishing a corporation or entering a partnership, syndicate, or investment trust which owns property. Such forms offer tax benefits and limited liability which could be critical to the fulfillment of the investor's objectives, although the magnitude and quality of property ownership rights are not affected by the interjection of the separate holding entity.

For the investor to make sound decisions concerning ownership, he must be aware of the types of situations which might arise when he considers potential investment properties. He cannot acquire a greater ownership right than that of the existing owner, so he must obtain complete information about those rights before he undertakes the venture. This requires that he have a familiarity with the types of ownership rights which exist and the means available for transferring them.

There are several ownership rights such as fee tail and qualified fee estates which rarely appear and which are generally in disfavor with courts of law and with investors in general. However, the individual investor must analyze the minimum ownership rights which he needs to make use of a given property before condemning a particular right. He might find that a determinable fee estate or a lease from period to period

144

is adequate for his purpose. In any event, he should be cognizant of all possible types of rights so that he has a basis for deciding whether or not he should enter a specific transaction.

The investor's option to join with others in an investment situation also requires careful attention to ownership form. Ownership with others can be effected in a manner that the various owners can freely deed or will their individual rights to others, or ownership can be established with a right of survivorship where the surviving owners acquire the share of any owner who dies. The first form, tenancy in common, is by far the more frequently used. It grants the investor more freedom of action, and it permits him to use the property ownership to provide for his heirs in the event of his death. The second form, joint tenancy, leads to continuity of the ownership venture by preventing the heirs of a deceased owner from interfering with the plans of the surviving owners. Here again, the specific plans of the investor(s) dictate the ownership form to be used.

The development of a proper group ownership form is one of the most important decisions that must be made in any real estate investment. The corporation and the trust permit the loss liability of investors to be limited to their cash or property investment in the project. The partnership, tenancy in common, and joint tenancy forms fail to limit liability, but they permit individual investors to obtain personal income tax deductions. The limited partnership form allows liability limitation for one category of partners while retaining the full tax deduction status for all partners. The strategy implications of selecting a group ownership form are considered in this chapter.

A different type of multiple ownership situation arises through special legislation providing for married couples. Some states recognize a special form known as tenancy by the entireties wherein the right of survivorship exists between the married partners. Upon the death of one partner, title to all properties held in tenancy by the entireties automatically passes to the other, a situation which is true even if one of the partners sells his or her share to a third party (without the signature of the other partner). State laws vary considerably in this area; tenancy by the entireties and other forms such as community property and condominium require state enabling laws. For the investor this means two things: (1) he must be familiar with the possible forms of ownership in each state where he considers investments, and (2) he must decide which forms he prefers when an option is available.

WORKING DEFINITION OF REAL ESTATE, REALTY, AND REAL PROPERTY

An awareness of the distinction between the terms *real estate* and *real property* is essential to an understanding of property ownership rights.

As mentioned in chapter 1, real estate can usually be defined as land and anything permanently attached to land. A parcel of real estate is tangible; it is described in terms of size, shape, and location, and it extends from a point at the center of the earth outward to the outermost layer of the earth's atmosphere. Mineral, oil, and water contained in the land, and air rights above the land, are included. Anyone standing upon the parcel or on an adjoining parcel can physically view it. *Real property, on the other hand, is an embodiment of intangible ownership rights.* These ownership rights are available to individuals in a free enterprise economy such as that of the United States, and they are retained by sovereign government in directed economies such as the U.S.S.R. They are described in terms of extent of ownership, considering factors of possession, control, enjoyment, and disposition.[1]

Given a society in which private property prevails, ownership rights can range from virtually absolute to highly limited. An individual is entitled to own a parcel of real estate "outright," with complete rights to possession, control, enjoyment, or disposition in whole or in part. The government which permits private ownership imposes only one restriction—to refrain from creating conditions which could be harmful to public health and/or welfare. Limited ownership usually occurs by contract, where one individual acquires part of the ownership rights of the outright owner. Examples are leasing agreements, public utility easements, and mineral rights purchases.

PERSONAL PROPERTY AND FIXTURES

Our definition of real estate in terms of land and its permanent attachments is very vague insofar as the word *permanent* is involved. Items not permanently attached to land are considered to be personal property, personalty, or moveables. They are not real estate, and they can be removed from the real estate at any time by the holder of the personal property rights.

A fixture is an item that was once personal property but later attached to real estate in a permanent manner. Fixtures go to the buyer in a sale of real property, and they cannot be removed from the real estate without the permission of the real estate owner. The law of fixtures is one of the most complex areas in the study of real estate law, with every case having unique considerations. In general, the courts apply four tests to determine whether or not an article is permanently attached to real estate.[2]

1. *Intention of the parties.* The most important test is whether or not the article was intended to be permanently attached at the time of attach-

---

[1] Alfred A. Ring, *Real Estate Principles and Practices* (Englewood Cliffs, N.J.: Prentice-Hall, Inc., 1972), p. 46.

[2] Robert Kratovil, *Real Estate Law* (Englewood Cliffs, N.J.: Prentice-Hall, Inc., 1969), p. 9.

ment. This is a commonsense approach which attempts to determine whether or not a reasonable person would consider an item to be a fixture.

2. *Manner of attachment.* In general, an item is permanently attached if its removal damages the real estate.

3. *Character of the article and its adaptation to the real estate.* Articles built especially for a particular building are normally considered fixtures.

4. *Relation of the parties.* Courts tend to favor certain parties in disputes, primarily on the grounds that their adversaries should know better than to permit fixture disputes to arise. For example, buyers tend to be favored over sellers where sales agreements are indefinite, and tenants are normally favored over landlords in gaining permission to remove personal property they may have inadvertently attached to the landlord's property.

Residential property transactions create many problems of defining personal property and fixtures. Buyers sometimes assume that they are buying houses completely equipped with storm windows, carpets, elaborate light fixtures, special plumbing attachments, etc., which the sellers do not wish to sell. A deal is closed, and the buyer learns to his dismay that the items which were so instrumental in his decision to buy are gone when he prepares to take possession. Thus, the investor must question all fixtures and personal property items to determine whether or not they are part of the sales agreement. When he is in doubt as to the permanence of any item, he should state in the offer to buy that he plans to acquire it. The seller then has an opportunity to reject the offer, but no confusion or misunderstanding is likely to arise. The two parties agree as to the items included in the price, and the sale is either consummated or cancelled.

REAL PROPERTY OWNERSHIP RIGHTS

The interest that an individual holds in real estate is referred to as an estate. Estates are of two types: estates in possession and estates not in possession. Estates in possession are by the far the more common, being divided into freehold estates and estates of less than freehold. Freeholds represent substantial ownership rights and are treated as real property by the law; estates of less than freehold, i.e., leaseholds, are considered personal property. Estates not in possession represent future interests in property which convert to estates in possession upon the occurrence of a specified event. The relationship between types of estates is presented in Figure 8–1.

Freehold estates of inheritance

The most complete forms of ownership are those which can be enjoyed by the owner during his lifetime and then passed on to designated heirs or lineal descendants. Fee simple absolute and fee tail estates endure

FIGURE 8–1

Estates in land

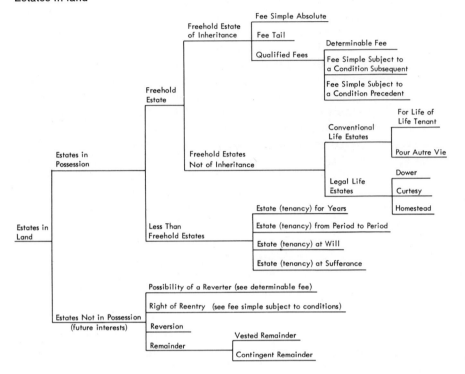

Source: William Velman, the Ohio State University lecture handout, 1963.

throughout the lifetime of the owner. He can change the form of the estate by grant or by will, such as the establishment of a life estate for his wife with the property to go to specified heirs upon her death, but the estate remains fee simple or fee tail in absence of such actions. Qualified fee estates endure either indefinitely or until a specified event occurs— this event not normally being the death of the estate holder.

Fee simple estates.   One who holds real property as fee simple owner is entitled to do whatever he wishes with the property as long as his actions are lawful and do not conflict with public interest. He may improve it in any manner he wishes, lease it to whomever he wishes, give it away, sell it, remove or plant trees, or remove or add soil and minerals. Fee simple ownership can be restricted by law through zoning, where only specified uses of the land are permitted, or by voluntary deed restrictions which specify permitted uses. Nuisances cannot be maintained, such as a deep hole which could endanger children; the public welfare is harmed by jeopardizing the health and safety of others.

Fee tail estates. The concept of fee tail is a carryover from feudal times where the ownership of property was granted to an individual and the heirs of his body. Early common law held that the property reverted back to the original grantor when the blood line of the grantee terminated, but modern (U.S.) statutory law either refuses to recognize a fee tail or limits it to lives in being at the time of the original grant. Fee tail estates are rarely encountered today, but the investor must be aware of what they are and be certain that he can derive a fee simple ownership from the seller's fee tail.

Qualified fee estates. A qualified, determinable, or base fee estate is one which terminates upon the occurrence of a specified event. Words such as "as long as" or "during" are used in its creation.[3] An example of a determinable fee estate is where an individual grants property to a peace-promoting charity for as long as the United States remains a member of the United Nations. If the United States later withdraws from the United Nations, ownership reverts back to the grantor or his heirs. His right in the property between the time of grant and the time of U.S. withdrawal is called a *possibility of a reverter* rather than a *reversion,* since the United States might never withdraw from the United Nations. If an event had been stated which is reasonably certain to occur, such as granting the property until January 1, 2000, the grantor would possess an outright reversion. The charity's right to the property prior to U.S. withdrawal is a fee simple right, since ownership could possibly continue forever. The charity can sell the property, but the buyer obtains only the determinable fee subject to the possibility of a reverter.

Two other forms of qualified fee estates, fee simple subject to a condition subsequent and fee simple subject to a condition precedent, work the same way as a determinable fee, except that a condition must be fulfilled by the grantee. In the U.S.–U.N. situation, ownership reverts back to the grantor following an action taken by the U.S. government. The grantee has no control over this action, and the reversion occurs automatically at the time of U.S. withdrawal. The fee simple subject to a condition subsequent requires action (or lack of action) on the part of the grantee, such as where a grantor grants his property to a school as long as it is used for school purposes. If the school sells the property or converts it to a nonschool use, the grant becomes void and the grantor or his heirs have the right to re-enter the property and assume absolute ownership. However, in recent years courts have held that sales of land owned under qualified fee is permitted if the proceeds are put to a use which fulfills the conditions of the agreement with the grantor. This would be where the school sells land held under qualified fee and uses the proceeds to buy a parcel of land better suited for school business.

---

[3] Ibid., p. 48.

The fee simple subject to a condition precedent is identical to the fee simple subject to a condition subsequent except for the timing of the condition. To use the above example, a condition precedent would arise if the property owner were to grant his property to the charity *as of* the date the United States withdraws from the United Nations. If the United States withdraws, fee simple absolute passes to the charity. The grantor retains ownership as long as the United States remains a member. Obviously, the condition precedent fits few practical situations. Most states have abolished estates on condition precedent.

The qualified fee estate has been in disfavor with courts for many years. It provides a vehicle for unusual situations which inevitably require court action before the rightful owner of a property can gain possession. An individual might grant property to his distant nephew so long as the nephew refrains from drinking alcoholic beverages, while another man might devise a grant in which the grantee must follow a specified religious faith. The extent to which conditions of this type are upheld is impossible to measure, and the courts tend to interpret the law in a manner that the fee simple character of the grantee's right outweighs the conditions imposed. However, the investor must be very careful whenever a deed contains pecularities of this type. An attorney should be consulted to ascertain whether or not fee simple absolute could be achieved in the purchase.

Freehold estates not of inheritance

A life estate is an interest in real property granted to an individual for the duration of his (or someone else's) lifetime. At the time of death of the designated person, the property reverts back to the original owner or his heirs.

Life estates are of two types: conventional and legal.[4] Conventional life estates are created by the grantor and grantee(s) involved in the estate. In most cases the life tenant receives the property right for the duration of his own lifetime. If he retains his right for the lifetime of another person, such as would be the case where a man grants his son the rights to a property for the lifetime of his (the grantor's) wife, the estate is known as a life estate *pour autre vie*.

A life estate can be sold or leased, but the buyer or lessee must realize that he might have to surrender the property on short notice after the death of the life estate holder. Thus, the economic value of a life estate is normally based on personal utilization or a composite of short-term leases.

Legal life estates are created by operation of law. They are of three types:

---

[4] Harold F. Lusk, *Law of the Real Estate Business* (Homewood, Ill.: Richard D. Irwin, Inc., 1965), p. 69.

1. *Dower.* The ownership rights of a wife in her husband's property during her lifetime. As long as the husband is alive, dower is said to be "inchoate," which means that the wife has only the possibility of a right rather than the right itself. Upon the husband's death, the dower right becomes consummate. Under the laws of many states, the dower ripens into a life estate in one third of the real property owned by the husband during the marriage. All real property owned by the husband during the marriage is included, even though part or all might have been sold prior to his death.

Dower right, in those states which recognize it, is an important consideration for the purchaser of real property. To obtain an unencumbered title, he must be certain that the seller's wife relinquishes her dower right to the subject property in writing. Otherwise, she is entitled to a life estate upon her husband's death, although the property is not a part of his estate.

As in any life estate, property acquired by a wife through her dower right is hers to use in any manner she pleases during her lifetime. Upon her death, the property passes on to a party named by the husband in his will, or to his natural heirs on succession, if he died intestate (without a will). The party named by the husband or his heirs holds the *right of remainder.* This right is normally vested (i.e., absolute and definite; cannot be taken from them), but it is contingent in situations where a remainderman cannot be ascertained at the time of transfer. Some people still retain the practice in wills of naming "my oldest son" or "my first-born child" where no such son or child had been born at the time the life estate is created. A remainder exists in either the vested or contingent situation, however, and the property eventually passes on to the remainderman. Even in those rare cases when a man dies with no heirs or assigns, the government is a contingent remainderman through the power of escheat.

Dower provides the wife a claim to real property superior to claims of the husband's debtors. Dower is terminated by divorce in nearly all states; a few states terminate dower only where the wife is at fault in the divorce proceedings.

2. *Curtesy.* Curtesy is a man's right in real property owned by his wife during their marriage. Very few states recognize curtesy today, and where it exists it is usually treated the same as dower. The laws of some states grant the husband dower rather than curtesy. Other states grant curtesy only where the wife is survived by a child of the marriage to the surviving husband. Regardless of the requirements imposed on curtesy, a buyer of real property should obtain a release of curtesy in the same manner as dower to be certain of obtaining an unencumbered title.

3. *Homestead.* The laws of a few states permit a family to declare either a specified amount of land or a specified dollar value of property

as a homestead.[5] A properly declared and recorded homestead is exempt from foreclosure by creditors to the extent of the legal maximum amount of area or dollar value. The family cannot be evicted from the land during the husband's lifetime, and his widow is protected after his death. The states' laws which provide for homestead generally require that a family exists, that the homestead be used as the family's residence, and that the head of the family possesses an ownership interest in the property.[6] Most states also require that the family file for homestead and have it recorded in the county records.

The right of homestead is actually a protection of other ownership rights rather than an independent estate in land. Homesteads are owned either in fee simple or fee tail, with the homestead right granting protection of ownership. The homesteader's widow receives substantial protection through this right; the husband cannot convey clear title during his lifetime without the wife's permission, and the wife's right to the homestead is prior to the claims of the husband's creditors upon his death.

Less than freehold estates

Earlier in this chapter, we noted that an individual does not have to be absolute owner of a parcel of real estate in order to derive valuable benefits. Many business firms have found that they can create extra profits by selling their business realty and obtaining long-term leases. Physical use of the property is not disturbed by this financing arrangement, but fee simple ownership is transferred into the hands of an absentee landlord. The former owner no longer has capital tied up in realty and he can deduct all rents for tax purposes. The new owner acquires an investment which should yield a satisfactory return.

A leasehold can be defined very simply as the right to use the property of another. Complete utilization with no restrictions is rarely granted; the most common situation is one in which the use to which the land can be put by the lessee and the manner in which the use is carried out are regulated by contract between lessor and lessee. Leases generally can be classified by duration of lease. Four types of estates can be created by varying the length of time for which the property is leased:

1. *Estate for years—beginning and ending point of lease specified.* Leases of this type are usually measured in periods extending over several years, but they can be for any specified period—even less than a year. The key distinguishing factor is that the exact duration of the lease must be specified.

---

[5] No choice is involved; each state determines how the homestead is to be established.

[6] Harold F. Lusk, *Law of the Real Estate Business* (Homewood, Ill.: Richard D. Irwin, Inc., 1965), p. 80.

2. *Tenancy from year to year.* As in the estate for years, the period of measurement can be something other than a year. A tenancy from year to year (actually period to period) is automatically renewed every period until one of the parties gives sufficient notice of termination.

3. *Tenancy at will.* A tenancy at will exists without a definite agreement among parties. It can be terminated at any time (without notice) by either party. A tenancy at will frequently arises where the tenant holds over without objection by the landlord after the expiration of his lease.

4. *Tenancy at sufferance.* This final form of tenancy arises when a tenant continues to use property after his agreement with the landlord has completely expired. It is a wrongful tenancy, and it cannot exist if the owner exercises his right of repossession. Tenancy at sufferance also arises where a person moves onto a property owned by someone else without the owner's knowledge or consent.

The differences in the four types of leasehold described here are significant to both lessors and lessees. Lessees must beware of the last two forms if a fairly permanent lease is contemplated. Where termination without notice is possible, unscrupulous landlords can let a tenant build up a successful business and then cancel the lease in order to take over the business. Lessees of homes can find themselves evicted if they fail to comply with unreasonable rent demands. From the lessor's standpoint, some degree of certainty of income is required for sound planning. The "midnight movers" who leave under the cover of darkness on the day the rent is due create significant management problems for the landlord. For either party, a temporary arrangement may be desired for a test period. However, the benefits of a lease of known duration outweigh the disadvantages, and a test arrangement should be replaced in a reasonable time if trouble is to be avoided.

Incorporeal property rights

The owner of an estate in land can, if he wishes, grant the privilege of using his land to others without surrendering any of his property ownership rights. Such privileges do limit his freedom of use, however, and they normally must be included in the definition of his ownership. They are of three types: (1) easement, (2) license, and (3) profit.

Easements. An easement is a nonpossessory interest one person holds in the real estate of another. It is not considered to be an estate in land, although it cannot be revoked by the landowner. The most common form of easement is the *commercial easement in gross,* such as a right-of-way for a pipeline, electric line, telephone line, or railroad. An easement in gross also exists as an individual's personal right. The commercial form can be assigned, conveyed, or inherited, but the individual form is granted to a single individual for his lifetime only. Few courts recognize the individual, noncommercial easement in gross today, since the easement appurtenant and the license are defined broadly enough to include nearly every situation which may arise.

The easement appurtenant is a grant made by the owner of one parcel of property, the *servient tenement,* to permit his land to be used in some manner by the owner of an adjoining parcel, the *dominant tenement.* The most common easement appurtenant is a right-of-way granted to a neighbor for ingress and egress. Once granted, the benefits attach to the dominant tenement and the obligation to permit use attaches to the servient tenement. Both dominant and servient tenements exist in an easement appurtenant, while only the servient land is involved in an easement in gross.

Most easements are formed through express grants in writing, although they can arise by will, by implication, or by prescription. Easements established by grant are normally part of a conveyance by deed, although they can be created by written contract. Implied easements arise where a landowner sells a portion of his parcel which is completely surrounded by other land that he owns. The buyer can safely imply that he is entitled to establish a right-of-way across the seller's land, although the seller is entitled to select a reasonable location for the right-of-way. An easement by prescription arises where a person's land is used by another on an adverse, visible, open, notorious, and continuous basis under claim of right by the user for an uninterrupted period of time as prescribed by law. The owner of the property in question can stop the running of the prescribed period by interrupting use of the easement for a short time, thereby making the prescribed easement exceptionally difficult to obtain. He may also grant permission for the use at one point in time, thereby eliminating the essential requirement of adverse use. Easements by prescription arise almost exclusively in the case of vehicular right-of-ways, although courts tend to include nonadverse party driveways under this procedure.

License. A license is a privilege granted to a single individual permitting him to go upon the servient land. Permission to hunt or fish is one example; another is the sale of admission tickets for theatrical or sporting performances. Licenses can be made orally, and they are revocable by the owner of the servient land.

Profit. A profit, or *profit a pendre,* is the right to remove soil or minerals from the servient tenement. Profits are personal rights which can be assigned, conveyed, or inherited, although they can be established in favor of a single dominant tenement.

OWNERSHIP BY MORE THAN ONE PERSON

Many parcels of real estate are owned by more than one individual. The total parcel is usually owned in fee simple, so the problems of multiple owners arise in determining how to divide interests among the various owners. The following types of multiple ownership are prevalent in the United States.

1. *Tenancy in common.*   Ownership in the form of tenancy in common works like a common stock corporation. A single parcel of real property, undivided in the sense that each owner exercises the rights of ownership of the entire parcel rather than a staked-off portion, is operated by the owners exactly as though it were a business firm. Each owner has a say in making decisions about the parcel, and he can sell his interest, give it away, or grant it to his heirs as he wishes.

2. *Joint tenancy.*   A tenancy in common is created automatically whenever two or more people acquire concurrent ownership of a parcel of real estate. Joint tenancy, on the other hand, requires a formal written instrument evidencing the desire to create an ownership situation different from that of tenancy in common. In a joint tenancy, all owners have equal ownership rights. The ownership rights of each owner pass upon his death to the other owners—again being split equally among them.

A joint tenancy between two or more persons is enforced by the courts only where four "unities" exist. These unities, or common bonds, are:

1. Unity of interest. The ownership rights of each of the parties must be equal and endure for the same length of time.
2. Unity of time. The interests of each of the parties must be acquired at the same time.
3. Unity of title. All joint tenants must receive their interest through a single conveyance of title.
4. Unity of possession. All joint tenants must have equal rights of possession, although these rights do not have to be exercised by any of the parties.

The unique characteristic of joint tenancy is that it can exist for either the entire parcel or part of the parcel. For example, a group of five men pool their money to buy an investment property. Each man supplies 20 percent of the money for an undivided 20 percent ownership right. A tenancy in common is formed among the five men. Three of the men wish to form a joint tenancy as to their 60 percent combined interest, so they prepare a binding legal agreement to that effect. They have their wives sign the agreement in order to avoid any claim of dower right, and they make use of the property with their two partners by tenancy in common. If one of the three men dies, his two joint tenant partners each receive 10 percent additional ownership—the property now being owned 30 percent by each of the two joint tenants and 20 percent by each of two tenants in common.

If one of the three joint tenants does not die, but grants his 20 percent interest to an outside party, the joint tenancy is upset as far as his share is concerned. His 20 percent falls back into the tenancy in common status. However, the other two joint tenants can continue the joint tenancy on the 40 percent.

Joint tenancies have created many problems over the years and are currently in disfavor with the courts. An ironclad agreement must exist for the joint tenancy to be recognized over the rights of the surviving spouse of a joint tenant.

3. *Tenancy by the entireties.* Tenancy by the entireties is a special form of joint tenancy in some states which can be employed only by husband and wife. Any real property acquired by them during their marriage can be established as a tenancy by the entireties, thereby guaranteeing each partner a right of survivorship to the other's share. The right of survivorship continues even when one of the partners conveys his or her share to a third party. Like joint tenancies, tenancy by the entireties is held in disfavor by many states, and they require a binding written agreement for the tenancy to be enforced.

4. *Community property.* The concept of community property is of Spanish origin, and it is prevalent in several western states. It holds that husband and wife each own 50 percent of all real property purchased after their marriage. The only property excluded is that which is purchased with funds which are clearly owned by only one of the married partners. Both owners must sign transfer papers on community property.

5. *Condominium.* Many state laws have been passed in recent years to permit the development of condominium apartment units. Each owner holds a fee simple interest in an apartment and a tenancy in common in halls, elevators, lawns, etc. The separate ownership forms have been discussed previously, but the condominium combination is unique. Condominiums are discussed in chapter 14.

6. *Corporation, trust, and partnership.* A parcel of real estate can be owned by a single legal entity that is in itself an aggregation of individual owners. The legal framework that unites the owners also defines the manner in which ownership interests are divided. The use of corporations, trusts, and partnerships is considered here in terms of property ownership strategy.

PROPERTY OWNERSHIP STRATEGY

The goals of investors and the risks associated with individual properties determine the proper form of ownership structure in each investment situation. In general, high-risk projects are more properly structured as corporations or trusts. These two forms are also excellent choices for situations in which large numbers of investors are called upon to provide equity capital.

Partnerships and tenant in common structures are well suited for tax shelter investments and other investments that involve small numbers of investors. The limited partnership is particularly popular as a vehicle for syndicators to use in assembling equity money from small numbers of investors who seek limited liability and freedom from management decisions.

The major consideration in selecting an ownership form is the objectives of investor groups. Small-scale investors frequently fear the partnership form in which the ownership shares have no active market and cannot be sold easily. Larger investors at times find the corporation and trust forms useful for those projects that are to be subdivided and sold at ordinary income rates or for those projects that are to be operated to yield tax-sheltered cash income. The same investors might prefer the partnership form for projects yielding tax deductions via depreciation or those yielding capital gains through sale.

The variables in the ownership decision are (1) avoidance of double taxation when using a corporation; (2) avoidance of personal liability for investors; (3) marketability of shares; and (4) acquisition of maximum income tax deduction benefits. These variables are reflected in the four basic ownership forms as follows.

Corporation.   The corporate form is designed for easy transfer of small portions of ownership, and it offers total limitation of liability for investors. However, it creates a taxable entity that pays tax in addition to that which must be paid by investors individually. Also, the corporate form fails to permit investors to deduct net taxable losses from their personal income tax returns.

The corporate form is of maximum value to investors who place a much higher priority upon easy transferability of ownership and liability limitation than on income tax minimization. However, careful tax planning can lead to a need for one or more corporations in achieving desired salaries, pension plans, medical plans, deductibility of automobiles and other expenditures, etc. These issues go beyond the basic real estate planning and are not considered in this text.

Tax-free real estate investment trust.   The tax-free real estate investment trust has become popular as a vehicle for achieving a single tax on income plus the desired liability limitation. However, tax losses cannot be passed through to investors. To retain its tax-free status, the trust must pay 90 percent or more of its income to investors, and it must follow numerous rules regarding the percentage of investments that must be in real estate and the length of time that investments must be held. Virtually all income must be passive in nature rather than the result of direct project operation by a trust's management.

Partnership.   The partnership form avoids double taxation and allows tax losses to be deducted by individual investors. Liability is unlimited for all investors in the general partnership, but it can be limited in the limited partnership for partners who are not involved in project management. Broadly based markets for partnership shares rarely exist, but shares are easily transferred and purchasers can usually be found for shares in a quality offering.

Most states have securities registration laws that affect partnership interests (as well as trusts and tenancies in common). When out-of-state investors are involved, the Securities and Exchange Commission requires registration of partnerships. These laws frequently have exemptions for those entities that stay intrastate and maintain small ownership groups. Registration is time consuming and expensive, and the form of ownership and size of share is often kept small to achieve exemption from registration laws.

Tenancy in common.   The tenancy in common shares most of the features of the partnership. Liability is more difficult to limit, but an agreement among tenants in common can be devised in which one owner assumes all liability incurred by the owners. If the other owners pay off a partnership debt to an outside party, they can secure reimbursement from the managing (liable) owner.

Summary regarding strategy.   The proper ownership form for a group of individuals or for a combination of individuals, trusts, partnerships, and corporations is a function of investor objectives and project characteristics. Tax implications, transferability of shares, and liability limitations must be considered; and compromise solutions can lead to an optimal ownership structure. These compromises must be minor in nature; investors with widely divergent objectives usually should not invest together. Anyone structuring a real estate ownership arrangement should learn everything possible about the objectives of his investors and carefully place each investor in a project that best meets his objectives.

Sophisticated real estate syndicators frequently attempt to construct large files of investors in which those investors having a common interest are brought together. This has been an exceptionally effective approach for Realty Research Corporation in Atlanta, Georgia.

Large-scale developers tend to develop a successful joint-venture arrangement with one or more financial institutions that can be used repeatedly on different projects. Cousins Properties, Incorporated, of Atlanta, Georgia, has followed this pattern in several major developments with Fidelity Mutual Life Insurance Company. U.S. Steel Realty Company has joint ventured projects with Connecticut Mutual Life Insurance Company, and John Hancock Life Insurance Company has devised a successful joint-venture format that has been used in conjunction with many developers throughout the nation. The limited partnership tends to be the most popular form for these joint ventures, but any of the other forms could meet investor objectives.

TRANSFER OF OWNERSHIP RIGHTS

The term *estate* is used to define the characteristics of an interest in land. Formal government recognition of an estate is expressed in terms of *title*. An individual may hold title to both personal and real property, given that his government holds claim of original title through discovery, conquest, occupancy, or cessation. The government has the power to cancel his title, such as: (1) condemnation: his land is needed for public purposes; (2) forfeiture: he fails to pay taxes or he commits treason; (3) confiscation: he is an enemy during time of war; or (4) escheat; he dies without heirs or assigns.

Obviously, government cancellation of real estate titles rarely occurs. Individuals are free to enjoy their property, and they can transfer it to others in a number of ways. The most common means of transferring property are discussed here.

Private grant

A voluntary transfer of real property during the grantor's lifetime is known as a private grant. The grantor *deeds* his property right to another party, the grantee, either by sale or by gift.[7] The property deeded can represent anything from the right to enter the property and fish in its waters to complete fee simple ownership.

Devise or descent

The second most common means of transferring title is by will (devise) or, in the absence of a will, by legal statute specifying the manner in which property passes to descendants (descent).

Foreclosure

The holder of a valid lien on real property is entitled to request that the property be sold at public sale when the fee simple owner defaults in satisfying the claim which caused the lien to arise. The fee simple owner's rights of ownership are cut off at the time of sale by a court-appointed official, and the buyer at the sale receives a fee simple title. The court does not guarantee the quality of this title; the buyer takes it subject to any defects that existed in the hands of the former owner.

Adverse possession

An individual can take away the title of another person if he uses that person's property on an actual, continuous, hostile, visible, and exclusive

---

[7] Deeds are discussed in chapter 9.

basis for a period of time prescribed by law. This change of title is based upon the concept that land should be used rather than left idle. In other words, anyone who owns property for the prescribed period—usually 10 to 21 years—and fails to use the property or assert a claim of ownership against the adverse possessor should lose his property where the adverse possessor did make profitable use of the land.

Prescription

Where an individual uses the land of another for a period of time stated by law, such as using a roadway across a neighbor's land, the user obtains a right of easement in the neighbor's land. This use must have most of the attributes of adverse possession, except that it need not be exclusive.

Title from nature

As will be seen in the following chapter, recorded deeds contain a detailed description of the owner's parcel of property. Many descriptions are expressed in terms of natural boundaries, and natural boundaries can change. Where a body of water washes land into the described area, title is obtained through *accretion*. Where boundary water recedes and leaves dry land, *reliction* adds to the title holder's land. The only time natural causes do not change title is where a boundary river or stream changes course (avulsion). The dry bed is still the boundary.

SUMMARY

The ownership form selected for a real estate investment situation determines the relationship among investors; between investors and lenders; and between investors and their officers or partners. Many forms of legal protection for all parties involved can be created in corporate charters, trust agreements, partnership agreements, or agreements among tenants in common.

When real estate is owned by only one person, fee simple ownership is the most desirable form. It provides the maximum ownership rights. However, some property titles are encumbered with conditional titles, life estates, and other limitations which prevent the investor from gaining the maximum bundle of ownership rights.

At times, an investor might prefer to lease, rather than own outright, a parcel of property. Leases can be established for any period of time and on several renewal bases, and most state laws are quite articulate about what constitutes an enforceable clause or an act of renewing a lease.

Given many alternatives of ownership form and structure, the investor must plan a workable strategy for his projects that optimizes his protection from liability, his income tax deduction status, and his protection against lenders, officers, and other investors. The corporate and trust forms offer excellent liability protection, but they limit opportunities for investors to obtain income tax deductions. A tenancy in common form offers excellent income tax liability deductibility, but unlimited liability for debts of all types. The limited partnership form provides liability limitation, tax deductions, and protections among limited partners, but it requires that the limited partners refrain from making managerial decisions, thereby causing them to lose ownership control. Thus, the investor must devise the optimal structure for each project based upon his goals and the project's risks.

QUESTIONS FOR REVIEW

1. What is "real estate"? How does this term differ from "real property"?
2. How does one determine whether an asset is a fixture or an item of realty?
3. Distinguish between estates in possession and estates not in possession.
4. Distinguish between freehold estates of inheritance and freehold estates not of inheritance.
5. What are the three types of incorporeal rights to real property?
6. What are the four unities of a joint tenancy?
7. Indicate the ownership form that appears to be most practical for a joint venture. Defend your choice.
8. Indicate the six ways in which property ownership can be transferred.

REFERENCES

Kratovil, Robert. *Real Estate Law.* Englewood Cliffs, N.J.: Prentice-Hall, Inc., 1969.

Lusk, Harold F. *Law of the Real Estate Business.* Homewood, Ill.: Richard D. Irwin, Inc., 1965.

Ring, Alfred A. *Real Estate Principles and Practices.* Englewood Cliffs, N.J.: Prentice-Hall, Inc., 1972, Chapters 5 and 12.

Semenow, Robert W. *Questions and Answers on Real Estate.* Englewood Cliffs, N.J.: Prentice-Hall, Inc., 1972.

Unger, Maurice A. *Real Estate Principles and Practices.* Cincinnati: Southwestern Publishing Company, 1969, Chapters 3, 21, and 22.

chapter 9

REAL ESTATE
CONVEYANCING

THE LAWS pertaining to real estate conveyancing require that formal procedures be followed in all types of transactions. Offers, contracts, closings, title transfers, rentals, and many other activities are framed in legal terms with precisely worded documents evidencing them. Many of these documents appear to be cumbersome, but less precise terminology leads to ambiguity, and failure to insert the many clauses can easily cause disagreement among the parties at a later date.

Nearly all real property transactions are governed by the Statute of Frauds, a law requiring that all transactions other than short-term leases must be in writing. Oral clauses or oral agreements pertaining to the writings are not enforceable until they have been set down in writing and incorporated properly into the document. This is a reasonable statute; many disagreements are avoided where oral testimony is not permitted, and people tend to plan more carefully when everything must be stated in writing.

Investors who enter written agreements concerning real property should have all pertinent documents examined by an attorney to be certain that agreement is reached on all essential points and to provide a measure of protection against undesirable provisions. However, the attorney cannot do the entire job. The investor is the man who is planning to bind himself by the agreement, and only he is in a position to know exactly what his objectives are and what clauses can meet them best. For example, a land contract containing a forfeiture clause (which states that failure to make a payment causes the land to revert back to the seller) might be advantageous for a speculator who would like to withdraw from the investment if it were not profitable. The same clause would be disadvantageous for a person having a low income who is buying his home under land contract to avoid making a large downpayment. The speculator knows that the decision to forfeit or not forfeit is his own; the man who could not afford the downpayment is at the mercy of the seller, if illness or other problems cause him to miss one or more payments.

The frequent investor in real estate must learn to read documents thoroughly in a short period of time. He must be able to determine whether or not all pertinent items are included, and he must analyze his objectives to determine the clauses that he definitely would and would not like to have inserted. Other clauses are subject to negotiation, and he must know enough about them to determine that an agreement is equitable, given his particular objectives.

The first step in preparing a document for a real estate transaction is to determine whether or not it is proper for his purpose. Warranty deeds, deeds of bargain and sale, and quitclaim deeds all transfer ownership rights, but only the warranty deed employs wording that calls for the seller to guarantee the quality of the ownership right which is transferred. A quitclaim deed conveys only the seller's interest, no matter how encumbered. The use of these and other documents varies among the states, and the investor must become familiar with all practices within his realm of operation.

Many of the documents involved in real property transactions are preprinted in standard form. Offers to purchase, deeds, closing statements, mortgages, liens, leases, trading agreements, trust agreements, escrow agreements, and brokers' listing contracts are examples of documents that are typically prepared en masse by trade groups and individual firms. Local boards of Realtors usually prescribe a certain set of forms for their members, but each board can prescribe a different form, and not all members of a particular board adhere to the entire package of prescribed forms. Also, many brokers do not have access to Realtor-approved forms. Lenders normally develop their own forms, as do escrow agents, trustees, and landlords.

Many functions must be performed in even the least complicated conveyancing transaction. The most frequently encountered activities are considered here, presented in chronological order from the initial purchase offer to the listing agreement employed in selling.

CONVEYANCING FUNCTIONS

Making an offer

[Upon finding a desirable property, the investor normally prepares a formal, written offer to submit to the owner] This offer ripens into a contract for sale if it is accepted by the owner, and it permits the owner to make a counter offer if he desires a change in terms. As a practical matter, the investor usually learns of the property's availability through a broker who holds a listing contract with the seller. The investor thus has a statement of the owner's desired terms to guide him in preparing his offer.

Two points are worth noting about the offer to purchase: (1) The buyer should be specific as to exactly what he is offering to buy. He should specify that storm windows and screens, light fixtures, carpets, and so on are to be included in or excluded from the sale. Anything he wishes to receive which might be considered personal property should be listed. (2) The seller might wish to state the terms of the listing contract in a general enough manner that he can retain his right to reject offers to buy because of certain specific items they contain. On the other hand, he might wish to make his listing extremely specific and hold that the listing must be agreed upon exactly by a buyer. Either way, the seller may accept any offer he chooses, even if the terms deviate widely from the listing.

Once an offer to buy is tendered to the seller, the potential buyer and the seller can negotiate as to the price and what the sale includes until they make a satisfactory arrangement or terminate negotiations. The offer to buy is merely an offer; many counteroffers and counter-counteroffers might be necessary to effect a sale.

The offer must state formally that an offer is being made, and it must indicate clearly each of the following items. A standard offer form approved by the Atlanta Real Estate Board is presented as Figure 9–1 to indicate the manner in which these factors are commonly considered.

1. Name of offeror, offeree, and broker.
2. Detailed description of property and fixtures, including a listing of all items that are to be made part of the transaction.
3. Amount to be paid and terms of payment. The offer can be worded to make it contingent upon obtaining a specific financing arrangement.
4. Type of deed to be received and specific ownership restrictions and encumbrances that will be permitted.
5. Manner in which expenses, taxes, rentals, and so on are to be prorated between buyer and seller.
6. Options available to the offeror if the property is damaged or destroyed before the final closing and statements evidencing the insurable interests of the parties.
7. Duration of offer.
8. Time and place of closing and length of time permitted for title search and removal of objections to title.

9. Manner in which earnest money deposits are to be handled and provision for the broker's commission.
10. Statement of how the broker's commission is to be computed.
11. A complete agreement clause that excludes all facts and material items not considered in the writing. This clause requires that oral agreements be incorporated in the document.
12. Offeror's witnessed signature, owner's acceptance of the offer, and receipt for deposit.

The offer to purchase is designed to meet the needs of the offeror. The standard clauses contained in Figure 9–1 avoid most of the problems that could arise in the event of damage to the property, failure to obtain clear title or proper financing at closing, failure to pay the broker's commission, and so forth. Other clauses can be inserted to meet any type of need, such as those regarding an exchange of properties, a sale of previously owned properties, or the establishment of a corporation or syndicate to hold the real estate assets. The standard form is a logical and desirable instrument for most transactions, but specialized activities call for individualized provisions. The wording of these provisions must be precise, and an attorney should normally be consulted in preparing them.

Reaching agreement

When a buyer and seller agree as to the exact terms of a real property transaction, a written contract is prepared that describes the property and all extras, states the price to be paid, and indicates the time at which title is to pass. A contract of sale does not have to be a very formal document to be legally enforceable. It is frequently represented as an accepted offer to purchase. Kratovil [1] provides an example of a contract similar to the following that was enforced by one court, indicating that the contract does not even have to state the specific details of transfer:

> New York, February 29, 1908
> Received of John Smith $200 on said purchase of property 2293 Jones Avenue, New York, New York at a price of $18,000.
> T. Wilson

Obviously, this is not good practice. The contract should identify clearly the parties, the property to be transferred, including personal property, if any, and the type of deed to be granted. It should specify that a merchantable title is to pass, and should contain the signatures of both parties.

---

[1] Robert Kratovil, *Real Estate Law* (Englewood Cliffs, N.J.: Prentice-Hall, Inc., 1969), p. 110.

FIGURE 9–1

ATLANTA REAL ESTATE BOARD
Residential Sales Contract
September, 1972

(YOUR FIRM NAME)
REALTORS
Atlanta, Georgia

As a result of the efforts of _____ YOUR FIRM NAME _____ ,
a licensed Broker, the undersigned Purchaser agrees to buy, and the undersigned Seller agrees to sell, all that tract or parcel of land, with such improvements as are located thereon, described as follows:

together with all electrical, mechanical, plumbing, air-conditioning, and any other systems or fixtures as are attached thereto and all plants, trees, and shrubbery now on the premises.

The purchase price of said property shall be:

_____ DOLLARS, $_____

to be paid as follows:

Purchaser has paid to the undersigned _____ , Broker,
$_____ ( ) cash ( ) check, receipt whereof is hereby acknowledged by Broker, as earnest money, which earnest money is to be promptly deposited in Broker's escrow account and is to be applied as part payment of purchase price of said property at the time sale is consummated.

Seller warrants that he presently has title to said property, and at the time the sale is consummated, he agrees to convey good and marketable title to said property to Purchaser by general warranty deed subject only to (1) zoning ordinances affecting said property, (2) general utility easements of record serving said property, (3) subdivision restrictions of record, and (4) leases, other easements, other restrictions and encumbrances specified in this contract. In the event leases are specified in this contract, the Purchaser agrees to assume the Seller's responsibilities thereunder to the tenant and to the Broker who negotiated such leases.

The Purchaser shall move promptly and in good faith after acceptance of this contract to examine title and to furnish Seller with a written statement of objections affecting the marketability of said title. Seller shall have reasonable time after receipt of such objections to satisfy all valid objections and if Seller fails to satisfy such valid objections within a reasonable time, then at the option of the Purchaser, evidenced by written notice to Seller, this contract shall be null and void. Marketable title as used herein shall mean title which a title insurance company licensed to do business in the State of Georgia will insure at its regular rates, subject only to standard exceptions unless otherwise specified herein.

Seller and Purchaser agree that such papers as may be necessary to carry out the terms of this contract shall be executed and delivered by such parties at time the sale is consummated.

Purchaser, its agents, or representatives, at Purchaser's expense and at reasonable times during normal business hours, shall have the right to enter upon the property for the purpose of inspecting, examining, testing, and surveying the property. Purchaser assumes all responsibility for the acts of itself, its agents, or representatives in exercising its rights under this paragraph and agrees to hold Seller harmless for any damages resulting therefrom.

Seller warrants that when the sale is consummated the improvements on the property will be in the same condition as they are on the date this contract is signed by the Seller, natural wear and tear excepted. However, should the premises be destroyed or substantially damaged before the contract is consummated, then at the election of the Purchaser: (a) the contract may be cancelled, or (b) Purchaser may consummate the contract and receive such insurance as is paid on the claim of loss. This election is to be exercised within ten (10) days after the Purchaser has been notified in writing by Seller of the amount of the insurance proceeds, if any, Seller will receive on the claim of loan; if Purchaser has not been notified within forty-five (45) days subsequent to the occurance of such damage or destruction, Purchaser may, at its option, cancel the contract.

In negotiating this contract, Broker has rendered a valuable service for which reason Broker is made a party to enable Broker to enforce his commission rights hereunder against the parties hereto on the following basis: Seller agrees to pay Broker the full commission when the sale is consummated and in the event the sale is not consummated because of Seller's inability, failure or refusal to perform any of the Seller's covenants herein, then the Seller shall pay the full commission to Broker, and Broker, at the option of Purchaser, shall return the earnest money to Purchaser. Purchaser agrees that if Purchaser fails or refuses to perform any of Purchaser's covenants herein, Purchaser shall forthwith pay Broker the full commission; provided that Broker may first apply one-half of the earnest money toward payment of, but not to exceed, the full commission and may pay the balance thereof to seller as liquidated damages of Seller, if Seller claims balance as Seller's liquidated damages in full settlement of any claim for damages, whereupon Broker shall be released from any and all liability for return of earnest money to Purchaser. If this transaction involves exchange of real estate, the full commission shall be paid in respect to the property conveyed by each party to the other and notice of the dual agency is hereby given and accepted by Seller and Purchaser. The commission on an exchange shall be calculated on the amount on the basis of which each property is taken in such exchange, according to the contract between the parties, and if no value is placed on any property exchanged, then according to the reasonable value thereof. In the event of an exchange, each party shall be regarded as Seller as to the property conveyed by each party.

Commission to be paid in connection with this transaction has been negotiated between Seller and Broker and shall be _____

Time is of essence of this contract.

This contract shall inure to the benefit of, and be binding upon, the parties hereto, their heirs, successors, administrators, executors and assigns.

The interest of the Purchaser in this contract shall not be transferred or assigned without the written consent of Seller.

This contract constitutes the sole and entire agreement between the parties hereto and no modification of this contract shall be binding unless attached hereto and signed by all parties to this agreement. No representation, promise, or inducement not included in this contract shall be binding upon any party hereto.

The following stipulations shall, if conflicting with printed matter, control:

FIGURE 9–1 (*Continued*)

SPECIAL STIPULATIONS

1. Real Estate taxes on said property shall be prorated as of the date of closing.
2. Seller shall pay State of Georgia property transfer tax.
3. Sale shall be closed on or before _____ .
4. Possession of presmises shall be granted by Seller to Purchaser no later than _____ .

    This instrument shall be regarded as an offer by the Purchaser or Seller who first signs to the other and is open for acceptance by the other until _____O'clock ___ M., on the _____ day of_____,19___ ;by which time written acceptance of such offer must have been actually received by Broker, who shall promptly notify other party, in writing of such acceptance.

The above proposition is hereby accepted
this _____ day of _____ , 19 ____.

_____
(Purchaser)

_____
(Purchaser)

_____
(Seller)

_____
(Seller)

_____
(Broker)

YOUR FIRM NAME, Etc.

REALTOR

Tucker-Castleberry Ptg., Inc.
226 Luckie Street, N. W.
Atlanta, Ga. 30303

These forms made to your
Specifications available from

To

From

Commerical Sales Contract

ATLANTA REAL ESTATE BOARD
September, 1972

One of the most important functions of the contract of sale is to stipulate the time for title to be passed from seller to buyer. If the time is not specified, the law holds that title must be conveyed within a reasonable time after the signing of the sale contract. Adequate time is allowed to permit the buyer to ascertain the seller's ownership rights and determine whether or not any encumbrances exist that could prevent a clear title from passing. Both parties must work out their financial arrangements within this time.

Closing the sale

The contract for sale is a binding legal contract that states the manner in which ownership rights are to be transferred. At the time of transfer, a statement is prepared indicating the manner in which expenses are to be prorated, the costs to be paid by the buyer, and the costs to be paid by the seller. All expenses are subject to negotiation, but the purchaser normally is required to pay: (1) appraisal fees, survey fees, and photograph costs, (2) title search charges or title insurance premiums, (3) recording and transfer fees, (4) attorney fees, and (5) costs incidental to obtaining a new mortgage such as a credit report, mortgage origination fees, and the cost of special title insurance fees to protect the lender. The seller typically pays: (1) broker's commission, (2) repair costs needed to improve the property to the condition specified in the contract for sale, (3) federal and state revenue stamps, (4) attorney fees, and (5) discounts charged the buyer by lenders on Federal Housing Administration (FHA) and Veterans Administration (VA) mortgages. The most important items to be prorated are property taxes, prepaid home owner's insurance premiums, and prepaid tenant rent. Utility bills can be prorated when it is not convenient to obtain a special billing at the date of closing.

Closing costs vary widely among transactions, as would be indicated by the nature of the charges. A small, single-family home in an established subdivision typically requires much less work in preparing an appraisal, a title search, a survey, or a cost proration than would a farm property or a high-rise apartment building. Nearly every service performed does have a minimum charge, however, making the minimum total cost several hundred dollars in most cases. Certain services such as the appraisal can be eliminated at times, but the title search and attorney fee are almost inescapable. Thus, closing costs must be anticipated in nearly every real estate investment transaction.

The closing statement is the final accounting in a real property conveyance. All costs, services, and prorated expenses are listed in the closing statement so that each party understands his responsibilities and the flow of funds that results from these responsibilities. See Figures 9–2, 9–3, and 9–4 for examples of closing documents.

FIGURE 9–2

CLOSING STATEMENT

Property

Seller

Broker   C. A. BAKER REAL ESTATE
Purchaser

Date of Contract _____   Date of Closing _____

	Credit Purchaser	Credit Seller
PURCHASE PRICE		
EARNEST MONEY		
FIRST MORTGAGE		
INTEREST		
SECOND MORTGAGE		
INTEREST		
GENERAL TAXES		
GENERAL TAXES — Pro Rated		
SPECIAL ASSESSMENTS		
INSURANCE PREMIUMS (Unearned — Pro Rated)		
RENTS		
COAL OR OIL		
SERVICES		
WATER		
GAS AND LIGHT		
REVENUE STAMPS		
. . . .		
CHECK OR CASH TO BALANCE		
TOTAL . . .		

Buyer Acceptance	Seller Acceptance

SETTLEMENT	Debit	Credit
BALANCE FROM ABOVE		
EARNEST MONEY		
ABSTRACT OR GUARANTY POLICY		
RECORDING FEES		
COMMISSION		
BALANCE		
TOTAL . . .		

FIGURE 9–3

Form 10-1-1

_____

Escrow Agent

SETTLEMENT STATEMENT

Closed by No._____   (As of:_____)   Title or Escrow No._____
Date

_____   _____
Seller   Purchaser

_____(Location of Property)

	Credit to Purchaser	Due to Seller
1. Purchase Price:_____	• • • • • • •	
2. Earnest Money (Paid to_____):		• • • • • • •
3. Outstanding Liens assumed by purchaser:		
(a) First Loan: Prin. $_____Int. $_____ : Total		• • • • • • •
(b) Second Loan: Prin. $_____Int. $_____ : Total		• • • • • • •
4. Purchase money notes executed by purchaser to seller_____		• • • • • • •
5. Adjusted (Pro-rated) Items:		
(a) City taxes for present year: Assmt. $_____Amt. $_____		
(b) S.&C. taxes for present year: Assmt. $_____Amt. $_____		
(c) Insurance Premiums (Paid to_____)		
Amount $_____Agent_____		
(d) Rent: (Paid to_____at $_____per month)_____		
(e) Water Bill: (Paid to_____) _____		
(f) Reserves for taxes, Ins., etc., in escrow with mortgagee_____	• • • • • • •	
(g) F. H. A. Insurance paid in advance (Paid to_____)_	• • • • • • •	
6. Miscellaneous Items:_____		
_____		
_____		
7. Balance due seller as per statement on back hereof:_____		• • • • • • •
TOTALS		

READ AND APPROVED:

_____   _____
Seller   Purchaser
(over)

Transferring ownership

A deed is a written instrument that evidences transfer of ownership.
(See Figure 9–5.) Whether property rights are sold outright, given away,
or sold at public auction to satisfy a lien, every exchange requires a
properly prepared and properly recorded deed in order for a legally

FIGURE 9–4

ESCROW MEMORANDUM

Received of the PURCHASER the following amounts for the following purposes:

1. Balance due the seller as per statement on reverse side (Item 7) _____ $ _____
2. Title fee and Escrow fee (Includes "Lawyers Title" Insurance) _____ $ _____
3. Clerk's fee for recording Warranty Deed _____ $ _____
4. _____ $ _____

                    Total _____ $ _____

Received of the SELLER the total amount as shown below,
    for the following purposes:

1. Internal Revenue Stamps on Warranty Deed _____ $ _____
2. Recording fees and cancellations _____ $ _____
3. Agent's Commission: To: _____ $ _____
4. Taxes: _____ $ _____
5. Payment of loans on property not assumed by purchaser:

    To: _____ $ _____

    _____ $ _____

6. Payment of other items as follows: _____ $ _____

    _____ $ _____

    _____ $ _____

                    Total _____ $ _____

Check to seller for balance of purchase price _____ $ _____

                    Total $ _____

Date _____   _____   **Escrow Agent**

                    By

REMARKS AND EXPLANATIONS:

---

recognized exchange to occur. There are numerous types of deeds, including (1) general warranty deed, (2) quitclaim deed, (3) deed of bargain and sale, (4) special warranty deed, and (5) officer's deed.

The most desirable type of deed from the buyer's viewpoint is the general warranty deed. In such a deed, the seller normally makes three guarantees or covenants:

FIGURE 9–5

Form 10–8

BRANCH OFFICE

WARRANTY DEED

STATE OF   COUNTY OF

THIS INDENTURE, Made the   day of   , in the year
one thousand nine hundred   .   , between

of the County of   , and State of Georgia, as party or parties of the
first part, hereinafter called Grantor, and

as party or parties of the second part, hereinafter called Grantee (the words "Grantor" and
"Grantee" to include their respective heirs, successors and assigns where the context requires or
permits).
        WITNESSETH that: Grantor, for and in consideration of the sum of
                                          (   ) DOLLARS
in hand paid at and before the sealing and delivery of these presents, the receipt whereof is hereby
acknowledged, has granted, bargained, sold, aliened, conveyed and confirmed, and by these presents
does grant, bargain, sell, alien, convey and confirm unto the said Grantee,

TO HAVE AND TO HOLD the said tract or parcel of land, with all and singular the rights,
members and appurtenances thereof, to the same being, belonging, or in anywise appertaining, to the
only proper use, benefit and behoof of the said Grantee forever in FEE SIMPLE.
        AND THE SAID Grantor will warrant and forever defend the right and title to the above
described property unto the said Grantee against the claims of all persons whomsoever.

        IN WITNESS WHEREOF, the Grantor has signed and sealed this deed, the day and year above
written.

        Signed, sealed and delivered in presence of:

_____   _____(Seal)

_____   _____(Seal)

_____   _____(Seal)

1. That he possesses a legally recognizable title to the property conveyed. This is known as the covenant of seizin.
2. That there are no encumbrances against the title other than those stated therein. This is the covenant against encumbrances.
3. That he will protect the grantee against persons claiming to have superior title to the conveyed property. This is the covenant for quiet enjoyment.

The buyer must keep in mind that the seller's guarantees are worthless when the seller is financially irresponsible, but they do provide grounds for legal action when the buyer finds that a good title did not pass, when unknown encumbrances arise, or when claims are made against the property. Aside from this margin of protection, the guarantees in a warranty deed give the buyer a feeling that he is acquiring property from a seller having no fear of outside parties who may make claims against it.

A quitclaim deed passes the seller's ownership rights to the buyer without guarantees. Buyers are, and should be, suspect of such deeds. They are definitely meant to be advantageous to sellers. However, they are used frequently in situations where partial ownership rights are involved. A woman who possesses dower right in a parcel of real estate sold by her husband might be willing to sign a quitclaim deed after the sale in order that the buyer can pass unencumbered title to other parties. Heirs of former owners of property who might wish to bring claims against the property due to slight legal technicalities in title transfer will often sign a quitclaim deed for a price. Many nuisance situations of this type arise, and the quitclaim deed is an effective means of handling them.

A third type of deed, the deed of bargain and sale, is worded in a manner that the land itself is said to be conveyed rather than the ownership interest therein. A fine line of distinction exists between the deed of bargain and sale and the other two forms, but there are times when a seller wishes to convey ownership without warranties but also without using the quitclaim deed which a buyer might not accept. Corporations frequently use the deed of bargain and sale to effect such an arrangement.

The special warranty deed is one in which the grantor covenants only against claims arising from the time during which he owned the property. It is typically used when title has an old encumbrance that cannot be cured but is not expected to create a difficulty for subsequent purchasers.

Officer's deeds are used in conjunction with mortgage foreclosure sales and to convey tax titles. They record transfers from a public official to an auction purchaser, with the ownership rights of the foreclosed owner being cut off after a stated redemption period. No warranties are made.

Regardless of which type of deed is employed, the following requirements must be met:

1. There must be a grantor, and the grantor's legal name must appear

in the body of the deed. He must be of full age and sound mind, and he must be acting without duress.

2. There must be a grantee. The deed must state to whom the property is to be conveyed.

3. Words of conveyance from grantor to grantee.

4. A description of the conveyed property that is adequate to permit identification.

5. A statement of consideration—i.e., something to be paid in exchange for the real estate. The amount paid for the property need not be stated, the usual consideration being "one dollar plus other valuable consideration."

6. The grantor must sign the deed, and in some states he must affix a seal. The grantee is not required to sign or seal, although it is usually customary for him to do so.

7. The deed must be delivered to the grantee. Further, delivery must be accomplished in a manner that the grantor and grantee have a meeting of minds that the transaction is consummated. Improper delivery, such as when the grantee picks up the deed from the grantor's secretary without the grantor's knowledge, does not result in a valid transaction.

The above list represents the absolute minimum requirements for a valid deed. Some states also require that the deed be dated, witnessed, and acknowledged, and the parties involved may agree that it should contain warranties of title and statements of encumbrances. The investor should note that the law only partially protects him in deed transactions; he must make an individual effort to bring out the warranties and statement of debts or liens.

A final requirement to have a deed recorded is that it must contain an adequate number of state (or county) revenue stamps where required. A federal tax formerly was imposed on all deeds conveying real estate, except in the case of gifts or other transactions where there was no monetary consideration. Federal revenue stamps are not required on deeds recorded after December 31, 1967, but a number of state governments require state revenue stamps. Georgia, for example, requires stamps at a rate of 10 cents per $100 valuation on all deeds recorded after January 1, 1968.

A few essentials on deeds can save the investor many legal problems:

1. He should always sign his full legal name (middle initial is satisfactory). The other party to the contract should do the same.

2. Words, phrases, or clauses that are uncertain, unneeded, or ambiguous should not be used. Many phrases which sound very legal and impressive do not further the purpose of the deed and can raise legal questions.

3. A deed form that is recognized by the state in which the real estate is located must be used. Ownership rests in the state containing the

property, rather than the owner's state of residence (where different), and variations in state laws can affect the validity of the deed.

Searching title

A deed conveys title, but it can convey a bad title as well as a good one. The investor seeks a good title in every transaction, as evidenced by one of the following: (1) abstract or certificate of title; (2) title insurance policy; (3) Torrens certificate.

Abstract and attorney's opinion. The most common evidence of title in the United States is the *abstract and attorney's opinion.* An abstract is a summary of all deeds, liens, land contracts, or any other recorded instruments that may affect ownership. If lost or destroyed, it can be replaced by a certificate of title. Many abstracts are lengthy when a property has changed hands frequently, but fortunately, the attorney who traces title can update it from the last transfer and review earlier documents effectively in a short period of time. He then expresses an opinion as to the probability that the buyer will encounter claims against the property. This opinion is not legally binding against the attorney unless he is negligent in his research. However, an expert researcher's opinion is usually quite reliable, especially when the property has changed hands infrequently and is purchased from a person who has owned it for a long period of time.

Title insurance. The investor will usually find that lending institutions require that he provide them with a title insurance policy which protects their interests against most possible claims. The mortgagee policy does not protect the investor's equity in the property, but he can obtain a separate equity policy at a cost lower than that of the mortgagee's policy. The title insurance company searches the title through the abstract and the public records, granting a policy only when the probability is low that the company will have to pay a claim. If a policy is issued, a single premium is charged to the property buyer at the initiation of coverage. After that time, the insurance company handles any claims or lawsuits relating to title.

Torrens certificate. The Torrens certificate involves a formal land registration approach to title verification. The landowner develops a list of persons from his abstract who could have an interest in his property. This list is submitted to a county registrar of Torrens certificates with an application for a certificate. The application serves as a lawsuit against those named on the list, requiring them to contest any claims they might have to prevent issuance of the certificate. The registrar also publishes the application in local newspapers, advertising for claims against the property. If no claims arise, a certificate is issued declaring the applicant to be the owner of the land. The declared owner need have little worry about future claims after this procedure has been followed, but he must defend himself if one should arise. Indemnity funds are provided by counties for paying claims, but these accumulated funds are often insufficient into provide complete indemnity.

The Torrens certificate is an inexpensive means of obtaining freedom from fear as to title claims, but it is a time-consuming and complicated procedure. Further transfers require both a deed passage and a certificate transfer, thereby adding further complications. For these reasons, and because (1) covered property cannot be removed from the system without court permission, and (2) the system has not been tested for constitutional validity, Torrens certificates are not widely employed.

Securing funds

Owners of real estate can normally earn a higher return on invested dollars by borrowing a high percentage of value from professional lenders at a fixed interest rate than they can by providing 100 percent financing. Thus, most transactions involve debt financing. Two closely related agreements are typically involved in this process: one in which the owner borrows the needed funds, while the other pledges the real estate as collateral for the obligation. The first is evidenced by a note, the latter by a mortgage.

The note.   The promissory note is a formal, written acknowledgment of a debt. Matters relating to the amount of the lebt, the rate of interest to be paid, manner of repayment, and the conditions which constitute default are considered in the note. An example of a promissory note is shown in Figure 9–6. The mortgaged property is usually referred to in the note to cross-reference the note and the mortgage.

Mortgage loans can be classified by manner of repayment. The "norm" today is the *fully amortized loan* in which payments are made each month and interest computed on the outstanding balance at the end of the month. This is an alternative to a *straight term loan,* in which no payments are made until the due date, or to the *partially amortized loan,* in which some payments are made periodically and a large payment is made at the end of the term. The partial amortization form has been abused substantially. Unscrupulous lenders in the past would establish a low monthly payment level with an unexpected "balloon" payment at the end. This practice is not permitted to most lenders today on long-term mortgage loans.

The investor should familiarize himself with four clauses that are frequently found in the mortgage indenture. First, lenders normally insist upon an *acceleration clause* which makes the entire debt due and payable upon default (default being defined in the agreement). Without the acceleration feature, the lender would have to bring a separate lawsuit for each

FIGURE 9-6

Promissory note

ATLANTA, GA., _____ 19___ $_____

_____ AFTER DATE, THE UNDERSIGNED PROMISES TO PAY TO THE ORDER OF

The Citizens & Southern National Bank (HEREAFTER, TOGETHER WITH ANY HOLDER HEREOF, CALLED "HOLDER"), AT ATLANTA, GEORGIA, OR AT SUCH OTHER PLACE AS THE HOLDER MAY DESIGNATE AND NOTIFY UNDERSIGNED.

DOLLARS

with interest from date until maturity at _____ per cent per annum, and with interest after maturity until paid at eight per cent (8%) per annum, together with all costs of collection, including fifteen per cent (15%) of the principal and interest as attorney's fees if collected by law or through an attorney at law. To secure the payment of this Note and all other indebtedness or liability of the undersigned to Holder, however and whenever incurred or evidenced, whether direct or indirect, absolute or contingent, or due or to become due (hereafter with this Note, collectively called "Liabilities"), undersigned transfers and conveys to Holder any and all balances, credits, deposits, accounts, items and monies of the undersigned now or hereafter with the Holder, and the undersigned agrees that the Holder shall have a lien upon, security title to and a security interest in all property of the undersigned of every kind and description now or hereafter in the possession or control of the Holder for any reason, including all dividends and distributions on or other rights in connection therewith.

In the event of nonpayment when due of any amount payable on any of Liabilities, or if the Holder shall feel insecure for any reason whatsoever (1) any and all of Liabilities may, at the option of Holder and without demand or notice of any kind, be declared and thereupon immediately shall become due and payable, (2) the Holder may exercise from time to time any of the rights and remedies available to Holder under the Uniform Commercial Code as in effect at that time in Georgia, or otherwise available to Holder and (3) the Holder may, at any time, without demand or notice of any kind, appropriate and apply toward the payment of such of Liabilities, and in such order of application as the Holder may from time to time elect, any balances, credits, deposits, accounts, items or monies of the undersigned with the Holder.

Undersigned transfers, assigns and conveys to the Holder a sufficient amount of homestead and exemption which undersigned or undersigned's family may have under or by virtue of the Constitution or laws of Georgia or any other State of the United States as against Liabilities and to pay them. In case of bankruptcy, undersigned authorizes and directs the Trustee to deliver to the Holder a sufficient amount of property or money claimed as exempt to pay Liabilities and the Holder is appointed attorney in fact for undersigned to claim any and all homestead exemptions allowed by law.

If more than one party shall execute this Note, the term undersigned as used herein shall mean all parties signing this Note and each of them, who shall be jointly and severally obligated hereunder.

Given under the hand and seal of each of the undersigned.

DUE _____ NO. _____

ADDRESS _____ (SEAL)

TELEPHONE NO. _____ (SEAL)

CREDIT LIFE INSURANCE

DATE OF BIRTH OF PERSON TO BE INSURED

15-542 NOTE REV. 1-64

payment missed during the life of the debt. This is a reasonable feature that should not be objectionable to the investor.

The second common clause is the *prepayment clause*. Unless a statement is made in the note that the debtor is entitled to pay more than the scheduled payment in any period, he is not entitled to prepay. Prepayment is a matter of contract—not an inherent right. The prepayment clause states the manner in which prepayment is permitted, usually specifying (1) whether a penalty is to be charged by the lender, (2) whether extra payments directly reduce the principal upon which interest is computed or serve to eliminate the final payment, and (3) whether the size of extra payments or the amount of extra payments per year are restricted. Some lenders, such as life insurance companies, wish to place their funds for the maximum length of time possible, and they frequently impose a penalty for higher-than-agreed-upon payments during the first few years. Savings and loan associations and commercial banks, on the other hand, encourage prepayment by subtracting all principal payments from the outstanding balance upon which they compute interest. Thus, the policies of lending institutions vary with regard to prepayment. The investor should select that lender whose prepayment policy agrees with the investor's most optimistic repayment schedule.

The third clause to be considered is the *cognovit*, or confession of judgment, clause. This clause authorizes any attorney at law to obtain from the court a judgment lien against the debtor. The debtor gives up his "day in court," even in situations when he might have valid grounds for contesting the creditor's claims. The cognovit clause can be abused easily by unscrupulous lenders, and few states uphold it. However, in those states that consider it valid, it is used widely and the investor may be forced to accept it if he is to obtain needed financing.

Notes may also contain an *escalator clause* that permits the lender to vary the interest rate as money market conditions change. If the rate of interest in the current market increases, the rate charged on the specific loan would increase. If the going rate falls, the rate on the specific loan falls. This arrangement is rarely employed today. A similar plan that is used when rates must be fixed calls for the establishment of a high stated rate, representing the maximum the lender expects to charge under adverse conditions. The going rate is then charged as long as it is lower than the stated rate.

Another variant of the escalator clause is the variable rate mortgage. It *requires* the interest rate to vary according to a previously specified index of interest rates. The rate is adjusted upward or downward by (1) increasing or decreasing the loan's maturity and/or (2) increasing or decreasing the monthly payment.

The mortgage. A mortgage is written evidence of the right of a creditor to have property of a debtor sold upon default of the debt. This right, or lien, is exercised through the judicial system under modern law, with the creditor requesting that a court foreclose the property, sell it at sheriff's auction sale, and apply the proceeds toward repayment of the debt. A deed to secure debt is shown in Figure 9–7. The debtor is permitted to correct his default prior to the sheriff's sale, a privilege known as the right or equity of redemption. In some states, an additional period after the sale is permitted, known as the statutory redemption period.

The various states distinguish between *title theory* and *lien theory* in the format of mortgages, a distinction which years ago determined whether or not the creditor, or mortgagee, could assume possession of the mortgaged property without formal foreclosure proceedings. The title theory states held that the mortgage is an actual passage of title to the mortgagee, and that the mortgagee, as actual owner, could assume possession whenever he wished. The lien theory states reasoned that the mortgage passes only equitable title, requiring proper foreclosure. Obviously, a strict interpretation of the title theory can create unjust situations. A property owner who mortgages his property does not intend to transfer ownership for any purpose other than to secure a debt, and he should not be subject to ejectment from the premises when a minor default occurs.

One of three approaches has been taken by nearly every title theory state (for example, Alabama, Maine, Maryland, and Tennessee) to eliminate inequities. A few states have adopted an intermediate title theory (Illinois, New Jersey, North Carolina, and Ohio, for example) which requires foreclosure proceedings, but which permits the mortgagee to assume possession of the property between the time of the debtor's default and the time of the sheriff's sale. This protects the mortgagee against waste that might be committed by the mortgagor who knows that foreclosure is in process and that he is to be removed soon, and it protects the mortgagor from removal without due process of law. A similar alternative used mainly in California (not a title theory state) is to employ a *trust deed in the nature of a mortgage.* The owner conveys a contingent title to a trustee who holds it as security for the lender. The trustee is empowered to sell the property if the debtor defaults.

The third means of tempering the effects of the title theory is for the courts of the title theory states to hold that foreclosure proceedings must be followed in the same manner as the lien theory states. This equates the title theory and the lien theory except for the formal wording on documents. Currently, fewer than 20 states follow the title theory, with all others following the lien theory.

Regardless of which theory is followed, a mortgage is terminated when the debt which created it is satisfied. In addition nearly all mort-

FIGURE 9–7

BRANCH OFFICE

DEED TO SECURE DEBT

STATE OF

County.

THIS INDENTURE, Made the   day of   ,in the year
one thousand nine hundred   , between

of the County of   , and State of   , as party or parties of
the first part, hereinafter called Grantor, and

as party of the second part, hereinafter called Grantee
WITNESSETH, That Grantor, for the consideration hereinafter set forth, in hand paid at and
before the sealing and delivery of these presents, the receipt whereof is hereby acknowledged, has
granted, bargained, sold, aliened, conveyed and confirmed, and by these presents does grant, bargain, sell, alien, convey and confirm unto the said Grantee, all that tract or parcel of land lying and
being in

THIS CONVEYANCE is made under the provisions of the existing Code of the State of Georgia
to secure a debt (and interest thereon and other indebtedness as described herein) evidenced by
                      note   dated   made by Grantor to order of Grantee, for
the principal sum of   ($) Dollars

FIGURE 9–7 (*Continued*)

The title, interest, rights and powers granted herein by Grantor to Grantee, particularly the power of sale granted herein, shall inure to the benefit of anyone to whom Grantee shall assign the indebtedness herein secured, and/or convey the property herein described, as well as to the successors and legal representatives of Grantee.

In case the debt hereby secured shall not be paid when it becomes due by maturity in due course, or by reason of a default as herein provided, Grantor hereby grants to Grantee, the following irrevocable power of attorney: To sell all or any part of the said property at auction, at the usual place for conducting sales at the Court House in the County where the land or any part thereof lies, in said State, to the highest bidder for cash, after advertising the time, terms and place of such sale once a week for four weeks immediately preceding such sale (but without regard to the number of days) in a newspaper published in the County where the land or any part thereof lies, or in the paper in which the Sheriff's advertisements for such County are published, all other notice being hereby waived by Grantor, and Grantee (or any person on behalf of Grantee) may bid and purchase at such sale and thereupon execute and deliver to the purchaser or purchasers at such sale a sufficient conveyance of said property in fee simple, which conveyance may contain recitals as to the happening of the default upon which the execution of the power of sale herein granted depends, and Grantor hereby constitutes and appoints Grantee the agent and attorney in fact of Grantor to make such recitals, and hereby covenants and agrees that the recitals so made by Grantee shall be binding and conclusive upon Grantor, and that the conveyance to be made by Grantee shall be effectual to bar equity of redemption of Grantor in and to said property, and Grantee shall collect the proceeds of such sale, and after reserving therefrom the entire amount of principal and interest due, together with the amount of taxes, assessments and premiums of insurance or other payments theretofore paid by Grantee, with eight per centum per annum thereon from date of payment, together with all costs and expenses of sale and ten per centum of the aggregate amount due for attorney's fees, shall pay any over-plus to Grantor as provided by law.

AND Grantor further covenants that in case of a sale as hereinbefore provided, Grantor, or any person in possession under Grantor, shall then become and be tenants holding over and shall forthwith deliver possession to the purchaser at such sale, or be summarily dispossessed, in accordance with the provisions of law applicable to tenants holding over.

The power and agency hereby granted are coupled with an interest and are irrevocable by death or otherwise and are granted as cumulative to the remedies for collection of said indebtedness provided by law.

It is agreed that the Grantee shall be subrogated to the claims and liens of all parties whose claims or liens are discharged or paid with the proceeds of the loan secured hereby.

Whenever the terms "Grantor" or "Grantee" are used in this deed such terms shall be deemed to include the heirs, administrators, executors, successors and assigns of said parties. All rights and powers herein granted to the Grantee shall inure to and include his, her or its heirs, administrators, executors, successors and assigns, and all obligations herein imposed on the Grantor shall extend to and include Grantor's heirs, administrators, executors, successors and assigns.

IN WITNESS WHEREOF, Grantor has caused this instrument to be executed and sealed the day and year first above written.

Signed, sealed and delivered in the presence of

.... (L. S.)
(UNOFFICIAL WITNESS)

.... (L. S.)
NOTARY PUBLIC

.... (L. S.)

FORM L2 5M

gages contain a provision known as a *defeasance clause* stating that the mortgagee cannot foreclose so long as the debtor upholds the conditions of the mortgage.

A mortgage conveys an interest in real estate, so it must be in writing to be enforceable. This writing must meet most of the requirements of a valid deed,[2] except that the statement of consideration might be a reference to a separate document, the note, that evidences the debt which caused the mortgage lien to arise. The mortgage itself is a *lien*—not evidence of a debt.

The owner or buyer of a parcel of real estate might find that one lender will not provide as great a sum of money as he needs to acquire or retain ownership. The major lender demands a first lien on the property, i.e., the right to be paid before others if foreclosure becomes necessary, but the owner may be able to obtain additional funds from others on a second or third lien basis if his credit rating is favorable. These lower level liens are called "junior mortgages." A junior mortgage is usually a second mortgage having only one senior lien existing at the time it is created. However, tax liens, mechanics liens, or other liens can demand priority over existing senior or junior mortgages, thereby reducing the second mortgage to third or fourth lien priority. If the first mortgage is paid off, the second mortgage automatically achieves top priority.

The only time priority of liens becomes important is when the mortgagor is in financial difficulty. The importance of priority cannot be over-emphasized at that time because the debt may have to be satisfied by selling the property. Several instances where priority planning is important to the investor are:

1. When the investor owns land and is asked by a developer to accept a purchase money mortgage that is subordinated in lien to future construction loans. The investor is more concerned about his role as an investor than as a creditor in this case, since he is willing to grant a first priority lien to the lenders who supply cash for improvements even though he is entitled to the first lien himself.

2. When the investor is buying on land contract and the seller wishes to borrow against the property deed. The investor must agree (in writing) to subordinate his equitable title to the claims of the new lender if the seller is to succeed in getting the money he desires.

3. When the borrower has a second mortgage and he wishes to renegotiate with the first mortgage lender for a larger sum. The first mortgage lender wishes to retain a first lien basis on all sums loaned, yet the existing second mortgage would have rights that are prior to additional loans. To avoid this situation, some lenders have promoted the "open-end" mortgage that permits several sums to be loaned at different times on a first lien basis.

---

[2] Deed requirements are discussed on pp. 173–74 of this chapter.

Second mortgages can be employed profitably by investors in two ways. First, these mortgages can often be purchased at a price that provides an attractive yield. Extreme caution must be exercised by an investor in selecting lenders and properties, but the rates of interest can run as high as three times the first mortgage rate. Second, he might wish to become a second mortgage debtor in periods of tight mortgage money to provide a large downpayment that would secure the best possible interest rates. A second mortgage obtained from family or friends can provide this downpayment, usually at rates low enough to make that dual borrowing operation worthwhile. Second mortgage borrowing from most professional second mortgage lenders should be avoided whenever possible, however, due to their prohibitively high cost.

Mortgages are usually liens against fee ownership interests, but many interests are mortgageable. Long-term leaseholds are frequently mortgaged in commercial properties. Mineral rights, air rights, and life estate interests also may have mortgaging possibilities. If the owner can establish a verifiable value in his ownership, he likely would be able to borrow against it.

Mortgage by purpose. Mortgage forms have been devised to accomplish many purposes. Subdividers of large tracts employ a "blanket" mortgage on the entire tract which permits small portions of the land to be paid off, released from the mortgage, and sold. The lender usually requires that an amount greater than the pro rata share be paid to secure the release, but the ability to retain financing until lots are sold makes the blanket mortgage ideal.

Financial institutions offer homeowners a "package" mortgage secured both by real estate and certain home equipment items such as a range, refrigerator, dishwasher, and airconditioner. Low real estate mortgage interest rates apply to the appliances as well as the real estate, and lenders are able to increase the sum of money invested profitably with no additional lending costs and little additional risk.

As mentioned above, lenders also offer an open-end mortgage which permits additional sums to be lent on a single mortgage. This insures a safe priority position for the lender, and it permits the homeowner to obtain low-cost financing for improvements and replacements.

Participation mortgage. From 1966 to 1970, mortgage interest rates were the highest in recent history. In some instances, a conflict arose between returns required by lenders and state usury laws, which state the ceiling interest rate that an individual may legally pay. Constant annual loan payments as high as 11.5 percent of the original loan balance were not uncommon, and many borrowers competed for funds regardless of the high interest rates. However, few projects could afford to pay fixed mortgage cost at these high levels, and lenders devised plans wherein a lower fixed rate of interest is charged on money advanced, accompanied by a percentage of gross or net income. This is a participation mortgage arrangement.

The most widely used form of participation mortgage is a variation in which the lender receives his normal loan amortization payment plus a small percentage of gross income in excess of a stated amount. The stated amount is usually the current gross income level, and the excess represents inflation in rents after the loan is made. This permits the lender to realize a satisfactory return based on current rentals and an increasing return as rents go up.

Mortgage loans that call for a percentage of net income offer the lender the highest possible return potential. However, this provision is unpopular with borrowers, and it is used only in periods of tight money.

Conventional, insured, and guaranteed mortgages. The majority of mortgages today are conventional, that is, they are agreements between borrower and lender in which only the borrower's credit worthiness and property as collateral support the obligation to pay. Lenders prefer conventional mortgages for three reasons: (1) they can impose their own individual requirements upon borrowers and properties, thereby permitting individualized programs that best meet the needs of both parties; (2) they are not required to submit reports to insuring or guaranteeing institutions that increase costs of administration; and (3) they do not have to charge discount points, that is, charges necessary to increase yields from rates fixed by insuring and guaranteeing institutions to competitive market rates. Discount points are required for conventional mortgages only in those states such as New York, Delaware, and Maryland in which state usury rates are so low that competitive market rates may exceed them. Georgia, for example, does not permit mortgage lenders to charge more than 9 percent interest, thereby requiring lenders to "discount" loans when competitive rates exceed that figure.

The Federal Housing Administration insures mortgage loans against lender default by agreeing to compensate lenders against losses resulting from forced foreclosure sales. A charge of 0.5 percent per annum is made against the borrower for the privilege of obtaining FHA insurance. Property values covered by this insurance vary between $15,000 and $30,000, depending upon money market conditions. The FHA exercises substantial control over both borrowers and properties, maintaining strict loan-to-income restrictions and construction requirements. These restrictions and requirements vary slightly as market conditions change, but they are enforced strictly at all times.

The borrower derives one basic advantage from FHA insurance: Lenders will loan a higher percentage of appraised value with the insurance than under conventional terms, running as high as 97 percent for properties valued at $15,000–$20,000 or less. It is true that the lender cannot charge more than the maximum interest permitted by the FHA, usually varying between 6¼ percent and 7½ percent, and the borrower is not permitted to pay the discount points that arise in periods of high conventional interest rates. However, sellers of properties that qualify for FHA financing normally increase their selling price to include these charges. This system in which discounts must frequently be charged is controversial and has been attacked by some economists. Recently, several proposals to change the system of fixed interest rates have emanated from several sources, including the secretaries of the Treasury and the Department of Housing and Urban Development and several trade organizations. These proposals would do one of the following: (1) eliminate the fixed FHA ceiling rates; (2) peg FHA rates to rates on selected U.S. government securities; or (3) permit the ceiling rates to vary among regions of the country.

The Veterans Administration offers qualified veterans a guarantee program that is, in effect, a loan cosigned by the government. No premium charge is made, however, and requirements imposed upon borrowers and properties are less severe. Upon default, the VA will pay up to $12,500 of any loss incurred by the lender. Many VA loans are 100 percent of the selling prices, with the borrowers paying only the loan closing costs. An eligible veteran is normally entitled to only one VA loan, although in some cases the loan may be transferred to another eligible veteran in a manner that the original borrower's VA right is restored.

Transferring partial ownership rights

The investor might arrange with the owner of a selected parcel of real estate to obtain only partial ownership rights. Those who desire mineral rights, air rights, or surface use rights might find leasing arrangements more advantageous than fee simple ownership. Leases permit minimal capital investment and tax deductibility of the rental payments. Leases can be established in any manner desired by the parties. Short-term oral leases are enforced by law in most states.

Typical lease contents. Long-term leases must be in writing to be enforced, and agreement must normally be reached on all the following matters to protect the parties against unforeseen contingencies:

1. Repairs and landlord's right to enter. Any obligation imposed upon the landlord to repair and maintain the property must be accompanied by a statement of his right to enter. He normally would like to be able to inspect the property for damage or excess wear, and would designate certain times that he may be permitted to do so.

2. Use and care of the premises.

3. Payment of taxes, utilities, and insurance premiums. Related to this is a statement of insurable interests of the parties.

4. Construction of buildings and changes of improvements.

5. Assignments of the lease or subletting by the lessee-tenant.

6. Subordination of the lessee's lien rights to subsequent mortgages obtained by the fee owner or lessor. The lessee jeopardizes his rights upon mortgage default, but this clause may be required by the lessor. Otherwise, it is disadvantageous to the lessee.

7. Right of the lessee to mortgage his leasehold interest.

8. Restrictions prohibiting objectionable occupancy or illegal activities.

9. Requirement that municipal ordinances be obeyed.

10. Rights of the parties in the event that one of them enters bankruptcy or that the property is condemned.

11. Rights and penalties if liens arise or waste is incurred.

12. Rights of the parties regarding termination, public use condemnation, renewal, or purchase by lessee. Arbitration procedures should be established to protect against disagreements regarding renewals.

These requirements are representative of the many different problems that may be considered. Most lease situations are unique; therefore, each lease is usually a highly individualized document.

Lease payment plans. Lease payment plans are generally one of three types:

1. Flat lease. Constant monthly, quarterly, or annual payments are made during the life of the lease.
2. Graduated lease, graded lease, or step-up lease. A formula is established regarding the rental to be paid during the first five years, the second five years, and so on.
3. Reappraisal lease. A procedure is stated for reviewing and adjusting rentals at fixed intervals.

A lease may also be gross, in which the lessor, or fee owner, pays taxes, insurance premiums, and upkeep or net, in which the lessee, or tenant, pays these costs.

Specialized leasing arrangements. Leases are frequently designed to accommodate sale-and-leaseback arrangements, large land purchases through lease and release, and long-term ground leases when sales cannot be effected by law. Sale-and-leaseback arrangements permit property owners to sell without sacrificing possession, thereby releasing funds for other purposes. Lease rentals are fully tax deductible on income-producing property when the property is transferred irrevocably, while building depreciation is expensable when the property is owned.

Land developers normally find that many thousands of dollars are needed to acquire a tract of land and make the minimum improvements necessary to sell or build upon the land. One means of minimizing the land investment employed by residential subdividers is to lease a large parcel of land with a provision in the lease that individual lots will be released from the lease and sold as buyers are found. The subdivider acts as a middleman insofar as transfers go, but he pays more than 100 percent of the agreed-upon price for lots until he pays off the entire parcel. His lease establishes the price of both the entire parcel and the individual lots, and he makes a profit on all revenues in excess of his original cost.

Long-term ground leases are employed in lieu of land sales in many eastern states and in Indian lands that by law cannot be sold. Ground leases must be extremely precise and irrevocable when they are used to acquire land upon which expensive improvements are to be placed. They are usually drawn for 21 or 99 years with a "renewable forever" clause being common. State laws vary the form of these leases, the "Baltimore" and "Pennsylvania" systems being most common, but the long-term and irrevocability features are contained in all.

Minimizing equity investment: The land contract

Many real estate transactions are consummated in a manner that the seller is called upon to wait for his money for a substantial period of time. He might accept a second mortgage, or he might prefer a land contract for deed. Under the latter plan, the seller retains title until a substantial portion of the purchase price, frequently 50 percent to 75 percent, is paid by the buyer. The price paid under land contract is usually higher than the cash price. In addition, the seller can often obtain an installment sales [3] arrangement in which taxable profits are recognized in small amounts over many years.

The land contract must incorporate all of the provisions of a mortgage-note combination. In addition, the seller and buyer must work out agreements regarding:

1. Time of passing of title.

2. Whether or not the land contract is to be recorded. The seller would prefer not to record the contract, but the buyer's interest is protected by doing so.

3. Whether or not the deed is to be placed in escrow during the land contract period. The seller cannot dispose of the property easily when the deed is in escrow; an additional measure of protection is thereby added for the buyer.

4. The extent to which the seller may mortgage the property during the land contract period. The buyer can find himself in a dilemma if he pays off the contract and finds that the seller has a large mortgage against the property that he cannot retire. As a general rule, the land contract agreement should not permit the mortgage debt to exceed the amount owed by the buyer to the seller. The buyer should also specify that he retains the right to approve any new loans against the property.

---

[3] See chapter 7 for installment sales rule.

5. Buyer's and seller's rights in the event of rescision or forfeiture of the contract. The seller would wish to retain payments made by the buyer in the event of default and rescind the buyer's interest. Conversely, the buyer would like to be able to forfeit his rights at will and walk away from the project if it should turn out to be unproductive. A mutually satisfactory balance of the two forces should be developed.

The land contract is an expert land speculator's tool. It requires a high degree of specialized knowledge, and the investor who uses this tool must feel that every agreement must be strongly in his favor. He will usually have to negotiate with the seller on such items as interest rates, recording, escrows, and mortgages; and he must be able to hold firm to his forfeiture rights and other essential clauses while convincing the seller of the desirability of some other aspects of the contract—usually the interest rate and selling price.

Selling the property

One who wishes to divest himself of a real estate holding frequently lists the property with a real estate broker. A listing contract is an agreement between a real estate broker and a person who plans to sell his property stipulating the price to be asked for the property, the amount (usually a percentage of the selling price) the broker is to receive for finding a buyer, and the length of duration of the agreement. There are three basic types of listing contracts: (1) open listing, (2) exclusive listing, and (3) exclusive right to sell. A fourth type, net listing, is mentioned frequently in the literature but is frowned upon in practice, and a fifth, multiple listing, is a subtype of the exclusive right to sell contract.

Open listing. The open listing contract is one which permits the seller to grant a similar contract to all brokers who will accept. No broker has an exclusive right to sell, and the first broker to produce an acceptable offer for the property is entitled to the commission. All others get nothing. If the owner sells the property without the help of a broker, no commission is paid.

Open listings require a minimum commitment by the seller, but they rarely occur because few brokers will accept them. In most cases, the broker must cultivate a potential buyer for days or even weeks to convince him to buy. With an open listing, he might find the buyer just after another broker effected the sale. One might say that open listings "keep brokers honest," but the rationale for brokers not accepting such contracts is strong.

Exclusive agency listing. In an exclusive listing, the seller hires only one broker but retains the right to sell the property through his own efforts without paying a commission. Even if another broker sells the property, the broker holding the exclusive listing is entitled to his com-

FIGURE 9–8

		Rooms	Bdrms	Baths	Suburb	Price
	Address					

C. A. BAKER
REAL ESTATE

PHONE SY 8-8000
CHICAGO PHONE PU 5-0760
18661 DIXIE HIGHWAY
HOMEWOOD, ILLINOIS

				REMARKS		
Type property		Carpeting				
Construction		Draperies				
Lot size		Ven. blinds				
Taxes		Fireplace				
Age-Condition		Tiled bath				
Why selling		Tiled kitchen				
Possession		Dishwasher				
Foundation		Disposal				
Basement		Softener				
Utility Rm.		Exhaust		**ROOMS**	**SIZE-1st FLOOR**	
Floors		Built in		Living room		
Walls		Air cond.		Dining room		
Heat		Storm win.		Kitchen		
Water Heater		Screens		Cabinet		
Garage		TV antenna		Family room		
Rec. Rm.		Fenced yard		Baths		
Patio		Storm sewer		Bedroom		
Porch		San. sewer		Bedroom		
Catholic school		Septic tank		Bedroom		
Churches		Gas			**SIZE-2nd FLOOR**	
Public school		Water		Bedroom		
Title		Well		Bedroom		
Sign		Paved street		Bedroom		
Owner		Driveway		Bedroom		
Tenant		No. of closets		Baths		

Information herein is not warranted and subject to change without notice. We assume no liability for errors

(a)

FIGURE 9–8 *(Continued)*

EXCLUSIVE SALES CONTRACT   PREPARED BY   **No. 4-S**   COPYRIGHT 1949
       MAXIM HIRSCH   UNIVERSITY PRINTING COMPANY
         1410 EAST 62ND ST.   CHICAGO

_____, 19____

TO_____

In consideration of your promise to list as of this date and exhibit the realty of the address noted below and in further consideration of your promise to advertise it at your expense for sale ____hereby give you the sole and exclusive right to sell through your efforts or with any brokers cooperating with you the property located at and known as_____

in the City of_____, County of_____,

State of_____, for the period of

_____from the date hereof at a price of $_____

or any less sum that_____may hereafter accept, subject to the incumbrances of record this date in the

amount of $_____, due_____. Terms to be

_____cash and balance payable____.

Thereafter this agreement shall automatically renew itself for a like term but may be terminated by either party by personally notifying the other party in writing of such intention 30 days in advance of such intended termination date.

In the event said property is sold or title conveyed while this agreement is in force by you or the undersigned or anyone else. _____agree to pay you_____% commission in such sale price. In the event said property is sold or title conveyed within 90 days after termination date to any prospective purchaser previously procured through or by you, you shall likewise have earned your commission hereunder.

You have the privilege of purchasing this property, if you so desire, title to said realty to be conveyed to the name of anyone you may designate.

_____agree to furnish upon demand, as quickly as possible, satisfactory evidence of title brought down to date of contract with purchaser, and convey title by warranty deed with release of dower and homestead rights, and pay all unpaid installments of special assessments for improvement completed, and pro-rate, on customary basis, taxes, interest and all other items of income and expense to date of delivery of deed.

_____further agree to protect you by quoting a selling price of $_____and referring all inquiries to you during the time covered hereby.

It is understood that this agreement is irrevocable during above stated period and that you make no guarantee of sale.

You are hereby authorized to advertise the said property "For Sale" and to place a "For Sale" sign on the same.

Accepted:

C. A. BAKER REAL ESTATE _____ _____(SEAL)

By_____ _____(SEAL)

(b)

mission. This type of contract is more common than an open listing, but brokers are somewhat reluctant to accept a contract when they must compete with the seller.

Exclusive right to sell. The contract type which grants the major legal advantage to the broker is the exclusive right to sell. Regardless of who sells the property—owner included—the broker with an exclusive right to sell listing is entitled to receive his commission. (See Figure 9–8.) Obviously, brokers prefer the exclusive right to sell listing arrangement, and sellers are frequently satisfied to accept it, particularly after they have failed to sell their properties through their own efforts. Under this contract type, the broker can proceed in obtaining contacts without fear of being too late to make the sale.

Net listing. The net listing contract is one in which the seller specifies a price he wishes to receive from the sale, and the broker keeps everything in excess of that amount. Obviously, this would encourage brokers to attempt to establish low net prices for sellers, and it would encourage them to inflate prices. Thus, sellers would tend to become dissatisfied with the arrangement, and a few unscrupulous brokers would give the brokerage profession a bad name.

Multiple listing. One arrangement that has been very satisfactory for sellers, buyers, and brokers is the multiple listing in which the seller grants an exclusive right to sell listing to a broker who agrees to put the property in a pool operated by an organized group of brokers. All of the brokers work to sell the property, and all or part of the commission is shared by the participating members of the group. Sellers find the multiple listing advantageous because the prospective buyers being serviced by several brokers become potential buyers for the subject property. Brokers find that a rapid turnover of properties brings in more business and promotes greater profit and greater efficiency than is possible through individual operation. However, the multiple listing concept does have two problems which keep it from being used more widely: (1) some brokers tend to rely upon their coparticipants to bring in most or all of the listings and (2) some brokers withhold choice listings for their individual sale. The latter problem can be quite serious; "vest-pocket" listings can dissolve a multiple listing arrangement very quickly. The first problem can also cause serious difficulties with the multiple listing service and particularly in small organizations may ultimately cause its downfall.

Establishing a reasonable duration for listing contracts is an important problem faced by brokers. Many legal actions have been brought by brokers who introduced a buyer to seller only to find that the two of them conspired to wait until the listing contract terminated so that they could transact a sale without paying a commission. Today, the courts generally hold that a broker is entitled to his commission when: [4]

1. The deal falls through because the owner changes his mind and refuses to sign the deed to the purchaser or a contract to sell. The rule is the same when the land has increased in value and the owner rejects the broker's buyer for this reason. If the seller refuses to sign, giving as his only reason the fact that he has changed his mind, he cannot thereafter shift ground and claim that the buyer's offer was not in compliance with the listing. *Russell* v. *Ramm,* 200 Cal. 348, 254 Pac. 532.

2. The deal falls through because the owner's wife refuses to sign the contract or deed. *Pliler* v. *Thompson,* 84 Okla. 200, 202 Pac. 1016.

3. The deal falls through because of defects in the owner's title. *Triplett* v. *Feasal,* 105 Kan. 179, 182 Pac. 551.

4. The deal falls through because of the owner's fraud. *Hathaway* v. *Smith,* 187 Ill. App. 128.

5. The deal falls through because the owner is unable to deliver possession within a reasonable time.

---

[4] Kratovil, *Real Estate Law,* p. 92.

6. The deal falls through because seller insists on terms and provisions not mentioned in the listing contract, as where the seller insists on the right to remain in possession after the deal has been closed. *Brown* v. *Ogle* 75 Ind. App. 90, 130 N.E. 147.

7. After the contract of sale has been signed, the seller and buyer get together and cancel the contract. *Steward* v. *Brock* 60 N.M. 216, 290 P. 2d. 682.

Even when there is no reluctance on the part of the seller to pay the broker his commission, a question arises as to the point in time when the commission is earned. In general, the broker has earned his commission when he introduces the seller to a buyer who is ready, willing, and able to buy the property according to the terms specified in the listing. *Ready* and *willing* mean that the buyer wishes to purchase immediately; *able* indicates that he has financial means to acquire the property. A sale need not result from this union of seller and buyer in order for the commission to be earned; the seller must pay the commission even though he refuses to consummate the deal (unless he refuses due to the buyer's being other than ready, willing, and able). If the seller and potential buyer both sign a contract of sale but later cancel for any reason, the commission must be paid. This is true even if the *buyer* fails to fulfill the contract, the seller's remedy being to sue the buyer for damages because of breach of contract —the damages being primarily the commission.

To avoid the possibility of paying a commission without his property being sold, a seller may specify in the listing contract that the broker is entitled to his commission only if the property is sold to a buyer introduced by the broker.[5]

Other functions

Purchasing an option.   An option is an agreement between buyer and seller in which the seller agrees to hold an offer open for a specified time and the buyer agrees to pay a sum of money as consideration. No real property ownership rights pass at the time the option is granted. The buyer is merely purchasing the right to buy at a fixed priced within a stated period. If he accepts the offer, a purchase contract results. The consideration paid for the option is kept by the seller regardless of the buyer's decision.

Employing an escrow agent.   An escrow operation is one in which a person is asked to serve as a neutral third party to a business transaction. The usual situation is when a banker or other lending institution official

---

[5] Under such a provision the buyer may be introduced *indirectly* by the broker, such as when a newspaper advertisement leads to a sale; the broker is still entitled to his commission. Such a provision cannot be specified in an exclusive right to sell listing, however, since the broker gets his commission regardless of who sells the property.

is employed to hold a seller's property deed and a buyer's purchase money until the property title is cleared. The third party, referred to as an escrow agent, escrow company, or escrow holder, requires a detailed set of instructions regarding provisions such as when title is to pass, how delivery is to occur, and actions to be taken if impediments of title or other complications arise. Both parties to the business transaction can work together to terminate the escrow arrangement, but neither party can terminate it by himself. Since the agreement is legally binding, it should be composed in a manner that little or nothing is subject to interpretation by the escrow holder. The instructions should be complete and thorough, and provisions should be made for both parties to reach agreement upon any item of uncertainty.

Exchanging properties. Current tax laws concerning capital gains frequently make it desirable to trade one parcel of real estate for another rather than to effect separate sale and repurchase transactions. Most realtors have a contract form for this that specifies the exact nature of each property and the manner in which the commission is to be paid. The exchange contract contains most of the aspects of the contract for sale discussed previously in this chapter.

The commission on an exchange is agreed to by all parties to the transaction. The amount is often determined by charging a flat percentage of the exchange value of each property (actually two commissions), although wide variations in practice are found. Most brokers who specialize in selling homes do not operate as middlemen between two trading parties. In the residential real estate market very few cases arise in which a person wishing to trade his home would desire to trade his home for the exact home which another person wishes to trade. Therefore, the broker acts as a principal for both parties, buying their old homes and selling them new ones. The "pure" exchange arrangement in which the broker does not acquire title to either property is more commonly used in business and investment real estate.

Other income tax issues. Income taxes are an especially important consideration in disposing of property ownership. Depreciation methodology, timing of disposition, and manner of disposition, e.g., cash sale, installment sale, tax-free exchange, or credit sale, should all be planned with the help of an income tax expert. The basic income tax issues of conveyancing were presented in chapter 7.

SUMMARY

Basic conveyancing functions examined in this chapter include (1) making offers; (2) settlement of property transactions; (3) securing funds; and (4) transferring partial ownership rights. A minimum of eight kinds of legal documents are presented, and the important elements of each are discussed. The important point to be made in the chapter is that planning for investment return, income taxation, and liability protection can be the most productive use of time only when the investor achieves skill at conveyancing. He must learn to minimize his time in activities that facilitate his basic task, and developing skills in conveyancing is the only way that he can avoid losing a great deal of time in working with deeds, mortgages, contracts, and other documents.

Attorneys can relieve the investor of much of his conveyancing burden, but only he can evaluate documents in terms of his varied objectives. A carefully drawn statement of objectives, coupled with sound ownership and tax planning, should help him develop a sound pattern of action to follow in conveyancing.

QUESTIONS FOR REVIEW

1. What is the Statute of Frauds?
2. Indicate 10 provisions normally covered in an offer for sale.
3. What costs are to be paid by the buyer and the seller in a normal closing statement?
4. What are the basic deed forms?
5. How are titles searched? What evidence of a good title can one obtain?
6. Distinguish clearly between a note and a mortgage.
7. What is a participation mortgage?
8. What is the difference between a VA and an FHA mortgage?
9. Indicate three types of lease payment plans.
10. What is a land contract?
11. What is an option on real estate?
12. Describe the various forms of listing contracts used by real estate brokers.

REFERENCES

Friedman, Milton R. *Contracts and Conveyances of Real Property.* New York: Practicing Law Institute, 1972.

Gray, Charles D. and Steinberg, Joseph L. *Real Estate Sales Contracts: From Preparation Through Closing.* Englewood Cliffs, N.J.: Prentice-Hall, Inc., 1970.

Harvey, David C. B. *Harvey Law of Real Property Title and Closing.* New York: Clark Boardman Company, Inc., 1972, 3 vols.

Kratovil, Robert. *Real Estate Law.* Englewood Cliffs, N.J.: Prentice-Hall, Inc., 1969.

Lusk, Harold F. *Law of the Real Estate Business.* Homewood, Ill.: Richard D. Irwin, Inc., 1965.

Ring, Alfred A. *Real Estate Principles and Practices.* Englewood Cliffs, N.J.: Prentice-Hall, Inc., 1972, Chapters 5, 8, 9, 10, and 11.

Semenow, Robert W. *Questions and Answers on Real Estate.* Englewood Cliffs, N.J.: Prentice-Hall, Inc., 1972.

Unger, Maurice A. *Real Estate Principles and Practices.* Cincinnati: South-Western Publishing Company, 1969, Chapters 4, 21, and 22.

PRODUCTIVITY ANALYSIS

THE INVESTMENT CALCULATION in chapter 6 naturally leads to the question of what factors are responsible for producing the investment value. Modern value theory discussed in chapter 4 emphasizes the role of productivity in relation to scarcity as the essential cause of real estate's ability to produce income. Chapter 5 dealt with the measurement of the market value of a parcel of real estate. Chapters 7–9 have been concerned with the legal and tax constraints on real estate investment. In this chapter, we are concerned with identifying and understanding the elements of real estate productivity. This understanding is essential if the investor is to attain insight into all the important factors that may affect a property's income-producing ability.

NATURE OF PRODUCTIVITY

The concept of productivity involves obtaining a greater output than the inputs which produced the output. Usually this phenomenon is accomplished by a rearranging of the inputs into a final product or service that has greater value than the sum total of the inputs. For example, various materials (such as steel, glass, and rubber), machines, labor, and managerial talent go into the production of automobiles. The materials are purchased, machines are depreciated, and workmen's wages and managers' salaries are paid. Yet the automobile company may end up with a surplus above the payment of all costs. This surplus is a profit, and over the long run it represents the productivity of the firm.

Elements of productivity

Real estate can have value because it too enters into the productive process. It is combined with other factors of production to yield services and other goods, the sum total of which have a greater value than that of the factors added together. In the automobile example real estate should also be listed as one of the input factors. The land provides a location for assembling the automobiles, and a building provides shelter for the employees and a base for the machines used in the production process.

Location is an important element in the productivity of real estate because of the transportation and communication necessary between a parcel and other parcels of real estate. In the manufacturing of automobiles the factory's access to raw materials and labor inputs and to consumer markets partially determines whether the manufacturer makes a profit. Similarly, the ability of a parcel of real estate to fulfill certain physical requirements is a determinant of its income-producing ability. If the automobile factory had been built on marshy land, or if the building were too small, the company's profit position would be impaired.

Thus real estate can be productive in two general ways: first, in a parcel's convenience or location relative to other parcels of real estate and second, in a parcel's physical capacity to provide desirable materials or services. We shall term these two types of factors transfer characteristics and physical characteristics.[1] Hoover has called them transfer costs and processing costs and has described them as follows:

In some uses the value of a site depends primarily on the access the site affords to other parties with whom the occupant may want to trade. A good site in this sense is one entailing low *transfer costs*. For downtown urban land uses in general, transfer costs are the important locational factor, and land is rented, bought, and sold on the basis of its positional advantages alone.

At the other extreme are types of land use for which transfer costs are unimportant compared with differences in *processing costs* at good and bad sites. The more valuable the product in relation to its distribution costs per mile the greater is the significance of resource quality as against access to markets.[2]

---

[1] Other authors have also used two basic categories for analysis of productivity but have named them differently. For example, Ratcliff calls them location and physical characteristics. This seems to lead to some confusion in Ratcliff's classification of productivity factors. He includes exposure to view, sun, breeze, and offensive influences under location factors. Hoover labels such factors more correctly, we believe, processing costs—which is analogous to our physical characteristics. Therefore, because of the confusion engendered by the everyday meaning of the word *location* and because the term *processing costs* is not such a meaningful term for improved urban real estate, we prefer to label these categories "transfer characteristics" and "physical characteristics."

[2] Edgar M. Hoover, *The Location of Economic Activity,* paperback ed. (New York: McGraw-Hill Book Co., 1963), pp. 90–91.

Significance of the distinction between transfer characteristics and physical characteristics

Too often in current real estate administration a less-than-incisive analysis of a parcel's productivity results from an unclear distinction between physical factors involving processing costs and location factors involving transfer costs. As pointed out in the passage by Hoover, the relative importance of these types of factors to each other depends upon the purpose for which the real estate is used. For mining, processing advantages are much more important than transfer advantages. But to attach the same importance to processing advantages in analyzing a site for a parking lot is obviously absurd. In less obvious situations, however, how many small retail establishments have been opened in a particular place simply because a suitable building was available? How many substandard dwellings are occupied by persons who could obtain better accommodations at the same rental in a different location? How many industries are operated in the founder's home town, incurring higher than required transfer costs? All such situations are examples of uneconomic weighting being applied to the relative importance of physical and locational factors.

Implications of the distinction between transfer characteristics and physical characteristics

The ability of each parcel of real estate to enter the productive process can differ according to the favorable or unfavorable geographic relationship it has with other parcels of real estate. Differences in future productivity expectations—whether due to physical or transfer factors—usually result in different values among properties.

Another implication, however, which we hasten to emphasize, is that similarities in transfer characteristics in urbanized areas where physical factor differentials are unimportant result in land use patterns that are both discernible and predictable. Similarities in the transfer advantages of a number of sites cause supply competition to take place, thus refuting the idea that land income is more of a monopolistic rent than is the income to other factors of production.[3] Certainly elements of monopoly

---

[3] See Edward Chamberlain, *Monopolistic Competition* (Cambridge: Harvard University Press, 1939), Appendix D, "Urban Rent as a Monopoly Income," pp. 214–17, for the viewpoint that income to real estate represents a monopoly return. This viewpoint derives from the contention that each parcel of land is unique in its locational characteristics and, therefore, cannot be considered as in direct competition with other parcels of real estate in supplying specific locational needs. According to Chamberlain, the locational characteristic of urban land is different from that of agricultural land. Urban land carries its market with it, and the rent paid represents the value of the monopoly privilege of providing retail services *at that particular place.*

may be motivating factors in producing land income, but no more so than for the return to labor or capital. When any commodity or service is in short supply, the owners thereof have some monopolistic control over it. A general theory of factor income would impute no difference between land and other production factors with respect to whether the income was caused by monopoly.

PHYSICAL CHARACTERISTICS

The processing advantages specified by Hoover are the chemical and physical makeup of the site (e.g., ore mining), availability of water, suitability of the soil and climate for agriculture, the natural flora and fauna (for trapping, fishing, hunting, forestry, or grazing), the amenities of the site (climate, view, and terrain), and those features of the site which determine construction and maintenance cost (primarily terrain, soil structure, and climate).[4]

Although Hoover's definition of processing advantages concerns only land, we extend this concept to include any and all improvements. Rather than dealing in sites alone, the real estate analyst deals with parcels of land which have been greatly modified. The site itself may have been leveled, graded, had storm and sanitary sewers installed, drives and walks paved, and the entire lot landscaped. In addition, a building may have been erected on the land which is several times as valuable as the land itself.

Even when no detectable improvements have been made to the site itself, public improvements (off-site improvements or improvements in common) serve to make the land more valuable. Streets, the lighting system, public sewers, parks, and sidewalks are all important value-determining characteristics. All such improvements, as well as on-site improvements, represent applications of labor, capital, and managerial talent to the parcel of land. They become wedded in an inseparable marriage in which the contribution of one factor cannot be separated from the others. In almost every instance of urban land analysis, it must be recognized that much more is involved than simply the original and indestructible qualities of land only. In this sense, then, real estate is, as Ratcliff has emphasized, a manufactured product.[5]

All such characteristics and modifications of urban land may be thought of as imparting processing advantages. They determine the efficiency and capacity with which real estate can perform services and provide benefits. They determine how well a parcel of real estate provides the amenities of home ownership, how much corn another parcel can

---

[4] Hoover, *Location of Economic Activity*, p. 91.

[5] Richard U. Ratcliff, *Real Estate Analysis* (New York: McGraw-Hill Book Co., 1961), pp. 1, 43, 54–55.

produce, how well an office building performs its function, how many cattle can be supported on a range, how many automobiles can be produced in a factory, and how many lobsters can be caught in a particular oceanic area. The real estate analyst must examine and consider each characteristic or feature of a given parcel that would have a bearing on its future processing advantage. Poor construction, inadequate utilities, inappropriate style, and insufficient lighting would be examples of unfavorable factors that would influence the processing advantage of a parcel of real estate relative to other, competing parcels. Such characteristics obviously would tend to reduce future net income or services in relation to other properties and thus to reduce its value.

Analysis of physical characteristics—the site

The physical characteristics of a parcel of real estate determine the property's processing costs. Characteristics of the site are usually analyzed separately from those of major on-site improvements. The major improvement will often dictate the type of analysis performed for the site, although this distinction would be unrealistic for some types of improvements. For example, an intensive analysis of the agricultural fertility of a parcel of real estate that is already improved with an appropriate, costly commercial structure would be inappropriate. Beginning with the site, then, analysis of the processing characteristics includes the following possible categories of factors: (1) geological characteristics, (2) agricultural fertility, (3) surface characteristics, and (4) facilitating improvements.

Geological characteristics. Subsurface characteristics of the soil are important in determining support which can be provided to buildings, drainage and seepage, and the possibility of mineral extraction. The degree to which the latter would be profitable can be analyzed only by competent specialists.

Subsurface soil characteristics also may impose strict limitations to the type of improvement that can be erected on the surface. Marshy, swampy areas or areas subject to volcanic activity require more costly construction techniques to support buildings, although in most cases suitable structures can be built if costly, specialized techniques are used. The Imperial Hotel in Tokyo, designed by Frank Lloyd Wright, is a foremost example of how potential damage from earthquakes can be overcome. It was erected in the years 1916 to 1922, using a revolutionary, floating cantilever construction to provide the required flexibility to absorb shocks. A tremendous earthquake shortly after the construction left the structure standing unaffected, while almost every other building in Tokyo was destroyed.

In Chicago, where land is marshy, huge piers must be sunk to bedrock to support tall buildings. The costs of this additional construction requirement limited the height of Chicago's skyscrapers to fewer than 45 stories until the mid-1960s when newer construction techniques allowed the 100-story John Hancock Center and the 60-story First National Bank Building to be constructed. Now even taller structures are being built in Chicago. Sometimes the culprit is quicksand. An adequate number of borings to test for the presence of quicksand and other geological characteristics should always be made before construction contracts are signed.

Where rock is close to the surface of the land additional costs for excavation are encountered. Basements are much costlier, and subsurface sewage, electrical, and telephone placements are more difficult and costly. Also, impervious soils and subsurface rock may affect the drainage and seepage of the land. The area may be subject to flooding, precluding the proper drainage of storm and sanitary sewage. The elevation of the surface in relation to surrounding land can also be a determinant of drainage.

Agricultural fertility. This factor should obviously be considered when a prospective real estate investment will involve agronomic endeavors. Appropriate agricultural experts should be employed to perform such analysis. A resort to do-it-yourself analysis, opinion by the owner or neighbors, or other nonscientific approaches will usually yield unreliable results.

Surface characteristics. The terrain, size, shape, vegetation, and exposure are characteristics of the surface of a parcel of real estate which may possibly influence value. Hilly terrain and woods require costly modifications for commercial, industrial, or low-cost residential uses. Long, narrow lots are not suitable in today's market for single-family residences. Extreme irregularity in shape of a residential lot is undesirable, while pleasant views and attractive neighborhood structures are important advantages. Additionally, the freedom from obnoxious odors and noises is a virtual necessity for middle and upper class residential neighborhoods. Having adequate foot traffic and exposure to appropriate clientele is necessary for commercial uses.

Sometimes a lot is of insufficient size to accommodate a desired use, and two or more parcels are combined to produce the desired size. When the several parcels together have a greater value than the sum of the individual parcels before being combined, the difference is called *plottage* value.

Facilitating improvements. These represent capital expenditures on *and* off the site for such improvements as utilities, paving, subsidiary buildings (e.g., a garage), and landscaping. The analyst should identify all such improvements and consider their adequacy or the cost of installing adequate facilities. For well-established uses the amount of analysis may be relatively small; facilitating improvements would have been needed and installed already. New uses, however, may require significant attention to such items. For example, before Anheuser Busch located a new brewery near Columbus, Ohio, a great deal of analysis was required to determine whether the water supply would be adequate to meet the great needs of a large brewery.

Analysis of physical characteristics—the major improvement

Analysis of the major improvement must be tailored to the specific type of structure. Often experts are required to judge the quality and condition of the construction of large, steel-frame buildings or of special-purpose structures, such as a grain elevator or refinery. For any building the following items should be examined relative to their physical characteristics: (1) construction, (2) functional capability, and (3) subsidiary systems.

Construction. Quality and condition of the structural components are the criteria to be considered in evaluating construction. Studs, rafters, joists, subflooring, foundations, footings, and the roof are examples of such components. Quality of the physical components should be judged relative to their original character and workmanship, while condition should indicate how much physical deterioration has occurred. A 10-year-old bathtub that was of high quality when installed and is in good condition may contribute more to a home than a new tub of lesser quality. If the 10-year-old tub is functionally less desirable than a new tub, that penalty should be reflected under the following category.

Functional capability. The degree to which the size, shape, arrangement, lighting, and general appropriateness of the building and its component rooms are adequate determines functional capability. Such considerations can be of overriding importance to the financial success of a real estate venture. For example, a large, high-rise, luxury apartment building in a midwestern city experienced financial difficulty because of the small size of the rooms and apartments. Persons seeking that type of housing were unwilling to accept the small quarters even at reduced rents. The investors lost their shirts, and the Federal Housing Administration, which insured the mortgage, was forced to take over the building.

Subsidiary systems. Heating, air-conditioning, electrical, plumbing, and elevator systems contribute to the overall productivity of the property. These systems should be examined with respect to their *future* capacity and efficiency. Usually the analyst must estimate the age of these components, their condition, and their capacity to continue to perform their intended functions. These systems will normally have to be replaced one or more times over the life of a building.

Use of checklists

To lessen the likelihood of omitting small but important details, the analyst should develop a checklist for use in analyzing a major improvement. In single-family residential buildings, for example, one should begin in the basement, examining such items as the floor, walls, foundation, plumbing, furnace, water heater, laundry facilities, subflooring, windows, and stairs. Upper floors should be examined in respect to room size, layout, shape, decorating, condition of walls, floors, and ceilings, electrical outlets, heating ducts, and for condition and adequacy of fixtures such as the kitchen sink, disposal, and bath appliances. The attic should be examined with respect to rafters, sheathing, insulation, ventilation, and general condition. Obviously, an analysis of larger commercial, industrial, and apartment buildings would be more complex.

Lastly, the exterior of a building should be examined. The siding, foundation, chimneys, porches, and windows should be noted for quality and condition. Aspects of the site, such as landscaping and paving, will have been considered under site processing advantages or costs discussed above.

TRANSFER CHARACTERISTICS

The second category of factors influencing the productivity of real estate involves the costs of transferring people, information, goods, and services from one site to other locations. Transfer characteristics are concerned with a property's geographic relationship to other parcels of real estate. As Ratcliff puts it:

The essence of location derives from one of the elemental physical facts of life, the reality of space. We cannot conceive of existence without space; if there were no such thing, all objects and all life would have to be at one spot. If this happened to be the case real estate would have no such quality as location; all real estate would be in the same place, equally convenient to every other piece of real estate and to every human activity and establishment. But under the physical laws of the universe, each bit of matter—each atom, molecule, stone, dog, house, and man—takes up space at or near the surface of the earth. As a result no two objects can be at the same place at the same time. Necessarily, then, all people, animals, and objects are distributed in a spatial pattern.[6]

From this explanation we can realize that transfer costs arise because the user of a parcel of real estate is not in immediate proximity to users of other parcels of real estate. The conveyance of people, information, goods, and services is hindered by the geographic barrier or *friction of space*. An analysis of transfer advantages is thus concerned with the cost associated with a parcel of real estate in overcoming this friction relative to such costs associated with competing parcels.

The use assumption

The use to which real estate is put is an important determinant of its transfer costs. For example, the transfer costs of a single-family residence will differ greatly from that of a retail store. Therefore, an assumption

---

[6] Richard U. Ratcliff, *Real Estate Analysis*, p. 62.

must be made as to the future use of a parcel of real estate. In some cases the future use is already determined. The zoning ordinance, for example, may limit the usage to single-family residential or to light industrial. Also, many parcels of real estate include a costly improvement component. A building that is several times as valuable as the land will ordinarily not be torn down even if some other improvement would be a better use of the land; the costs of demolition and erection of a new structure usually outweigh the benefits to be gained. The analyst has little choice but to assume that the existing land use will be continued into the foreseeable future.

In cases where land use determination has considerable leeway—for example, vacant, unzoned land or land improved with structures having relatively low value and not subject to stringent zoning regulations—the analyst cannot necessarily assume that the current usage will continue. Instead, he must decide what use will provide the greatest return on investment after both processing and transfer costs have been deducted. Conceptually this is done by holding constant the income and processing costs of several potential uses to see how the transfer costs vary among them. When one finds several uses having low transfer costs, he then examines the total income expected less anticipated expenses, or processing costs. The combination yielding lowest transfer costs and highest income after process costs is the financially justified use to which the land should be put.

Analysis procedure

Transfer costs can be regarded as linkages with other parcels of real estate. The term *linkage* implies that there is a need or desire for communication or conveyance of goods, services, or persons between the subject parcel and other parcels of real estate. To the extent that one parcel of real estate is more favorably located with respect to the linkages for the use to which it is likely to be put than other parcels having similar use expectations, the subject parcel enjoys transfer advantages.

Several examples of the relationship between location and linkages can be cited. In the retailing business, location in terms of other compatible or incompatible businesses within the same trading center will affect the level of business volume. A drugstore located near a supermarket, bakery, or hardware in a large shopping center would likely attract 10 to 20 percent more customers than if the surrounding businesses were gardening or household repair shops; its location near auto repair services or eating drive-ins would have a negative effect.[7] Trade and professional organiza-

---

[7] Richard Lawrence Nelson in *The Selection of Retail Locations* New York: McGraw Hill Book Co., 1958), pp. 70–77, lists tables predicting the degree of compatibility, or interchange, between various types of stores in rural trading centers, neighborhood convenience centers, large shopping centers, and the central business district.

tions and unions frequently locate near state capitals or in Washington, D.C., to conduct lobbying activities with state legislators or congressmen and senators. They also may require ready access to state and federal agencies, such as a state banking regulatory authority (by a state banker's association) or the U.S. Department of Labor (by a national labor union). Fire departments locate along major arteries close to the center of the area to be served.

An identification of expected linkages, judgment as to their relative importance to each other, and comparison between the expected linkages of the subject parcel and linkages of other parcels having the same use potential are the steps necessary to carry out an analysis of transfer advantages.

Identification of expected linkages. Linkages arise because of the need for persons, goods, services, or information to come to the subject parcel or to go from the subject parcel to other locations. When the people, goods, services, or information come to the subject parcel they are termed inputs factors; when they go from the property they can be regarded as outputs. Thus, a manufacturing plant receives people (managers and laborers), goods (raw materials), capital (buildings and machines), and information as inputs. It processes all these factors and puts out manufactured products or services.

A residential property typically has inputs of capital (the structure and other improvements), people (the occupants), goods (groceries, clothes, furniture, and so on), and information; its outputs are people who have been sheltered, clothed, maintained, and pleasantly comforted. The output of residential services, as well as the produce of the manufacturing plant, must be transferred to (have linkages with) schools, stores, place of work, churches, and so forth. In a like way commercial establishments, public service facilities, and other land uses have inputs and outputs. Both types of transfer needs must be analyzed.

The significance of the input-output distinction lies in the determination of the most desirable location and physical situation for a particular function. If we think of input markets on one side and output markets on the other, we may graph the relative desirability of potential sites in terms of their total transfer costs, as shown in Figure 10–1.

There is an optimal location, assuming equal physical facilities, between the two markets. This optimal location is usually much closer to one market or the other, depending on whether the product is weight-gaining or weight-losing. A weight-gaining product is one such as beer or soft drinks which by the addition of material (water) gain weight in their processing. Obviously the transportation of water is very expensive relative to the value of the product; therefore, the choice between locating a brewery at the source of raw materials and at the consumption market should be made in favor of the latter.

Some products, iron for example, lose weight in processing. When

FIGURE 10–1

Input, output, and total transfer costs

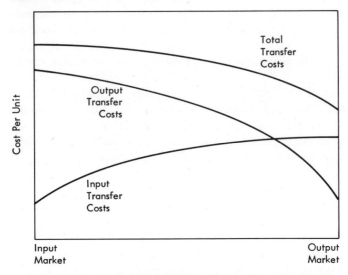

Source: Colberg, Forbush, and Whitaker, *Business Economics Principles and Cases* (3d ed.; Homewood, Ill., Richard D. Irwin, Inc., 1964), p. 451; and Hoover, *The Location of Economic Activity*, paperback ed. (New York: McGraw-Hill Book Co., 1963), p. 39.

relatively valuable material must be separated from other, heavy waste material, as in the case of separating iron ore from the earth, the location dictated is near the source of raw materials. Sometimes such a decision is determined by the presence of a vital input, such as cheap labor, in one location but not in others. This factor, however, is a physical factor involving processing costs and does not properly fall under the category of transfer costs.

When identifying linkages which he believes will be important in the expected future use of a particular location, the analyst can often usefully employ a mapping technique such as that shown in Figure 10–2 for a residential property. The advantages of visualizing expected linkages are twofold: the analyst is less likely to omit important linkages, and in viewing the total linkage situation, he can better assess their relative importances. Only the important linkages need be shown. Minor linkage requirements will tend to even out in terms of relative advantage among prospective sites.

Judging relative importance of expected linkages. The importance of the various linkages must often be judged for the average or typical user of the real estate. For example, in deciding whether to invest in an apartment project, the investor must consider the places to which the typical occupant will desire to commute. If adequate facilities are not

FIGURE 10–2

Linkages with single-family residence

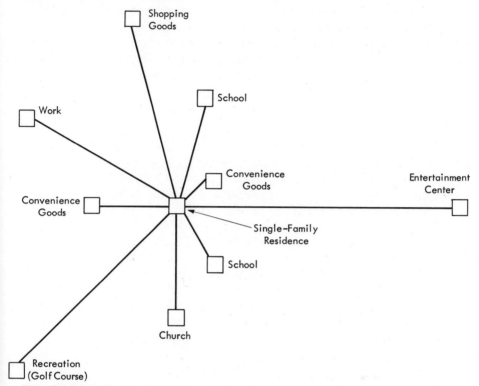

Note: The linkage lines are effective distances; i.e., they account for difficulty as well as distance between the site and linked establishments.

available for some necessary linkages, such as shopping centers and schools, the project should be rejected or means should be found to provide these services in nearby locations. Similarly, in analyzing linkages for a speculative housing development, the analyst must consider what linkages most people in the market the developer hopes to serve will find desirable.

The prospective buyer-occupant also can analyze the linkages with respect to his own specific requirement. Unless he has definite plans to stay permanently, however, he should also consider the linkages other possible purchasers would find desirable.

Comparison of transfer costs. Advantages of transfer provided by competing sites should be analyzed for the obvious reason that another site may have lower total transfer costs for the desired linkages. If the other important variables (income or benefits, processing costs, and price) are equally favorable, a decision to reject the subject site in favor of the competing site is required by financial sanity. The real estate specialist (broker, salesman, investor, appraiser, or consultant) who works in a fairly small market area usually knows the relative advantages of all or most sites for fulfilling various functional requirements. Although his analysis may not be written or specified in the above manner, it is performed nonetheless. The person less familiar with the site and its surroundings would do well to perform the steps prescribed here in a definite, detailed manner.

SUMMARY

Productivity of real estate consists of two elements—physical characteristics and location (transfer characteristics). The physical characteristics of a property determine how well the property can be used for its intended purpose. Transfer characteristics determine how conveniently a property is situated in relation to other properties. The criterion for deciding whether some aspect (such as building design, convenience to a bus stop, or view) is a physical characteristic or a locational factor is whether the transfer of people, goods, or messages is involved. If transfer is involved, the factor under consideration is location; if not, it is a physical characteristic.

The distinction between transfer and physical characteristics facilitates analysis of the productivity of a parcel of real estate. Although the physical characteristics of a property might be quite attractive, its location could be detrimental to the property's intended use. Conversely, a well-located property might be much less valuable than other equally well-located properties because of an unattractive, poorly constructed, or disfunctional building.

The analysis procedure for physical characteristics requires identification and evaluation of each principal physical aspect of a property. In analyzing transfer characteristics all important linkages must be identified and their time-distances compared with competing properties.

QUESTIONS FOR REVIEW

1. What is meant by location?
2. What is meant by processing costs? Why is the term *physical characteristics* more applicable for improved real estate?
3. Is the view from an apartment overlooking San Francisco Bay a physical characteristic or location? What about an attractive neighborhood in relation to a single-family residence? Why?
4. Why is the financial center of the United States concentrated around Wall Street at the southern tip of Manhattan?
5. Why did Pittsburgh and Gary develop into steel-producing centers?

6. Several older, tall hotel buildings have been torn down in recent years (the Park Plaza in New York, the Morrison in Chicago). Why? Did your answer concern physical characteristics or location?

7. The authors know of a small, attractive shopping plaza containing a dinner-type restaurant, a beer and wine carryout, a barber shop, and a pizza parlor that was constructed a few years ago along a four-lane highway leading to the center of a large midwestern city. Although traffic counts along the highway were high, a real estate consultant counseled against the project. The sketch shows the relationships between the plaza and surrounding land uses.

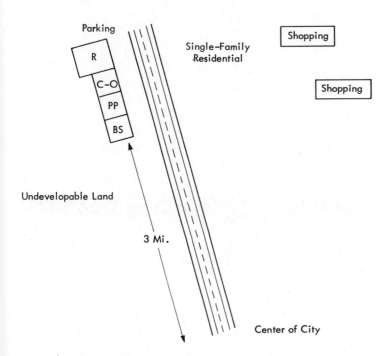

The experience of the plaza confirmed the consultant's advice. Although the restaurant's volume was sufficient to remain in business, the other three establishments went out of business within a year after opening. The turnover of tenants has continued to be high, and the developer sold out for less than his investment cost.

a) Why did the consultant recommend against the project? What factors do you believe he considered?

b) Might his recommendation have been different for an office building? Why?

c) Was the failure of the shopping plaza the result of locational factors or physical characteristics?

REFERENCES

Haggett, Peter. *Locational Analysis in Human Geography.* New York: St. Martin's Press, 1966.

Hoover, Edgar M. *The Location of Economic Activity.* New York: McGraw-Hill Book Co., Inc., 1963.

Lawrence, Richard L. *The Selection of Retail Locations.* New York: McGraw-Hill Book Co., Inc., 1958.

Ratcliff, Richard U. *Real Estate Analysis,* Chap. 4. New York: McGraw-Hill Book Co., Inc., 1961, pp. 62–80.

chapter 11

ANALYZING REAL ESTATE MARKETS

THE EXTENT to which any parcel of real estate is productive and thus has value is determined by the market within which it is bought and sold. Any decision about a property's most productive use or its most likely use, whether to buy, sell, improve, let deteriorate, what type of building to construct, how many stories a building should have, internal features of a building, and the timing of all of these decisions, can only be determined within a market framework. This chapter thus deals with the nature of real estate markets, the many types of forces influencing decision makers within a market, and the methods of analysis for estimating and predicting market decisions and trends.

A market may be conceptualized as including all of the people, both potential buyers and potential sellers, and all of the influences which tend to determine the price for which a property will be transacted. Beckman and Davidson define the term *market* as "a sphere within which price-making forces operate and in which exchanges of title tend to be accompanied by the actual movement of the goods affected . . . . On a more general plane, the market is the mechanism by which the valuable resources of our society are allocated among the various alternative ends that compete for their use." [1] In analyzing a market, one must at least conceptually consider the types and characteristics of people on both the buying and selling side of the market and all of the activities, actions, and opinions occurring within society that may play a role in influencing the decisions of potential buyers and sellers. Obviously, there are so many

---

[1] Theodore N. Beckman and William R. Davidson, *Marketing*, (8th ed.; New York: Ronald Press Co., 1967), pp. 3–6.

potential influences on the motivations of human beings that all considerations can never be completely identified and measured. The reactions of people in the market to some new government policy or to a decision on land use control by a city council can never be known with certainty. The influence on a community of the plans of a major industry to expand can never be predicted with complete accuracy. Nor can the actions of a foreign government or an institution, such as a bank, be translated into some precise effect upon the value of an individual parcel of real estate. Nevertheless, the analyst's job is to attempt to discern which influences are important and what approximate effect such influences may have upon real estate productivity, decisions, and value.

Also, it must be pointed out that although important influences may be correctly identified, the quantification of these influences may be extremely difficult and their translation into value changes extremely hazardous and qualitative. Social trends occurring in our society are some of the most important considerations that will influence long-run real estate values. The trend toward industrialization and urbanization, for example, has been one of the most important conditioners of life in our society. Industrial growth indicates new development of industrial real estate resources, which in turn leads to increased needs for commercial and residential resources. The effects of the trend toward industrialization, however, can be shown only in the most general terms, such as a general determination of which areas will grow, which areas will grow faster than others, and what type of growth to expect.

Social or behavioral trends may be of interest and value by themselves; however, the real estate analyst attempts to relate them to the market with which he is dealing. A behavioral approach to the analysis of real estate would place primary reliance upon social and psychological variables. Only incidentally would social trends and psychological analysis result in economic measures of productivity. Since the purpose of this book, however, concerns the investment decision-making process, social and psychological variables in this chapter and the next are placed within an economic framework. They are regarded as constituting some of the determinants of market prices. One of the most fertile areas for further research in real estate is the relation of behavioral (social and psychological) variables to real estate values and trends.

This chapter first examines some economic models of market behavior. The purpose of this section is to allow the reader to understand the alternative models that are available and to build a case for one model, that of monopolistic competition, as being the most relevant for the economic good of real estate. Identification of a relevant market model allows the analyst to gain insight into the types of influences that may prevail in a market and what implication these influences may have upon potential buyers and sellers. Next, the chapter deals with the important types of influences on market behavior. These are divided into forces influencing demand and those influencing supply. A systematic identification and analysis of these forces is necessary in any market analysis. Lastly, the chapter deals with market analysis and feasibility analysis. The actual steps in each of these types of analysis is presented, and a step-by-step procedure is outlined for completing a market study.

MARKET FUNCTIONS AND MODELS

Although one may employ different models or concepts of a market, all markets perform the basic task of allocating resources among various uses in the economy. This allocation process involves the accomplishment of several functions by a market. Weimer, Hoyt, and Bloom identify three such functions: (1) apportioning existing quarters among those who need them, (2) contracting or expanding the space available in order to meet changed conditions, and (3) determining land use.[2] Ratcliff adds a fourth market function—price establishment[3] which could be included in Weimer, Hoyt, and Bloom's first function. The market conditions associated with the first function can be illustrated with a graph of short-run supply-demand relationships as shown in Figure 11–1.[4]

In the short-run the supply of housing space is shown to be price inelastic. Over a period of one to six months, or even a year, rents and prices may advance because of an increased demand. Such an increase may have been caused by a new employment source locating in the city or an expansion in an existing one. Although the demand may increase, as shown in Figure 11–1, from D_1 to D_2, the supply of housing available cannot increase proportionately. The market thus serves to allocate the available space among those who need it. Such a lag in housing construction usually lasts six months to a year, partly because the construction process will take in many cases at least six months or longer. Additionally, however, it should be recognized that potential investors in new housing to be made available for sale or rental must be convinced that the increased demand will be a long-term rather than a temporary phenomenon.

Sometimes builder-investors produce additional housing units in anticipation of future increases in demand. Sometimes builder-investors continue to add new units after demand has slackened. For example, in a speech to the Biennial Congress of the International Fraternity of Lambda Alpha and the Land Economic Foundation on October 7, 1971, James

---

[2] Weimer, Hoyt, and Bloom, *Real Estate* (6th ed.; New York: Ronald Press Co., 1972), p. 126.

[3] Ratcliff, *Real Estate Analysis* (New York: McGraw-Hill Book Co., 1961), p. 229.

[4] Weimer, Hoyt, and Bloom, *Real Estate*, p. 128.

FIGURE 11–1

Short-run supply-demand relationships

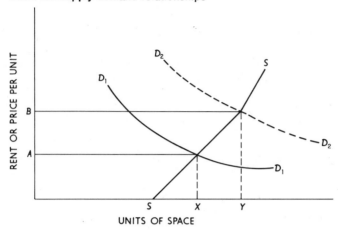

Downs, Chairman of the Board of Real Estate Research Corporation, stated that "the effective demand is not there to absorb units at today's construction costs . . . . residential vacancy in the effective market is going up very rapidly and is going to continue to go up very rapidly until we cut the amount of building which we're doing next year." [5] Most desirably, however, increases in supply will occur when builder-investors correctly forecast additional demand for the immediate future. Ideally, the builder wants to be Johnny-on-the-spot with available housing when new long-term demand appears. This is the raison d'être for market analysis by suppliers of housing units.

The production of new units of housing space involves longer run adjustments in the quantity and quality of space—function 2 of the real estate market. This function operates during a time period long enough to allow new units to be created (usually six months and longer). Conceptually, the time period is not so long as to allow a shift in the usage to which the land can most profitably be put.

The third market function—land use determination—operates over a sufficiently long time period for all factors to vary. Buildings can be torn down, and new ones constructed in their place. Although the market forces of competition must operate within the constraints of the zoning law, the market determines over a long period of time what land use is the most profitable. Presumably the most profitable land use (highest and best use) will provide the greatest service to the community, since people will pay more for that usage than for alternative uses.

---

[5] *Appraisal Briefs*, Society of Real Estate Appraisers, October 1971.

Market imperfections

As we discussed in chapter 5, the concept of a perfect market contains several assumptions or inherent conditions of participant behavior. In the model of pure competition, shown graphically in Figure 11–2, the

FIGURE 11–2

Short-run pure competition

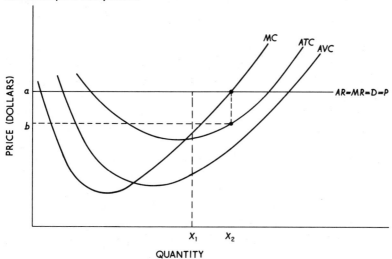

seller can sell all of a product he desires at the market price, average revenue (AR). He will receive for each additional (or marginal) unit the same additional or marginal revenue (MR) that he received for every other unit. He will strive to operate at that level of output where marginal cost (MC) equals marginal revenue (X_2), since at that level his total profit will be the highest possible. Note that this is not necessarily the level where average total cost (ATC) is lowest. Average total cost is lowest at X_1, but operating at this level will not maximize total profit, since the marginal revenue produced by each additional unit is greater than its marginal cost. The profit resulting in this situation is $a–b$. In long-run pure competition, profits would be minimized.

The wheat market might be visualized as an example of the most nearly competitive market. Each kernel of wheat is nearly like every other kernel (at least within a grade), most sellers must accept the going market price when they sell their wheat, and there are many buyers and sellers who actively bid in a well-organized market. Even here, however, the imperfections are evident. The product is not homogeneous; there are several grades of wheat. Some buyers and sellers are large enough to affect market price by withholding from or bringing to the market their wheat or bids. Entry to the market is not free or easy; considerable capital is required. And knowledge about the potential worth of the wheat is subject to disagreement. In fact, an active futures market for grain has developed. In this market, buyers bid to purchase grain which will be delivered at a future date. If the price goes up in the meantime, they will profit; if the price goes down, they will lose. On the other side, sellers are betting that the price of wheat will go down and thus agree to sell wheat they will obtain later at the present price, which they believe to be high.

In contrast with the wheat market, the real estate market is one of the least perfect markets we could identify. The product (a parcel of real estate) is highly differentiated. Large owners or buyers can sometimes affect market price. Entry to the market usually requires a sizeable amount of capital, and knowledge about the potential productivity and value of real estate is subject to a lack of information as well as disagreement. Because of these market imperfections, some economists have stressed the monopolistic characteristics of urban real estate. According to this view, each parcel of real estate is a monopoly for its particular group of characteristics; no other parcel will substitute equally well. Just as in the classical theory of land value and rent, greater profits will accrue to some parcels than to others. These profit differentials result because the elements of productivity (transfer and physical characteristics) are superior in some parcels and inferior in others. Thus, a well-located office building will produce more income than an equally attractive poorly located one. A dime store located on a "100 percent" site will do better than one located a block away. And a residential property having desirable architectural and design qualities will tend to sell for a higher price than another property that is equally well located, but which has less desirable physical characteristics.

If each parcel of real estate were a true monopoly, we know from economic theory that the monopolist-owner would be assured of a profit —at least in the long run. In pure monopoly where there is only one producer or seller, he chooses that level of output that will maximize his total profit, given market demand conditions. Although the monopolist may lose money or do no better than break even in the short run, the fact that he may choose his level of output is assumed to insure in the long run that the monopolist will operate at a level that will provide a profit. This is shown graphically in Figure 11–3. The monopolist depicted in Figure 11–3, as any other firm, operates at the level where marginal revenue equals marginal cost. At this level average total costs are less than average revenue. (If they were not, the monopolist would not continue to operate.) The amount of profit is measured by *a–b*.

FIGURE 11–3

Long-run pure monopoly

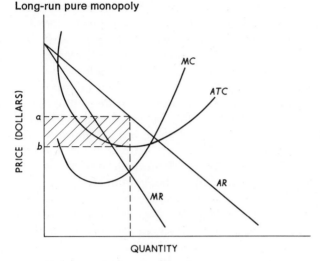

It should be noted from Figure 11–2 that the incurrence of profit in short-run pure competition is just as likely as under conditions of pure monopoly. As shown by Figure 11–4, the only difference between long-

FIGURE 11–4

Long-run pure competition

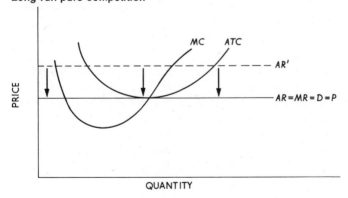

run pure competition and short-run pure competition is that profits disappear in the long-run situation. The firm, as always, operates where $MC = MR$, and at this point in long-run pure competition, average total costs equal average revenue. (It should be realized that total costs include a wage for the owner-operator in this analysis.) The average and marginal revenue curves are pushed to the tangent position with total costs because of the large number of small firms seeking to sell the same product in pure competition. In other words, the *AR'* curve of Figure 11–3 that might exist under short-run pure competition is pushed to the *AR* curve.

It should be evident that the case for urban real estate's falling under the classification of pure monopoly is no stronger than its falling under the model of pure competition. To refute the long-standing emphasis on the monopolistic aspects of urban land, Ratcliff has emphasized the "economic mobility" of urban land.[6] In this view, perfect substitutability is not required for effective competition. Woolworth or Kresge *can* accept a 98 percent location, particularly when obtainable at a disproportionately lower price than a 100 percent location. Thus, the fact that many parcels of urban land are to some extent in competition with each other for a given usage would seem to refute the idea of monopolistic control of urban land. As pointed out in chapter 10, Chamberlain includes this product within the vast majority of commodities whose markets contain aspects of both competition and monopoly.[7] Since the real estate market is far from being a perfect market, we could conclude, by definition, that it contains elements of monopoly. Whether these are greater or less than the monopoly elements in other markets makes little difference. But the concept of monopolistic competition does seem appropriate in describing the operation of real estate markets. In monopolistic competition, the firm decides at what level of output to operate in the same way as does the monopolist. Given a demand function, the firm operates at the level where $MC = MR$ and where AR is greater than the average total costs (ATC). This condition is depicted in Figure 11–5, and it results in profit *a–b*.

However, monopolistic competition differs from pure monopoly because there is no true market demand for a product. Every firm or entity differentiates its product or service by producing a different brand or type of the economic good. Nevertheless, each brand or type is related to the other brands and types of the same commodity. That is, each is a close substitute (not perfect substitute) for the others. For example, Gleem toothpaste is a close substitute for Crest and Colgate. Thus, the level of output each firm can sell depends upon the prices and types of close substitutes, as well as its own price.

The way that the relationship between a firm's output and the prices of other competing products in the market is established is depicted in

---

[6] Ratcliff, *Urban Land Economics* (New York: McGraw-Hill Book Co., 1949), chap. 12.

[7] Edward Chamberlain, *Monopolistic Competition* (Cambridge: Harvard University Press, 1939), appendix D.

FIGURE 11–5

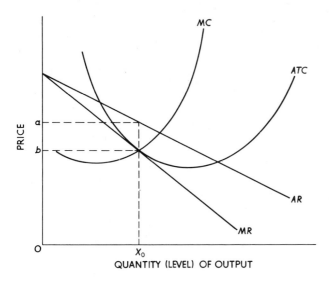

QUANTITY (LEVEL) OF OUTPUT

the following figures. Figure 11–6 shows the revenue and cost curves for two firms producing competitive products. Firm A produces at the point where $MC=MR$, which is the level of maximum profit. Its average revenue curve is the one appropriate to existence of Firm B, which charges a price (P_2) for the competitive product. Firm A's price, however, is lower than Firm B's, and if the products are close substitutes, this price differential will result in the demand for Firm B's product being reduced. In other words, as shown in Figure 11–7, Firm B's average

FIGURE 11–6

Short-run monopolistic competition

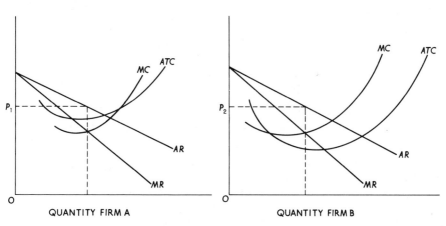

FIGURE 11–7

Shifting demand curve

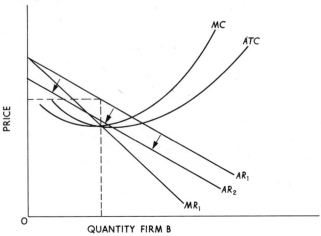

revenue curve will tend to drop because of a loss of sales to Firm A. When Firm B realizes that Firm A is gaining sales at the expense of Firm B, it will lower its price to be competitive. And in time, Firm A may adjust its price and output to the new condition; thus, Figures 11–6 and 11–7 do not depict market equilibrium. Rather, market equilibrium for the firm in monopolistic competition is the same type of situation as it is in pure monopoly. In monopolistic competition the firm can change its plant capacity over the long run, just as can firms in pure competition or pure monopoly. In making adjustments in output capacity, the monopolistic competitor follows the same rules as does the pure monopolist. That is, he operates at the level where $MR = MC$ and $AR \geqq ATC$.

There is an important difference between pure monopoly and monopolistic competition, however. The firm in monopolistic competition does not have a monopoly over the ability to satisfy the market, as does the pure monopolist. In pure monopoly, firm equilibrium is the same situation as market equilibrium. In monopolistic competition, however, the presence of profits will lead to new firms coming into the market with closely substitutable products. The demand curves (*AR* curves) for the older firms in the market will shift to the left, representing the fact that the new firms gain a share of the market at the expense of the old firms. Assuming that market demand remains unchanged, profit levels in the industry shrink as new firms continue to enter the industry. Thus, in long-run equilibrium, profit levels of monopolistically competitive firms shrink to 0. The graphic result, as shown in Figure 11–8, is closely akin

FIGURE 11–8

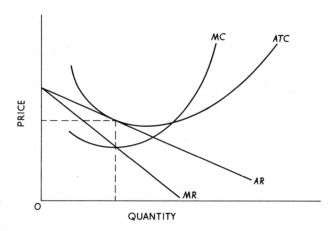

to pure competition. The difference is the downward sloping demand curve of monopolistic competition, as contrasted with the perfectly elastic demand curve of pure competition.

Implications of theory

The real estate market's lack of qualification for being a perfect market implies justification for the role of middlemen in the market. The existence of relatively few buyers and sellers at any one time for a given type of parcel of real estate, the incomplete knowledge and lack of agreement about future market conditions, the potential for any one buyer or seller to influence the market, and the lack of mobility into and out of the market necessitate the facilitating function of the real estate broker.

Nevertheless, the competitive aspects of real estate imply that investors must realize that with a few possible exceptions, there are always substitutable parcels of real estate for any other parcel. If there is an active, viable market, an owner cannot expect to extract an unreasonable price from informed, intelligent potential buyers. At the same time, potential buyers can take comfort from the knowledge that there are normally a number of parcels of real estate that will serve a given need equally well. Some may be better than others, however, and a buyer must expect to pay a premium for those parcels having the greatest productivity potential. The point is that true monopoly profits are almost never attainable in real estate. Large profits will attract competitors, who will tend to drive prices and profits down.

On the other hand, it should be recognized that each parcel of real estate holds some—be it ever so small—degree of monopoly advantage.

One parcel of residential real estate is located nearer the corner than other similar parcels. One house has a more desirable floor plan than another house in a comparable location. One commercial property is located at the center of pedestrian traffic patterns, while another is not. One industrial property has more complete docking and storage facilities than other comparably located properties. Price reflecting these monopolistic advantages can be expected to be paid—but only in proportion to the degree of advantage perceived by the market. True monopoly prices reflecting total market demand will not be attainable.

DETERMINANTS OF DEMAND

The various types of influences on market behavior and prices can for convenience and for purposes of analysis be divided between the demand and supply sides of the market. The determinants of demand are all of those forces or influences that tend to cause real estate to be needed or desired plus the conditions making it possible for people to purchase and own property. Influences tending to cause real estate to be produced or supplied are all of those forces and conditions which motivate the suppliers of real properties to create and construct new real estate resources. Thus, this section of the chapter deals with the demand side of the market, and the next section deals with the supply side.

Although we make the distinction between demand and supply determinants, in reality it may be very difficult to separate the two. The fact that the population is growing is usually considered to be a demand factor, although realistically the growing population is a major determinant of supply as well. Similarly, the availability and relative prices of materials and labor are usually regarded as supply factors. They also influence demand, however, because of the competition of real estate with other economic goods. If the prices of real estate rise relative to other goods, demand will tend to be decreased, while if the prices of real estate decrease relative to other goods, the demand for real estate will tend to increase. We recognize the difficulties of arbitrarily assigning the various forces to the demand or the supply side of the market; however, it must be recognized that this classification is for convenience and analysis, and anyone else is welcome to change the classification to fit his own needs.

Need for housing and other types of real estate

The productivity and the value of real estate are derived from its ability to be used beneficially by human beings. Many types of real estate are needed or desired to satisfy and fulfill the human condition. A broad classification of types of properties consists of residential, commercial, and industrial properties. The value of all of these types of properties is dependent upon the presence of people to utilize them effectively. Thus, housing is needed to provide shelter and a measure of privacy for individuals and groups. Commercial properties are needed and desired because they provide the means by which other economic goods are made available to people. Industrial real estate is needed and desired because it provides shelter and a base for the production of other economic goods.

In considering the demand for residential real estate, the need for shelter must be regarded as basic. Protection from the elements, however, is only one of the functions which most housing in the United States provides today. Housing is much more than shelter; it involves all of the emotional needs and desires, as well as the need for pure shelter. Most housing today is a luxury good which attempts to fulfill the psychological and sociological, as well as physical, needs of people. Housing, as distinguished from shelter, includes architecturally pleasing designs, divided interior space, attractive wall and floor coverings, indoor plumbing, attractive kitchen and bathrooms, conditioned air circulating systems, space that may go unused for substantial periods of time, and many appliances and gadgets that make living more comfortable and more socially fulfilling.

People make a market and therefore the first determinant of demand must be people, or population. Population is important not only in terms of sheer size, but also in terms of characteristics (or subgroupings) of the total population, such as age groupings, educational levels, race, and occupation. Migratory patterns, indicating where people are moving to and where they came from, are a further dimension of population trends that determine the need or demand for real estate.

Marketing analysis begins with identifying broad characteristics and movements, including studying and analyzing national trends in population growth, movements of people to and from different regions of the country, and identifying the characteristics of the people moving, as well as hypothesizing reasons for such movements. Regional population changes can then be more accurately predicted and the impact of population mobility translated to the community and neighborhood levels. The prime source of demographic information comes from census data.

Data from the "100 percent coverage" portion of the 1970 Census reveals some of the current trends which are potentially useful to real estate market analysts. These trends include:

1. Internal migration—shifts of the population:
   a) From rural to urban areas
   b) From central cities to suburbs
   c) Into white and nonwhite concentrations in large central cities

    d) From central geographic divisions of the nation to the coasts
    e) From South to North in the case of Negroes
    f) Among the states resulting in changes in size-rankings of the states.
2. Differing decade-rates of growth among racial groups, including:
    a) Reduced fertility and total growth rate of white populations
    b) Greater fertility and total growth rate of Negro population
    c) Extremely high total growth rates of other non-white populations.
3. Younger population.
4. Smaller family size, and reduced importance of male family heads.[8]

Shifts in population among states and regions may have dramatic effects for real estate marketeers operating in those states experiencing significant shifts. Table 11–1 shows that shifts of considerable magnitude

TABLE 11–1

Ten largest states

State	Rank: 1970	Rank: 1960	Amount	Percent of U.S. total 1970	Percent of U.S. total 1960	Percent increase, 1970 from 1960
California	1	2	19,953,134	9.8	8.8	+27.0
New York	2	1	18,190,740	9.0	9.4	8.4
Pennsylvania	3	3	11,793,909	5.8	6.3	4.2
Texas	4	6	11,196,730	5.5	5.3	16.9
Illinois	5	4	11,113,976	5.5	5.6	10.2
Ohio	6	5	10,652,017	5.2	5.4	9.7
Michigan	7	7	8,875,083	4.4	4.4	13.4
New Jersey	8	8	7,168,164	3.5	3.4	18.2
Florida	9	10	6,789,443	3.3	2.8	37.1
Massachusetts	10	9	5,689,170	2.8	2.9	10.5
Total, 10 largest states			111,422,366	54.8	54.3	+14.7

Source: *Bulletin of Business Research*, vol. 46, no. 9.

have occurred among the 10 largest states. Two of the largest, Florida and California, are also among the 10 fastest growing states (Table 11–2). In proportion to the total U.S. population, some regions are remaining stable (East North Central and West South Central regions) or are declining (Middle Atlantic, West North Central, East South Central, and New England) (see Table 11–3). The trend for increasing urbanization held true for all regions of the United States.

    The total percentage of nonwhites increased substantially during the 20-year period from 1950 to 1970, a reflection of the higher than average rate of increase in the birthrate for nonwhite as compared with the white

---

[8] James C. Yocum, "Population Changes in Two Decades," *Bulletin of Business Research*, vol. 46, no. 9, The Ohio State University (September 1971), p. 1.

TABLE 11–2

Ten fastest growing states

| | | | | Increase, 1970 from 1690: | |
State	Rank, 1970	Amount	Percent of U.S. total	Percent change	Percent of U.S. total
Nevada	48	488,738	0.3	+71.3	0.8
Florida	9	6,789,443	3.3	37.1	7.7
Arizona	33	1,772,482	0.9	36.1	2.0
Alaska	51	302,173	0.1	33.6	0.3
California	1	19,953,134	9.8	27.0	17.7
Maryland	18	3,922,399	1.9	26.5	3.5
Colorado	30	2,207,259	1.1	25.8	1.9
Delaware	47	548,104	0.3	22.8	0.4
Hawaii	40	769,913	0.4	21.7	0.6
New Hampshire	42	737,681	0.4	21.1	0.6
Total, 10 fastest growing states		37,491,326	18.5	+29.2	35.5

Source: *Bulletin of Business Research*, vol. 46, no. 9.

population. Blacks and other minorities have migrated from the southern states to the more industrialized states of the North.

The age composition of the United States during the 20 years shifted to a lower average age. Although the higher age groups also increased proportionately, the lower average age is attributable to the even higher proportions of the population in the young age categories. The age composition of the U.S. population will remain low relative to former years for several years into the future; however, the longer run prospect is for an increasing average age of the population. The rate of population growth is already decreasing, and the number of children below the age of five has dropped dramatically. As the rate of increase of the population slows, the average age of the population will increase. As the relatively large numbers of younger people in the 10 to 20 age category become older, they will tend to cause the average age to increase also.

The effects of these trends can already be noted in the real estate market, particularly in the larger cities. The increased percentages of apartments being constructed in almost every large city attests to the growing numbers of young people entering the housing market at this time. It reflects the trend of younger people waiting longer to get married, married couples waiting longer to have children and having fewer of them. The advent of apartments for singles only or for young married couples without children is simply a manifestation of these population changes. In fast-growing regions of the country, such as Florida, California, and Arizona, complete new communities are being developed with increased emphasis on apartments and condominiums

TABLE 11-3

Resident * population of United States, and geographic divisions, 1970, 1960, and 1950

| Area | (No. of states) | Total Population | | | | | | | | | | | | | Negro population: Percent of U.S. | |
| | | Number 1970 | Percent increase | | Percent of U.S. total | | | Percent urban | | | Percent nonwhite | | | | |
			1970 from 1960	1960 from 1950	1970	1960	1950	1970	1960	1950	1970	1960	1950	1970	1960
Divisions:															
E. North Central	(5)	40,252,678	11.1	19.3	19.8	20.2	20.1	74.8	73.0	69.7	10.2	8.2	6.1	17.1	12.0
Middle Atlantic	(3)	37,152,813	8.7	13.3	18.3	19.0	19.9	81.7	81.4	80.5	11.5	8.5	6.4	17.4	12.5
South Atlantic	(9)	30,671,337	18.1	22.6	15.1	14.5	14.0	63.7	57.2	49.1	21.5	22.8	24.3	28.3	33.9
Pacific †	(5)	26,525,774	25.1	40.2	13.1	11.8	10.0	86.0	81.1	74.4	11.1	8.9	5.2	6.7	3.4
W. South Central	(4)	19,322,458	14.0	16.6	9.5	9.5	9.6	72.6	67.7	55.6	16.3	16.9	17.2	13.4	16.2
W. North Central	(7)	16,324,389	6.0	9.5	8.0	8.6	9.3	63.7	58.8	52.0	5.1	4.2	3.4	3.1	2.8
E. South Central	(4)	12,804,552	6.3	5.0	6.7	6.7	7.6	54.6	48.4	39.1	20.5	22.5	23.6	11.5	17.9
New England	(6)	11,847,186	12.7	12.8	5.8	5.9	6.2	76.4	76.4	76.2	3.8	2.5	1.6	1.7	0.9
Mountain	(8)	8,283,585	20.8	35.1	4.1	3.8	3.3	73.1	67.1	44.9	5.8	5.0	4.5	0.8	0.4
U.S. Total †	(51)	203,184,772	13.3	18.5	100.0	100.0	100.0	73.5	69.9	64.3	12.6	11.4	10.7	100.0	100.0

* Total U.S. population, 1970, including U.S. citizens stationed abroad (U.S. armed forces and federal employees, and their dependents), 204,765,770.
† All 1950 figures derived from totals including Alaska and Hawaii.
Source: *Bulletin of Business Research*, vol. 46, no. 9.

which provide smaller sized units with more complete services and facilities for the occupants.

Societal trends

Many changes occur in society which result in changing living patterns, changes in class structure, changes in work conditions and life styles, and changes in the way that people use their time. Most of these changes are a result of the increasing capabilities of technology. In the area of transportation and communication, improved technology has resulted in the beginnings of mass transit systems in some cities that formerly did not have them, new road systems allowing people to live further away from their work, and better communications among all parts of the country. As new transportation systems or additions to old systems are made, real estate values in the areas affected are changed often dramatically. As many people have made the move to suburbia, their entire life style has changed or at least it has been different from what it would have been had they lived in an apartment close to the center of a city. This trend, while much maligned, would seem to offer advantages in the minds of many people, or they would not have made the decisions to live in the outlying areas. It is not surprising that many people desire to have green space, trees, and desirable surroundings for their children when they can afford it. Without the ability to transfer themselves to and from important destinations, such as work, schools, and cultural centers, few people would have had the opportunity for these types of advantages.

Improved technology has also resulted in the greater use of machines and correspondingly increasing levels of efficiency. The requirement of fewer man-hours to produce the same amount of output as previously has led to more and more people obtaining greater amounts of time free from work. Greater emphasis upon leisure living and informality has created entire new markets for outdoor recreational equipment. Color TVs, picnic tables, and charcoal grills are but a few of the products demanded to satisfy this type of living pattern. Similarly, new houses are expected to contain patios, sliding glass doors, attractive yards and recreational areas, and often a pleasant view with green areas for recreation and relaxation. Bowling alleys, golf courses, and other recreational facilities have proliferated.

The new technology has made available for many housewives such gadgets as self-cleaning ovens, dishwashers, built-in vacuum systems, automatic ice makers, electronic ranges, and many others. In short, changes in technology have shifted the society from an agricultural one to an industrialized one. An industrialized society has produced an urban society, where even rural residents have adopted and pursued the goals of their urban counterparts.

Values and attitudes

The values and attitudes adopted by a society change over time, and these changes, as well as the values and attitudes themselves, can have an important bearing upon the types of commodities, goods, and housing that people demand. Some values are associated with the entire society, while some are characteristic of subgroups or subcultures within a society. Religious groups, racial groups, members of social classes, and ethnic groups are some of these subcultures that may form their own values which vary somewhat from the overall society's values.

From the standpoint of society as a whole, some of the more important values and attitudes that seem to prevail are that leisure time is important in obtaining the benefits of the good life. One's home, and possibly his office, is an important measure of his social status. Informality in daily life and a willingness to make change are more characteristic of families today than was the case before World War II. These attitudes and values are interrelated, of course, since the importance of leisure time is reflected in the type of home that one purchases. Greater informality is reflected in smaller living rooms, larger family rooms, and patios. Also, as people are willing to make changes—to move from one section of the country to another, to change houses within the same city, and to change sources of employment—these trends are reflected in the emphasis placed upon new housing and new office buildings of every type. Only the new structures can adequately reflect the new tastes and preferences.

One of the most important types of subgroups that is important in determining demand is social class. Lloyd Warner's work in identifying social classes in U.S. cities showed that four characteristics are important in explaining class differences. These variables are income, occupation, house type, and area of residence; they produce a class structure as follows:

1. Upper class (0.9 percent of the population)
   a) Upper upper—old line, wealthy families
   b) Lower upper—socially prominent, newly rich families
2. Upper middle class (7.2 percent of the population)
   Professionals and highly successful businessmen
3. Lower middle class (28.4 percent of the population)
   Teachers, technicians, most salesmen, white-collar workers
4. Upper lower class (44.0 percent of the population)
   Skilled workers, production workers, service workers, local politicians, and labor leaders
5. Lower lower class (19.5 percent of the population)
   Unskilled laborers, racial immigrants, and people in unrespectable occupations

Social class, as any other subgrouping, holds significance for the real estate market analyst because people within one group have different needs and desires than people in the other groups. Studies by Martineau and others have shown that people in different social classes respond differently to advertising media, have differing levels of interest in products and brands, and want to be treated differently by sales personnel. Given the same number of dollars to spend, they will spend the money differently.

Implications for real estate market analysts and real estate marketers are that as the size and composition of social classes in the society and within a community change, the types of housing and other real estate demanded will change.

Values attributed to different social classes are translated into different housing needs. Upper middle class families, for example, place high value on privacy whereas upper lower class families value friendliness and openness to the community. In the first instance, high fences around yards are acceptable, while in a lower class community such physical barriers would be rejected and, in cases where erected, would be interpreted as an act of snobbishness. Dobriner illustrates in *Class in Suburbia* how hostilities arose in a new community as a result of value clashes (and in particular how values were interpreted into everyday living patterns) between two differing social classes moving into the same neighborhood.[9] Friction between the two classes ultimately led to members of one social class moving from the community.

While suburbia typically has been portrayed as an upper middle class phenomenon, in actuality the metropolis is a network of suburbs of the several class groups, with the exception of the lower lower class. Suburbs exist which are identical economically, in terms of property values and income levels of the residents, but which differ in class structure and mode of living. In the Dobriner study cited above the intermixture of two classes residing in the same community was temporary. The community, a new development, was the first Levittown constructed at the end of World War II at a time when demand for housing was exceptionally great. The houses appealed to two diverse groups, one the young middle class families who traditionally were home owners and found at that stage of the life cycle Levittown to be what they could afford, and second the working class families who accumulated enough savings during the war years to escape the crowded city and achieve for the first time the all-American dream of home ownership. While studies indicate class differences do exist, assessing their effects upon real estate development is difficult, offering a potentially fertile area for investigation.

---

[9] William M. Dobriner, *Class in Suburbia* (Englewood Cliffs, N.J.: Prentice-Hall, Inc., 1963).

National income

Along with people, who are the ultimate source of demand for real estate, must be income. Income turns potential demand into effective demand. If the people are there and they have the ability with income to purchase real estate, properties will be sold and purchased in the market. As with population, at least three levels of income must be considered and analyzed. Income trends at the national, regional, and local levels ultimately determine the effective demand for an individual parcel of real estate. To analyze income trends at the national level, one may refer to three types of accounting systems. Each of these systems is designed to provide a different type of information and is useful for different purposes. It is likely that the greatest weight in analyzing market demand will be placed upon the first system to be discussed—the gross national product/national income accounts—since the other two systems do not deal directly with income. Nevertheless, the other two systems can be useful for specialized types of analyses. As discussed in the real estate financing chapter, the flow of funds system is particularly useful in analyzing financial transactions. Similarly, the input-output accounts can be useful to an industrial real estate broker in analyzing industry trends.

Gross national product/national income accounting system. The gross national product/national income accounts provide a broad picture of national production and income. Predictions about the economic health of the country are made in terms of the gross national product (GNP). Trends in the components of GNP and national income can be analyzed to detect changing patterns of production and income. While it is not consistent with the purpose of this book to describe in detail the GNP and income accounts, several trends illustrating the use of this accounting system can be cited. Within the GNP accounts, the services category of personal consumption expenditures has been the fastest growing component. This trend is in part a result of the growing affluence of a large part of the population, combined with the relatively mature characteristic of the economy in being able to produce and provide physical goods. Investment in residential structures has been growing comparatively slowly with other categories of private investment. In fact, there was an actual decline in constant dollars in this category between 1969 and 1970. State and local government purchases of goods and services have been growing rapidly. While national defense and other federal government expenditures have held fairly level in recent years, the state and local category has increased dramatically from $79 billion in 1966 to $122.2 billion in 1970. Personal income increased very slightly from 1969 to 1970 compared with years immediately preceding.

However, personal income was considerably higher in 1971 and expanded even more during 1972. Rates of personal saving were unusually high during 1970 and 1971 but declined somewhat during 1972, as people began to buy more consumer goods.

Flow of funds. The flow of funds accounting system describes how funds or assets have been used in the economy and the sources from which they came. This system is particularly useful in analyzing financial changes in the economy, and is considered more fully in chapter 14. Some interesting trends that could be discerned from the flow of funds accounts, however, can be cited. The first of these is that the greatest percentage of funds in the economy have been used by real estate mortgages, during the decade of the 1960s. During the latter five years of the decade, however, this percentage dropped significantly. Corporate bonds and stocks increased in the percentage of funds used. Nevertheless, real estate mortgages continue to be the single most important use of funds, although the decline in importance is one that needs to be watched and analyzed by real estate market analysts. On the supply side, commercial banks have furnished the greatest proportion of funds. Savings and loan associations, while for several years being the fastest growing suppliers of funds, have leveled out in total dollar supply and have decreased in recent years in the percentage of the funds being supplied.

Input-output analysis. Input-output analysis involves the use of a table which quantifies the use of goods and services among major sectors or industries in the economy. For example, the amount of manufactured goods being used in agriculture and the amount of agricultural goods being utilized in manufacturing would show up in an input-output table. One can then trace through the amount and types of goods being used in each industry and from where they came.

Input-output tables are not available in series at the present time. However, there is increasing interest in this type of analysis, and when federal agencies are able to accumulate the type of data needed on a continuing basis, input-output tables may become available on a regular basis.

Regional income

Real estate productivity and values also depend upon the level of income within a region. The regional income and economic prospects may differ significantly from national trends. Low per capita incomes in the Appalachian region, the demise of coal mining as a major industry in southern Illinois and the consequent depression of economic activity in that area, and the great growth and prosperity in southern California during the 1960s are but a few examples of regional trends that have varied substantially from the national experience. Real estate values in depressed regions have suffered commensurately with the decline in economic activity, while values in areas experiencing greater than average growth and prosperity have increased faster than the national average.

Although it is important for the real estate market analyst to keep abreast of regional economic trends, measures of these trends are less readily attainable than for trends either at the national or local levels. Two reasons for this lack of data can be cited. First, there is no standard delineation of regions. A region has been defined as varying in size from a group of states to a section of a city. A regional breakdown for one analyst or for one government agency would not be functionally useful for another analyst or another agency. Thus, there has not been agreement on how to divide up the country for the collection of regional data.

The second reason is that the boundaries of regions are much less meaningful as determinants of economic activity. It is much easier to identify the production of goods and services within the United States and to keep track of products and services flowing into and out of the country than it is to keep track of these same flows among regions. The federal government has shown much more interest in data collection for the entire country rather than the identification of differences among regions of the country. In recent years, however, many groups have become concerned about regional analysis, and government agencies, as well as academic and professional groups, have devoted more attention to the understanding and collection of regional data.

Input-output analysis.   Input-output analysis would seem to hold some of the greatest potential as a tool for analyzing regions. While no regional input-output analysis is done on a series basis, the idea has been advocated, and indeed input-output analysis has been performed for a state. Hopefully, this tool may become operative and useful for states, and the state data could then be combined into regional groupings.

Other measures.   Without a regular system of measuring regional income and production, a market analyst must keep track of other indicators of economic activity. Personal income and buying income are estimated for states. Personal income measures can be found in *Business Week* magazine, while *Sales Management* magazine publishes estimates of buying income for states and other geographic areas in its annual "Buying Power" issue. The bureaus of business research of many state universities are also valuable sources of data on regional economic trends and prospects. State departments of development and chambers of commerce are other potential sources of statewide information.

Community income

The principal tool or method for analyzing community income and economic prospects is economic base analysis. In its original concept, economic base analysis was designed as a tool to predict future population for a community. This prediction was accomplished by identifying all sources of employment in a community and dividing the number of employees between two categories—basic and service (or primary and secondary). Basic employment is recognized as the type for which products and services are exported beyond the community's borders. Service employment redistributes the income within the community. Examples of the former type are the automobile industry in Detroit, wherefrom the community derives much of its income by the shipment of automobiles out of the city, and a large university within a city which brings income from students who come from beyond the borders of a city. Examples of the second category, or service employment, are barber shops, beauty parlors, real estate and insurance offices, and other types of service businesses that do not draw customers primarily from outside of the community. Figure 11–9 shows the various components of total community income.

A ratio is obtained between the number of basic and service employees, and then the basic sources of employment are surveyed to attempt to determine whether increases in this type of employment will be taking place in the future. Increases in service employment are then predicted in relation to the ratio between service and basic employment existing previously in the community. The total increase in population deriving from the increase in basic employment can then be projected on the basis of the ratio of total employment to total population existing in the community. For example, each new job of both basic and service types may result in an increased population of three persons. If total employment increases were estimated to be 5,000 persons for the coming year in a given community, the total population increase would be projected as 15,000 persons.

The process of surveying basic employment sources to determine planned increases in employment has proven to be an unreliable predicting method for determining future basic employment. Therefore, in carrying out economic base analyses, usually several techniques are employed to project employment in various industry classifications. In a mammoth study of the Columbus, Ohio, economic base performed during the 1960s, The Ohio State University Bureau of Business Research utilized three projection techniques. County share of U.S. total value added per employee was determined for each industry classification, and ratios were projected into the future on the basis of projected total U.S. industry projections. Secondly, manufacturers were surveyed to determine future employment expectations according to the amount of sales expected outside the community and within the community. Thirdly, input-output tables were constructed to show the interrelationships among the various industries in metropolitan Columbus. Projected sales of each in-

FIGURE 11-9

How the community earns its living

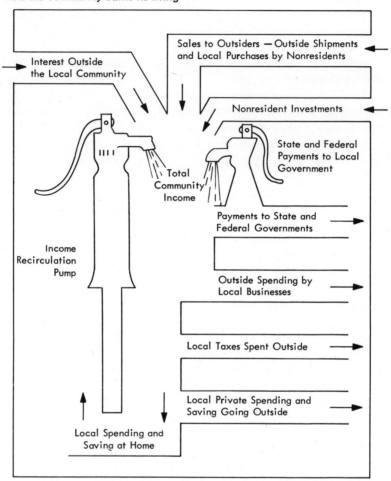

Source: Bank of America, Area Development Service, San Francisco.

dustry was then computed from the coefficients developed in the input-output matrix. Projected sales were then converted to projected employment. This large study of the Columbus economic base projected employment at various intervals 20 years into the future to 1985. A summary of this large study is contained in Appendix F.

Other measures. Buying income is estimated by *Sales Management* for metropolitan areas. The magazine also estimates the number of people in various income categories. The analyst can use these data both in comparing a community with other similar communities and in developing trends for the community under analysis. Chambers of commerce also usually maintain data on incomes and numbers of households in a community, as well as information on the number and types of industries, the number and types of commercial establishments, current and expected development in the community, and other economic measures.

The Federal Housing Administration periodically performs market analyses for metropolitan areas. These studies can be extremely useful in analyzing a real estate market. Trade and professional organizations within a community, such as a home builders association or an apartment owners and managers association, may also maintain useful data and perform market studies.

Price structure

The prices of real estate in a community also help determine the demand for real estate. The price structure refers to the relationships among prices of properties within the community and to the relationship between prices of real estate and other economic goods. If real estate prices rise relative to other goods, people who would otherwise be in the market may refrain from buying until prices seem to be more reasonable. By the same token, if people expect the prices of real estate to increase in the future relative to other goods, they may decide to purchase now rather than later.

In addition to total price, other elements of price must be considered also. The downpayments required on real estate may become more liberal or more rigorous. As money conditions tighten in the overall economy, for example, lenders often require larger downpayments than during periods of relatively easy money. Also, sometimes institutional regulations are adjusted to allow smaller downpayments. When these happenings occur, the demand for real estate is likely to be affected.

The monthly housing expense can be regarded as part of the price mechanism for residential real estate. Families must budget their housing expense, and the extent to which monthly housing expense is expected to increase can affect the willingness of families to purchase homes.

DETERMINANTS OF SUPPLY

Anticipations of demand

Perhaps the single most important determinant of supply of new real estate resources is the expectation that suppliers have of demand. If developers and builders are optimistic about the future demand, they will tend to bring forth newly created resources. If, however, they are relatively pessimistic about the coming year's demand, they will tend to hold back the level of development and construction activity. These anticipations result from forecasts of national economic activity, regional changes, and community income and economic activity.

Utilization of existing real estate resources

If the existing stock of real estate resources is not being utilized at close to its capacity, the suppliers of new real estate resources will be hesitant to bring new properties onto the market. The degree of utilization of existing resources is usually measured by the vacancy rate in residential property, the vacancy rate in office buildings, the number of square feet utilized per employee in office buildings and other commercial buildings, the sales per square foot in commercial property, and the number of employees per square foot or the income generated per square foot of floor space for industrial property. If these ratios indicate an unusually high level of unused or underused space, developers and builders will tend not to supply new properties. For residential property, the normal or average vacancy rate may run around 5 percent; this rate may go as low as 2 percent, and it may go considerably higher than 5 percent. When the rate is much above 5 percent, however, suppliers tend to reduce the amount of new development and construction.

Availability and prices of land and utilities

Suitable land must be available for development; furthermore, land must be available at reasonable prices or development will be impeded. Land by itself, however, is not sufficient. Sewage facilities, storm drains, water mains, and power sources must be available. Some of the stickiest problems of real estate development today revolve around the obtaining of proper and adequate facilities of all types. Many communities have resisted the further provision of utilities without the payment of higher fees by developers. At the same time, communities have become cognizant of the ecological damage that can potentially be done by septic tanks, the use of private water systems, and the unregulated development of new projects. Suppliers of new real estate resources today must work carefully with city planning commissions, zoning boards, city councils, other administrative bodies of local governments, and private groups of interested citizens.

Availability and price of financing

The importance of financing in real estate markets is indicated by its position as both a determinant of demand and of supply. On the supply side of the market, financing for land development and construction are at least of equal importance with the availability and relative prices of financing for long-term mortgage commitments. Most developers and contractors operate with relatively small amounts of their own capital. If development and construction financing are not available, or are available only at relatively high prices, new development and construction will be unresponsive to any needs that exist.

Availability and prices of materials and labor

In normal times, materials and labor are available to real estate developers and contractors. During times of war, however, materials may be in short supply because they are diverted to a war effort. Very little building took place in this country of nonstrategic resources during World War II and during the Korean War. The Vietnam War has seen little constriction of the supply of materials because this most recent war has been much less of a drain on our national economic resources. Undoubtedly, even this war has helped to inflate the prices of building materials above what they would be otherwise.

The prices of labor, or wages, in the construction industry have been one of the country's severe unresolved economic problems. As discussed in the chapter on real estate production, the structure for bargaining between the construction industry and the labor unions is not ideal. Unions have not received the assurances of security that their members want and need. As a substitute for security, unions have demanded wage rate increases consistently above the national average. Thus, the prices for labor in the construction industry have been inordinately high, helping to push prices of housing and other types of real estate beyond the reach of many below-average income people. Only wholesale reform in the relationships between unions and industry and in the provision of adequate security for construction workers will resolve this problem and serve to make real estate more realistically priced relative to other economic goods.

Taxes

The real estate tax and the federal income tax play an important role in influencing both the demand and supply of real estate resources. The real estate tax serves as the principal means of financing for local communities, and faced with increasing demands, these communities have continually increased the levels of real estate taxation. In recent years there has been a revolt against the payment of higher and higher real estate taxes. Furthermore, the tax has served to discourage improvements in existing properties and desirable changes in land uses.

The federal income tax has an influence on both the form and financing of capital investment. Rules governing the deductions of various expenses applicable to real estate may produce favorable or unfavorable conditions for real estate investment. Deductions for interest on a mortgage loan and for depreciation of the improvements in a real estate investment and for other legitimate expenses may make some properties relatively desirable and others less desirable. Changes in the income tax laws, as discussed in chapter 7, have changed the relative attractiveness of various types of real estate projects. No properties other than apartments today receive the benefits of the most rapid form of depreciation allowed for computing income tax—200 percent declining balance. Before the Tax Reform Act of 1969, however, other properties received this advantage.

MARKET AND FEASIBILITY ANALYSES

Market and feasibility analyses are the end results of the consideration of all the factors discussed heretofore in this chapter.[10] These studies attempt to relate all of the determinants of supply and demand to the problem of anticipating future real estate needs in a community. As such, they represent the practical application of the theory of market behavior. Whether market studies and feasibility analyses are reliable and useful is thus a function of two considerations—validity of the theory and ability to attach accurate measures to the elements and relationships of the theory.

To be reliable, market and feasibility analyses must be painstaking and thorough. Past trends and relationships may not hold for the future. The analyst may have to dig beneath the surface to find qualitative indicators of future quantitative changes. Household size may not remain steady but may decline because of a declining birthrate, greater financial independence of older and younger persons (leading to undoubling), older marriage ages, and an increasing divorce rate. To predict such a change, the market analyst must understand social trends and changes in values and attitudes, as well as economic conditions and trends.

Market analysis

A market analysis is a study designed to determine the types and quantities of additional real estate resources which can be absorbed by

---

[10] Although we discuss only market studies and feasibility studies, other types of economic studies are sometimes useful. For a discussion of a number of different types of studies, including highest and best use studies, land use studies, land utilization studies, marketability studies, reuse appraisals, and cost-benefit studies, see Anthony Downs, "Characteristics of Various Economic Studies," *The Appraisal Journal* (July 1966), pp. 329–38.

the market over a reasonable period of time. Typically, market studies are limited to an analysis of a particular type of real estate, such as housing, industrial, or commercial real estate. The predominant type of study concerns housing.

Individual businesses; industry trade groups; and governmental agencies at local, state, and federal levels have interest in market studies. Businesses with markets of national scope, such as lumber and hardware suppliers, appliance manufacturers, and home furnishers, base their budgeting procedures on the estimated aggregate demand for new real estate for the coming year. Home builders' associations usually engage in market research to help their members plan the types, styles, and price ranges of new homes to produce during the coming year. And governmental agencies need to understand the economic and social needs of their constituencies in order to formulate policies that will encourage the proper amounts and types of housing and other real estate to be produced. In short, market analysis is a planning or budgeting tool. As one well-known analyst has said, "Market analysis is a study of the reasons why prices are being paid. It has far more to do with the future than with either the present or the past." [11]

Perhaps the organization most concerned with housing market analysis is the Federal Housing Administration (FHA) of the U.S. Department of Housing and Urban Development. The FHA has developed comprehensive techniques and instructions for the undertaking of market analyses in local communities across the country.[12] The purpose of an FHA market study is to identify and measure the housing needs in a community. The FHA then uses the market study in determining which projects that it has been requested to underwrite can be absorbed by the market. Each FHA market analysis is concerned with the following broad subject areas:[13]

1. Delineation of the market area—the area within which dwelling units are competitive with one another.
2. The area's economy—principal economic activities, basic resources, economic trends.
3. Demand factors—employment, incomes, population, households, family size.
4. Supply factors—residential construction activity, housing inventory, conversions, demolitions.
5. Current market conditions—vacancies, unsold inventory, marketability

---

[11] W. A. Bowes, "What Is Market Analysis?," *The Real Estate Appraiser* (July–August 1968), p. 11.

[12] *F.H.A. Techniques of Housing Market Analysis*, FHA Economic and Market Analysis Division, U.S. Dept. of Housing and Urban Development, 1970.

[13] Ibid., p. 5. (Note: A detailed outline for FHA housing market analyses is shown in Appendix E.)

of sales and rental units, prices, rents, building costs, mortgage defaults and foreclosures, disposition of acquired properties.
6. Quantitative and qualitative demand—prospective number of dwelling units that can be absorbed economically at various price and rent levels under conditions existing on the "as of" date.

Some of the end results of a housing market analysis can be seen in Tables 11–4 and 11–5. They were compiled in a 1971 FHA housing market analysis of the Gainesville, Florida, housing market.

TABLE 11–4
Estimated annual demand for nonsubsidized housing
Gainesville, Florida, housing market area (April 1, 1971–April 1, 1973)

A. Single family

Sales price	Number of units	Percent of total
Under $22,499	85	17
$22,500– 24,499	85	17
25,000– 29,999	145	29
30,000– 34,999	100	20
35,000 and over	85	17
Total	500	100

B. Multi-famliy

Gross monthly rent *	Efficiency	One bedroom	Two bedrooms	Three bedrooms
Under $130	15	—	—	—
$130– 149	5	85	—	—
150– 169	—	40	50	—
170– 189	—	15	60	5
190– 209	—	5	35	10
210– 229	—	5	20	5
230– 249	—	—	10	5
250– 269	—	—	5	5
270– 290	—	—	5	5
290 and over	—	—	5	5
Total	20	150	190	40

* Gross rent is shelter rent plus the cost of utilities.
Source: FHA Housing Market Analysis of Gainesville, Florida.

As can be seen from the tables, housing demand is broken down between nonsubsidized and subsidized housing needs, between single-family and multifamily needs and the price classes of each, and between programs and among unit sizes for subsidized housing. By keeping track of any changes in the conditions upon which these forecasts were made and the numbers and types of units supplied during the two-year period,

TABLE 11–5

Estimated annual occupancy for subsidized rental housing
Gainesville, Florida, housing market area (April 1, 1971–April 1, 1973)

	Section 236 * *exclusively*	*Eligible for both programs*	*Public housing exclusively*	*Total for both programs*
A. Families				
1 bedroom	30	0	60	90
2 bedrooms	90	20	120	230
3 bedrooms	70	0	90	160
4+ bedrooms	40	0	50	90
Total	230	20†	320†	570
B. Elderly				
Efficiency	20	30	25	75
1 bedroom	20	10	15	45
Total	40	40‡	40‡	120

* Estimates are based upon exception income limits.
† 47 percent of these families also are eligible under the rent supplement program.
‡ All of the elderly couples and individuals also are eligible for rent supplement payments.
Source: FHA Housing Market Analysis of Gainesville, Florida.

the FHA, local builders, lending institutions, and local government agencies can determine whether housing demand is being fulfilled, whether shortages continue to exist, or whether overbuilding is occurring.

In the above example an apparent oversupply of some types of housing was being constructed. Compared with the predicted annual housing demand of 1,590 units (nonsubsidized and subsidized), 3,484 housing units were constructed during the first 50 weeks of 1971. The FHA analysis indicated an annual need for 500 single-family units and 400 multifamily units. By contrast, building permit data for 1971 showed projected construction of 760 single-family units and 2,769 multifamily units. In 1970, only 555 single-family and 105 multifamily unit building permits were issued. Certainly the evidence suggests that (1) the conditions upon which the FHA analysis was based had changed, (2) the FHA analysis was incorrect, or (3) an oversupply was developing. The FHA, local builders, and other interested organizations would want to determine which of these alternative reasons (or combination) explain the situation and to identify more precisely any submarkets that were experiencing overbuilding.

Feasibility analysis

While closely related to market analysis, feasibility analysis differs in that it deals with the acceptability and desirability of a particular real estate project. Market analysis may establish the need for more apartments of a particular type and price class in a community; whether a specific apartment project is sufficiently desirable to be absorbed by the market is another question. This question can be answered only by an intensive examination of the property's ability to meet various requirements and its relative desirability to prospective consumers.

A feasibility study involves one of three basic types of problems: [14]

1. A site or building in search of a user.
2. A user in search of a site or certain improvements.
3. An investor looking for an opportunity.

A specific hypothesis is usually advanced as to how each type of problem may be solved. A site may be analyzed to determine whether an apartment project would be a desirable type of use; an oil company may analyze an available site to determine whether a service station would be a profitable investment for the company; or an analyst may study the desirability of a shopping center investment for a client wishing to liquidate his stock holding in favor of a real estate venture. In short, a feasibility study attempts to forecast whether a particular course of action regarding a parcel of real estate fulfills the objectives of an owner-investor and meets externally or internally imposed conditions or requirements.

One of the most common objectives of an investor is that a project must produce a specified or desired rate of return. If the specified rate is the market rate of return, the capitalized value of the project will be its market value. And, as G.I.M. Young points out, if this value equals or exceeds cost, the project is prima facie justified.[15] However, prima facie justification of feasibility is not the end of a feasibility study. Other conditions and objectives may have to be met, and income may be further maximized.

The requirements which must be met by a real estate use are economic, political, legal, physical and ethical in nature. A proposed use must be consistent with market needs; may depend on convincing community officials to provide water or sewer service; and must be within the realm of permissible uses and conform to space, site planning, and design standards imposed by zoning and planning commissions. Furthermore, the site must be capable of supporting the proposed improvements; and the proposed use must meet the ethical requirements of environmental concerns, the requirements of prospective tenants and employees, and the self-imposed standards of conduct of the investor himself in providing resources that will be used usually for many years. Failure on any one of the counts is sufficient to render a proposed project "unfeasible."

---

[14] James A. Graaskamp, *A Guide to Feasibility Analysis*, Society of Real Estate Appraisers, 1970, p. 11.

[15] G.I.M. Young, "Feasibility Studies," *The Appraisal Journal* (July 1970), p. 379.

The following examples illustrate how each of these types of conditions or requirements may affect a project's feasibility:

1. A proposed 60-story office building in Cincinnati was nixed before design work was begun because a market study showed that the projected demand for high-quality office space was amply supplied for the next five years.

2. An apartment project on the outskirts of Orlando, Florida, was stymied because sewer facilities were not available to the project, and the City Commission had ruled that septic tanks were unacceptable.

3. A low-rent housing project to be constructed in a section of $20,000 to $30,000 homes in a medium-size southern city was unacceptable because the number of square feet of living space in each unit was less than required by the zoning ordinance.

4. Before the 1960s the height of Chicago's skyscrapers was limited to about 50 stories because the subsoil conditions would not support taller buildings. Newer technology developed after World War II allowed caissons to be sunk to bedrock economically, so that taller buildings could be supported. Today several buildings, including John Hancock Center, First National Bank Building, Standard Oil Building, Lakepoint Tower Apartments, and Marina Towers all exceed 60 stories. The Sears Building when completed will be the world's tallest.

5. An oil refinery which was thought to be of great economic benefit to Maine was nixed by the state because of the potential for ecological damage that would occur from oil spills and leaks.

6. A high-rise public housing building for families in Columbus, Ohio, was converted to other uses because of social and physical problems that tenants experienced by being grouped into small areas with only one elevator for access to the entire building.

In addition to meeting certain conditions and requirements, a project must be feasible in meeting other objectives, in addition to a desired rate of return. A project that does not produce tax shelter for a high-income investor would not be feasible from his standpoint. Cash flow may be important to another investor, while maximizing return on total investment may be important to another investor. Generally, the investor's objective for an overall rate of return on the total investment can be incorporated into an appraisal of the property. As one well-known real estate analyst puts it, "An apartment project is economically feasible when its projected future net income affords an investor an appropriate rate of earnings on capital and provides for its recapture." [16]

The necessity of identifying objectives of the potential owner-investor suggests that criteria need to be established to judge whether the objec-

---

[16] James E. Gibbons, "Apartment Feasibility Studies," *The Appraisal Journal* (July 1968), p. 326. Gibbons further develops the point that a carefully prepared appraisal constitutes a feasibility study—a viewpoint that would be contested by some others.

tive will be obtained. Minimum requirements should be established for tax shelter, cash flow, return on equity, or return on total investment. Sometimes, however, the objective may be less definable and the criteria less specific. One firm was willing to spend up to $1 million for a relatively small office building if the building would enhance the firm's image. It is difficult enough to define image, let alone to measure its enhancement. Nevertheless, criteria were established calling for an "air of quality" about the building, its access to view by many passing motorists, aesthetically enriching landscaping, hidden parking, and proximity to a body or stream of water. In this instance cash flow, tax shelter, and return on investment were relatively unimportant.

Sometimes it may be desirable to develop a mathematical model to measure the returns produced by alternative uses or by differing intensities of development. Singer develops such a model for identifying that intensity which provides the maximum rate of return on overall investment.[17] The model is built around the relationships between profit, value, and costs; rentable building area, gross building area, and building efficiency; and development costs, developer's profit, and investment profit.

In any type of feasibility study, the analyst should understand that his client has a problem for which he needs help in solving. A feasibility analysis that does not identify the client's objectives or establish meaningful decision criteria will produce meaningless results. A study that has not analyzed in depth the relevant variables for measuring the criteria may produce erroneous results. And a study that is undertaken with a prior positive conclusion helps neither the client nor the analyst's reputation for objectivity. Unfortunately, many feasibility studies that the authors have seen could be accused of one or all of these defects.

If the situation warrants, one of the most valuable types of advice an analyst can give a client is *not* to undertake a project—or at least how to modify a project to render it feasible. Any positive bias should be toward helping the client, not toward a proposed project. In turn, the client should grant an analyst complete freedom of objectivity. Without this freedom, the investor will likely be misled, and the analyst will find that his professional integrity is undermined.

SUMMARY

The analysis of real estate markets is facilitated by a concept or model of the way in which the market functions. An examination of the models of pure competition and pure monopoly shows that neither is applicable to real estate markets. Rather, the model of monopolistic competition, we contend, best explains how the forces of price determination operate.

---

[17] Bruce Singer, "Determining Optimum Developmental Intensity," *The Appraisal Journal* (July 1970), pp. 406–17.

Market activity can be analyzed and forecast through the determinants of demand and supply. Market analyses can be carried out that are national, regional, community, or district in scope. Markets can also be divided into submarkets on the basis of various characteristics, such as price class of property, income class of buyers, ethnic and racial composition, legal tenure of occupants (owners versus renters), and geographic location. Although a direct relationship between national economic and social trends and the value of an individual parcel of real estate is often difficult to demonstrate, careful evaluation of these factors can often provide clues about broad patterns of demand that may be developing.

Market and feasibility studies are the most commonly useful types of economic studies requiring market analysis. While market studies attempt to analyze and predict the future demand for various types of real estate and to relate the demand to existing supply, feasibility studies attempt to determine whether a particular use will fulfill the objectives of a potential investor. Additionally, a project must meet externally and internally imposed physical, legal, political, ethical, and financial conditions or requirements. One of the requirements normally is that a project be absorbable by the market.

QUESTIONS FOR REVIEW

1. What is a market? How many potential buyers and sellers must there be before a market can exist?
2. What is the role of social class in real estate markets? Can you think of some examples of the way social class affects housing patterns?
3. Are real estate markets efficient? Why or why not? How do you measure and judge efficiency?
4. Consider the population mobility trends cited in the chapter. What implications for real estate values do these trends have? What changes in the mobility trends do you anticipate in the coming 10 years?
5. How has the change from a rural to an urban society affected real estate markets and values? What do you see as the future trend of urbanization?
6. Would a proposed project that met every condition but which produced a low (say 2 percent) rate of return for the investor be considered unfeasible? Why or why not?
7. What is the relationship between a market analysis and a feasibility study? What is the viewpoint of each?
8. How is economic base analysis used in analyzing communities? What possible weaknesses do you see in using this technique?

PROBLEMS

1. Sketch diagrams reflecting pure competition and total monopoly.
2. Indicate the elements of the housing market in the U.S. that draw the mar-

ket toward each extreme, and comment upon the placement of this market on a scale between the two extremes.

3. Outline the table of contents for each of the following market feasibility studies:
    a) An apartment complex in a Chicago suburb
    b) A high-rise office building in downtown Saint Louis
    c) A shopping mall in a Houston suburb
4. Identify the major points of difference between the three study types delineated in problem 3.

REFERENCES

Beckman, Theodore N. and Davidson, William R.   *Marketing,* 8th ed. New York: The Ronald Press Co., 1967.

Dobriner, William M.   *Class in Suburbia.* Englewood Cliffs, N.J.: Prentice-Hall, Inc., 1963.

Federal Housing Administration.   *FHA Techniques of Housing Market Analysis.* Washington, D.C.: U.S. Department of Housing and Urban Development, 1970.

Graaskamp, James A.   *A Guide to Feasibility Analysis.* Chicago: Society of Real Estate Appraisers, 1970.

McCarthy, E. Jerome.   *Basic Marketing,* 4th ed., Chaps. 4 and 5. Homewood, Ill.: Richard D. Irwin, Inc., 1971, pp. 89–164.

—————————————PART IV

Development
functions

chapter 12

MARKETING REAL ESTATE

MARKETING is one of the essential functions that must be performed by every business firm. A useful good or service may be produced and financed, but if it is not distributed to the proper people or firms who will pay a fair price, the cycle of business activity has not been completed. One view (propounded mostly by marketing people) is that marketing is the most important business function of all. Marketing, this view holds, is the drive wheel of every economic enterprise. If a firm cannot identify and serve a particular demand in the economy, the other functions of producing and financing will be to no avail; the firm is doomed to failure. Of course, the same observation could be made with regard to producing and financing.

Consistent with the view of marketing as a broad, important business function is the following definition of marketing. "Marketing is the process by which the demand structure for economic goods and services is anticipated or enlarged and satisfied through the conception, promotion, exchange, and physical distribution of such goods and services." [1]

This definition implies or assumes several characteristics about markets and how to serve them. First, it suggests that demand is not creatable by a marketer. It can be magnified or pushed forward in time, but every demand function exists prior to a marketer's exploitation of it. Therefore, it is crucially important to a marketer to be able to "read" the demand structure. He must collect relevant data and analyze the data to determine what products and services can be marketed successfully.

---

[1] Marketing faculty of The Ohio State University, *Statement of the Philosophy of Marketing,* College of Commerce and Administration, The Ohio State University, May 1964.

249

Second, an existing demand structure must result from fundamental economic, social, and psychological forces all serving to mold an individual's wants and desires. Part of the job of understanding and reading markets is to understand and project the nature of the basic demand-creating forces. Knowledge about the role of society and culture and shifts in values and attitudes should assist the marketer in analyzing quantitative data.

The third implication from the definition is that the activities of marketing are extremely broad in nature. They include the formulation of ideas of new goods and services that will meet the expected demand. Ways in which the availability of these products can be made known to the public and methods by which the public can be convinced of their desirability are all part of the marketing function. Finally, the marketer is concerned with the legal and physical arrangements for the transfer of title and possession to a purchaser.

The marketing of real estate is a major function of real estate brokerage firms, land developers, and builders. Brokerage firms specialize in bringing together buyers and sellers of existing properties; land developers convert unused or agricultural land to residential or business uses, usually holding title to the land and selling parcels from their own account; and builders construct residences or business structures for sale to ultimate purchasers. Variations in the activities of these types of firms may occur. A builder may construct a building which he does not own but for which he is paid a builder's fee. A brokerage firm may have a building constructed for speculative resale from its own account. And a land development company may also do construction work and have a brokerage division. Nevertheless, they all engage in the marketing of real properties.

Other types of real estate firms—management, appraisal, counseling, and financing companies—also have a marketing function to perform. They must market the services provided by their firms. They differ from brokerage, development, and construction firms, however, in that they do not create or maintain an inventory of real properties for sale. Our analysis of the marketing function is oriented to those firms maintaining an inventory of properties, although marketing principles are applicable to other types of firms as well. Brokerage firms are the focus of analysis because marketing is the principal business function of these firms; marketing is even more important to them; it is their reason for existence.

Nevertheless, the term *marketing* carries a much broader connotation than does the term *brokerage*. Brokerage usually refers to the legal relationships—rights and obligations—among the parties to a real estate transaction. These relationships are covered in depth in chapter 9. While a knowledge of these relationships may be regarded as prerequisite to a viable marketing effort, they are not the whole story—or even most of it. Marketing, as we said before, deals with the entire process of enlarging and satisfying needs in society. It is the process by which resources are allocated in the economy.

MARKETING STRATEGY

Since a marketer cannot hope to fulfill all the needs in society, he must limit the market he hopes to serve. He must decide which needs he will try to meet, who the people are who have those needs, where they are, and when they will likely experience the need. Note that the decisions focus upon the needs and people having the needs—not upon a particular service or product.

Failure to focus upon needs has been termed marketing myopia.[2] Many examples could be cited of businesses that failed because of marketing myopia. Automobile companies such as Studebaker Corporation that did not provide those types of styling, design, engine performance, or other features the market desired have gone out of business. Ford Motor Company lost its market dominance in the 1930s because it failed to modify its styles, designs, and colors to meet market desires. *Esquire* magazine lost its dominance of the would-be sophisticate male reader-ship market to *Playboy* by not providing the desired mix of features, interviews, stories (and photographs). Railroad companies have experienced great difficulties because they did not realize they should be in the general transportation business.

In the world of real estate, many builders have failed because the properties they constructed did not have the features desired. Many apartment buildings lose tenants to other properties because the owners or managers did not regard themselves as purveyors of housing services. They did not provide the features and services desired by the market. Brokerage firms have failed because they did not project the image of security, trustworthiness, or adequate service desired by home purchasers.

Our purpose is not to emphasize the negative—to dwell on how or why firms fail. We do want to point out that failures can occur without proper attention to the marketing concept. Failures can occur from other sources as well, of course. Improper management of the production, financing, organization, or personnel functions are just as likely to produce unfavorable results. Nevertheless, marketing myopia leads to a high proportion of failures and may be difficult to diagnose.

The best defense against marketing myopia is a marketing strategy. A strategy identifies long-range objectives and the general means for achieving those objectives. In marketing, the development of a strategy requires the identification and delineation of the market or submarket

---

[2] Theodore Levitt, "Marketing Myopia," *Harvard Business Review*, vol. 38, no. 4 (July–August 1960), pp. 45–56.

that exhibits needs or desires the firm believes it can serve and the types, quantities, and prices of products or services to fulfill those needs.

Market segmentation

Identifying and delineating the market to be served involves the process of market segmentation—carving out submarkets from larger, more general markets. This process recognizes that needs and desires of consumers are not homogeneous. In the extreme, each individual would have his own private preference for any type of want-satisfying product or service. Fortunately, however, preferences can usually be grouped into market segments, or submarkets. For example, some groups of consumers prefer tooth-decay preventing toothpaste, some consumers prefer a breath sweetening product, and still others prefer a tooth whitening product. Crest, Close-up, and Pearldrops toothpastes attempt to serve each of these segments or submarkets of the larger market for toothpaste.

Similarly, real estate marketers should segment their markets. A builder cannot realistically expect to construct houses of every architectural style, size, and design in every price range for every type of purchaser in every section of the country, region, or community. A real estate broker cannot effectively serve every category of seller or purchaser. An apartment developer-owner cannot expect his building to appeal to all groups of prospective tenants.

Identification of potential submarkets should be undertaken in a systematic way. One of the best ways of undertaking this process is to construct a marketing grid.[3] Ideally, such a grid contains characteristics of one dimension on one axis and characteristics of another dimension along another axis. For example, a construction firm seeking to identify potential markets for office buildings might construct the grid in Figure 12–1 showing desired features among several types of owners or occupants.

Such a grid focuses upon the needs of potential customers, not upon specific ways of fulfilling those needs. For example, the need for variable space patterns in offices might be met with movable partitions, removable walls, or added units in modular construction. The desirability of a pleasant view might be met with an interior courtyard, a site with a natural view, or height. And climate conditioning would require a different mix of heating, cooling, and purification in New York, Miami, and Fairbanks.

A grid identifying possible submarkets for a residential brokerage firm might appear as shown in Figure 12–2.

---

[3] For a more thorough treatment of the development and construction of marketing grids, see E. Jerome McCarthy, *Basic Marketing: A Managerial Approach*, (4th ed.; Homewood, Ill., Richard D. Irwin, Inc., 1971), chaps. 2, 6–9.

FIGURE 12–1

Market grid for new office needs

Real estate and insurance officers	Attorneys	Physicians	Accounting firms	Finance companies	
X	X		X	X	Variable space patterns
		X			Special plumbing and fixtures
X	X		X		View
X			X	X	Informational service
				X	Special security arrangements
	X		X	X	Central location
X	X	X	X	X	Climate conditioning

FIGURE 12–2

Market grid for real property marketing services

Center city	North	South	East	West	NW	NE	SW	SE	
	X	X	X	X	X		X	X	Single-family residences (owner market)
		X	X	X		X	X	X	Multi-family units (rental market)
	X		X		X				High income
	X	X	X	X			X	X	Medium income
		X	X	X					Low income

A firm wishing to provide marketing services to purveyors and consumers of real estate services would find that he could serve the market for single-family residences, most of which are owner-occupied, in all sections of the city except the center and northeast areas. Multi-family units are available in all sections except the center, north, and northwest areas. High-income buyers and properties are located in the north, east, and northwest areas of the city. And the low-income market is concentrated in the south, east, and west sections. Thus, a broker wishing to serve the high-income, single-family residence market could operate in the north, east, and northwest sections of the city. He might further wish to specialize by limiting his operation to one of those areas.

The marketing mix

The second phase of a marketing strategy is development of the appropriate mix of products and/or services to be offered. After identifying markets with specific needs that can be satisfied, enlarged, or pushed forward in time, the marketer must decide how best to accomplish the marketing job. The marketing mix in some cases may be largely determined by the market and its needs. If the real estate marketer finds a low medium-income market in dire need of modern, safe, sanitary housing, he may find that the only way of economically attempting to serve this market would be through a government program, such as the Sec. 235 or 236 subsidized occupancy programs.

Usually, however, the marketer will have several alternative products and services to offer. Deciding what these products and services are and in what proportions to be offered is the objective of this step in developing a marketing strategy. The builder may offer homes of standard design in various styles and interior decoration. Or he may offer custom design and architecture in his higher priced homes. He may offer some combination—say 75 percent standard and 25 percent custom—depending upon his analysis of market needs.

The brokerage firm may specialize in the type, location, or price range of homes it lists and attempts to sell. Or it may offer a variety in each category. The decision as to the combination, however, should be made only after and in consideration of an analysis of market needs.

In addition to the types of properties to attempt to offer and sell, the brokerage firm has a choice among services to offer. It may offer only selling services for its own listings. Or it may participate in a multiple listing service and attempt to sell the listings of other firms as well. A firm may offer insurance along with its marketing service. It may also offer other real estate services, such as appraisal, management, or counseling. Its marketing service could include financial analyses for income properties, inspection and appraisal services for prospective purchasers, or a trade-in program for sellers wishing to purchase another property. Other possible services may come to mind. Whether they are provided or not should be a conscious decision of the firm's marketing strategy.

Marketing properties or service?

The discussion relating to the development of a marketing strategy suggests that there is more involved to the marketing of real estate than simply listing properties for sale and making the list available for public perusal. Indeed, with multiple listing services, all brokerage firms in a community have essentially the same list of properties for sale as does one's favorite firm. Within a given market, every firm has the same function—to help expedite and consummate transactions of real properties. For fulfilling this function a commission is paid.

Since a number of firms within a market attempt to achieve the same objective, the degree of success of any individual firm will be largely dependent upon *how* it goes about its pursuit of the objective, first in terms of internal management of the firm and second in ability to attract buyers and sellers. The first type of activity involves recruitment and training of personnel, cost accounting, control procedures, and so forth. A firm may be able to consummate a high volume of sales, and yet receive a small return for its services because of unwise expenditures of time and money in the running of the business. The second type of activity, attracting buyers and sellers, is crucial to the survival (or maintenance) of the business and is the focus of this chapter. The nature of the competition suggests that the firm itself must be marketed. The firm must convince potential customers through deed and word that it provides a better service—or at least a different service—than other firms serving the same market.

Through previous discussion in the book and in what follows we are saying that two markets are relevant to the real estate middleman—the market for the product and the market for the services of real estate middlemen. Real estate markets and the marketing function presumbly would exist even without broker-middlemen. The broker-middleman's role should be viewed as a facilitating, expediting, convenience-rendering function which causes the market to work *better,* but which in itself does not "make the market."

Firms as monopolistic competitors. The economic analysis of the product in chapter 11 developed the contention that the real estate market, whereby the product is land and its improvements, best fits the model of monopolistic competition. Many parcels of real estate are sold and purchased each day, and each parcel is different from every other parcel. Each parcel is imperfectly substitutable for others, but each parcel usually is in competition with other parcels that are to some degree substitutable for it. Since there is effective competition among various parcels, the demand curve for one parcel may shift left as other substitutable parcels are brought onto the market. True monopoly prices will not be available in a well-functioning market, but purchasers will pay for perceived differential advantages of one property over another.

The model of monopolistic competition would seem also to fit many of the markets for the services of real estate firms. Particularly in the field of residential brokerage, this model realistically describes the market structure: many small firms in a community, each seeking to differentiate its service, vie for a share of the market. To a limited extent a firm may build up a loyal clientele; but as other firms enter the market (in a static economy), an individual firm's demand curve will shift to the left.

Firms as oligopolists.   Some real estate markets, particularly those in-volving large, special purpose properties, are served by fewer, larger, more specialized firms. Commercial and industrial brokerage firms typi-cally are more specialized, larger, and fewer in number than are resi-dential brokerage firms. These markets and some residential markets, both for the product and for the services of the firms, may more ap-propriately be described by the model of differentiated oligopoly.

FIGURE 12–3

Differentiated Oligopoly

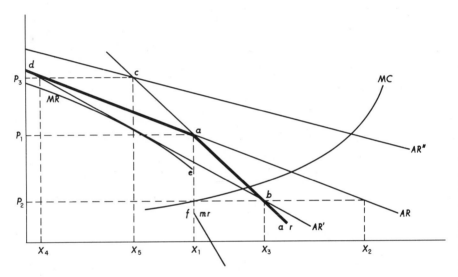

Differentiated oligopoly may be regarded as a special case of mono-polistic competition. The difference is that there is even greater inter-dependence among the larger firms. This interdependence leads to the belief by a firm that if it lowers its price, other firms will follow suit. If, however, it raises its price, other firms will not. Whether in fact other firms behave according to these beliefs is irrelevant to the way in which a firm perceives its demand function. Its pricing policy and determina-tion of level of operation will be decided on the basis of its assumptions about the actions other firms will take in response to its own pricing policy and level of operation. These assumptions lead to the perception of a kinked demand curve, as shown in Figure 12–3, and lead to a stable pricing policy even in the face of changing costs, changing demand, or changing competitive conditions.

The demand curve of Figure 12–3, *AR*, assumes equilibrium with other firms. If the firm reduces its price, however, other firms are expected to follow suit, so that the firm's demand function is shifted left to *AR′*. Thus, the firm can sell only X_3 units of output rather than X_2. By similar analysis, a price rise by the firm to P_3 would result in the firm's being able to sell only X_5 units—*if* other firms followed suit and the new demand function *AR″* were developed. The points *a, b, c* produce the firm's effective demand curve—the curve relevant to the assumptions of competitors' responses to price changes.

The firm believes, however, that competing firms will not raise prices in response to a price increase. Rather, competing firms would hold prices and increase profits by capturing a much larger share of the total market. The demand curve *AR″* would not occur and thus the relevant demand curve for the firm is the kinked line, *d a b*. *MR* is the marginal revenue curve relevant to *AR* and *m r* is the marginal revenue curve relevant to *a r*. The firm will operate at level X_1 because *MC* (marginal cost curve) intersects the discontinuous portion of the *MR–m r* curve.

Since the discontinuity in the *MR* function offers a range of values for the *MC* curve to intersect, costs can change and the firm will still operate at the same level and charge the same prices as previously; *MC* will still intersect the *e f* discontinuity. Furthermore, the demand function may increase and leave price unchanged. So long as the *MC* curve intersects the new discontinuity, the firm can continue to charge the same price and sell more units of output.

These characteristics of differentiated oligopoly explain the market behavior of many real estate firms. Average total costs can vary substantially without inducing a firm to alter its level of operation. Advertising, telephone, transportation, entertainment, and other expenses can be higher than normal for several months before the real estate firm would decide to reduce its sales force or move to a less desirable location. Increased demand will result in increased business at the same price structure. The firm can take advantage of the demand change at the same commission rate(s); but it believes that if it increased rates, other firms would not follow suit and most of the brokerage business would go to them.

Price fixing. To avoid the traumatic results of price competition, many real estate firms formerly adhered to a schedule of suggested commission rates promulgated by a local trade or professional group—usually a board of Realtors. Recently the practice of requiring or even suggesting a standard structure of commission rates has been attacked by the U.S. Department of Justice and by private individuals. Suits to require an end to such practices have been filed under both the Sherman Anti-Trust Act and the Clayton Act against boards of Realtors and groups of brokers in a number of cities.

Two outstanding examples of such actions are the suits against all real estate brokers in Los Angeles County and the Atlanta Real Estate Board. The Los Angeles suit was filed by a private couple as a $750 million antitrust class action, seeking damages for themselves and all other home buyers. The Atlanta suit was filed by the U.S. Department of Justice.

A typical result of these suits is probably indicated by the agreement in early 1972 of the Atlanta Real Estate Board to accept a consent judgment from the Department of Justice. The judgment prohibits the fixing or recommending of commission rates or fees. It further requires the Board not to take any punitive action against anyone for failing or refusing to charge any particular commission or fee in connection with the sale, lease, or management of real estate.[4]

Developing monopolistic advantage

The theories of monopolistic competition and differentiated oligopoly, as well as the need for a marketing strategy, suggest that a real estate marketing firm should attempt to carve out an area of operation that it can serve as well or better than any other firm. Realization that the firm must market its own services, not just a list of properties, also suggests the need for specialization and differentiation of its services. In other words, the firm needs to offer that combination of products and services that will be most useful to its target submarket.

The purpose of specializing and differentiating markets and services is, of course, to develop a monopoly advantage in one area of operation. A monopoly advantage will produce a profit above the minimum wage level as long as the firm is able to maintain its market position. As one real estate analyst has stated, "The ultimate objective of the firm within a free enterprise system is to create a monopoly to some extent either in fact or in the mind of the consumer."[5] Or as a marketing expert has put it, "The real dough is in what economists call monopoly profits. I don't mean in a restrictive sense. I mean being first, the guy who skims the cream."[6]

As demonstrated in the previous section, the firm engaged in real estate marketing competes in a market for services, as well as in a market for real properties. Therefore, marketing strategy should be formulated with respect to the functions involved in the firm's entire operation. Through advertising, public relations, quality of personnel, management efficiency, and selling techniques (as well as by segmenting markets), the firm can be different or more efficient than other firms performing the

---

[4] *Realtor's Headlines,* Washington, D.C., National Association of Real Estate Boards (January 10, 1972).

[5] James A. Graaskamp, *A Guide to Feasibility Analysis* (Chicago: Society of Real Estate Appraisers, 1970), p. 35.

[6] Theodore Levitt, *Sales Management* (October 1, 1965), p. 32.

same economic function. The job of top management, including marketing management, in a real estate firm is to perform the long-range planning necessary to identify target submarkets of properties and services, and to determine the appropriate mix of properties and services for these markets. Developing the appropriate mix of services can be accomplished by analyzing each of the following areas.

Advertising. This activity is one which every businessman must engage in to some extent or another. Good advertising practices and techniques can often mean the difference between a successful firm and one that is less than successful. In the advertising function, as we will maintain for the remaining four areas, the marketer of real estate products and services should keep in mind that his objective is to establish a monopolistic advantage. That is, he wants to formulate his advertising program and the content and nature of the advertising in such a way that perspective clients will tend to prefer his firm over others.

In carrying out that advertising function, the principal purposes of the advertising will be to gain attention for the firm and to present specific properties which the firm has listed for sale to the public. These two types of advertising are called firm advertising and specific advertising. Another type of advertising, institutional advertising, has as its purpose the popularizing of real estate in general. It is usually carried on by a trade or professional group. For example, the National Association of Real Estate Boards carries on a fairly extensive advertising campaign to promote real estate and the term *Realtor*. Similarly, local real estate boards often promote real estate activity and the dealing with members of the local board when purchasing or selling real estate.

In seeking to establish a monopolistic advantage in this area of activity, the broker-manager should consider how to use the various advertising media available to him. Most real estate firms rely heavily upon newspapers and signs for their advertising efforts. However, other media such as radio, television, posters, direct mail, streetcar and bus cards, calendars, office displays, letterheads, pencils, and matchbooks are additional possible media that can be used. Newspaper advertising is most appropriate for specific advertising, where the broker-manager wishes to present various properties that he has for sale to public notice. This type of advertising, however, also provides an important opportunity for the broker to engage in name advertising. A unique name or initials can be used for effective public identifications. For example, through successful advertising and promotion, the Harley E. Rouda Company in Columbus, Ohio, has become known as HER. This symbol has become identified with a fast-growing, progressive firm. The initials appear in bold print on all advertising media used by this firm.

The choice of advertising media will also depend upon the market segment that the firm wishes to exploit. For example, brokers dealing in very expensive residential properties may want to advertise in the *Wall*

Street Journal, where executives with high incomes may be likely to notice the advertisement. Firms catering to particular ethnic groups may advertise in newspapers serving those groups. Some firms in university cities seek to serve university-related personnel and may advertise heavily in the campus newspaper. In all of these kinds of advertising efforts, an effective analysis of the objectives and the media to accomplish those objectives will often mean the difference between a favorable public image being developed in the public mind and a lack of public identification.

Public relations. Public relations can be defined as constituting all of those activities in which the businessman and firm come in contact with the public. The real estate marketer needs to realize that a public image of himself and his business is built up over a period of time in the public mind. All external activities of the firm, such as advertising, attendance at public meetings, statements made on public issues, his and the firm's dealing with clients, quality of the sales force, attractiveness and neatness of the office facilities, and manner of dress and personal appearance all blend together to create a public image of the businessman and his firm. The businessman should consider all of these activities and whether they are helping to create the type of public image desired. Is the image desired, for example, that of a dynamic, progressive, fast-growing firm, or is the desired image one of stability—an old line, conservative firm?

In attempting to establish a public image, the use of a theme, as well as a unique name or initials, may be helpful. Such a theme might emphasize the friendliness or courteousness of the firm's staff. Or it might emphasize the high volume of sales created by the firm. In a subtle way, a theme can quickly and efficiently help establish the public image desired.

Quality of personnel. The real estate broker-manager needs to consider the capacity and efficiency of his sales force. How well educated and trained are the sales associates who meet with and deal with the public? This question needs to be considered in relation to the market being served. For example, an extremely high level of education may not be required to perform the sales function efficiently. A Ph.D. degree, or even a master's degree is certainly not required in most brokerage operations—unless the office or the salesman specializes in a clientele of physicians, lawyers, or college professors!

Too often sales personnel are chosen on the basis of the number of people they presumably know. Little thought or attention is traditionally given to a prospective salesman's education level, his knowledge of art and music, his level of success in other fields, or even his aptitude for sales work. With the growing sophistication of real estate investors, however, a background that includes a good education and the ability to converse intelligently on a variety of subjects is becoming more important than the number of people that a particular salesman can call by their first names. It is often possible, we contend, to train and develop a good salesman from a well-educated, personable background; the reverse process is much more difficult.

The objective of personnel policies in a real estate marketing office should be to attract, train, and retain competent people who will take a *professional* approach to the sales function. This approach requires that sales personnel analyze prospective buyers, as well as the properties that they have listed for sale. It means that they should be aware of and should use the steps in the buying process as described later in this chapter. It means that they must be aware of investment principles and what constitutes good investment and bad investment practice. It requires a desire to study continually to upgrade one's competence in helping clients solve their real estate problems. It takes a longer run point of view than many salesmen seem to have. It should emphasize the buildup of a clientele over a period of time, rather than maximizing the number of sales in any one month. If the sales person develops an attitude of trying to help people solve real estate problems, he will indeed be successful over the long run.

Management efficiency. Very few firms can be successfully and profitably operated for long without fairly good reporting and control. A sizeable portion of the broker-manager's time should be spent in analyzing the performance of his firm as it relates to forecasted performance levels. Thus, budgeting and meaningful reports are essential.

Sales performances by individual sales personnel should be analyzed regularly. Such items as the number of hours spent by each salesman in the office, the time spent in transportation, the time spent in open houses, the time spent in analyzing potential customers, the geographic locations served by the salesman, the length of time that he has been with the firm, and his educational level are all important items that should be correlated to the sales performance being rendered.

This type of analysis should be undertaken with the view of helping the sales force to do a better, more professional job of marketing real estate. Reports and control devices should not be used with the objective of checking up on or taking punitive action. A salesman who has been employed by a firm for more than a probationary period should be considered a permanent part of the firm, and should not be subject to dismissal except in very unusual circumstances. Thus, the objective of management efficiency should be positive rather than negative; it should seek to develop ways in which greater service and more productivity can be attained but should not be a tool for penalizing members of the sales force.

Selling techniques. The development of selling techniques can be overemphasized. A book answer to every possible objection, a canned sales approach, and a particular time schedule for increasing the pressure on every prospect will all lead to an unthinking, unprofessional approach to real estate marketing. Rather, selling techniques should be related to the roles played by various parties in a real estate transaction, as described later in this chapter. The salesman needs to understand these roles and seek to analyze potential buyers in terms of whether they are actual buyers, influencers, users, or a combination of several. Furthermore, the salesman needs to analyze potential buyers in terms of the stage in the buying process in which they happen to be. Some buyers will be going through the stage of prepurchase activity. It would be a mistake to ask such a person to close a sale when he has not completed this stage of activity and is not yet ready to make a purchase decision. Furthermore, the professional salesman needs to consider the long-run needs of the client relative to the properties available for sale and also relative to what the potential buyer says that his needs are. It may be, for example, that a family says that it needs a three-bedroom house. And such a house might be adequate for one or two years. If the salesman has reason to believe that the family may have need for a larger house within a couple of years, he should point this out and attempt to have the family upgrade the size of house they consider for purchase. Similarly, if he believes that a client needs a smaller or less expensive property than he is considering, the sales person should encourage the prospective buyer to scale down his desires.

Books have been written about the ways that sales personnel can overcome objections of buyers. Such an approach has little to commend it for two reasons: first, a buyer may have legitimate reasons why he does not consider any particular property appropriate for him. He may not like the design, the architecture, or the interior arrangement of the property. To try to overcome such an objection when it is real and legitimate does not serve the buyer in a professional manner. Second, such an approach assumes that a stock answer to an objection will be satisfactory to everyone. Obviously, no stock answer will satisfy all potential buyers, and a great injustice is done to the art of salesmanship in trying to get by on stock answers. Again, if the philosophy of trying to help people solve real estate problems prevails, the salesman will attempt to discuss the disadvantages as well as the advantages of a property with a potential buyer. By gaining the confidence of the buyer, the salesman will ultimately be able to consummate a transaction with a happy, satisfied client. To high pressure a buyer into a purchase which he is regretful about afterwards is to win a battle but lose the war.

THE BUYING PROCESS

The goal of the marketing effort is to produce a consummated transaction with a satisfied buyer. After developing a viable, consistent marketing strategy in both the market for properties and the market for marketing services, the marketing executive hopes the sales force will be able to convince individual members of the market that the services and properties offered by the firm are worthy of purchase. The analysis to this point helps to identify these individuals and their needs; it does not help in developing an approach to consummating a transaction. This step results from completion of the stages in the buying process.

Stages in the buying process [7]

Every buyer experiences several phases during the time that he is considering a major purchase. Each phase may be short lived or extended over weeks or even months. Nevertheless, the successful completion of each stage is prerequisite to a successful transaction.

Felt need. The buying process begins when a consumer experiences a need. He realizes for one reason or another that he may require a new home, office, or commercial facility. The need for a different home may be felt because of an impending family addition, a job transfer to another city, or the desire to upgrade or change location. Whatever the source, experiencing the need produces a state of tension in the potential buyer—a feeling that a problem requires resolution.

Prepurchase activity. The person, as a result of a felt need, becomes sensitive to advertising, bits of news, educational programs, experiences of others, and other cues in his environment which may bring him closer to satisfying the need. During the stage of prepurchase activity, the potential buyer's perception becomes tuned in to differences in sizes, styles, designs, location, price, and other characteristics; he learns and accumulates experience.

This is the stage during which the real estate marketer should provide information—not only about available properties, but about the entire purchase process. For most new buyers, and many older buyers as well, the purchase of a home is a traumatic experience. The more they can learn about the process, the greater will be the possibility of overcoming their fears and consummating the sale.

Prepurchase activity can be used to create a sequence of changes in the buyer's state of mind that bring the buyer closer to the act of purchase. The buyer proceeds from a state of awareness of his need and the necessity to satisfy it to knowledge about various alternative properties that could fulfill the need. He then begins to like one or several properties and develops a preference for one over the alternatives. The preference ripens into a conviction that one property can best satisfy the need and relieve his state of tension. Conviction leads to purchase.

---

[7] For a thorough analysis of buyer behavior, see Philip Kotler, *Marketing Management: Analysis, Planning, and Control* (Englewood Cliffs, N.J.: Prentice-Hall, Inc., 1967), Chap. 4.

Purchase decision. The decision to purchase is made in relation to the amount of risk perceived by a consumer. This depends on the degree of subjective certainty that he will do well by making the purchase. One tries to reduce this risk by gathering information and making comparative judgments as to the amount of risk involved among various alternatives. The purchase decision is in effect the manifestation of favorable prepurchase activity.

Use behavior. The buying process is not completed by the purchase decision. In some respects the consumer's "buying" has just begun. He must study and learn how to use the property just purchased; he must learn various aspects of its use, such as how the dishwasher works, when to pay taxes, how to get the porch fixed, and so on. The broker can be very helpful during this stage by anticipating the types of questions a buyer will have and taking the initiative in providing that type of information. The property purchased should be viewed as part of the consumption system; it is the means by which the purchaser of the property attempts to meet his needs.

Postpurchase feelings. A buyer usually sees his purchase as both a reward and a punishment. It is a reward because it helps to satisfy his felt need. He has gone through a lengthy process of buying the property, and the new home is the end result of all the time, effort, and money expended. But it is also punishment because the purchaser continues to have doubts as to the wisdom of the purchase. He wonders whether he should have gone so far into debt, whether the house will be adequate for a growing family, whether the family should have gotten along a little longer in an apartment and gotten into better financial shape before purchasing a home. He becomes aware of the opportunity costs—the passing up of alternative uses of his resources—during the postpurchase stage.

The anxiety experienced during this stage has been termed cognitive dissonance. The dissident feelings that occur following a purchase can be allayed by an effective real estate broker, and will produce a satisfied customer—and a potential client for the future. The broker should reassure the buyer by visiting him, introducing him to the neighbors, pointing out the favorable aspects of the property, and perhaps giving him a housewarming gift. This should be regarded as one of the most effective ways of building a satisfied clientele—people who will recommend the broker to others and who will call the broker when they wish to sell.

Buying process roles

Different roles may be assumed by the various parties concerned with a real estate purchase. In a home-buying situation, one member of the family may dominate and be the principal decider. Yet, if one member dominates in that decision (say, the wife), another member (the husband) may dominate in another decision—e.g., the city where the family will live.[8] In the purchase of business real estate, the company president may be the final decider but only after receiving advice from others in the firm. Other functions in the process may be undertaken by different persons. Kotler groups these activities into the roles of influencers, deciders, buyers, and users.[9]

Influencers are those who provide information, persuade, or stimulate a buyer during any stage of the buying process. Salesmen, advertising media, and friends are examples of some influencers. Some part of the real estate advertising budget should be aimed at those who will influence buyers. Children are often important influencers of parents who are deciding whether or which home to purchase. Yet, how often do real estate salesmen discourage children from speaking up or expressing their opinions? Sometimes they are encouraged to remain outdoors while the parents tour the property. The salesman may be passing up an opportunity to direct some marketing effort toward some important influencers!

Deciders make the actual decision. It may be the wife who decides she likes one house better than another. It may be the husband's decision; or it may be a democratically formed family decision. The real estate marketer would do well to try to identify the decision maker(s) in every buying situation and address a great deal of effort to that person or persons.

Those who make the actual purchase are termed the buyers. The buyer may be a different person than the decider, for example, a child sent to the store to buy a carton of milk for her mother. For most real estate transactions both husband and wife are the buyers, since both usually sign the contract and/or deed. If, however, the buyers are different from the deciders, more attention should be directed to the deciders.

If someone uses or consumes a product or service, he is a user. As with the buyer, the user may be someone different from the decider. The person who receives a gift or the employee who uses the facilities provided by his employer is a user but not a decider. The user, however, may be a strong influencer, and marketing effort directed to the user who is also an influencer may pay off handsomely. Apartment dwellers who complain to the landlord about the noise level between apartments will induce the landlord to desire better soundproofing in his next apartment building investment. Workers who experience difficulty in performing tasks in a building with inadequate lighting will likely influence their employer to modify the lighting system. Supportive communication should be addressed to such users-influencers to make them aware of the availability of more adequate facilities.

---

[8] James F. Engel, Hugh G. Wales, and Martin R. Warshaw, *Promotional Strategy* (Homewood, Ill.: Richard D. Irwin, Inc., 1967), p. 62.

[9] Kotler, *Marketing Management*, pp. 79–80.

Benefits of buying process analysis

Analysis of the stages in the buying process through which a buyer progresses and the roles played by various parties to a real estate purchase can be quite rewarding. Perceptive insight can tell the salesperson who the decider is, who the influencers are, and who the users are likely to be. He can then direct the appropriate sales message to each person.

By attempting to understand which stage of purchase a prospective buyer is in, the salesperson will be better able to direct the appropriate type of information to the prospect. If the prospect is still in the prepurchase activity stage, the prospect will likely be turned off if the sales person attempts to close the sale; the buyer has not yet completed the information gathering and analysis necessary to make a decision.

Similarly, the salesperson may gain many new clients if he understands the significance of postpurchase feelings. By allaying fears and concerns after a purchase, the salesperson makes a satisfied, convinced buyer who will use that salesperson the next time he needs to buy or sell and who will recommend the salesperson and firm to his friends. It should be realized that a postpurchase gift by itself does not perform the function of allaying cognitive dissonance.

The selling job

Development of a marketing strategy, understanding the stages of buyer behavior, and analyzing the roles that individuals play in the buying process are all important, and even crucial, to a successful marketing effort. However, they do not accomplish the actual job of selling—finding individual buyers, persuading them to purchase, and seeing that they are satisfied. This is the job of the individual salesman.

The actual techniques of selling are as varied as individual salesmen. Each salesman must develop his own selling approach based upon his own personality, philosophy, and training. Nevertheless, we can identify the steps that a real estate salesman should go through. They include:

1. Find and meet prospective buyers and sellers of properties.
2. Orient selling techniques to concerns of the individual buyer or seller.
3. Provide information and advice—help the seller list or the buyer buy.
4. Answer questions and objections.
5. Provide assurance about doubts
6. Show several acceptable properties to a buyer—help him compare.
7. Help indecisive buyers make up their minds.
8. Close the sale—ask the buyer to sign a contract.
9. Suggest steps the buyer should take before closing the transaction.

Include the purchase of complementary items, such as insurance, that the buyer may purchase from the brokerage firm.
10. Assure the buyer's satisfiaction; allay cognitive dissonance after the purchase.

These steps may seem obvious; but how many purchases can you recall in which the salesperson did not follow them? Unfortunately, they are all too often ignored or misapplied. Some sales personnel have never been exposed to them or have not been instructed in how to implement them. These responsibilities must also be borne by marketing management.

LEGAL FRAMEWORK OF REAL ESTATE MARKETING

Most real estate transactions are effected by middlemen, licensed by the state, whose relationship to their principals is that governed by the law of agency. The law of agency requires that an agent, such as a real estate broker, in effect stand in the shoes of his employing principal. Thus, a real estate agent must be careful to protect the interests of his client and do nothing that would compromise the probability of consummating a transaction. He must exercise the restraint of a "prudent man" in protecting the interests of his client. He cannot, for example, purchase the property from his client and then resell the property at a higher price, pocketing both the commission and the profit on the transaction.

A real estate agent's principal to whom the agent owes legal fealty is normally the owner of the property. As discussed in chapter 9, the owner hires a real estate broker to attempt to sell his property. And it is the owner who agrees to pay a commission to the broker if he is successful in finding a buyer who is "ready, willing, and able" to buy the property on the terms specified by the seller or on terms he agrees to accept. In most cases a transaction is not actually required to take place before the seller is liable for the commission.

The terms of the sale that the seller is willing to accept and other aspects of the relationship between the seller and agent are usually spelled out in a written listing contract. The listing is the legal document that gives the broker the right to attempt to sell the property. Upon agreement by a seller and purchaser, each signs a contract verifying and legalizing the agreement. The contract must be in writing to be enforceable and should cover all the important concerns to both buyer and seller. Listings and contracts, as well as other important documents and legal requirements are discussed thoroughly in chapter 9.

SUMMARY

Intelligent marketing is crucial to the success of every business firm. For those firms operating in a market characterized by effective competition, intelligent marketing requires the development of a marketing strategy. Identifying markets or submarkets having needs and devising the proper services or products to meet those needs are the components of strategy development.

Although the real estate market, including the market for properties and the market for the services of marketing firms, often fits the model of monopolistic competition, the marketing of larger, more specialized types of properties may better fit the model of differentiated oligopoly. Price leadership and inflexibility are characteristic of these firms. To avoid the ravages of price competition, oligopolists often attempt to adhere to previously agreed upon price schedules. Such practices in the real estate business are currently under attack by the federal government.

The job of marketing real estate can be analyzed in terms of buyer behavior and the roles that individuals play during the buying process. The stages of felt need, prepurchase activity, purchase decision, use behavior, and postpurchase feelings are sequential steps through which a purchaser of a major item progresses. It is helpful to a real estate marketer to know which stage a buyer may be in and to know what roles are played in a group purchase. In addition to the final decision maker, there may be influencers, an actual purchaser (as distinguished from the decision maker), and users.

A marketing strategy and analyses of buying stages and roles are useful, often indispensable, components of the marketing function. They do not guarantee success however. Only effective implementation of them by each member of the sales force can produce the desired results. To implement strategy and analysis, the real estate sales person should carry through several basic steps, tailoring them to the individual customer with whom he is dealing. His selling techniques should be determined by his own personality and his firm's policies and training procedures.

Real estate marketers operate within the legal framework of the law of agency and use several types of documents and procedures described at length in chapter 9.

QUESTIONS FOR REVIEW

1. What is the difference between real estate marketing and brokerage?
2. What is a general definition or concept of strategy? Are other types of strategy relevant to real estate firms? If yes, what are they?
3. What kinds of information would be required to identify appropriate submarkets for a new construction firm? for a new brokerage firm? for a new appraisal-investment analysis firm? for a new property management firm?
4. What would be some potential different marketing mixes for a residential construction firm? a residential brokerage firm? an industrial brokerage firm?
5. How would a salesperson's approach differ between a buyer who is believed

to be in the prepurchase activity stage and the same buyer who is in the felt need stage?

6. How would a salesperson's approach differ between a decider and a buyer (assuming they are different individuals)?

7. What do you believe should be the role of a "sales manager" in a real estate marketing firm?

8. What types of analyses might a sales manager want to make and what types of information would he need to make such analyses? What types of reports from the sales personnel would he require for these analyses?

PROBLEMS

1. Diagram graphically the buying process.

2. Comment upon problems of the selling job that appear to be unique to the real estate sales person.

3. Identify the actions of real estate boards that have led recently to charges of price fixing.

4. Indicate three bases upon which a real estate broker can negotiate commissions effectively.

REFERENCES

Case, Fred E. *Real Estate Brokerage.* Englewood Cliffs, N. J.: Prentice-Hall, Inc., 1965.

Engel, James F., Kollat, David T., and Blackwell, Roger D. *Consumer Behavior.* New York: Holt, Rinehart & Winston, Inc., 1968.

Hadar, Josef. *Elementary Theory of Economic Behavior,* Chaps. 5, 6, 7 and 8. Reading, Mass.: Addison-Wesley Publishing Co., 1966, pp. 53–158.

Kotler, Philip. *Marketing Management: Analysis, Planning, and Control,* Chaps. 3–5. Englewood Cliffs, N. J.: Prentice-Hall, Inc., 1967, pp. 43–123.

McCarthy, E. Jerome. *Basic Marketing: A Managerial Approach,* 4th ed. Homewood, Ill.: Richard D. Irwin, Inc., 1971.

chapter 13

REAL ESTATE PRODUCTION

THE REAL ESTATE INVESTOR usually can choose among properties that already are in existence or properties that can be created to his specifications. The principles and procedures governing any type of real estate investment, along with the legal and market framework, discussed previously, are now brought to bear upon the production of new properties.

Real estate production can conveniently be classified into two principal phases—land development and construction. Land development concerns all those steps taken to prepare raw land for building or improvement. Included in this phase are land procurement, land planning, land preparation, installation of utilities, and installation of streets and curbs. Construction of buildings can then follow. Included in the construction phase are plannng the building, contracting for its construction, and managing the construction process. In most production operations both phases must be financed; typically each phase is financed separately. Administration of the financing function is discussed in chapter 14.

Economic significance

Real estate production is one of the most important segments of the national economy. New construction in the United States (including land development) was 10.6 percent of gross national product (GNP) in 1965 and 9.4 percent in 1970 (see Table 13-1). In addition to new construction, maintenance and repair on existing structures serves to raise the value of total construction to about 15 percent of GNP. Investment in new residential and nonresidential structures is the principal component

TABLE 13–1

Value of construction and gross national product (in billions)

	1965	1970
GNP	684.9	974.1
Total new construction	72.3	91.3
Percent of GNP	10.6	9.4
New private construction	50.3	63.1
Percent of GNP	6.9	6.5

Source: *Federal Reserve Bulletins*, October 1971, pp. A65, A71, and November 1969, p. A68; U.S. Bureau of the Census, *Statistical Abstract of the United States: 1971* (92d ed.; Washington, D.C., 1971) pp. 657, 660.

of gross private domestic investment in the GNP accounts (see Table 13–2). Also, a measure of the importance of the construction industry is the fact that roughly 3.5 million people are employed in the production of real estate resources and several million more are employed in related industries that manufacture products that become components of new properties.

Implications of theory

Elasticity of supply. Chapter 11 was concerned with the interaction of demand and supply forces in the market. It was pointed out that the

TABLE 13–2

Value of new construction put in place in the United States: 1955–1970

Type of construction	Value in millions of dollars			
	1955	1960	1965	1970
Total new construction	46,419	53,941	72,319	91,266
Private construction	34,804	38,078	50,253	63,079
Percent of total	(74.8)	(70.6)	(69.5)	(69.1)
Residential buildings (nonfarm)	21,877	21,706	26,268	29,273
Nonresidential buildings	7,611	10,149	16,592	22,292
Farm construction	1,385	1,321	189	—*
Public utilities	3,770	4,621	5,788	—*
All other private	161	281	416	946
Public construction	11,715	15,863	22,066	28,187
Percent of total	(25.2)	(29.4)	(30.5)	(30.9)
Buildings	4,462	5,511	7,875	10,657
Highways and streets	3,852	5,437	7,550	9,989
Military facilities	1,287	1,366	852	791
Conservation and development	701	1,175	2,019	1,919
Other public construction	1,413	2,374	3,770	4,831

* Not available.
Source: U.S. Bureau of the Census, *Statistical Abstract of the United States: 1971* (92d ed.; Washington, D.C., 1971), p. 657.

supply of real estate is inelastic relative to price increases in the short run. In other words, because of the length of time required in the marshaling of resources to produce new real estate resources, an upward shift in the demand curve will result in relatively greater increases in rents and prices than in the additional units of space supplied. As the time period of analysis lengthens, however, the supply curve becomes relatively more elastic.

The clear implication for those in the construction industry is that forecasting is of paramount importance to successful business operations. Because of cyclical fluctuations in demand conditions, it will often be too late to take full advantage of an increased demand situation after it has arrived. By the time the builder gets tooled up, his resources organized, and construction well along, a period of six months to one year may have elapsed and either demand conditions may have slackened or other builders will have provided the needed units. Furthermore, by the time the builder gets his workers laid off and his construction activities diminished, cyclical variations are apt to produce another upturn, with the builder being once again out of phase. Unfortunately, this description is not atypical of the average builder today.

We must realize, however, the difficulties and uncertainties with which the construction demand forecaster is faced. Unfortunately, the federal government's housing policies are more in the nature of short-run expedient tactics rather than long-run strategies for significantly upgrading American housing. Shifts from tight money to loose money and back again are promulgated periodically by the Federal Reserve Board. Sometimes such shifts are reinforced and sometimes mitigated by actions of the Federal Home Loan Bank Board, the Federal Home Loan Mortgage Corporation, the Federal National Mortgage Association, and the Government National Mortgage Association. In addition, fiscal policy and actions by the Federal Housing Administration and the Veterans Administration serve at times to run the forecasting art into little more than a guessing game. Myrdal points out the need for longer range planning in the United States.

. . . the main thing (needed) in long-range planning is all the separate pieces of the jigsaw should be integrated into a single comprehensive plan for the development of the economy as a whole. Such a plan, specifying not only the speed but also the main direction of economic growth, is vital for the framing of government policy. It is equally vital as a basis for planning in private business, which must otherwise operate with a complex of important parameters in the form of mere guesses, based on no real knowledge.[1]

Certainly, however, within the limits of forecasting ability, a six-months to one-year forecast is crucial to construction firms.

---

[1] Gunnar Myrdal, *Challenge to Affluence* (New York: Pantheon Books, 1965), p. 84.

Filtering. Filtering is the movement of people of one income group into homes that have recently dropped in price and which were previously occupied by those in the next higher income group. The implication of the filtering phenomenon is that for the continual improvement of housing standards, even in a static economy or community, new construction must occur to maintain a surplus of supply at each family income level. To stand still in the production of housing even when economic conditions are static means to regress. Urban development and community progress require a continuing supply of new housing above and beyond that level needed to house an increasing population.

LAND DEVELOPMENT

Although land development is normally undertaken by private real estate developers and entrepreneurs, it is one of the most socially significant types of business activity. The individual or firm that converts raw, agricultural land to urban usage establishes land use patterns and other physical arrangements that often prevail into the future for 100 years or longer. Productivity of the real estate after development will depend upon the extent to which the developer has made wise decisions and has established land use patterns that will protect and enhance long-run values.

Much criticism has been leveled at land developers in recent years. Too often the land developer and builder is one who has failed in other businesses and who then tries his hand in the field of real estate production. Too often his motives have not been concerned with the long-run best interest of the community; instead, he has in many cases subdivided small acreages with inefficient layouts—small lots, narrow streets, insufficient services, unattractive designs—having little relation to previously established subdivisions, road systems, and utility services. Many times the land developer-builder has had no education in real estate. He is unknowledgeable about economic analysis, social trends, legal influences, and administrative concepts and tools. In more cases than not real estate production has been performed by a carpenter or other tradesman who has attempted to go into business for himself or to expand a limited operation. Clearly, with America's urban problems becoming increasingly crucial with each passing month and year, society cannot long tolerate the luxury of nonprofessional dominance in this field.

In order to bring some control and efficiency to land development, many communities have established various regulations and agencies which govern new real estate development. The developer legally must comply with some of these controls and should coordinate his development planning with other community plans and agencies whether there is a legal obligation or not. The plans and limitations that may be involved are briefly discussed below.

Zoning.   As discussed in chapter 2, zoning is an exercise of the community's police power in regulating land usage, and the height, width, bulk, and density of buildings. Zoning laws are well established in most communities and compliance is mandatory, although not infrequently the laws have been subverted through political influence. Appointees to a planning commission are sometimes pressured to repay political debts or favors by voting favorably on a requested zoning change. Still, a change in the law or a "variance" is required to defeat the purpose of a zoning ordinance. Misinterpretations of the law or blatant favoritism will be overturned by the courts. In a few cases of noncompliance developers and builders have been forced to tear down buildings and realign subdivisions. Obviously, the developer and builder should know and thoroughly understand the zoning laws applicable to his development. Appendix A contains a description of a typical administrative structure for planning and zoning.

Master plan.   Many communities have developed a master plan, often on a metropolitan area or regional basis. The Franklin County Regional Planning Commission, for example, has prepared a plan (known as the Blue Plan) for the entire Columbus, Ohio, metropolitan area. The plan concerns a number of municipalities and attempts to forecast and to plan for future land development. The plan itself is not legally enforceable; however, most of the communities encompassed by the plan have developed their own city plans and zoning ordinances in conformity with the regional plan. Certainly the professional real estate developer should coordinate his developments with the plan so as to promote sound, long-run growth.

Building and housing codes.   These local codes regulate, respectively, construction standards and housing conditions and maintenance. Normally the latter would not be of concern to a developer except insofar as construction could influence future housing conditions. The builder obviously must be concerned with the building code and comply with it.

Transportation plans and facilities.   Various governmental levels (city, county, and state) may have plans for street and highway development and expansion of other public transportation facilities. Many cities, for example, have airport expansion plans which could drastically influence land development plans in the area. The large amount of freeway construction in recent years has cut through many existing and planned real estate developments. Plans for extending city streets into newly developing areas in many cases will determine the basic street layout for a new subdivision.

Sewer extensions.   As a community expands, both sanitary sewers and storm sewers should be extended to serve new areas. The developer must be aware of such plans. In some housing developments subdivisions have been established without storm sewers with disastrous results. In some other situations the facilities were inadequate or the land was too low for adequate drainage.

Activities in land development

Land development encompasses all those steps taken from the inception of the decision to undertake a development project to the construction phase. In other words, it involves all those activities necessary to procure and prepare land for construction of a building. Each of these activities is discussed below.

Land procurement. Although the necessity of this activity is obvious, the execution and problems associated with it can be quite complex. Furthermore, the considerations vary depending upon whether land acquisition is for the purpose of combining already improved parcels into a more intensive use or for the development of agricultural land into single-family residential lots. Land should be procured for either purpose only after an adequate market analysis has been performed to determine the feasibility of the proposed undertaking.

In procurring previously developed land within an urbanized area, complex problems often arise from two sources: (1) the existence of improvements on the individual parcels and (2) having to deal with multiple owners of the several parcels needed. For example, the acquisition of land in a downtown area for the purpose of constructing a new, larger building usually requires the developer to acquire a number of older, smaller parcels having structures of various ages and sizes. The owners of these parcels may for various reasons have inflated opinions of the value of their parcels or may even refuse to sell at any price—particularly when they realize that it is imperative for the developer to obtain a given parcel to complete his land procurement plan. This problem has been especially knotty in large-scale, private redevelopment efforts. Mr. William Zeckendorf, Jr., has proposed that developers of such extensive projects be given the right to eminent domain.[2]

Land preparation. Most tracts of land that are to be developed from agricultural to urban uses require the application of a considerable amount of labor and capital. Redevelopment projects in urbanized areas typically require much greater costs for land preparation. In either case the land must be cleared of unwanted debris, old buildings, and trees that hinder construction.

Subdividing. For residential developments, which typically involve the conversion of rural to urban land, the site must be further developed after the land has been cleared. This phase is known as subdividing and usually involves the plotting of lots; the grading of the cleared site; and the installing of utilities, drainage facilities, and roads. Many substeps involving various kinds of costs are of course involved in this process. Surveying charges; preparation of blueprints for the subdivision; installa-

---

[2] Paper delivered to Annual Meeting of American Real Estate and Urban Economics Association in New York City, December 28, 1965.

tion of curbs, catch basins, and sewers; and providing for water lines are but a few of such steps and costs.

In addition to the above type cash outlays, a land developer must also consider the property taxes he will incur during the time he owns the lots and also his equity cost that accrues because his capital is tied up. From an economic point of view, all of these costs plus the developer's profit must be considered the cost of society's obtaining the newly developed real estate.

Financing. Rarely can the land developer pay cash for the land to be developed. Rather, he must usually finance the property by one of several methods. He might borrow from the seller (with a purchase money mortgage serving as security), obtain an option from the owner to purchase the lots one at a time as he sells previously developed lots (with or without a house constructed on the lot), form a syndicate or corporation to obtain equity capital from other individuals, or obtain a land development loan from a financial institution. In all such cases, the developer must usually convince the lender (whether he be owner, investor, or financial institution) of the feasibility of the project. Therefore, the developer needs to have specific plans and budgets for the land development and construction that is to take place on the land. A market survey showing the demand expected for the completed units can be helpful in convincing a seller or financial institution to advance the necessary funds.

Significance to urban development

Our purpose is not to describe in detail the steps and processes involved in land development. Rather, we wish to identify and analyze some of the important considerations that should concern developers and society in the production of profitable and socially desirable real estate projects. Society has the responsibility of providing incentives to the developers who perform their function by creating the long-term utility that is to society's advantage; i.e., developers who subdivide in accordance with future requirements and long-term values should be rewarded more than those who are in business to turn a quick dollar and get out. Developers, on the other hand, have a responsibility to understand their social responsibility as well as their financial reward. They should be educated in the area of long-run aesthetics and values. Too often they are not, and the zoning regulations are not intended or sufficient to preclude developments that may produce short-term profits, but long-term slums.

Integrated development. The modern approach to land development is to assure proper relationships among the various land uses. Martin defines an integrated development as "one in which many kinds of land improvements are planned in relation to each other and constructed as a unit, as a whole." [3] Subdivisions which provide for shopping facilities, entertainment and recreational areas, public parks, and churches are integrated developments. A shopping center, in which the various land uses are planned ahead of time and are related to each other, is another example of an integrated development. Integrated developments are related to existing and future land uses, utilities, and streets that now or in the future will border the development.

Integrated development contrasts with the so called add-on type, in which individual lots are developed and improved one at a time. Development of this type, however, usually results in too much consideration being given existing bordering uses which are probably obsolescent. It also fails to provide for needed services and utilities. The ultimate result is unplanned, uncoordinated, nonhomogeneous land uses which do not retain their values as long as integrated developments.

Integrated development requires large-scale development and construction operations. The large firms that can engage in this type of development usually experience economies of scale in their business operations, making large-scale, integrated developments generally more profitable. Workmen can be assigned to specialized functions, materials can be bought in large quantities, advertising is more rewarding, and managerial talent is equally applied to all phases of the job.

The benefits to planned, systematic urban development of the integrated approach are obvious. Compliance with a master plan and the implementing provisions of the zoning regulations have become crucial in the effort to stem unplanned, topsy-turvy urban sprawl.

Land planning and control. To plan for the allocation and control of land uses within an integrated development requires an understanding of desirable and undesirable locational relationships. It is one thing to state simply that adequate shopping facilities should be provided in a residential development; it is quite another to decide the actual layout and thus the relationship between the residential properties and the shopping area. In general, the shopping area should be convenient enough so that residents can travel there within 5 or 10 minutes, but it must be located so as not to spoil the view or access of the residences. Consideration must be given relationships between number, types, and sizes of various stores and the number of people and their income characteristics who are to be served.

The residential lots themselves must be developed so that the homes to be constructed will have adequate space and will be in pleasing relationships with neighboring properties and views, while being shielded from nuisances such as dumps, railroads, and highways. Street patterns

---

[3] Preston Martin, *Real Estate Principles and Practices* (New York: Macmillan Co., 1959), p. 96.

should be planned to avoid monotony and high-speed traffic, yet should provide convenient access. The natural contours of the land and other natural advantages such as streams, trees, and views should be considered.

Once the subdivision has been planned and developed, steps should be taken to insure its continued existence as a planned, integrated development. The zoning laws may provide some control, but as discussed previously, these laws serve only to provide a broad framework within which many variations may occur. The developer of an integrated subdivision may well decide that more precise controls are needed. These usually take the form of deed restrictions.

Deed restrictions operate in addition to the zoning laws. The restrictions are placed on every parcel in the subdivision being developed, with provision for termination in 20 or 30 years unless extended by the property owners. Typically the restrictions should place minimum limitations on the size or ground area of the structures, restrict the land use and type of structure that can be constructed, provide adequate setback lines, and provide for architectural control through an architectural control committee of subdivision property owners. Formerly, restrictions limiting the cost of structures to those above a given dollar level were often placed in deeds, but they have become meaningless with the increasing price level over the years. Restrictions involving measures that are subject to change such as prices and costs should generally be avoided. Similarly, restrictions that run for indefinite periods should be avoided. Land uses change, and adequate flexibility as well as the desired degree of control should be provided.

Role of the developer-investor

The land developer is an investor who commits his equity, equipment, labor force, and managerial talent to the conversion of land from one use to another. The role of the developer is to conceptualize, plan, organize, and carry out the development of land resources. The social responsibility of the developer must be regarded as of highest importance when one considers the vast amount of wealth represented by the land and the fact that society must usually live with the developer's accomplishments many years. As such, then, the economic rationale for land development and redevelopment should be understood by the developer so that he can carry out his function in the best interest of both society and himself.

Most simply, land development or redevelopment is justified when the present value of the expected benefits are equal to or greater than the cost of obtaining those benefits. The developer should predict future income levels and patterns that are obtainable under various uses. He should then estimate the costs necessary to develop the land for those purposes and compare the results. The costs for redevelopment projects should, of course, include the costs of demolishing existing uses and the forgoing of income from the existing use. In either development or redevelopment projects, the developer's cost of capital should be the point below which he will not undertake the project. The returns afforded by alternative uses above the cost of capital should be ranked, and the use showing the highest overall return should be chosen.

This suggests that the developer-investor must be intimately familiar with costs, income estimation procedures, and capitalization concepts. Income estimation requires knowledge of market analysis techniques, and these require knowledge and understanding of data sources and research methodology. Certainly the development field should be no place for an unsophisticated, nonanalytically oriented person. It should command the highest level of competence in business decision-making techniques.

The role of the developer is also that of risk bearer. His tie-up of capital and labor subject him to interest rate risk, and the project in which he has his capital and labor committed is subject to business risk (failure of the undertaking) and market risk (the possibility that the project will decline in value). In most cases the financial risk associated with borrowed funds will also be incurred. The developer must know and understand these risks and be prepared to accept some, avoid some, and pass some along to insurers. As a risk manager, he must be aware of the alternative courses of action that are possible.

The role of the land developer can be illustrated by the considerations involved in a decision by one large land development firm. The firm, Winter and Company, purchases land for subsequent resale—either developed or undeveloped. All of the land purchased by the company is located in or around a large metropolitan area in the Southwest. The area has a well-diversified economic base, with major categories of basic employment being heavy manufacturing, national defense, state government, and education. The area has a population of about one million persons and has been growing at a rate of about 10 percent per year. In short, the demand for well-located, high-quality raw acreage is expected to continue strong.

A tract of 55 acres of land has been offered for sale and is being considered for purchase by Winter and Company. The land is now zoned for agricultural and rural residential uses. Winter and Company believes the land can be rezoned for urban residential usage (single family), with perhaps some part of the tract zoned for apartment residential usage. The land is located about one-half mile outside a recently completed circumferential highway, part of the interstate highway system.

The asking price for land is $825,000—$15,000 per acre. If the land is developed for single-family residences, Winter and Company estimate development costs will run approximately $4,500 per acre, based on the following unit estimates.

Per lineal foot

Curbing	$ 2.50
Blacktop paving	15.00
Storm sewers	2.50
Sanitary sewers	5.00*
Water mains	5.00†

* Plus $130 per lot per additional bath.
† Plus $100 per water meter, plus $100 per fireplug.

It is believed that the lots can be sold within five years for an average price of $13,000, with about four lots per acre. A bank line of credit will finance 75 percent of the purchase price at 8 percent. Real estate taxes are expected to amount to 1 percent of the purchase price per year. The company's marginal tax bracket is 50 percent, and its return is calculated in Figure 13–1.

As can be seen in Figure 13–1, a discount rate of 25 percent comes close to equating the present value of the cash intake from the sale of

FIGURE 13–1

Winter and Company calculation of rate of return land investment project

	Actual dollars at time of incurrence	Operation	Present value discounted at 25%
Sales price (in 5 years)	$2,800,000		
Less: Costs of sales			
Real estate commissions (5%) .$140,000			
Title matters 5,000			
Surveys 3,000	148,000		
Net sales price	$2,652,000	× .328 =	$869,856
Less: Adjusted cost basis			
Acquisition cost $825,000		loan	
Development cost 247,500	1,072,500	−618,750 =	453,750
Taxable gain	$1,579,500		$416,106
Less: 25% capital gain tax ..	394,875	× .328 =	129,519
Aftertax gain	$1,184,625		$286,587
Less: Repayment of loan	618,750	× .328 =	202,950
	$ 565,875		$ 83,637
Less: Sum of 5-year expenses, adjusted for 50% tax deductibility Interest expenses ($49,500 ×			
.50)5 = $24,750 × 5 = ...	123,750	× 2.69 =	66,578
	$ 442,125		$ 17,059
Real estate tax ($8,250 ×			
.50)5 = $4,125 × 5 = ...	20,625	× 2.69 =	11,096
	$ 421,500		$ 5,963*

* Net present value above a 25 percent rate of return.

lots with the present value of the cash outlays and expenses. The exact rate of return is somewhat more than 25 percent.

Several questions arise from this analysis. First, how reliable and accurate are the expected sale prices of lots? Second, are all the expenses that will actually be incurred included? Third, are the financing assumptions valid and realistic? Obviously, any variation of substantial proportion will cause the yield to be different from that calculated. There is always some probability that the lot prices will be lower than expected or that sales cannot be made at the expected prices at the time anticipated. Are these risks adequately compensated by a 25 percent rate of return? Although a 25 percent return may seem high, the risks associated with land holding and development are high.

To state the problem differently, the land should not be purchased and developed unless the expected rate of return is above the firm's cost of capital. Its cost of capital is a weighted average of the cost of debt capital and equity. Since equity capital in land development will require a high rate of return to compensate for the risks, the weighted cost of capital will be relatively high—probably at least 15 percent. Winter and Company thus must consider its cost of capital in relation to the project's expected return. It should be confident that its predictions of sale prices, costs, and expenses are as complete and reliable as they can be. The company is then in a position to make a judgmental decision about whether to proceed with the project.

CONSTRUCTION

The building or construction process is carried on by an industry which, when considered in total, is our largest single industry. Although the economic significance of the construction industry was discussed earlier, Table 13–3 shows total construction and its principal categories projected to 1980 and 2000. The projected figures represent an increase of roughly 300 percent in total construction, which is a faster rate of growth than that expected for GNP.

Size alone—present and future—however, is not the only consideration that is expected to enhance the place of the construction industry in the national economy. Increases in efficiency and productivity of the industry may well occur at a faster rate than formerly and at faster rates than increases in other productive segments of the economy. Heretofore, the construction industry has been regarded as the least progressive of our major industries. Although productivity has increased, the gains have been lower than productivity increases in other fields. As Weimer, Hoyt, and Bloom point out,

The industry suffers from restrictive building codes, restrictive labor practices, and from its dependence on the development of regional supporting

TABLE 13–3

Principal categories of construction, 1950, 1960, and medium projections
for 1980, 2000 (billion 1960 dollars)

			Medium projection	
	1950	*1960*	*1980*	*2000*
Total construction	58.6	76.2	166.3	348.4
New construction	42.2	56.6	130.1	280.9
Maintenance and repair	16.4	19.6	36.2	67.5
for residential construction	6.2	7.2	10.8	14.7
Residential new construction including				
additions and alterations	19.6	22.6	54.7	126.4
Nonresidential new construction	22.7	34.1	75.4	154.5
Private new construction	32.8	40.6	90.2	196.8
Public new construction	9.4	16.0	39.9	84.1
Components of public new nonresidential				
construction:	9.1	15.3	37.2	77.8
Schools and hospitals	2.3	3.2	5.0	7.4
Highways	2.6	5.5	16.1	34.6
Military and industrial	.6	1.8	5.1	12.3
All other (water, sewerage, etc.)	3.6	4.8	11.0	23.5

Source: "Resources in America's Future," Appendix Table A4-3. Reprinted in Weimer and Hoyt, *Real Estate* (5th ed.; New York: Ronald Press Co., 1966), p. 370.

facilities by government to allow for new land development. Many builders, of course, continue to follow outmoded practices. Informal agreements sometimes result in price fixing and the reduction of competition.[4]

To the extent that productivity gains in construction have not kept pace with other industries, the construction industry has contributed less growth to our total national wealth than other segments of the economy. If productivity gains can be increased significantly, however, construction will contribute an even greater share of increase to our national resources. Weimer, Hoyt, and Bloom also point out that the building industry may be having its industrial revolution, which suggests that the industry may shortly take off in productivity relative to (1) its past performance and (2) other industries.[5]

Structure of the industry

Construction firms range in size all the way from very small to very large companies that engage in building operations in several countries. However, most of today's builders are small-time operators who are often dropouts from other small business failures. In home building even the

---

[4] Arthur M. Weimer, Homer Hoyt, and George F. Bloom, *Real Estate* (New York: Ronald Press Co., 1972), p. 367.

[5] Weimer, Hoyt, and Bloom, *Real Estate*, p. 371.

large builders such as Levitt and Sons, Inc., and Ryan Homes, Inc., are small in relation to the total market; in 1966 Levitt accounted for only about 0.5 percent of total production.

Also characteristic of the industry are the small outlays on research and development expended by construction firms and industry groups. Little research and development effort is undertaken by private firms, with the result that little new knowledge is obtained or distributed about construction materials and methodologies. Prefabrication techniques are considerably further advanced in European countries, and laborsaving techniques are employed more extensively. The conclusion is that profit squeezes will be felt increasingly by smaller firms and that increases can be expected in the number of large-scale regional and national builders.

The construction process

Many steps and operations are involved in the construction of any major improvement to the land—whether the improvement be a home, apartment building, commercial structure, factory, or hydroelectric dam. Construction concerns the conversion of prepared but vacant land to a usable, productive parcel of real estate. It represents the creation of economic resources by the combining of various components into new time, form, and place relationships—both among themselves and with the land.

Functions

Planning. As with every complex task, the management functions of planning, organizing, and controlling must be performed in the construction process. In the planning function, provisions must be made for designing the structure, specifying the materials and components that will make up the structure, arranging for the purchase and timely availability of materials and components, arranging for the labor force required to assemble the materials and components, and providing for financing adequate to support these activities. Typically, an architect and contractor are hired to perform all except the financing activity for the investor-builder.

The planning objective of the architect is to design a building that will serve most appropriately the functions or uses to which the building will be put. To do this the architect must thoroughly understand the requirements of the owner or user of the property, whether the property is to serve as a home or an industrial plant. As Ratcliff points out,

Design involves space planning, engineering design, and aesthetics. Space planning includes site planning—the disposition of the structure on the land —and interior planning—the distribution of the space within the building;

engineering design relates to the structural features of the building, the floor and wall construction, roof framing, stairways, footings, and other features that determine the structural strength of the building. From an aesthetic standpoint, the architect endeavors to impart a pleasing appearance to the structure through the arrangement of masses and proportions and the selection of materials and architectural details.[6]

Also, under the planning function, the architect specifies the quality, grade, brand name, or model number (hence, the term *specification* or *specs*) of the exact materials and component assemblies that are to go into the building. The architect must keep abreast of new materials, building techniques, and local building codes in writing the specifications. He must have every subsurface aspect as well as surface aspect of the structure designed and integrated in his plans. He must be able to visualize the finished product and convert this visualization to a step-by-step plan for achieving it.

Organizing. Except for arranging for suitable financing, other activities involved in the organizing function are usually performed by the architect and/or contractor. In addition to designing and specifying the structure and its components, an architect may usually be engaged to supervise the building process. He controls the activities of the builder to insurance conformance with the plans and specifications. He checks the construction process to ascertain that the quality of workmanship is acceptable.

Although architects are not ordinarily employed in the construction of single-family homes costing under $40,000, it seems likely that professional architectural services could profitably be used for the construction of many homes above the $30,000 level. The typical fee for full architectural service runs about 10 percent of the cost, and for this figure the advantages of architectural design and supervision may more than make up for the cost in higher priced homes. Studying the functional requirements of the family that is to occupy the dwelling and incorporating a design and features into a structure that will best meet these needs is ordinarily not work for an amateur.

For his fee the architect attempts to provide an aesthetically pleasing environment and building, yet one which conforms to the pocketbook constraints of his employer. Since each family's makeup, age structure, personalities, and interests are different from every other's, it stands to reason that individual attention to the design of a home would be desirable for most families that can afford a relatively high-priced structure.

The purchase of a house that has been built for speculative resale (although constituting the largest source of new home purchases) may

---

[6] Richard U. Ratcliff, *Urban Land Economics* (New York: McGraw-Hill Book Co., 1949), p. 177.

not offer the best compromise between the desirable attributes of efficiency and beauty and the cost expended. Indeed, the disadvantages may extend even further to inferior workmanship, materials, and components. To their credit, many of the larger, more experienced speculative builders now offer reliable warranties on ready-built houses. Furthermore, some recent court decisions have enforced the concept of vendor (builder-seller) warranty and in some cases have even extended the concept to financial institutions that have significant control over the building process. Nevertheless, the larger issue between architectural cost and advantage will not be resolved by the courts—only by the service provided.

Financing of the construction process is ordinarily organized by the owner or contractor. The owner may be a speculative builder who is erecting a large number of houses for resale or he may be an individual who has contracted for the building of a home for his own occupancy. In the construction of multi-family residential buildings, commercial buildings, or industrial structures the owner may be an individual investor, a partnership syndicate, a corporation, or another type of organization. In almost all cases, however, the individual or organization doing the actual construction must obtain the financing. Because of the large and unusual risks involved in this type of financing, a number of special safeguards and arrangements have evolved for construction financing.

The need for construction financing arises because the person who has contracted to have a building constructed will not pay for the work until it is completed, and the builder is not able or does not want to pay the bills for labor and materials out of his own pocket before receiving payment from his employer. The builder thus borrows by means of a short-term (usually two to nine months), secured loan from a financial institution. Security for the loan is the land and a nonexistent building. Because of the risk that the building will not be built or will not be completed according to plans and specifications in the time period forecasted, the financial institution will typically not pay out the loan before construction has begun. Rather, the loan is usually paid out in stages after specified portions of the building have been completed—for example, after the foundation is in, after the roof is on, after the plumbing and electrical work are completed, and when the building is finished. The financial institution will pay out portions of the loan, the total of which are smaller than the value of the security or the percentage of the job accomplished. For example, one third of the loan might be paid out after the roof is on although the building would be approximately 50 percent complete. Also, the lender will require the builder to show proof of payment of bills and to provide lien waivers from contractors and subcontractors.

Controlling. The controlling function for the construction process is performed by the owner, architect, contractor, and sometimes the financier. As discussed above, an architect representing the owner may control the construction process by supervising the builder. The owner, of course, could perform this function if he is qualified, but usually he is not capable of adequate supervision. Typically for small, single-family home construction jobs, the owner employs a contractor who is entrusted with the controlling function, as well as the actual building process. The owner periodically checks major aspects of the job such as general layout, brand names of components, and general construction quality. It would be quite easy in most cases, however, for a dishonest contractor to get by with inferior materials and workmanship.

For large-scale development and construction projects, a team of engineers and inspectors representing the general contractor maintain constant supervision of the actual work. Spot checks by the owner, his architect, or the financial institution could cause nonpayment to the contractor. In large residential developments the speculative builder's team of inspectors is charged with maintaining certain minimum standards of materials and workmanship. If the builder wishes to be able to sell houses on a continuing basis, the buying public must have a favorable image of the builder's capability and product. Also, in order to sell the houses, the builder may have to rely on government underwritten financing for buyers and must therefore meet the standards required by the FHA and VA.

Role of the builder

Although various aspects of the functions of planning, organizing, and controlling are performed by parties other than the builder, he is the crucial element in the construction process. More of the construction process is performed by the builder than anyone else. The builder's role consists of a number of activities. He must estimate construction costs, submit bids on building jobs that will allow him an acceptable rate of return, assemble and organize materials and labor, arrange for construction financing, disburse payments to workers and subcontractors, supervise actual construction, and work with the owner.

The key to success for a builder is his ability to estimate costs realistically and accurately. A reliable cost estimate and breakdown will allow him to submit acceptable bids, obtain materials and labor, cover his overhead, and make a profit. Figure 13–2 is a builder's house for which there is a detailed description and a cost breakdown in Figures 13–3 and 13–4. As shown in Figure 13–4, the costs are usually categorized according to the labor and materials going into the main structure, with heating, plumbing, and electric systems considered separately from the main structure. If the builder has heating men, plumbers, and electricians on his work force, they would do this work. Often, however, the smaller

FIGURE 13-2

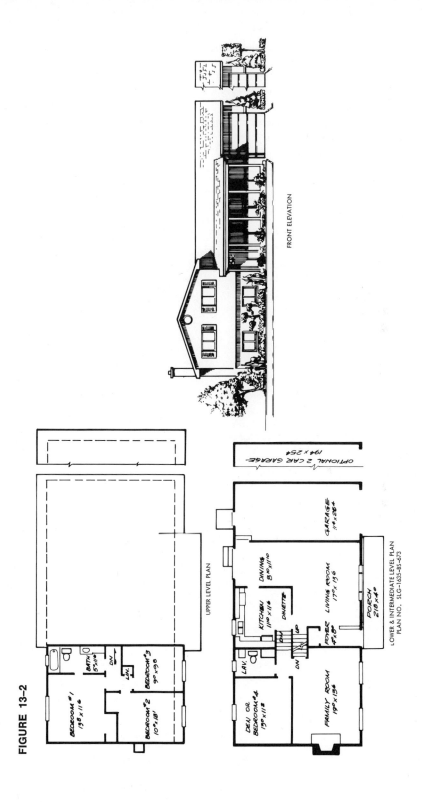

BEDROOM #1
13'8 x 11'6

BEDROOM #2
10'8 x 18'

BATH
5' x 11'0

BEDROOM #3
9'0 x 9'8

DN

LIN.

UPPER LEVEL PLAN

DEN OR
BEDROOM #4
13'0 x 11'8

LAV.

FAMILY ROOM
19'0 x 13'6

DN

UP

FOYER
5'0 x 8'0

KITCHEN
11'0 x 11'6

DINETTE

DINING
8'0 x 11'0

LIVING ROOM
17'0 x 13'6

PORCH
21'8 x 4'0

GARAGE
11'4 x 26'4

OPTIONAL 2 CAR GARAGE
19'4 x 25'4

LOWER & INTERMEDIATE LEVEL PLAN
PLAN NO. SLG-1635-B5-673

FRONT ELEVATION

FIGURE 13–3

Builder's house (detailed description)

Description:

Three-bedroom, brick and stucco, side split-level home.

Seven rooms, 1½ baths.

Built-ins in kitchen.

Partial basement under living area.

Brick fireplace in family room.

Two-car garage.

Structure:

Excavation and clay gravel: 11 courses, 8″ C.B., waterproofing; termite protection; metal windows.

Chimney: C.B. with brick facing fireplace flue size 12″ × 12″, gas vented into 8″ × 12″ flue; water heater vented.

Fireplace (in family room): Firebrick lining; stone hearth; ceiling high mantle.

Exterior walls: Sheathing Gyplap, ½″, 4′ × 8′, solid; face brick; frame backup, 2′ × 4′; door sills concrete; stone window sills; exterior painting lead and oil.

Floor framing: #1 fir, 2″ × 8″—16″ O.C.; 1″ × 3″ bridging; joist anchors concrete slab basement floor.

Fill under slab: 4″ gravel.

Subflooring: ⅜″ plywood.

Finish flooring: #1 oak, ²⁵⁄₃₂″ thick, 2¼″ wide; sanded, filled, shellacked and waxed.

Partition framing: #1 fir, 2″ × 4″—16″ O.C.

Ceiling framing: #1 fir, 2″ × 6″—16″ O.C.; bridging 1″ × 3″.

Roof framing: #1 fir, 2″ × 6″ O.C.; collar beams #1 fir, 2″ × 4″ —24″ O.C.

Roofing: Asphalt shingle #210, size 12″ × 36″; tin flashing 26 ga.

Gutters: Galvanized iron, 26 ga., 5″ o.g.

Downspouts: Galvanized iron; 26 ga.; 3″ o.g.; number 4; connected to tile and to curb.

Drywall: Walls and ceiling; ½″ thick; tape and sanded; joints cemented.

Decorating: Kitchen and baths—3 coats I. & O. (1 flat—2 enamel); living room, hall, and bedrooms—flat oil base paint, 2 coats; recreation room—paneled.

Interior doors and trim: Doors—slab, flush; door trim—modern; finish—doors and trim. Stain shellac, varnish.

Windows: Aluminum sliding—glass, single strength. Trim—molding W.P., painted 3 coats; screens—full aluminum; basement windows—Truscon or equal steel.

Entrance and exterior detail: Main entrance door—3′ wide 1¾″ thick; other entrance doors—W.P., head flashing 26 ga.; screen doors 1¼″ thick; shutters—fixed; railings and louvers, exterior millwork, redwood-plywood under overhang painted 3 coats.

Cabinets and interior detail: Westinghouse kitchen; base units, birch; Formica counter top, stainless steel edging, 4″ back splash; medicine cabinet; all cabinets fruit wood stain—1 sealer, 1 filler, 1 finish shellac.

Special floors and wainscot: Kitchen & bath—Armstrong inlaid linoleum, rubber base ⅝″ plywood underfloor; bath—ceramic tile recess 4½″ high.

Plumbing: 1 kitchen double bowl sink, Westinghous disposer and dishwasher; 2 single bowl sinks in bathrooms (tinted fixtures); 2 water closets (2 white fixtures); 1 bathtub (tinted fixture); 1 shower over tub (ceramic tile recess 4½′); 1 40-gallon glass-lined automatic water heater.

Heating: Gas forced air (100,000 Btu input—80,000 output capacity); kitchen exhaust hood.

Electric wiring: Circuit breaker—110–220 volts.

Hardware: Chrome and brass.

FIGURE 13-4
Builder's house (cost estimate)

Cost breakdown

Excavation and grading .... $	668
Masonry (brick and stucco)	2,693
Concrete (concrete block and other surface	1,581
Carpenter labor	1,634
Lumber, millwork and other (carpenter materials)	3,798
House package (hardware, etc.)	653
Kitchen cabinets	424
Insulation	185
Drywall	1,121
Painting	857
Floor covering and ceramic tile	764
Floor finishing	120
Water proofing	23
Screens, windows	509
Appliances	404
Sheet metal and spouting	301
Cleaning	67
Total basic cost	$15,802
Minus garage ($1,986)	$13,816

Square foot estimate

25.7' × 41' = 1,054 sq. ft.
Total cost of structure = $21,775
Cost per square foot = $20.66
Land size: 65' × 132'
Land cost: $5,060
Garage (2 car) cost: $1,986
  Area 20' × 25.4' = 508 sq. ft.
  Cost per sq. ft. = $3.91

	Dollar cost	Cost per sq. ft.	Percent of total cost
Main structure (above)	$13,816	$13.11	63.45
Heating (includes labor and materials)	633	.60	2.90
Plumbing (includes labor and materials)	1,142	1.08	5.24
Electric (includes wiring, fixtures, labor, and materials)	693	.67	3.19
Indirect costs (includes building permit, survey, misc. and utilities)	316	.30	1.45
Overhead and profit (includes loan fee, interest, closing costs, office expense, selling expense)....	5,175	4.91	23.77
Total cost of structure	$21,775	$20.67	100.00

Site improvements

Blacktop base and asphalt (1,090 sq. ft. @ $.33 per sq. ft.) $360
Sod (6,750 sq. ft. @ $.0383 per sq. ft.) 259
Landscaping (shrubs) 80

  Total site improvements $699

Total site improvement cost expressed as a cost per sq. ft. of building area = $.66
Total site improvement cost expressed as a percentage of total cost of construction = 3.69%

Total finished cost = $29,520

builder subcontracts the heating, plumbing, and electrical work to specialized firms in these fields. The heating, plumbing, and electrical installations make up relatively small components percentage wise in the total cost of the house. (Together, they total 11.33 percent.)

Another small category is indirect costs. This type of cost is for items that pertain to the entire property but that are not functionally identifiable. Costs of utilities are lumped together in this category, together with such items as the building permit, survey expense, and other similar costs.

A much larger category is overhead and profit. A normal builder's profit of about 10 percent of total costs in included here. Overhead normally includes the builder's expenses that are not directly related to any particular job. Office expense and selling expenses (such as advertising and sales force) are the two principal components of this type. The breakdown in Figure 13–4 also shows the loan fee, interest expense on the construction loan, and closing costs in the overhead category. It can be argued that these costs might be shown more logically in the indirect cost category.

Site improvements are shown separately from the structure costs, as is the garage cost. These items can be included or omitted as desired by the builder (if the property is not sold) or the owner, and the unit costs are more easily controllable when shown separately. The land cost to the builder is then added to obtain the total cost of the property. Presumably, this cost (including a fair profit) would be the price that the builder would be willing to accept for the completed property.

The possibility or, more accurately, the likelihood of being in error on the cost estimate, together with the vagaries inherent in the real estate market, should point up the hazards to the small builder. A small underestimation of costs can easily wipe out most of his profit. Or, if the demand for the type of property he has produced is not strong, he may not be able to sell it at the desired price or at the time of completion. The supply of mortgage money may become tighter, an industry may leave town, employment levels may drop, or the market just may not react favorably to the new property. Relative to the profit, the structure may be too large, too small, unattractive, poorly designed, or low in quality. Thus, we find that many small builders go bankrupt or leave the business each year.

Administrative problems and considerations

Labor unions and productivity.   Labor unions have frequently been attacked as a principal cause of the high costs and slow productivity advances in the construction industry. Certainly in an industry which requires large inputs of hand work, labor costs are bound to be high and the role of unions highly visible. In residential construction, for example, on-site labor costs typically run about 50 percent of the total. In pre-fabrication of buildings the input of hand labor is still relatively high—both in the assembling of components at the site and in the manufacturing process. Undoubtedly labor practices have added to the rocketing costs of construction; however, in the overall picture too much of the blame for the industry's problems probably has been attributed to unions.

One method by which unions impede productivity in the construction industry is the attempt to dictate supply terms to the market by placing limitations on the number of new workers admitted to a trade; the effect, of course, is to maintain high wage rates. High initiation fees and trade examinations are sometimes used to control entrance to a trade. The degree to which unions are able to manipulate the labor supply varies from community to community.

Restrictive entrance requirements have had as one objective and effect the exclusion of racial minority groups to union membership. Such practices came under strong attack in the late 1960s with the push for civil, social, and economic rights. Today requirement by federal and state governments for more than token employment has resulted in increasing employment of blacks in the building trades; many business firms building large structures specify that a certain percentage of the work force must belong to minority groups.

Another difficulty occurs because trade and craft unions are highly specialized, resulting in jurisdictional disputes and work stoppages where specific areas of work are unclear. Some unions demand jurisdiction in activities which do not involve specialized talent, such as the right to clean paint spots by the painters' union.

Perhaps the greatest negative effect in limiting production comes from unions' efforts, often violent, to fight the use of laborsaving devices and new materials that threaten the need for skilled labor. As one example, the use of plastic pipe has been resisted forcefully in many communities with arguments that the new type of pipe is inferior to cast iron or copper, which is untrue. Plumbers' unions have also argued that plastic pipe is a cheap substitute requiring no ability to install—arguments which are irrelevant to accomplishing the job. Some other examples are forbidding the use of paint spray guns, limiting the size of paint brush used, and forbidding the use of premixed concrete.

It should be pointed out that the real underlying motivation for unions to engage in restrictive practices is the concern for job security. The nature of the construction industry and the construction process has produced quite unstable employment. Neither social legislation nor approaches by employers have allowed unions to take a positive viewpoint toward labor saving innovations.

It seems likely, however, that labor unions have been criticized too harshly and assigned too much of the responsibility for the construction industry's slow productivity advances. The basic culprit must be identified as the structure of the industry itself, since a structure of larger firms would allow more effective dealings with unions. A situation in which small, weak, unsophisticated firms must deal with larger, more powerful unions is not the ideal model for collective bargaining.[7]

Market analysis. Data available regarding demand are the same whether an existing or new structure is being contemplated, but changes in supply require consideration of possible adjustments in activity patterns that might result. A development of new retail shopping facilities might reroute traffic, causing great demand in the new shopping area and a deterioration of demand in the old area. Property values follow consumer demand, the problem being one of determining whether a new development can pull business from old ones. The investors in the older structures have a proven record, providing them with a sound base for holding their business.

A closely related problem is that of attempting to produce a product that offers a competitive advantage over existing land uses in the vicinity. An apartment builder might find a strong demand for three-bedroom apartments, the meeting of which might draw families out of two-bedroom units located in the area. A residential subdivider might choose to specialize in $40,000–$50,000 homes for a given tract, even though the surrounding area is improved with homes of substantially lesser value. In all such cases it is much easier to determine the demand experience of existing uses than the proposed new one. Market research studies under these circumstances thus must be of two types: (1) analyses of demand for the proposed use and (2) analyses of demand for existing uses in the area. The latter studies might indicate that a greater advantage could be gained by developing land in the same manner that surrounding properties are developed.

Financing. The cost of money changes frequently, and new construction is subject only to current costs. This places new structures at a distinct, long-range disadvantage as compared to existing structures when current money costs are high. A 7½ percent market requires $2,000 more net income per year than a 5½ percent market on a $100,000 apartment building, an amount that normally would require higher rental charges than those received by the older buildings. Of course, a low interest rate market has the opposite effect in terms of interest cost.

Aside from the interest expense of money, the investor must consider the downpayment required and the terms of repayment possible in the present market. Real estate investments normally involve loans that comprise a high percentage of appraised value.

---

[7] Halbert C. Smith, "Housing: Are We Paying More and Getting Less?" *Business Horizons* (Winter 1967), pp. 7–20.

Leverage, that is, the use of borrowed money to earn a sum greater than the cost of that money, provides a higher percentage return on investment than would be possible with 100 percent equity financing. Financing terms requiring high down payments and 20-year amortized repayments require a much higher net income than would be necessary with lower down payments and 40-year amortization. This increased net income would not be forthcoming where competing investments have competitive financing advantages. The importance of the fact is emphasized by a statement of an Atlanta mortgage banker:

Several apartment building owners have been in to see me recently about refinancing their buildings. They want 7½% loans rather than their existing 5¾% loans, the important point being that they can borrow large sums based upon today's high rental market. Some have been able to borrow nearly 100% of their original investment.

Taxation. A common practice in recent years has been for developers to establish rapid depreciation techniques that minimize taxes in the first few years of operations. Reported profits are low or nonexistent, yet the cash flow from the investment is substantial. After about 10 years the annual write-off is reduced, thereby increasing the annual income tax, but the investor has withdrawn much of his capital and, supposedly, has reinvested it elsewhere in a manner that he has earned more than he would have done using a more gradual depreciation form.

The important point regarding the use of the concept is that investors look toward sources other than reported income to justify new improvements. A tax advantage today is more beneficial than an advantage gained after several years, and past exchanges of investment properties have indicated a tendency for different types of investors to operate in the short-run construction arena and the long-run operational arena. The former looks toward cash flow and capital gain through property sales for this return; the latter looks toward net income.

A significant point to note in this regard is that the taxing authorities periodically change those tax laws which offer the benefits desired by real estate developers. The 7 percent investment credit tax feature developed in 1962 offered a cash flow benefit to some industrial developers. Its termination in 1966 was a detriment to them. The 1966 moratorium on several of the commonly used rapid depreciation methods was a hindrance upon apartment builders and commercial developers. Thus, the investor who specialized in the production of improvements must examine his depreciation alternatives before he attempts to compare his investment with those already existing in his area of activity.

Zoning. New structures frequently do not fit the existing zoning plan. Zoning is nearly always a hindrance rather than a help to land developers. Existing structures operate under innumerable forms of former zoning regulations or variances. When a new use is contemplated that requires rezoning or granting of a variance, the potential competitors are able to fight it through the city council or zoning board. The competitors' position is more secure when new competition is thwarted.

SUMMARY

The production of new real estate resources is one of the country's most important economic functions, with new construction in the United States averaging about 10 percent of the GNP. The construction industry holds added significance for economic forecasters and related industries because of the difficulty of predicting future activity. Forecasting is difficult because supply lags demand, the industry is composed of primarily small, unsophisticated firms, and labor unions can interrupt work and increase costs after a project has been started.

The two main types of real estate production are land development and construction. Both of these activities must operate within a framework of social controls such as zoning, building codes, community plans, and local regulations pertaining to streets, sewers, and utilities. Effective performance of the management functions of planning, organizing, and controlling are required in the construction field to minimize cost overruns which are often disastrous to small builders. Important roles may be played in some or all of these functions by the owner, architect, contractor, and financier.

At the micro administration level, the business administrator-investor needs to estimate accurately all costs to be incurred in evaluating the desirability of a land holding and development project or a construction project. He must then estimate gross and net proceeds to be obtained, placing all proceeds and costs on a present-value basis. A rate of return may then be calculated which can be compared with the firm's cost of capital.

QUESTIONS FOR REVIEW

1. How can zoning affect a land developer's rate of return?
2. Is the holding of land a useful economic function? Why? Can land holding be socially undesirable? How?
3. Do you believe that great increases in productivity in the construction industry are possible. Why or why not?
4. If you were to build a new home for your family, would you employ an architect? Why or why not?
5. Why does the structure of the construction industry contribute to an inefficient handling of labor disputes?

6. How could greater job security be provided for construction workers while taking full advantage of laborsaving machines?

7. How does the development of single-family residential areas favorably affect the already existing metropolitan area? What are the disadvantages or costs of such development?

8. What social controls over development and construction do you believe are necessary? Why?

PROBLEMS

1. Diagram the relationship between housing market construction cycles and the general business cycle.

2. Comment upon reasons why the two cycles are likely to be parallel but different.

3. Devise a critical path type of chart in which development process steps are shown in chronological order.

4. Identify those steps that appear to be of maximum importance to the developer.

REFERENCES

Beaton, William R. *Real Estate Investment.* Englewood Cliffs, N. J.: Prentice-Hall, Inc., 1971.

David, Philip. *Urban Land Development.* Homewood, Ill.: Richard D. Irwin, Inc., 1970.

Martin, Preston. *Real Estate Principles and Practices.* New York: The Macmillan Co., 1959.

Ratcliff, Richard U. *Real Estate Analysis,* Chap. 11. New York: McGraw-Hill Book Co., Inc., 1961, pp. 269–305.

Ring, Alfred A. *Real Estate Principles and Practice,* Chaps. 25 and 26. 7th ed. Englewood Cliffs, N. J.: Prentice-Hall, Inc., 1972, pp. 425–55.

Unger, Maurice A. *Real Estate,* Chap. 25. 4th ed. Cincinnati: Southwestern Publishing Co., 1969, pp. 649–70.

Weimer, Arthur M., Hoyt, Homer, and Bloom, George F. *Real Estate,* chaps. 15 and 16. 6th ed. New York: Ronald Press Co., 1972, pp. 335–73.

FINANCING REAL ESTATE

EPIC HOMES CORPORATION, a medium-size builder, began development of a 74-acre tract of land. Its objective was to create a well-planned subdivision of $30,000 to $40,000 homes at the edge of a medium-size city. As preliminary work began at the site, an observer could not see and perhaps would not comprehend the importance of financing to this project. Neither Mr. James Randolph, president of Epic, nor Epic Homes Corporation had invested any cash in the project. The land was purchased, development was begun, and homes would be constructed entirely with funds borrowed from others.

While most development projects require some financial input by the investor-entrepreneur, almost all real estate developments rely on a preponderant proportion of borrowed funds. The complex structure of institutions that lend money, the legal instruments and arrangements, the methods of evaluating risk, and many specialized conventions and techniques of the mortgage market form a system that is essential to real estate development. It is a system that must be studied one part at a time, yet for effective understanding should be visualized in toto. The arrangements in any given real estate venture will constitute a unique combination; no two financing transactions are identical. However, the successful real estate entrepreneur understands thoroughly each component part of the system and is able to combine them in creative ways.

In the case of Epic Homes, the land was provided by the land owner in exchange for 25 percent of the profit to be derived from the project plus a 10 percent interest in the stock of Epic Homes Corporation. On the basis of the planned layout, engineering studies, and home designs, a local bank extended a loan for development and agreed to provide con-

"If you think the floor plan is complicated, you should see the financing!"

Source: *Grin and Bear It* by Lichty. *Courtesy Publishers-Hall Syndicate.*

struction financing for up to one third of the homes. The bank also agreed to make long-term mortgage loans on prevailing terms for up to one third of the homes in the development to home purchasers who qualify under the bank's requirements. Other local lending institutions had expressed interest in financing both the construction and long-term purchases of the remaining two-thirds of the homes. Mr. Randolph was confident that with the successful completion and sale of one-eighth to one-fourth of the homes, public acceptance of the project would insure that the remaining financing could be obtained.

The financing pattern for the Epic Homes project could have been quite different. Epic might have owned or purchased the land with its own capital—all or part of which might have been equity. Epic might have purchased the land partially with its own capital and partially with a loan from the landowner. The land development loan might have been obtained from the land owner at market interest rates or the land owner might have been given a larger share of the profits to make the loan. Both the land development loan and the construction financing might have been obtained from a mortgage investment trust or a savings and loan association. Or one loan might have been obtained from one institution and the other loan from another institution. A permanent financing commitment might have been obtained for all of the new homes from a savings and loan, a mutual savings bank, a mortgage banker, or directly from a life insurance company. The terms—including interest rates, discounts and fees, maturities, privileges, and penalties—of the various loans could differ greatly among lenders. Thus, financing as an element in the real estate development process is subject to greater variation than almost any other factor.

In addition to making real estate development possible, financing often determines whether a project is profitable. If the interest rate on a major loan is too high or a discount too great, a project's profit may be eaten away. If a loan must be repaid before other funds are obtained, the entire project may be forfeited. If a lender exerts too much control over the project, unpopular designs and inefficient methods may be required or too much effort in paper work may result. All of these considerations point up the great importance of financing to the production of new real estate resources and the significance of understanding the role of financing to every real estate investor.

Flow of funds to finance real estate

Funds may be defined as cash or any resource having value which is capable of being sold in order to buy some other asset. We may think of funds as being composed of deposits in banks and savings and loan associations, reserves built up in life insurance policies,[1] equity interests in investments such as stocks, bonds, or real estate, or other noninvestment assets such as homes, paintings, oriental rugs, automobiles, or any item of value. The great bulk of funds used for real estate originate from two sources: (1) equity buildup in real estate and (2) cash savings of individuals and businesses in financial institutions.

Equity buildup in real estate is a continuous source of financing for the owner of real estate. Equity buildup occurs because (1) the real estate may increase in value and/or (2) the mortgage debt is paid down gradually, leaving more value to the owner or equity interest. Equity value results from legal ownership rights—the right to use the real estate in any legal manner, the right to sell it, and the right to convey title upon death. The cost of equity funds, however, may be high. This cost must be measured primarily by the opportunity of investing in other assets which might be higher yielding. Also, an equity interest in real estate may be relatively illiquid and unmarketable—and there may not be enough equity funds to finance the real estate. Because of the disadvantages of having to rely totally on equity funds, then, real estate users, as well as other capital users, use borrowed funds extensively.

Figure 14–1 suggests that the principal sources of borrowed funds are the financial institutions, including banks, savings and loans, mutual savings

---

[1] Savings or reserves build up in nonterm life insurance policies because a purchaser pays a higher premium than would be required for pure protection. Part of the premium of an ordinary life, limited pay life, or endowment policy thus accumulates as "cash value" and is available to the owner of the policy.

banks and life insurance companies. They are regarded as sources even though they depend on savings by individuals and companies. The institutions decide how the funds will be used and allocated among loan applicants. Of course, when individuals loan funds directly for real estate usage, they are also regarded as a source.

Tables 14–1 and 14–2 show the uses and sources of funds in the U.S. economy during 1971 and 1972. As can be seen in Table 14–1, real estate mortgages constitute the single largest use of funds, with government securities (U.S. and state and local) being second. Although the importance of real estate credit in the employment of funds is great, the percentage of funds applied in this way declined in the latter half of the 1960s from the early 1960s when real estate mortgages used about 35

TABLE 14–1

Uses of funds in the U.S. economy (in billions of dollars)

	1971 (est.) *amount*	*Percent* *of total*	*1972 (proj.)* *amount*	*Percent* *of total*
Investment uses:				
Real estate mortgages	48.3	30.82	47.1	27.48
Corporate bonds	19.1	12.19	15.5	9.04
Corporate stocks	11.1	7.08	9.5	5.53
State and local government securities...	21.0	13.40	17.5	10.21
Foreign securities	1.1	0.70	.5	0.29
Term loans by banks	2.3	1.47	3.2	1.87
Funds raised by financial intermediaries.	4.9	3.13	15.3	8.93
Total investment uses	107.8	68.79	108.6	63.36
Short-term uses:				
Open market paper	0.1	0.06	2.0	1.17
Consumer credit	10.0	6.38	12.5	7.29
Policy loans	1.0	0.64	1.5	0.86
Loans of federally sponsored agencies...	.9	0.57	2.2	1.28
Bank loans on securities	—.9	—0.57	1.0	0.58
Bank loans to nonfinancial business	4.6	2.94	8.6	5.02
Other bank loans	4.0	2.55	2.4	1.40
Net trade credit of nonfinancial corps...	7.5	4.79	8.5	4.96
Finance company loans	2.3	1.47	2.5	1.46
Total short-term uses	29.5	18.83	41.2	24.04
U.S. government uses:				
U.S. government securities (publicly held)	20.1	12.83	21.3	12.43
Budget agency securities	—.7	—0.45	—.2	—0.12
Total U.S. Government and agency use	19.4	12.88	21.6*	12.60*
Total uses	156.7	100.00	171.4	100.00

* Total includes $0.5 B U.S. Postal Service financing.
  Source: Economics Division, Bankers Trust Company, New York, N.Y., Annual Report, *The Investment Outlook for 1972*, Tables 2, 3 and 4, pp. 11–13, 1972.

TABLE 14–2

Sources of funds in the U.S. economy in 1971 and 1972 (in billions of dollars)

	1971 (est.) amount	*Percent of total*	*1972 (proj.) amount*	*Percent of total*
Savings institutions—deposit type:				
Savings and loan associations	27.2	17.36	21.7	12.66
Mutual savings banks	9.4	6.00	7.2	4.20
Credit unions	2.7	1.72	2.5	1.46
Commercial banks	43.8	27.95	59.6	34.77
Savings institutions—contractual type:				
Life insurance companies	11.2	7.15	11.6	6.77
Private noninsured pension funds	6.7	4.28	7.5	4.38
State and local government				
retirement funds	7.5	4.78	8.6	5.02
Fire and casualty insurance companies ..	4.7	3.00	4.5	2.63
Mutual funds	—	—	1.8	1.05
Total savings institutions	113.2	72.24	125.0	72.93
Others:				
Nonfinancial corporations	11.7	7.47	16.9	9.86
Financial corporations	4.7	3.00	5.7	3.33
U.S. government	.2	0.13	5.7	0.35
Federally sponsored agencies	4.8	3.06	8.5	4.96
State and local general funds	1.1	0.70	3.5	2.04
Federal Reserve banks	.2	0.13	.1	0.05
Noncorporate business	.5	0.32	.6	0.35
Foreign investors	28.3	18.06	−1.5	−0.86
Residual: Individuals and others	−8.0	−5.11	12.0	7.00
Total	43.5	27.76	46.4	27.07
Total sources	156.7	100.00	171.4	100.00

Source: Economics Division, Bankers Trust Company, New York, N.Y., Annual Report, *The Investment Outlook for 1972*, Table 1, p. 10, 1972.

percent of the total funds supplied. This development reflects the increased demand for funds by large corporations and government agencies. Higher interest rates prevailing during the latter period allowed securities other than mortgages to have relatively more attractive yields.

Commercial banks are the most important source of funds, as shown in Table 14–2. Savings and loans are the second largest source, having decreased in importance in 1966, 1969 and 1970 but regaining their position in 1971. Traditionally, they have supplied 15 to 16 percent of total funds. Interestingly, individuals and others were expected to become an important source in 1972 after having been a net negative source during 1971 and the early 1960s.

In essence, then, the problem of the real estate investor is to be able to tap into the flow of funds at the best time and source to obtain the

FIGURE 14–1

Model of flow of funds into real estate

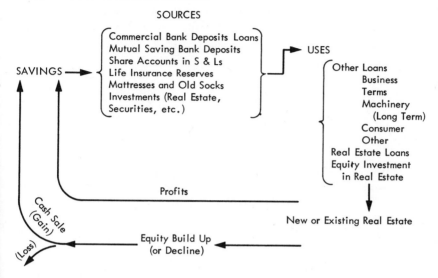

needed amount of funds at the least expense. A model of the flow of funds into real estate is depicted in Figure 14–1. Mr. Randolph and Epic Homes were able to tap the funds flow, although we cannot say without further information (nor can we ever be certain—except with hindsight) whether the best mix of equity and debt funds was used, whether the least expense was incurred, and whether the time was correct in relation to beginning the project. Perhaps a different mix of types of funds, a different combination of sources, or different terms would have been more advantageous to Epic Homes. The problem of determining best mix, terms, and cost is a part of the return on investment calculus and is reserved for more thorough treatment later in this chapter.

It is often the explicit or implicit strategy on the part of a real estate investor to attempt to tap the funds flow on whatever terms fund suppliers will offer. Although not usually stated so bluntly, it is felt that no lender will grant a loan that is beyond the limit of reasonable risk. Furthermore, given a fairly high level of risk, which most real estate projects contain, the cost and terms among the various potential sources will not vary a great deal. Thus, for large, unique projects, the developer too often simply tries to obtain financing at whatever cost or terms are required. Rather than accepting the terms that are offered by one or two lenders, the developer should shop around thoroughly and be prepared, if possible, to wait until better terms can be obtained.

The inability to be selective or to have bargaining power in the borrowing process is a resultant of weakness in the equity position and should be avoided with three exceptions: (1) when the investor has relatively little (in funds, reputation, or other commitments) to lose, while at the same time has a great profit potential, (2) in spite of a slim profit potential and costly financing, there is little risk of default, and (3) when the project is so large that a chunk of borrowed funds will be required even with a sizeable chunk of equity.

Of course, the risks and profit potentials are difficult to assess. In periods of growth and/or inflation, risks are underestimated and profit potentials overestimated. During recessions the opposite assessments are likely to prevail. The real estate investor needs to look beyond the immediate period to the long-run future.

In any event—whether merely to try to obtain a loan on any terms available or to bargain for funds—the investor-borrower should understand the funds flow concept. Where to go to tap the flow and what to expect after he gets there are items of information equally important to the real estate entrepreneur as is the knowledge of construction technique. Thus, we now move to a brief analysis of the principal sources, their characteristics, and legal restraints in making real estate loans.

Savings and loan associations

A type of thrift institution which accumulates savings from individuals, savings and loan associations specialize in lending funds to purchasers of single-family homes. The lender obtains a personal note evidencing the debt and a first mortgage lien on the property. Savings and loans may also loan a portion of their funds on other types of properties such as commercial, industrial, mobile homes, and apartment buildings, but the greatest bulk of their loans must be in one- to four-family residences and government bonds. As shown in Tables 14–3 and 14–4, savings and loans hold twice as much of the outstanding mortgage debt as the next largest institutional holder and by far the largest percentage of mortgage debt to savings of these same institutions.

Savings and loan associations may be either state or federally chartered. State-chartered associations may be either stock-owned companies or mutually owned by the savers. All federally chartered associations must be mutually owned. Federally chartered associations must belong, and many state-chartered associations elect to belong to the Federal Home Loan Bank System and the Federal Savings and Loan Insurance Corporation. This agency insures savings by investors and periodically examines loans made by the associations to determine whether there is any excess risk. The Federal Home Loan Bank Board establishes liquidity requirements, enforces rules and regulations, and maintains a source of funds at district Federal Home Loan Banks which can be borrowed by member savings and loan associations.

TABLE 14–3

Mortgage debt outstanding by type of holder, 1950–1971 (selected years)
(in millions—percentages in brackets)

Year	Total	Mutual savings banks	Commercial banks	Savings and loans	Life insurance companies	Others *
1950	72,800	7,054	10,431	13,657	16,102	25,536
	(100.0)	(9.6)	(11.0)	(18.8)	(22.1)	(38.5)
1955	129,988	17,457	21,004	31,461	29,445	30,621
	(100.0)	(13.4)	(16.2)	(24.2)	(22.7)	(23.6)
1960	206,800	26,935	28,806	60,070	41,771	49,218
	(100.0)	(13.0)	(13.9)	(29.0)	(20.2)	(23.8)
1965	326,100	44,617	49,675	110,306	60,013	61,489
	(100.0)	(13.7)	(15.2)	(33.8)	(18.4)	(18.9)
1970	450,400	57,948	72,882	150,562	74,345	94,686
	(100.0)	(12.8)	(16.2)	(33.4)	(16.5)	(21.0)
1971	499,900	61,978	82,515	174,385	74,700	106,322
	(100.0)	(12.4)	(16.5)	(34.9)	(14.9)	(21.3)

* Government agencies, individuals and other institutions (pension funds mortgage bankers, et al.)
Source: National Association of Mutual Savings Banks, *National Fact Book of Mutual Savings Banking*, New York, 1972, p. 52.

TABLE 14–4

Mortgage loans as a percentage of savings by institution, 1950–1971 (selected years)

Year	Mutual savings banks	Commercial banks	Savings and loans	Life insurance companies
1950	35.5	29.6	97.7	30.0
1955	62.0	45.4	97.8	39.9
1960	74.1	42.9	96.6	43.6
1965	85.0	37.0	99.9	48.8
1967	83.8	35.0	97.8	49.9
1969	83.8	39.9	103.4	48.8
1970	81.0	36.0	102.7	47.5
1971	76.1	34.4	100.0	45.3

Source: National Association of Mutual Savings Banks, *National Fact Book of Mutual Savings Banking*, New York, 1972, pp. 45 and 52; Board of Governors, *Federal Reserve Bulletin*, Washington, D.C., February 1972, pp. A39, A40, A52; Institute of Life Insurance, *Life Insurance Fact Book*, New York, 1971, p. 80.

Although the policies and operations of the individual savings and loans vary greatly, legal requirements and common practices direct savings and loan lending into patterns that are describable in general terms.

Associations are limited as to the loan-to-value ratio and maturity period for mortgage loans they may grant. Since 1971 savings and loans have been empowered to make 95 percent loans, which have replaced much of the FHA lending. Additionally, savings and loan limitations have been somewhat more liberal with respect to loan maturity than other types of institutions. FHA and VA regulations govern the limits on government-underwritten loans, and prior to 1971, these were generally more liberal than terms for conventional loans.

Most (but not all) savings and loans prefer to make conventional loans. They have not been constrained by ceilings on interest rates or the extensive paper work required by the FHA and VA. As shown by Tables 14–5 and 14–6, savings and loans have obtained somewhat higher interest rates on their loans than have most other lenders but have given more liberal terms to borrowers.

Savings and loans have been limited to the direct making of loans within 100 miles of the main office and 100 miles of each branch office,

TABLE 14–5

Interest rates on conventional mortgage loans made by major lenders and comparable yields on FHA loans and selected types of bonds, 1965–1971

	1965	1966	1967	1968	1969	1970	1971
Conventional mortgage loans							
Savings and loans	5.97	6.70	6.59	7.06	7.88	8.50	7.78
Commercial banks	5.64	6.30	6.38	6.82	7.56	7.99	7.42
Mutual savings banks	5.53	6.19	6.25	6.76	7.56	7.98	7.45
Life insurance companies	5.57	6.48	6.46	6.81	7.73	8.72	7.84
Other debt obligations							
FHA* loans	5.83	6.40	6.53	7.12	7.99	8.52	7.70
U. S. government bonds	4.21	4.66	4.85	5.25	6.10	6.59	5.74
State and local bonds	3.34	3.90	3.99	4.48	5.73	6.42	5.62
AAA corporate bonds	4.49	5.13	5.51	6.18	7.03	8.04	7.39

* 30 year maturity and 90 % loan to value ratio.
Source: Board of Governors, *Federal Reserve Bulletin*, Washington, D.C., September, 1972, p. A36; Federal Home Loan Bank Board, *Federal Home Loan Bank Board Journal*, Washington, D.C., November, 1972, p. 31; National Association of Mutual Savings Banks, *National Fact Book of Mutual Savings Banking*, New York, 1972, p. 58; 1970, p. 49.

TABLE 14–6

Maturities and loan to value ratios on conventional loans made by major institutions, 1965–1971

	1965	1966	1967	1968	1969	1970	1971
Savings and loans							
Maturity	25.3	24.9	25.8	24.4	24.5	24.7	25.8
Loan to value ratio	76.1	75.4	75.0	75.7	74.4	73.8	76.5
Commercial banks							
Maturity	20.5	20.6	21.8	20.9	20.5	20.4	22.2
Loan to value ratio	67.3	66.2	66.4	66.7	65.0	65.0	66.3
Mutual savings banks							
Maturity	24.7	22.5	25.0	24.0	23.9	23.0	24.5
Loan to value ratio	69.9	66.1	68.4	68.5	67.4	67.5	69.6
Life insurance companies							
Maturity	25.2	23.5	25.2	26.4	26.1	26.4	27.0
Loan to value ratio	69.0	66.3	69.0	70.1	70.3	70.5	74.1

Source: National Association of Mutual Savings Banks, *National Fact Book of Mutual Savings Banking*, New York, 1969 and 1970, p. 49; 1971 and 1972, p. 58.

provided the territory around a branch office does not cross a state boundary. Thus, savings and loans are considered to be localized lending institutions. This limitation often results in greater specialized knowledge of the local area by the savings and loans, enabling them to fulfill more effectively their role of making loans on residential properties.

Life insurance companies

Historically, the second largest source of funds for mortgages has been the approximately 1,500 life insurance companies. However, as shown by Table 14–8, life insurance companies are no longer a large source of *new* mortgages. Most of the mortgage lending has been done by the large companies; many smaller life insurance companies do not make mortgage loans. Some life insurance companies, including the largest ones, until the late 1960s invested over one-half of their assets in mortgage loans, although just following World War II life insurance companies held less than 15 percent of their assets in such loans. The great increases in real estate lending by life insurance companies occurred principally because mortgages (especially FHA-insured mortgages) provided the right combination of safety and attractive yields, whereas prior to World War II less government underwriting of risk and lower yields made mortgages less desirable. In the early 1970s, however, mortgage yields (particularly on residential properties) have not been so attractive to insurance companies as securities and equities.

Large insurance companies have much greater flexibility in making loans over wide geographic areas than any other type of lender. Most of the large companies are qualified to do business in most or all states, and they utilize a network of mortgage bank correspondents to obtain and service loans.[2] Since the large insurance companies have vast amounts of funds to invest, they prefer to make large loans. The larger loans typically carry higher interest rates, and, as a result of fewer loans, less analysis and paper work is involved. The correspondent typically continues to service the loan for the insurance company, usually receiving a fee of about one-half of one percent of the outstanding balance.

For these reasons, loans on large commercial, industrial, and apartment properties are the dominant type made by insurance companies. When mortgage interest rates are favorable, life insurance companies also lend on entire groups (or packages) of single-family homes that are assembled by mortgage bankers. Because of their unfamiliarity with local real estate markets, the large national lenders usually demand that single-family home loans be underwritten by the FHA or VA.

---

[2] See Halbert C. Smith, *Interregional Mortgage Placement: Lenders' Policies, Practices and Characteristics* (Storrs, Conn.: Center for Real Estate and Urban Economic Studies, 1969) for a critical analysis of life insurance companies' operations in this field.

Commercial banks

Although primarily a lender of short-term business loans, commercial banks in recent years have expanded into the mortgage lending field. These institutions currently hold about 14 percent of the outstanding mortgages; their real estate loans average about 14 percent of their assets. While these percentages indicate that banks are not nearly as important in absolute or relative terms to the mortgage market as are savings and loans and insurance companies, their influence as a source of funds is keenly felt. The reasons for this influence are that (1) banks have attempted to expand their role in mortgage lending, (2) banks have fluctuated in the extent to which they have been active in the mortgage market, and (3) FHA and VA mortgages are not counted in the limits placed by law on the level of mortgages that banks may hold.

In recent years the most progressive commercial banks have attempted to become the department stores of finance. Competitive pressures for savings by other institutions and the need for profitable investment outlets for funds have encouraged banks to offer a wide variety of financial services and to make other types of loans in addition to short-term commercial loans. Mortgage loans (as well as consumer loans, construction and development loans, and business term loans) are now made by most banks.

Mortgages have been attractive investment outlets for banks, particularly during periods of "easy money" and relatively low interest rates. During these periods the yield on mortgages has been high relative to yields on government and municipal bonds and business loans. While mortgage yields typically suffer in comparison with other yields during "tight money" times, the large commercial banks that have gotten into the mortgage loan business have continued to grant mortgage loans during these periods. Nevertheless, the level of all banks' activity in mortgage lending has decreased substantially during periods of monetary restraint.

Banks are limited in the volume of mortgage loans they may have. Current regulations limit holdings of mortgage loans to no more than 70 percent of savings or 100 percent of invested capital, whichever is greater. Since FHA and VA loans are insured and guaranteed by the government, the risk of loss to a bank is very low on these loans, and they do not fall under the mortgage loan limitation.

Because of their background of conservative lending policies and more stringent regulations, banks typically grant less liberal loans than savings and loans. However, the interest rate charged has often been lower. Mortgage terms usually involve lower loan-to-value ratios and shorter maturities than savings and loans.

Banks strive to please their good customers. Consequently they will often grant a mortgage loan to a good customer when they would not make such a loan to a noncustomer. They typically prefer loans in the middle to upper value range in housing or larger loans on commercial and industrial property. Sometimes commercial banks grant a loan in order to service a good customer but then sell the loan to another financial institution, continuing to service the loan. This practice allows the bank to maintain a desirable liquidity position while maintaining the goodwill of customers.

Commercial banks are also good sources of construction and development loans. The regulations for banks' lending in this area have been less stringent than those imposed on savings and loans. These loans are usually short term and are not counted in the bank's portfolio of mortgage loans. Often a bank makes a construction loan when another institution has agreed to make the long-term mortgage loan.

Many banks indirectly make mortgage lending possible by "warehousing" loans for mortgage bankers. The mortgage banker often needs short-term financing while he accumulates a package of loans to sell to a life insurance company. The mortgage company obtains the funds from a commercial bank, pledging mortgages held in the firm's inventory as security for the loan.

Because of these activities and the volatility of banks' activity in the mortgage market, their influence is quite important. Additionally, however, the absolute amount of mortgage lending by banks is significant. The role of banks in providing funds for construction and development is crucial for the creation of new real estate resources to occur.

Mutual savings banks

From their depression-era image as perhaps the most staid and conservative type of lending institution, mutual savings banks have become some of the most imaginative and aggressive lenders. Regarded as something of a cross between commercial banks and savings and loan associations, mutual savings banks have wider investment powers than savings and loans but do not have the capability of creating money, as do commercial banks. Their relatively wide investment power has enabled mutual savings banks to grant mortgage loans on all types of real estate as well as to purchase stocks and bonds of private corporations and all levels of government. In contrast, savings and loans have been limited primarily to granting first mortgage loans on one- to four-family residential real estate and U.S. government securities.

As shown by Table 14–3, mutual savings banks as of December 31, 1971, held almost $62 billion in mortgage loans. This compares with the approximate amounts of $82 billion and $174 billion in mortgage loans held by commercial banks and savings and loans at the same date. Of the total assets held by mutual savings banks, mortgages are by far the most important. Mortgages are almost five times as large as the next largest investment—corporate securities.

Compared with the other major institutional lenders, the volume of mortgages held by mutual savings banks would not appear impressive. However, the concentration of these institutions in New York and New England emphasizes their importance as mortgage lenders in those states. In terms of savings held, New York is by far the largest state, while Massachusetts has the largest number of savings banks. (See Table 14–7.)

TABLE 14–7

Number of and savings held in mutual savings banks by states, December 31, 1971

State	Number	Savings (in millions)
Massachusetts	170	$12,673
New York	120	46,271
Connecticut	68	6,094
Maine	32	1,057
New Hampshire	30	1,178
New Jersey	20	3,662
Washington	9	1,538
Pennsylvania	8	4,971
Rhode Island	7	1,255
Vermont	6	339
Maryland	5	977
Indiana	4	129
Wisconsin	3	40
Alaska	2	67
Delaware	2	424
Minnesota	1	674
Ohio	1	6
Oregon	1	122
Puerto Rico	1	4
Total	490	$81,440

Source: National Association of Mutual Savings Banks, *National Fact Book of Mutual Savings Banking*, New York, 1972, pp. 14 and 46.

Mortgage bankers

Mortgage companies, or mortgage bankers, originate mortgage loans to individuals and firms but do not normally continue to hold the mortgage loan as an asset. Rather, the mortgage banker usually sells the mortgage paper to a large lender, such as a savings and loan association, a life insurance company or a mutual savings bank. (Savings and loans were the largest outlet for mortgage bankers in 1971 and 1972.) Typically, the mortgage banker continues to service the loan for the purchaser of the loan and is compensated for this service by the purchaser. The servicing fee usually runs about one-fourth to one percent of the outstanding balance of the loan. Servicing is defined as taking all steps necessary to make certain the loan provisions are carried out; the most obvious servicing procedure is to collect the monthly payments from the debtor and forward these to the lender.

Mortgage companies sometimes have continuing arrangements with large institutional lenders to obtain loans for them. A large lender will sometimes commit itself to purchase a specified amount of mortgage-secured loans from a mortgage company during a certain time period. Or a lender may let a mortgage banker know what types of loans it would like to purchase. The mortgage banker is then invited to submit such loans to the lender to determine whether to purchase the loan. This procedure is usually followed for large loans. When a mortgage company has a continuing arrangement or commitment to sell loans to an institutional investor, the mortgage banker is known as a correspondent.

Summary of the flow of funds into real estate finance

In summary, we can see from Table 14–8 the uses of credit funds supplied to real estate and the sources from which they came in 1971 and 1972. The largest amount of funds was placed in conventional home mortgages followed by multi-family and commercial loans, second and third respectively. The bulk of these loans (66 percent) was supplied in order of decreasing importance by savings and loans, commercial banks and mutual savings banks. Mortgage companies do not appear in the table because most of the mortgages they originate are sold to other institutional lenders.

The lending and borrowing decisions

With an understanding of the roles that the various institutional lenders play in financing real estate, a real estate investor-entrepreneur can set about to tap into the flow of funds. The entrepreneur usually wants to obtain financing at the lowest cost and under the most reasonable terms possible. The lender wants to believe that the loan will be safe, that is, it will be repaid according to schedule by the borrower, and that the yield obtained from the loan is consistent with yields on investments of comparable risk. Additionally, in recent years lenders have increasingly demanded protection from the risk of inflation through participation in any increased profits generated by the real estate.

Because of the objectives and requirements of lenders, real estate entrepreneurs must submit a total plan for any development to a lender for approval, modification, or rejection. The lender wants to examine such aspects as street layout, subdivision design, adequacy of utilities, lot sizes, location, architecture, and the attractiveness of buildings. Whether the

TABLE 14–8

Real estate mortgage financing summary for 1971 and 1972
(dollar amounts in billions)

	1971 (estimated)	*Percent of total*	*1972 (projected)*	*Percent of total*
Uses:				
Home mortgages:				
Government backed:				
FHA-insured	$ 7.0	14.49	$ 6.5	13.80
VA-guaranteed	4.2	8.70	4.0	8.49
Conventional	16.3	33.75	16.0	33.97
Total	$27.5	56.94	$26.5	56.26
Multi-family mortgages	$ 9.8	20.29	$ 9.5	20.17
Commercial mortgages	8.7	18.01	9.0	19.11
Farm mortgages	2.3	4.76	2.1	4.46
Total	$48.3	100.00	$47.1	100.00
Sources:				
Life Insurance Companies	$ 1.2	2.48	$ 1.9	4.03
Private Noninsured Pension Funds..	.6	−1.24	—	—
State and Local Gov't. Retirement Funds	.4	.83	.5	1.06
Savings and Loans	25.3	52.38	21.8	46.29
Mutual Savings Banks	4.5	9.32	4.0	8.49
Credit Unions	.5	1.04	.4	.85
Commercial Banks	9.0	18.63	7.5	15.92
Financial Corporations	1.5	3.11	1.5	3.19
U.S. Government	.1	.21	.2	.43
Federal Agencies	3.7	7.66	6.1	12.95
State and Local Gov't.	2.5	5.18	2.5	5.31
Other	.4	.83	.7	1.49
Total	$48.3	100.01	$47.1	100.01

Source: Economics Division, Bankers Trust Company, New York, N.Y., Annual Report, *The Investment Outlook for 1972*, Tables 7, 8 and 9, pp. 16–18, 1972.

local market will absorb a new building or development in terms of each of these aspects is the primary concern of the lender. Thus, cost to the developer and the prices he must sell or rent units to the public for must be related to a project's desirability. The entrepreneur must demonstrate that costs are reasonable and realistic, that materials, labor, land, and capital can be combined to produce a marketable project, and that the income from the project will allow the borrower to repay the loan with interest and do so with an adequate safety factor.

Financial analysis

In applying for a loan from an institutional lender, the borrower-developer will be required to submit an estimation of expected costs and a projection of future income and expenses. Examples of such schedules are shown in Tables 14–9 and 14–10. The lender will analyze the financial plan to determine whether it is accurate and realistic. An appraisal will be made either by the lender's appraisal staff or an independent appraiser. The lender may accept the plans and projections, suggest modifications, or reject them. Of course, a lender may believe that a proposed development has merit, yet not grant a loan because of a current lack of loanable funds or because of the availability of other desirable projects.

One large apartment project recently proposed to a life insurance company contained the following estimates of cost.

TABLE 14–9

Presidential Manor Apartment project estimated costs

Land:	
15.043 acres, or 655,263 sq. ft. @ $.46/sq. ft.	$ 301,420
Improvements:	
29 apartment buildings, 252,000 sq. ft. @ $14.50/sq. ft.	3,654,000
Blacktop, 191,000 sq. ft. @ $.40/sq. ft.	76,400
Laundry and maintenance building, 1,350 sq. ft. @ $11/sq. ft.	14,850
Estimated total cost	$4,046,670

The builder should have the building costs itemized for all materials, assemblies, parts, and labor. The costs should include the costs involved in drawing plans and blueprints, obtaining permits, paying city fees, the construction financing expense, legal fees, the marketing expense, overhead and profit, as well as the direct materials and labor costs. If the lender is convinced that the buildings as planned, the land, and other improvements can be obtained for the estimated costs, he will proceed with an analysis of income and expense projections. The project referred to above contained the income and expense projections shown in Table 14–10.

If the lender agrees with this projection of income and expense, he can capitalize the net income stream to estimate the property's value. If a capitalization rate of 10 percent is appropriate and an economic life of the improvements of 40 years is used, the level annuity factor of 9.8 produces an estimated value of 4,220,624, or approximately $4,220,600. To this is added the land reversion ($3,000,000 × .046) of $13,800 for a total value of $4,234,400. On the basis of this value, a life insurance company in this state legally can lend 80 percent, or $3,387,840. The borrower has requested this amount from the insurance company in the form of a 20-year, annually amortized mortgage loan, bearing a 9 percent interest rate.

Assuming that the insurance company is satisfied that the income and expense projections are as realistic and accurate as can be determined, the lender will still want to examine other factors and may propose an alternate financing arrangement to the developer. Important additional con-

TABLE 14–10

Presidential Manor projected income and expenses

Unit type	Number of units	Monthly rental	Sq. ft./ unit	Mo. rent/ sq. ft.	Number of rooms	Rent/room/ month	Total
1-BR Flat	80	$160	620	25.8¢	3	$53.33	$153,600
2-BR Flat	152	185	812	22.8	4	46.25	337,440
2-BR TH	76	200	928	21.6	4	50.00	182,400

Total Projected Annual Rental Income	$673,440
Other income: Laundry @ $25/unit	7,700
Gross annual income	681,140
Less: Vacancy and collection allowance @ 5%	34,072
Effective Gross Income	$647,068
Less expenses:	
Operating:	
Management @ 4½% .... $ 29,118	
Custodial 17,000	
Heat and air conditioning @ $25/room 28,900	
Electric (common areas only) 6,000	
Maintenance @ $12/room 13,872	
Painting and redecorating @ $12/room 13,872	
Miscellaneous 5,000	
Total Operating Expenses $113,762	
Fixed:	
Real estate taxes @ $200/unit .... $ 60,160	
Insurance @ $40/unit 12,320	
Reserve for replacements 30,150	
Total Fixed Expenses $102,630	
Total Operating and Fixed Expenses	216,392
Net Operating Income	$430,676

siderations are (1) the relation of the cash flow to be generated from the property to the financing payments and (2) the effect of the federal income tax on the stream of earnings.

The income projection of Table 14–10 can be extended as follows:

Net cash inflow before payment of financing and income tax		
(first year)		$430,676
Less annual depreciation (40 years straight line on		
building only)	$ 93,665	
Less interest (first year)	304,906	398,571
Net Taxable Income		$ 32,105
Income tax (50%)		16,052
Net Income (after depreciation, interest expense,		
and income tax)		16,053
Add: Depreciation	$ 93,665	
Deduct: Mortgage principal payment (first year)	66,218	27,447
Net Cash Flow (first year)		$ 43,500
Total mortgage payment (9%)	$371,124	
Interest (first year)	304,906	
Principal payment (first year)	$ 66,218	

By dipping into the funds earmarked for depreciation, it is evident that the borrower would be able to meet his mortgage payment and have some cash ($43,500) left over. The margin is not great, however, and both borrower and lender should consider the possibility that the rental estimates may be optimistic. If rents should turn out to be less than anticipated, the borrower might not be able to meet his mortgage commitment. The lender therefore proposed a different financing arrangement.

The new arrangement proposed that the lender grant a loan of $3 million for 25 years at 10 percent interest (amortized annually) and purchase the land for $300,000. The borrower would lease back the land for $30,000 per year (10 percent), this amount being deductible by the borrower for income tax purposes. Additionally, to protect itself against the risk of inflation, the lender wanted a kicker. The kicker took the form of additional rent on the ground tied to net operating income. The lender would be entitled to 25 percent of any additional operating income above that obtained in the current rental schedule. The kicker would continue for the length of the lease on the ground, although the mortgage would in all probability be paid off much sooner. Additionally, the lender stipulated that the property could not be sold or refinanced without its permission for 12 years.

The cash flow generated by the new financing arrangement was estimated as shown in Figure 14–2.

FIGURE 14–2

Estimated cash flow produced by bank-proposed financing arrangement (first year)*

Net Operating Income		$430,676
Less:		
Rent	$ 30,000	
Interest	300,000	
Depreciation	93,665	423,665
Taxable income		$ 7,011
Income tax (50%)		3,505
Net income after tax		$ 3,506
Add depreciation		93,665
		$ 97,171
Deduct mortgage principal payment (1st year)		30,504
Cash Flow (first year)		$ 66,667

* Loan terms: Amount—$3,000,000; Term—25 years; Amortization—Annual; Annual payment—$330,504; Constant—.110168; Interest rate—10 %.

Although the interest rate on the lender's proposed loan is higher than for the loan requested by the developer, the cash flow is greater. The better cash position results because of two factors: (1) the term of the loan is longer, reducing the annual mortgage payment and (2) the ground rent is tax deductible, producing a lower income tax liability for the developer.

If rental income did not increase or if expenses increase as much as income, of course the lender would obtain no increased yield from the kicker. In its projections, however, the lender assumed that net operating income (gross income less vacancy and operating expenses) would increase 3 percent per year. The property's cash flow would increase each year under the assumption, and both the lender's and developer's yields would increase, as shown in Tables 14–11 and 14–12. Thus, for the second year

TABLE 14–11

Lender's rate of return for 12-year locked-in period*

Year	Net operating income	Additional income over previous year	Kicker (25% of additional income)	Interest + Ground rent + Kicker	Lender's investment (Mortgage balance + Land)	Lender's rate of R.O.I.†
1	$430,676	—0—	—0—	$330,000	$3,300,000	10.00%
2	443,596	$12,920	$3,230	330,180	3,269,496	10.09
3	456,896	13,308	3,327	326,921	3,235,942	10.10
4	470,204	13,705	3,426	323,329	3,199,032	10.10
5	484,310	14,106	3,527	319,370	3,158,431	10.11
6	498,839	14,529	3,632	315,009	3,113,770	10.11
7	513,804	14,965	3,741	310,205	3,064,643	10.12
8	529,218	15,414	3,854	304,914	3,010,603	10.12
9	545,095	15,877	3,969	299,085	2,951,159	10.13
10	561,448	16,353	4,088	292,665	2,885,771	10.14
11	578,291	16,843	4,211	285,585	2,813,744	10.14
12	595,640	17,349	4,337	277,798	2,734,614	10.15

* Amount of loan—$3,000,000; Term—25 years; Interest rate—10 %; Amortization—Annual; Mortgage constant—.110168; Annual payment—$330,504.

† Return on Investment = $\dfrac{\text{Total Income}}{\text{Outstanding Investment}}$

$12,920 additional operating income would be generated, the lender receiving $3,230 and the developer receiving the remainder. The rates of return for each year are calculated by adding the total inflows to each party—the lender and developer—and dividing by the total investment of each. Income to the lender consists of mortgage interest, ground rent, and kicker income.

The developer's before-tax cash return to invested equity is calculated by deducting from net operating income ground rent and total debt service (mortgage interest plus principal payments) and adding the expected increases in net operating income, after subtracting the kicker paid to the lender. Although the mortgage principal payments serve to build up equity in the property, it can be assumed that depreciation equals the annual principal payments. The resulting rate of return is equal to in-

TABLE 14–12

Developer's before-tax rate of return for 12-year locked-in period

Year	Developer's additional NOI	Total income to developer	Developer's ROI *
1	—0—	$ 70,172 †	9.41%
2	$ 9,690	79,862	10.71
3	9,981	89,843	12.05
4	· 10,279	100,122	13.43
5	10,579	110,701	14.85
6	10,897	121,598	16.31
7	11,224	132,822	17.82
8	11,560	144,382	19.37
9	11,908	155,290	20.83
10	12,265	167,555	22.48
11	12,632	180,187	24.17
12	13,012	193,199	25.92

$$* \text{ Return on Investment} = \frac{\text{Total Income}}{\text{Outstanding Investment}}$$

Developer's investment calculated as follows:

Cost of improvements:	$3,745,250	
Less mortgage:	3,000,000	
	$ 745,250	

† Income to developer = 1st year's NOI − Ground rent and debt service
= $430,676 − ($30,000 + $330,504)
= $70,172

creasing the developer's investment each year by the amounts of the principal payment and increasing the developer's cash by the same amount of depreciation.

From the example it is clear that the developer of the apartment complex is able to obtain the financing necessary to produce the project and to realize an extremely attractive rate of return. The rate of return, however, is dependent upon the assumption of an annual, compounded growth rate of net income by 3 percent. The requirement that he pay a higher interest rate (10% vs. 9%) and extend the maturity five years has worked to his advantage. His annual mortgage payments are lower, thus giving him a greater cash flow. If the apartment project is successful, the higher interest rate and longer maturity will not be burdensome, whereas he will have gained a more secure financial position. On the other hand, the insurance company will have gained a higher rate of return, which to it is very important.

Obviously, any number of different financing schemes could be worked out. Interest rates, maturities, amortization schedules, and kickers could be changed to reflect the best combination for one or both parties. In recent years the field of income property financing has experienced almost every conceivable financing arrangement. There is no such thing as a "standard" or even "preferred" type of loan package.

The clear implication for the real estate developer is that he needs to understand the various instruments and techniques of real estate finance. He needs to realize that he can and should shop around for a lender who will put together a financing package suitable for his requirements. Even better, he needs to be able to suggest financing arrangements to lenders that will meet the lender's requirements for legality and safety, yet which provide the required amount of funds at the proper place and time. The key to most successful real estate developments is financing.

INSTRUMENTS OF REAL ESTATE FINANCE

The principal instruments, or legal arrangements, used in financing real estate are the note, the mortgage, the deed of trust, the land contract, and the lease. They are described in chapter 9, and it may be helpful to review them in conjunction with this chapter. In a review of these instruments, three questions should be kept in mind: (1) what is their essential nature? (2) what legal responsibilities do they create? and (3) how are they used in real estate transactions?

If the investor, as well as the lender, understands the implications of these three questions, he should be able to structure creative financing arrangements for proposed investment opportunities. For example, an investor may find that an advantageous method of financing an investment is to create a split ownership situation by selling the land and leasing it back. Another investor with little or no capital may be able to obtain control of a property by purchasing on a land contract. A home builder may increase sales by having obtained prior agreement from a lender to finance major appliances in a package mortgage. An investor may decrease his tax liability by making an installment purchase. And yet another investor may be able to finance properties by forming syndicates and selling limited partnership shares. These arrangements require the creation of legal rights and obligations appropriate for each party to a transaction. Such arrangements and combinations (as well as others) are created by the basic instruments of real estate finance, tailored to the individual situation and purpose.

SPECIALIZED TYPES OF REAL ESTATE FINANCE

Several types of ownership or purchase arrangements of parcels of real estate have developed in recent years. Several reasons can be hypothesized for the growth of these arrangements. First, demographic characteristics of the country have greatly increased the need for the services of real estate. The great population increase, the density of population in our cities, and the large numbers of population in the older and younger categories have all resulted in great demands being placed upon housing and commercial and industrial establishments that serve housing and related industries. The young and old age groups have been particularly significant in increasing the demand for apartments. Housing construction costs have risen in the last several years at a faster rate than have other costs in the economy. Thus, the necessity for financing these needs has shown that the traditional purchase of a single-family residence by means of a large downpayment mortgage loan has been inadequate.

Additionally, investors have not had the same kinds of opportunities to purchase small shares or interests in real estate as have investors in securities. In an effort to gain the capacity to attract the savings of small investors, interests in real estate have been divided up and sold in relatively small shares.

Condominiums

The condominium arrangement differs from traditional real estate ownership arrangements in that a single property is divided into several physical portions, usually apartments or office spaces, with each unit being owned by a different owner. The purchaser of a condominium can pay cash or finance his purchase in any of the traditional ways. As with any property ownership, the owner must pay real estate taxes and all other costs and expenses associated with his property. Additionally, however, he must pay a monthly charge for the management and maintenance of the common areas of the property, such as hallways and the lawn. The advantage to this arrangement, as contrasted with some other possibilities, is that a condominium owner has long-term possession and control of the property, and any value increases will be reflected in equity buildup for the owner. If he vacates rented property, of course, his rent receipts would not reflect any increased real estate value.

Condominiums are particularly attractive arrangements for large apartment buildings and are being used to a great extent in Florida, California, and large cities in some other states. Condominiums are also attractive to builders in that the builder is able to get out from under the responsibilities of owning and continuing to manage and maintain the property. These functions are usually turned over to professional managers by the condominium owners.

Cooperatives

In their practical effect, cooperatives are similar to condominiums. A building's space is divided up, and owners of partial interest occupy the space. Unlike condominiums, however, the cooperative owners do not own real estate; they own stock in a corporation which owns the real estate. The main result of this difference is that the purchaser-owner must purchase stock and finance it by means other than a mortgage loan. Since he does not own the fee simple title, he cannot mortgage his real estate ownership. His right to equity buildup and possession and control of the premises would be similar to that of condominiums.

Like the condominium owner, the cooperative owner must also pay monthly charges for maintaining common areas and other common expenses such as janitorial service, management, and maintenance. Whereas a condominium owner can sell his interest in real estate, a cooperative owner can sell his stock and the occupancy rights which accompany his ownership.

Real estate investment trusts

In 1960 the federal income tax law was amended to recognize the real estate investment trust as a passive investment vehicle whose income that is passed on to beneficiaries is not taxed. This provision gave investors in real estate investment trusts the same tax advantage that investors in mutual funds have. To obtain this tax advantage, a real estate investment trust must distribute at least 90 percent of its taxable income in dividends, 75 percent of the value of the trust's assets must be in real estate, first mortgages, cash, or government securities, and the trust must not hold property owned primarily for sale to customers as a dealer. Funds to purchase investment real estate are obtained from many investors (there must be at least 100 or more persons to qualify for the tax advantage) in the same way that a corporation obtains capital by selling stock. The real estate investment trust sells shares, which are really certificates of beneficial interest in the trust. The shares are freely transferable and are limited in liability to the amount paid. A board of trustees runs the investment trust for the benefit of the share owners.

Real estate investment trusts are a vehicle by which a relatively small investor can own a share of a much larger property. Actually share owners in a real estate investment trust own shares of many properties in most cases. Thus, there is a great amount of diversification through trust ownership of several properties. The share owner is usually paid a regular dividend on his shares coming from the income produced by the real estate and by the depreciation expense charged on the books. If the property accumulates in value at a rate greater than the depreciation rate, the share owners' equity capital may appreciate in value. An additional advantage to the small investor is that he obtains the benefits of professional management which he would not have if he saved his funds and invested them in a property on his own. Also, he may benefit from the use of leverage by the investment trust. That is, the trust may borrow funds from a financial institution to help finance properties that it purchases.

Real estate syndicates

As emphasized in chapter 7, syndicates are not a separate form of business organization. Rather, the term refers to the fact that several investors in real estate accumulate their capital within one of the traditional forms of business organization for a particular purpose—such as the purchase of a parcel of real estate.

A syndicate is usually formed as a corporation or a limited partnership. If it is formed as a corporation, the investors receive shares as evidence of their interest in the venture. If the syndicate is formed as a limited partnership, the investors receive limited partnership interests. In the limited partnership arrangement there is at least one general partner with unlimited liability; however, most of the investors will have limited liability. There will be supplementary agreements among the members outlining the rights and responsibilities of various interest holders. Although the limited partners have no voice in the management of the syndicate or the property, they do have the right to a proportional share in the earnings of the syndicate as they are distributed. When the venture for which the syndicate is formed is completed, the syndicate is dissolved.

RISK IN REAL ESTATE FINANCING

Risk in using borrowed funds to help purchase and own real estate can be viewed from the standpoint of either the owner-investor or the lender. In the case of the investor, the principal risk associated with financing is that the monthly or annual cash flow will not be sufficient to meet the mortgage payments. In such a case, the owner must be prepared to obtain funds from other sources to pay the mortgage loan or to forfeit the property. The chart on page 36 shows the relationship between cash flow and mortgage payment on a month by month basis for a year. It is evident that during the months of April and June the owner must be prepared to obtain additional funds from other sources in order to meet his debt obligation. If he cannot do this, it is likely that he will not be able to retain the property.

It is evident therefore that an investor and a lender should carefully consider the factors that would cause the projected income and cash flow not to be realized and to try to evaluate the likelihood that external events would influence any projected income flows. Vacancies, deaths, illnesses, and external economic, political, and social considerations must be analyzed. Final determination as to safety of the loan will of necessity be subjective. Nevertheless, such an analysis is crucial to successful real estate lending and investment.

GOVERNMENT INFLUENCE ON REAL ESTATE FINANCE

Government influence on real estate finance is pervasive, although largely indirect. The influence is indirect in the sense that governmental agencies do not become directly involved in the financing operations of real estate transactions. Rather, they establish and operate a framework of interest rates, insurance, regulation of secondary markets, and special purpose assistance. The framework, however, is pervasive in that every real estate transaction is affected by government activity. Since it has hopefully been demonstrated earlier in this chapter that financing is a major determinant of the profitability of real estate investments, the significance of government influence on financing arrangements and terms can hardly be overemphasized.

One may analyze the structure and operations of government activity through the various agencies or through the functions they perform. The primary agencies affecting real estate finance are (1) the Federal Reserve System, (2) the Federal Home Loan Bank System, (3) the U.S. Treasury, (4) the Department of Housing and Urban Development, and (5) the Veterans Administration. Abbreviated organization charts are shown in Figures 14–3 to 14–5 of three of these agencies. As can be seen from these charts, several subagencies or organizations affiliated with these agencies are important components of the total picture. While it is not our purpose to describe in detail the nature of these agencies and subagencies, we do

FIGURE 14–3

Federal Reserve System organization structure

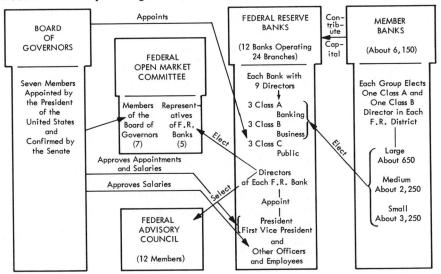

Source: Board of Governors, *The Federal Reserve System: Purposes and Functions* (Washington, D.C. 1963), p. 23.

FIGURE 14–4

Federal Home Loan Bank System organization structure

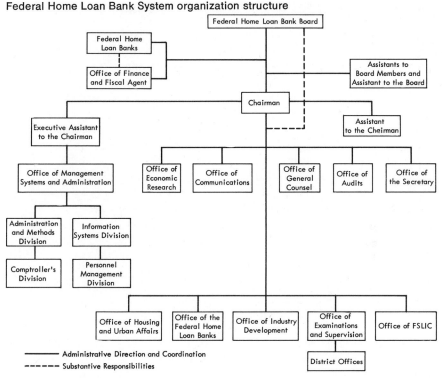

Source: *Federal Home Loan Bank Board Annual Report, 1969*, p. 91.

need to examine the ways in which they affect the financing of real estate. In order to do this we refer to Table 14–13, which identifies six major functions and the agencies and organizations that carry out each function. It is hoped that this manner of presentation will emphasize the complexity of the bureaucratic web which plays such an important role in determining the attractiveness of real estate transactions and investments.

Regulation of the supply of funds and interest rates

The supply of funds and the level of interest rates in the economy are influenced by several factors, including Federal Reserve policy, debt management policies of the U.S. Treasury, the financing of new plants and equipment, purchases by large corporations, and the financing needs of individual investors and consumers. The Federal Reserve System is perhaps the most important one of these determinants. Its function is to establish, maintain, and supervise the monetary system for the country. It has direct control of the supply of money in the economy and of certain interest rates, which influence all interest rates. This control is exercised

FIGURE 14–5

Department of Housing and Urban Development organization structure

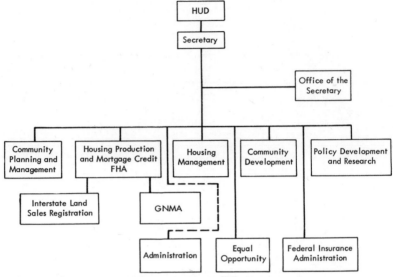

Source: *U.S. Department of Housing and Urban Development Annual Report, 1969.*

through the instruments of monetary regulation—the discount rate, reserve requirements, and open market operations. Through the operation of these instruments, the Board of Governors of the Federal Reserve System can effectively increase or decrease the rate of growth of the money supply and can drive interest rates upward or downward.

The important point for our consideration in considering the Federal Reserve System is that the policies adopted by its Board of Governors influence real estate to a greater extent than any other economic good. If the Board of Governors decides to slow the rate of growth of the money supply and to drive interest rates upward, the effect is to make real estate financing for many would-be purchasers more difficult and costly. With the decreased availability of funds and higher interest rates, many persons will stay out of the market. On the other hand, during periods of monetary ease, when the money supply is growing at an ample rate and interest rates are relatively low, financing is more readily available to a greater number of people. Marginal buyers will be able to obtain financing, and real estate activity will tend to increase.

Obviously, this analysis is much oversimplified. Other factors may at times be equal in importance or perhaps even more important to real estate financing than Federal Reserve policy. For example, if there is general pessimism about the future of the economy, an increased rate of growth of the money supply and lower interest rates will not by them-

TABLE 14–13

Functions and government agencies associated with real estate finance

Function	*Government agency*
Regulation of the supply of funds and interest rates	1. Federal Reserve System 2. U.S. Treasury (debt management)
Secondary market activities	1. Federal National Mortgage Association 2. Federal Home Loan Mortgage Corporation 3. Government National Mortgage Association—Department of Housing and Urban Development
Supervision and insurance	1. Federal Reserve System 2. Federal Deposit Insurance Corporation 3. Federal Home Loan Bank Board 4. Federal Savings and Loan Insurance Corporation 5. State Regulatory Agencies
Special aid for low-income housing and urban renewal	1. Offices for Housing Production and Mortgage Credit, Housing Management, and Community Development—Department of Housing and Urban Development 2. Government National Mortgage Association
Mortgage loan insurance and guarantee	1. Federal Housing Administration—Department of Housing and Urban Development 2. Veterans Administration
Taxation	1. U.S. Internal Revenue Service 2. Local Taxing Authorities (real estate tax)

selves overcome this factor. Also, if the demand for funds increases greatly on the part of the government or by private industry for non-real estate purposes, an increase in the total availability of funds would perhaps not benefit real estate interests. Nevertheless, the influence of Federal Reserve policies must be considered both in terms of their own effects on real estate finance and in relation to other considerations that we have just discussed. The importance of financing to almost every real estate transaction means that Federal Reserve policy will often mean the difference between whether a buyer desires and can afford to complete a transaction.

The financing of the national debt of the United States is also an important consideration to the financing of real estate. The amount which the U.S. government owes holders of short-term and long-term debt is well over $400 billion. Since the amount of the debt continues to grow and there is no thought that the debt will be paid off to any significant extent, the Treasury must continually refinance the debt. As this refinancing takes place, the amounts of funds drained from the capital market and the interest rates paid on the securities that are issued have a significant impact upon the amount of funds available and interest rate levels in the economy. In general, as interest rates rise and government bonds become relatively more attractive, funds are siphoned off from potential real estate usage. When funds become more readily available and interest rates on government securities are relatively low, mortgage investment is more attractive and funds flow into real estate finance.

Secondary market activities

Two government-related agencies operate to provide a market for those wishing to sell previously originated mortgage loans. Such an operation provides liquidity for mortgage loans and thus stimulates a large flow of funds for financing real estate. The Federal National Mortgage Association (known as Fanny May) has specialized in buying and selling mortgages that are insured by the Federal Housing Administration or guaranteed by the Veterans Administration. Its intent is to develop secondary market operations in nongovernment underwritten (conventional) mortgages as well, however. The Federal National Mortgage Association (FNMA) tends to be a net buyer of mortgage loans, as it unpopularly tightens the mortgage market when it sells loans. It buys loans by periodically announcing a dollar amount of mortgages that it will purchase. Those who wish to sell mortgages to it, typically mortgage companies, then auction their mortgages to Fanny May on the basis of yield. Fanny May will buy those mortgages up to the indicated amount that are offered to it at the lowest prices offered. FNMA obtains its funds to buy mortgages by selling capital stock to those who sell mortgages to the association, by the sale of mortgage-backed debentures, short-term discount notes, and U.S. Treasury borrowing.

The second organization is the Federal Home Loan Mortgage corporation (FHLMC). This is a relatively new organization, having been established by an act of Congress in 1970. Capital stock of FHLMC of $100 million was acquired by the 12 Federal Home Loan Banks. It is closely associated with the Federal Home Loan Bank System, since the three directors of the Federal Home Loan Bank Board also serve as the directors of the FHLMC, and policy is coordinated with the credit policies of the 12 regional Federal Home Loan banks. The FHLMC will buy FHA- and VA-backed mortgages and will acquire up to an 85 percent interest in a group of nongovernment-backed mortgages. It is likely that FHLMC will purchase whole conventional loans in the near future.

Another organization, the Government National Mortgage Association also serves as a secondary market for mortgages granted under special purpose government programs. It will purchase mortgages made under sections of the National Housing Act designed to help particular needy groups. For example, it might purchase a mortgage loan made to a sponsor of an apartment project for low-income families who are under a government subsidy program.

Supervision and insurance

The Federal Reserve System, the Federal Home Loan Bank Board, state regulatory agencies, the Federal Deposit Insurance Corporation (FDIC), and the Federal Savings and Loan Insurance Corporation (FSLIC) all have a supervisory role over banking and thrift institutions under their jurisdictions. The Federal Reserve System supervises member commercial banks—all national banks and state banks which are members of the system. The Federal Home Loan Bank System supervises savings and loan associations that are members—all federally chartered associations and state-chartered member associations. State regulatory agencies for both banks and savings and loan associations that are chartered by the states and that are not members of the Federal Reserve System or the Federal Home Loan Bank System supervise the operations of these institutions. All of these institutions are required to abide by specific regulations and standards in regard to the loans that they make. The supervisory function is for the purpose of assuring that the standards and regulations are observed by the various institutions.

The Federal Deposit Insurance Corporation and the Federal Savings and Loan Insurance Corporation insure deposits or accounts in banks or savings and loans up to a maximum of $20 thousand each. By so doing, the agencies provide real relief in the rare instances where a financial institution goes bankrupt, and they insure public confidence as to the safety of funds placed in financial institutions. Public confidence had been greatly shaken during the Great Depression of the 1930s, leading to the formation of the FDIC and the FSLIC.

Mortgage loan insurance and guarantee

The Federal Housing Administration is an agency under the Department of Housing and Urban Development. This agency, which was also born in the depth of the Great Depression, and the Veterans Administration insure and guarantee, respectively, loans that might otherwise be considered too risky by lending institutions. The terms on FHA-insured loans and VA-guaranteed loans are usually considerably more liberal than those allowed by conventional lenders. The U.S. government, however, backs the loans which qualify thus giving added capacity for borrowing to veterans and others who could not otherwise purchase a home. In order to obtain a government backing, both the borrower and the property which he intends to purchase must meet specified standards. Insurance premiums to pay for the backing are made in the monthly mortgage payment.

Special aid for low-income housing and urban renewal

The Department of Housing and Urban Development's functional offices for Community Development, Housing Management, and Housing Production and Mortgage Credit—FHA are primarily responsible for the government effort in the fields of low-income housing and urban renewal. The Assistant Secretary for Community Development is responsible for administering loans and grants to local public agencies engaged in urban renewal. Through this office of HUD the U.S. government will pay a large proportion of the cost of urban renewal projects which meet the standards imposed by HUD.

The Assistant Secretaries for Housing Management and Housing Production and Mortgage Credit supervise a number of programs to enable low-income people to occupy safe, sanitary housing. Traditional public housing programs, whereby the government subsidizes local housing authorities in providing low-income housing was the first concern of HUD. Newer efforts include various Turnkey programs, a leasing program, and an elderly housing program. The Turnkey programs involve the purchase or leasing of new or rehabilitated units by a local housing authority for the purpose of renting or selling the units to low-income families. A builder or owner constructs or rehabilitates units in accordance with plans approved by the FHA and HUD and then turns the key over to the housing authority. The owner, of course, receives either the purchase price or the agreed upon rental from the housing authority.

Turnkey III is a home ownership program for low-rent public housing tenants. If the tenant pays rent and maintains and repairs the property for 20 to 21 years, he may obtain ownership of the unit. The federal government, through annual contributions, pays the mortgage principal and interest.

The Section 23 Leasing program is similar in concept to Turnkey leasing. An owner can lease apartments to a local housing authority for occupancy by low-income tenants. Market rents and no vacancy are assured the owner for the duration of the lease contract.

Section 202, Elderly Housing, is a program of direct, 3 percent interest rate, 100 percent loan-value ratio loans for a term of up to 50 years for housing for elderly individuals or heads of households 62 years or older. The loans are made to a nonprofit sponsor for the construction or rehabilitation of the units.

Taxation

Although the manner in which taxes influence a particular real estate investment was described and analyzed in chapter 7, it should be recognized here that income, state, and gift taxes exert a great influence on real estate decisions. Tax rates applied to various types and amounts of income, and the rules promulgated to calculate the tax burden must be considered when analyzing an investment decision. Rules regarding allowable economic lives and rates of depreciation are particularly important in this regard. When the rules governing these matters are changed, the relative attractiveness of real estate investments may be altered drastically. For example, the Tax Reform Act of 1969 eliminated the double-declining balance method of calculating depreciation for new, nonresidential property. Investment in new commercial and industrial properties thus became considerably less desirable than had formerly been the case.

SUMMARY

Obtaining financing on favorable terms and at a reasonable cost is an important aspect of creating successful real estate projects. Although some amount of equity funds will normally be required in the production or purchase of real estate, the bulk of funds usually will be borrowed; these funds constitute the debt capital committed to a project.

In seeking debt capital, the real estate investor attempts to tap into the flow of funds available for such financing. The principal sources of debt capital are savings and loan associations, commercial banks, life insurance companies, and mutual savings banks. Mortgage bankers play a facilitating role by granting loans for real estate use and then selling the loans to institutional lenders. When shopping for loans, the real estate investor needs to understand the legal framework, characteristics, and practices of the institutional lenders. In bargaining with lenders, he can often be prepared to concede a point of relatively small importance to him (such as a somewhat higher interest rate) in order to obtain a feature of great importance to him but of less importance to the lender (such as a higher loan-to-value ratio).

In analyzing a proposed real estate project, the developer should compute his expected rate of return by relating forecasted net income to his required capital investment. Expenses, as well as rental income, should be evaluated carefully and projected as realistically as possible for the expected life of the investment. Vacancy rates, management expense, and replacement reserves must be included in the expense forecast.

Some basic legal documents used in real estate finance—the note, the mortgage, the deed of trust, the land contract, and the lease—are discussed in terms of their significance to the investor. By knowing the possible relationships that can be established by these documents, one can be creative in designing financing arrangements that meet the needs of both the providers of equity capital and the providers of debt capital.

In recent years several specialized types of real estate finance have gained prominence. Condominiums and cooperatives have made it possible for occupants of apartments and offices to obtain the advantages of ownership (and for condominium owners to obtain the advantages of mortgage financing) over the leasing arrangement. In both the condominium and cooperative arrangement, any increases in value of the properties accrue to the owners. Real estate investment trusts and syndicates are designed to allow investment in real estate by relatively small investors and offer the potential advantages of expert analysis and professional management.

Lastly, the chapter deals with the pervasive influence of government on real estate finance. While government agencies normally do not become directly involved in private financing transactions and arrangements, their influence plays a prominent role in determining the quantity and types of financing available. The Federal Reserve System, the Federal Home Loan Bank System, the U.S. Treasury, the U.S. Department of Housing and Urban Development, and the Veterans Administration establish and operate a framework for real estate finance of interest rate determination, institutional supervision and regulation, secondary mortgage market activity, loan insurance, and special purpose assistance.

QUESTIONS FOR REVIEW

1. In what ways is financing real estate different from financing corporate securities? Why?

2. Why are mortgage bankers not shown as an important source of mortgage funds in the U.S. flow of funds accounting system?

3. What are the advantages and dangers of purchasing and selling by land contract? How would you protect yourself against the dangers?

4. How do you explain the fact that savings and loan associations dropped in the percentage of funds supplied in the U.S. economy from an average of about 16 percent per year in the early 1960s to less than 10 percent in the late 1960s?

5. Why do savings and loans and mutual savings banks lend a much higher percentage of their savings on mortgages than do commercial banks?

6. What is a "kicker"? Do you believe kickers will continue to exist during periods of lower interest rates?

7. How does financing influence a developer's expected return on investment? How does financing influence cash flow? What role is played by principal repayments?

8. Look up an annual report of the U.S. Department of Housing and Urban Development. What are the principal kinds of programs carried on by this agency?

9. What are the advantages of condominium ownership of an apartment over leasing the same apartment? What are the advantages of leasing over ownership? Which do you prefer?

10. Why are the effects of monetary policies of the Board of Governors of the Federal Reserve System so keenly felt in the field of real estate finance?

PROBLEMS

1. Indicate the cash flow and taxable income associated with the following facts:

Gross Income	$500,000
Vacancy allowance	5% of gross
Operating expenses plus fixed expenses	37% of effective gross
Mortgage (new)	$1,800,000
Debt Service constant	.0967
Interest rate on mortgage	8½%
Depreciation—1st year	$100,000

2. Prepare a numerical example that shows an after-income tax advantage of owning a condominium apartment over renting the same apartment. Incorporate the following data into your example:

Rental level if rented	$300 per month
Purchase price	$35,000
Mortgage	90% of price
Marginal income tax rate	40%
Utilities and maintenance	$800 per year
Real Estate taxes	$700 per year

REFERENCES

Hoagland, Henry E. and Stone, Leo D. *Real Estate Finance,* 3d ed. Homewood, Ill.: Richard D. Irwin, Inc., 1965.

Ricks, R. Bruce and McElhone, Josephine T. "A Five-Year Plan of Asset-Liability Restructuring for S&L's," *Federal Home Loan Bank Board Journal,* March 1971, pp. 3–8 and 27.

Smith, Halbert C. "Institutional Aspects of Interregional Mortgage Investment," *Journal of Finance,* Vol. 23, No. 2 (May 1968), pp. 349–58.

Smith, Halbert C. *Interregional Mortgage Placement: Lenders' Policies, Practices and Characteristics.* Storrs, Conn.: University of Connecticut, Center for Real Estate and Urban Economic Studies, 1969.

Smith, Halbert C. "Regional Placement of Mortgage Funds by Life Insurance Companies and Mutual Savings Banks," *Journal of Risk and Insurance,* Vol. 31, No. 3 (September 1964) pp. 429–36.

Smith, Halbert C. "The Savings and Loan Business in 1973," *Federal Home Loan Bank Board Journal,* January 1973, pp. 1–4.

Smith, Halbert C. and Tschappat, Carl J. "Monetary Policy and Real Estate Values," *Appraisal Journal,* Vol. 34, No. 1 (January 1966), pp. 18–26.

—————————————PART V

Real estate administration in the public sector

—————————————— chapter **15**

REAL ESTATE ADMINISTRATION IN THE PUBLIC SECTOR

REAL ESTATE decision-making and implementation of decisions have been analyzed in previous chapters as processes within the private sector of the economy. The decision maker as an individual, household, or firm was assumed to collect relevant information, engage in rational problem-solving behavior, and reach a decision based upon his objectives and priorities. The term, micro administration, was used to describe this individual decision-making process and its implementation. The functions of real estate production (chapter 13), marketing (chapter 12), and financing (chapter 14) resulted from the collective implementation of these separate decisions in the private sector.

Subsequent chapters focus on decision making and implementation by the public sector, which are major aspects of macro administration, and reflect the breadth and magnitude of public sector decisions. Decisions made at the level of the federal government can affect cities and communities throughout the nation or within an entire region, such as Appalachia. Federal mortgage insurance, subsidized housing, federal tax policies, and other federal programs have a pervasive impact on all urban housing. At the level of local government, a decision to improve an urban arterial route sets in motion repercussions throughout the community. Travel patterns are affected, the demand for transit can be altered, linkages among urban land uses are realigned, and ultimately, the configuration of urban land uses and topography of urban land values can change.

Macro administration of urban real estate resources also produces a widespread impact because of the relatively large-scale investment undertaken. Investors in the private sector continually demolish existing structures and construct new improvements, but rarely, if ever, is reconstruction undertaken in the magnitude of an urban renewal project. The scale of public investment produces a macro effect by becoming an input in the micro administration of real estate situated in areas remote from the public project.

This chapter provides an overview of the process of decision making in the public sector. It is concerned with identification of decision makers, their decision-making processes, and the manner in which alternatives are generated. Subsequent chapters are concerned with the criteria or objectives used to select the best alternative action, the manner in which the action is implemented, the end results, and the effect of these results upon the decisions and actions of other decision makers in both the public and private sectors. For the most part, attention is deliberately focused on the expenditure decisions in the public sector. It must be recognized that all actions taken by the public sector require expenditures, including regulatory action, such as the formulation of the master plan and its implementation through zoning.

How much government?

When the economist debates the relative magnitudes of expenditure and investment to be made by the public sector of our economy, he becomes just another citizen. At the heart of the decision are the value judgments that influence the individual in his selection of goals and the means for meeting them. Economists differ in their interpretation of goals and selection of means, as do other citizens. As a nation, we are committed by tradition and philosophy to the tenets of capitalism, individual freedom, and equality of opportunity. We advocate a competitive market, free enterprise, and the sovereign consumer. An individual often defines these goals differently, or he may repudiate one or more of them entirely. Indeed, our collective goal of individual freedom sanctions this right to disagree.

Regardless of the personal philosophy of the economist, economic principles in their most abstract form are universal and apply in any culture. The following principle can be stated for any nation: Our national resources and production should be distributed between the public sector and private sector in such a manner that the marginal satisfaction from the last dollar spent (invested by) the public sector just equals the marginal satisfaction from the last dollar spent (invested by) the private sector. Furthermore, total welfare will be maximized when the resources controlled by each sector of the economy are utilized in the most efficient manner. Application of these principles could produce government budgets of different magnitude in nations equal in total resources and technology. Our nation might obtain a lesser quantum of satisfaction from a dollar spent by the public sector than another country which embraces goals of government ownership of the means of production and a high degree of income equality among its citizens.

Our society accepts public expenditures for the purchase of goods and services from the private sector, investment in social overhead capital, and transfer payments. The provision of public services requires that persons be paid as administrators, legislators, civil servants, and judges and that materials and consumer goods be purchased (primarily from the private sector) for the national defense, space exploration, housing programs, and other government activities. Bridges, schools, public buildings, housing projects, highways, and parks are constructed and become public investments in social capital. Social security payments, unemployment compensation and partial payments of rent or mortgage payments are examples of transfer payments that redistribute income.

Transfer payments. Some government expenditures are the result of perceived need, with perception being influenced by our values and attitudes. The transfer programs of old age assistance, veteran's cash bonuses, housing subsidies, unemployment compensation, farm subsidies, and many aspects of the "war on poverty" belong in this category. These programs transfer income among groups in our society and do not necessarily cause resources to bypass the market, but simply redistribute command over resources among our citizens. On the other hand, the present housing subsidy program transfers income in kind in the form of standard housing, rather than giving cash income to the lower income family and allowing them to control resources by voting their preferences in the market. The value judgment has been made in this case that the national welfare would be maximized by providing safe, sanitary, and adequate housing to lower income families, even though a subsidized family may be at a lower level of total satisfaction than if it had been able to vote equivalent dollars in the marketplace for housing, automobiles, food, and other goods and services.

Technical monopolies. Other public expenditures for social overhead capital and for the purchase of goods and services from the private sector are justified because of the existence of a "technical monopoly." [1] Efficient allocation of our public transit facilities, for instance, may result in negative profits, requiring a subsidy in the public interest. In these situations, government may intervene as a regulator of a private monopoly, or the service may be provided by a publicly owned enterprise, or the private industry may be both regulated and subsidized.

Public goods. The so-called public good is the extreme case of a decreasing cost situation, where the marginal cost of extra use is zero.

---

[1] A technical monopoly is a strongly decreasing cost industry with a high original fixed cost and very low variable unit cost. Electric power and public transit are among these industries.

Once produced, the goods can be divided among innumerable users; the benefits received by each user do not detract from the benefits received by others. The national defense is close to being a pure public good. All citizens benefit equally, and the benefit obtained by one of us does not reduce the benefits available to all. Many goods are more or less public goods. Schools, parks, highways, street lighting, police protection, sanitation facilities, public health programs, and urban renewal are examples. If provided, they are available to everyone, and it is not feasible to charge any particular users for their benefits.

Public goods have "neighborhood" or spillover effects. It is not possible to identify the effects on users and nonusers, respectively, or at least the magnitude of the effect cannot be measured sufficiently to charge accordingly. Friedman points out that neighborhood effects cut both ways.[2] When the government provides the public good or intervenes in the market which provides the good, a different set of neighborhood effects arises. An urban renewal project, for instance, removes a neighborhood effect that existed because of the blighted condition of the area. Blight exists because a property owner cannot economically improve his property to standard condition. Net income after improvement is not sufficient to generate the additional value necessary to cover the costs of the improvement. The individual inaction on the part of separate owners in the blighted area, when considered in total, creates a neighborhood effect. Each individual is a prisoner because of the inaction of his neighbors. Residents elsewhere in the community suffer because of higher costs of police protection, fire protection, schooling, and other public services provided residents in the blighted area.

Urban renewal removes the neighborhood effect. It may be held to have elements of a public good, in that it is very difficult to identify the beneficiaries of the action and to charge them according to the benefits received. The renewal action itself produces a pattern of benefits and disbenefits among groups in the community. These groups do not necessarily bear the cost of the public action in proportion to their respective net benefits. Friedman points out in such a case that the social costs of the neighborhood effects prior to and following public intervention must be carefully weighed. Once again, our preferences and goals influence our decision concerning the propriety of public action and the magnitude of action needed. If one felt as Friedman, that any government intervention in the free operation of the market reduces the sphere of individual freedom, then he might add a large increment to social costs following renewal.

---

[2] Milton Friedman, "The Role of Government in a Free Society," in Edmund S. Phelps (ed.), *Private Wants and Public Needs* (New York: W. W. Norton and Co., Inc., 1965), pp. 104–17. Also see: *Capitalism and Freedom* (Chicago: The University of Chicago Press, 1962).

The problem of "how much government" will continue to be debated. Some individuals believe as J. K. Galbraith that our national affluence permits more government activity than presently exists in our society. Their contention is supported with both economic and philosophical arguments. In contrast, Professor Friedman would restrict government activity when the persons benefited can be identified and charged. Friedman would classify a city park and a general city street as public goods that justify government expenditures. The national park and the limited access freeway, however, would not be public goods, and users would pay directly for their construction and maintenance.

Public sector decision makers

The atomistic decision maker in the public sector is the public servant, perhaps a government executive, an elected or appointed administrator, a judge, or a legislator. These elected or appointed officials can be classified into four government institutions: the legislature, the executive branch, the judiciary, and the bureaucracy. The legislature, executive, and judicial branches are commonly recognized as the primary sources of power and decision making in our government. The bureaucracy, comprised of the regulatory or administrative agencies, is sometimes regarded as politically neutral and subordinate to the other three institutions, each of which exercises some control over agency policy and operations. The bureaucracy, however, is better viewed as an active participant in decision making in the public sector.[3] At times, an administrative agency acts in an advisory capacity to other decision-making units. Congressional committees and government executives call upon the professional expertise of administrators when proposing legislation pertaining to the area of policy administered by, say, the Department of Housing and Urban Development (HUD) and its constituent agencies, or other administrative agencies. The administrative agency also makes and implements policy at the operational level where it functions within limits as a decision-making unit in its own right.

The decision-making process in the public sector

Behavioral aspects. Micro administration of real estate in the private sector assumes that the decision-making unit acts rationally to maximize personal profit, satisfaction, or utility. Utility maximization by individuals

---

[3] The concept of the administrative agency as an active participant in government decision making, rather than simply an extension of the executive branch, has been developed by Millett. See: John D. Millett, *Organization for the Public Service* (New York: D. Van Nostrand Co., Inc., 1966), p. 159.

also can explain how decisions are reached in the public sector.[4] The public servant arrays the benefits and costs associated with each decision as he perceives them, assesses the subjective probabilities of their realization, and makes the trade-offs necessary to reach his preferred position, that is, the decision and course of action that maximizes his net satisfaction. The concept of benefit can be defined broadly enough to include all alternatives that produce satisfaction for the individual. A decision made "for the public good" (as the individual legislator perceives it) may result in enough personal satisfaction to the legislator to overcome a result which he may consider to be distasteful or damaging in some way (a cost to that legislator). For instance, a man harboring racial prejudice may vote in favor of open housing for the public good.

Another explanation of the decision-making process in government has been termed by Downs as the "economic theory of democracy." The central premise in this theory is that each political party designs its budget, both revenues and expenditures, to maximize its chances of winning the next election.[5] The budget is a mix of expenditure programs and the taxation or borrowing proposals to finance these programs. The voter acts rationally by deciding which budget produces the greatest net benefit for him. Each election, the citizen-voter casts his ballot for the candidates who, in his estimation, will maximize his personal satisfaction. The victorious candidates have until next election to demonstrate to the voter their ability to perform as expected.

The ultimate decision or policy made in the public sector represents the end result of a complex bargaining process. Compromises and trade-offs are arranged among individuals and interest groups. Finally, however, the executive, the legislature, or the judiciary all speak with a single voice, although a minority opinion may be written by a dissenting justice. The bargaining process preceding a decision in the public sector performs the function of the marketplace in the private sector. "Both mechanisms tend to substitute voluntary exchange for direct coercion and induce decision-makers to take into account many of the indirect or external impacts of their decisions." [6]

Power and influence. Decisions made at the community level reflect basic characteristics of the community and its leadership and decision-

---

[4] Roland N. McKean, *Public Spending* (New York: McGraw-Hill Book Co., 1968), p. 13. Also: "The Unseen Hand in Government," *The American Economic Review,* vol. 40, no. 3 (June 1965), pp. 496–506.

[5] Anthony Downs, *An Economic Theory of Democracy* (New York: Harper and Row, 1957). Our respected mentor, Robert O. Harvey, was fond of asking his principles classes: "Which has the longer-run planning horizon, private enterprise or the government?" The temptation is to reply, "the government," since the public sector establishes national parks, builds dams, and sponsors other programs having an impact for generations. The answer sought, however, was private enterprise, on the premise that the time horizon of government is constrained by the next election.

[6] Roland N. McKean, *Public Spending* (New York: McGraw-Hill Book Co., 1968), p. 19.

making structure.[7] Sociologists attempt to relate these decisions to the demographic, economic, legal-political, and cultural characteristics of the community. The integrating functions performed by local political and voluntary organizations also are important in deriving the final decision. The activities of these organizations permit groups of individuals in the community to have a voice in the decision process.

Power and influence are involved in the analysis of leadership and the structure of decision making. Power is defined as the "potential ability of an actor or actors to select, to change and to attain the goals of a social system," and influence is the "exercise of power that brings about change in a social system." [8] Power can be thought of as a static distribution of resources at a point in time. Clark identifies resources providing power as: (1) money and credit, (2) control over jobs, (3) control of mass media, (4) high social status, (5) knowledge and specialized technical skills, (6) popularity and esteemed personal qualities, (7) legality, (8) subsystem solidarity, (9) the right to vote, (10) social access to community leaders, (11) commitments of followers, (12) manpower and control of organization, and (13) control over the interpretation of values. The exercise of influence is a dynamic process which relates the existing distribution of power to the final decision.

Nuttall, Scheuch, and Gordon report an example of power and influence culminating in the final decision on an urban renewal project in Cambridge, Massachusetts.[9] The authors identify four separate decision processes occurring over time. The first decision process was the planning stage, begun in 1957, involving the Cambridge Redevelopment Authority, the Housing and Home Finance Agency (predecessor to HUD), the mayor and city manager, major local businessmen and bankers, and the CIO union, which was to be the eventual owner and operator of the new buildings. Following the lengthy administrative planning process, the first public hearing was held in 1961. At this point, new actors were able to exercise their influence, including families and small businessmen in the renewal area, a church in the area, and low-income groups residing outside the area. The spokesman for the church emphasized that persons in the renewal area would pay more for the new low-income housing than they presently paid for rent. Blacks and low-income families elsewhere in the community were fearful of future displacement if renewal was begun in Cambridge.

The second decision process occurred in the political arena when the city council had to ratify the proposed project. The dissident groups

---

[7] Terry N. Clark (ed.), *Community Structure and Decision-Making: Comparative Analyses* (San Francisco: Chandler Publishing Co., 1968), pp. 15–24, 57–58.

[8] Ibid., pp. 46–47.

[9] Ronald L. Nuttall, Erwin K. Scheuch, and Chad Gordon, "On the Structure of Influence," in Terry N. Clark (ed.), *Community Structure and Decision-Making: Comparative Analyses*, pp. 349–80.

possessed power and the ability to exercise influence in this arena. On the other hand, the Housing and Home Finance Agency (HHFA), the local redevelopment authority, the CIO union, and the large businessmen and bankers found their influence limited in the political debate. The second decision process resulted in defeat of the proposed renewal plan.

The third decision process involved reformulation of the plan. This time, the administrative process included a Citizens Advisory Committee representing residents and small businessmen in the renewal area and the church. The reformulated plan received the greatest opposition in public hearings from large businessmen who held property in the area and from two city councilmen whose constituents were black and low-income persons in other parts of the city. A threat of legal action by the large businessmen resulted in the mayor's effecting a compromise in their behalf before the city council finally approved the plan in 1965. This approval was the fourth decision process.

The case study of the Cambridge, Massachusetts, urban renewal project demonstrates the bargaining and compromise occurring in all public decision making that is not routine and institutionalized. The influence of certain individuals and groups was brought to bear on the issue over time, and although not all groups were appeased by the final decision (the black and low-income elements outside the renewal area), they were able to exercise whatever influence their power base permitted.

Institutional aspects.   Decisions made in the public sector and their implementation depend in large part upon the institutional structure of our government. Power, influence, and political factors are channeled through these institutions in the bargaining process that culminates in the final decision. Primary institutions in government are the executive branch, the legislature, and the judiciary, which divide governmental power among them. The administrative agencies comprising the bureaucracy are an extension of the executive branch and also possess influence to affect government decisions, but their power is delegated by the legislature. Our system of government incorporates this separation of power among institutions, but it also involves a sharing of power between the federal, state, and local governments. The Constitution enumerates the powers of central government, and the states have the residual powers, including the police power.

Today, the state and local governments can best be described as exercising a concurrent power with the federal government.[10] The exercise of these concurrent powers necessitates a system of shared administrative activity. Federal, state, and local administrative agencies are concerned with a particular activity but are not formally subordinate to each other. For example, the U.S. Department of Housing and Urban Development ad-

---

[10] Millett, *Organization for the Public Service,* pp. 19–20.

ministers the public housing program, but a state also may have a Division of Housing to oversee the activities of communities participating in the program, and each community or county has its own local housing authority that owns and operates the public housing. The interagency problems are to define their respective spheres of influence and to resolve conflicts of authority.

It is through the administrative agency that public policy is translated into highways and streets, subsidized housing, the city plan, zoning enforcement, and other public sector activities. The operating policies and regulations established by the agencies in carrying out the broad policies determined by the legislature have the force of law and control the character of the public good or service provided. Control over operations of the agency to insure that it continues to fulfill its policy objectives is exercised by budgetary review and, in extreme instances, by congressional investigation. At the federal level, the administrator must submit his requests for operating funds to the president, who reviews the request in context with all other needs and sources of funds for operation of the government. Broad national goals must be considered, including the need for economic growth, full employment, and price stability. The budget is then sent to Congress where it is reviewed once again. The administrator is called upon to inform congressional committees of programs and policies. The authorization of funds and their ultimate appropriation for administrative activity will depend upon the ability of the administrator and other expert witnesses to convince the legislature that a public need will be met. The size of the government budget determines the extent to which the government participates in the total economy, and the administrative agencies play important roles in determining both the total budget and the proportion devoted to housing, national defense, and other public needs.

Economic analysis in the decision-making process

The broadest goal our government could attain would be to maximize the welfare of all citizens collectively by assuming control only over functions delegated by our citizens and by organizing to carry out its assigned roles efficiently. McKean points out that several levels of decision making are involved in this process.[11] First, there is the problem of how much control over national resources should be given to the government. Second, resources available to the government must be allocated among perceived needs. Third, after it has been decided to support transit, housing, welfare, and so on, in varying proportions, the policy maker is

---

[11] Roland N. McKean, *Efficiency in Government through Systems Analysis* (New York: John Wiley & Sons, Inc., 1958). The following problems in the economic analysis of public expenditures are among those discussed by McKean.

faced with almost infinite alternatives for carrying out each program. A choice must be made among these alternative courses of action. Fourth, given a course of action for each program, the most efficient organization for producing the desired results must be developed.

These decisions are not independent of each other. For example, the case for giving more control over our resources to government may rest upon an argument that a centralized entity will be more efficient in producing desired results. The demonstrated or expected ability of one government agency to get more utility from its appropriations can influence the division of the total budget. The ability of an administrator to select the most appropriate program for translating policy into action and the organizational efficiency of his agency can enhance its image with the policy maker and influence the share of the budget devoted to its programs. Political factors, judgment, and personal bias influence decision making at all levels, particularly in determining government control over resources and the allocation of these resources among perceived needs. Analytical tools become more useful at the third and fourth levels of decision making, where the problems are to select an alternative course of action for carrying out the policy decision and to organize to achieve the goal.

Economic analysis at the third level of decision making, where alternative programs are considered, may demonstrate program efficiency in the form of benefits minus costs, a ratio of benefits to cost, cost minimization given a specified goal, or benefit maximization given cost. A continual difficulty in the economic analysis of government programs is the inability to quantify all costs and benefits. Not only are spillover effects too numerous to identify completely, but social costs and benefits often defy measurement in dollars and cents. What is the dollar value of the human lives saved by improvement of a city street?

Another inescapable problem arises from the fact that the public program can affect different groups in our society. Higher income groups may experience a net disbenefit to provide subsidized housing for a lower income group, who experience a net benefit. A value judgment must be made that society will experience a net benefit before the program is undertaken. Still another problem in the economic analysis of public programs is that alternative programs available to meet a perceived need are too numerous to consider each of them separately. Consequently, the analysis of an expenditure decision often is suboptimal or partial analysis.

Analysis also should be made of the impact of the financing decision that makes the expenditure possible, that is, the incidence of the tax, the effect of borrowing to finance the expenditure, and the effect of expanding the money supply. In many instances, the financing side of government decision making is not explicitly considered in the analysis of program alternatives. Most often, the budget for the program is considered as given, with the problem being how to spend the money most efficiently.

Viewed in this manner, the problem of scale is not adequately considered. Significant cost savings or net benefits could perhaps be achieved by expanding the scale of expenditure in a given program. Government programs also are interrelated, and expenditure for one program may affect the costs and benefits of another. Spending for public housing or other subsidized housing, for instance, may enhance worker productivity and affect the costs and benefits of the welfare program. Tracing and quantifying these side effects usually is beyond the scope of the analysis.

Economic analysis, whether it is cost-benefit analysis, systems analysis or simulation, admittedly will not replace the public decision maker. The analysis of alternative programs, however, does provide the decision maker with better understanding and permits more rational choice. Subsequent chapters summarize types of economic analyses performed for various public expenditure decisions.

SUMMARY

The physical attributes of our urban areas are the end product of decisions and expenditures made by both the private and public sectors of our economy. Individuals and organizations in the private sector make decisions concerning the financing, development, and marketing of urban real estate. The physical product is produced, and the ownership rights are apportioned. Decisions are then made periodically to spend for maintenance or to allow the improvements to deteriorate. Less frequently, a decision will result in renovation, conversion, or demolition and replacement with a more profitable use. Ownership and financing are continually reviewed and modified in response to changing economic factors and the needs and objectives of investors. These separate and collective decisions in the private sector have been termed micro administration of our urban real estate resources.

Decisions in the private sector are not made in a vacuum. Factors considered in the micro administration of our real estate resources include the results of public sector decision making, such as zoning, the street and utility system, and urban renewal and housing subsidies. If such factors are taken as given, micro administration in the private sector is partial analysis, where the problem typically is to maximize profit and satisfaction within the constraints imposed by government regulation and programs and by working with existing social overhead capital in the form of streets, schools, and utility systems. Preceding chapters have described tax laws, zoning, and other government activities when necessary to provide information pertinent to decision making in the private sector.

A general analysis of the production and use of our urban real estate resources would consider decisions, actions, and results in both the private and public sectors and their interrelation. To borrow two current "buzz" words, the interfaces between systems would be examined. A circular system would be formulated in which the decisions, actions, and results in the private sector become inputs to the public sector, which in turn generates outputs affecting micro administration in the private sector.

This chapter examines some of the attributes of administration in the public sector. The extent of involvement of the government in the economy is constrained by our values. Any government regulation or expenditure reflects this value system as well as our institutional framework of government, political factors, and the exercise of power and influence. Our values and perception of need influence the selection of programs involving transfer payments that redistribute income among segments of our society. Government actions in dealing with technical monopolies and in the provision of a public good do not escape the influence of these factors. Economic analyses of government programs and expenditures decisions are useful in generating alternative courses of action for implementation of policy and in quantifying at least some of the costs and benefits. Economic analysis may contribute to a more rational choice being made by the public sector decision maker, but it is, once again, partial and suboptimal analysis.

Subsequent chapters review selected government programs and expenditure decisions in housing, transportation, community renewal, and conservation. The problems in the private sector that result in these public sector decisions are mentioned, and the impacts of macro administration on the private sector are described. An effort is made not only to show the effect of public sector activities on the profitability of investment in urban real estate, but to take the analysis to a more general level by pointing out the income redistribution effects and noneconomic factors involved.

QUESTIONS FOR REVIEW

1. How does micro administration differ from macro administration?
2. How can you justify government spending for transfer payments? Technical monopolies? Public goods?
3. What are the roles of power and influence in the decision-making processes of government?
4. What is the role of economic analysis in the government decision-making process?
5. What is meant by cost-benefit analysis? Is it comparable to investment analysis discussed in preceding chapters?

REFERENCES

Clark, Terry N. (ed.). *Community Structure and Decision-Making: Comparative Analyses*. San Francisco: Chandler Publishing Co., 1968.

Due, John F. *Government Finance: Economics of the Public Sector.* 4th ed. Homewood, Ill.: Richard D. Irwin, Inc., 1968.

McKean, Roland N. *Efficiency in Government through Systems Analysis.* New York: John Wiley & Sons, Inc., 1958.

————. *Public Spending.* New York: McGraw-Hill Book Co., 1968.

Margolis, Julius (ed.). *The Analysis of Public Output.* New York: National Bureau of Economic Research, 1970.

Millett, John D. *Organization for the Public Service.* New York: D. Van Nostrand Co., 1966.

Phelps, Edmund S. (ed.) *Private Wants and Public Needs.* New York: W. W. Norton & Co., Inc., 1965.

chapter 16

THE GOVERNMENT IN HOUSING, RENEWAL, AND CONSERVATION

FEDERAL HOUSING

FEDERAL GOVERNMENT INVOLVEMENT in the provision of housing for low- and moderate-income families reflects increasing concern with our national housing problem. The home building industry and the private housing market have been unable to place adequate housing within the financial means of all American families. The Report of the President's Committee on Urban Housing estimated the need for new and rehabilitated housing units at about 26 million from 1968 to 1978.[1] Of this total, 6 million units would need to be subsidized. Housing construction and rehabilitation of this magnitude is expected at least to permit lower income families to occupy physically standard units, although overcrowding could persist.

A history of federal housing

Recognition of a need for improving the housing condition of lower income families began much earlier than 1968. The present federal programs intended to encourage production of such housing are somewhere on a continuum of evolving legislation that originated in the Great Depression. A brief chronology of federal involvement in subsidized housing suggests that current programs will be further modified before our national housing needs are met.

1937–1960. Milestones in the history of government housing programs

---

[1] Report of the President's Committee on Urban Housing (Kaiser Report), *A Decent Home* (Washington, D.C.: U.S. Government Printing Office, 1969), p. 39.

include the formation of the Public Housing Administration in 1937, which was initially authorized to permit construction of a total of 810,000 low-rent, government-owned housing units. The National Housing Act of 1949 stated our often-quoted national housing policy of "a decent home and a suitable living environment for every American family." Private enterprise was encouraged to provide the needed housing with government assistance only when required to make the projects economically feasible. The Housing Act of 1954 broadened the scope of the 1949 act by adding conservation and rehabilitation programs for housing in renewal areas. The 1954 act also required a "workable program" to be approved by the Housing and Home Finance Agency prior to funds being obtained by a community for renewal or subsidized housing. The workable program contains a survey of present housing and community facilities and a statement of feasible goals, together with a coordinated plan for attainment of these objectives. The workable program requirement was eliminated in 1969 for provision of low-rent housing in private accommodations, public housing, and other subsidized housing.

1961–1971. The 1961 Housing Act initiated the Sec. 221(d)(3) BMIR (below-market interest rate) program, permitting development of subsidized housing for moderate-income families by both limited dividend and nonprofit organizations. The interest rate for an FHA-insured mortgage on a Sec. 221(d)(3) BMIR project was to be no higher than an average rate on the federal debt. In 1965, the rate was fixed at 3 percent.

The Housing Act of 1965 introduced the Sec. 101 rent supplement program, under which low-income families pay no more than 25 percent of family income for rent, with a subsidy paid to the landlord in an amount equal to the difference between the fair market rent for the unit and the rent payment made by the family. The 1965 act also permitted public housing units to be leased from private owners. In 1966, Sec. 203 loans, which are the standard FHA-insured mortgages, were allowed for one- to four-family housing in blighted areas. In 1967, a Home Counseling Service was begun in selected FHA field offices. Prospective home owners could obtain information on housing opportunities under the various FHA programs and could have FHA procedures explained.

The Housing Act of 1968 was particularly concerned with subsidized housing. This act created the Sec. 235 home ownership program and the Sec. 236 multi-family rental housing for lower income families. The Sec. 236 program replaced the Sec. 221(d)(3) program. The 1968 act initiated Sec. 237 home mortgage insurance for families who are special credit risks and created the National Housing Partnership. Sec. 237 mortgage insurance is available to finance single-family homes when the family would not be able to meet the credit requirements under other sections of the act. The National Housing Partnership is a profit-motivated organization that was conceived to induce industry and other firms to invest in and to produce subsidized housing. A corporate general partner appointed by the president would join with local builders and investors, as well as large private companies, in providing subsidized housing of a magnitude sufficient to experience economies of scale. Expertise in development would be obtained, which is often absent in smaller organizations and companies not in the housing field.

The 1968 act also provided Sec. 221(h), Sec. 221(d)(2), Sec. 221(d)(4), and Sec. 106 programs. Sec. 221(h) permits nonprofit organizations to rehabilitate single-family or multi-family housing for subsequent resale to low-income families. Low-income buyers of units released from a Sec. 221(h) project may obtain a 100 percent loan with an interest rate as low as 1 percent, depending upon the borrower's income. Families displaced by urban renewal or other government action and low- or moderate-income families can obtain mortgage insurance under Sec. 221(d)(2). The mortgage carries the going market rate on FHA-insured mortgages. New or rehabilitated multi-family projects for low- and moderate-income families can be financed with a Sec. 221(d)(4) mortgage. Priority for admission to occupancy is given to families displaced by urban renewal or other government action. The mortgage carries the current FHA market interest rate, and consequently, families occuping the project need not report their income to the FHA. The attractiveness of the 221(d)(4) mortgage to the developer results from the 90 percent loan-to-value ratio and its 40-year term. Sec. 106(b) provides nonprofit sponsors with a two-year, interest-free loan for organizational expenses, legal fees, architect fees, site engineering, land options, FHA and Federal National Mortgage Association (FNMA) application fees, and construction loan fees necessary for the development of subsidized housing. The loan is repaid when the permanent financing is obtained.

Emerging trends. An overview of the history of federal housing assistance shows that the emphasis has shifted from government-owned and operated housing to private ownership of subsidized units. The 1949 act affirmed our present position of encouraging private industry and private initiative to meet the housing needs of disadvantaged families. Government subsidies are used only when necessary to make construction and rehabilitation economically feasible. The subsidies themselves are paid to the developer, the landlord, or the lending institution in the private sector.

Another trend developing in the subsidy programs has been recognition that rehabilitation and conservation of the existing stock of housing can provide needed housing at lower cost to the taxpayer. The major subsidy programs, Sec. 221(d)(3), Sec. 236, Sec. 235, and rent supplements, are all available for rehabilitated units, in addition to programs exclusively for rehabilitation. The reliance on rehabilitated units in meeting our national housing goals is indicated in Table 16–1, which summarizes estimated new subsidized housing starts and rehabilitations by program. For each

TABLE 16–1

Projected subsidized starts and rehabilitation by program, fiscal years 1969–78
(thousands of housing units)

Program	Total starts 1969–78	New starts	Rehabili- tations
Rental-type units			
Low-rent public housing	1226	1058	168
Rent supplement*	297	263	34
Sec. 221(d)(3) BMIR	98	88	10
Sec. 202, elderly and handicapped	27	27	
Sec. 236	1291	1111	180
USDA programs	67	64	3
Subtotal	3006	2611	395
Owner-occupied units			
Sec. 235	1386	1192	194
One-time grants and loans, rehabilitations	190		190
Sec. 221(h), rehabilitations	4		4
USDA programs	1420	1202	218
Subtotal	3000	2394	606
Total subsidized new starts and rehabilitations †	6006	5005	1001

* Units subsidized solely with rent supplements; BMIR units combined with rent supplements
and other combinations are listed under major program.
  † These estimates were revised from previous projections of 4 million new starts and 2 million
rehabilitations.
  Source: "Second Annual Report on National Housing Goals," 1970. Message from the President
of the United States, Appendix A, pp. 44–52. Table reproduced from R. L. Racster, H. C. Smith, and
W. B. Brueggeman, "Federal Housing Programs in the Local Housing Market," *The Appraisal Journal*,
vol. 34, no. 3 (July 1971), p. 397.

five new subsidized units constructed between 1969 and 1978, one unit is
expected to be rehabilitated. The final mix of units by type and program
is of course, apt to vary markedly from the projected totals in Table
16–1. For instance, the most recent innovation in subsidy, the housing
allowance program, is presently in an experimental stage and may replace,
or greatly reduce, provision of housing "in kind."

PUBLIC HOUSING

"Conventional" public housing

The original type of public housing project was owned and operated
by a local housing authority. The Department of Housing and Urban
Development renders technical aid and advice to local housing authorities,
contracts to provide federal financial assistance, and supervises project
development and administration to assure compliance with statutory requirements. However, the local housing authority has the primary responsibility for initiation and administration of a project. HUD can give

assistance only when there has been a local determination of need for low-rent housing, a locally made and approved plan for fufilling the need, and local initiation of the project.

Demonstration of need. The process of project development begins with the local housing authority's examining the community's housing to determine the extent of need. Assistance from HUD is provided upon request for these surveys. In larger cities, the survey is made by a professional consulting firm, but smaller communities often conduct their own study. The amount of substandard housing (rental and owned), the extent of overcrowding, identification of blighted areas, determination of the number and characteristics of low-income families in the community, vacancies available for occupancy by low-income families, and other available vacancies are among data included in the study. If housing for the elderly is requested, data are collected that show the number of elderly families, their incomes and housing conditions. On the basis of the study of housing need, the local housing authority submits to HUD a request for allocation of a specific number of dwelling units to the community and reservation of federal funds. HUD approves and issues a program reservation to the local authority, citing the number of units being set aside and the government's intention to hold the necessary funds in readiness. In general, housing need and condition are the basis of allocation of units to a community after consideration of applications from all localities.

Project planning. The local housing authority then proceeds to the planning stage, at which time HUD may make a preliminary loan to cover planning costs. Site plans, dwelling plans, land acquisition costs, development cost estimates, income limits for admission and continued occupancy, rent schedules, and the estimated operating budget are submitted for HUD review and approval. Upon HUD approval of the general scheme of the project, the annual contribution contract is entered into and capital loans, if any, are made.

Project financing. Federal financial assistance to local housing authorities can take the form of loans, capital grants, and annual contributions, all of which are made under contract between HUD and the local authority. Long-term financing usually is provided by issuance of bonds by the local authority, with the federal government guaranteeing repayment of principal and interest. Annual contributions are then made to insure retirement of the debt. Loans are made to assist in development of the project and project administration. Although capital grants are an alternative to long-term debt financing, but they have not been utilized in the past by HUD.

The most important form of federal assistance to local authorities is annual contributions to assist in achieving and maintaining low rentals.

Annual contributions, unlike loans, depend upon congressional authorizations and are used to insure that there will be no default on the long-term debt. HUD contracts with the local authority to provide fixed annual contributions over a specified number of years. The maximum duration of an annual contribution contract is 40 years. Annual contributions can equal 100 percent of the total cost of development and operation of the project.

Until recently, HUD has limited the subsidy to no more than the annual debt service on the bonds issued to finance the project. This limitation meant that other revenues, primarily project rents, had to be sufficient to cover operating expenses. However, there was an exception to this limitation. Fixed annual contributions can be increased up to $120 per year for each project until occupied by an elderly family or a displaced family when they cannot pay the average rental that would have been charged if the units had been rented to other low-income families. This additional contribution can be used for operating expenses.

In 1972, local housing authorities were prohibited from charging low-income families more than 25 percent of income as rent. Consequently, a subsidy of operating expenses was initiated to insure project solvency. Any excess of project revenues and subsidy over the debt service and operating expenses is used to reduce the amount of subsequent annual contribution. Rising operating costs and the accumulation over time of lower income tenants (who pay less in rent) have acted to insure that such a surplus of revenues over expenses will not occur.

The use of annual contributions to finance low-rent public housing helped make the program acceptable to Congress. The appropriations are made in relatively small amounts over 40 years, rather than a single large sum, and the long-term contract has made continuous federal supervision possible.

The changing character of public housing

Public housing was initially developed in high-density projects located in or near the central city. Typically, these projects provided only minimum amenities for tenant families. The social and economic problems experienced by these early developments have led to a policy of lower density projects scattered throughout the city. A local housing authority presently has alternatives to the development of the former conventional project.

The Turnkey I program, begun in 1966, permits the local housing authority to purchase a project from a private developer. The developer must be approved by the housing authority and must agree to sell the project to the authority upon completion. Turnkey II permits private management of the government-owned project. Turnkey III allows the local housing authority to buy an existing single-family or multi-family development from a private developer without approval of either developer or project plans prior to purchase, although such approval normally is secured. These properties may be either new or rehabilitated.

The local housing authority can lease privately owned single-family or multi-family housing under Sec. 23 of the housing act. The subsidy paid to the owner of a leased unit is the difference between a fair market rent for the unit and the rent paid by the public housing tenant, less an allowance for management and administration expenses incurred by the local housing authority. The owner is required to maintain and repair the unit and continues to pay the property tax. He also retains the ability to depreciate the improvements for tax purposes. Leased units also may either be new or rehabilitated. Finally, the local housing authority can provide home ownership for selected public housing tenants by arranging a lease-purchase agreement with the low-income family. The units usually are obtained by the Turnkey III method and are financed by 25-year bonds issued by the housing authority. The subsidy covers the difference between the contribution made to equity by the low-income family and the debt service. The family must maintain the unit and pay the property tax and insurance.

SEC. 221(d)(3) BMIR AND SEC. 236 PROGRAMS

The Sec. 221(d)(3) below market interest rate program required projects to be developed and owned by a "limited dividend" or a nonprofit organization. The projects were financed with an FHA-insured mortgage carrying a 3 percent interest rate. These mortgages were then sold to FNMA by the financial institution making the loan at a price permitting the lender to realize the going market rate of return on conventional mortgages. Profit-seeking owners could borrow 90 percent of total replacement cost and receive a maximum 6 percent pay-out on stated equity. A $1 million project with a mortgage of $900,000 and a stated equity of $100,000 could pay out only $6,000 in after-financing cash flow to the investor (6 percent of $100,000). Nonprofit organizations could borrow 100 percent of total replacement cost.

The total replacement cost upon which the mortgage amount is calculated is the end result of the "cost-plus-allowances" contract between the builder and the FHA. The builder must certify all costs before final approval by the FHA. Total replacement cost is the cost of the structure, on-site improvements such as streets, job overhead for field engineering, building permits, and other job-related expenses during construction (a percentage of total cost, depending upon the size of the job). Total replacement cost also includes either a builder's general overhead allowance and builder's profit, or a builder's-sponsor's profit and risk allowance (BSPRA).

The builder's general overhead allowance is a percentage of total improvement costs, exclusive of architect fees, bond premium, and builder's profit. Builder's profit is a percentage of total cost normally expected by a general contractor for a project of that type. Both the general overhead allowance and builder's profit rates decrease with the size of the project. They are used when the builder and owner-sponsor are separate entities. When the builder and sponsor have an identity of interest (the builder has an ownership interest in the project, or the sponsor has a proprietary interest in the builder), a 10 percent builder's-sponsor's profit and risk allowance is used. BSPRA is 10 percent of total improvement cost, which omits land and off-site improvements.

A Sec. 236 project is developed and mortgaged under regulations similar to the Sec. 221(d)(3) projects, except that the mortgage carries the current FHA interest rate. Tenants pay 25 percent of their income for rent and the government pays the difference between the fair market rent for their unit and the tenant's contribution. The maximum subsidy for a Sec. 236 project, however, is no more than the difference in debt service between the payment on the mortgage carrying the market rate of interest and the amount that the payment would have been if the mortgage had been written with a 1 percent contract rate of interest.

Profitability considerations

Subsidized housing must be at least as profitable for private developers-owners as unsubsidized projects if the needed 6 million plus subsidized units are to be provided for lower income families. Allowances for builder's profit and overhead expenses must be adequate. The cost-plus-allowances formula for computing these amounts, of course, rewards efficiency in construction. The 6 percent limited-dividend cash flow after financing, together with depreciation of improvement value and interest on the 40-year mortgage, can provide an adequate after-financing, after-tax return to the investor. The benefit of depreciating the buildings in such a project can increase returns to high-bracket taxpayers to a level well in excess of 20 percent per annum on an after-tax basis. A highly simplified example of this rate of return calculation is shown in Figure 16–1.

Another advantage for the investor is the exculpatory clause in the mortgage, which makes the property sole security for the debt. The investor escapes personal liability for the mortgage in the event of foreclosure and subsequent sale of the property for a price less than the outstanding debt. This provision permits the owner to depreciate over the investment holding period both his equity and mortgage in an amount equal to the cost of the improvements (land remains nondepreciable). A

FIGURE 16–1

First year after-tax return on equity: Section 236 project

Project total replacement cost $3,000,000
FHA-insured loan 2,700,000
Owners' stated equity 300,000
Net operating income 58,000
Debt service (1½% of $2,700,000) 40,500

Cash Flow to Equity (6% of $300,000) ....$ 18,000

Taxable income:
  Net operating income ....$ 58,500
  Less interest (1% of $2,700,000) 27,000

                                                        $ 31,500
  Less depreciation (5% of $2,700,000 building cost) 135,000
Net Taxable Income ....$ (103,500)

After-tax return to investor:
  $18,000 Cash flow
  51,750 Tax loss ($103,500 × .50 assumed marginal tax rate)

  $69,750 Return to Equity

  $$\frac{\$ 69{,}750 \text{ Return to Equity}}{\$300{,}000 \text{ Book Equity}} = 23.2\% \text{ After-tax Return}$$

building in which the investor has a $100,000 equity and a $900,000 mortgage has a depreciable basis for tax of $1 million.

Furthermore, the stated equity on which the 6 percent maximum after-financing cash flow is calculated may not be the actual cash investment in the project. For instance, the 10 percent BSPRA is part of total replacement cost upon which the 90 percent mortgage is calculated, but it does not represent an actual cash outlay by the builder-sponsor. The site is included in total replacement cost at fair market value, which may be above actual acquisition cost, particularly when there has been a change in zoning that produced an increase in market value. Also, the working capital requirement included in the stated equity may be met with a letter of credit rather than cash.

Provision was made in the 1968 housing act to allow resale of a project to a cooperative or nonprofit organization, with the purchaser's obtaining a new FHA-insured mortgage adequate to permit the seller to retire the existing mortgage, pay the tax on capital gain, and recover his equity investment. These projects still are relatively new, however, and the ability to resell the project when tax shelters are failing remains a risk for the owner. The investor could suffer a substantial reduction in return on investment over the holding period if the after-tax cash reversion is inadequate. The exculpatory clause in the mortgage raises a specter of foreclosure if the investor is not permitted to sell the project profitably, with the FHA subsequently reselling the property.

SEC. 235 PROGRAM

The ownership of a single-family home under the Sec. 235 program is subsidized in the same manner as a Sec. 236 project, with the FHA paying a portion of the debt service. Purchasers must pay at least $200 down and more if their income warrants.

The developer, in the case of new construction, obtains FHA approval for inclusion of the homes in the Sec. 235 program. The builder obtains his profit from an overhead and profit allowance of 12–13 percent of total replacement cost. The FHA-determined value for mortgage lending purposes considers lot value, closing costs, sales expense (broker's commission), structure cost, and on-site improvements. The builder's profit and overhead allowance is included in the value, which can be adjusted up or down within limits to reflect the quality of construction. The final value estimated by FHA usually is very close to sales price.

The builder's profit and overhead allowance provides adequate profitability. The builder also widens his market for the homes in his development, since a prospective buyer unable to meet normal FHA requirements may qualify under the Sec. 235 program, enabling a sale to be made that otherwise would be lost. A potential risk for the subdivider is the reaction of nonsubsidized families seeking homes. Will they accept subsidized families in nearby Sec. 235 homes? Will the amenities of the neighborhood be affected by lower income families occupying homes scattered throughout the area?

RENT SUPPLEMENT PROGRAM

The landlord placing units in the rent supplement program enters into a 40-year contract with the Department of Housing and Urban Development (HUD), in which the latter agrees to pay the difference between the fair market rent for a unit and 25 percent of the tenant family's adjusted income. Deductions are permitted from total family income for secondary wage earners, continuing medical expenses, and child care if needed to permit a family member to work. Rent supplement units may be in both subsidized or nonsubsidized projects and may be either new or rehabilitated. To insure that the program would not subsidize uneconomical construction or excessively elaborate projects, cost limitations and fair market rent limits are imposed upon units. These limitations have often made new construction of rent supplement units in larger cities infeasible. The maximum subsidy payment in this program can be no more than 70 percent of the fair market rent for the unit, requiring families to have sufficient income to bear at least 30 percent of the cost of keeping the project economically sound.

ELIGIBILITY FOR OCCUPANCY

Each of the subsidized housing programs has family eligibility controlled by legislation and administrative policy. Public housing, for instance, is for families of low income. Congress has never defined *low income* except to state that the family's income will not permit them to obtain safe, sanitary, and decent housing within their financial means. The local housing authority, with HUD approval, determines income limits for its community.

Income limits for families in the Sec. 235 program can be no more than 135 percent of the local public housing limits for a family of that size. In urban communities with a high cost of living, some families can be admitted who exceed this income limit, but in no event can their income be greater than 90 percent of the Sec. 221(d)(3) BMIR limits. Sec. 221(d)(3) BMIR income limits are the lower of: (1) median family income for families of a given size in the community or (2) income great enough to pay rent for a standard unit needed for a family of that size, without paying a disproportionate share of income for housing expense (no more than 25 percent). The rent charged a family in a Sec. 221(d)(3) BMIR unit must be sufficient to pay operating expenses, including the property tax, and carry a 3 percent mortgage. In addition, this rent is fixed by the FHA at 20 percent below fair market rent for a unit of that type in the community.

Income limits for the rent supplement program are defined as gross family income (family income from all sources) and are not greater than income limits for admission to public housing. Public housing income limits, however, are defined as adjusted family income (gross income less certain expenses required for the occupation of the family head, a portion of the income contributed by secondary wage earners, child care needed to permit income to be earned, continuing medical expenses, and other deductions). Public housing, therefore, can admit families with a higher total family income from all sources. Families eligible for rent supplements also must have one of the following characteristics: (1) be over 62 years of age, (2) be living in substandard housing, (3) be physically handicapped, or (4) be displaced by government action or by natural disaster.

Families are eligible for the Sec. 236 program if their adjusted family income (total income less $300 per child) is no more than 135 percent of public housing limits for a family of that size. In higher cost areas, a portion of the families admitted may have incomes exceeding the 135 percent limit, but in no event can their income be greater than 90 percent Sec. 221(d)(3) BMIR limits. An example of maximum income limits for families eligible for the various federal housing programs in Franklin County, Ohio, is shown in Table 16–2. Income limits for eligibility are

TABLE 16–2

Income limits by federal housing program, Franklin County, Ohio, 1971

No. of persons	Public housing and rent supplement *	Sec. 235 and Sec. 236 Regular †	Sec. 235 and Sec. 236 Exceptional ‡	Sec. 221(d)(3) BMIR §
1	$3,000	$4,050	$5,200	$ 5,500
2	4,000	5,400	6,250	6,650
3	4,600	6,210	7,400	7,850
4	5,000	6,750	7,400	7,850
5	5,300	7,155	8,500	9,050
6	5,600	7,560	8,500	9,050
7	5,900	7,965	9,600	10,200
8	6,200	8,370	9,600	10,200
9	6,500	8,775	8,600	10,200
10	6,800	9,180	9,600	10,200
11	7,100	9,180	9,600	10,200
12	7,300	9,180	9,600	10,200

* Income limits for continued occupancy are higher, i.e., $3,700 for one-person family, $5,000 for two-person family, etc. Minimum income for families in the public housing home ownership program are $3,240 (three-bedroom unit) and $3,720 (four-bedroom unit).

† Adjusted family income (gross family income less $300 per minor child, all income from minors and unusual or temporary income). Families of more than 10 persons can have no more than $9,180 adjusted family income.

‡ Used in communities when the family's adjusted annual income is greater than 135 percent of the public housing limit, but less than 90 percent of the Sec. 221(d)(3) BMIR limits. Families of more than seven persons can have no more than $9,600 adjusted family income.

§ Families of more than seven persons can have no more than $10,200 family income.

Source: William B. Brueggeman, "The Impact of Private Construction and Government Housing Programs in a Local Housing Market," unpublished doctoral dissertation (The Ohio State University, 1970), pp. 34, 40, 43.

defined as gross family income (rent supplement), adjusted family income (public housing Sec. 235 and Sec. 236) or in another manner (Sec. 221(d)(3) BMIR). Consequently, the actual total income of families admitted to the several programs may vary from the reported maximum income limits for eligibility.

The various federal housing programs also have asset limits in different amounts. Generally, these limits are set low enough that the family could not afford standard housing in the community by supplementing family income with asset liquidation. The rent supplement and public housing programs have the lowest asset limits, followed by Sec. 235 and Sec. 236. The Sec. 221(d)(3) BMIR program permits the greatest amount of assets. Elderly families are allowed larger amounts of assets in recognition of future needs for health care and their inability to replenish possible depletion of their estates.

Operators of subsidized housing projects cannot discriminate in the selection of tenants without risking loss of financial assistance from the federal government. An executive order issued in 1962, entitled "Equal Opportunity in Housing," is designed to assure integration of all residential property and related facilities owned or operated by the federal government or where the government participated in financing.[2] Executive Order 11063 is still in effect to control discrimination on the basis of creed. The order was superceded, however, by the Civil Rights Act of 1964, which stated that "no person in the United States shall, on the ground of race, color, or national origin, be excluded from participation in, be denied the benefits of, or be subjected to discrimination under any program of activity receiving federal financial assistance.[3] The 1968 Federal Fair Housing Law and U.S. Supreme Court decisions promoting equal opportunity in housing are summarized in Appendix A.

FEDERAL HOUSING IN THE LOCAL HOUSING MARKET

Federal housing programs are available to families that vary not only in size, income, and assets, but also in tastes and preferences, stage in the family cycle, and other characteristics. Some families have more than one wage earner, others have none. Moreover, their places of employment can be widely distributed over the urban area. These characteristics determine the location and type of unit occupied in the private housing market by families eligible for subsidized housing. Since the subsidized programs admit families having different income distributions (and different distributions of other characteristics), it can be expected that each program would admit families from units in the housing market that vary in type (single-family residence or apartment), size, physical condition, location, rent, and value. In Columbus, Ohio, for instance, families moving into federal housing generally come from the inner city, from apartments, from deteriorating and dilapidated units, and from low-rent units, but the various programs differ with respect to the proportion of occupants coming from the inner city or from various types of housing units.[4]

New housing developed under the federal programs conceptually is a factor contributing to the filtering process when it provides a net increase in the number of units available in the market. The vacancy rate in the nonsubsidized portion of the local housing market would rise, in this instance, contributing to the potential for a decline in the level of rents in submarkets affected and permitting lower income families to better their housing condition at the same or less expense. In reality, separation of the net impact of units provided by the federal programs from other forces operating in the market to influence the demand for and supply of housing would, indeed, be very difficult. The net increase in total housing units represented by these programs and the rise in the level of vacancies

---

[2] Executive Order No. 11063, November 20, 1962, 27 F.R. 11527.

[3] U.S. Congress, Civil Rights Act of 1964, Public Law 88–352, July 2, 1964, 78 Stat. 241, Sec. 601, Title VI.

[4] Ronald L. Racster, Halbert C. Smith, and William B. Brueggeman, "Federal Housing Programs in the Local Housing Market," *The Appraisal Journal*, vol. 39, no. 3 (July 1971), pp. 402–6.

in the housing submarkets affected can only be viewed as a marginal change that may be swamped by in-migration of households, undoubling of existing households, new household formations, and loss of units from demolition and conversion, all of which simultaneously affect this part of the local housing market.

Rehabilitated units supplied by the federal programs improve the quality of the housing stock, but do not increase the number of units available in the market. Large-scale rehabilitation could increase prices of properties in lower quality submarkets as investors and public agencies bid for suitable units to place in the federal programs. This increase in market prices could give incentive to owners of better quality units to allow their properties to filter down into the lower quality housing stock by foregoing maintenance and repair.[5] Better quality submarkets lose units to the lower quality submarkets that are experiencing relatively higher prices. Prices, in turn, rise in these better quality submarkets, attracting units from still higher value submarkets. The process repeats itself until it reaches those submarkets which are competitive with new properties and calls forth new construction.

POLICY FOR THE PROVISION OF ADEQUATE HOUSING

The decision to improve the housing condition of the ill-housed is a higher level government decision, where the problem is to allocate the national budget among broad categories of perceived needs. At a lower level of decision making, methods of meeting the need must be determined. Our present federal housing programs are the result of past decisions at this level. However, there are unresolved problems that deserve consideration and further analysis. For example, should income supplements be provided to lower income families rather than subsidizing the development and operation of their housing? Our national housing policy, to date, has provided housing developed specifically for disadvantaged families. An alternative solution would be to give income to these families, which they could spend for housing if they choose, or for other goods and services. The negative income tax is one proposal for this purpose. Another variation on income supplements is the housing allowance program presently being tried experimentally in selected cities. The housing allowance is tied to expenditure for housing, but it may be spent on any standard unit in the private market. The final form which the housing allowance program will take is not yet known, but the concept seems to have the capabilities of replacing present federal housing programs that provide new and rehabilitated housing for low- and moderate-income families.

---

[5] Edgar O. Olsen, "A Competitive Theory of the Housing Market," *American Economic Review,* vol. 59, no. 4 (September 1969), pp. 612–22.

If the decision is to subsidize lower income families by providing housing directly, what form of subsidized program should be used? Should housing be subsidized for only low-income families, or should moderate-income families also be provided housing? What mix of subsidized housing should be provided? The present policy permits simultaneous development of all types of subsidized housing in a community. Public housing directly admits low-income families, improving their housing condition and at the same time reducing their housing expense. However, the subsidy cost per public housing unit is relatively large. Units available to moderate-income families in Section 235, 236, and other programs can be supplied at a lower subsidy cost per unit. Federal appropriations for housing subsidies are limited. Therefore, should a greater number of moderate-income program units be supplied from a given appropriation or should fewer low-income program units be supplied? The solution may depend, in part, upon the ability of units in moderate-income programs to initiate filtering, enabling low-income families to improve their housing condition in the private market at the same or less housing expense.

INCOME REDISTRIBUTION EFFECTS

The economic analysis of subsidized housing can involve examination of broader income redistribution effects. In one analysis of income redistribution, Nourse uses the example of development and operation of conventional public housing.[6] A schematic presentation of the potential shifts in income from this housing program is depicted in Figure 16–2. His analysis notes a potential increase in national income if construction workers otherwise were unemployed, or a shift from the development of other types of real estate to public housing (with no change in national income) if workers would have been employed elsewhere. If the program places additional demand upon the construction industry during full employment, wage and construction cost increases are to be expected, with income shifting to favor persons in the building industry. Otherwise, it is noted that raising funds by issuing bonds to finance public housing shifts income from other investment. A local government may get more or less tax revenue from the housing project (which pays 10 percent of rent collected in lieu of the property tax) than from the properties condemned for project construction, depending upon the relative intensity of use of the site before and after project development. Whether or not the slum landlord, whose property was taken for the project, experiences a net benefit or disbenefit will depend upon his condemnation award. If he is paid more than fair market value of his property, he benefits at the ex-

---

[6] Hugh O. Nourse, "Redistribution of Income from Public Housing," *National Tax Journal*, vol. 19, no. 1 (March 1966), pp. 27–37.

FIGURE 16-2

Channels of potential income redistribution in the development and operation of Public Housing

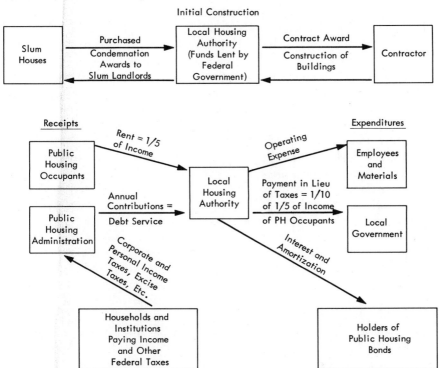

Source: Hugh O. Nourse, "Redistribution of Income from Public Housing," *National Tax Journal*, vol. 19, no. 1 (March 1966), p. 37.

pense of the taxpayer. The most important shift of income is from the taxpayer to the public housing tenants.

The point made by Nourse and other economists must be kept in mind during any discussion of income redistribution from public expenditure decisions. The economist can trace potential income redistribution effects, but it is not possible to state objectively that the total national welfare has been increased following redistribution. The decision to provide public housing or any form of subsidized housing remains a value judgment.

URBAN RENEWAL

Nature of the subsidy

The National Housing Act of 1949 initiated slum clearance and urban redevelopment that evolved to our present urban renewal program. Urban renewal has been accomplished in our cities by the local renewal agency condemning (if necessary) and purchasing properties in the blighted area, demolishing existing improvements, and providing or improving streets, utilities, schools, and municipal buildings as planned in the reuse of the area. Sites in the renewal area are sold to private developers who agree to build improvements suggested by the renewal plan. The site is sold at a price sufficient to induce the desired development.

From the viewpoint of the investor, development on the renewal site must be at least as profitable as investment elsewhere in similar properties. Building in a renewal area has substantial risk because of the character of the surrounding neighborhoods. There is uncertainty about the ability to attract tenants to the renewal area. The time elapsing before complete redevelopment also is a hazard, which can result in a new structure being isolated in a large vacant tract. Consequently, renewal sites may be sold below the price of alternate sites in the community that are suitable for a similar use.

The subsidy in urban renewal is the difference between proceeds realized from resale of sites and the costs of purchasing the blighted properties, razing them, and supplying the required municipal improvements. The federal government supplies two thirds of this subsidy and the local government provides one third, which may be in the form of labor and municipal improvements. Other federal loans and grants are available for feasibility studies, planning, engineering, and relocation payments.

Rationale for renewal

The rationale for urban renewal includes the contention that removal of neighborhood externalities permits improvement of an area that could not occur in normal operation of the market. Each property owner in a blighted area is faced with the "prisoner's dilemma." [7] Renovating his property or constructing a new building would not be profitable because of the character of the immediate neighborhood. The additional rent needed to justify the cost of improvement could not be obtained. Only by removing the blighted condition of the neighborhood can families be attracted who are willing and able to pay the necessary rents. Other reasons given for urban renewal include the attraction of the middle-class family back to the central city, increasing the city's property tax base and tax revenues, removal of aesthetically unattractive structures, and reduction of the cost of police and fire protection, health services, and education by eliminating the slum conditions making provision of these services so costly.

---

[7] Otto A. Davis and Andrew B. Whinston, "Economics of Urban Renewal," *Law and Contemporary Problems,* vol. 26, no. 1 (Winter 1961), pp. 105–17.

Problems, costs, and benefits

Urban renewal has been beset by problems. Blighted areas have to be identified, and concerned citizens protest certain neighborhoods being classified as "blighted" and, therefore, eligible for renewal. At what point does an area contain sufficient substandard properties to be blighted? The relocation of families displaced from the renewal areas has presented continual complications. Before an urban renewal program is authorized, the local agency must demonstrate that sufficient standard housing is available in the community within the financial means of families to be displaced and reasonably close to their place of work. At times, public housing had to be provided before renewal was begun. The local public agency must provide counseling and relocation assistance to displaced families. Families forced to move, however, do not have to take advantage of this service. Urban renewal has been accused of shifting slum conditions from the renewal area to another low-income neighborhood. The broad generalization that renewal merely shifts slum conditions to other neighborhoods in all instances is not supported by empirical evidence, although in some communities displaced families did concentrate in other neighborhoods.[8] Each local public agency is required to trace the displaced families and assess their new housing condition and housing expense. A summary of several of these relocation studies concludes that relocated families generally were better housed, but were paying more in housing expenses.[9]

The reuse of urban renewal sites for offices, commercial and other nonhousing purposes has been severely criticized. Similarly, replacement of low-rent housing with units priced for higher income families has been questioned. A decrease in the supply of units within the financial means of lower income families is a disbenefit for all such families in the community. Presently, in situations where units containing low- and moderate-income families are demolished, and there is a demonstrated need for adequate housing for these families, a unit within the financial reach of the displaced family must be provided somewhere in the community for each unit demolished in the renewal area. When a project has a proposed residential reuse plan, 50 percent of the units provided must be for moderate- and low-income families, and at least 20 percent of the units provided must be for low-income families.

Reuse of the renewal area for higher priced residential units can be viewed as less of a problem than reuse for nonresidential purposes. The higher rent units could result in vacancies elsewhere in the market as

---

[8] Chester Hartman, "The Housing of Relocated Families," *Journal of the American Institute of Planners,* vol. 30, no. 4 (November 1964), pp. 266–86.

[9] Ibid.

families move to the new housing, precipitating the filtering process. Ultimately, better quality units than they are occupying may be available to lower income families at the same or less housing expense.

Filtering, however, is a slow and uncertain process, which can be impeded by net in-migration, undoubling of households, and new household formations that absorb vacancies. The cost of moving, unwillingness to move because of neighborhood ties, lack of knowledge about the availability of better housing, and prejudice that restricts freedom of choice in the housing market further hamper the process. Rents and prices in the market can be slow to fall as landlords tolerate marginal increases in vacancy rates and property owners accept longer waiting periods for sale of their properties. If blight exists because people are poor, filtering down of better quality housing will not prevent blight from reoccurring.[10] Properties which filter down may have maintenance and repair foregone over time because of insufficient rental income to induce normal upkeep. Eventually, the property will become physically substandard.

Urban renewal has the potential of increasing land values in the renewal area and increasing the property tax base of the central city. Land values in the vicinity of the renewal area also may appreciate. When the metropolitan area is considered as a whole, however, the net long-term effect on land values may be minimal.[11] If aggregate land value is some multiple of aggregate rent, the total value of land following urban renewal increases to the extent that households pay more in total rent after renewal. This increase in aggregate rent may be very small. Land values increase in the renewal area because new residents can afford to pay more rent than the displaced families. However, the rental income realized by landlords in the renewal area was lost by owners of competitive properties elsewhere in the market, who are experiencing a higher vacancy loss. Displaced families moving elsewhere in the market and faced, perhaps, with higher rents may choose to buy less housing by doubling up or by otherwise reducing the quantity and quality of housing purchased. Certainly, they are limited in the amount of additional housing expense they can tolerate. The renewal project may alter the topography of land values in the metropolitan area, but not appreciably affect the aggregate value.

Increases in land value resulting from commercial and other land uses locating in the renewal area can be counted as a net increase in aggregate land value only if these establishments would not have located elsewhere in the community. Renewal may increase the community's aggregate income and the demand for goods and services since the federal subsidy dollars can be, in part, a net gain to the community. These dollars are

---

[10] Hugh O. Nourse, "The Economics of Urban Renewal," *Land Economics,* vol. 42, no. 1 (February 1966), p. 67.

[11] Ibid., pp. 68–69.

acted upon by the local income multiplier to produce a greater regional or community income. This amount would be small, and the additional derived demand for commercial and other nonresidential improvements generated by this increased local purchasing power should not be expected to call forth construction of any magnitude.

Empirical studies of the costs and benefits of urban renewal have been attempted by Messner and Mao.[12] Rothenberg, however, notes that the benefits from urban renewal may be the reduction in the social costs of slum living.[13] Fire hazards and crime may be lessened; health hazards are reduced; and the conditions fostering personality problems are removed. These items are difficult to quantify in rigorous cost-benefit analysis.

REHABILITATION AND CONSERVATION

Disenchantment with urban renewal has resulted in programs designed to rehabilitate deteriorating properties and to conserve "gray" areas that might further deteriorate. The model cities program initiated in 1966 provides grants and technical assistance to municipalities or other government bodies which propose an acceptable comprehensive plan for dealing with the social, economic, and physical problems of selected neighborhoods. Grants to assist in carrying out a model cities program must indicate that several social and economic criteria will be met (see Figure 16–3).

Rehabilitation of deteriorating properties in urban renewal areas and in neighborhoods designated for conservation is facilitated by strict code enforcement. When the landlord is told to improve his property to code or face condemnation, he will decide to make the necessary improvements if the cost is no greater than the loss of value experienced by abandoning his property. Some landlords, however, seem capable of inordinately extending the period of compliance. Furthermore, declaring units unfit for human habitation and boarding the windows does not solve the housing problem of the occupants who must seek housing elsewhere. Nor does an increase in rent following improvement of the property aid low-income families to achieve adequate housing within their financial means. If strict code enforcement is effectively to encourage rehabilitation, the availability of credit and other incentives must make rehabilitation the viable alternative to abandonment without unduly increasing the rent of the units.

The federal government is active in providing credit for rehabilitation both directly as grants and loans and indirectly in the form of mortgage

---

[12] J. C. T. Mao, *Efficiency in Public Urban Renewal Expenditures through Capital Budgeting*, Research Report No. 27 (Berkeley: University of California, Center for Real Estate and Urban Economics, 1965); and Stephen D. Messner, "Urban Redevelopment in Indianapolis: A Benefit-Cost Analysis," *The Journal of Regional Science*, vol. 8, no. 2 (Winter 1968), pp. 149–58.

[13] Jerome Rothenberg, *Economic Evaluation of Urban Renewal* (Washington, D.C.: The Brookings Institution, 1967), p. 175.

FIGURE 16–3

Program criteria for model cities

1. Remove or arrest blight or decay and make a substantial impact on the physical and social problems in entire sections or neighborhoods.
2. Contribute to the sound development of the entire city.
3. Make marked progress in reducing social and educational disadvantages, ill health, underemployment, and enforced idleness.
4. Provide educational, health, and social services necessary to serve the poor and disadvantaged in the area.
5. Involve widespread citizen participation.
6. Create maximum opportunities for training and employing area residents in all phases of the program.
7. Provide a substantial increase in the supply of low- and moderate-income housing.
8. Assure maximum opportunities in housing choices for all citizens.
9. Provide adequate public and commercial facilities to serve the residents of the area.
10. Provide ease of access to the residential areas and center of employment.
11. Use high standards of design.
12. Incorporate the preservation of natural and historic sites and distinctive neighborhood characteristics.
13. Make maximum use of new and improved technology and cost reduction techniques.
14. Have reasonably prompt initiation of the projects and activities.
15. Have, or will have, adequate local resources to carry out the projects.
16. Use private initiative and enterprise to the fullest extent possible.
17. Have an adequate relocation plan to serve displaced persons.
18. Be consistent with comprehensive planning in the entire urban and metropolitan area.

insurance or rehabilitation loans. Rehabilitated units are accepted in the principal federal housing programs (Sections 235, 236, and leased or owned public housing). In addition, rehabilitation grants up to $1,500 are available from the Federal Housing Administration for low-income home owners in urban renewal areas and areas of concentrated code enforcement. The FHA also can make direct, low-interest rate loans for rehabilitation to owners of residential and business properties in renewal areas, and can provide insurance for loans made by private lenders for housing, both in renewal areas and outside those areas. HUD can provide grants to cities for two thirds of the cost of planning and carrying out programs of concentrated code enforcement in deteriorating areas. Grants also can be made for citywide surveys of rehabilitation needs and for planning rehabilitation projects.

Further incentive to provide rehabilitated units for low- and moderate-income families was incorporated in the 1969 Tax Reform Act. The act permits a maximum of $15,000 of rehabilitation expenditures per unit to be written off using straight line depreciation over five years. To prevent prolonging improvement of the property and to insure that renovation will be more than cosmetic, at least $3,000 must be spent per dwelling unit within a two-year period. Eligible expenditures must be made after

July 24, 1969, and before January 1, 1975, at which time the program will be evaluated.

The rapid write-off of rehabilitation expenditures should improve the profitability of providing such units. One study, however, suggests that rent for the rehabilitated unit will be increased although the tax incentive will abate the increase necessary to provide an adequate return on investment in these properties.[14] Also, landlords using this tax incentive do not have to accept tenants from the entire spectrum of lower income families and may be disposed to take only families who barely qualify for the program. The tax incentive remains even though the tenants subsequently become over-income, although new tenants must be eligible low-income families.

SUMMARY

Our national housing policy is to provide a decent home and suitable living environment for every American family. In pursuit of this goal, several federal housing programs have been initiated. Public housing was a depression-born program designed to provide adequate housing for low-income families. Over time, public housing has evolved from high-rise projects to less intensive developments and to lease or purchase programs and the public housing home ownership program. The rent supplement program enables low-income families to occupy adequate housing without paying a disproportionate share of their income for rent. Housing for families of moderate income has been made available through the Sec. 221(d)(3) BMIR, Sec. 236, and Sec. 235 programs. Both new and rehabilitated housing are included in these programs. Other federal programs provide grants and loans for renovation and rehabilitation of housing in renewal and conservation districts.

The emerging intent of these programs has been to encourage private enterprise to construct, own, and operate the needed housing. Federal subsidy is provided when necessary to encourage development. The subsidy permits below-market rents and housing expense to be charged and, at the same time, gives the developer and investor satisfactory profits. With the exception of the rent supplements, present federal programs focus upon the provision of housing units for the underhoused. Other alternatives are possible, such as the housing allowance program, which can supplement the income of poor families, although the subsidy still will be earmarked for housing expense. Proposals for unrestricted income supplements have not been well received.

Employment, education, and equality of opportunity will, in the longer

---

[14] John D. Heinberg and Emil M. Sunley, Jr., "Tax Incentives for Rehabilitating Rental Housing," *Proceedings of the American Real Estate and Urban Economics Association*, vol. 6 (1971), pp. 197–218.

run, alleviate the social and economic problems besetting our minority groups and lower income families. In the interim, provision of decent housing directly for some of these disadvantaged families and, hopefully, indirectly for others through the filtering process can only be a partial solution.

All levels of government—federal, state, and local—must be involved in the effort to provide decent housing. It is now recommended that programs which subsidize new and rehabilitated units must be accompanied by strict code enforcement, neighborhood conservation and renewal programs, social work designed to assimilate disadvantaged families into socially acceptable life styles, and professional management of subsidized projects.

Urban renewal and more recent programs emphasizing rehabilitation and conservation of "gray" areas are part of the continuing effort to find incentives necessary for private enterprise to develop and maintain a satisfactory living environment in our cities. Urban renewal provides a subsidy which permits the purchase and demolition of blighted properties and the profitable reuse of the land in accordance with a master plan. Recognition of the need to conserve gray areas which could further deteriorate in a freely competitive housing market, together with the problems besetting urban renewal, resulted in designation of neighborhood conservation districts and in the creation of the comprehensive model cities program. Rehabilitation and conservation have been facilitated by programs of strict code enforcement, grants and loans to property owners in code enforcement and renewal areas, and tax incentives. The effort continues to find the means of reorienting developers, investors, and home owners to the inner city, which has been unable to compete effectively with more desirable areas in our cities.

QUESTIONS FOR REVIEW

1. How does the developer-investor profit from a Sec. 236 project?
2. Should we be concerned with the effects on the local housing market of the simultaneous provision of housing units in the various programs? Discuss.
3. Not every low- or moderate-income family can be provided with a subsidized housing unit. Given a total allocation for subsidy, what factors are involved in an analysis of the alternatives of providing fewer units requiring a higher subsidy cost per unit directly to low-income families versus providing a larger number of units to moderate-income families?
4. What prevents the economist from stating that federal housing programs increase the total national welfare?
5. Explain the rationale for urban renewal.
6. Do you agree with the statement: "Blight exists because people are poor?" Is this contention a complete analysis of the problem?

REFERENCES

Brueggeman, William B.; Racster, Ronald L.; and Smith, Halbert C. "Research Report: Multiple Housing Programs and Urban Housing Policy," *Journal of the American Institute of Planners,* vol. 38, no. 3 (1972), pp. 161–67.

Grigsby, William G. *Housing Markets and Public Policy.* Philadelphia: University of Pennsylvania Press, 1963.

Lansing, J. B.; Clifton, C. W.; and Morgan, J. N. *New Homes and Poor People: A Study of Chains of Moves.* Ann Arbor: University of Michigan, Institute for Social Research, 1969.

O'Block, Robert P. and Kuehn, Robert H., Jr. *An Economic Analysis of the Housing and Urban Development Act of 1968.* Boston: Harvard University, Graduate School of Business Administration, Division of Research, 1970.

Report of the President's Committee on Urban Housing, *A Decent Home.* Washington, D.C.: U.S. Government Printing Office, 1969.

Rothenberg, Jerome. *Economic Evaluation of Urban Renewal.* Washington, D.C.: The Brookings Institution, 1967.

Smith, Wallace F. *Housing: The Social and Economic Elements.* Berkeley: The University of California Press, 1970.

U.S. Department of Housing and Urban Development, *Digest of Insurable Loans and Summaries of Other Federal Housing Administration Programs.* Washington, D.C.: HUD, March 1970.

chapter 17

URBAN TRANSPORTATION

CITIES began when there was sufficient surplus agricultural production to support an urban population, when sanitary facilities permitted a dense aggregation of persons to survive, and when transportation had progressed sufficiently to provide the urban population with a market for its goods and services. As transportation became more efficient and less costly, the market increased in size and the city grew in population and area. At the same time, the internal structure of the urban area was reflecting changes in transportation technology. The city and transportation evolved simultaneously to their present state. Our urban transportation problem today is, in large part, the result of improved transportation struggling with a city developed in response to yesterday's technology.

Each of us can recount the major symptoms of our urban transportation problem: traffic jams, insufficient parking, mass transit that is deficient in both quality and quantity of service, air pollution, and so on. The problem has instigated legislation, experimentation, and considerable analysis, some of which is summarized in this chapter.

The urban transportation system

Urban transportation should be viewed as an integrated system. The physical components of the system are streets, highways, railways, airways, and ancillary structures such as parking facilities, airports, and transit terminals. These facilities are used by automobiles, mass transit, and aircraft in moving persons and goods within the city and among cities in the metropolitan region.

Analysis of urban transportation as an integrated system involves considering all modes of transportation used to move goods and persons from their origin to final destination in the urban area. The system is a "market" in which the supply of transportation service and the demand for its use could conceptually reach equilibrium. In the short run, the equilibrium is constrained by a fixed transportation network. In the long run, the equilibrium would be attained when the overall level of service generated by the system is balanced by the willingness to pay by all beneficiaries. Users, property owners, and other taxpayers would be willing to pay the cost entailed by this system, but would not be willing to pay for further improvements.

Manheim points out that the transportation system is not an end in itself.[1] The system exists to fulfill policy decisions made in both the private and public sectors of our economy. Policy decisions typically relate to only one subsystem or component of the system, such as rapid rail transit or improvement of a single arterial highway route. These policy decisions must be made after considering the repercussions throughout the system, including traffic diversion and traffic generation. In making these decisions, the direct and indirect impacts of transportation on both users and nonusers of the system should be recognized.

User benefits

Improvement in highways provides user benefits such as increased safety, lower vehicle operating costs, time saving, and reduced strain and annoyance of driving. Viewed in another manner, accidents, vehicle operating expenses, time spent in travel, and the discomforts associated with travel are user disbenefits in that they represent real costs to the private motorist and to the commercial user. The social costs of accidents, loss of time, and discomfort defy exact valuation in dollars. Accidents involving personal injury or property damage, however, will result in loss to society of productive capacity which otherwise would be available. Medical expenses and payments for property damage express the cost of accidents to the individuals and concerns involved.

The value of time losses is another intangible cost. Estimates of time saving involve consideration of two factors: (1) the actual total amount of time lost by various classes of vehicles because of traffic conditions and (2) the value of the unit of time. The mobility of the motor vehicle and the ability to vary its speed and path of movement in accordance with the whims and objectives of certain classes of drivers makes measurement of time loss difficult. There is also the problem, especially for the noncommercial driver, of assigning a dollar value to the loss of time. Certain

[1] Marvin L. Manheim, "Principles of Transport Systems Analysis," *Papers—Seventh Annual Meeting: Transportation Research Forum, 1966* (Oxford, Ind.: The Richard B. Cross Co., 1966), p. 11.

measurable costs which enter into the operation of the vehicle, such as fuel and the wages of drivers in commercial vehicles, are directly affected by loss of time.

Even more difficulties have blocked attempts to assign a dollar value to the intangible benefits of reduced discomfort and strain experienced by the motorist traveling a freeway or other highway-type facility. Although quantification is impractical, limited-access highways and other highway improvements theoretically increase the comfort and pleasure of the motorist in some proportion to increases in average speed and to decreases in the frequency and magnitude of necessary changes in speed resulting from stops, turns, and slow traffic.

Vehicle operating costs are the most directly and easily measured user costs. Vehicle operating costs can be separated into fixed costs, such as interest, depreciation, license fees and taxes, insurance, driver's wages and supervision, and variable costs such as gasoline, oil, tires, and maintenance. Only the costs that vary directly with distance and speed of travel, such as gasoline and oil consumption and maintenance expenses, are typically used to indicate vehicle operating costs. Fairly dependable estimates can be made of these costs.

Other user benefits are attained by diversion of traffic from alternate routes. Diversion of traffic and consequent relief of congestion on alternative routes give benefits to users of the latter routes that otherwise would not have been obtained.

Benefit-cost ratios have been developed and used by engineers to determine the feasibility of construction of highways and the order of priority of construction. These ratios are concerned mostly with the user, or direct benefits discussed above. Benefit-cost ratios provide part of the information needed for policy decisions in community planning, but additional information must be obtained, such as the value which the community attaches to savings in travel time and reduced accident risks, the capital costs of the improvement, and the opportunity costs forgone by investment in a highway facility instead of some other form of social capital. Wingo has pointed out that social income from the project must be matched with social costs, and these may not be identical to money savings or money costs.[2]

Transportation and the value of urban sites

The value of an urban site depends upon the type and intensity of use to which it can be put. Accessibility is a determinant of the type and intensity of use of urban sites, and accessibility, in turn, is inversely re-

---

[2] Lowdon Wingo, Jr., *Transportation and Urban Land* (Washington, D.C.: Resources for the Future, Inc., 1960), p. 112.

lated to the sum of transport costs from other sites in the urban area. These transport costs reflect user benefits that depend upon the urban transport system.

The value of an urban site is determined by the amount that must be paid to hire it from its next best use. Its value, then, is an opportunity cost. Once a site has become a location for a retail store, a warehouse, or residence, however, it may earn a surplus above the price paid for its use. A retail store in an area served by a new traffic artery may receive this surplus or abnormal profit because of its increased accessibility.

Whether the value of the urban site increases because of its greater accessibility will depend upon the monopoly position enjoyed by that site. If the site contributed to the abnormal profit and the landlord has a strong bargaining position by virtue of an inelastic supply of sites of that type and a definite need for the service of the site, then he can claim the excess profit by raising the rent and site value will increase. An apartment owner may be able to raise the rent of a tenant who has experienced reduced transportation costs. The owner of a single-family residence may find that his home has increased in value for the same reason.

In a dynamic world, these abnormal profits continually arise as relative accessibility changes for particular sites. However, these profits can vanish as more firms enter the market or as the character of the neighborhood or trade area changes. An improvement in transportation can make alternative sites available and, thus, destroy the "monopoly" position of certain areas of the community, such as the central business district. The intensity of use of such areas and the value of sites would be reduced in response to the changing supply conditions.

Empirical studies. The conception and implementation of the national system of interstate and defense highways by the federal-aid highway acts of 1944 and 1956 greatly accelerated interest in the economic influence of motor transportation on urban communities. A large number of empirical studies of the impact of highway improvements have been completed since the inception of the interstate system.[3] These empirical studies differed in objective, type of highway improvement studied, geographic area analyzed, data used to measure the changes attributed to the highway improvement, methodology used in the process of measurement, and their findings. Consequently, no definitive statement can be made concerning the effect of a particular type of highway improvement on property values in its vicinity. However, there is evidence to support a

---

[3] Research on highway impact has been summarized in: Massachusetts Department of Public Works, *Social and Economic Aspects of Highways*, Publication No. 2: "Review of Important Studies and Selected Bibliography" (Boston, April 1961); and Warren A. Pillsbury, *The Economic and Social Effects of Highway Improvement: An Annotated Bibliography* (Charlottesville: Virginia Council of Highway Investigation and Research, May 1961).

generalization that increased urban land values are associated with a highway improvement.

One synopsis of 183 separate observations encompassing all types of land uses showed that only 20 observations exhibited a decline in annual percentage change of urban property value (in constant dollars) following a highway improvement.[4] The studies summarized in the 183 observations vary in methodology and type of highway facility analyzed. Some were only "before and after" analyses, which makes it difficult to separate the effect of the highway on land values from other factors in the local economy. Other investigations use study and control areas or correlation and regression analysis to isolate the effect of the highway. Some of the studies dealt with the location of an intraurban freeway or expressway, while other studies examined the impact of bypasses.

A study considered typical of the more rigorous and thorough empirical studies examined the economic impact of Massachusetts Route 128, a 55-mile limited-access highway around Boston.[5] Surveys were made of industrial and commercial developments in an area one-mile wide on either side of the highway. As "controls," industries which were located in the area before the new highway was opened were studied to determine benefits they might receive fom the highway. A second control group was comprised of plants built after the highway had opened in areas not influenced by Route 128.

The industrial survey disclosed that of the new plants on Route 128, 22 percent were either new companies or new branches, and 78 percent were relocated from other areas. The relocated plants came predominately from in-town areas. The industrial expansion along the route was significant and strengthened the tax base of the communities; there was an in-

---

[4] U.S. Department of Commerce, *Final Report of the Highway Cost Allocation Study*, Part VI: *Data Concerning the Economic and Social Effects of Highway Improvement* (Washington, D.C.: U.S. Government Printing Office, 1961), Table VI–1, p. 7. Nineteen of the 20 observations experienced a decline of 1 to 5 percent, while only one observation experienced a fall of 5 percent; 137 of the observations fell between a zero increase in value and an increase of 20 percent. When the 183 observations are classified as to type of land use and a median annual percentage change of property value is determined in constant dollars, the ranking of median change shows: (1) a median annual percentage increase in value of about 18 percent for industrial land use (11 observations); (2) a median increase of almost 13 percent for unimproved land (22 observations); (3) a median increase of over 10 percent for commercial land (33 observations); and (4) a median increase of over 8 percent for residential land (85 observations). The total of all classified uses had a median annual percentage increase of slightly less than 10 percent (151 observations), and unspecified types of land use had a median increase of less than 6 percent (32 observations). The type of land use evidently is a determinant of the amount of value change experienced. Speculation could account for the large value change experienced by unimproved land. Conversion of land to industrial and commercial uses could account for the greater median percentage changes in value experienced by the industrial and commercial land.

[5] A. J. Bone, *Economic Impact Study of Massachusetts Route 128* (Cambridge: Massachusetts Institute of Technology, December 31, 1958).

crease in the value of land for industrial uses from $1,000–$1,500 per acre prior to the highway to $8,000–$26,000 per acre afterwards.

Companies gave a number of reasons for locating on Route 128, including the need for land for expansion, accessibility for commercial purposes, an attractive site, labor market considerations, accessibility for employees, advertising value of the site, and adequate parking facilities. A factor that was very important in motivating these industries was the desire for ease of regional access, implying desire for freedom from traffic and parking congestion prevalent in downtown areas. The urge to decentralize is evident. Companies representing more than half of the total investment on Route 128 considered only suburban locations as being feasible.

The effect which Route 128 had upon residential development was examined, particularly in the towns of Lexington and Needham. The study method considered residential development in an area close to the highway both before and after the highway had been built, and trends before and after in a control area having similar characteristics. This study area divided Lexington into two parts. An area one-half mile from Route 128, and running parallel to it, was the study area and the remainder of the town was the control area.

Access distance zones were established to determine the effects of access to Route 128 upon residential growth. These zones contain privately owned land within 250 feet of a street which could be reached by driving less than one and one-half miles from the nearest Route 128 interchange. The control zone included all privately owned and public land within 250 feet of streets more than one and one-half miles from the interchanges. Three access zones were studied in the belief that highway influence is related to ease of access to the highway. Zone 1 was up to one-half mile from the interchange. Zone 2 was from one half to one mile, and Zone 3 from one to one and one-half miles.

In Lexington, a bedroom city for Boston, assessed valuation increased 180 percent in the land area adjacent to the Route 128, compared to only 83 percent in the rest of the town. The cumulative number of occupancy permits issued in the adjacent band increased 538 percent, and house density increased 112 percent, compared with 383 percent and 58 percent respectively in the control area. The number of residential real estate sales also showed a greater increase in the adjacent band than in the control area. However, the average prices of the houses sold were less along Route 128. In comparing access distance and control zones, a somewhat similar, but less marked difference between Route 128 and the other areas was observed. Activity was especially spirited in the zero to one-half mile zone around the interchange. In the city of Needham, more building occurred in the area adjacent to the highway than in the control area. The rate of increase in building permits in residential sales also exceeded that of the control area. In both Lexington and Needham, some part of the residential development took place because of the convenience offered by Route 128.

The methodology used in the Route 128 study is typical of a large number of empirical studies completed after construction of the interstate system. The findings of these several studies, however, vary significantly. Furthermore, many of the impact investigations using study and control areas mention that changes in land or property values in the study area can only be considered as net benefits if the economic activity producing the change, such as industry moving to the area, would not have located elsewhere in the community in the absence of the highway improvement.

Regional effects

Transportation innovations and improvements free resources needed to overcome the cost of movement and permit these resources to be used otherwise for production. The changes in national product following a highway improvement between regions have been examined by Tinbergen [6] and Bos and Koyck.[7] Their analyses emphasize direct and indirect increases in productivity following the improved transport route and suggest that user benefits are only one form of the total benefit to the regional economy. Further investment in productive capacity may be made following a reduction in transportation costs.

Empirical studies. Studies that assess the intraregional influence of new, improved, or relocated transportation routes on relatively large areas, such as a county, state, or larger region, typically find net benefits accruing to the area. In one study of the Sunshine State Parkway in Florida, the potential impact on the basic determinants of the economic growth in the state were studied.[8] The geographic area affected by the highway was delineated and divided into five districts, each composed of several counties. The authors concluded that: (1) Tourism will benefit most from the highway. The volume of tourists will increase and there will be greater dispersion of tourists throughout the state. Seasonal fluctuations in the tourist industry should be reduced. (2) The highway is not expected to increase population migration to Florida, but the dispersion of population within the state may be affected. (3) The market structure of the state will become more integrated and the spatial arrangement of wholesaling and industry will be affected. (4) The volume of agricultural output will not

---

[6] J. Tinbergen, "The Appraisal of Road Construction: Two Calculation Schemes," *The Review of Economics and Statistics* (August 1957), pp. 241–49.

[7] H. C. Bos and L. M. Koyck, "The Appraisal of Road Construction Projects: A Practical Example," *The Review of Economics and Statistics* (February 1961), pp. 13–26.

[8] First Research Corporation, *An Economic Study on the Proposed Florida Sunshine State Parkway* (New York: First Research Corporation, 1956).

be appreciably increased, but truck transportation will experience a competitive advantage over rail. The new route was expected to affect volume only where tourists were concerned, but was expected to alter the pattern of organization of economic activities within the state.

Another regional study analyzing the economic benefits of two possible locations of an interstate highway between Phoenix and Brenda, Arizona, considered gains and losses in business volume, agricultural production, gasoline and sales tax revenues, real estate taxes, and highway user costs savings.[9] The net gain for the new route to be constructed 35 miles south of the alternate, existing route was estimated to exceed $39 million. The principal contribution to this gain would be additional agricultural production resulting from increased accessibility to relatively uncultivated land.

Once again, empirical studies measuring the net benefits accruing to a region may fail to reflect losses of population and industry from places outside the chosen area of influence. In this respect, the size of the area analyzed can influence the extent of net benefits realized. When the size of the area is enlarged, net benefits attributed to a smaller area could disappear. For benefits to exist, the increase in regional economic activity must be the result of an investment that otherwise would not occur; using resources that otherwise would be unemployed.[10] A transportation route that makes previously unused resources or agricultural land available could produce significant benefits. Even if increased volumes of business activity or population in the region are not forthcoming, however, rearrangement of existing economic activity would be expected.

Transportation and urban land use

Generalized explanations of the spatial dimensions of urban activities include the concentric circle hypothesis and the sector hypothesis discussed in chapter 2. Transportation is a factor in these descriptive schemes of urban land use, together with other economic, social, and physical factors.

Concentric circle hypothesis. Transportation is a central force in the concentric circle hypothesis. The central business district, for instance, is near the center of the zones of land uses because it is the area of optimum accessibility, where transportation facilities tend to converge. The "zone of working men's homes" is located near their place of work, in part, to minimize transport costs. Zones of more expensive apartments, and single-

---

[9] Stanley Womer Associates, *Economic Study of Alternate Proposals for the Construction of Route I–10 between Phoenix and Brenda, Arizona* (Phoenix: Arizona Highway Department, December 1958).

[10] Herbert Mohring and Mitchell Harwitz, *Highway Benefits: An Analytical Framework* (Chicago: Northwestern University Press, 1962), p. 143.

family residences appear further from the center, in part, because of the lower sensitivity of their occupants to transport costs. Expansion of the city occurs from the inner zones and depends primarily upon the mobility of the population. Land values are indices of mobility, with the highest land values found at the point of greatest mobility. The urban transportation system permits and channels mobility and, therefore, is a major determinant of land values.

Sector theory. The sector theory of urban land use is primarily concerned with the pattern and determinants of residential land use. The reasonably homogeneous sectors typically grow outward to the periphery of the city. Automobile transportation can cause the outward movement to skip over undeveloped land. Generally, high-quality residential areas follow lines of most rapid transportation and are pulled to areas of natural beauty or other advantageous residential sites. Intermediate and some low-quality residential areas are drawn along. Other low-price residential areas develop around places of work to minimize commuting costs.

Systems of activities. Another descriptive scheme of urban land patterns views urban land uses as systems of activities.[11] In this explanation, the physical structure of cities reflects the institutionalized activities of groups and individuals, each of whom is engaged in routine actions and random movements. Once institutions evolve, they interact in numerous cross-relationships. The repetitive activities of individuals in groups create establishments, which use specific locations for carrying on that activity. Establishments occupy the physical structure and give concrete evidence of institutionalized activities and their cross-relationships. Establishments are linked together by the movement of persons, goods, and information that are, in turn, reflections of the linkages between firms and individuals. The "pulls" exerted by the multitude of linkages with other establishments determine the spatial arrangement of urban land uses.

Transportation is an establishment of the systems-of-activity explanation of urban land use patterns. Transportation is connected with the activities of all urban establishments and provides the means of movement between locations. Transportation facilities develop in response to the need for them, but the new patterns of land use which evolve require yet additional needs.

The system-of-activities scheme shows that the relationship between land use and transportation is reciprocal and that the cause and effect between increased differentiation of urban activity systems and accompanying developments in transportation cannot be ascertained. Market

---

[11] John Rannells, *The Core of the City: A Pilot Study of Changing Land Uses in the Central Business District* (New York: Columbia University Press, 1956); Robert B. Mitchell and Chester Rapkin, *Urban Traffic: A Function of Land Use* (New York: Columbia University Press, 1954).

imperfections, together with the relatively fixed transport system and physical structures, cause establishments to adapt to the existing physical arrangement, even though the internal activities and relationships among these establishments might be better served by some other arrangement.

Hypothesis of median location. The hypothesis of median location has been advanced as an explanation of the tendency for nonprofit urban land uses, retail stores, office buildings, wholesaling outlets, financial institutions, industrial uses, and residences to locate at the geographical median in a time-cost sense with respect to: (1) the resources utilized by a particular urban activity; (2) the people or businesses to which the activity is related; and (3) the customers that it serves.[12] For each particular land use, the median responds to different factors. The type of clientele, their incomes, the goods and services produced or sold, the market area served, the type of workers employed, and the shopping areas and work places of home owners determine the median applicable to each particular urban land use. The concept of median location has been used to describe the tendency of natural areas to form within the urban community as land uses of the same general type respond to similar sets of locational determinants.[13] Median location involves the concept of minimization of costs or maximization of profit or net satisfaction, which, in turn, lies behind location theory and other explanations of urban land use structure.

Empirical studies. The value of an urban site is determined by its most profitable use. An improvement in the transportation system can result in a site's becoming more valuable because it now generates a larger net income or greater amenities. The site may be utilized more intensively for its original purpose, or it may have become suitable for a different use. The greatest change in value typically results from a change in land use, perhaps from residential to commercial or from rural to urban use. Since conversion of use often is impeded by zoning and other factors, the change in site value may precede actual redevelopment.

Generalizations from empirical studies of the effects of transportation on urban land use suffer because of the diversity of route improvements and urban areas affected. Improvements may be a bypass, an outerbelt, an arterial route through the city, a limited-access freeway, an expressway without limited access, or a one-way street. Each of these improvements may have its effects on land use determined in part by existing development and zoning in the area traversed.

Several studies indicate that if other circumstances are favorable, there will be a conversion of existing uses and development of vacant land to

---

[12] James A. Quinn, "The Hypothesis of Median Location," *American Sociological Review* (April 1943), pp. 148–56.

[13] Paul Hatt, "The Concept of Natural Area," *American Sociological Review* (August 1946), pp. 423–27.

commercial and business use following a highway improvement.[14] Studies have found commercial and business uses developing more rapidly near downtown and along the highway improvement. Another study found these land uses developing most rapidly along the major access routes and feeder streets to a limited-access freeway. In many studies, the time needed for conversion was believed to be too long to allow the full impact of the highway improvement to be felt.

Surveys of businessmen indicate that highways are important in the location decisions of commercial and business land uses. One survey of 52 establishments engaged in retailing or wholesaling and distribution activities showed that 19 of the respondents considered factors of highway access and highway exposure to be the dominant criteria in the selection of a location.[15] Fourteen other respondents indicated factors related to the highway network were important. A Dallas study found that advantages for businesses located along the expressway included accessibility, freedom from congestion, expansion potential, and advertising and parking advantages.[16]

The location of industry along or near a highway improvement is often observed in highway impact studies.[17] All types of highway improvements seem to attract industrial development, but circumferential or beltline highways and interchanges may be particularly attractive. Beltlines allow

---

[14] The following studies are indicative of the research in this area, but are not inclusive: William G. Adkins, *Effects of the Dallas Central Expressway on Land Values and Land Use*, Bulletin 6 (College Station, Tex.: Transportation Institute, September 1957); Bone, *Economic Impact Study of Massachusetts Route 128;* Donald D. Carroll et al., *The Economic Impact of Highway Development upon Land Use and Values: Development of Methodology and Analysis of Selected Highway Segments in Minnesota* (Minneapolis: University of Minnesota, 1958); George W. Childs, *The Influence of Limited Access Highways on Land Value and Land Use: The Lexington, Virginia, By-pass* (Charlottesville: Virginia Council of Highway Investigation and Research, 1958); Richard Duke, "The Effects of a Depressed Expressway—A Detroit Case Study," *The Appraisal Journal* (October 1958); John C. Frey et al., *The Economic and Social Impact of Highways: A Process Summary of the Monroeville Case Study* (University Park: Pennsylvania State University, Agricultural Experiment Station, 1960); James H. Lemly, *Expressway Influence on Land Use and Value, Atlanta, 1941–1956,* Paper No. 10 (Atlanta: Georgia State College of Business Administration, Bureau of Business and Economic Research); David R. Levin, "Land Use Development and the Highway Interchange," mimeographed (Washington, D.C.: Bureau of Public Roads, 1960).

[15] Real Estate Research Corporation, *Highway Network as a Factor in the Selection of Commercial and Industrial Locations* (Chicago: RERC, 1958), p. 18.

[16] Adkins, *Effects of the Dallas Central Expressway.*

[17] The following references are suggestive of the many studies reporting this type of highway impact: Donald Bowersox, *Influence of Highways on Selection of Six Industrial Locations*, Bulletin 268 (Washington, D.C.: Highway Research Board, 1960); Bureau of Business Research, *The Effect of the Louisville-Watterson Expressway on Land Use and Land Values and Lexington Northern Belt Line* (Lexington: University of Kentucky, 1960); John R. Bochert, *Beltline Commercial-Industrial Development: A Case Study in the Minneapolis-St. Paul Metropolitan Area* (St. Paul: University of Minnesota, 1960).

access to the highway net, while making space available for one-story plants, parking, and expansion. Determination of the relative importance of highways in interregional and intraregional plant location decisions is hampered by the complexity of the decision and the variation among industries with respect to labor needs, market and material orientation, plant requirements, and need to maintain contact with other businesses. A survey of 68 manufacturing and processing firms found that a single highway was rarely the foremost consideration in the location and success of an industrial enterprise.[18] A more important factor is the entire network of highways, of which the particular road is but a part. The transportation network determines access to markets, to the labor force, and to needed materials.

Highway improvements can make land available for residential use, and several studies indicate that residential development occurred along the highway or within its area of influence.[19] Other studies, however, did not find residential development stimulated by the highway.[20] Zoning, the degree of development of the area prior to the highway improvement, business uses along the facility, traffic volume and noise have been advanced as reasons for lack of residential development. Opinion surveys were used in several studies to determine whether the highway was an important influence on the residential land use.[21] Considerable diversity of opinion existed with respect to whether or not the highway was a material consideration when buying; whether the noise was bothersome; and whether the facility depressed or enhanced the value of their property. In general, a majority felt that the facility had little or no adverse effect on property values. Opinions of home owners were found to be conditioned by factors such as proximity to the highway, with more residents approving as their distance from the facility increased; by the type of facility, with a parkway preferred to a freeway and a depressed highway preferred to an elevated

---

[18] Real Estate Research Corporation, *Highway Network as a Factor.*

[19] The following studies are indicative of research in this area, but are not inclusive: *Traffic Impact: A Study of the Effects of Selected Roads on Residential Living in Southern Westchester* (White Plains, N.Y.; Westchester County Dept. of Planning, 1954); Bone, *Economic Impact Study of Massachusetts Route 128,* William Adkins and Alton Tieken, *Economic Impacts of Expressways in San Antonio* (College Station, Tex.: Transportation Institute, 1958); Bayard O. Wheeler, "The Effect of Freeway Access upon Suburban Real Property Values," Part V, *Allocation of Road and Street Costs* (Seattle: University of Washington, 1956).

[20] Duke, "The Effects of a Depressed Expressway"; Dale Gustafson and Everett G. Smith, Jr., *A Highway Change in Changing Faribault* (Minneapolis: University of Minnesota, 1959); Norris & Elder, consulting engineers, *A 15-Year Study of Land Values and Land Use along the Gulf Freeway in the City of Houston, Texas* (Houston, 1956).

[21] Adkins, *Effects of the Dallas Central Expressway;* Adkins and Tieken, *Economic Impacts of Expressways in San Antonio;* Bone, *Economic Impact Study of Massachusetts Route 128;* Maryland State Roads Commission, *Three Economic Impact Studies on a Portion of the Baltimore Beltway* (Annapolis, 1960).

highway; and by the presence of children in the household. The question can be asked, of course, as to whether the opinions of people who bought or owned homes in an affected area are representative of the attitudes of the entire population.

The traffic artery as an urban land use

The location of urban streets and highways ideally is based in large part upon the criterion of greatest efficiency in movement of people and goods, although the exercise of political and various environmental factors may have significant roles in site selection. The preservation of historical landmarks and cemeteries, for instance, may affect route location. The relatively high cost of a route in areas already developed with valuable residential, commercial, or industrial property may result in the facility traversing blighted or vacant tracts. Urban arterial routes in many American cities have served to accomplish at least the demolition aspect of urban renewal.

Several alternate locations for an arterial route usually are considered. Origin and destination surveys indicate major desire lines of the urban traffic pattern and the corridors in which arterial routes should be located. Assignment of traffic to the route determines whether a major street, expressway, freeway, or parkway is required. Prediction of the volume and type of traffic involves estimating: (1) the normal growth of traffic; (2) the additional traffic generated by the new or improved facility; (3) traffic resulting from land uses which will locate near the facility; (4) the number of zone-to-zone trips that each type of expected land development will produce; and (5) the comparative advantage of the route for zone-to-zone traffic considering travel distance, travel times, economies and ease of operation of vehicles, and safety of operation on alternate routes. Estimates of the cost of right-of-way and construction, user benefits, the feasibility of construction of the facility in stages, and the ease of handling traffic during construction also are considered in choosing between alternate locations.

The reciprocal nature of urban land uses and street and highway location is evident. The land use pattern creates a demand for routes by generating traffic. The predicted volume and character of future traffic influences the type of facility to be constructed, and the present and prospective land use pattern typically dominates the choice of location.

The urban transportation problem

The most vexing urban transportation problem is moving people to and from areas of high population and work place density, i.e., the twice-a-day rush "hour," which in many American cities should be "hours." [22] The increasing number of cross-haul and reverse commuter trip patterns has aggravated the rush hour problem. Cross-haul trips arise from dispersion of places of origin and destination, resulting in people's wishing to traverse the central city during periods of peak load on the system.

The problem is further aggravated by declining use of mass transit, which is caught in the vicious circle of lower patronage as people elect to use the automobile, rising operating costs, declining level of service, still lower levels of patronage and higher operating costs, and further reductions of service. The decentralization of American cities has rendered mass transit relatively uneconomical in many areas of the community. Decentralization has at least been permitted by the advent of the automobile, but cannot solely be attributed to the changing transportation technology. Some dispersion of the population would be expected, given our increasing urban population. Certainly many families have been attracted by the provision of relatively inexpensive, good quality single-family housing in the outskirts of the city and the tax concessions promoting home ownership.

Mass transit also has suffered from the changing character of downtown, which has become the location for offices and other activities of a professional nature requiring face-to-face contact. Office workers and professional persons comprise one group of demanders wishing access to the central city. At the other extreme is the low-income service worker employed in the supporting retail and service establishments remaining in the central city. It may be difficult to get these contrasting groups to accept the same quality of transportation service or even to travel together. Social stratification may hinder joint use of transit, as it alters the spatial pattern of demand.

The automobile has made parking a part of the urban transportation problem. Inadequacy of parking is believed to be associated with decentralization of the central business district functions, with the volume of retail sales in the central business district, and, consequently, with the level of central business district land values. Shopping centers, office buildings, and industrial plants have located in suburban areas to accommodate, in part, customers and workers seeking adequate parking. Dispersion of retail stores has slowed the rate of growth in central business district retail sales and land values.

Fragmentation of government in our metropolitan areas contributes to the urban transportation problem. Historically, there has been an inability to plan for the urban region or to coordinate municipal efforts in

---

[22] John Meyer, John Kain, and Martin Wohl, *The Urban Transportation Problem* (Cambridge, Mass.: Harvard University Press, 1966), pp. 360–67.

providing an integrated transportation system. The fact that investment in the urban transportation system is made by federal, state, and local governments is a further complication. The interstate system is administered by the Federal Highway Administration, and the federal government provides 90 percent of the cost of the constructing of these facilities. Other arterial routes in the urban area include state or federal highways, with part of the cost of construction and maintenance being shared between these governments and the municipalities. Mass transit often is privately owned but regulated by the state. Once again, there is a problem of shared administrative authority, with federal, state, and local agencies struggling to define their respective spheres of influence in providing an adequate transportation system.

Alleviation of the urban transportation problem

Technological development. The urban transportation problem may be alleviated in the longer run by technological advances that permit a greater level of service at the same cost. Several promising transportation innovations are presently in various stages of development and experimentation. These improvements center around making mass transit more attractive to the user and improving the efficiency of the urban transportation system.

The limited-stop express bus, complete with stewardess, perhaps traveling on its own restricted highway, is an effort to improve both attractiveness and efficiency. High-speed rail transportation traveling up to 150 miles per hour is now in limited use. V/STOL (vertical and short take-off and landing aircraft) are in use in a few cities.[23] V/STOL permits connection between major air terminals and the central city or suburb and can serve short-haul traffic between central cities within the urban region. V/STOL will be less costly and less complex than the helicopter presently used to provide the link between air terminal and destination. The major requirements for a workable V/STOL system are slow-flying dependable aircraft capable of a short approach and take-off and V/STOL ports in or near the central city, perhaps on parking structures, docks, or over rail yards. Other innovations are TACV (the tracked air-cushion vehicle), a magnetic suspension vehicle in the 400-mile per hour class, and tube vehicles employing electric power or using a gravity vacuum tube.[24] All of these very rapid facilities are in the theoretical-experimental stage.

---

[23] P. Y. Davoud and W. T. Heaslip, "The Prospect of V/STOL Aircraft in Future Airline Operations," *Papers of the Transportation Research Forum* (1967), pp. 55–56.

[24] Edward J. Ward, "A Progress Report on High Speed Ground Transportation (R & D)," *Papers of the Transportation Research Forum* (1967), pp. 297–309.

In addition to equipment innovations, techniques for improving the flow of traffic within the system are being explored. CARS (computer aided routing system), for instance, is an attempt to provide economical mass transit to low-density population areas such as the suburb.[25] Both the distribution and collection problems are aided by dynamic routing and scheduling of the evening and morning rush hours. In the evening, persons arriving on a train must be dispersed to available vehicles, which follow an optimal route to distribute the commuter to his home. In the morning rush hour, the commuter must be picked up at different times and places and brought to the transit station.

Project CARS also is known as Dial-A-Ride, a personalized door-to-door public transportation service.[26] The Dial-A-Ride experiment used a fleet of small vehicles to serve customer requests as they were received. There were no fixed routes and schedules. Customers called the local Dial-A-Ride number and informed the operator that he wanted to make a trip, giving such information as his origin, desired destination, and number of passengers. A computer takes this information and develops the optimum routes as well as sequencing the stops for the vehicles. Dial-A-Ride is adaptable both for the "many-to-one" situation, where travelers come from a variety of points of origin to a single destination, and the more complex "many-to-many" situation.

Intergovernmental cooperation. The manifest inability of local governments to coordinate their planning and actions resulted in federal legislation promoting a coordinated urban transportation system. The Department of Transportation was established in 1966 for the purpose of developing national transportation policies and programs conducive to the provision of expedient, safe, efficient, and convenient transportation service at reasonable cost.[27] The department has the responsibility of coordinating federal transportation programs and projects involving federal, state, and local governmental agencies. Federal agencies engaged in various aspects of transportation prior to 1966 either were transferred to the department or had their functions placed under the jurisdiction of the department. The Department of Transportation presently has six operating agencies: (1) U.S. Coast Guard, (2) Federal Aviation Administration, (3) Federal Highway Administration, (4) Federal Railroad Administration, (5) Urban Mass Transportation Administration, and (6) St. Lawrence Development Corporation. Although the Federal Highway Administra-

---

[25] Nigel H. M. Wilson and Daniel Roos, "CARS: Computer Aided Routing System," *Papers of the Transportation Research Forum* (1966), pp. 129–40.

[26] Daniel Roos et al., *The Dial-A-Ride Transportation System: Summary Report* (Cambridge, Mass.: MIT, March 1971).

[27] Grant M. Davis, *The Department of Transportation* (Lexington: Heath Lexington Books, 1970), pp. 152–58.

tion, primarily through the Bureau of Public Roads, and the Federal Railroad Administration, through its Office of High Speed Ground Transportation, are active in research and development affecting the urban transportation system, it is the Urban Mass Transportation Administration which has the principal impact on our urban transportation problem.

The Urban Mass Transportation Administration administers the Urban Mass Transportation Act of 1964 and the Urban Mass Transportation Assistance Act of 1970. The Urban Mass Transportation Act of 1964 provided federal assistance for acquisition or improvement of facilities or equipment associated with mass transportation; for research, development, and demonstration projects related to urban mass transportation; engineering, planning, and designing mass transportation systems; and training personnel in managerial, technical, and professional positions related to urban mass transportation.[28]

The 1964 act authorized federal grants for up to two thirds of the "net project cost" of a coordinated urban mass transit system that otherwise could not be financed. Net project cost is gross cost less the amount that could be financed from operating revenues. The applicant must be a public body with areawide responsibility for an urban system.

The Urban Mass Transportation Act of 1970 furthers federal assistance to urban mass transit.[29] The Secretary of Transportation was authorized to incur additional obligations up to $5 billion to finance grants and loans to state and local agencies for acquisition, construction, reconstruction, and improvement of mass transit. Loans can be made for advance acquisition of facilities, right-of-way, station sites, and related items, including payments for relocating families and businesses and the net cost of property management to cover the holding period. Facilities purchased must be used within a reasonable time (no longer than 10 years), and the original loan may be repaid using part of a federal grant made at that time for construction of the system. The local share (one third) of the net project cost of construction can come from public sources or from a local private transit system.

Congress has recognized that the nation's mass transportation needs will require a federal commitment of at least $10 billion over a 12-year period. The 1970 act is the first major step toward making this commitment. The funds, however, are for acquisition and construction of plant and equipment; mass transit operating deficits are not federally subsidized. Applicants for federal assistance under the 1970 act are to have a comprehensive transportation planning agency, encouraging a coordinated transport system for the urban region.

Planning for transportation. More rational use of land would promote in a more efficient, less costly transportation system. Proper planning and

---

[28] U.S. Congress, Public Law 88-365, 88th Congress, 2d session, 1964.
[29] U.S. Congress, Public Law 91-453, 91st Congress, 2d session, 1970.

zoning, by controlling the density of development and preventing urban sprawl, contribute to alleviation of the transportation problem. Planning for an efficient structure of urban land uses for the sole purpose of minimizing transportation costs, however, misplaces priorities. The transportation system exists to serve urban areas, which grow and change in response to a great number of determinants, only one of which is transportation.

Regional transportation planning. Comprehensive planning for the transportation system in the urban region copes with a critical aspect of the transportation problem. Areawide transportation planning exists in most metropolitan areas, although the experts' recommendations may not be implemented. The availability of federal funds for urban areas having a comprehensive plan, however, provides the coordinating agency with considerable power in debates over arterial route locations, mass transit programs, and other improvements.

The Northeast Corridor project is an example of large-scale coordinated transportation planning for a region. The Northeast Corridor project was initiated by the Northeast Corridor Act of 1964 and is presently administered by the Department of Transportation. The project involves planning a transportation system for the megalopolis stretching from southern New Hampshire to Virginia and from the Coast to Appalachia. All modes of transportation are considered, with the planning horizon extending to 1980 and 1990.

The number of alternate transportation systems available for this region and the number and variety of impacts precluded using a single model for predictive purposes. Consequently, a "PSP" (problem-solving process) model was developed, which structured the analysis in seven levels (see Figure 17–1).[30] Analysis proceeds from policy decisions at Level I through successive levels to the design and operation of the transportation system. At each level of analysis, a number of alternatives are considered, and the results of their implementation are determined. These consequences are evaluated and the preferred results serve as the beginning point for analysis at the next level. Detailed analysis is performed at the seventh level, which uses a "forward-seeking model system" to test a relatively small number of alternative transportation systems (see Figure 17–2). The forward-seeking model predicts outcomes, which are ranked according to preference. The methodology of the Northeast Corridor project reflects the enormous complexity of a planning process that must consider all modes of transportation, route configurations, levels of service, pricing policies, and the impact of alternative actions on users and nonusers.

Pricing alternative modes. The urban transportation problem may require pricing alternative modes of transportation to discourage the use of

---

[30] H. W. Bruck, Marvin L. Manheim, and Paul W. Shuldiner, "Transportation Systems Planning as a Process: The Northeast Corridor Example," *Annals of the Transportation Research Forum* (1967), pp. 67–98.

FIGURE 17–1

Multi-level structure of the problem-solving process

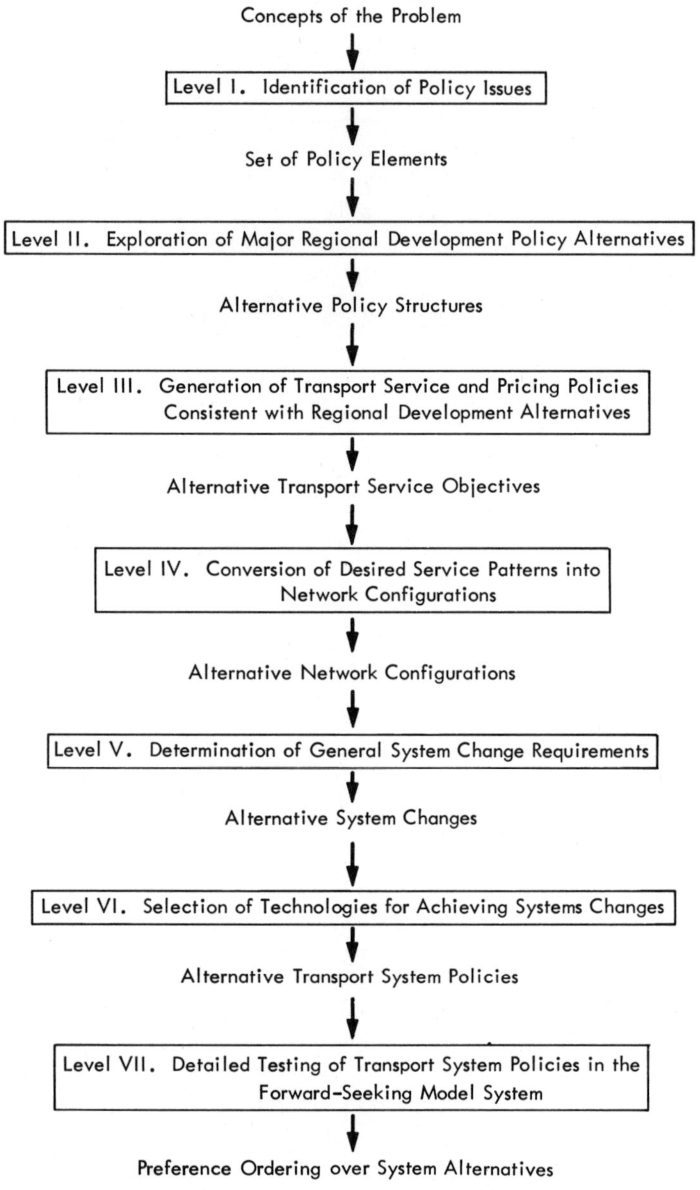

Concepts of the Problem

Level I. Identification of Policy Issues

Set of Policy Elements

Level II. Exploration of Major Regional Development Policy Alternatives

Alternative Policy Structures

Level III. Generation of Transport Service and Pricing Policies
Consistent with Regional Development Alternatives

Alternative Transport Service Objectives

Level IV. Conversion of Desired Service Patterns into
Network Configurations

Alternative Network Configurations

Level V. Determination of General System Change Requirements

Alternative System Changes

Level VI. Selection of Technologies for Achieving Systems Changes

Alternative Transport System Policies

Level VII. Detailed Testing of Transport System Policies in the
Forward–Seeking Model System

Preference Ordering over System Alternatives

Source: Bruck, Manheim, and Shuldiner, "Transportation Systems Planning
as a Process: The Northeast Corridor Example," *Annals of the Transportation Research Forum*, p. 82.

FIGURE 17–2

Northeast Corridor Project (sequence of operations in a run of the forward-seeking model system)

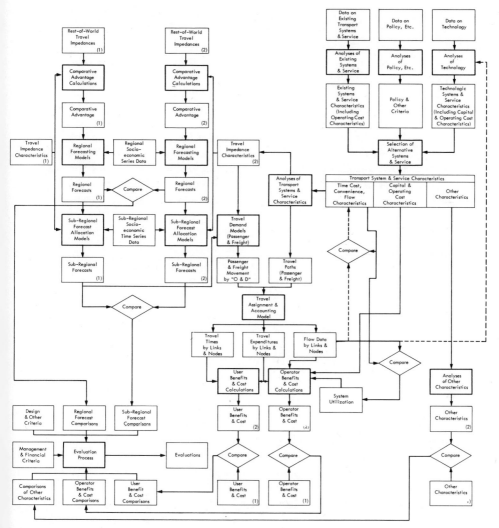

Source: Bruck, Manheim, and Shuldiner, "Transportation Systems Planning as a Process: The Northeast Corridor Example," *Annals of the Transportation Research Forum*, p. 86.

the automobile and to utilize mass transit more efficiently. Vickrey suggests a two-pronged approach: (1) increase the cost of automobile usage in urban areas and (2) use differential fares for mass transit, with a lower fare during off-peak travel periods.[31] Differential fares for peak and off-peak periods should permit transit to operate more efficiently, with less overcapacity in nonrush hours and a higher quality of service during rush hours. Pricing street use sufficiently high would reduce automobile congestion, allowing rapid transit to provide a better level of service.

SUMMARY

The urban transportation system encompasses all modes of transportation, the network of streets and highways, parking facilities, railways, airways and terminal facilities, and the vehicles that move over the transportation network. The system is in continuous evolution, but it fails to adapt as rapidly as changing needs. Budgetary constraints permit only certain components of the system to be altered at any one time. A rapid transit route is initiated or extended, new vehicles are placed in service, a revised timetable for transit is developed, a new highway is located, streets are widened or converted to one-way traffic, additional parking facilities are provided in the central business district—the list of improvements to the system is endless.

Each change in a component of the system can affect other parts and can have an impact upon users and nonusers, and upon urban property values and land use. User benefits often are expressed in benefit-cost analyses employed to determine the feasibility and priority of transportation improvements, although benefit-cost ratios represent only partial analysis of the problem. Empirical studies have been made on the effects of highways and parking on urban land values, retail sales, and urban land use. Unfortunately, the results of these studies provide only broad generalizations of the expected direction of impact.

The complexity of the urban transportation system and its slowness to adapt to changing needs are reflected in our multifaceted urban transportation problem. Dimensions of the problem include rush-hour demands upon the system, the mass transit dilemma, inadequacy of parking facilities in congested areas, interagency cooperation in coping with areawide transportation problems and, of course, the means of financing an acceptable level of service.

Public agencies and private organizations are involved with all aspects of the problem. Technological developments in equipment and the transportation network are being explored. Governmental cooperation is encouraged by formation of regional transportation planning agencies and

---

[31] William S. Vickrey, "Pricing in Urban and Suburban Transport," *American Economic Review, Papers and Proceedings*, vol. 53, no. 2 (May 1963), pp. 452–65.

by centralization of federal activities in the Department of Transportation. Methodologies for analyzing complex systems are being developed, such as the Northeast Corridor Project discussed in this chapter. Consideration is being given to pricing policies that would promote the use of transit relative to the private automobile. The urban transportation problem is persistent, but abatement of the more critical aspects is on the foreseeable horizon. Ultimately, the condition of our urban transportation will depend upon the willingness of beneficiaries to finance it.

QUESTIONS FOR REVIEW

1. The urban transportation system should be designed solely to minimize the costs of movement of persons and goods. Discuss.
2. What are user benefits? Why is consideration of user benefits only partial analysis of the feasibility of a highway improvement?
3. How is an improvement in transportation related in theory to the value of an urban site?
4. What highway-related factors are considered important in industrial location?
5. Why is it impossible to generalize from empirical studies of highway benefits?
6. Itemize the components of the urban transportation problem in a particular urban area. What are the current programs for alleviation of these local problems? What will be the effects of these programs on the entire system? On urban land values? On urban land use?

REFERENCES

Alonso, William. *Location and Land Use: Toward a General Theory of Land Rent.* Cambridge, Mass.: Harvard University Press, 1965.

Meyer, John et. al. *The Urban Transportation Problem.* Cambridge, Mass.: Harvard University Press, 1966.

Mills, Edwin S. *Urban Economics.* Glenview, Ill.: Scott, Foresman and Co., 1972. Chap. 11, pp. 192–217.

Mohring, Herbert and Harwitz, Mitchell. *Highway Benefits: An Analytical Framework.* Chicago: Northwestern University Press, 1962.

Thompson, Wilbur R. *A Preface to Urban Economics.* Baltimore: John Hopkins Press for Resources for the Future, Inc., 1965. Chaps. 9 and 10, pp. 333–79.

Vickrey, William S. "Pricing in Urban and Suburban Transport," *American Economic Review,* Papers and Proceedings, vol. 53, no. 2 (1963), pp. 452–65.

Wingo, Lowdon, Jr. *Transportation and Urban Land.* Washington, D.C.: Resources for the Future, Inc., 1960.

chapter 18

OVERVIEW

THE READER who has perused this volume from the beginning may have become very impatient with the authors. "When," he may ask, "are they going to discuss the important aspects of real estate?" Most of our readers, we suspect, became acquainted with our book as the result of curiosity about the real estate business or because they heard that real estate might be a profitable investment. The successful ventures of real estate investors and operators appear daily in the popular press. Syndication, joint ventures, tax-free income, and other terms have become part of our vocabulary. Books such as Nickerson's, *How I Turned $1,000 into a Million in Real Estate in My Spare Time*,[1] are not uncommon. The reader, whose eagerness has been whetted by this material, may wonder when the authors will explain the secrets of how to make a killing in real estate.

The authors believe that they have discussed the attributes which cause real estate to be a profitable and satisfying investment for many persons and a successful occupation for others. There would be no real estate success stories without the basic want-satisfying power of the economic good. Consequently, a portion of this treatise has been devoted to the characteristics of real estate that give it productivity and value.

Analytical approach. An analytical approach to real estate investment is proposed in which market value and investment value are central concepts. Appraisal methodologies provide techniques for estimating market value, which can be adapted to computations of investment value or justified investment price. Other return on investment calculations were examined as additional criteria for ranking investment alternatives.

---

[1] William Nickerson, *How I Turned $1,000 into a Million in Real Estate in My Spare Time* (New York: Simon and Schuster, 1959).

These measurements of the relative value or worth of a real estate investment in chapters 5 and 6 are only the mathematical end product of the many factors affecting the future productivity and risk of the investment. These physical, locational, economic, and social determinants are too numerous to recount in detail in this brief overview. However, among major factors affecting real estate value are: the physical characteristics of land and improvements; the character of the neighborhood or district in which the property is located; the market conditions in which the property is competing; the economic strength and stability of the local, regional, and national economies; property rights transferred and other legal aspects; form of ownership; financing; tax factors; and the public actions, controls, and regulations affecting the property and its future productivity.

Real estate business. Another section of this basic text is devoted to real estate business. In the minds of most people, the real estate business is most closely associated with real estate brokerage. The broker and his sales persons are the most visible occupation in the real estate business. Most of us have or will utilize their services in buying or selling our homes and other properties. The real estate business, however, encompasses a variety of occupations in the private and public sectors related to land development and construction, financing, management, law, appraisal, consulting, and brokerage. Each of these occupations has its specialties. Real estate brokerage, for instance, includes persons who specialize in one type of real estate (such as single-family residences or industrial properties), in negotiating leases, in arranging exchanges, and in effecting transactions.

The real estate business utilizes the economic and institutional aspects of real estate in organizing for the production, financing, and marketing of the product. When persons in the business are creative in combining the various determinants of value, a windfall profit materializes. The real estate business has always offered great potential for creativity and resultant imitation as others attempt to duplicate successful ventures. We can all recount the history of several recent "innovations," such as the resurgence of real estate investment trusts, condominiums and quadraminiums, planned unit developments, new towns, resort communities and ranchettes for $10 down and $10 a month, wrap-around mortgages, equity participations, joint ventures and syndications, prefabrication and modular units; the list continually lengthens. These newsworthy developments in the real estate business obtain the most publicity. Many of these developments have been mentioned in this text, although the authors believe that detailed treatment should be reserved for advanced courses.

Administrative processes. Another major emphasis of this text has been on the decision-making process. In this regard, the authors have chosen to differentiate between micro administration and macro administration of our real estate resources. Micro administration occurs in both the private and public sectors of our economy. Individuals and firms in the private sector combine land and improvements to create useful properties and valuable assets that are attractive to investors. The functions of production, financing, marketing, and management in the real estate business are manifestations of micro administration. Micro administration in the public sector by the executive branch, the legislature, the judicial branch, and the bureaucracy result in laws, regulations, and programs which have macro effects. Zoning regulations, building codes, federal housing, urban renewal, model cities, the property tax, and the transportation system are examples of publicly enacted rules and programs which become inputs to the micro administration of our real estate resources. They comprise part of the list of determinants of real estate productivity and value. We have chosen to call these results of public sector decision making, macro administration, to reflect their far-reaching and pervasive effects.

PROGNOSIS

The excitement of real estate as an academic field of study comes from two principal sources. First, there is the challenge of adapting the theory, concepts, and analytical methods from several disciplines in the process of analyzing the production of real estate and its investment qualities. Then, there is the need to impose ever-changing institutional factors upon the analytical framework.

Theory and concepts.   Real estate "principles," removed of their institutional wrappings, are economic principles. Economic models are used to analyze urban economies and local housing markets. Recent developments in regional and urban economics blend with materials often included in real estate courses, particularly in the analyses of urban economies and the location of firms and households. The analysis of real estate investments claims kinship with the financial analysis of the firm, capital budgeting, and security analysis. General marketing and management theories and concepts are applicable to the real estate business. City planning, sociology, psychology, and geography make their contribution. Advancements in the state of the art in real estate investment analysis and appraisal; in housing market research; in understanding the motivations of investors, home buyers, and renters; in the organization for efficient production and marketing of the product; and in other aspects of the field of real estate undoubtedly will come from continued adaptation of work in related fields to real estate problems.

Institutional factors.   The study of real estate is differentiated from other academic fields by the institutional aspects of the subject. Legal aspects, for instance, are a large part of these institutional characteristics. The law mirrors the attitudes and mores of our society. In recent years, statutory law and court interpretations have combined in a manner that will affect real estate investment and the actions of persons involved in the real estate business. Civil rights legislation, open housing, and court decisions in antitrust cases are in the forefront of the evolution of the law.

The provision of new housing in our cities is primarily dependent upon the economic and demographic factors underlying the demand for shelter. However, enabling legislation permitting ownership of condominium units has created a new housing submarket. Legislation permitting the formation of real estate investment trusts has enabled the small investor to enjoy the benefits of real estate investments and provided a new source of equity capital to the developer. Enactment of each new federal tax bill has repercussions on the profitability of real estate investments. The so-called tax shelters available to real estate investors were created initially to stimulate investment in needed social capital. Now, in response to continued inflation, Congress seems willing to pare away some of the shelters it previously created.

The real estate cycle is wasteful of our precious human and natural resources and has been ruinous to many individuals and firms in the real estate business. To a large extent, the fluctuations in real estate construction have been attributable to monetary conditions. New channels for the flow of funds into the mortgage market are opening through innovations under the auspices of the Federal Home Loan Bank Board, the Federal Home Loan Mortgage Corporation, the Federal National Mortgage Association, and the Government National Mortgage Association. Federal housing (Sec. 235, Sec. 236, and so on) has continued in quantity even in periods of tight monetary policy. The combined impact of these actions has the potential of containing fluctuations in housing starts within tolerable limits. Further efforts to stabilize the availability of credit and construction are to be expected.

The physical character of the housing unit is progressing to modular components and modular units, and further innovations in construction techniques and materials are being encouraged by government programs. Concomitant with new construction techniques is the industrialization of housing, applying the concept of mass production to the housing industry. Large-scale developments worthy of being called "new towns" are becoming more common. The profitability of real estate development has attracted insurance companies into joint ventures with developers who obtain the needed long-term commitments of equity capital for very large-scale developments. American industry also is experimenting with large-scale real estate development as potentially profitable activity and, in some instances, as a market for their products. The scale of developments in general has become larger. Real estate development firms are often merged or controlled by industrial corporations, providing them with the capital necessary to undertake larger projects. The scale of development is reflected in the diversification of the firms in the real estate business. A single firm and its subsidiaries may include a mortgage company, a brokerage company, a construction company, an investment company to buy and hold land and other properties, and a property management company.

Government involvement with real estate is increasing. Our nation is experiencing changes in social attitudes as we become more wealthy and urbanized. Acquisition of the means to obtain a better quality of life and increased interdependency in an urban environment reduce our tolerance for nuisances, for inequities in the distribution of opportunities, and for self-seeking actions considered to be detrimental to the social welfare. At the same time, our falling level of tolerance has been met by the rising intensity of certain nuisances, such as congestion and pollution. Government regulation, subsidies, and other actions are invoked by these conditions. Hopefully, our democratic form of government permits the will of the majority of our citizens to be reflected in these actions. The authors of this basic text find that, over time, a larger part of their courses in real estate principles is devoted to what we have called "macro administration" of our real estate resources. This trend is expected to continue.

Appendixes

LAWS PROHIBITING
DISCRIMINATION IN HOUSING

FEDERAL FAIR HOUSING LAW—APRIL 11, 1968

Title VIII of the Civil Rights Act of 1968, which is better known as the Federal Fair Housing Law, bans discrimination in the sale, rental, and leasing of housing in the United States because of race, color, religion, or national origin.

Under this law the following are typical discriminatory acts which are declared illegal:

1. Refusing to sell, rent, or deal with any person.
2. Making different terms and conditions for buying or renting housing.
3. Advertising housing as available to only certain buyers.
4. Denial of availability of housing for inspection for sale or rental when it actually is available.
5. Persuading someone to sell housing by telling him minority groups are moving in—commonly called blockbusting.
6. Denying or making different home loan terms by lender.
7. Denying or limiting the use of real estate services to anyone.
8. Coercing, intimidating, or interfering with any person in the exercise or enjoyment of these federal rights.

Enforcement procedures and penalties are as follows:

1. An aggrieved person may file a complaint with HUD which can attempt to conciliate after investigation.
2. A civil suit may be filed by an individual in federal or state court.
3. The U.S. Department of Justice can investigate and bring suit if the Attorney General has reasonable cause to believe there is a pattern or

practice of resistance to the act, or if the Attorney General believes that the case is one of general public importance.

4. The court may issue an injunction requiring or preventing the home or apartment sale or rental.
5. *Damages may be assessed against the defendant.*

Properties and people covered by this law include all housing in the United States except the rental of apartments up to four families if the owner occupies one, religious organizations and private clubs, and home owners who do not use the services of a real estate broker or advertise discriminatorily in the sale of a single-family home.

These exemptions are negated by the Ohio Fair Housing Act of 1969 and a provision of the Federal Civil Rights Act of 1866 as interpreted by the U.S. Supreme Court in a case known as *Jones* v. *Mayer Co.,* decided in 1968.

U.S. SUPREME COURT DECISION

Jones v. *Mayer Co.* (June 17, 1968)

In a case charging racial discrimination in the sale of housing emanating from St. Louis known as *Jones* v. *Mayer Co.,* the U.S. Supreme Court ruled that a law, enacted at the close of the Civil War in 1866 and reenacted in 1870 to protect the freed slaves and assure them equal citizenship, was applicable today in housing.

The law "bars all racial discrimination, private as well as public, in the sale or rental of property."

This law and its present-day application make it clear that racial discrimination by anyone in the sale or rental of property is illegal.

Under this mandate, no exemptions such as are permitted under the 1968 Federal Fair Housing Act can exist. No discrimination on a racial basis in housing can exist.

This ruling is enforceable by the federal district court or an appropriate state court.

STATE OF OHIO FAIR HOUSING LAW (HOUSE BILL 432)

As of November 12, 1969, when sections 4112.01 and 4112.99 of the Ohio Revised Code became effective, discrimination in the sale, rental, or leasing of housing on the basis of race, color, religion, national origin, or ancestry became illegal.

This law prohibits the following actions or activities in housing in Ohio by property owners or their agents.

1. Falsely denying availability.
2. Refusing to show.

3. Refusing to sell, rent, etc., because of race, religion, or ethnic background of any actual or prospective owner, occupant, or user of the property.
4. Inquiring into the keeping of records relating to property sales or rentals concerning race, religion, or ethnic origin.
5. Advertising or circulating any statement indicating a preference or limitation based on race, religion, or ethnic origin in connection with sales or rentals.
6. Aiding or abetting the commitment of any unlawfully discriminatory act or obstructing another person from complying with the law.
7. Induce or solicit real estate activity by representing that the presence or anticipated presence of persons of any race, religion, etc., will have any of the following effects:
    a) Lowering of property value.
    b) Change the race, religious, or ethnic composition of the area.
    c) An increase in criminal or antisocial behavior.

Real estate agents, following the mandates of this law, are protected from harassment and intimidation. Threats by neighbors for retaliation against real estate brokers in the event a home is sold to unwanted neighbors are not allowed and are violations of the law.

All real property in the State of Ohio is covered by this law. There are no exceptions! From single-family homes to vacant lots—from hotel rooms to graveyards.

Courses of action open to aggrieved persons:

1. The court may order affirmative action.
2. The court may issue an injunction if it finds a discriminatory practice has occurred or is about to occur.
3. Temporary or permanent injunctions may be granted by the court.
4. Actual damages and court costs may be assessed against the guilty party.
5. A penalty fine of not less than $100 nor more than $500 may be assessed.

Other provisions of the Ohio law are:

1. The accused may not be compelled to testify against himself.
2. Attorneys will be provided for plaintiffs if they don't have the money to hire one.
3. A bond must be posted by the plaintiff before temporary relief or a restraining order will be issued.

ADMINISTRATIVE STRUCTURE FOR PLANNING AND ZONING IN GAINESVILLE, FLORIDA

The top level in the administrative decision-making structure of Gainesville is the City Commission. The Commission is composed of five members elected by the citizens of the city at large. It is the legislative body of the city and thus must approve any changes in the zoning ordinance.

Directly below the City Commission is the City Planning Commission, or Plan Board, which is the main advisory body to the City Commission. Its function is to provide advice to the City Commission in the areas of current and future planning. The Plan Board is composed of seven lay members appointed by the City Commission. The appointive system presumably minimizes political pressure to which elected officials might be subject from constituent groups, thus allowing them to act more independently in reviewing controversial issues. In appointing these members, the legislative body is required to select a cross-section of citizens in order to prevent minority interest from being suppressed.

To assist it in carrying out its functions, the Planning Commission hires a full-time, paid Plan Board staff. At present the staff is composed of nine professionally trained urban planners, most of whom hold masters degrees in urban planning. The staff performs the research and analysis required in the formulation of planning concepts and developments. Its two main functions are (1) to plan for current needs and (2) to develop and continually update the city's Comprehensive Development Plan.

Current planning primarily involves zoning and ordinance changes. This phase is subdivided into three functions: A. Small area land use plans; B. Zoning; C. Site plan approval.

Small area land use plans

These are land use plans for small areas which the Comprehensive Plan does not include. When adopted by the City Commission, the plans are used for determining land uses in the area in the immediate future. Small area land use plans were used extensively before the city adopted a Comprehensive Plan several years ago. Since that time, these plans have generally not been needed.

Zoning

In this function, a request is filed by a property owner or his representative to change a zoning classification. The filing fee is $112. The professional staff analyzes requests in light of the city's Comprehensive Plan and small area land use plans. The Planning Commission then establishes a time and place for a public hearing on the zoning request. For this hearing, the public must be notified at least 16 days prior to the hearing. Notification is given by three methods. The first method involves publishing in a newspaper an agenda of items to be covered at the hearing and stating the change in zoning (e.g., "RI-A to Mobile Home Park"). The second method is to place a sign on the subject property stating the agenda and zoning change request. Third, all property owners within 300 feet of the site to be rezoned must be notified by mail. If more than 20 percent of these owners object to the rezoning, the vote of the City Commission must be 4 out of 5 to accomplish the zoning change.

Then comes the public hearing. The Plan Board listens to the advice of the staff, arguments of the property owner, and anyone who is against the zoning change. The request is then voted upon by the Board. If the decision confirms the zoning change, it is passed on to the City Commission for final consideration.

Site plan approval

The approval of site planning and development by the Plan Board is required for multiunit residential developments of four or more units and for shopping centers. The Board's decision about a site plan is final; if there is any appeal, it must be made directly to the courts. Site planning includes all the physical aspects of the development. It involves matters such as architectural style, layout of the land, location of buildings on the site, access to parking areas, landscaping, etc.

PLANNING FOR THE FUTURE

The second major function of the planning staff is to develop a future planning guide. This guide is better known as the Comprehensive Plan.

It is a land use plan for the growth of an area figured usually 10 years ahead of the present. It includes present and proposed land uses such as the type and number of recreational areas to be located in the city, proposed highways, police and fire stations, schools, and areas designated for residential, commercial, and industrial use.

Six background studies support the Comprehensive Plan. First and most important is the population study, designed to provide present population data and future growth statistics. Second is the economic base study, which analyzes the city's economy. These two studies attempt to predict the size and economic needs of the city 10 years hence. Third is the land use study, providing a physical inventory of all land in the area at the present time. Fourth is a recreation study, which provides an inventory of the recreational areas and attempts to relate the city's recreational needs to its future size and geographic distribution. Fifth is a physiographic study showing all soil conditions and qualities. Last is the land use and transportation study.

Another important agency in the zoning process is the Board of Adjustment. It is a semijudicial body appointed by the City Commission for the purpose of providing flexibility in the zoning ordinances. Its decisions are final; the only appeal is to the courts. It provides flexibility in two ways. First, the Board of Adjustment has the power to vary the strict letter of the zoning ordinance, i.e., to grant a variance. Although a variance does not involve changing the zoning law, it does involve changing the use requirements. To obtain a variance, the owner must show that he has a hardship (not caused by himself) which prevents him from following the normal zoning requirements. The Board will consider the request for a variance in accordance with criteria established by the Board.

The second method used in providing flexibility is through special exceptions to the zoning law. Under this method, the Board has the power to allow a use that is not a matter of right in a given area. By applying criteria established by the Plan Board, the Board of Adjustment can change the zoning limitations to allow a prohibited type of use for a given parcel.

BLUEPRINT FOR ACTION TO ATTAIN PROFESSIONAL STATUS FOR THE REAL ESTATE PRACTITIONER IN OHIO

1969

1. Announce finalized plans to attain, in a ten-year period, professional status for the real estate practitioner.
2. Circulate information re plans to give broad exposure and general acceptance of objectives.
3. Organize program designed to increase real estate educational facilities throughout the state.
4. Survey sales associates and conduct other needed studies in order to ascertain the obstacles to be overcome in reaching a point that anyone who is qualified to be in contact with the public in a real estate transaction should qualify for professional designation and be a Realtor member.

1970

1. Execute all-out effort to encourage colleges and universities to make available real estate educational courses.
2. Continue program to publicize objective of professional status for real estate practitioners.
3. Encourage Member Boards to permit *qualified* sales people to hold Realtor membership.
4. Draft legislation that would:
    a) Require broker license applicants to have completed a 30-hour course in both Real Estate Practices and Legal Aspects of Real Estate; and

  b) Submit to a special examination in Real Estate Appraisal and in Real Estate Finance; unless
  c) Applicant has completed 30-hour course in these subjects.

1971

1. Seek legislative action to adopt legislation as drafted (1970) with effective date 1973.
2. Continue efforts to increase real estate educational facilities throughout the state.

1972

1. Draft legislation that would:
  a) Eliminate partnership and corporation licenses;
  b) Permit one with a broker's license to affiliate with another broker as an independent contractor sales person;
  c) Require broker license applicants to have previously completed the four basic courses; and
  d) Require applicants for salesmen licenses to have completed two basic courses and two additional or submit to an examination covering two additional subjects.

1973

1. 1971 legislation becomes effective.
2. Seek legislative action to adopt legislation as drafted in 1972 (effective 1975).

1974

1. Seek legislation to phase out inactive licenses.
2. Encourage boards to extend Realtor membership to all who have completed the courses irrespective of type of license held.
3. Draft legislation that would:
  a) Require completion of two years of college including the four basic courses as a condition to receiving a broker's license (effective 1977).
  b) Require completion of four basic courses as a prerequisite to a salesman's license (effective 1977).

1975

1. 1973 legislation becomes effective:
  a) Four college courses as a prerequisite to broker's license;
  b) Two college courses plus two, or an exam for salesman's license;

c) No more corporate or partnership licenses;

d) One broker can affiliate with another as an independent contractor.

2. Seek legislative action on legislation drafted in 1974—to be effective in 1977.

1976

1. Amend Association and Member Board Constitution and By-Laws to require Realtor membership for all licensees who are members.

2. Draft legislation requiring:

   a) Four years of college (bachelor's degree) including the basic real estate courses as a prerequisite to receiving a broker's license (effective 1979);

   b) Two years of college including the basic courses as a prerequisite to receiving a salesman's license (effective 1979).

1977

1. 1975 legislation becomes effective:

   a) A broker applicant must have had two years of college, including four basic real estate courses; and

   b) A salesman applicant must have had the four basic courses.

2. Seek legislative action to pass legislation as drafted in 1976 (effective 1979).

1978

1. Draft legislation that:

   a) Would eliminate the further issuance of salesman's licenses; and

   b) Set a date to cause all salesmen's licenses to cease to exist or as an alternative permit existing licenses to gradually phase out.

1979

1. 1977 legislation becomes effective:

   a) Four years of college (bachelor's degree) including the basic real estate courses as a prerequisite to receiving a broker's license;

   b) Two years of college including the basic real estate courses as a prerequisite to receiving a salesman's license.

2. Seek legislative action to pass legislation drafted in 1978 (effective 1980).

1980

1. One license concept in existence.

2. Professional designation in force.

CASE SITUATION: QUEENSWORTH APARTMENTS

Mr. Queensworth recently purchased an obsolete, deteriorating factory building on 14.5 acres of land near the central business district. He hoped to use the building, a 160,000 sq. ft., three-story building, as a boutique-oriented shopping center.

A market analysis showed a lack of demand for the shopping center, but it suggested that the salvage market would accept the building's materials at high prices. The land was shown to be ideal for apartment usage in a strong apartment market.

Mr. Queensworth paid $175,000 for the property. Within two months thereafter, he sold two small commercial frontage sites for $60,000 and netted $120,000 from the sale of scrap metal, hard pine, water tank, air-conditioner, etc. Thus, he more than recaptured his initial cash investment, and he owned an excellent apartment site of 9.5 acres (net of internal streets) plus commercial frontage sites of approximately 2.5 acres.

The financial analysis indicated as Projection I shows the return that would result for apartment investors under market-based financing, rental, and expense projections. A net after-tax return of approximately 16 percent per year is shown for year 1, a return that is low for apartment investors.

Not shown in the projection are the following case facts:

1. The land is sold to the partnership at a substantial profit to Mr. Queensworth.
2. Mr. Queensworth absorbs all risks of construction cost overrun and slow rent-up. His $180,000 land sales income funds this risk.
3. Mr. Queensworth retains 80 percent of any funds remaining in the con-

Proposed Queensworth Apartments economics of apartment offering,
Projection I (October 1974)

Gross annual rental income:

25 1-BR @ 700 sq. ft. @ $135/mo.	$ 40,620
75 2-BR @ 950 sq. ft. @ $175/mo.	157,500
	$ 198,120
Vacancy and collection loss allowance—5%	9,906
	$ 188,214
Operating expenses @ 33% (tenants pay elec., gas)	62,738
Net Operating Income	$ 125,476
Value (net income capitalized at 10.5%)	1,195,010
say	$1,200,000
Loan—75%	$ 900,000
Loan constant, 8.5% interest, 25 years	.0967

Cash flow analysis:

Net income	$ 125,476
Debt service (.0967 × $900,000)	87,030
Net Cash Flow	$ 38,446

Cash equity required:

Improvement cost (90,000 sq. ft. @ $11.00)	$ 990,000
Land at cost	175,000
	$1,165,000
Deduct loan proceeds	900,000
Cash Equity Required	$ 265,000

Tax loss or shelter:

Interest at 8.5%	$ 76,500
Depreciation—double-declining balance, 33 yr.	59,400
Total	$ 135,900
Net income before interest and depreciation	$ 125,476
First-year Tax Loss or Income Shelter	($ 10,424)

Investment position: Total equity

Sell 80% of total project for cash—20 shares at $13,250 each	$ 265,000
Distribute first-year cash flow pro rata 80% of $38,446	$ 30,957

Distribute first-year tax loss pro rata 80% of $10,424 = $8,340

Benefit for 40% taxpayer	3,336
Benefit for 50% taxpayer	4,170

Distribute first-year mortgage equity payments pro rata

80% of $10,530 = $8,424	8,424

Return on investment:

40% bracket taxpayers:

$$\frac{\$30,957 + 3,336 + 8,424}{\$265,000} = 16.1\% \text{ after tax}$$

50% bracket taxpayers:

$$\frac{\$30,957 + 4,170 + 8,424}{\$265,000} = 16.4\% \text{ after tax}$$

struction loan accounts at the time the permanent loan is closed. He draws no developer's fee.

4. Mr. Queensworth sells 80 percent of the equity for cash and retains 20 percent of the equity for his services.
5. The project is structured as a limited partnership.
6. All profits, losses, refinancing, and sales proceeds are distributed on a pro rata basis to investors and Mr. Queensworth based upon ownership share.

Mr. Queensworth did not think that his partnership shares would sell well based upon a 16 percent after-tax total earning and a cash flow of less than 12 percent. Thus, he worked out Projection II to improve the earnings picture.

Projection II utilizes the same market-based revenue and expense data, but it is premised upon a gross cost per sq. ft. of buildings of $10.50 as compared with $11.00 in Projection I. It also assumes an 80 percent mortgage rather than a 75 percent mortgage. This situation leads to an after-tax earning of approximately 24 percent, but it requires a higher-than-market mortgage amount and it reduces the project cost to a level that offers little or no protection from cost overruns.

Realizing the difficulties associated with Projection II, Mr. Queensworth reduced the loan amount to 75 percent and increased the cost of construction to $10.75. In reviewing market conditions, he also increased the loan interest rate from 8.5% to 9% and reduced the capitalization rate from 10.5% to 10%. This led to Projection III, which he decided was a sound structure for his project. He then prepared his pro forma financial statements upon this basis.

Throughout the three sets of calculations, Mr. Queensworth consistently retained a price of $175,000 for his land input. This was a profit to him, and it provided the financial assets needed to underwrite the risk of cost overruns.

The amount of equity money needed in the project varied from a high in Projection I of $265,000 to a low in Projection II of $165,000. The latter amount was insufficient to pay the full land price, thereby requiring that Mr. Queensworth draw $15,000 from loan proceeds at the end of the construction period. In Projection III, the equity cash of $187,000 appeared to be adequate to make the project work.

Proposed Queensworth Apartments economics of apartment offering, Projection II (October 1974)

Gross annual rental income:

25 1-BR @ 700 sq. ft. @ $135/mo.	$	40,620
75 2-BR @ 950 sq. ft. @ $175/mo.		157,500
	$	198,120
Vacancy and collection loss allowance—5%		9,906
	$	188,214
Operating expenses @ 33% (tenants pay elec., gas)		62,738
Net Income before Interest and Depreciation	$	125,476
Value (net income capitalized at 10.5%)		1,195,010
	say	$1,200,000
Loan—80%	$	960,000
Loan constant, 8.5% interest, 25 years		.0967

Cash flow analysis:

Net income	$	125,476
Debt service (.0967 × $900,000)		92,732
Net Cash Flow	$	32,744

Cash equity required:

Improvement cost (90,000 sq. ft. @ $10.50)	$	945,000
Land at cost		175,000
	$1,120,000	
Deduct loan proceeds		960,000
Cash Equity Required	$	160,000

Tax loss or shelter:

Interest at 8.5%	$	81,600
Depreciation—Double-declining balance, 33 yr.		56,700
Total	$	138,300
Net income before interest and depreciation	$	125,476
First-year Tax Loss or Income Shelter	($	12,824)

Investment position: Total equity

Sell 80% of total project for cash—20 shares at $8,000 each	$	160,000
Distribute first-year cash flow pro rata 80% of $32,744	$	25,995

Distribute first-year tax loss pro rata 80% of $12,824 = $10,259

Benefit for 40% taxpayer		4,104
Benefit for 50% taxpayer		5,130

Distribute first-year mortgage equity payments pro rata

80% of $11,132 = $8,906		8,906

Return on investment:

40% bracket taxpayers:

$$\frac{\$25,995 + 4,104 + 8,926}{\$160,000} = 24.4\% \text{ after tax}$$

50% bracket taxpayers:

$$\frac{\$25,995 + 5,130 + 8,926}{\$160,000} = 25.0\% \text{ after tax}$$

Proposed Queensworth Apartments first-year return on investment, Projection III (October 1974)

Gross annual rental income:

25 1-BR @ 700 sq. ft. @ $135/mo.	$ 40,620
75 2-BR @ 950 sq. ft. @ $175/mo.	157,500
Laundry, telephone, misc. income	2,500
	$ 200,620
Vacancy and collection loss allowance—5%	10,031
	$ 190,589
Operating expenses (tenants pay elec., gas)	63,300
Net Income before Interest and Depreciation	$ 127,289
Value (net income capitalized at 10%)	$1,272,890
Loan—75%	$ 955,000
Loan constant, 9% interest, 25 years	.1018

Cash flow analysis:

Net income	$ 127,289
Debt service ($955,000 × .1018)	97,219
Net Cash Flow	$ 30,070

Cash equity required:

Improvement cost (90,000 sq. ft. @ $10.75)	$ 967,500
Land at cost	175,000
Total Cost	$1,142,500
Deduct loan proceeds	955,000
Cash Equity Required	$ 187,500

Tax loss or shelter:

Interest at 9%	$ 85,950
Depreciation—double-declining balance, 33 years	58,050
Total	$ 144,000
Net income before interest and depreciation	127,289
First-year Tax Loss or Income Shelter	($ 16,711)

Investment position: Total equity

Sell 80% of total project for cash—20 shares at $9,375 each	$ 187,500
Distribute first-year cash flow pro rata 80% of $30,070	$ 24,056

Distribute first-year tax loss pro rata 80% of $16,711 = $13,369

Benefit for 40% taxpayer	5,347
Benefit for 50% taxpayer	6,684
Distribute first-year mortgage equity payments pro rata 80% of $11,269..	9,015

Return on investment:

40% bracket taxpayers:
$$\frac{\$24,056 + 5,347 + 9,015}{\$187,500} = 20.5\% \text{ after tax}$$

50% bracket taxpayers:
$$\frac{\$24,056 + 6,684 + 9,015}{\$187,500} = 21.2\% \text{ after tax}$$

Proposed Queensworth Apartments pro forma statement of revenue and expenses

	Year 1	Year 2	Year 3	Year 4	Year 5	Year 6	Year 7	Year 8	Year 9	Year 10
Gross Annual Rental Income:										
25 1-BR @ 700 sq. ft.	$ 40,620	$ 40,620	$ 40,620	$ 41,850	$ 41,850	$ 41,850	$ 43,100	$ 43,100	$ 43,100	$ 43,100
75 2-BR @ 950 sq. ft.	157,500	157,500	157,500	162,289	162,289	162,289	167,238	167,238	167,238	167,238
Laundry, telephone, misc.	2,500	2,500	2,500	2,500	2,500	2,500	2,500	2,500	2,500	2,500
Total	$200,620	$200,620	$200,620	$200,639	$206,639	$206,639	$212,838	$212,838	$212,838	$212,838
Vacancy and collection loss allowance—5%	10,031	10,031	10,031	10,332	10,332	10,332	10,642	10,642	10,642	10,642
Effective Gross Income	$190,589	$190,589	$190,589	$196,037	$196,307	$196,307	$202,196	$202,196	$202,196	$202,196
Operating Expenses:										
Water and sewer	$ 7,000	$ 7,000	$ 7,000	$ 7,158	$ 7,150	$ 7,150	$ 7,300	$ 7,300	$ 7,300	$ 7,300
Trash service	2,500	2,500	2,500	2,650	2,650	2,650	2,800	2,800	2,800	2,800
Janitor/yard man	4,500	4,500	4,500	4,650	4,650	4,650	4,800	4,800	4,800	4,800
Painting and decorating	5,000	5,000	5,000	5,150	5,150	5,150	5,300	5,300	5,300	5,300
General repairs	2,500	2,500	2,500	2,650	2,650	2,650	2,800	2,800	2,800	2,800
Reserve for replacements	4,000	4,000	4,000	4,150	4,150	4,150	4,300	4,300	4,300	4,300
Supplies	1,000	1,000	1,000	1,150	1,150	1,150	1,300	1,300	1,300	1,300
Resident manager	8,000	8,000	8,000	8,150	8,150	8,150	8,300	8,300	8,300	8,300
Cable TV	1,300	1,300	1,300	1,450	1,450	1,450	1,600	1,600	1,600	1,600
Insurance	7,500	7,500	7,500	7,650	7,650	7,650	7,800	7,800	7,800	7,800
Property taxes	10,000	10,000	10,000	10,250	10,250	10,250	10,553	10,553	10,553	10,553
Management fee	10,000	10,000	10,000	10,150	10,150	10,150	10,300	10,300	10,300	10,300
Total Expenses	$ 63,300	$ 63,300	$ 63,300	$ 65,200	$ 65,200	$ 65,200	$ 67,153	$ 67,153	$ 67,153	$ 67,153
Net Operating Income	$127,289	$127,289	$127,289	$131,107	$131,107	$131,107	$135,043	$135,043	$135,043	$135,043

Proposed Queensworth Apartments 10-year return on investment

	Year 1	Year 2	Year 3	Year 4	Year 5	Year 6	Year 7	Year 8	Year 9	Year 10
Total Return on Investment:										
Gross revenue	$200,620	$200,620	$200,620	$206,639	$206,639	$206,639	$212,838	$212,838	$212,838	$212,838
Less vacancy and collection loss allowance—5%	10,031	10,031	10,031	10,332	10,332	10,332	10,642	10,642	10,642	10,642
Effective Gross Income	$190,589	$190,589	$190,589	$196,307	$196,307	$196,307	$202,196	$202,196	$202,196	$202,196
Less operating expenses	63,300	63,300	63,300	65,200	65,200	65,200	67,153	67,153	67,153	67,153
Net Income before Interest and Depreciation	$127,289	$127,289	$127,289	$131,107	$131,107	$131,107	$135,043	$135,043	$135,043	$135,043
A. Deduct:										
Interest	85,950	84,936	83,830	82,625	81,312	79,880	78,320	76,619	74,765	72,744
Depreciation	58,050	54,567	51,293	48,215	45,323	42,603	40,047	37,644	35,385	33,262
Net Taxable Income	$(16,711)	$(12,214)	$(7,834)	$267	$4,472	$8,624	$16,676	$20,780	$24,893	$29,037
B. Deduct:										
Debt service	$97,219	$97,219	$97,219	$97,219	$97,219	$97,219	$97,219	$97,219	$97,219	$97,219
Cash Throw Off	$30,070	$30,070	$30,070	$33,888	$33,888	$33,888	$37,824	$37,824	$37,824	$37,824
Principal Payments on Mortgage	$11,269	$12,283	$13,389	$14,594	$15,907	$17,339	$18,899	$20,600	$22,454	$24,475
Return on 80% Investors' Shares:										
Cash flow return on investment	12.8%	12.8%	12.8%	14.5%	14.5%	14.5%	16.1%	16.1%	16.1%	16.1%
Adjust for tax benefit (detriment) for 40% bracket taxpayer	2.9	2.1	1.3	(0.1)	(0.8)	(1.5)	(2.8)	(3.5)	(4.2)	(5.0)
Add mortgage payment value (assumes constant property value)	4.8	5.3	5.7	6.2	6.8	7.4	8.1	8.8	9.6	10.5
Total After-tax Effective Return on Investment (property value does not change)	20.5%	20.2%	19.8%	20.6%	20.5%	20.4%	21.4%	21.4%	21.5%	21.6%

Thus a single 5% share costing $9,375 would receive $1,203 cash plus a tax refund of $267 plus a mortgage equity value of $450 in Year 1 if the above projections are correct. Note that these are only projections, even though they are based upon current market information.

FHA HOUSING MARKET
ANALYSIS OUTLINE

The following outline is indicative of the scope and sequence of subject matter to be considered in an overall market analysis. It does not reflect geographic submarket considerations; these can be incorporated by the analyst at appropriate points wherever feasible and to the extent required by each analysis. An abbreviated form of analytical treatment is adaptable from these components.

Preface

If a brief statement of the purpose of the analysis, i.e., the specific problem which occasioned the need for the market study, is desired, it could be included as a preface. Alternatively, it may be omitted or incorporated into a letter or memorandum of transmittal as a substitute for the preface.

Summary and conclusions

Generally, a summary is desired to provide a quick, overall perspective on the principal findings and conclusions of the analysis, preferably at the beginning rather than at the end of the report. The summary is not intended to be a résumé of the entire analysis. To achieve its purpose most effectively it should be limited to the salient statistical findings and major conclusions and presented concisely in a series of brief paragraphs in the same sequence of subject matter followed in the text. Specific page references to parallel subject matter in the text may be utilized to facilitate ready access to pertinent details.

Housing market area

1. Definition (delineation), including identification of entire area encompassed and principal cities; geographic submarkets discussed and defined.
2. Description, including:
   a. Size (total population)
   b. Major topographical features
   c. Principal transportation arteries (highway, rail, water) and distance to other urban areas
   d. General urban structure and direction of growth
   e. Special features, characteristics, or considerations
   f. Major community developments in process or planned which are germane to the present analysis
   g. Net (in or out) commutation; significance
3. Map of area.

Economy of the housing market area

1. Economic character and history
   a. General description
   b. Principal economic activities and developments—past and present
2. Employment—total, wage and salary, other
   a. Current estimate
   b. Past trend (last 8–10 years)
   c. Distribution by major industry
      (1) Current
      (2) Comparison with previous years
   d. Female employment participation rate
   e. Trend of employment participation rate
3. Discussion of principal employers
   a. Manufacturing
   b. Nonmanufacturing
   c. Military, if any (history and mission)
   d. Other
4. Unemployment
   a. Current level and composition
   b. Past trend
5. Estimated future employment
   a. Total and annual increments
   b. Analytical exposition
6. Income
   a. Average weekly wages of manufacturing workers

      (1) Current level

      (2) Trend since last census

   b. Other data from state estimates for counties, if available

   c. Estimates of current famil income distribution after tax) for all families, for renter households, and for other segmental groups, if necessary

Demographic analysis

1. Population
   - *a.* Current estimate
   - *b.* Past trend
   - *c.* Estimated future population—total and annual increments
   - *d.* Net natural increase and imputed migration
   - *e.* Distribution by age
   - *f.* Trend of military and military-connected civilian strength, if applicable
   - *g.* Trend of college enrollment, if applicable
2. Households
   - *a.* Current estimate
   - *b.* Past trend
   - *c.* Estimated future households—total and annual increments
   - *d.* Household size trends
   - *e.* Military and military-connected civilian households, if applicable
     - (1) Present—on-base and off-base with distribution by minor civil divisions
     - (2) Projected
   - *f.* College-oriented households, faculty and student, present and projected

Housing stock and market conditions

1. Housing supply
   - *a.* Current estimate
   - *b.* Past trends, including last census date
   - *c.* Principal characteristics: last census and current estimates
     - (1) Type of structure
     - (2) Year built
     - (3) Condition
     - (4) Plumbing facilities
2. Residential building activity, by type
   - *a.* Annually, last 10 years
   - *b.* Monthly, January to latest month for current and previous year

    c. Units under construction
    d. Demolition and conversion trends and projections
 3. Tenure of occupancy
    a. Current estimate
    b. Past trends
 4. Vacancy
    a. Last census—net available
       (1) Overall, home owner, and rental
       (2) Number of units lacking one or more plumbing facilities
    b. Postal vacancy surveys—current and previous, if any, and conversion and adjustment to census concepts of owner and renter unit vacancy
    c. Other occupancy-vacancy indicators and surveys, including surveys of FHA-insured projects
    d. Current estimates—net available (qualified for units lacking one or more plumbing facilities)
       (1) Owner
       (2) Renter
       (3) Quality differentials
       (4) Evaluation
 5. Mortgage market
    a. Sources and availability of funds
    b. FHA participation
    c. Interest rates and terms of mortgages
    d. Mortgage and deed recordings
 6. Sales market
    a. General market conditions—strong and weak points
    b. Major subdivision activity
    c. Speculative versus contract building
    d. Marketing experience—new and existing
    e. Price trends—new and existing
    f. Unsold inventory of new houses
       (1) Price
       (2) Months unsold
       (3) Comparison with previous period, if available
    g. Houses under construction—volume and quality
    h. Foreclosures
       (1) Overall trend
       (2) FHA and other
       (3) Sales versus acquisitions
    i. Outlook
 7. Rental market
    a. General market conditions—strong and weak points
    b. New rental housing, FHA and other, by years, type, and rents

      (1) General marketing experience
      (2) Competitive status with existing rental housing
    c. Rental housing under construction
      (1) Volume, type, and quality
      (2) Probable marketing schedule
    d. Rental housing committed but not started—volume, type, and quality
    e. Foreclosures—FHA and other
  8. Urban renewal activity, if applicable (federal, state, and local)
    a. Summation: Overall renewal plan and progress
    b. Urban renewal areas
      (1) Identification and location (street boundaries)
      (2) Description and renewal plans of areas
      (3) Environment (surrounding area)
      (4) Housing unit demolitions and replacements
      (5) Present status and time schedule
  9. Military housing, if applicable
    a. Housing available to military (including military-connected civilians, i.e., civil service and contractor employees)
      (1) Number of units by type and construction status, on- and off-base
      (2) Physical adequacy
      (3) Occupancy status
    b. Current and projected housing requirements and deficits
      (1) Eligible military personnel
      (2) Ineligible military personnel
      (3) Civilians, including contractor employees
10. Subsidized housing, Section 221(d)(3), rent-supplement, Section 235, Section 236; quantity, (existing, under construction, and planned), rents, income limits, vacancy

Demand for housing

1. Quantitative demand (annual basis)
    a. Projected increase in households
    b. Adjustments
    c. Net quantitative demand
      (privately financed), by tenure
    d. Net quantitative demand by geographic submarkets
    e. Occupancy potentials for subsidized types, with submarket proportions
2. Qualitative demand
    a. Demand for single-family housing (nonsubsidized)
    b. Demand for multi-family housing (nonsubsidized)

  c. General locations favorable to market absorption

  d. Qualitative occupancy potential for subsidized housing: Section 221(d)(3), rent-supplement, Section 235, Section 236, public housing.

  e. Geographic demand distribution for nonsubsidized housing and subsidized potential

3. Submarkets of demand—At times, the purpose of the housing market analysis may require an estimate of demand for one or more submarkets identified in chapter 7. Subject matter pertinent to a particular submarket may be integrated with the discussion of the broader scope of the respective subject matter in the comprehensive analysis; or it may be consolidated and presented as a supplement following the overall estimates of qualitative demand for housing.

Statistical appendix

The statistical appendix is intended to contain the detailed tables of only the key data used in the analysis. It should not be used as a catchall for extensive statistical material of less than primary importance in the analysis.

Much of the data used in the analysis can be included in text tables or the narrative in the body of the report Text tables, maps, and charts, serve a helpful purpose when used effectively. They provide sharp focus on important facts, relationships, and trends which require special emphasis otherwise achievable only by lengthy narration. Text tables, however, must be carefully selected and strategically integrated with the discussion; they must be simple and highly condensed; and they must be minimized rather than maximized in usage. The accompanying text must be analytical and interpretative to reveal the significance of the data shown in the tables rather than a mere repetition of these data in narrative form. Caution must be exercised, of course, to avoid overloading the text with statistics—thus rendering the report difficult to read and distracting from the salient facts and findings.

THE COLUMBUS AREA ECONOMY
Structure and growth, 1950 to 1985*

By James C. Yocum

This article presents some highlights of an intensive, 3-volume economic base study of the Columbus Area, with detailed projections to 1985. The study was undertaken by the Bureau of Business Research for The Comprehensive Regional Plan of Columbus and Franklin County, Ohio, and required the assembly of a special research staff,[1] including members of the Bureau Staff and other faculty from the College of Commerce and Administration.

The long-term economic and demographic projections developed by this study are primarily for use in the preparation of a comprehensive, long-range Master Plan for Franklin County. The projections, and the historical and structural analysis of the economy of the Area, are useful as well in gaining a better understanding of the workings of the Area's economy as it has been in the recent past and as it is likely to be in the future, and provide a basis for assessing the viability of the Area's industrial location factors in the light of changing technology and U.S. regional trends in the location of population and industry

Volume I, Employment, and Value Added by Manufacture, analyzes the economic structure of the Columbus Area, its historic and recent

---

* Reprinted from *Bulletin of Business Research,* College of Commerce and Administration, The Ohio State University, vol. 41, no. 11 (November 1966), pp. 1, 6–9.

[1] Members of the staff were: James C. Yocum, Professor of Business Research and Director, Bureau of Business Research; Richard A. Tybout, Professor of Economics; Henry L. Hunker, Professor of Geography; Gilbert Nestel, Assistant Professor of Business Research and Economics; and Wilford L'Esperance, Associate Professor of Economics and Business Research. Kent P. Schwirian, Associate Professor of Sociology, was also a member of the staff as Principal Investigator for the population segment of the study.

421

growth, and its interrelationships both internally and with the rest of the world, and makes projections to 1985 of number employed, by 33 major industry classifications, and of dollar value added by manufacture, by 17 SIC 2-digit manufacturing industry classifications and for manufacturing industry classifications not now in the Columbus Area.

Volume II, Income, Trade, Housing, provides projections to 1985 of other economic parameters for the Columbus Area, including personal income, income distribution, retail sales, household automobile population, number of households by household type, and housing demand by housing unit tenure.

Volume III, Population and Labor Force, develops projections to 1985 of population and labor force of the Columbus Area and of some principal population characteristics.

Volume I is the basic work (comprising 466 pages) since it deals with the recent growth and industry distribution of employment and output, and their projection to 1985 in the light of changes in technology and productivity likely for the Columbus Area economy. The employment projections underlie and are the principal determinants of the projected levels of population, labor force, households, income, and other economic variables developed in the other volumes.

For this reason, and because of space limitations, the highlights presented here, and the summary of the projection methodologies employed, are chiefly from Volume I, and relate to number employed.

The Columbus area—location and growth

Although Ohio for decades has been one of the nation's leading manufacturing states, Columbus, despite its location, for many years was principally a capital city, education, transportation, and finance-and-trading center.

By 1940, when the population of Ohio was 6,908,000, the Franklin County population was 388,700; Franklin County had 138,662 employed, of which only 23.6 percent were employed in Manufacturing. World War II, however, brought new industrial activity to the Area and was the catalyst to an industrial expansion that continues to the present and that has changed the character of the Area's economy. With the war's end, the Columbus Area had the labor, space, facilities and the recognized location to attract new manufacturing firms. The dynamic growth of the Columbus Area's economy in the 1940s continued in the 1950s. By 1960, the population of Franklin County had risen to 683,000 and resident employment to 256,684.

The Area's growth in these two decades was the result of two main forces: the surging industrial expansion, especially in durables manufacture, that stemmed from a somewhat belated recognition of the locational advantages of the Area for many kinds of manufacturing; and the continuing growth of elements related to the strong and long-established orientation of the Columbus Area as a political, educational, and financial-and-trading center.

Present economic structure

By 1960 the industrial growth of the Columbus Area had proceeded to the point where Manufacturing accounted for 27.2 percent of total resident employment (adjusted), compared to 25.6 percent in 1950 and approximately 23.6 percent in 1940. The general pattern of industry composition of the Columbus Area in 1960 more closely resembled that of the United States than that of Ohio—e.g. Manufacturing accounted for 28.3 percent of total employment in the United States, 38.3 percent in Ohio. The principal departures of the Columbus Area from the United States pattern are the substantially lower proportions of Agricultural employment, and higher percentages of employment in Professional Services (including Education), in Services generally, in Government, and in Insurance.

The makeup of Columbus Area Manufacturing, however, is less diversified than the United States or than Ohio but more nearly resembles Ohio than the United States.

The growth of Manufacturing in the Columbus Area since 1940 was primarily in durable goods, with five durable goods industry classifications accounting for almost 90 percent of the total increase in Manufacturing employment. Increasingly, therefore, Franklin County has become oriented to durable goods production, so that in 1960 durable goods manufacturing represented 67 percent of its total Manufacturing employment.

By 1965, although Manufacturing employment had increased 7.2 percent from 1960, larger increases in other industry classifications resulted in a decline to 26.0 percent in the Area's ratio of Manufacturing-to-all employment. In economic base terms, in which "Basic Industries" and "Local Industries" are defined on the basis of an external (exogenous)-internal (endogenous) dichotomy with respect to the source of their demands (with Basic Industries selling primarily to buyers outside the Area and generating activity whose multiplicative and cumulative effects are conceived as determining the demands (internal) of the Local Industries), the Columbus Area economy, despite the industrial expansion of the previous 25 years, still retains the advantage of a relatively large reliance on Local Supporting Industries, as the following table shows:

Classification	Percent of total employment, 1965
Basic Industries—Total	46.0
Products (Manufacturing, Construction, Quarrying, Agriculture)..	(31.8)
Services (Exogenous)	(14.2)
Local Supporting & Services Industries	54.0
Total	100.0

Employment in the Local Industries and Basic Services is notably more stable, much less cyclically sensitive, than in Manufacturing and Construction.

Projections

The central concern of the study was with the rate of growth at which the Area's economy can be expected to proceed in the future, the probable nature and dimensions of the changes among the principal divisions of the economy, and the structure of the economic base, at five-year intervals, 1970 through 1985.

The projections of number employed by industry classifications were critical to the projections of all the other variables, and special pains were taken, therefore, in their preparation. Rather than relying on a *single* methodology and accompanying assumptions, a pluralistic research design was employed. As a safeguard, to minimize the deviations of the projected values from true future values, it might be said that redundancy was deliberately incorporated in the research design.

Thus, projections of employment for each industry classification were made by several methods. For the (existing) Manufacturing industry classifications these methods were:

a. Franklin County Share of U.S. Total

For each industry classification, ratios of Franklin County/U.S. value added by manufacture, and of Franklin County/U.S. value added per employee, were developed from historical data; subjective determinations of the possible range ("High," "Intermediate," and "Low") of these two ratios in the projection period were made; and projected High, Intermediate, and Low Franklin County industry employment was derived from the projected ratios using the National Planning Association's projections of U.S. value added and number employed, by industry.

b. Manufacturers' Markets

Empirical data were obtained by questionnaire from Franklin County manufacturers showing the distribution of their 1963 sales by industry (industrial goods) and/or by U.S. region (consumer goods). Sales were then projected to 1985, using NPA's projections of U.S. gross output by manufacturing industry classifications, and of personal income by U.S. regions; projected employment of each industry classification was then obtained by dividing the projected sales by the respective projected sales/employee ratios.

c. Input-Output

A table of Franklin County 1958 inter-industry transactions and external sales was specially constructed, which, for each industry expresses its total output (sales) as the sum of the purchases of its output by every other category of local business, plus its output exported outside Franklin County. A matrix of technical coefficients, representing for each industry, for each dollar of its output, the value of its inputs from each other Franklin County industry, was computed. The matrix was inverted, and projected total sales of each Franklin County industry were computed by multiplying the inverse matrix by the matrix of projected exports. Projected sales were then converted to projected employment as in (b.) above.

The projections from these separate methods were then compared (as illustrated in Chart 1, reproduced from Chart C.4, Volume I of the study)

CHART 1

Manufacturing industries (SIC 33 and 34) establishment employment: Projections by three methods, and final projections (high, judgment intermediate, and low), Franklin County, 1963, and projected 1965–1985

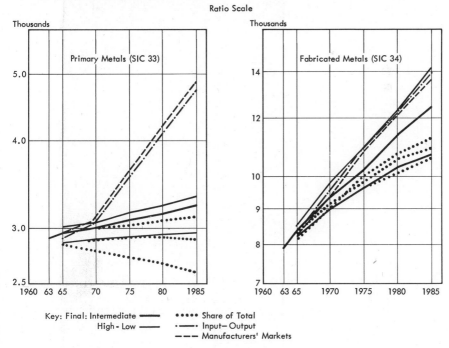

CHART 2

Major industry classifications: Franklin County resident employment, 1950, 1960, and 1965, and projected (judgment intermediate), 1970–1985

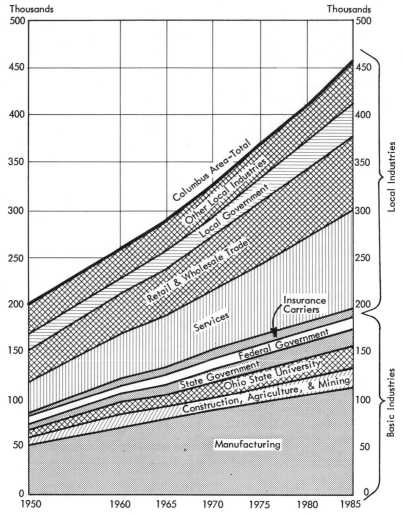

and used to develop a "Judgment Intermediate" (or implicitly a "most likely") level, and upper and lower bounds, which may be taken as "possible high" and "possible low." Where the projections by the various methods were closely confirming, the range between the upper and lower bounds is relatively small (as in the case of the Fabricated Metals industry in Chart 1). In a few industries in which the projections showed substantial dispersion (as in the case of the Primary Metals industry in Chart

1) the assumptions underlying the projection methods and subjective evaluations of the future prospects of the industry were restudied, and if a firm basis for decision among the alternatives was available, judgmental determinations were made; or if not, the range between the upper and lower bounds was left commensurately larger.

Historical and projected employment for all major industry classifications is shown in Chart 2 (reproduced from Chart 9.1, Volume I).

In summary it may be noted that on the basis of these projections no major structural changes in the employment of the Columbus Area are anticipated. Continuing large gains in manufacturing per-employee productivity, however, will limit the employment growth in this principal segment of the Basic Industries, so that by 1985 it will account for 23.6 percent of the total Area employment compared to 26.1 percent in 1965.

The rate of growth of employment projected for the Columbus Area, 1965–1985, compared with its recent historic rate, and with the United States as projected by NPA, is summarized in the following table:

	Average annual percent increase	
Area	*1950–1965*	*1965–1985*
Columbus Area total civilian resident employment		
High	—	2.7
Judgment Intermediate	2.5	2.3
Low	—	1.7
U.S. civilian employment	1.2	1.8

Projections of other selected economic variables are summarized in the accompanying table.

Columbus Area population, employment, and selected other economic and demographic measures, 1950 and 1960, and projected, 1965–1985

Item	1950	1960	1965	1970	1975	1980	1985
Total population (civilian) (thousands)*							
High			777.8	906.6	1,015.1	1,137.5	1,290.0
Intermediate	503.4	683.0	775.7	881.8	974.9	1,063.1	1,193.7
Low			774.2	849.5	922.6	978.8	1,068.3
Total labor force (civilian) (intermediate) (thousands)†	210.6	269.0	298.6	346.7	380.0	418.7	468.7
Total employment (civilian) (resident, adjusted) (thousands)‡							
High			288.4	339.3	383.1	432.2	488.9
Judgment Intermediate	200.0	256.7	288.2	327.0	367.9	408.8	453.6
Low			288.0	318.5	349.5	378.9	406.9
Total households (thousands)§							
High			218.0	263.3	286.7	316.4	364.1
Intermediate	145.7	200.8	217.9	254.9	277.7	299.1	345.5
Low			217.6	238.4	263.8	284.4	309.7
Total personal income (billion 1960 $s)‖							
High			$2.089	$2.664	$3.347	$4.193	$5.269
Judgment Intermediate	$1.030	$1.699	2.088	2.564	3.199	3.944	4.838
Low			2.086	2.492	3.026	3.633	4.310
Retail sales (intermediate) (billion 1960 $s)#	$ .610	$ .904	$1.097	$1.309	$1.591	$1.923	$2.321
Automobile ownership (households) (thousands)**							
High			255.8	307.7	354.2	403.5	483.5
Intermediate	n.a.	217.4(e)	254.2	305.7	351.6	400.3	479.5
Low			249.3	299.7	344.0	390.7	467.4

Source:
* The Columbus Area Economy: Structure and Growth, 1950 to 1985—Vol. III—Population and Labor Force, Bureau of Business Research, The Ohio State University, 1966, Tables 7 and 23.
† Ibid., Vol. III, Tables 13 and 23.
‡ Ibid., Vol. I—Employment and Value Added by Manufacture, Table 9.1.
§ Ibid., Vol. II—Income, Trade, Housing, Table 2.1 and Appendix Table B.13.
‖ Ibid., Vol. II, Appendix Table A.8.
Ibid., Vol. II, Table 5.1.
** Ibid., Vol. II, Table 4.1.

———————————————— appendix **G**

INTEREST TABLES

	1 AMOUNT OF $1 AT COMPOUND INTEREST	2 ACCUMULATION OF $1 PER PERIOD	3 SINKING FUND FACTOR	4 PRESENT VALUE REVERSION OF $1	5 PRESENT VALUE ORD. ANNUITY $1 PER PERIOD	6 INSTALMENT TO AMORTIZE $1	
MONTHS							
1	1.002500	1.000000	1.000000	0.997506	0.997506	1.002500	
2	1.005006	2.002500	0.499376	0.995019	1.992525	0.501876	
3	1.007519	3.007506	0.332501	0.992537	2.985062	0.335001	
4	1.010038	4.015025	0.249064	0.990062	3.975124	0.251564	
5	1.012563	5.025063	0.199002	0.987593	4.962718	0.201502	
6	1.015094	6.037625	0.165628	0.985130	5.947848	0.168128	
7	1.017632	7.052719	0.141789	0.982674	6.930522	0.144289	
8	1.020176	8.070351	0.123910	0.980223	7.910745	0.126410	
9	1.022726	9.090527	0.110005	0.977779	8.888524	0.112505	
10	1.025283	10.113253	0.098880	0.975340	9.863864	0.101380	
11	1.027846	11.138536	0.089778	0.972908	10.836772	0.092278	
12	1.030416	12.166383	0.082194	0.970482	11.807254	0.084694	
YEARS							**MONTHS**
1	1.030416	12.166383	0.082194	0.970482	11.807254	0.084694	12
2	1.061757	24.702818	0.040481	0.941835	23.265980	0.042981	24
3	1.094051	37.620560	0.026581	0.914034	34.386465	0.029081	36
4	1.127328	50.931208	0.019634	0.887053	45.178695	0.022134	48
5	1.161617	64.646713	0.015469	0.860869	55.652358	0.017969	60
6	1.196948	78.779387	0.012694	0.835458	65.816858	0.015194	72
7	1.233355	93.341920	0.010713	0.810797	75.681321	0.013213	84
8	1.270868	108.347387	0.009230	0.786863	85.254603	0.011730	96
9	1.309523	123.809259	0.008077	0.763637	94.545300	0.010577	108
10	1.349354	139.741419	0.007156	0.741096	103.561753	0.009656	120
11	1.390395	156.158171	0.006404	0.719220	112.312057	0.008904	132
12	1.432686	173.074254	0.005778	0.697990	120.804069	0.008278	144
13	1.476262	190.504855	0.005249	0.677386	129.045412	0.007749	156
14	1.521164	208.465626	0.004797	0.657391	137.043486	0.007297	168
15	1.567432	226.972690	0.004406	0.637986	144.805471	0.006906	180
16	1.615107	246.042664	0.004064	0.619154	152.338338	0.006564	192
17	1.664232	265.692670	0.003764	0.600878	159.648848	0.006264	204
18	1.714851	285.940350	0.003497	0.583141	166.743566	0.005997	216
19	1.767010	306.803882	0.003259	0.565928	173.628861	0.005759	228
20	1.820755	328.301998	0.003046	0.549223	180.310914	0.005546	240
21	1.876135	350.454000	0.002853	0.533011	186.795726	0.005353	252
22	1.933199	373.279777	0.002679	0.517277	193.089119	0.005179	264
23	1.992000	396.799821	0.002520	0.502008	199.196742	0.005020	276
24	2.052588	421.035250	0.002375	0.487190	205.124080	0.004875	288
25	2.115020	446.007823	0.002242	0.472809	210.876453	0.004742	300
26	2.179350	471.739961	0.002120	0.458852	216.459028	0.004620	312
27	2.245637	498.254766	0.002007	0.445308	221.876815	0.004507	324
28	2.313940	525.576044	0.001903	0.432163	227.134679	0.004403	336
29	2.384321	553.728325	0.001806	0.419407	232.237341	0.004306	348
30	2.456842	582.736885	0.001716	0.407027	237.189382	0.004216	360
31	2.531569	612.627767	0.001632	0.395012	241.995247	0.004132	372
32	2.608570	643.427810	0.001554	0.383352	246.659253	0.004054	384
33	2.687912	675.164665	0.001481	0.372036	251.185586	0.003981	396
34	2.769667	707.866827	0.001413	0.361054	255.578310	0.003913	408
35	2.853909	741.563657	0.001349	0.350397	259.841368	0.003849	420
36	2.940714	776.285408	0.001288	0.340054	263.978590	0.003788	432
37	3.030158	812.063254	0.001231	0.330016	267.993688	0.003731	444
38	3.122323	848.929318	0.001178	0.320274	271.890268	0.003678	456
39	3.217292	886.916698	0.001128	0.310820	275.671828	0.003628	468
40	3.315149	926.059501	0.001080	0.301646	279.341764	0.003580	480

*Tables on pages 430–59 are taken from Paul Wendt and Alan R. Cerf, *Tables for Investment Analysis* (Berkeley, Calif.: The Center for Real Estate and Urban Economics, Institute of Urban and Regional Development, the University of California), © 1966, The Regents of the University of California, Pages 22, 25, 54, 57, 70, 73, 78, 81, 86, 89, 94, 97, 102, 105–6, 109–10, 113–14, 117–18, 121, 126, 129, 138, 141, 158, 161, 178, and 181.

3.00% ANNUAL COMPOUND INTEREST TABLES 3.00%
EFFECTIVE RATE 3.00

	1 AMOUNT OF $1 AT COMPOUND INTEREST	2 ACCUMULATION OF $1 PER PERIOD	3 SINKING FUND FACTOR	4 PRESENT VALUE REVERSION OF $1	5 PRESENT VALUE ORD. ANNUITY $1 PER PERIOD	6 INSTALMENT TO AMORTIZE $1
YEARS						
1	1.030000	1.000000	1.000000	0.970874	0.970874	1.030000
2	1.060900	2.030000	0.492611	0.942596	1.913470	0.522611
3	1.092727	3.090900	0.323530	0.915142	2.828611	0.353530
4	1.125509	4.183627	0.239027	0.888487	3.717098	0.269027
5	1.159274	5.309136	0.188355	0.862609	4.579707	0.218355
6	1.194052	6.468410	0.154598	0.837484	5.417191	0.184598
7	1.229874	7.662462	0.130506	0.813092	6.230283	0.160506
8	1.266770	8.892336	0.112456	0.789409	7.019692	0.142456
9	1.304773	10.159106	0.098434	0.766417	7.786109	0.128434
10	1.343916	11.463879	0.087231	0.744094	8.530203	0.117231
11	1.384234	12.807796	0.078077	0.722421	9.252624	0.108077
12	1.425761	14.192030	0.070462	0.701380	9.954004	0.100462
13	1.468534	15.617790	0.064030	0.680951	10.634955	0.094030
14	1.512590	17.086324	0.058526	0.661118	11.296073	0.088526
15	1.557967	18.598914	0.053767	0.641862	11.937935	0.083767
16	1.604706	20.156881	0.049611	0.623167	12.561102	0.079611
17	1.652848	21.761588	0.045953	0.605016	13.166118	0.075953
18	1.702433	23.414435	0.042709	0.587395	13.753513	0.072709
19	1.753506	25.116868	0.039814	0.570286	14.323799	0.069814
20	1.806111	26.870374	0.037216	0.553676	14.877475	0.067216
21	1.860295	28.676486	0.034872	0.537549	15.415024	0.064872
22	1.916103	30.536780	0.032747	0.521893	15.936917	0.062747
23	1.973587	32.452884	0.030814	0.506692	16.443608	0.060814
24	2.032794	34.426470	0.029047	0.491934	16.935542	0.059047
25	2.093778	36.459264	0.027428	0.477606	17.413148	0.057428
26	2.156591	38.553042	0.025938	0.463695	17.876842	0.055938
27	2.221289	40.709634	0.024564	0.450189	18.327031	0.054564
28	2.287928	42.930923	0.023293	0.437077	18.764108	0.053293
29	2.356566	45.218850	0.022115	0.424346	19.188455	0.052115
30	2.427262	47.575416	0.021019	0.411987	19.600441	0.051019
31	2.500080	50.002678	0.019999	0.399987	20.000428	0.049999
32	2.575083	52.502759	0.019047	0.388337	20.388766	0.049047
33	2.652335	55.077841	0.018156	0.377026	20.765792	0.048156
34	2.731905	57.730177	0.017322	0.366045	21.131837	0.047322
35	2.813862	60.462082	0.016539	0.355383	21.487220	0.046539
36	2.898278	63.275944	0.015804	0.345032	21.832252	0.045804
37	2.985227	66.174223	0.015112	0.334983	22.167235	0.045112
38	3.074783	69.159449	0.014459	0.325226	22.492462	0.044459
39	3.167027	72.234233	0.013844	0.315754	22.808215	0.043844
40	3.262038	75.401260	0.013262	0.306557	23.114772	0.043262
41	3.359899	78.663298	0.012712	0.297628	23.412400	0.042712
42	3.460696	82.023196	0.012192	0.288959	23.701359	0.042192
43	3.564517	85.483892	0.011698	0.280543	23.981902	0.041698
44	3.671452	89.048409	0.011230	0.272372	24.254274	0.041230
45	3.781596	92.719861	0.010785	0.264439	24.518713	0.040785
46	3.895044	96.501457	0.010363	0.256737	24.775449	0.040363
47	4.011895	100.396501	0.009961	0.249259	25.024708	0.039961
48	4.132252	104.408396	0.009578	0.241999	25.266707	0.039578
49	4.256219	108.540648	0.009213	0.234950	25.501657	0.039213
50	4.383906	112.796867	0.008865	0.228107	25.729764	0.038865

5.00%   MONTHLY COMPOUND INTEREST TABLES   5.00%
                                      EFFECTIVE RATE 0.417

	1	2	3	4	5	6	
	AMOUNT OF $1 AT COMPOUND INTEREST	ACCUMULATION OF $1 PER PERIOD	SINKING FUND FACTOR	PRESENT VALUE REVERSION OF $1	PRESENT VALUE ORD. ANNUITY $1 PER PERIOD	INSTALMENT TO AMORTIZE $1	
MONTHS							
1	1.004167	1.000000	1.000000	0.995851	0.995851	1.004167	
2	1.008351	2.004167	0.498960	0.991718	1.987569	0.503127	
3	1.012552	3.012517	0.331948	0.987603	2.975173	0.336115	
4	1.016771	4.025070	0.248443	0.983506	3.958678	0.252610	
5	1.021008	5.041841	0.198340	0.979425	4.938103	0.202507	
6	1.025262	6.062848	0.164939	0.975361	5.913463	0.169106	
7	1.029534	7.088110	0.141081	0.971313	6.884777	0.145248	
8	1.033824	8.117644	0.123188	0.967283	7.852060	0.127355	
9	1.038131	9.151467	0.109272	0.963269	8.815329	0.113439	
10	1.042457	10.189599	0.098139	0.959272	9.774602	0.102306	
11	1.046800	11.232055	0.089031	0.955292	10.729894	0.093198	
12	1.051162	12.278855	0.081441	0.951328	11.681222	0.085607	

YEARS							MONTHS
1	1.051162	12.278855	0.081441	0.951328	11.681222	0.085607	12
2	1.104941	25.185921	0.039705	0.905025	22.793898	0.043871	24
3	1.161472	38.753336	0.025804	0.860976	33.365701	0.029971	36
4	1.220895	53.014885	0.018863	0.819071	43.422956	0.023029	48
5	1.283359	68.006083	0.014705	0.779205	52.990706	0.018871	60
6	1.349018	83.764259	0.011938	0.741280	62.092777	0.016105	72
7	1.418036	100.328653	0.009967	0.705201	70.751835	0.014134	84
8	1.490585	117.740512	0.008493	0.670877	78.989441	0.012660	96
9	1.566847	136.043196	0.007351	0.638225	86.826108	0.011517	108
10	1.647009	155.282279	0.006440	0.607161	94.281350	0.010607	120
11	1.731274	175.505671	0.005698	0.577609	101.373733	0.009864	132
12	1.819849	196.763730	0.005082	0.549496	108.120917	0.009249	144
13	1.912956	219.109391	0.004564	0.522751	114.539704	0.008731	156
14	2.010826	242.598299	0.004122	0.497308	120.646077	0.008289	168
15	2.113704	267.288944	0.003741	0.473103	126.455243	0.007908	180
16	2.221845	293.242809	0.003410	0.450076	131.981666	0.007577	192
17	2.335519	320.524523	0.003120	0.428170	137.239108	0.007287	204
18	2.455008	349.202022	0.002864	0.407331	142.240661	0.007030	216
19	2.580611	379.346715	0.002636	0.387505	146.998780	0.006803	228
20	2.712640	411.033669	0.002433	0.368645	151.525313	0.006600	240
21	2.851424	444.341787	0.002251	0.350702	155.831532	0.006417	252
22	2.997308	479.354011	0.002086	0.333633	159.928159	0.006253	264
23	3.150656	516.157528	0.001937	0.317394	163.825396	0.006104	276
24	3.311850	554.843982	0.001802	0.301946	167.532948	0.005969	288
25	3.481290	595.509709	0.001679	0.287250	171.060047	0.005846	300
26	3.659400	638.255971	0.001567	0.273269	174.415476	0.005733	312
27	3.846622	683.189213	0.001464	0.259968	177.607590	0.005630	324
28	4.043422	730.421325	0.001369	0.247315	180.644338	0.005536	336
29	4.250291	780.069922	0.001282	0.235278	183.533283	0.005449	348
30	4.467744	832.258635	0.001202	0.223827	186.281617	0.005368	360
31	4.696323	887.117422	0.001127	0.212933	188.896185	0.005294	372
32	4.936595	944.782889	0.001058	0.202569	191.383498	0.005225	384
33	5.189161	1005.398630	0.000995	0.192709	193.749748	0.005161	396
34	5.454648	1069.115587	0.000935	0.183330	196.000829	0.005102	408
35	5.733718	1136.092425	0.000880	0.174407	198.142346	0.005047	420
36	6.027066	1206.495925	0.000829	0.165918	200.179632	0.004996	432
37	6.335423	1280.501402	0.000781	0.157843	202.117759	0.004948	444
38	6.659555	1358.293140	0.000736	0.150160	203.961555	0.004903	456
39	7.000270	1440.064850	0.000694	0.142852	205.715609	0.004861	468
40	7.358417	1526.020157	0.000655	0.135899	207.384291	0.004822	480

5.00%   ANNUAL COMPOUND INTEREST TABLES   5.00%
                            EFFECTIVE RATE 5.00

	1 AMOUNT OF $1 AT COMPOUND INTEREST	2 ACCUMULATION OF $1 PER PERIOD	3 SINKING FUND FACTOR	4 PRESENT VALUE REVERSION OF $1	5 PRESENT VALUE ORD. ANNUITY $1 PER PERIOD	6 INSTALMENT TO AMORTIZE $1
YEARS						
1	1.050000	1.000000	1.000000	0.952381	0.952381	1.050000
2	1.102500	2.050000	0.487805	0.907029	1.859410	0.537805
3	1.157625	3.152500	0.317209	0.863838	2.723248	0.367209
4	1.215506	4.310125	0.232012	0.822702	3.545951	0.282012
5	1.276282	5.525631	0.180975	0.783526	4.329477	0.230975
6	1.340096	6.801913	0.147017	0.746215	5.075692	0.197017
7	1.407100	8.142008	0.122820	0.710681	5.786373	0.172820
8	1.477455	9.549109	0.104722	0.676839	6.463213	0.154722
9	1.551328	11.026564	0.090690	0.644609	7.107822	0.140690
10	1.628895	12.577893	0.079505	0.613913	7.721735	0.129505
11	1.710339	14.206787	0.070389	0.584679	8.306414	0.120389
12	1.795856	15.917127	0.062825	0.556837	8.863252	0.112825
13	1.885649	17.712983	0.056456	0.530321	9.393573	0.106456
14	1.979932	19.598632	0.051024	0.505068	9.898641	0.101024
15	2.078928	21.578564	0.046342	0.481017	10.379658	0.096342
16	2.182875	23.657492	0.042270	0.458112	10.837770	0.092270
17	2.292018	25.840366	0.038699	0.436297	11.274066	0.088699
18	2.406619	28.132385	0.035546	0.415521	11.689587	0.085546
19	2.526950	30.539004	0.032745	0.395734	12.085321	0.082745
20	2.653298	33.065954	0.030243	0.376889	12.462210	0.080243
21	2.785963	35.719252	0.027996	0.358942	12.821153	0.077996
22	2.925261	38.505214	0.025971	0.341850	13.163003	0.075971
23	3.071524	41.430475	0.024137	0.325571	13.488574	0.074137
24	3.225100	44.501999	0.022471	0.310068	13.798642	0.072471
25	3.386355	47.727099	0.020952	0.295303	14.093945	0.070952
26	3.555673	51.113454	0.019564	0.281241	14.375185	0.069564
27	3.733456	54.669126	0.018292	0.267848	14.643034	0.068292
28	3.920129	58.402583	0.017123	0.255094	14.898127	0.067123
29	4.116136	62.322712	0.016046	0.242946	15.141074	0.066046
30	4.321942	66.438848	0.015051	0.231377	15.372451	0.065051
31	4.538039	70.760790	0.014132	0.220359	15.592811	0.064132
32	4.764941	75.298829	0.013280	0.209866	15.802677	0.063280
33	5.003189	80.063771	0.012490	0.199873	16.002549	0.062490
34	5.253348	85.066959	0.011755	0.190355	16.192904	0.061755
35	5.516015	90.320307	0.011072	0.181290	16.374194	0.061072
36	5.791816	95.836323	0.010434	0.172657	16.546852	0.060434
37	6.081407	101.628139	0.009840	0.164436	16.711287	0.059840
38	6.385477	107.709546	0.009284	0.156605	16.867893	0.059284
39	6.704751	114.095023	0.008765	0.149148	17.017041	0.058765
40	7.039989	120.799774	0.008278	0.142046	17.159086	0.058278
41	7.391988	127.839763	0.007822	0.135282	17.294368	0.057822
42	7.761588	135.231751	0.007395	0.128840	17.423208	0.057395
43	8.149667	142.993339	0.006993	0.122704	17.545912	0.056993
44	8.557150	151.143006	0.006616	0.116861	17.662773	0.056616
45	8.985008	159.700156	0.006262	0.111297	17.774070	0.056262
46	9.434258	168.685164	0.005928	0.105997	17.880066	0.055928
47	9.905971	178.119422	0.005614	0.100949	17.981016	0.055614
48	10.401270	188.025393	0.005318	0.096142	18.077158	0.055318
49	10.921333	198.426663	0.005040	0.091564	18.168722	0.055040
50	11.467400	209.347996	0.004777	0.087204	18.255925	0.054777

6.00%   MONTHLY COMPOUND INTEREST TABLES   6.00%
                                  EFFECTIVE RATE 0.500

	1	2	3	4	5	6	
	AMOUNT OF $1 AT COMPOUND INTEREST	ACCUMULATION OF $1 PER PERIOD	SINKING FUND FACTOR	PRESENT VALUE REVERSION OF $1	PRESENT VALUE ORD. ANNUITY $1 PER PERIOD	INSTALMENT TO AMORTIZE $1	
MONTHS							
1	1.005000	1.000000	1.000000	0.995025	0.995025	1.005000	
2	1.010025	2.005000	0.498753	0.990075	1.985099	0.503753	
3	1.015075	3.015025	0.331672	0.985149	2.970248	0.336672	
4	1.020151	4.030100	0.248133	0.980248	3.950496	0.253133	
5	1.025251	5.050251	0.198010	0.975371	4.925866	0.203010	
6	1.030378	6.075502	0.164595	0.970518	5.896384	0.169595	
7	1.035529	7.105879	0.140729	0.965690	6.862074	0.145729	
8	1.040707	8.141409	0.122829	0.960885	7.822959	0.127829	
9	1.045911	9.182116	0.108907	0.956105	8.779064	0.113907	
10	1.051140	10.228026	0.097771	0.951348	9.730412	0.102771	
11	1.056396	11.279167	0.088659	0.946615	10.677027	0.093659	
12	1.061678	12.335562	0.081066	0.941905	11.618932	0.086066	
YEARS							**MONTHS**
1	1.061678	12.335562	0.081066	0.941905	11.618932	0.086066	12
2	1.127160	25.431955	0.039321	0.887186	22.562866	0.044321	24
3	1.196681	39.336105	0.025422	0.835645	32.871016	0.030422	36
4	1.270489	54.097832	0.018485	0.787098	42.580318	0.023485	48
5	1.348850	69.770031	0.014333	0.741372	51.725561	0.019333	60
6	1.432044	86.408856	0.011573	0.698302	60.339514	0.016573	72
7	1.520370	104.073927	0.009609	0.657735	68.453042	0.014609	84
8	1.614143	122.828542	0.008141	0.619524	76.095218	0.013141	96
9	1.713699	142.739900	0.007006	0.583533	83.293424	0.012006	108
10	1.819397	163.879347	0.006102	0.549633	90.073453	0.011102	120
11	1.931613	186.322629	0.005367	0.517702	96.459599	0.010367	132
12	2.050751	210.150163	0.004759	0.487626	102.474743	0.009759	144
13	2.177237	235.447328	0.004247	0.459298	108.140440	0.009247	156
14	2.311524	262.304766	0.003812	0.432615	113.476990	0.008812	168
15	2.454094	290.818712	0.003439	0.407482	118.503515	0.008439	180
16	2.605457	321.091337	0.003114	0.383810	123.238025	0.008114	192
17	2.766156	353.231110	0.002831	0.361513	127.697486	0.007831	204
18	2.936766	387.353194	0.002582	0.340511	131.897876	0.007582	216
19	3.117899	423.579854	0.002361	0.320729	135.854246	0.007361	228
20	3.310204	462.040895	0.002164	0.302096	139.580772	0.007164	240
21	3.514371	502.874129	0.001989	0.284546	143.090806	0.006989	252
22	3.731129	546.225867	0.001831	0.268015	146.396927	0.006831	264
23	3.961257	592.251446	0.001688	0.252445	149.510979	0.006688	276
24	4.205579	641.115782	0.001560	0.237779	152.444121	0.006560	288
25	4.464970	692.993962	0.001443	0.223966	155.206864	0.006443	300
26	4.740359	748.071876	0.001337	0.210954	157.809106	0.006337	312
27	5.032734	806.546875	0.001240	0.198699	160.260172	0.006240	324
28	5.343142	868.628484	0.001151	0.187156	162.568844	0.006151	336
29	5.672696	934.539150	0.001070	0.176283	164.743394	0.006070	348
30	6.022575	1004.515043	0.000996	0.166042	166.791614	0.005996	360
31	6.394034	1078.806895	0.000927	0.156396	168.720844	0.005927	372
32	6.788405	1157.680906	0.000864	0.147310	170.537996	0.005864	384
33	7.207098	1241.419693	0.000806	0.138752	172.249581	0.005806	396
34	7.651617	1330.323306	0.000752	0.130691	173.861732	0.005752	408
35	8.123551	1424.710299	0.000702	0.123099	175.380226	0.005702	420
36	8.624594	1524.918875	0.000656	0.115947	176.810504	0.005656	432
37	9.156540	1631.308097	0.000613	0.109212	178.157690	0.005613	444
38	9.721296	1744.259173	0.000573	0.102867	179.426611	0.005573	456
39	10.320884	1864.176825	0.000536	0.096891	180.621815	0.005536	468
40	10.957454	1991.490734	0.000502	0.091262	181.747584	0.005502	480

6.00%   ANNUAL COMPOUND INTEREST TABLES   6.00%
                              EFFECTIVE RATE 6.00

	1	2	3	4	5	6
	AMOUNT OF $1 AT COMPOUND INTEREST	ACCUMULATION OF $1 PER PERIOD	SINKING FUND FACTOR	PRESENT VALUE REVERSION OF $1	PRESENT VALUE ORD. ANNUITY $1 PER PERIOD	INSTALMENT TO AMORTIZE $1
YEARS						
1	1.060000	1.000000	1.000000	0.943396	0.943396	1.060000
2	1.123600	2.060000	0.485437	0.889996	1.833393	0.545437
3	1.191016	3.183600	0.314110	0.839619	2.673012	0.374110
4	1.262477	4.374616	0.228591	0.792094	3.465106	0.288591
5	1.338226	5.637093	0.177396	0.747258	4.212364	0.237396
6	1.418519	6.975319	0.143363	0.704961	4.917324	0.203363
7	1.503630	8.393838	0.119135	0.665057	5.582381	0.179135
8	1.593848	9.897468	0.101036	0.627412	6.209794	0.161036
9	1.689479	11.491316	0.087022	0.591898	6.801692	0.147022
10	1.790848	13.180795	0.075868	0.558395	7.360087	0.135868
11	1.898299	14.971643	0.066793	0.526788	7.886875	0.126793
12	2.012196	16.869941	0.059277	0.496969	8.383844	0.119277
13	2.132928	18.882138	0.052960	0.468839	8.852683	0.112960
14	2.260904	21.015066	0.047585	0.442301	9.294984	0.107585
15	2.396558	23.275970	0.042963	0.417265	9.712249	0.102963
16	2.540352	25.672528	0.038952	0.393646	10.105895	0.098952
17	2.692773	28.212880	0.035445	0.371364	10.477260	0.095445
18	2.854339	30.905653	0.032357	0.350344	10.827603	0.092357
19	3.025600	33.759992	0.029621	0.330513	11.158116	0.089621
20	3.207135	36.785591	0.027185	0.311805	11.469921	0.087185
21	3.399564	39.992727	0.025005	0.294155	11.764077	0.085005
22	3.603537	43.392290	0.023046	0.277505	12.041582	0.083046
23	3.819750	46.995828	0.021278	0.261797	12.303379	0.081278
24	4.048935	50.815577	0.019679	0.246979	12.550358	0.079679
25	4.291871	54.864512	0.018227	0.232999	12.783356	0.078227
26	4.549383	59.156383	0.016904	0.219810	13.003166	0.076904
27	4.822346	63.705766	0.015697	0.207368	13.210534	0.075697
28	5.111687	68.528112	0.014593	0.195630	13.406164	0.074593
29	5.418388	73.639798	0.013580	0.184557	13.590721	0.073580
30	5.743491	79.058186	0.012649	0.174110	13.764831	0.072649
31	6.088101	84.801677	0.011792	0.164255	13.929086	0.071792
32	6.453387	90.889778	0.011002	0.154957	14.084043	0.071002
33	6.840590	97.343165	0.010273	0.146186	14.230230	0.070273
34	7.251025	104.183755	0.009598	0.137912	14.368141	0.069598
35	7.686087	111.434780	0.008974	0.130105	14.498246	0.068974
36	8.147252	119.120867	0.008395	0.122741	14.620987	0.068395
37	8.636087	127.268119	0.007857	0.115793	14.736780	0.067857
38	9.154252	135.904206	0.007358	0.109239	14.846019	0.067358
39	9.703507	145.058458	0.006894	0.103056	14.949075	0.066894
40	10.285718	154.761966	0.006462	0.097222	15.046297	0.066462
41	10.902861	165.047684	0.006059	0.091719	15.138016	0.066059
42	11.557033	175.950545	0.005683	0.086527	15.224543	0.065683
43	12.250455	187.507577	0.005333	0.081630	15.306173	0.065333
44	12.985482	199.758032	0.005006	0.077009	15.383182	0.065006
45	13.764611	212.743514	0.004700	0.072650	15.455832	0.064700
46	14.590487	226.508125	0.004415	0.068538	15.524370	0.064415
47	15.465917	241.098612	0.004148	0.064658	15.589028	0.064148
48	16.393872	256.564529	0.003898	0.060998	15.650027	0.063898
49	17.377504	272.958401	0.003664	0.057546	15.707572	0.063664
50	18.420154	290.335905	0.003444	0.054288	15.761861	0.063444

6.50%   MONTHLY COMPOUND INTEREST TABLES   6.50%
                              EFFECTIVE RATE 0.542

	1	2	3	4	5	6	
	AMOUNT OF $1 AT COMPOUND INTEREST	ACCUMULATION OF $1 PER PERIOD	SINKING FUND FACTOR	PRESENT VALUE REVERSION OF $1	PRESENT VALUE ORD. ANNUITY $1 PER PERIOD	INSTALMENT TO AMORTIZE $1	
MONTHS							
1	1.005417	1.000000	1.000000	0.994613	0.994613	1.005417	
2	1.010863	2.005417	0.498649	0.989254	1.983867	0.504066	
3	1.016338	3.016279	0.331534	0.983924	2.967791	0.336951	
4	1.021843	4.032618	0.247978	0.978624	3.946415	0.253395	
5	1.027378	5.054461	0.197845	0.973351	4.919766	0.203262	
6	1.032943	6.081839	0.164424	0.968107	5.887873	0.169841	
7	1.038538	7.114782	0.140552	0.962892	6.850765	0.145969	
8	1.044164	8.153321	0.122649	0.957704	7.808469	0.128066	
9	1.049820	9.197485	0.108725	0.952545	8.761014	0.114142	
10	1.055506	10.247304	0.097587	0.947413	9.708426	0.103003	
11	1.061224	11.302811	0.088474	0.942309	10.650735	0.093890	
12	1.066972	12.364034	0.080880	0.937232	11.587967	0.086296	
YEARS							MONTHS
1	1.066972	12.364034	0.080880	0.937232	11.587967	0.086296	12
2	1.138429	25.556111	0.039130	0.878404	22.448578	0.044546	24
3	1.214672	39.631685	0.025232	0.823268	32.627489	0.030649	36
4	1.296020	54.649927	0.018298	0.771593	42.167488	0.023715	48
5	1.382817	70.673968	0.014149	0.723161	51.108680	0.019566	60
6	1.475427	87.771168	0.011393	0.677770	59.488649	0.016810	72
7	1.574239	106.013400	0.009433	0.635227	67.342623	0.014849	84
8	1.679669	125.477348	0.007970	0.595355	74.703617	0.013386	96
9	1.792160	146.244833	0.006838	0.557986	81.602576	0.012255	108
10	1.912184	168.403154	0.005938	0.522962	88.068500	0.011355	120
11	2.040246	192.045460	0.005207	0.490137	94.128569	0.010624	132
12	2.176885	217.271134	0.004603	0.459372	99.808260	0.010019	144
13	2.322675	244.186218	0.004095	0.430538	105.131446	0.009512	156
14	2.478229	272.903856	0.003664	0.403514	110.120506	0.009081	168
15	2.644201	303.544767	0.003294	0.378186	114.796412	0.008711	180
16	2.821288	336.237756	0.002974	0.354448	119.178820	0.008391	192
17	3.010235	371.120256	0.002695	0.332200	123.286152	0.008111	204
18	3.211836	408.338901	0.002449	0.311348	127.135675	0.007866	216
19	3.426938	448.050147	0.002232	0.291806	130.743570	0.007649	228
20	3.656447	490.420930	0.002039	0.273490	134.125004	0.007456	240
21	3.901326	535.629362	0.001867	0.256323	137.294192	0.007284	252
22	4.162605	583.865486	0.001713	0.240234	140.264456	0.007129	264
23	4.441382	635.332073	0.001574	0.225155	143.048282	0.006991	276
24	4.738830	690.245473	0.001449	0.211023	145.657372	0.006865	288
25	5.056198	748.836525	0.001335	0.197777	148.102695	0.006752	300
26	5.394821	811.351528	0.001233	0.185363	150.394529	0.006649	312
27	5.756122	878.053277	0.001139	0.173728	152.542509	0.006556	324
28	6.141620	949.222165	0.001053	0.162823	154.555664	0.006470	336
29	6.552936	1025.157366	0.000975	0.152603	156.442457	0.006392	348
30	6.991798	1106.178087	0.000904	0.143025	158.210820	0.006321	360
31	7.460052	1192.624917	0.000838	0.134047	159.868185	0.006255	372
32	7.959665	1284.861250	0.000778	0.125633	161.421521	0.006195	384
33	8.492739	1383.274822	0.000723	0.117748	162.877357	0.006140	396
34	9.061513	1488.279333	0.000672	0.110357	164.241813	0.006089	408
35	9.668379	1600.316190	0.000625	0.103430	165.520625	0.006042	420
36	10.315889	1719.856364	0.000581	0.096938	166.719167	0.005998	432
37	11.006763	1847.402364	0.000541	0.090853	167.842480	0.005958	444
38	11.743906	1983.490356	0.000504	0.085151	168.895284	0.005921	456
39	12.530417	2128.692413	0.000470	0.079806	169.882006	0.005886	468
40	13.369602	2283.618920	0.000438	0.074797	170.806793	0.005855	480

6.50%

ANNUAL COMPOUND INTEREST TABLES
EFFECTIVE RATE 6.50

6.50%

	1 AMOUNT OF $1 AT COMPOUND INTEREST	2 ACCUMULATION OF $1 PER PERIOD	3 SINKING FUND FACTOR	4 PRESENT VALUE REVERSION OF $1	5 PRESENT VALUE ORD. ANNUITY $1 PER PERIOD	6 INSTALMENT TO AMORTIZE $1
YEARS						
1	1.065000	1.000000	1.000000	0.938967	0.938967	1.065000
2	1.134225	2.065000	0.484262	0.881659	1.820626	0.549262
3	1.207950	3.199225	0.312576	0.827849	2.648476	0.377576
4	1.286466	4.407175	0.226903	0.777323	3.425799	0.291903
5	1.370087	5.693641	0.175635	0.729881	4.155679	0.240635
6	1.459142	7.063728	0.141568	0.685334	4.841014	0.206568
7	1.553987	8.522870	0.117331	0.643506	5.484520	0.182331
8	1.654996	10.076856	0.099237	0.604231	6.088751	0.164237
9	1.762570	11.731852	0.085238	0.567353	6.656104	0.150238
10	1.877137	13.494423	0.074105	0.532726	7.188830	0.139105
11	1.999151	15.371560	0.065055	0.500212	7.689042	0.130055
12	2.129096	17.370711	0.057568	0.469683	8.158725	0.122568
13	2.267487	19.499808	0.051283	0.441017	8.599742	0.116283
14	2.414874	21.767295	0.045940	0.414100	9.013842	0.110940
15	2.571841	24.182169	0.041353	0.388827	9.402669	0.106353
16	2.739011	26.754010	0.037378	0.365095	9.767764	0.102378
17	2.917046	29.493021	0.033906	0.342813	10.110577	0.098906
18	3.106654	32.410067	0.030855	0.321890	10.432466	0.095855
19	3.308587	35.516722	0.028156	0.302244	10.734710	0.093156
20	3.523645	38.825309	0.025756	0.283797	11.018507	0.090756
21	3.752682	42.348954	0.023613	0.266476	11.284983	0.088613
22	3.996606	46.101636	0.021691	0.250212	11.535196	0.086691
23	4.256386	50.098242	0.019961	0.234941	11.770137	0.084961
24	4.533051	54.354628	0.018398	0.220602	11.990739	0.083398
25	4.827699	58.887679	0.016981	0.207138	12.197877	0.081981
26	5.141500	63.715378	0.015695	0.194496	12.392373	0.080695
27	5.475697	68.856877	0.014523	0.182625	12.574998	0.079523
28	5.831617	74.332574	0.013453	0.171479	12.746477	0.078453
29	6.210672	80.164192	0.012474	0.161013	12.907490	0.077474
30	6.614366	86.374864	0.011577	0.151186	13.058676	0.076577
31	7.044300	92.989230	0.010754	0.141959	13.200635	0.075754
32	7.502179	100.033530	0.009997	0.133295	13.333929	0.074997
33	7.989821	107.535710	0.009299	0.125159	13.459088	0.074299
34	8.509159	115.525531	0.008656	0.117520	13.576609	0.073656
35	9.062255	124.034690	0.008062	0.110348	13.686957	0.073062
36	9.651301	133.096945	0.007513	0.103613	13.790570	0.072513
37	10.278636	142.748247	0.007005	0.097289	13.887859	0.072005
38	10.946747	153.026883	0.006535	0.091351	13.979210	0.071535
39	11.658286	163.973630	0.006099	0.085776	14.064986	0.071099
40	12.416075	175.631916	0.005694	0.080541	14.145527	0.070694
41	13.223119	188.047990	0.005318	0.075625	14.221152	0.070318
42	14.082622	201.271110	0.004968	0.071010	14.292161	0.069968
43	14.997993	215.353732	0.004644	0.066676	14.358837	0.069644
44	15.972862	230.351725	0.004341	0.062606	14.421443	0.069341
45	17.011098	246.324587	0.004060	0.058785	14.480228	0.069060
46	18.116820	263.335685	0.003797	0.055197	14.535426	0.068797
47	19.294413	281.452504	0.003553	0.051828	14.587254	0.068553
48	20.548550	300.746917	0.003325	0.048665	14.635919	0.068325
49	21.884205	321.295467	0.003112	0.045695	14.681615	0.068112
50	23.306679	343.179672	0.002914	0.042906	14.724521	0.067914

7.00%   MONTHLY COMPOUND INTEREST TABLES   7.00%
                              EFFECTIVE RATE 0.583

	1 AMOUNT OF $1 AT COMPOUND INTEREST	2 ACCUMULATION OF $1 PER PERIOD	3 SINKING FUND FACTOR	4 PRESENT VALUE REVERSION OF $1	5 PRESENT VALUE ORD. ANNUITY $1 PER PERIOD	6 INSTALMENT TO AMORTIZE $1	
MONTHS							
1	1.005833	1.000000	1.000000	0.994200	0.994200	1.005833	
2	1.011701	2.005833	0.498546	0.988435	1.982635	0.504379	
3	1.017602	3.017534	0.331396	0.982702	2.965337	0.337230	
4	1.023538	4.035136	0.247823	0.977003	3.942340	0.253656	
5	1.029509	5.058675	0.197680	0.971337	4.913677	0.203514	
6	1.035514	6.088184	0.164253	0.965704	5.879381	0.170086	
7	1.041555	7.123698	0.140377	0.960103	6.839484	0.146210	
8	1.047631	8.165253	0.122470	0.954535	7.794019	0.128304	
9	1.053742	9.212883	0.108544	0.948999	8.743018	0.114377	
10	1.059889	10.266625	0.097403	0.943495	9.686513	0.103236	
11	1.066071	11.326514	0.088288	0.938024	10.624537	0.094122	
12	1.072290	12.392585	0.080693	0.932583	11.557120	0.086527	
YEARS							**MONTHS**
1	1.072290	12.392585	0.080693	0.932583	11.557120	0.086527	12
2	1.149806	25.681032	0.038939	0.869712	22.335099	0.044773	24
3	1.232926	39.930101	0.025044	0.811079	32.386464	0.030877	36
4	1.322054	55.209236	0.018113	0.756399	41.760201	0.023946	48
5	1.417625	71.592902	0.013968	0.705405	50.501993	0.019801	60
6	1.520106	89.160944	0.011216	0.657849	58.654444	0.017049	72
7	1.629994	107.998981	0.009259	0.613499	66.257285	0.015093	84
8	1.747826	128.198821	0.007800	0.572139	73.347569	0.013634	96
9	1.874177	149.858909	0.006673	0.533568	79.959850	0.012506	108
10	2.009661	173.084807	0.005778	0.497596	86.126354	0.011611	120
11	2.154940	197.989707	0.005051	0.464050	91.877134	0.010884	132
12	2.310721	224.694985	0.004450	0.432765	97.240216	0.010284	144
13	2.477763	253.330789	0.003947	0.403590	102.241738	0.009781	156
14	2.656881	284.036677	0.003521	0.376381	106.906074	0.009354	168
15	2.848947	316.962297	0.003155	0.351007	111.255958	0.008988	180
16	3.054897	352.268112	0.002839	0.327343	115.312587	0.008672	192
17	3.275736	390.126188	0.002563	0.305275	119.095732	0.008397	204
18	3.512539	430.721027	0.002322	0.284694	122.623831	0.008155	216
19	3.766461	474.250470	0.002109	0.265501	125.914077	0.007942	228
20	4.038739	520.926660	0.001920	0.247602	128.982506	0.007753	240
21	4.330700	570.977075	0.001751	0.230910	131.844073	0.007585	252
22	4.643766	624.645640	0.001601	0.215342	134.512723	0.007434	264
23	4.979464	682.193909	0.001466	0.200825	137.001461	0.007299	276
24	5.339430	743.902347	0.001344	0.187286	139.322418	0.007178	288
25	5.725418	810.071693	0.001234	0.174660	141.486903	0.007068	300
26	6.139309	881.024426	0.001135	0.162885	143.505467	0.006968	312
27	6.583120	957.106339	0.001045	0.151904	145.387946	0.006878	324
28	7.059015	1038.688219	0.000963	0.141663	147.143515	0.006796	336
29	7.569311	1126.167659	0.000888	0.132112	148.780729	0.006721	348
30	8.116497	1219.970996	0.000820	0.123206	150.307568	0.006653	360
31	8.703240	1320.555383	0.000757	0.114900	151.731473	0.006591	372
32	9.332398	1428.411024	0.000700	0.107154	153.059383	0.006533	384
33	10.007037	1544.063557	0.000648	0.099930	154.297770	0.006481	396
34	10.730447	1668.076622	0.000599	0.093193	155.452669	0.006433	408
35	11.506152	1801.054601	0.000555	0.086910	156.529709	0.006389	420
36	12.337932	1943.645569	0.000514	0.081051	157.534139	0.006348	432
37	13.229843	2096.544450	0.000477	0.075587	158.470853	0.006310	444
38	14.186229	2260.496403	0.000442	0.070491	159.344418	0.006276	456
39	15.211753	2436.300456	0.000410	0.065739	160.159090	0.006244	468
40	16.311411	2624.813398	0.000381	0.061307	160.918839	0.006214	480

ANNUAL COMPOUND INTEREST TABLES 7.00%
EFFECTIVE RATE 7.00

	1	2	3	4	5	6
	AMOUNT OF $1 AT COMPOUND INTEREST	ACCUMULATION OF $1 PER PERIOD	SINKING FUND FACTOR	PRESENT VALUE REVERSION OF $1	PRESENT VALUE ORD. ANNUITY $1 PER PERIOD	INSTALMENT TO AMORTIZE $1
YEARS						
1	1.070000	1.000000	1.000000	0.934579	0.934579	1.070000
2	1.144900	2.070000	0.483092	0.873439	1.808018	0.553092
3	1.225043	3.214900	0.311052	0.816298	2.624316	0.381052
4	1.310796	4.439943	0.225228	0.762895	3.387211	0.295228
5	1.402552	5.750739	0.173891	0.712986	4.100197	0.243891
6	1.500730	7.153291	0.139796	0.666342	4.766540	0.209796
7	1.605781	8.654021	0.115553	0.622750	5.389289	0.185553
8	1.718186	10.259803	0.097468	0.582009	5.971299	0.167468
9	1.838459	11.977989	0.083486	0.543934	6.515232	0.153486
10	1.967151	13.816448	0.072378	0.508349	7.023582	0.142378
11	2.104852	15.783599	0.063357	0.475093	7.498674	0.133357
12	2.252192	17.888451	0.055902	0.444012	7.942686	0.125902
13	2.409845	20.140643	0.049651	0.414964	8.357651	0.119651
14	2.578534	22.550488	0.044345	0.387817	8.745468	0.114345
15	2.759032	25.129022	0.039795	0.362446	9.107914	0.109795
16	2.952164	27.888054	0.035858	0.338735	9.446649	0.105858
17	3.158815	30.840217	0.032425	0.316574	9.763223	0.102425
18	3.379932	33.999033	0.029413	0.295864	10.059087	0.099413
19	3.616528	37.378965	0.026753	0.276508	10.335595	0.096753
20	3.869684	40.995492	0.024393	0.258419	10.594014	0.094393
21	4.140562	44.865177	0.022289	0.241513	10.835527	0.092289
22	4.430402	49.005739	0.020406	0.225713	11.061240	0.090406
23	4.740530	53.436141	0.018714	0.210947	11.272187	0.088714
24	5.072367	58.176671	0.017189	0.197147	11.469334	0.087189
25	5.427433	63.249038	0.015811	0.184249	11.653583	0.085811
26	5.807353	68.676470	0.014561	0.172195	11.825779	0.084561
27	6.213868	74.483823	0.013426	0.160930	11.986709	0.083426
28	6.648838	80.697691	0.012392	0.150402	12.137111	0.082392
29	7.114257	87.346529	0.011449	0.140563	12.277674	0.081449
30	7.612255	94.460786	0.010586	0.131367	12.409041	0.080586
31	8.145113	102.073041	0.009797	0.122773	12.531814	0.079797
32	8.715271	110.218154	0.009073	0.114741	12.646555	0.079073
33	9.325340	118.933425	0.008408	0.107235	12.753790	0.078408
34	9.978114	128.258765	0.007797	0.100219	12.854009	0.077797
35	10.676581	138.236878	0.007234	0.093663	12.947672	0.077234
36	11.423942	148.913460	0.006715	0.087535	13.035208	0.076715
37	12.223618	160.337402	0.006237	0.081809	13.117017	0.076237
38	13.079271	172.561020	0.005795	0.076457	13.193473	0.075795
39	13.994820	185.640292	0.005387	0.071455	13.264928	0.075387
40	14.974458	199.635112	0.005009	0.066780	13.331709	0.075009
41	16.022670	214.609570	0.004660	0.062412	13.394120	0.074660
42	17.144257	230.632240	0.004336	0.058329	13.452449	0.074336
43	18.344355	247.776496	0.004036	0.054513	13.506962	0.074036
44	19.628460	266.120851	0.003758	0.050946	13.557908	0.073758
45	21.002452	285.749311	0.003500	0.047613	13.605522	0.073500
46	22.472623	306.751763	0.003260	0.044499	13.650020	0.073260
47	24.045707	329.224386	0.003037	0.041587	13.691608	0.073037
48	25.728907	353.270093	0.002831	0.038867	13.730474	0.072831
49	27.529930	378.999000	0.002639	0.036324	13.766799	0.072639
50	29.457025	406.528929	0.002460	0.033948	13.800746	0.072460

7.50%   MONTHLY COMPOUND INTEREST TABLES   7.50%
                                    EFFECTIVE RATE 0.625

	1 AMOUNT OF $1 AT COMPOUND INTEREST	2 ACCUMULATION OF $1 PER PERIOD	3 SINKING FUND FACTOR	4 PRESENT VALUE REVERSION OF $1	5 PRESENT VALUE ORD. ANNUITY $1 PER PERIOD	6 INSTALMENT TO AMORTIZE $1	
MONTHS							
1	1.006250	1.000000	1.000000	0.993789	0.993789	1.006250	
2	1.012539	2.006250	0.498442	0.987616	1.981405	0.504692	
3	1.018867	3.018789	0.331259	0.981482	2.962887	0.337509	
4	1.025235	4.037656	0.247668	0.975386	3.938273	0.253918	
5	1.031643	5.062892	0.197516	0.969327	4.907600	0.203766	
6	1.038091	6.094535	0.164081	0.963307	5.870907	0.170331	
7	1.044579	7.132626	0.140201	0.957324	6.828231	0.146451	
8	1.051108	8.177205	0.122291	0.951377	7.779608	0.128541	
9	1.057677	9.228312	0.108362	0.945468	8.725076	0.114612	
10	1.064287	10.285989	0.097220	0.939596	9.664672	0.103470	
11	1.070939	11.350277	0.088104	0.933760	10.598432	0.094354	
12	1.077633	12.421216	0.080507	0.927960	11.526392	0.086757	
YEARS							**MONTHS**
1	1.077633	12.421216	0.080507	0.927960	11.526392	0.086757	12
2	1.161292	25.806723	0.038750	0.861110	22.222423	0.045000	24
3	1.251446	40.231382	0.024856	0.799076	32.147913	0.031106	36
4	1.348599	55.775864	0.017929	0.741510	41.358371	0.024179	48
5	1.453294	72.527105	0.013788	0.688092	49.905308	0.020038	60
6	1.566117	90.578789	0.011040	0.638522	57.836524	0.017290	72
7	1.687699	110.031871	0.009088	0.592523	65.196376	0.015338	84
8	1.818720	130.995147	0.007634	0.549837	72.026024	0.013884	96
9	1.959912	153.585857	0.006511	0.510227	78.363665	0.012761	108
10	2.112065	177.930342	0.005620	0.473470	84.244743	0.011870	120
11	2.276030	204.164753	0.004898	0.439362	89.702148	0.011148	132
12	2.452724	232.435809	0.004302	0.407710	94.766401	0.010552	144
13	2.643135	262.901620	0.003804	0.378339	99.465827	0.010054	156
14	2.848329	295.732572	0.003381	0.351083	103.826705	0.009631	168
15	3.069452	331.112276	0.003020	0.325791	107.873427	0.009270	180
16	3.307741	369.238599	0.002708	0.302321	111.628623	0.008958	192
17	3.564530	410.324766	0.002437	0.280542	115.113294	0.008687	204
18	3.841254	454.600560	0.002200	0.260332	118.346930	0.008450	216
19	4.139460	502.313599	0.001991	0.241577	121.347615	0.008241	228
20	4.460817	553.730725	0.001806	0.224174	124.132131	0.008056	240
21	4.807122	609.139496	0.001642	0.208025	126.716051	0.007892	252
22	5.180311	668.849794	0.001495	0.193039	129.113825	0.007745	264
23	5.582472	733.195558	0.001364	0.179132	131.338863	0.007614	276
24	6.015854	802.536650	0.001246	0.166227	133.403610	0.007496	288
25	6.482880	877.260872	0.001140	0.154252	135.319613	0.007390	300
26	6.986163	957.786129	0.001044	0.143140	137.097587	0.007294	312
27	7.528517	1044.562771	0.000957	0.132828	138.747475	0.007207	324
28	8.112976	1138.076109	0.000879	0.123259	140.278506	0.007129	336
29	8.742807	1238.849131	0.000807	0.114380	141.699242	0.007057	348
30	9.421534	1347.445425	0.000742	0.106140	143.017627	0.006992	360
31	10.152952	1464.472331	0.000683	0.098494	144.241037	0.006933	372
32	10.941152	1590.584339	0.000629	0.091398	145.376312	0.006879	384
33	11.790542	1726.486751	0.000579	0.084814	146.429801	0.006829	396
34	12.705873	1872.939621	0.000534	0.078704	147.407398	0.006784	408
35	13.692263	2030.762007	0.000492	0.073034	148.314568	0.006742	420
36	14.755228	2200.836555	0.000454	0.067773	149.156386	0.006704	432
37	15.900715	2384.114432	0.000419	0.062890	149.937560	0.006669	444
38	17.135129	2581.620647	0.000387	0.058360	150.662457	0.006637	456
39	18.465374	2794.459783	0.000358	0.054155	151.335133	0.006608	468
40	19.898889	3023.822174	0.000331	0.050254	151.959350	0.006581	480

7.50%   ANNUAL COMPOUND INTEREST TABLES   7.50%
                                  EFFECTIVE RATE 7.50

	1	2	3	4	5	6
	AMOUNT OF $1 AT COMPOUND INTEREST	ACCUMULATION OF $1 PER PERIOD	SINKING FUND FACTOR	PRESENT VALUE REVERSION OF $1	PRESENT VALUE ORD. ANNUITY $1 PER PERIOD	INSTALMENT TO AMORTIZE $1

YEARS

1	1.075000	1.000000	1.000000	0.930233	0.930233	1.075000
2	1.155625	2.075000	0.481928	0.865333	1.795565	0.556928
3	1.242297	3.230625	0.309538	0.804961	2.600526	0.384538
4	1.335469	4.472922	0.223568	0.748801	3.349326	0.298568
5	1.435629	5.808391	0.172165	0.696559	4.045885	0.247165
6	1.543302	7.244020	0.138045	0.647962	4.693846	0.213045
7	1.659049	8.787322	0.113800	0.602755	5.296601	0.188800
8	1.783478	10.446371	0.095727	0.560702	5.857304	0.170727
9	1.917239	12.229849	0.081767	0.521583	6.378887	0.156767
10	2.061032	14.147087	0.070686	0.485194	6.864081	0.145686
11	2.215609	16.208119	0.061697	0.451343	7.315424	0.136697
12	2.381780	18.423728	0.054278	0.419854	7.735278	0.129278
13	2.560413	20.805508	0.048064	0.390562	8.125840	0.123064
14	2.752444	23.365921	0.042797	0.363313	8.489154	0.117797
15	2.958877	26.118365	0.038287	0.337966	8.827120	0.113287
16	3.180793	29.077242	0.034391	0.314387	9.141507	0.109391
17	3.419353	32.258035	0.031000	0.292453	9.433960	0.106000
18	3.675804	35.677388	0.028029	0.272049	9.706009	0.103029
19	3.951489	39.353192	0.025411	0.253069	9.959078	0.100411
20	4.247851	43.304681	0.023092	0.235413	10.194491	0.098092
21	4.566440	47.552532	0.021029	0.218989	10.413480	0.096029
22	4.908923	52.118972	0.019187	0.203711	10.617191	0.094187
23	5.277092	57.027895	0.017535	0.189498	10.806689	0.092535
24	5.672874	62.304987	0.016050	0.176277	10.982967	0.091050
25	6.098340	67.977862	0.014711	0.163979	11.146946	0.089711
26	6.555715	74.076201	0.013500	0.152539	11.299485	0.088500
27	7.047394	80.631916	0.012402	0.141896	11.441381	0.087402
28	7.575948	87.679310	0.011405	0.131997	11.573378	0.086405
29	8.144144	95.255258	0.010498	0.122788	11.696165	0.085498
30	8.754955	103.399403	0.009671	0.114221	11.810386	0.084671
31	9.411577	112.154358	0.008916	0.106252	11.916638	0.083916
32	10.117445	121.565935	0.008226	0.098839	12.015478	0.083226
33	10.876253	131.683380	0.007594	0.091943	12.107421	0.082594
34	11.691972	142.559633	0.007015	0.085529	12.192950	0.082015
35	12.568870	154.251606	0.006483	0.079562	12.272511	0.081483
36	13.511536	166.820476	0.005994	0.074011	12.346522	0.080994
37	14.524901	180.332012	0.005545	0.068847	12.415370	0.080545
38	15.614268	194.856913	0.005132	0.064044	12.479414	0.080132
39	16.785339	210.471181	0.004751	0.059576	12.538989	0.079751
40	18.044239	227.256520	0.004400	0.055419	12.594409	0.079400
41	19.397557	245.300759	0.004077	0.051553	12.645962	0.079077
42	20.852374	264.698315	0.003778	0.047956	12.693918	0.078778
43	22.416302	285.550689	0.003502	0.044610	12.738528	0.078502
44	24.097524	307.966991	0.003247	0.041498	12.780026	0.078247
45	25.904839	332.064515	0.003011	0.038603	12.818629	0.078011
46	27.847702	357.969354	0.002794	0.035910	12.854539	0.077794
47	29.936279	385.817055	0.002592	0.033404	12.887943	0.077592
48	32.181500	415.753334	0.002405	0.031074	12.919017	0.077405
49	34.595113	447.934835	0.002232	0.028906	12.947922	0.077232
50	37.189746	482.529947	0.002072	0.026889	12.974812	0.077072

8.00%   MONTHLY COMPOUND INTEREST TABLES   8.00%
                              EFFECTIVE RATE 0.667

	1 AMOUNT OF $1 AT COMPOUND INTEREST	2 ACCUMULATION OF $1 PER PERIOD	3 SINKING FUND FACTOR	4 PRESENT VALUE REVERSION OF $1	5 PRESENT VALUE ORD. ANNUITY $1 PER PERIOD	6 INSTALMENT TO AMORTIZE $1	
MONTHS							
1	1.006667	1.000000	1.000000	0.993377	0.993377	1.006667	
2	1.013378	2.006667	0.498339	0.986799	1.980176	0.505006	
3	1.020134	3.020044	0.331121	0.980264	2.960440	0.337788	
4	1.026935	4.040178	0.247514	0.973772	3.934212	0.254181	
5	1.033781	5.067113	0.197351	0.967323	4.901535	0.204018	
6	1.040673	6.100893	0.163910	0.960917	5.862452	0.170577	
7	1.047610	7.141566	0.140025	0.954553	6.817005	0.146692	
8	1.054595	8.189176	0.122112	0.948232	7.765237	0.128779	
9	1.061625	9.243771	0.108181	0.941952	8.707189	0.114848	
10	1.068703	10.305396	0.097037	0.935714	9.642903	0.103703	
11	1.075827	11.374099	0.087919	0.929517	10.572420	0.094586	
12	1.083000	12.449926	0.080322	0.923361	11.495782	0.086988	

YEARS							MONTHS
1	1.083000	12.449926	0.080322	0.923361	11.495782	0.086988	12
2	1.172888	25.933190	0.038561	0.852596	22.110544	0.045227	24
3	1.270237	40.535558	0.024670	0.787255	31.911806	0.031336	36
4	1.375666	56.349915	0.017746	0.726921	40.961913	0.024413	48
5	1.489846	73.476856	0.013610	0.671210	49.318433	0.020276	60
6	1.613502	92.025325	0.010867	0.619770	57.034522	0.017533	72
7	1.747422	112.113308	0.008920	0.572272	64.159261	0.015586	84
8	1.892457	133.868583	0.007470	0.528414	70.737970	0.014137	96
9	2.049530	157.429535	0.006352	0.487917	76.812497	0.013019	108
10	2.219640	182.946035	0.005466	0.450523	82.421481	0.012133	120
11	2.403869	210.580392	0.004749	0.415996	87.600600	0.011415	132
12	2.603389	240.508387	0.004158	0.384115	92.382800	0.010825	144
13	2.819469	272.920390	0.003664	0.354677	96.798498	0.010331	156
14	3.053484	308.022574	0.003247	0.327495	100.875784	0.009913	168
15	3.306921	346.038222	0.002890	0.302396	104.640592	0.009557	180
16	3.581394	387.209149	0.002583	0.279221	108.116871	0.009249	192
17	3.878648	431.797244	0.002316	0.257822	111.326733	0.008983	204
18	4.200574	480.086128	0.002083	0.238063	114.290596	0.008750	216
19	4.549220	532.382966	0.001878	0.219818	117.027313	0.008545	228
20	4.926803	589.020416	0.001698	0.202971	119.554292	0.008364	240
21	5.335725	650.358746	0.001538	0.187416	121.887606	0.008204	252
22	5.778588	716.788127	0.001395	0.173053	124.042099	0.008062	264
23	6.258207	788.731114	0.001268	0.159790	126.031475	0.007935	276
24	6.777636	866.645333	0.001154	0.147544	127.868388	0.007821	288
25	7.340176	951.026395	0.001051	0.136237	129.564523	0.007718	300
26	7.949407	1042.411042	0.000959	0.125796	131.130668	0.007626	312
27	8.609204	1141.380571	0.000876	0.116155	132.576786	0.007543	324
28	9.323763	1248.564521	0.000801	0.107253	133.912076	0.007468	336
29	10.097631	1364.644687	0.000733	0.099033	135.145031	0.007399	348
30	10.935730	1490.359449	0.000671	0.091443	136.283494	0.007338	360
31	11.843390	1626.508474	0.000615	0.084435	137.334707	0.007281	372
32	12.826385	1773.957801	0.000564	0.077964	138.305357	0.007230	384
33	13.890969	1933.645350	0.000517	0.071989	139.201617	0.007184	396
34	15.043913	2106.586886	0.000475	0.066472	140.029190	0.007141	408
35	16.292550	2293.882485	0.000436	0.061378	140.793338	0.007103	420
36	17.644824	2496.723526	0.000401	0.056674	141.498923	0.007067	432
37	19.109335	2716.400273	0.000368	0.052330	142.150433	0.007035	444
38	20.695401	2954.310082	0.000338	0.048320	142.752013	0.007005	456
39	22.413109	3211.966288	0.000311	0.044617	143.307488	0.006978	468
40	24.273386	3491.007831	0.000286	0.041197	143.820392	0.006953	480

8.00%   ANNUAL COMPOUND INTEREST TABLES   8.00%
                                  EFFECTIVE RATE   8.00

	1 AMOUNT OF $1 AT COMPOUND INTEREST	2 ACCUMULATION OF $1 PER PERIOD	3 SINKING FUND FACTOR	4 PRESENT VALUE REVERSION OF $1	5 PRESENT VALUE ORD. ANNUITY $1 PER PERIOD	6 INSTALMENT TO AMORTIZE $1
YEARS						
1	1.080000	1.000000	1.000000	0.925926	0.925926	1.080000
2	1.166400	2.080000	0.480769	0.857339	1.783265	0.560769
3	1.259712	3.246400	0.308034	0.793832	2.577097	0.388034
4	1.360489	4.506112	0.221921	0.735030	3.312127	0.301921
5	1.469328	5.866601	0.170456	0.680583	3.992710	0.250456
6	1.586874	7.335929	0.136315	0.630170	4.622880	0.216315
7	1.713824	8.922803	0.112072	0.583490	5.206370	0.192072
8	1.850930	10.636628	0.094015	0.540269	5.746639	0.174015
9	1.999005	12.487558	0.080080	0.500249	6.246888	0.160080
10	2.158925	14.486562	0.069029	0.463193	6.710081	0.149029
11	2.331639	16.645487	0.060076	0.428883	7.138964	0.140076
12	2.518170	18.977126	0.052695	0.397114	7.536078	0.132695
13	2.719624	21.495297	0.046522	0.367698	7.903776	0.126522
14	2.937194	24.214920	0.041297	0.340461	8.244237	0.121297
15	3.172169	27.152114	0.036830	0.315242	8.559479	0.116830
16	3.425943	30.324283	0.032977	0.291890	8.851369	0.112977
17	3.700018	33.750226	0.029629	0.270269	9.121638	0.109629
18	3.996019	37.450244	0.026702	0.250249	9.371887	0.106702
19	4.315701	41.446263	0.024128	0.231712	9.603599	0.104128
20	4.660957	45.761964	0.021852	0.214548	9.818147	0.101852
21	5.033834	50.422921	0.019832	0.198656	10.016803	0.099832
22	5.436540	55.456755	0.018032	0.183941	10.200744	0.098032
23	5.871464	60.893296	0.016422	0.170315	10.371059	0.096422
24	6.341181	66.764759	0.014978	0.157699	10.528758	0.094978
25	6.848475	73.105940	0.013679	0.146018	10.674776	0.093679
26	7.396353	79.954415	0.012507	0.135202	10.809978	0.092507
27	7.988061	87.350768	0.011448	0.125187	10.935165	0.091448
28	8.627106	95.338830	0.010489	0.115914	11.051078	0.090489
29	9.317275	103.965936	0.009619	0.107328	11.158406	0.089619
30	10.062657	113.283211	0.008827	0.099377	11.257783	0.088827
31	10.867669	123.345868	0.008107	0.092016	11.349799	0.088107
32	11.737083	134.213537	0.007451	0.085200	11.434999	0.087451
33	12.676050	145.950620	0.006852	0.078889	11.513888	0.086852
34	13.690134	158.626670	0.006304	0.073045	11.586934	0.086304
35	14.785344	172.316804	0.005803	0.067635	11.654568	0.085803
36	15.968172	187.102148	0.005345	0.062625	11.717193	0.085345
37	17.245626	203.070320	0.004924	0.057986	11.775179	0.084924
38	18.625276	220.315945	0.004539	0.053690	11.828869	0.084539
39	20.115298	238.941221	0.004185	0.049713	11.878582	0.084185
40	21.724521	259.056519	0.003860	0.046031	11.924613	0.083860
41	23.462483	280.781040	0.003561	0.042621	11.967235	0.083561
42	25.339482	304.243523	0.003287	0.039464	12.006699	0.083287
43	27.366640	329.583005	0.003034	0.036541	12.043240	0.083034
44	29.555972	356.949646	0.002802	0.033834	12.077074	0.082802
45	31.920449	386.505617	0.002587	0.031328	12.108402	0.082587
46	34.474085	418.426067	0.002390	0.029007	12.137409	0.082390
47	37.232012	452.900152	0.002208	0.026859	12.164267	0.082208
48	40.210573	490.132164	0.002040	0.024869	12.189136	0.082040
49	43.427419	530.342737	0.001886	0.023027	12.212163	0.081886
50	46.901613	573.770156	0.001743	0.021321	12.233485	0.081743

8.50%   MONTHLY COMPOUND INTEREST TABLES   8.50%
                                 EFFECTIVE RATE 0.708

	1 AMOUNT OF $1 AT COMPOUND INTEREST	2 ACCUMULATION OF $1 PER PERIOD	3 SINKING FUND FACTOR	4 PRESENT VALUE REVERSION OF $1	5 PRESENT VALUE ORD. ANNUITY $1 PER PERIOD	6 INSTALMENT TO AMORTIZE $1	
MONTHS							
1	1.007083	1.000000	1.000000	0.992966	0.992966	1.007083	
2	1.014217	2.007083	0.498235	0.985982	1.978949	0.505319	
3	1.021401	3.021300	0.330983	0.979048	2.957996	0.338067	
4	1.028636	4.042701	0.247359	0.972161	3.930158	0.254443	
5	1.035922	5.071337	0.197187	0.965324	4.895482	0.204270	
6	1.043260	6.107259	0.163740	0.958534	5.854016	0.170823	
7	1.050650	7.150519	0.139850	0.951792	6.805808	0.146933	
8	1.058092	8.201168	0.121934	0.945098	7.750906	0.129017	
9	1.065586	9.259260	0.108000	0.938450	8.689356	0.115083	
10	1.073134	10.324846	0.096854	0.931850	9.621206	0.103937	
11	1.080736	11.397980	0.087735	0.925296	10.546501	0.094818	
12	1.088391	12.478716	0.080136	0.918788	11.465289	0.087220	
YEARS							**MONTHS**
1	1.088391	12.478716	0.080136	0.918788	11.465289	0.087220	12
2	1.184595	26.060437	0.038372	0.844171	21.999453	0.045456	24
3	1.289302	40.842659	0.024484	0.775613	31.678112	0.031568	36
4	1.403265	56.931495	0.017565	0.712624	40.570744	0.024648	48
5	1.527301	74.442437	0.013433	0.654750	48.741183	0.020517	60
6	1.662300	93.501188	0.010695	0.601576	56.248080	0.017778	72
7	1.809232	114.244559	0.008753	0.552721	63.145324	0.015836	84
8	1.969152	136.821455	0.007309	0.507833	69.482425	0.014392	96
9	2.143207	161.393943	0.006196	0.466590	75.304875	0.013279	108
10	2.332647	188.138416	0.005315	0.428698	80.654470	0.012399	120
11	2.538832	217.246858	0.004603	0.393882	85.569611	0.011686	132
12	2.763242	248.928220	0.004017	0.361894	90.085581	0.011101	144
13	3.007487	283.409927	0.003528	0.332504	94.234798	0.010612	156
14	3.273321	320.939504	0.003116	0.305500	98.047046	0.010199	168
15	3.562653	361.786353	0.002764	0.280690	101.549693	0.009847	180
16	3.877559	406.243693	0.002462	0.257894	104.767881	0.009545	192
17	4.220300	454.630657	0.002200	0.236950	107.724713	0.009283	204
18	4.593337	507.294589	0.001971	0.217707	110.441412	0.009055	216
19	4.999346	564.613533	0.001771	0.200026	112.937482	0.008854	228
20	5.441243	626.998951	0.001595	0.183782	115.230840	0.008678	240
21	5.922199	694.898672	0.001439	0.168856	117.337948	0.008522	252
22	6.445667	768.800112	0.001301	0.155143	119.273933	0.008384	264
23	7.015406	849.233766	0.001178	0.142543	121.052692	0.008261	276
24	7.635504	936.777024	0.001067	0.130967	122.686994	0.008151	288
25	8.310413	1032.058310	0.000969	0.120331	124.188570	0.008052	300
26	9.044978	1135.761595	0.000880	0.110559	125.568199	0.007964	312
27	9.844472	1248.631307	0.000801	0.101580	126.835785	0.007884	324
28	10.714634	1371.477676	0.000729	0.093330	128.000428	0.007812	336
29	11.661710	1505.182546	0.000664	0.085751	129.070487	0.007748	348
30	12.692499	1650.705711	0.000606	0.078787	130.053643	0.007689	360
31	13.814400	1809.091800	0.000553	0.072388	130.956956	0.007636	372
32	15.035468	1981.477780	0.000505	0.066509	131.786908	0.007588	384
33	16.364466	2169.101112	0.000461	0.061108	132.549457	0.007544	396
34	17.810936	2373.308640	0.000421	0.056145	133.250078	0.007505	408
35	19.385261	2595.566257	0.000385	0.051586	133.893800	0.007469	420
36	21.098742	2837.469426	0.000352	0.047396	134.485244	0.007436	432
37	22.963679	3100.754635	0.000323	0.043547	135.028655	0.007406	444
38	24.993459	3387.311862	0.000295	0.040010	135.527934	0.007379	456
39	27.202654	3699.198142	0.000270	0.036761	135.986665	0.007354	468
40	29.607121	4038.652333	0.000248	0.033776	136.408142	0.007331	480

8.50%   ANNUAL COMPOUND INTEREST TABLES   8.50%
                              EFFECTIVE RATE   8.50

---

	1 AMOUNT OF $1 AT COMPOUND INTEREST	2 ACCUMULATION OF $1 PER PERIOD	3 SINKING FUND FACTOR	4 PRESENT VALUE REVERSION OF $1	5 PRESENT VALUE ORD. ANNUITY $1 PER PERIOD	6 INSTALMENT TO AMORTIZE $1
YEARS						
1	1.085000	1.000000	1.000000	0.921659	0.921659	1.085000
2	1.177225	2.085000	0.479616	0.849455	1.771114	0.564616
3	1.277289	3.262225	0.306539	0.782908	2.554022	0.391539
4	1.385859	4.539514	0.220288	0.721574	3.275597	0.305288
5	1.503657	5.925373	0.168766	0.665045	3.940642	0.253766
6	1.631468	7.429030	0.134607	0.612945	4.553587	0.219607
7	1.770142	9.060497	0.110369	0.564926	5.118514	0.195369
8	1.920604	10.830639	0.092331	0.520669	5.639183	0.177331
9	2.083856	12.751244	0.078424	0.479880	6.119063	0.163424
10	2.260983	14.835099	0.067408	0.442285	6.561348	0.152408
11	2.453167	17.096083	0.058493	C.407636	6.968984	0.143493
12	2.661686	19.549250	0.051153	0.375702	7.344686	0.136153
13	2.887930	22.210936	0.045023	0.346269	7.690955	0.130023
14	3.133404	25.098866	0.039842	0.319142	8.010097	0.124842
15	3.399743	28.232269	0.035420	0.294140	8.304237	0.120420
16	3.688721	31.632012	0.031614	0.271097	8.575333	0.116614
17	4.002262	35.320733	0.028312	0.249859	8.825192	0.113312
18	4.342455	39.322995	0.025430	0.230285	9.055476	0.110430
19	4.711563	43.665450	0.022901	0.212244	9.267720	0.107901
20	5.112046	48.377013	0.020671	0.195616	9.463337	0.105671
21	5.546570	53.489059	0.018695	0.180292	9.643628	0.103695
22	6.018028	59.035629	0.016939	0.166167	9.809796	0.101939
23	6.529561	65.053658	0.015372	0.153150	9.962945	0.100372
24	7.084574	71.583219	0.013970	0.141152	10.104097	0.098970
25	7.686762	78.667792	0.012712	0.130094	10.234191	0.097712
26	8.340137	86.354555	0.011580	0.119902	10.354093	0.096580
27	9.049049	94.694692	0.010560	0.110509	10.464602	0.095560
28	9.818218	103.743741	0.009639	0.101851	10.566453	0.094639
29	10.652766	113.561959	0.008806	0.093872	10.660326	0.093806
30	11.558252	124.214725	0.008051	0.086518	10.746844	0.093051
31	12.540703	135.772977	0.007365	0.079740	10.826584	0.092365
32	13.606663	148.313680	0.006742	0.073493	10.900078	0.091742
33	14.763229	161.920343	0.006176	0.067736	10.967813	0.091176
34	16.018104	176.683572	0.005660	0.062429	11.030243	0.090660
35	17.379642	192.701675	0.005189	0.057539	11.087781	0.090189
36	18.856912	210.081318	0.004760	0.053031	11.140812	0.089760
37	20.459750	228.938230	0.004368	0.048876	11.189689	0.089368
38	22.198828	249.397979	0.004010	0.045047	11.234736	0.089010
39	24.085729	271.596808	0.003682	0.041518	11.276255	0.088682
40	26.133016	295.682536	0.003382	0.038266	11.314520	0.088382
41	28.354322	321.815552	0.003107	0.035268	11.349788	0.088107
42	30.764439	350.169874	0.002856	0.032505	11.382293	0.087856
43	33.379417	380.934313	0.002625	0.029959	11.412252	0.087625
44	36.216667	414.313730	0.002414	0.027612	11.439864	0.087414
45	39.295084	450.530397	0.002220	0.025448	11.465312	0.087220
46	42.635166	489.825480	0.002042	0.023455	11.488767	0.087042
47	46.259155	532.460646	0.001878	0.021617	11.510384	0.086878
48	50.191183	578.719801	0.001728	0.019924	11.530308	0.086728
49	54.457434	628.910984	0.001590	0.018363	11.548671	0.086590
50	59.086316	683.368418	0.001463	0.016924	11.565595	0.086463

MONTHLY COMPOUND INTEREST TABLES
                                  EFFECTIVE RATE 0.750

	1 AMOUNT OF $1 AT COMPOUND INTEREST	2 ACCUMULATION OF $1 PER PERIOD	3 SINKING FUND FACTOR	4 PRESENT VALUE REVERSION OF $1	5 PRESENT VALUE ORD. ANNUITY $1 PER PERIOD	6 INSTALMENT TO AMORTIZE $1
MONTHS						
1	1.007500	1.000000	1.000000	0.992556	0.992556	1.007500
2	1.015056	2.007500	0.498132	0.985167	1.977723	0.505632
3	1.022669	3.022556	0.330846	0.977833	2.955556	0.338346
4	1.030339	4.045225	0.247205	0.970554	3.926110	0.254705
5	1.038067	5.075565	0.197022	0.963329	4.889440	0.204522
6	1.045852	6.113631	0.163569	0.956158	5.845598	0.171069
7	1.053696	7.159484	0.139675	0.949040	6.794638	0.147175
8	1.061599	8.213180	0.121756	0.941975	7.736613	0.129256
9	1.069561	9.274779	0.107819	0.934963	8.671576	0.115319
10	1.077583	10.344339	0.096671	0.928003	9.599580	0.104171
11	1.085664	11.421922	0.087551	0.921095	10.520675	0.095051
12	1.093807	12.507586	0.079951	0.914238	11.434913	0.087451

YEARS							**MONTHS**
1	1.093807	12.507586	0.079951	0.914238	11.434913	0.087451	12
2	1.196414	26.188471	0.038185	0.835831	21.889146	0.045685	24
3	1.308645	41.152716	0.024300	0.764149	31.446805	0.031800	36
4	1.431405	57.520711	0.017385	0.698614	40.184782	0.024885	48
5	1.565681	75.424137	0.013258	0.638700	48.173374	0.020758	60
6	1.712553	95.007028	0.010526	0.583924	55.476849	0.018026	72
7	1.873202	116.426928	0.008589	0.533845	62.153965	0.016089	84
8	2.048921	139.856164	0.007150	0.488062	68.258439	0.014650	96
9	2.241124	165.483223	0.006043	0.446205	73.839382	0.013543	108
10	2.451357	193.514277	0.005168	0.407937	78.941693	0.012668	120
11	2.681311	224.174837	0.004461	0.372952	83.606420	0.011961	132
12	2.932837	257.711570	0.003880	0.340967	87.871092	0.011380	144
13	3.207957	294.394279	0.003397	0.311725	91.770018	0.010897	156
14	3.508886	334.518079	0.002989	0.284991	95.334564	0.010489	168
15	3.838043	378.405769	0.002643	0.260549	98.593409	0.010143	180
16	4.198078	426.410427	0.002345	0.238204	101.572769	0.009845	192
17	4.591887	478.918252	0.002088	0.217775	104.296613	0.009588	204
18	5.022638	536.351674	0.001864	0.199099	106.786856	0.009364	216
19	5.493796	599.172747	0.001669	0.182024	109.063531	0.009169	228
20	6.009152	667.886870	0.001497	0.166413	111.144954	0.008997	240
21	6.572851	743.046852	0.001346	0.152141	113.047870	0.008846	252
22	7.189430	825.257358	0.001212	0.139093	114.787589	0.008712	264
23	7.863848	915.179777	0.001093	0.127164	116.378106	0.008593	276
24	8.601532	1013.537539	0.000987	0.116258	117.832218	0.008487	288
25	9.408415	1121.121937	0.000892	0.106288	119.161622	0.008392	300
26	10.290989	1238.798494	0.000807	0.097172	120.377014	0.008307	312
27	11.256354	1367.513924	0.000731	0.088839	121.488172	0.008231	324
28	12.312278	1508.303750	0.000663	0.081220	122.504035	0.008163	336
29	13.467255	1662.300631	0.000602	0.074254	123.432776	0.008102	348
30	14.730576	1830.743483	0.000546	0.067886	124.281866	0.008046	360
31	16.112406	2014.987436	0.000496	0.062064	125.058136	0.007996	372
32	17.623861	2216.514743	0.000451	0.056741	125.767832	0.007951	384
33	19.277100	2436.946701	0.000410	0.051875	126.416664	0.007910	396
34	21.085425	2678.056697	0.000373	0.047426	127.009850	0.007873	408
35	23.063384	2941.784473	0.000340	0.043359	127.552164	0.007840	420
36	25.226888	3230.251735	0.000310	0.039640	128.047967	0.007810	432
37	27.593344	3545.779215	0.000282	0.036241	128.501250	0.007782	444
38	30.181790	3890.905350	0.000257	0.033133	128.915659	0.007757	456
39	33.013050	4268.406696	0.000234	0.030291	129.294526	0.007734	468
40	36.109902	4681.320272	0.000214	0.027693	129.640902	0.007714	480

9.00%   ANNUAL COMPOUND INTEREST TABLES   9.00%
                              EFFECTIVE RATE 9.00

	1 AMOUNT OF $1 AT COMPOUND INTEREST	2 ACCUMULATION OF $1 PER PERIOD	3 SINKING FUND FACTOR	4 PRESENT VALUE REVERSION OF $1	5 PRESENT VALUE ORD. ANNUITY $1 PER PERIOD	6 INSTALMENT TO AMORTIZE $1
YEARS						
1	1.090000	1.000000	1.000000	0.917431	0.917431	1.090000
2	1.188100	2.090000	0.478469	0.841680	1.759111	0.568469
3	1.295029	3.278100	0.305055	0.772183	2.531295	0.395055
4	1.411582	4.573129	0.218669	0.708425	3.239720	0.308669
5	1.538624	5.984711	0.167092	0.649931	3.889651	0.257092
6	1.677100	7.523335	0.132920	0.596267	4.485919	0.222920
7	1.828039	9.200435	0.108691	0.547034	5.032953	0.198691
8	1.992563	11.028474	0.090674	0.501866	5.534819	0.180674
9	2.171893	13.021036	0.076799	0.460428	5.995247	0.166799
10	2.367364	15.192930	0.065820	0.422411	6.417658	0.155820
11	2.580426	17.560293	0.056947	0.387533	6.805191	0.146947
12	2.812665	20.140720	0.049651	0.355535	7.160725	0.139651
13	3.065805	22.953385	0.043567	0.326179	7.486904	0.133567
14	3.341727	26.019189	0.038433	0.299246	7.786150	0.128433
15	3.642482	29.360916	0.034059	0.274538	8.060688	0.124059
16	3.970306	33.003399	0.030300	0.251870	8.312558	0.120300
17	4.327633	36.973705	0.027046	0.231073	8.543631	0.117046
18	4.717120	41.301338	0.024212	0.211994	8.755625	0.114212
19	5.141661	46.018458	0.021730	0.194490	8.950115	0.111730
20	5.604411	51.160120	0.019546	0.178431	9.128546	0.109546
21	6.108808	56.764530	0.017617	0.163698	9.292244	0.107617
22	6.658600	62.873338	0.015905	0.150182	9.442425	0.105905
23	7.257874	69.531939	0.014382	0.137781	9.580207	0.104382
24	7.911083	76.789813	0.013023	0.126405	9.706612	0.103023
25	8.623081	84.700896	0.011806	0.115968	9.822580	0.101806
26	9.399158	93.323977	0.010715	0.106393	9.928972	0.100715
27	10.245082	102.723135	0.009735	0.097608	10.026580	0.099735
28	11.167140	112.968217	0.008852	0.089548	10.116128	0.098852
29	12.172182	124.135356	0.008056	0.082155	10.198283	0.098056
30	13.267678	136.307539	0.007336	0.075371	10.273654	0.097336
31	14.461770	149.575217	0.006686	0.069148	10.342802	0.096686
32	15.763329	164.036987	0.006096	0.063438	10.406240	0.096096
33	17.182028	179.800315	0.005562	0.058200	10.464441	0.095562
34	18.728411	196.982344	0.005077	0.053395	10.517835	0.095077
35	20.413968	215.710755	0.004636	0.048986	10.566821	0.094636
36	22.251225	236.124723	0.004235	0.044941	10.611763	0.094235
37	24.253835	258.375948	0.003870	0.041231	10.652993	0.093870
38	26.436680	282.629783	0.003538	0.037826	10.690820	0.093538
39	28.815982	309.066463	0.003236	0.034703	10.725523	0.093236
40	31.409420	337.882445	0.002960	0.031838	10.757360	0.092960
41	34.236268	369.291865	0.002708	0.029209	10.786569	0.092708
42	37.317532	403.528133	0.002478	0.026797	10.813366	0.092478
43	40.676110	440.845665	0.002268	0.024584	10.837950	0.092268
44	44.336960	481.521775	0.002077	0.022555	10.860505	0.092077
45	48.327286	525.858734	0.001902	0.020692	10.881197	0.091902
46	52.676742	574.186021	0.001742	0.018984	10.900181	0.091742
47	57.417649	626.862762	0.001595	0.017416	10.917597	0.091595
48	62.585237	684.280411	0.001461	0.015978	10.933575	0.091461
49	68.217908	746.865648	0.001339	0.014659	10.948234	0.091339
50	74.357520	815.083556	0.001227	0.013449	10.961683	0.091227

9.50%   MONTHLY COMPOUND INTEREST TABLES   9.50%
                                     EFFECTIVE RATE 0.792

	1	2	3	4	5	6
	AMOUNT OF $1 AT COMPOUND INTEREST	ACCUMULATION OF $1 PER PERIOD	SINKING FUND FACTOR	PRESENT VALUE REVERSION OF $1	PRESENT VALUE ORD. ANNUITY $1 PER PERIOD	INSTALMENT TO AMORTIZE $1
MONTHS						
1	1.007917	1.000000	1.000000	0.992146	0.992146	1.007917
2	1.015896	2.007917	0.498029	0.984353	1.976498	0.505945
3	1.023939	3.023813	0.330708	0.976621	2.953119	0.338625
4	1.032045	4.047751	0.247051	0.968950	3.922070	0.254967
5	1.040215	5.079796	0.196858	0.961340	4.883409	0.204775
6	1.048450	6.120011	0.163398	0.953789	5.837198	0.171315
7	1.056750	7.168461	0.139500	0.946297	6.783496	0.147417
8	1.065116	8.225211	0.121577	0.938865	7.722360	0.129494
9	1.073548	9.290328	0.107639	0.931490	8.653851	0.115555
10	1.082047	10.363876	0.096489	0.924174	9.578024	0.104406
11	1.090614	11.445923	0.087367	0.916915	10.494940	0.095284
12	1.099248	12.536537	0.079767	0.909713	11.404653	0.087684

YEARS							**MONTHS**
1	1.099248	12.536537	0.079767	0.909713	11.404653	0.087684	12
2	1.208345	26.317295	0.037998	0.827578	21.779615	0.045914	24
3	1.328271	41.465760	0.024116	0.752859	31.217856	0.032033	36
4	1.460098	58.117673	0.017206	0.684885	39.803947	0.025123	48
5	1.605009	76.422249	0.013085	0.623049	47.614827	0.021002	60
6	1.764303	96.543509	0.010358	0.566796	54.720488	0.018275	72
7	1.939406	118.661756	0.008427	0.515622	61.184601	0.016344	84
8	2.131887	142.975186	0.006994	0.469068	67.065090	0.014911	96
9	2.343472	169.701665	0.005893	0.426717	72.414648	0.013809	108
10	2.576055	199.080682	0.005023	0.388190	77.281211	0.012940	120
11	2.831723	231.375495	0.004322	0.353142	81.708388	0.012239	132
12	3.112764	266.875491	0.003747	0.321258	85.735849	0.011664	144
13	3.421699	305.898776	0.003269	0.292253	89.399684	0.011186	156
14	3.761294	348.795027	0.002867	0.265866	92.732722	0.010784	168
15	4.134593	395.948628	0.002526	0.241862	95.764831	0.010442	180
16	4.544942	447.782110	0.002233	0.220025	98.523180	0.010150	192
17	4.996016	504.759939	0.001981	0.200159	101.032487	0.009898	204
18	5.491859	567.392681	0.001762	0.182088	103.315236	0.009679	216
19	6.036912	636.241570	0.001572	0.165648	105.391883	0.009488	228
20	6.636061	711.923546	0.001405	0.150692	107.281037	0.009321	240
21	7.294674	795.116775	0.001258	0.137086	108.999624	0.009174	252
22	8.018653	886.566731	0.001128	0.124709	110.563046	0.009045	264
23	8.814485	987.092874	0.001013	0.113450	111.985311	0.008930	276
24	9.689302	1097.595994	0.000911	0.103207	113.279165	0.008828	288
25	10.650941	1219.066282	0.000820	0.093888	114.456200	0.008737	300
26	11.708022	1352.592202	0.000739	0.085412	115.526965	0.008656	312
27	12.870014	1499.370247	0.000667	0.077700	116.501054	0.008584	324
28	14.147332	1660.715658	0.000602	0.070685	117.387195	0.008519	336
29	15.551421	1838.074212	0.000544	0.064303	118.193330	0.008461	348
30	17.094862	2033.035174	0.000492	0.058497	118.926681	0.008409	360
31	18.791486	2247.345541	0.000445	0.053216	119.593820	0.008362	372
32	20.656495	2482.925693	0.000403	0.048411	120.200725	0.008319	384
33	22.706602	2741.886606	0.000365	0.044040	120.752835	0.008281	396
34	24.960178	3026.548765	0.000330	0.040064	121.255097	0.008247	408
35	27.437415	3339.462955	0.000299	0.036447	121.712011	0.008216	420
36	30.160512	3683.433122	0.000271	0.033156	122.127671	0.008188	432
37	33.153870	4061.541498	0.000246	0.030162	122.505803	0.008163	444
38	36.444312	4477.176216	0.000223	0.027439	122.849795	0.008140	456
39	40.061322	4934.061676	0.000203	0.024962	123.162729	0.008119	468
40	44.037311	5436.291914	0.000184	0.022708	123.447408	0.008101	480

9.50%   ANNUAL COMPOUND INTEREST TABLES   9.50%
                        EFFECTIVE RATE 9.50

	1	2	3	4	5	6
	AMOUNT OF $1 AT COMPOUND INTEREST	ACCUMULATION OF $1 PER PERIOD	SINKING FUND FACTOR	PRESENT VALUE REVERSION OF $1	PRESENT VALUE ORD. ANNUITY $1 PER PERIOD	INSTALMENT TO AMORTIZE $1
YEARS						
1	1.095000	1.000000	1.000000	0.913242	0.913242	1.095000
2	1.199025	2.095000	0.477327	0.834011	1.747253	0.572327
3	1.312932	3.294025	0.303580	0.761654	2.508907	0.398580
4	1.437661	4.606957	0.217063	0.695574	3.204481	0.312063
5	1.574239	6.044618	0.165436	0.635228	3.839709	0.260436
6	1.723791	7.618857	0.131253	0.580117	4.419825	0.226253
7	1.887552	9.342648	0.107036	0.529787	4.949612	0.202036
8	2.066869	11.230200	0.089046	0.483824	5.433436	0.184046
9	2.263222	13.297069	0.075205	0.441848	5.875284	0.170205
10	2.478228	15.560291	0.064266	0.403514	6.278798	0.159266
11	2.713659	18.038518	0.055437	0.368506	6.647304	0.150437
12	2.971457	20.752178	0.048188	0.336535	6.983839	0.143188
13	3.253745	23.723634	0.042152	0.307338	7.291178	0.137152
14	3.562851	26.977380	0.037068	0.280674	7.571852	0.132068
15	3.901322	30.540231	0.032744	0.256323	7.828175	0.127744
16	4.271948	34.441553	0.029035	0.234085	8.062260	0.124035
17	4.677783	38.713500	0.025831	0.213777	8.276037	0.120831
18	5.122172	43.391283	0.023046	0.195230	8.471266	0.118046
19	5.608778	48.513454	0.020613	0.178292	8.649558	0.115613
20	6.141612	54.122233	0.018477	0.162824	8.812382	0.113477
21	6.725065	60.263845	0.016594	0.148697	8.961080	0.111594
22	7.363946	66.988910	0.014928	0.135797	9.096876	0.109928
23	8.063521	74.352856	0.013449	0.124015	9.220892	0.108449
24	8.829556	82.416378	0.012134	0.113256	9.334148	0.107134
25	9.668364	91.245934	0.010959	0.103430	9.437578	0.105959
26	10.586858	100.914297	0.009909	0.094457	9.532034	0.104909
27	11.592610	111.501156	0.008969	0.086262	9.618296	0.103969
28	12.693908	123.093766	0.008124	0.078778	9.697074	0.103124
29	13.899829	135.787673	0.007364	0.071943	9.769018	0.102364
30	15.220313	149.687502	0.006681	0.065702	9.834719	0.101681
31	16.666242	164.907815	0.006064	0.060002	9.894721	0.101064
32	18.249535	181.574057	0.005507	0.054796	9.949517	0.100507
33	19.983241	199.823593	0.005004	0.050042	9.999559	0.100004
34	21.881649	219.806834	0.004549	0.045700	10.045259	0.099549
35	23.960406	241.688483	0.004138	0.041736	10.086995	0.099138
36	26.236644	265.648889	0.003764	0.038115	10.125109	0.098764
37	28.729126	291.885534	0.003426	0.034808	10.159917	0.098426
38	31.458393	320.614659	0.003119	0.031788	10.191705	0.098119
39	34.446940	352.073052	0.002840	0.029030	10.220735	0.097840
40	37.719399	386.519992	0.002587	0.026512	10.247247	0.097587
41	41.302742	424.239391	0.002357	0.024211	10.271458	0.097357
42	45.226503	465.542133	0.002148	0.022111	10.293569	0.097148
43	49.523020	510.768636	0.001958	0.020193	10.313762	0.096958
44	54.227707	560.291656	0.001785	0.018441	10.332203	0.096785
45	59.379340	614.519364	0.001627	0.016841	10.349043	0.096627
46	65.020377	673.898703	0.001484	0.015380	10.364423	0.096484
47	71.197313	738.919080	0.001353	0.014045	10.378469	0.096353
48	77.961057	810.116393	0.001234	0.012827	10.391296	0.096234
49	85.367358	888.077450	0.001126	0.011714	10.403010	0.096126
50	93.477257	973.444808	0.001027	0.010698	10.413707	0.096027

10.00%   MONTHLY COMPOUND INTEREST TABLES   10.00%
                                     EFFECTIVE RATE 0.833

	1	2	3	4	5	6	
	AMOUNT OF $1	ACCUMULATION	SINKING	PRESENT VALUE	PRESENT VALUE	INSTALMENT	
	AT COMPOUND	OF $1	FUND	REVERSION	ORD. ANNUITY	TO	
	INTEREST	PER PERIOD	FACTOR	OF $1	$1 PER PERIOD	AMORTIZE $1	
MONTHS							
1	1.008333	1.000000	1.000000	0.991736	0.991736	1.008333	
2	1.016736	2.008333	0.497925	0.983539	1.975275	0.506259	
3	1.025209	3.025069	0.330571	0.975411	2.950686	0.338904	
4	1.033752	4.050278	0.246897	0.967350	3.918036	0.255230	
5	1.042367	5.084031	0.196694	0.959355	4.877391	0.205028	
6	1.051053	6.126398	0.163228	0.951427	5.828817	0.171561	
7	1.059812	7.177451	0.139325	0.943563	6.772381	0.147659	
8	1.068644	8.237263	0.121400	0.935765	7.708146	0.129733	
9	1.077549	9.305907	0.107459	0.928032	8.636178	0.115792	
10	1.086529	10.383456	0.096307	0.920362	9.556540	0.104640	
11	1.095583	11.469985	0.087184	0.912756	10.469296	0.095517	
12	1.104713	12.565568	0.079583	0.905212	11.374508	0.087916	
YEARS							**MONTHS**
1	1.104713	12.565568	0.079583	0.905212	11.374508	0.087916	12
2	1.220391	26.446915	0.037812	0.819410	21.670855	0.046145	24
3	1.348182	41.781821	0.023934	0.741740	30.991236	0.032267	36
4	1.489354	58.722492	0.017029	0.671432	39.428160	0.025363	48
5	1.645309	77.437072	0.012914	0.607789	47.065369	0.021247	60
6	1.817594	98.111314	0.010193	0.550178	53.978665	0.018526	72
7	2.007920	120.950418	0.008268	0.498028	60.236667	0.016601	84
8	2.218176	146.181076	0.006841	0.450821	65.901488	0.015174	96
9	2.450448	174.053713	0.005745	0.408089	71.029355	0.014079	108
10	2.707041	204.844979	0.004882	0.369407	75.671163	0.013215	120
11	2.990504	238.860493	0.004187	0.334392	79.872986	0.012520	132
12	3.303649	276.437876	0.003617	0.302696	83.676528	0.011951	144
13	3.649584	317.950102	0.003145	0.274004	87.119542	0.011478	156
14	4.031743	363.809201	0.002749	0.248032	90.236201	0.011082	168
15	4.453920	414.470346	0.002413	0.224521	93.057439	0.010746	180
16	4.920303	470.436376	0.002126	0.203240	95.611259	0.010459	192
17	5.435523	532.262780	0.001879	0.183975	97.923008	0.010212	204
18	6.004693	600.563216	0.001665	0.166536	100.015633	0.009998	216
19	6.633463	676.015601	0.001479	0.150751	101.909902	0.009813	228
20	7.328074	759.368836	0.001317	0.136462	103.624619	0.009650	240
21	8.095419	851.450244	0.001174	0.123527	105.176801	0.009508	252
22	8.943115	953.173779	0.001049	0.111818	106.581856	0.009382	264
23	9.879576	1065.549097	0.000938	0.101219	107.853730	0.009272	276
24	10.914097	1189.691580	0.000841	0.091625	109.005045	0.009174	288
25	12.056945	1326.833403	0.000754	0.082940	110.047230	0.009087	300
26	13.319465	1478.335767	0.000676	0.075078	110.990629	0.009010	312
27	14.714187	1645.702407	0.000608	0.067962	111.844605	0.008941	324
28	16.254954	1830.594523	0.000546	0.061520	112.617635	0.008880	336
29	17.957060	2034.847259	0.000491	0.055688	113.317392	0.008825	348
30	19.837399	2260.487925	0.000442	0.050410	113.950820	0.008776	360
31	21.914634	2509.756117	0.000398	0.045632	114.524207	0.008732	372
32	24.209383	2785.125947	0.000359	0.041306	115.043244	0.008692	384
33	26.744422	3089.330596	0.000324	0.037391	115.513083	0.008657	396
34	29.544912	3425.389448	0.000292	0.033847	115.938387	0.008625	408
35	32.638650	3796.638052	0.000263	0.030639	116.323377	0.008597	420
36	36.056344	4206.761236	0.000238	0.027734	116.671876	0.008571	432
37	39.831914	4659.829677	0.000215	0.025105	116.987340	0.008548	444
38	44.002836	5160.340305	0.000194	0.022726	117.272903	0.008527	456
39	48.610508	5713.260935	0.000175	0.020572	117.531398	0.008508	468
40	53.700663	6324.079581	0.000158	0.018622	117.765391	0.008491	480

10.00%   ANNUAL COMPOUND INTEREST TABLES   10.00%
                      EFFECTIVE RATE 10.00

	1 AMOUNT OF $1 AT COMPOUND INTEREST	2 ACCUMULATION OF $1 PER PERIOD	3 SINKING FUND FACTOR	4 PRESENT VALUE REVERSION OF $1	5 PRESENT VALUE ORD. ANNUITY $1 PER PERIOD	6 INSTALMENT TO AMORTIZE $1
YEARS						
1	1.100000	1.000000	1.000000	0.909091	0.909091	1.100000
2	1.210000	2.100000	0.476190	0.826446	1.735537	0.576190
3	1.331000	3.310000	0.302115	0.751315	2.486852	0.402115
4	1.464100	4.641000	0.215471	0.683013	3.169865	0.315471
5	1.610510	6.105100	0.163797	0.620921	3.790787	0.263797
6	1.771561	7.715610	0.129607	0.564474	4.355261	0.229607
7	1.948717	9.487171	0.105405	0.513158	4.868419	0.205405
8	2.143589	11.435888	0.087444	0.466507	5.334926	0.187444
9	2.357948	13.579477	0.073641	0.424098	5.759024	0.173641
10	2.593742	15.937425	0.062745	0.385543	6.144567	0.162745
11	2.853117	18.531167	0.053963	0.350494	6.495061	0.153963
12	3.138428	21.384284	0.046763	0.318631	6.813692	0.146763
13	3.452271	24.522712	0.040779	0.289664	7.103356	0.140779
14	3.797498	27.974983	0.035746	0.263331	7.366687	0.135746
15	4.177248	31.772482	0.031474	0.239392	7.606080	0.131474
16	4.594973	35.949730	0.027817	0.217629	7.823709	0.127817
17	5.054470	40.544703	0.024664	0.197845	8.021553	0.124664
18	5.559917	45.599173	0.021930	0.179859	8.201412	0.121930
19	6.115909	51.159090	0.019547	0.163508	8.364920	0.119547
20	6.727500	57.274999	0.017460	0.148644	8.513564	0.117460
21	7.400250	64.002499	0.015624	0.135131	8.648694	0.115624
22	8.140275	71.402749	0.014005	0.122846	8.771540	0.114005
23	8.954302	79.543024	0.012572	0.111678	8.883218	0.112572
24	9.849733	88.497327	0.011300	0.101526	8.984744	0.111300
25	10.834706	98.347059	0.010168	0.092296	9.077040	0.110168
26	11.918177	109.181765	0.009159	0.083905	9.160945	0.109159
27	13.109994	121.099942	0.008258	0.076278	9.237223	0.108258
28	14.420994	134.209936	0.007451	0.069343	9.306567	0.107451
29	15.863093	148.630930	0.006728	0.063039	9.369606	0.106728
30	17.449402	164.494023	0.006079	0.057309	9.426914	0.106079
31	19.194342	181.943425	0.005496	0.052099	9.479013	0.105496
32	21.113777	201.137767	0.004972	0.047362	9.526376	0.104972
33	23.225154	222.251544	0.004499	0.043057	9.569432	0.104499
34	25.547670	245.476699	0.004074	0.039143	9.608575	0.104074
35	28.102437	271.024368	0.003690	0.035584	9.644159	0.103690
36	30.912681	299.126805	0.003343	0.032349	9.676508	0.103343
37	34.003949	330.039486	0.003030	0.029408	9.705917	0.103030
38	37.404343	364.043434	0.002747	0.026735	9.732651	0.102747
39	41.144778	401.447778	0.002491	0.024304	9.756956	0.102491
40	45.259256	442.592556	0.002259	0.022095	9.779051	0.102259
41	49.785181	487.851811	0.002050	0.020086	9.799137	0.102050
42	54.763699	537.636992	0.001860	0.018260	9.817397	0.101860
43	60.240069	592.400692	0.001688	0.016600	9.833998	0.101688
44	66.264076	652.640761	0.001532	0.015091	9.849089	0.101532
45	72.890484	718.904837	0.001391	0.013719	9.862808	0.101391
46	80.179532	791.795321	0.001263	0.012472	9.875280	0.101263
47	88.197485	871.974853	0.001147	0.011338	9.886618	0.101147
48	97.017234	960.172338	0.001041	0.010307	9.896926	0.101041
49	106.718957	1057.189572	0.000946	0.009370	9.906296	0.100946
50	117.390853	1163.908529	0.000859	0.008519	9.914814	0.100859

12.00% MONTHLY COMPOUND INTEREST TABLES 12.00%
EFFECTIVE RATE 1.000

	1 AMOUNT OF $1 AT COMPOUND INTEREST	2 ACCUMULATION OF $1 PER PERIOD	3 SINKING FUND FACTOR	4 PRESENT VALUE REVERSION OF $1	5 PRESENT VALUE ORD. ANNUITY $1 PER PERIOD	6 INSTALMENT TO AMORTIZE $1	
MONTHS							
1	1.010000	1.000000	1.000000	0.990099	0.990099	1.010000	
2	1.020100	2.010000	0.497512	0.980296	1.970395	0.507512	
3	1.030301	3.030100	0.330022	0.970590	2.940985	0.340022	
4	1.040604	4.060401	0.246281	0.960980	3.901966	0.256281	
5	1.051010	5.101005	0.196040	0.951466	4.853431	0.206040	
6	1.061520	6.152015	0.162548	0.942045	5.795476	0.172548	
7	1.072135	7.213535	0.138628	0.932718	6.728195	0.148628	
8	1.082857	8.285671	0.120690	0.923483	7.651678	0.130690	
9	1.093685	9.368527	0.106740	0.914340	8.566018	0.116740	
10	1.104622	10.462213	0.095582	0.905287	9.471305	0.105582	
11	1.115668	11.566835	0.086454	0.896324	10.367628	0.096454	
12	1.126825	12.682503	0.078849	0.887449	11.255077	0.088849	
YEARS							**MONTHS**
1	1.126825	12.682503	0.078849	0.887449	11.255077	0.088849	12
2	1.269735	26.973465	0.037073	0.787566	21.243387	0.047073	24
3	1.430769	43.076878	0.023214	0.698925	30.107505	0.033214	36
4	1.612226	61.222608	0.016334	0.620260	37.973959	0.026334	48
5	1.816697	81.669670	0.012244	0.550450	44.955038	0.022244	60
6	2.047099	104.709931	0.009550	0.488496	51.150391	0.019550	72
7	2.306723	130.672274	0.007653	0.433515	56.648453	0.017653	84
8	2.599273	159.927293	0.006253	0.384723	61.527703	0.016253	96
9	2.928926	192.892579	0.005184	0.341422	65.857790	0.015184	108
10	3.300387	230.038689	0.004347	0.302995	69.700522	0.014347	120
11	3.718959	271.895856	0.003678	0.268892	73.110752	0.013678	132
12	4.190616	319.061559	0.003134	0.238628	76.137157	0.013134	144
13	4.722091	372.209054	0.002687	0.211771	78.822939	0.012687	156
14	5.320970	432.096982	0.002314	0.187936	81.206434	0.012314	168
15	5.995802	499.580198	0.002002	0.166783	83.321664	0.012002	180
16	6.756220	575.621974	0.001737	0.148012	85.198824	0.011737	192
17	7.613078	661.307751	0.001512	0.131353	86.864707	0.011512	204
18	8.578606	757.860630	0.001320	0.116569	88.343095	0.011320	216
19	9.666588	866.658830	0.001154	0.103449	89.655089	0.011154	228
20	10.892554	989.255365	0.001011	0.091806	90.819416	0.011011	240
21	12.274002	1127.400210	0.000887	0.081473	91.852698	0.010887	252
22	13.830653	1283.065278	0.000779	0.072303	92.769683	0.010779	264
23	15.584726	1458.472574	0.000686	0.064165	93.583461	0.010686	276
24	17.561259	1656.125905	0.000604	0.056944	94.305647	0.010604	288
25	19.788466	1878.846626	0.000532	0.050534	94.946551	0.010532	300
26	22.298139	2129.813909	0.000470	0.044847	95.515321	0.010470	312
27	25.126101	2412.610125	0.000414	0.039799	96.020075	0.010414	324
28	28.312720	2731.271980	0.000366	0.035320	96.468019	0.010366	336
29	31.903481	3090.348134	0.000324	0.031345	96.865546	0.010324	348
30	35.949641	3494.964133	0.000286	0.027817	97.218331	0.010286	360
31	40.508956	3950.895567	0.000253	0.024686	97.531410	0.010253	372
32	45.646505	4464.650519	0.000224	0.021907	97.809252	0.010224	384
33	51.435625	5043.562459	0.000198	0.019442	98.055822	0.010198	396
34	57.958949	5695.894923	0.000176	0.017254	98.274641	0.010176	408
35	65.309595	6430.959471	0.000155	0.015312	98.468831	0.010155	420
36	73.592486	7259.248603	0.000138	0.013588	98.641166	0.010138	432
37	82.925855	8192.585529	0.000122	0.012059	98.794103	0.010122	444
38	93.442929	9244.292938	0.000108	0.010702	98.929828	0.010108	456
39	105.293832	10429.383172	0.000096	0.009497	99.050277	0.010096	468
40	118.647725	11764.772510	0.000085	0.008428	99.157169	0.010085	480

12.00%   ANNUAL COMPOUND INTEREST TABLES   12.00%
                                EFFECTIVE RATE 12.00

	1 AMOUNT OF $1 AT COMPOUND INTEREST	2 ACCUMULATION OF $1 PER PERIOD	3 SINKING FUND FACTOR	4 PRESENT VALUE REVERSION OF $1	5 PRESENT VALUE ORD. ANNUITY $1 PER PERIOD	6 INSTALMENT TO AMORTIZE $1
YEARS						
1	1.120000	1.000000	1.000000	0.892857	0.892857	1.120000
2	1.254400	2.120000	0.471698	0.797194	1.690051	0.591698
3	1.404928	3.374400	0.296349	0.711780	2.401831	0.416349
4	1.573519	4.779328	0.209234	0.635518	3.037349	0.329234
5	1.762342	6.352847	0.157410	0.567427	3.604776	0.277410
6	1.973823	8.115189	0.123226	0.506631	4.111407	0.243226
7	2.210681	10.089012	0.099118	0.452349	4.563757	0.219118
8	2.475963	12.299693	0.081303	0.403883	4.967640	0.201303
9	2.773079	14.775656	0.067679	0.360610	5.328250	0.187679
10	3.105848	17.548735	0.056984	0.321973	5.650223	0.176984
11	3.478550	20.654583	0.048415	0.287476	5.937699	0.168415
12	3.895976	24.133133	0.041437	0.256675	6.194374	0.161437
13	4.363493	28.029109	0.035677	0.229174	6.423548	0.155677
14	4.887112	32.392602	0.030871	0.204620	6.628168	0.150871
15	5.473566	37.279715	0.026824	0.182696	6.810864	0.146824
16	6.130394	42.753280	0.023390	0.163122	6.973986	0.143390
17	6.866041	48.883674	0.020457	0.145644	7.119630	0.140457
18	7.689966	55.749715	0.017937	0.130040	7.249670	0.137937
19	8.612762	63.439681	0.015763	0.116107	7.365777	0.135763
20	9.646293	72.052442	0.013879	0.103667	7.469444	0.133879
21	10.803848	81.698736	0.012240	0.092560	7.562003	0.132240
22	12.100310	92.502584	0.010811	0.082643	7.644646	0.130811
23	13.552347	104.602894	0.009560	0.073788	7.718434	0.129560
24	15.178629	118.155241	0.008463	0.065882	7.784316	0.128463
25	17.000064	133.333870	0.007500	0.058823	7.843139	0.127500
26	19.040072	150.333934	0.006652	0.052521	7.895660	0.126652
27	21.324881	169.374007	0.005904	0.046894	7.942554	0.125904
28	23.883866	190.698887	0.005244	0.041869	7.984423	0.125244
29	26.749930	214.582754	0.004660	0.037383	8.021806	0.124660
30	29.959922	241.332684	0.004144	0.033378	8.055184	0.124144
31	33.555113	271.292606	0.003686	0.029802	8.084986	0.123686
32	37.581726	304.847719	0.003280	0.026609	8.111594	0.123280
33	42.091533	342.429446	0.002920	0.023758	8.135352	0.122920
34	47.142517	384.520979	0.002601	0.021212	8.156564	0.122601
35	52.799620	431.663496	0.002317	0.018940	8.175504	0.122317
36	59.135574	484.463116	0.002064	0.016910	8.192414	0.122064
37	66.231843	543.598690	0.001840	0.015098	8.207513	0.121840
38	74.179664	609.830533	0.001640	0.013481	8.220993	0.121640
39	83.081224	684.010197	0.001462	0.012036	8.233030	0.121462
40	93.050970	767.091420	0.001304	0.010747	8.243777	0.121304
41	104.217087	860.142391	0.001163	0.009595	8.253372	0.121163
42	116.723137	964.359478	0.001037	0.008567	8.261939	0.121037
43	130.729914	1081.082615	0.000925	0.007649	8.269589	0.120925
44	146.417503	1211.812529	0.000825	0.006830	8.276418	0.120825
45	163.987604	1358.230032	0.000736	0.006098	8.282516	0.120736
46	183.666116	1522.217636	0.000657	0.005445	8.287961	0.120657
47	205.706050	1705.883752	0.000586	0.004861	8.292822	0.120586
48	230.390776	1911.589803	0.000523	0.004340	8.297163	0.120523
49	258.037669	2141.980579	0.000467	0.003875	8.301038	0.120467
50	289.002190	2400.018249	0.000417	0.003460	8.304498	0.120417

15.00%   MONTHLY COMPOUND INTEREST TABLES   15.00%
                              EFFECTIVE RATE 1.250

	1 AMOUNT OF $1 AT COMPOUND INTEREST	2 ACCUMULATION OF $1 PER PERIOD	3 SINKING FUND FACTOR	4 PRESENT VALUE REVERSION OF $1	5 PRESENT VALUE ORD. ANNUITY $1 PER PERIOD	6 INSTALMENT TO AMORTIZE $1	
MONTHS							
1	1.012500	1.000000	1.000000	0.987654	0.987654	1.012500	
2	1.025156	2.012500	0.496894	0.975461	1.963115	0.509394	
3	1.037971	3.037656	0.329201	0.963418	2.926534	0.341701	
4	1.050945	4.075627	0.245361	0.951524	3.878058	0.257861	
5	1.064082	5.126572	0.195062	0.939777	4.817835	0.207562	
6	1.077383	6.190654	0.161534	0.928175	5.746010	0.174034	
7	1.090850	7.268038	0.137589	0.916716	6.662726	0.150089	
8	1.104486	8.358888	0.119633	0.905398	7.568124	0.132133	
9	1.118292	9.463374	0.105671	0.894221	8.462345	0.118171	
10	1.132271	10.581666	0.094503	0.883181	9.345526	0.107003	
11	1.146424	11.713937	0.085368	0.872277	10.217803	0.097868	
12	1.160755	12.860361	0.077758	0.861509	11.079312	0.090258	
YEARS							**MONTHS**
1	1.160755	12.860361	0.077758	0.861509	11.079312	0.090258	12
2	1.347351	27.788084	0.035987	0.742197	20.624235	0.048487	24
3	1.563944	45.115506	0.022155	0.639409	28.847267	0.034665	36
4	1.815355	65.228388	0.015331	0.550856	35.931481	0.027831	48
5	2.107181	88.574508	0.011290	0.474568	42.034592	0.023790	60
6	2.445920	115.673621	0.008645	0.408844	47.292474	0.021145	72
7	2.839113	147.129040	0.006797	0.352223	51.822185	0.019297	84
8	3.295513	183.641059	0.005445	0.303443	55.724570	0.017945	96
9	3.825282	226.022551	0.004424	0.261419	59.086509	0.016924	108
10	4.440213	275.217058	0.003633	0.225214	61.982847	0.016133	120
11	5.153998	332.319805	0.003009	0.194024	64.478068	0.015509	132
12	5.982526	398.602077	0.002509	0.167153	66.627722	0.015009	144
13	6.944244	475.539523	0.002103	0.144004	68.479668	0.014603	156
14	8.060563	564.845011	0.001770	0.124061	70.075134	0.014270	168
15	9.356334	668.506759	0.001496	0.106879	71.449643	0.013996	180
16	10.860408	788.832603	0.001268	0.092078	72.633794	0.013768	192
17	12.606267	928.501369	0.001077	0.079326	73.653950	0.013577	204
18	14.632781	1090.622520	0.000917	0.068340	74.532823	0.013417	216
19	16.985067	1278.805378	0.000782	0.058875	75.289980	0.013282	228
20	19.715494	1497.239481	0.000668	0.050722	75.942278	0.013168	240
21	22.884848	1750.787854	0.000571	0.043697	76.504237	0.013071	252
22	26.563691	2045.095272	0.000489	0.037645	76.988370	0.012989	264
23	30.833924	2386.713938	0.000419	0.032432	77.405455	0.012919	276
24	35.790617	2783.249347	0.000359	0.027940	77.764777	0.012859	288
25	41.544120	3243.529615	0.000308	0.024071	78.074336	0.012808	300
26	48.222525	3777.802015	0.000265	0.020737	78.341024	0.012765	312
27	55.974514	4397.961118	0.000227	0.017865	78.570778	0.012727	324
28	64.972670	5117.813598	0.000195	0.015391	78.768713	0.012695	336
29	75.417320	5953.385616	0.000168	0.013260	78.939236	0.012668	348
30	87.540995	6923.279611	0.000144	0.011423	79.086142	0.012644	360
31	101.613606	8049.088447	0.000124	0.009841	79.212704	0.012624	372
32	117.948452	9355.876140	0.000107	0.008478	79.321738	0.012607	384
33	136.909198	10872.735858	0.000092	0.007304	79.415671	0.012592	396
34	158.917970	12633.437629	0.000079	0.006293	79.496596	0.012579	408
35	184.464752	14677.180163	0.000068	0.005421	79.566313	0.012568	420
36	214.118294	17049.463544	0.000059	0.004670	79.626375	0.012559	432
37	248.538777	19803.102194	0.000050	0.004024	79.678119	0.012550	444
38	288.492509	22999.400698	0.000043	0.003466	79.722696	0.012543	456
39	334.868983	26709.518627	0.000037	0.002986	79.761101	0.012537	468
40	388.700685	31016.054774	0.000032	0.002573	79.794186	0.012532	480

15.00%   ANNUAL COMPOUND INTEREST TABLES   15.00%
                                EFFECTIVE RATE 15.00

---

	1 AMOUNT OF $1 AT COMPOUND INTEREST	2 ACCUMULATION OF $1 PER PERIOD	3 SINKING FUND FACTOR	4 PRESENT VALUE REVERSION OF $1	5 PRESENT VALUE ORD. ANNUITY $1 PER PERIOD	6 INSTALMENT TO AMORTIZE $1
YEARS						
1	1.150000	1.000000	1.000000	0.869565	0.869565	1.150000
2	1.322500	2.150000	0.465116	0.756144	1.625709	0.615116
3	1.520875	3.472500	0.287977	0.657516	2.283225	0.437977
4	1.749006	4.993375	0.200265	0.571753	2.854978	0.350265
5	2.011357	6.742381	0.148316	0.497177	3.352155	0.298316
6	2.313061	8.753738	0.114237	0.432328	3.784483	0.264237
7	2.660020	11.066799	0.090360	0.375937	4.160420	0.240360
8	3.059023	13.726819	0.072850	0.326902	4.487322	0.222850
9	3.517876	16.785842	0.059574	0.284262	4.771584	0.209574
10	4.045558	20.303718	0.049252	0.247185	5.018769	0.199252
11	4.652391	24.349276	0.041069	0.214943	5.233712	0.191069
12	5.350250	29.001667	0.034481	0.186907	5.420619	0.184481
13	6.152788	34.351917	0.029110	0.162528	5.583147	0.179110
14	7.075706	40.504705	0.024688	0.141329	5.724476	0.174688
15	8.137062	47.580411	0.021017	0.122894	5.847370	0.171017
16	9.357621	55.717472	0.017948	0.106865	5.954235	0.167948
17	10.761264	65.075093	0.015367	0.092926	6.047161	0.165367
18	12.375454	75.836357	0.013186	0.080805	6.127966	0.163186
19	14.231772	88.211811	0.011336	0.070265	6.198231	0.161336
20	16.366537	102.443583	0.009761	0.061100	6.259331	0.159761
21	18.821518	118.810120	0.008417	0.053131	6.312462	0.158417
22	21.644746	137.631638	0.007266	0.046201	6.358663	0.157266
23	24.891458	159.276384	0.006278	0.040174	6.398837	0.156278
24	28.625176	184.167841	0.005430	0.034934	6.433771	0.155430
25	32.918953	212.793017	0.004699	0.030378	6.464149	0.154699
26	37.856796	245.711970	0.004070	0.026415	6.490564	0.154070
27	43.535315	283.568766	0.003526	0.022970	6.513534	0.153526
28	50.065612	327.104080	0.003057	0.019974	6.533508	0.153057
29	57.575454	377.169693	0.002651	0.017369	6.550877	0.152651
30	66.211772	434.745146	0.002300	0.015103	6.565980	0.152300
31	76.143538	500.956918	0.001996	0.013133	6.579113	0.151996
32	87.565068	577.100456	0.001733	0.011420	6.590533	0.151733
33	100.699829	664.665525	0.001505	0.009931	6.600463	0.151505
34	115.804803	765.365353	0.001307	0.008635	6.609099	0.151307
35	133.175523	881.170156	0.001135	0.007509	6.616607	0.151135
36	153.151852	1014.345680	0.000986	0.006529	6.623137	0.150986
37	176.124630	1167.497532	0.000857	0.005678	6.628815	0.150857
38	202.543324	1343.622161	0.000744	0.004937	6.633752	0.150744
39	232.924823	1546.165485	0.000647	0.004293	6.638045	0.150647
40	267.863546	1779.090308	0.000562	0.003733	6.641778	0.150562
41	308.043078	2046.953854	0.000489	0.003246	6.645025	0.150489
42	354.249540	2354.996933	0.000425	0.002823	6.647848	0.150425
43	407.386971	2709.246473	0.000369	0.002455	6.650302	0.150369
44	468.495017	3116.633443	0.000321	0.002134	6.652437	0.150321
45	538.769269	3585.128460	0.000279	0.001856	6.654293	0.150279
46	619.584659	4123.897729	0.000242	0.001614	6.655907	0.150242
47	712.522358	4743.482388	0.000211	0.001403	6.657310	0.150211
48	819.400712	5456.004746	0.000183	0.001220	6.658531	0.150183
49	942.310819	6275.405458	0.000159	0.001061	6.659592	0.150159
50	1083.657442	7217.716277	0.000139	0.000923	6.660515	0.150139

20.00%   MONTHLY COMPOUND INTEREST TABLES   20.00%
                                     EFFECTIVE RATE 1.667

	1 AMOUNT OF $1 AT COMPOUND INTEREST	2 ACCUMULATION OF $1 PER PERIOD	3 SINKING FUND FACTOR	4 PRESENT VALUE REVERSION OF $1	5 PRESENT VALUE ORD. ANNUITY $1 PER PERIOD	6 INSTALMENT TO AMORTIZE $1	
MONTHS							
1	1.016667	1.000000	1.000000	0.983607	0.983607	1.016667	
2	1.033611	2.016667	0.495868	0.967482	1.951088	0.512534	
3	1.050838	3.050278	0.327839	0.951622	2.902710	0.344506	
4	1.068352	4.101116	0.243836	0.936021	3.838731	0.260503	
5	1.086158	5.169468	0.193444	0.920677	4.759408	0.210110	
6	1.104260	6.255625	0.159856	0.905583	5.664991	0.176523	
7	1.122665	7.359886	0.135872	0.890738	6.555729	0.152538	
8	1.141376	8.482551	0.117889	0.876136	7.431865	0.134556	
9	1.160399	9.623926	0.103908	0.861773	8.293637	0.120574	
10	1.179739	10.784325	0.092727	0.847645	9.141283	0.109394	
11	1.199401	11.964064	0.083584	0.833749	9.975032	0.100250	
12	1.219391	13.163465	0.075968	0.820081	10.795113	0.092635	
YEARS							**MONTHS**
1	1.219391	13.163465	0.075968	0.820081	10.795113	0.092635	12
2	1.486915	29.214877	0.034229	0.672534	19.647986	0.050896	24
3	1.813130	48.787826	0.020497	0.551532	26.908062	0.037164	36
4	2.210915	72.654905	0.013764	0.452301	32.861916	0.030430	48
5	2.695970	101.758208	0.009827	0.370924	37.744561	0.026494	60
6	3.287442	137.246517	0.007286	0.304188	41.748727	0.023953	72
7	4.008677	180.520645	0.005540	0.249459	45.032470	0.022206	84
8	4.888145	233.288730	0.004287	0.204577	47.725406	0.020953	96
9	5.960561	297.633662	0.003360	0.167769	49.933833	0.020027	108
10	7.268255	376.095300	0.002659	0.137585	51.744924	0.019326	120
11	8.862845	471.770720	0.002120	0.112831	53.230165	0.018786	132
12	10.807275	588.436476	0.001699	0.092530	54.448184	0.018366	144
13	13.178294	730.697658	0.001369	0.075882	55.447059	0.018035	156
14	16.069495	904.169675	0.001106	0.062230	56.266217	0.017773	168
15	19.594998	1115.699905	0.000896	0.051033	56.937994	0.017563	180
16	23.893966	1373.637983	0.000728	0.041852	57.488906	0.017395	192
17	29.136090	1688.165376	0.000592	0.034322	57.940698	0.017259	204
18	35.528288	2071.697274	0.000483	0.028147	58.311205	0.017149	216
19	43.322878	2539.372652	0.000394	0.023082	58.615050	0.017060	228
20	52.827531	3109.651838	0.000322	0.018930	58.864229	0.016988	240
21	64.417420	3805.045193	0.000263	0.015524	59.068575	0.016929	252
22	78.550028	4653.001652	0.000215	0.012731	59.236156	0.016882	264
23	95.783203	5686.992197	0.000176	0.010440	59.373585	0.016843	276
24	116.797184	6947.831050	0.000144	0.008562	59.486289	0.016811	288
25	142.421445	8485.286707	0.000118	0.007021	59.578715	0.016785	300
26	173.667440	10360.046428	0.000097	0.005758	59.654512	0.016763	312
27	211.768529	12646.111719	0.000079	0.004722	59.716672	0.016746	324
28	258.228656	15433.719354	0.000065	0.003873	59.767648	0.016731	336
29	314.881721	18832.903252	0.000053	0.003176	59.809452	0.016720	348
30	383.963963	22977.837794	0.000044	0.002604	59.843735	0.016710	360
31	468.202234	28032.134021	0.000036	0.002136	59.871850	0.016702	372
32	570.921630	34195.297781	0.000029	0.001752	59.894907	0.016696	384
33	696.176745	41710.604725	0.000024	0.001436	59.913815	0.016691	396
34	848.911717	50874.703013	0.000020	0.001178	59.929321	0.016686	408
35	1035.155379	62049.322767	0.000016	0.000966	59.942038	0.016683	420
36	1262.259241	75675.554472	0.000013	0.000792	59.952466	0.016680	432
37	1539.187666	92291.259934	0.000011	0.000650	59.961018	0.016678	444
38	1876.871717	112552.303044	0.000009	0.000533	59.968032	0.016676	456
39	2288.640640	137258.438382	0.000007	0.000437	59.973784	0.016674	468
40	2790.747993	167384.879554	0.000006	0.000358	59.978500	0.016673	480

20.00%   ANNUAL COMPOUND INTEREST TABLES   20.00%
                                    EFFECTIVE RATE 20.00

	1 AMOUNT OF $1 AT COMPOUND INTEREST	2 ACCUMULATION OF $1 PER PERIOD	3 SINKING FUND FACTOR	4 PRESENT VALUE REVERSION OF $1	5 PRESENT VALUE ORD. ANNUITY $1 PER PERIOD	6 INSTALMENT TO AMORTIZE $1
YEARS						
1	1.200000	1.000000	1.000000	0.833333	0.833333	1.200000
2	1.440000	2.200000	0.454545	0.694444	1.527778	0.654545
3	1.728000	3.640000	0.274725	0.578704	2.106481	0.474725
4	2.073600	5.368000	0.186289	0.482253	2.588735	0.386289
5	2.488320	7.441600	0.134380	0.401878	2.990612	0.334380
6	2.985984	9.929920	0.100706	0.334898	3.325510	0.300706
7	3.583181	12.915904	0.077424	0.279082	3.604592	0.277424
8	4.299817	16.499085	0.060609	0.232568	3.837160	0.260609
9	5.159780	20.798902	0.048079	0.193807	4.030967	0.248079
10	6.191736	25.958682	0.038523	0.161506	4.192472	0.238523
11	7.430084	32.150419	0.031104	0.134588	4.327060	0.231104
12	8.916100	39.580502	0.025265	0.112157	4.439217	0.225265
13	10.699321	48.496603	0.020620	0.093464	4.532681	0.220620
14	12.839185	59.195923	0.016893	0.077887	4.610567	0.216893
15	15.407022	72.035108	0.013882	0.064905	4.675473	0.213882
16	18.488426	87.442129	0.011436	0.054088	4.729561	0.211436
17	22.186111	105.930555	0.009440	0.045073	4.774634	0.209440
18	26.623333	128.116666	0.007805	0.037561	4.812195	0.207805
19	31.948000	154.740000	0.006462	0.031301	4.843496	0.206462
20	38.337600	186.688000	0.005357	0.026084	4.869580	0.205357
21	46.005120	225.025600	0.004444	0.021737	4.891316	0.204444
22	55.206144	271.030719	0.003690	0.018114	4.909430	0.203690
23	66.247373	326.236863	0.003065	0.015095	4.924525	0.203065
24	79.496847	392.484236	0.002548	0.012579	4.937104	0.202548
25	95.396217	471.981083	0.002119	0.010483	4.947587	0.202119
26	114.475460	567.377300	0.001762	0.008735	4.956323	0.201762
27	137.370552	681.852760	0.001467	0.007280	4.963602	0.201467
28	164.844662	819.223312	0.001221	0.006066	4.969668	0.201221
29	197.813595	984.067974	0.001016	0.005055	4.974724	0.201016
30	237.376314	1181.881569	0.000846	0.004213	4.978936	0.200846
31	284.851577	1419.257883	0.000705	0.003511	4.982447	0.200705
32	341.821892	1704.109459	0.000587	0.002926	4.985372	0.200587
33	410.186270	2045.931351	0.000489	0.002438	4.987810	0.200489
34	492.223524	2456.117621	0.000407	0.002032	4.989842	0.200407
35	590.668229	2948.341146	0.000339	0.001693	4.991535	0.200339
36	708.801875	3539.009375	0.000283	0.001411	4.992946	0.200283
37	850.562250	4247.811250	0.000235	0.001176	4.994122	0.200235
38	1020.674700	5098.373500	0.000196	0.000980	4.995101	0.200196
39	1224.809640	6119.048200	0.000163	0.000816	4.995918	0.200163
40	1469.771568	7343.857840	0.000136	0.000680	4.996598	0.200136
41	1763.725882	8813.629408	0.000113	0.000567	4.997165	0.200113
42	2116.471058	10577.355290	0.000095	0.000472	4.997638	0.200095
43	2539.765269	12693.826348	0.000079	0.000394	4.998031	0.200079
44	3047.718323	15233.591617	0.000066	0.000328	4.998359	0.200066
45	3657.261988	18281.309940	0.000055	0.000273	4.998633	0.200055
46	4388.714386	21938.571928	0.000046	0.000228	4.998861	0.200046
47	5266.457263	26327.286314	0.000038	0.000190	4.999051	0.200038
48	6319.748715	31593.743577	0.000032	0.000158	4.999209	0.200032
49	7583.698458	37913.492292	0.000026	0.000132	4.999341	0.200026
50	9100.438150	45497.190751	0.000022	0.000110	4.999451	0.200022

25.00%   MONTHLY COMPOUND INTEREST TABLES   25.00%
                                         EFFECTIVE RATE 2.083

	1 AMOUNT OF $1 AT COMPOUND INTEREST	2 ACCUMULATION OF $1 PER PERIOD	3 SINKING FUND FACTOR	4 PRESENT VALUE REVERSION OF $1	5 PRESENT VALUE ORD. ANNUITY $1 PER PERIOD	6 INSTALMENT TO AMORTIZE $1	
MONTHS							
1	1.020833	1.000000	1.000000	0.979592	0.979592	1.020833	
2	1.042101	2.020833	0.494845	0.959600	1.939192	0.515679	
3	1.063811	3.062934	0.326484	0.940016	2.879208	0.347318	
4	1.085974	4.126745	0.242322	0.920832	3.800041	0.263155	
5	1.108598	5.212719	0.191838	0.902040	4.702081	0.212672	
6	1.131694	6.321317	0.158195	0.883631	5.585712	0.179028	
7	1.155271	7.453011	0.134174	0.865598	6.451310	0.155007	
8	1.179339	8.608283	0.116167	0.847932	7.299242	0.137001	
9	1.203909	9.787622	0.102170	0.830628	8.129870	0.123003	
10	1.228990	10.991531	0.090979	0.813676	8.943546	0.111812	
11	1.254594	12.220521	0.081830	0.797070	9.740616	0.102663	
12	1.280732	13.475115	0.074211	0.780804	10.521420	0.095044	
YEARS							MONTHS
1	1.280732	13.475115	0.074211	0.780804	10.521420	0.095044	12
2	1.640273	30.733120	0.032538	0.609654	18.736585	0.053372	24
3	2.100750	52.835991	0.018926	0.476021	25.151016	0.039760	36
4	2.690497	81.143837	0.012324	0.371679	30.159427	0.033157	48
5	3.445804	117.398588	0.008518	0.290208	34.070014	0.029351	60
6	4.413150	163.831191	0.006104	0.226596	37.123415	0.026937	72
7	5.652060	223.298892	0.004478	0.176927	39.507522	0.025312	84
8	7.238772	299.461053	0.003339	0.138145	41.369041	0.024173	96
9	9.270924	397.004337	0.002519	0.107864	42.822522	0.023352	108
10	11.873565	521.931099	0.001916	0.084221	43.957406	0.022749	120
11	15.206849	681.928746	0.001466	0.065760	44.843528	0.022300	132
12	19.475891	886.842782	0.001128	0.051346	45.535414	0.021961	144
13	24.943389	1149.282656	0.000870	0.040091	46.075642	0.021703	156
14	31.945785	1485.397684	0.000673	0.031303	46.497454	0.021507	168
15	40.913975	1915.870809	0.000522	0.024442	46.826807	0.021355	180
16	52.399819	2467.191326	0.000405	0.019084	47.083966	0.021239	192
17	67.110102	3173.284913	0.000315	0.014901	47.284757	0.021148	204
18	85.950026	4077.601254	0.000245	0.011635	47.441536	0.021079	216
19	110.078911	5235.787733	0.000191	0.009084	47.563949	0.021024	228
20	140.981536	6719.113709	0.000149	0.007093	47.659530	0.020982	240
21	180.559502	8618.856102	0.000116	0.005538	47.734160	0.020949	252
22	231.248253	11051.916141	0.000090	0.004324	47.792431	0.020924	264
23	296.166936	14168.012922	0.000071	0.003376	47.837929	0.020904	276
24	379.310342	18158.896417	0.000055	0.002636	47.873455	0.020888	288
25	485.794726	23270.146862	0.000043	0.002058	47.901193	0.020876	300
26	622.172638	29816.286623	0.000034	0.001607	47.922851	0.020867	312
27	796.836134	38200.134414	0.000026	0.001255	47.939762	0.020860	324
28	1020.533185	48937.592880	0.000020	0.000980	47.952966	0.020854	336
29	1307.029059	62689.394819	0.000016	0.000765	47.963275	0.020849	348
30	1673.953366	80301.761578	0.000012	0.000597	47.971325	0.020846	360
31	2143.884907	102858.475544	0.000010	0.000466	47.977611	0.020843	372
32	2745.741063	131747.571026	0.000008	0.000364	47.982518	0.020841	384
33	3516.557237	168746.747367	0.000006	0.000284	47.986350	0.020839	396
34	4503.765838	216132.760226	0.000005	0.000222	47.989342	0.020838	408
35	5768.115051	276821.522428	0.000004	0.000173	47.991678	0.020837	420
36	7387.406991	354547.535558	0.000003	0.000135	47.993502	0.020836	432
37	9461.285285	454093.693657	0.000002	0.000106	47.994927	0.020836	444
38	12117.366668	581585.600079	0.000002	0.000083	47.996039	0.020835	456
39	15519.093924	744868.508353	0.000001	0.000064	47.996907	0.020835	468
40	19875.793381	953990.082294	0.000001	0.000050	47.997585	0.020834	480

25.00%   ANNUAL COMPOUND INTEREST TABLES   25.00%
                              EFFECTIVE RATE 25.00

	1	2	3	4	5	6
	AMOUNT OF $1 AT COMPOUND INTEREST	ACCUMULATION OF $1 PER PERIOD	SINKING FUND FACTOR	PRESENT VALUE REVERSION OF $1	PRESENT VALUE ORD. ANNUITY $1 PER PERIOD	INSTALMENT TO AMORTIZE $1
YEARS						
1	1.250000	1.000000	1.000000	0.800000	0.800000	1.250000
2	1.562500	2.250000	0.444444	0.640000	1.440000	0.694444
3	1.953125	3.812500	0.262295	0.512000	1.952000	0.512295
4	2.441406	5.765625	0.173442	0.409600	2.361600	0.423442
5	3.051758	8.207031	0.121847	0.327680	2.689280	0.371847
6	3.814697	11.258789	0.088819	0.262144	2.951424	0.338819
7	4.768372	15.073486	0.066342	0.209715	3.161139	0.316342
8	5.960464	19.841858	0.050399	0.167772	3.328911	0.300399
9	7.450581	25.802322	0.038756	0.134218	3.463129	0.288756
10	9.313226	33.252903	0.030073	0.107374	3.570503	0.280073
11	11.641532	42.566129	0.023493	0.085899	3.656403	0.273493
12	14.551915	54.207661	0.018448	0.068719	3.725122	0.268448
13	18.189894	68.759576	0.014543	0.054976	3.780098	0.264543
14	22.737368	86.949470	0.011501	0.043980	3.824078	0.261501
15	28.421709	109.686838	0.009117	0.035184	3.859263	0.259117
16	35.527137	138.108547	0.007241	0.028147	3.887410	0.257241
17	44.408921	173.635684	0.005759	0.022518	3.909928	0.255759
18	55.511151	218.044605	0.004586	0.018014	3.927942	0.254586
19	69.388939	273.555756	0.003656	0.014412	3.942354	0.253656
20	86.736174	342.944695	0.002916	0.011529	3.953883	0.252916
21	108.420217	429.680869	0.002327	0.009223	3.963107	0.252327
22	135.525272	538.101086	0.001858	0.007379	3.970485	0.251858
23	169.406589	673.626358	0.001485	0.005903	3.976388	0.251485
24	211.758237	843.032947	0.001186	0.004722	3.981111	0.251186
25	264.697796	1054.791184	0.000948	0.003778	3.984888	0.250948
26	330.872245	1319.488980	0.000758	0.003022	3.987911	0.250758
27	413.590306	1650.361225	0.000606	0.002418	3.990329	0.250606
28	516.987883	2063.951531	0.000485	0.001934	3.992263	0.250485
29	646.234854	2580.939414	0.000387	0.001547	3.993810	0.250387
30	807.793567	3227.174268	0.000310	0.001238	3.995048	0.250310
31	1009.741959	4034.967835	0.000248	0.000990	3.996039	0.250248
32	1262.177448	5044.709793	0.000198	0.000792	3.996831	0.250198
33	1577.721810	6306.887242	0.000159	0.000634	3.997465	0.250159
34	1972.152263	7884.609052	0.000127	0.000507	3.997972	0.250127
35	2465.190329	9856.761315	0.000101	0.000406	3.998377	0.250101
36	3081.487911	12321.951644	0.000081	0.000325	3.998702	0.250081
37	3851.859889	15403.439555	0.000065	0.000260	3.998962	0.250065
38	4814.824861	19255.299444	0.000052	0.000208	3.999169	0.250052
39	6018.531076	24070.124305	0.000042	0.000166	3.999335	0.250042
40	7523.163845	30088.655381	0.000033	0.000133	3.999468	0.250033

GLOSSARY OF TERMS

Chapter 1

Appraising. Estimating the magnitude of a predefined type of value for a parcel of real estate.

Macro administration. A study of the nature, organization, structures, interrelationships, and effects on resource allocation of business firms, governmental agencies, and private investors.

Macro economics. Analysis of economic functions from the viewpoint of the government, e.g., the decision maker for the economy as a whole.

Micro administration. Accomplishment of a given objective by working with people. The process is considered in terms of decision making and execution of required tasks.

Micro economics. Analysis of economic functions from the viewpoint of a single firm or decision maker.

Mortgage. Legal instrument evidencing the pledge of an asset to secure a debt.

Mortgagee. Holder of pledge on an asset; usually a lender of money.

Mortgagor. Borrower of money who pledges an asset to secure the debt.

Real estate. The physical "good" involved in the legal concept of real property.

Chapter 2

Building codes. Regulations regarding the quality and strength of materials for the purpose of controlling safety, fire prevention, and sanitation.

Eminent domain. The right of governments and designated private agencies to take private property (upon paying just compensation) for public use.

Escheat. Doctrine of law under which ownership of real property vests in the government when the legal owner dies and leaves no heirs.

Lien. Encumbrance of property ownership rights to protect a creditor.

Zoning. Division of a city, county, or other jurisdiction into districts for various types of land use.

Chapter 3

Amenities. Tangible and intangible benefits generated by a property.

Business risk. Possibility of losses caused by internal operating inefficiencies and external factors.

Cost of capital. Charge that must be paid to attract money into an investment project.

Depreciation. (1) loss in value from all causes; (2) apportionment of improvement cost to time periods.

Equity. Share of property possessed by residual owners after allowing for borrowed funds.

Equity funds. Capital invested to acquire a residual ownership interest in property.

Financial risk. Possibility of losses caused by the amount of and legal provisions concerning borrowed funds.

Gross income. Total dollars of revenue generated by an investment property.

Liquidity. Speed at which one is able to sell property.

Net operating income (NOI). Gross possible revenue minus an allowance for vacancies and for operating expenses.

Net (taxable) income. Gross possible revenue minus an allowance for vacancies; operating expenses; depreciation; and interest paid on borrowed funds.

Return on investment (ROI). A percentage relationship between the price an investor pays and the stream of income dollars he obtains from the investment.

Yield. Cash received by investors divided by the amount of their cash investment.

Chapter 4

Extensive margin. Extra benefits derived from adding increasing amounts of land to productive status.

Intensive margin. Extra benefits derived from adding increasing amounts of labor and capital to land.

Marginal utility. Worth of one extra unit of a good or a service that is produced.

Present value. Today's value derived by measuring all future benefits of an investment and converting those benefits into terms of today's dollars.

Price. The sum of money a purchaser actually pays for a property.

Residual techniques. Assignment of a portion of income to part of an asset, with the remainder (or residual) flowing automatically to the rest of the asset. Also, the assignment of part of the income to cover debt payments with the balance accruing to the equity.

Value. Present worth of benefits to be received in the future.

Value analysis. Determination of the present worth of future benefits to be derived from a property investment.

Value in exchange. Price an investment asset is expected to bring based upon comparable market transactions.

Value in use. Price an investor would pay based upon his personal assessment of the investment asset's merit.

Chapter 5

Amortization. Systematic apportionment of costs, loan principal, or other input to discrete periods of time such as months, years, etc.

Annuity capital recapture. Given a constant income in each time period, interest on unrecovered capital reduces and capital recapture increases. The sum of the two is constant, and an annuity schedule describes the pattern of change between the two elements.

Capital recapture. Expression of the manner in which the dollars of investment in a property are to be returned to investors. Stated as a rate or dollar amount per unit of time.

Capitalization. Process of converting a net operating income into value. Usually shown by the formula $V = \dfrac{I}{R}$ where R is a predetermined return rate.

Capitalization rate. Percentage of return required from an investment which provides for investor income, principal and interest on debts, and loss in value from depreciation.

Contract rent. Rental fixed by agreement among parties which may or may not be comparable to rentals of similar properties.

Curable penalty. Element of depreciation whose cost of repair or correction is offset by addition in value to the property caused by the repair or correction. Incurable penalty is charged when cost of repair adds less than itself to the property's value.

Discounting. Process of converting any cash flow into present value at a selected rate of return. Based upon the idea that one would pay less than $1 today for the right to receive $1 at a future date.

Estates in land. See Chapter 8 section of Glossary.

Functional obsolescence. Decline in value of property caused by changes in technology or by defects in design, layout, or size of building. Loss of a building's ability to perform its function.

Highest and best use. That use of property which results in maximum productivity or earning power.

Locational deterioration. Decline in value of property caused by deterioration in the quality of its neighborhood; also known as economic obsolescence.

Market rent. Rental level ascertained by seeking out similar properties in a selected market area.

Physical deterioration. Decline in value of property caused by wear, tear, or natural elements.

Quantity survey. Method of estimating building replacement cost in which all elements of labor, materials, and overhead are priced and totaled to obtain building cost.

Reconstructed operating statement. Set of operating revenue and expense figures that is adapted to a standard format which permits comparisons with similar properties.

Replacement reserves. Funds set aside to provide for replacement of building components, equipment, and so forth.

Reversion value. Worth of land at a time when improvements to that land have reached an economic value of zero. Usually expressed as a present worth of future reversion value.

Sinking fund capital recovery. Capital recovery in early time periods is higher than that which occurs under the annuity method by an amount set aside as a sinking fund. This sinking fund earns a rate of interest that compensates the property owner for earnings lost on funds recovered from the investment.

Straight line capital recapture. Amount of dollar investment recovery in each year is constant.

Unit in place costs. Method of estimating building replacement cost in which quanties of materials are costed on an in-place basis and summarized to obtain building cost.

Chapter 6

Cash flow after tax. Cash throwoff minus income taxes paid or plus income tax deduction benefits.

Cash throwoff. Net operating income minus debt service on mortgage for a given time period.

Debt service. Annual mortgage payment.

Debt service coverage. Requirement imposed by lender that earnings be a percentage or dollar sum higher than debt service.

Gross income multiplier. Expression of value based upon a multiple of project gross income.

Incremental income tax. Extra income tax caused by a given investment.

Internal rate of return. Predetermined earning rate requirement for a project. Usually established by comparison with other return opportunities available to the investor.

Investment calculation. Estimation of value for a particular investor/user.

Net income multiplier. Expression of value based upon a multiple of project net income.

Operating expense ratio. Relationship between operating expenses and project gross income.

Payback period. Length of time required for cash flow from project to equal amount of money invested.

Tax shelter. Net loss for income tax purposes.

Value calculation. Estimation of value that is recognized by buyers, sellers, lenders, and renters in the market place.

Chapter 7

Apportionment of basis. Division of income tax basis (or investment in asset) between depreciable improvements and nondepreciable land. This division must be acceptable to the Internal Revenue Service.

Boot. Cash or other assets exchanged for real property.

Collateral. Assets that are pledged to secure or guarantee the discharge of an obligation.

Conduit. A channel for conveying income from one entity to another wherein only the final recipient incurs the income tax consequences of the income.

Imputed interest. In an instalment sale, the Internal Revenue Service establishes an interest payment schedule even when the principals to a transaction mention no interest. This causes part of the seller's capital gain to be treated as ordinary interest income.

Investment property. An asset owned for the purpose of earning an investment return as opposed to one held as stock in trade or one held for operation in the ordinary course of business.

Nonmarketable securities. Usually notes taken in an instalment or deferred payment sale that contain restrictive clauses that hinder their marketability. This hinderance may be designed to reduce the seller's income tax liability.

Recapture (depreciation). The disallowance of a portion of rapid depreciation income tax deductions caused by disposing of the depreciable asset at a time when accumulative rapid depreciation exceeds the amount of depreciation that would have been taken during the holding period if straight line depreciation had been used. Only the amount by which accumulative depreciation exceeds straight line depreciation is disallowed.

Surcharge. An additional amount added to the usual charge.

Syndication. The formation of an association of individuals or corporations to carry out a financial venture.

Chapter 8

Accretion. Growth in size, especially by addition accumulation; (ex) the addition of soil to land by gradual, natural deposits.

Avulsion. The sudden transference of a piece of land from one person's property to another's without change of ownership, as by a change in the course of a stream.

Condemnation. A declaration that property is legally appropriated for public use; also, a declaration that something is unfit for use or service (example: the condemnation of a slum tenement).

Condominium. An arrangement under which a tenant in an apartment building or in a complex of multiple-unit dwellings holds full title to his unit and joint ownership in the common grounds.

Confiscation. That which is seized (private property) for the public treasury, usually as a penalty.

Dower. That part of a man's property which his widow inherits for life.

Easement. A right or privilege that a person may have in another's land, as the right of way.

Egress. A way out; exit.

Fixture. Fittings or furniture of a property attached to a building and ordinarily, and legally, considered to be a part of it.

Foreclosure. The act of depriving of the right to redeem a mortgage when regular payments have not been kept up.

Forfeiture. Anything lost or given up because of some crime, fault, or neglect of duty; specifically, a fine or penalty.

Freehold estate. An estate in land held for life or with the right to pass it on through inheritance.

Incorporeal rights. Easements, license to use property, and profit (right to remove minerals).

Ingress. A place or means of entering; entrance.

Joint tenancy. Special ownership situation in which two or more owners hold equal shares, acquire shares concurrently, and have equal rights of possession. The rights of one owner pass to the other owner upon his death.

Leaseholds. Less than freehold estates that are usually considered to be personal property.

License. A formal permission to do some specified thing, especially something authorized by law; also, a document, permit, and so on, indicating that such permission has been granted.

Occupancy. The period during which a house, and so forth, is kept in possession; in *law*, the taking possession of a previously unowned object, thus establishing ownership.

Prescription. One who uses the land of another for a period of time stated by law obtains the right of easement to the subject land.

Real estate. Land, including the buildings or improvements and its natural assets, as minerals, water, and so forth.

Reversion. The return of an estate to the grantor and his heirs by operation of law after the period of grant is over.

Right of way. Right of passage, as over another's property; also, land over which a public road, an electric power line, and so forth, passes.

Title. A document stating a right of ownership, especially of real estate; deed.

Chapter 9

Abstract of title. History of documents affecting title to real property.

Acceleration clause. Mortgage contract clause that makes all payments due immediately if a scheduled payment is missed.

Blanket mortgage. Mortgage lien secured by several land parcels.

Broker. One who, for a fee, buys, sells, rents, or advertises real property for sale.

Closing. Event at which title to real estate is transferred.

Cognovit clause. Borrower confesses judgment or authorizes lender to secure a judgment that can be attached to borrower's property as a lien.

Conventional mortgage. Mortgage not insured by a public or private agency.

Conveyancing. Passage of title or ownership to real estate.

Deed. Document evidencing title to real property.

Deed covenants. Warranties made by a seller of property to protect the buyer against items such as liens, encumberances, or title defects.

Earnest money. Money paid to evidence good faith when a contract of purchase is submitted to a property owner by a prospective purchaser.

Escrow agreement. Establishment of a fiduciary who holds documents, cash, or both until all elements of a transaction can be completed.

Exclusive listing.   Agreement between seller of property and broker in which broker is assured a commission if the seller's property is sold by anyone other than the seller.

Exclusive right to sell listing.   Agreement between seller of property and broker in which broker is assured a commission if the property is sold, no matter how it is sold or by whom it is sold.

Graduated lease.   Lease having payment levels that change at different volumes of sales.

Guaranteed mortgage.   Mortgage guaranteed (in part) by the Veterans Administration.

Insured mortgage.   Morgage insured by Federal Housing Administration, Farmers Home Administration, or a private insurance agency such as Mortgage Guaranty Insurance Corporation.

Lien theory.   State law permitting lenders to secure a lien against property as collateral for a loan. This is less protective to lenders than title theory.

Multiple listing.   Sharing of property sales listings by several real estate brokers.

Open listing.   Agreement between seller of property and broker which permits broker to receive a commission if he sells the seller's property. No exclusive protection is provided the broker.

Participation mortgage.   Lender participates in profits or ownership as well as receiving contract rents.

Plat.   Drawing that shows boundaries, shape, and size of a parcel of land.

Prepayment privilege.   Mortgage contract clause permitting borrower to pay loan payments in advance of their due date.

Proration.   Allocation of costs or revenues between buyer and seller of real property.

Quit claim deed.   Deed passing title with no warranties regarding quality and quantity of ownership passed by seller to buyer.

Reappraisal lease.   Lease having a clause calling for periodic reevaluation of rental levels.

Statement of consideration.   Statement in a deed that affirms the fact that the purchaser actually paid something for the property.

Statute of frauds.   Legal requirement that all matters affecting title to real estate must be in writing if they are to be enforced by a court of law.

Statutory redemption period.   Time permitted a delinqeunt borrower to cure his deficiencies before his property is taken permanently from him.

Title theory.   State law permitting lenders to secure title to property as collateral for a loan.

Trustee.   One who administers property held in trust for another.

Chapter 10

Linkage.   Time and distance relationship between a subject site and an important location such as a school, a shopping area, or a place of employment.

Plottage value.   Value added to land by assembling small parcels into large tracts.

Chapter 11

Economic base analysis. Study of a community's employment and income to identify the number of nonmanufacturing workers that can be afforded and to plan for future expansion of basic (manufacturing) and service (nonmanufacturing) employment.

Feasibility analysis. Study of the cash flow and profitability potential of a project.

Flow of funds accounts. Governmental system of accounting for movement of money throughout the economy.

Gross national product. Governmental system of accounting for annual output or production of the economy.

Input-output accounts. Measurement of products exported from a community and goods and services imported into the same community.

Marginal. Increment of change.

Marginal cost. Increment of cost resulting from a given business decision.

Marginal revenue. Increment of revenue resulting from a given business decision.

Market analysis. Study of the market into which a developer might thrust himself; study of the reason why prices are being paid.

Monopolistic competition. Control of a market by a number of parties who differentiate their services effectively.

Monopoly. Control of a market by one party.

100 percent site. Location past which the largest number of customers or space users pass (within a given market area).

Social class. Group of people delineated by selected social characteristics.

Chapter 12

Agency. Law governing the relationship between employer and his agent.

Firm advertising. Advertising intended to call attention to the firm and its specific offerings.

Institutional advertising. Advertising intended to popularize an industry such as real estate.

Market segmentation. Identification and delineation of the market to be served.

Marketer. Person engaged in the marketing of a product or service; deals with the satisfaction of human needs on a broad scale.

Marketing myopia. Failure to focus upon needs and people who have needs.

Oligopoly. Control of a market by a small number of participants.

Chapter 13

Debt capital. Borrowed money.

Deed restrictions. Land use constraints imposed in the deed passed from seller to buyer. These constraints then pass with the property in future transfers.

Elasticity. Ability of supply of real estate to respond to price increases over a short period of time.

Filtering. Movement of people of one income group into homes that have recently dropped in price and that were previously occupied by persons in the next higher income group.

Leverage. Use of money borrowed at a fixed rate of interest in an investment project; earnings (or losses) in excess of fixed debt costs accrue to the project owner.

Purchase money mortgage. Mortgage taken by the seller of property as part of the purchase price.

Specifications. Restrictions imposed on the quantity and quality of materials and labor to be used in a construction project.

Subdividing. Separation of a parcel of land into smaller parcels. Selling more than five parcels in a single year can cause investors to become dealers in real property.

Chapter 14

Certificates of beneficial interest. Ownership shares of a trust or mutual fund.

Condominium. Ownership form in which a single property, such as an apartment building, is divided into several portions (apartments) with each portion owned by a different person.

Cooperative. Ownership form in which a single property is divided into several use portions, with each user owning stock in a corporation that owns the property.

Deed of trust. Transfer of ownership interest to a trustee acting on behalf of a money lender. The trustee is usually instructed to supervise collection of the debt and return the trust deed to the borrower upon retirement of the debt.

Discount rate. Relationship between dollars transmitted from a lender to a borrower and dollars that must be repaid by the borrower. If a lender advances $960 and the borrower must repay $1,000, the discount rate is $\dfrac{\$40}{\$1,000} = 4\%$.

Funds. Cash or any resource having value which is capable of being sold in order to buy some other asset.

Kicker. Surcharge payment on a loan; any loan payment in excess of ordinary principal and interest.

Land contract. Purchase contract which conveys equitable title to a buyer with an agreement to transfer a deed when an event, such as payment of a debt, occurs.

Lease. Contract providing for the transfer of a right to use real estate.

Limited partnership. Ownership form in which a general partner performs all management functions and assumes all operating liabilities on behalf of passive investors known as limited partners.

Locked-in period. Time period in which a mortgage loan borrower is not permitted by contract to prepay any of the loan principal.

Mortgage bank correspondents. Mortgage bankers in local communities who serve as agents of lenders in placing and servicing loans.

Mortgage constant. Percentage of original loan balance represented by constant annual mortgage payment. A payment of $100,000 per year on a million dollar mortgage converts to a 10 per cent constant.

Mutual ownership.   Used in Chapter 14 to mean a financial institution that is owned by its depositors.

Note (promissory).   Document evidencing a debt and describing the terms by which the debt is to be paid.

Real estate investment trust.   A passive investment vehicle whose distributed earnings are taxed only to investors who receive them. Similar to a corporation in every way except for the permitted avoidance of double taxation of dividends.

Syndicate.   Group of individuals, corporations, or trusts who pool money to undertake economic ventures. The syndicate can take the form of a corporation, a trust, a partnership, a tenancy in common, or any other legal ownership form.

Warehousing (loans).   Provision of funds to a mortgage banker so that he may increase his inventory of mortgage loans. Typically a commercial bank does the warehousing of loans.

Chapter 15

Atomistic decision maker.   The public servant who acts on behalf of the public welfare.

Blight.   Decay caused by failure to maintain the quality of private land and buildings and the quality of government services.

Capitalism.   Economic system in which the government is committed to the tenets of private property ownership, individual freedom, and equality of opportunity.

Cost-benefit analysis.   Study of social and economic costs and benefits related to actions of governmental units.

Demographic characteristics.   Political, social, and economic qualities of a population of people.

Economic theory of democracy.   Each political party designs its budget, both revenues and expenditures, to maximize its chance of winning the next election.

Extra use.   Use (or activity) level in excess of a real or assumed normal level of use.

Macro administration.   See Glossary, Chapter 1.

Marginal cost.   Magnitude of cost associated with adding a new good or service.

Marginal satisfaction.   Change in level of satisfaction resulting from the occurrence of a given event.

Micro administration.   See Glossary, Chapter 1.

Public good.   Extreme case of decreasing cost industry in which the marginal cost of extra use is zero. A soldier's pay is essentially the same whether he fights or not.

Simulation.   Use of a controlled environment in which to test the impact of a decision.

Social overhead capital.   Investment by the government in public improvements such as bridges, roads, schools, and parks.

Sovereign consumer. Concept that the consumer is the decision maker who decides what goods and services are to be provided within the society.

Spillover effects. Addition of public goods in urban renewal might remove urban blight, but it also adds costs of new police and fire protection. These costs are a spillover effect.

Subsidized housing. Housing for low and moderate income families in which rentals are paid partly by the families and partly by the government or in which the government pays part of the developer's loan interest costs so that he can charge lower rentals.

Systems analysis. Study of private and public forces and their interrelationships in carrying out the objectives of society.

Chapter 16

Annual debt service. See **Debt service,** Glossary, Chapter 6.

BSPRA. Builder-sponsor's profit and risk allowance permitted in government subsidized housing projects.

Closing costs. Costs of settlement in transferring property ownership, such as recording fees, attorney fees, title insurance premium, etc.

Cost-plus-allowances contract. Builder must certify all costs and allowances to build a low income housing project that will be privately owned. Excess of costs plus allowances over certified level will not be included under the mortgage.

Exculpatory clause. Clause in a mortgage indenture that identifies only the property as collateral for the debt. No personal signatures are required.

FNMA (Fannie Mae). Federal National Mortgage Association, secondary market agency for FHA and VA loans.

Fair market value. Worth of a property that can be supported by an efficient market. In such a market, numerous transactions are made by knowledgeable parties who are under no duress.

Full face rate of interest. Rate of interest stated in indenture of obligation.

HAA. Housing Assistance Administration.

Identity of interest. Builder and sponsor of a housing project subsidized by the government have ownership interests in each other.

Lease-purchase agreement. A low income family can agree to rent a home with part of the rent applying toward a down payment. When the down payment is paid, the agreement transfers ownership to the family.

Negative income tax. Proposal that the government subsidize low income families by setting the minimum taxable income at a level such as $3,000, with anyone earning less than that amount receiving payments from the government rather than being obligated for taxes.

Sales expense. Costs associated with selling real property. Commissions to brokers, costs of advertising, and costs of preparing the property for sale are the most important of these expenses.

Straight-line depreciation. Amount of dollar investment deductible from income tax liability is constant each year.

Turnkey programs. Governmental housing projects built by private developers and sold to governmental housing authorities.

Chapter 17

Ancillary structures. Facilities to support the basic system under study; e.g., a transportation network is supported by parking facilities, transport terminals, and warehouse facilities.

Arterial highway. Major route into heavy traffic area.

Bedroom city. Suburban community in which a large number of the central city's workers reside.

Beltline highway. Limited access highway surrounding a city.

Benefit-cost ratio. Measure of social income (or benefits) to dollar cost.

CARS (dial-a-ride). Personalized door-to-door public transportation service.

Concentric circle hypothesis. Transportation is assumed to be a central force in community growth. Land values are highest where mobility is greatest.

Cross-haul trip. Movement of a traveller across town at a time when he enters the path of commuter and other traffic patterns.

Depressed highway. Highway cut into the earth so that it is depressed below the natural grade of the area.

Gravity vacuum tube. High-speed travel device operating within a vacuum tube.

Hypothesis of median location. A theory reflecting the tendency for businesses and other entities to locate at their lowest time/cost point.

Inversely related cost. Cost that declines as volume of activity to which it relates increases.

Limited access highway. Highway along which no traffic may stop. Entrance and exit opportunities are limited to predetermined intervals.

Megalopolis. Metropolitan area that results from two or more cities growing together.

PSP model. Problem-solving process model that structures an analysis in numerous levels.

Sector hypothesis. Sectors of land use arise in which the finest homes are in the most attractive locations, medium-priced homes follow traffic arteries, and lower-priced homes are near places of employment.

TACV. Tracked air cushion vehicle.

Tax base. Sum of property values in a community that underlies the financial strength of the government.

Urban sprawl. Spread of a city over a large geographical area.

V/STOL. Vertical and short take off and landing aircraft.

———————————Index

INDEX

This book has been set in 10 and 9 point Caledonia, leaded 2 points. Part numbers and titles are in 24 point Helvetica, chapter numbers are in 16 and 30 point Helvetica, and chapter titles are in 18 point Helvetica. The size of the type page is 27 x 45½ picas.